SIXTH EDITION

SUPERVISION

The Direction of People at Work

W. Richard Plunkett

WRIGHT COLLEGE
City Colleges of Chicago

Allyn and Bacon

Boston • London • Toronto • Sydney • Tokyo • Singapore

To my mother and father:
Mary C. and Paul M. Plunkett

Executive Editor: Rich Wohl
Series Editorial Assistant: Cheryl Ten Eick
Editorial-Production Service: The Book Company
Cover Coordinator: Linda Dickinson
Composition Buyer: Linda Cox
Manufacturing Buyer: Megan Cochran

Library of Congress Cataloging-in-Publication Data
Plunkett, W. Richard (Warren Richard)
    Supervision: the direction of people at work / W. Richard
Plunkett—6th ed.
     p. cm.
    Includes bibliographical references and index.
    ISBN 0-205-13656-7
    1. Supervision of employees.   I. Title.
HF5549.P564   1992
658.3′02—dc20   91-30620
                                      CIP

Printed in the United States of America
10 9 8 7 6 5 4 3 2 1   95 94 93 92 91

Photo credits: pp. 1, 172, 355, © Frank Siteman; p. 250 (all), © Bob Coyle; p. 505, Kay Chernush, The Image Bank.

Contents

PART II   YOU AND YOUR PEOPLE   172

Building Relationships with Individuals 245

Supervising Groups 284

PART III SHAPING YOUR ENVIRONMENT 355

Omit

Preface

This sixth edition of *Supervision: The Direction of People at Work* has been thoroughly updated and revised in light of the many helpful comments and suggestions of adopters and reviewers of the previous edition. Special care has been taken to preserve the "how to" and the "you" approaches of the previous editions, while enriching these features with additional application materials. As before, the text emphasizes how a supervisor can apply the major concepts introduced.

Intended Readers

This new edition is intended as a primary instruction tool for those who either want to become supervisors or want to improve the present levels of their supervisory skills and knowledge. Users will find this text an excellent introduction to management functions and principles as these apply to the supervisory level of management. It is designed for use in community colleges, in various in-house industry and trade association courses, and in supervisory management programs.

The text's primary goals are to keep the students' interest; to explain management principles and theories with examples, terms and situations that are understandable to beginners; and to translate these principles and theories into tools that can be used in the everyday practice of management. Management principles and their application to actual on-the-job situations are presented clearly and concisely.

New in This Edition

The major revisions in this sixth edition are as follows:

- A boxed feature, "News You Can Use," translates business headlines into practical applications for the supervisor. One appears at the middle of each chapter.
- Vocabulary terms have been highlighted in the margins next to the paragraphs in which they are first defined.

- An experiential exercise called "Incident" has been added to the back of each chapter between the questions for discussion and the case problems.

- The suggested readings at the end of each chapter include books and periodicals currently available in nearly all college libraries.

- Updated and new topics include communications, motivation, appraisals, applicant screening, discrimination in employment, time management, team management, security, coping with stress, new federal laws, and working with computers.

- Thanks to special arrangement between Allyn & Bacon and the Bureau of Business Practice, the *Supervisor's Bulletin* is available to both teachers and students with the adoption of this text. Qualified adopters are eligible for a free subscription for each term for which this text is used. Also available for students is a special edition of the text packaged with copies of the *Supervisor's Bulletin,* and a discounted subscription rate offer. Contact your Allyn & Bacon representative for full details.

In addition to the new features, each chapter continues to include the following pedagogical tools to aid students in the study and retention of the chapter's major concepts:

A topical outline that begins each chapter, showing the major and their minor headings.

Learning Objectives: specifications to aid the student in identifying and mastering the chapter's key concepts.

Key Terms: words and phrases listed at the beginning of each chapter, defined within the chapter, and contained in end-of-chapter and end-of-book glossaries.

Introduction: a brief highlight of the chapter's theme.

All visual representations of data are now called "Exhibits," eliminating the confusion between figures and tables.

Instant Replay: a list of the chapter's key concepts for review and study preparation.

Suggested Readings: books and articles for further explorations of chapter topics.

Glossary: key terms listed and defined in an end-of-chapter glossary.

Questions for Class Discussion: questions to help students review the chapter's learning objectives.

■ Case Problems: problems (nearly all of which are based on the actual experiences of supervisors) that allow students to apply the chapter's key concepts through real-world situations.

Supplementary Material

The Instructor's Manual includes chapter outlines, two additional cases for each chapter with suggested solutions, answers to the text's questions for class discussion and its cases, a vocabulary review for each chapter's key terms, thirty true/false and thirty multiple choice questions, with answers. The Allyn & Bacon Test Manager is also available for IBM and compatible systems in either a $5\frac{1}{4}''$ or $3\frac{1}{2}''$ format.

Acknowledgments

Various individuals have been most helpful in the development of this sixth edition, and all previous editions. Their reviews and suggestions have provided the insight needed to update and expand this text. I would like to acknowledge the following people for their help on this edition: Jerry Boles, Western Kentucky University; Carl F. Jenks, Purdue University; Win Chesney, St. Louis Community College; and Raymond F. Balcerzak, Jr., Ferris State University. Plus, I would like to acknowledge the help of the following people on the previous editions:

Ray Ackerman, East Texas State University; Thomas Auer, Murray State University; Richard Baker, Mohave Community College; Gregory Barnes, Purdue University; James Baskfield, North Hennepin Community College; Charles Beavin, Miami–Dade Community College; James Bishop, Arkansas State University; Frederick Blake, Bee County College; Raymond Bobillo, Purdue University; Arthur Boisselle, Pikes Peak Community College; Jerry Boles, Western Kentucky University; Terry Bordan, CUNY–Hostos Community College; Joe Breeden, Kansas Technical Institute; Robin Butler, Lakeshore Technical Institute; Leonard Callahan, Daytona Beach Community College; Donald Caruth, East Texas State University; Donald S. Carver, National University; Joseph Castelli, College of San Mateo; Joseph Chandler, Indiana–Purdue University at Fort Wayne; Jackie Conway, Lenoir Community College; Roger Crowe, State Technical Institute at Knoxville; E. Jane Dews, San Jacinto College–South; Michael Dougherty, Milwaukee Area Technical College; M. J. Duffey, Lord Fairfax Community College; C. S. "Pete" Everett, Des Moines Area Community College; Lawrence Finley, Western Kentucky University; Ethel Fishman, Fashion Institute of Technology; Jack Fleming, Moorpark College; Randall Scott Frederick, Delgado Community College; Daphne Friday, Sacred Heart College; Olene Fuller, San Jacinto College–North; Alfonso Garcia, Navajo Community College;

John Geubtner, Tacoma Community College; Tommy Gilbreath, University of Texas at Tyler; Cliff Goodwin, Indiana University–Purdue University; Edward Gott, Jr., Eastern Maine Vocational Technical Institute; Luther Guynes, Los Angeles City College; Ed Hart, Elizabethtown Community College; JoAnn Hendricks, City College of San Francisco; Steven Herendeen, Indiana–Purdue University at Fort Wayne; Ron Herrick, Mesa Community College; Karen Heuer, Des Moines Area Community College; Larry Hill, San Jacinto College; Larry Holliday, Southwest Wisconsin Vocational Technical Institute; Eugene Holmen, Essex Community College; David Hunt, Blackhawk Technical Institute; Tonya Hynds, Purdue University–Kokomo; Jim Jackson, Johnston Technical College; William Jacobs, Lake City Community College; Joseph James, Jr., Lamar University–Port Arthur; F. Mike Kaufman; George Kelley, Erie Community College–City Campus; Billy Kirkland, Tarleton State University; Steve Kirman, Dyke College; Jay Knippen, University of South Flordia; Thomas Leet, Purdue University; James Lewis, Gateway Technical Institute; Marvin Long, New River Community College; Doris Lux, Central Community College–Platte; Joseph Manno, Montgomery College; Manuel Mena, SUNY College at Oswego; Michael Miller, Indiana University–Purdue University at Fort Wayne; Jerry Moller, Frank Phillip's College; Sherry Montgomery, Saint Philip's College; Charles Moore, Neosho County Community College; Herff Moore, University of Central Arkansas; Jim Nestor, Daytona Beach Community College; Gerard Nistal, Our Lady of Holy Cross College; Carolyn Patton, Stephen F. Austin State University; Jean Perry, Contra Costa College; Donald Pettit, Suffolk County Community College; Jerome Pilewski, University of Pittsburgh at Titusville; Sharon Pinebrook, University of Houston; Peter Randrup, WorWic Technical Community College; Ed Raskin, Los Angeles Mission College; William Recker, Northern Kentucky University; Robert Redick, Lincoln Land Community College; James A. Reinemann, College of Lake County; Tom Reynolds, Southside Virginia Community College; Harriett Rice, Los Angeles City College; Ralph Rice, Mayland Technical College; Shirley Rickert, Indiana University–Purdue University at Fort Wayne; Charles Roegiers, University of South Dakota; Lloyd Roettger, Indiana Vocational Technical College; Pat Rothamel, Iowa Western Community College; Robert Sedwick, Fairleigh Dickinson University; Sandra Seppamaki, Tanana Valley Community College; David Shepard, Virginia Western Community College; David Shufeldt, Clayton State College; David Smith, Dabney Lancaster Community College; Carl Sonntag, Pikes Peak Community College; Frank Sotrines, Washburn University; William Steiden, Jefferson Community College Southwest; Greg Stephens, Kansas Tech; John Stepp, Greenville Technical College; Marge Sunderland, Fayetteville Technical Institute; George Sutcliffe, Central Piedmont Community College; Wes Van Loon, Matanuska–Susitan Community College; Mike Vijuk, William Rainey Harper College; Hal Ward, Temple Junior College; Willie Weaver, Amarillo

College; George White, Ohlone College; Ron Williams, Merced College; Willie Williams, Tidewater Community College; Bob Willis, Rogers State College; Ira Wilsker, Lamar University; Paul Wolff II, Dundalk Community College; Richard Wong, Olympic College; Robert Wood, Vance–Granville Community College; Charles Yauger, Arkansas State University.

Suggestions to the Students

I envy all of you for the fun and the challenge you are about to experience. I congratulate you on your ambition and foresight in choosing a very fascinating course of study: the management of people.

Do not hide your talents. Share your experiences with your class, and soon you will realize how valuable your personal experiences have been to yourself—and how valuable they may be to your classmates.

You can expect to find a frequent and almost immediate use for almost everything you learn in the management course. If you are already a manager, you can apply the lessons at work. If you are not one yet, study your boss. If your boss is highly qualified, you will soon be able to see why this is so. If he or she is not, you will learn what is wrong with his or her performance. More important, you will also know what mistakes you should *not* make. Often the example of a poorly qualified boss can provide an excellent learning experience.

Never seek to conceal your own ignorance about the task of being a supervisor. Admit to yourself that you have a lot to learn, as we all do. Only by recognizing a void in your knowledge can you hope to fill it. And the proper way to fill it is by studying and expanding your work experience. If you ask questions in class as they occur to you, you will avoid the old problem of missing out on important pieces of information. You must take the initiative. Quite possibly, some questions that are bothering you might also concern others in the class. The more you contribute to the course, the more you will receive from it.

From now on, you should think of yourself as a supervisor. Throughout this book, I will be talking to you as one supervisor to another. In the following pages you will find many tools—the tools of supervision. Their uses are explained in detail. A skilled worker knows his or her tools and knows which one is right for each task. When you complete this course, you will have the knowledge you need to be a successful supervisor. You should put this knowledge to use as soon as possible. During the course, you will probably have a chance to present one of the case problems to your classmates. This is a fine opportunity to test yourself on how to apply the principles of supervision to a concrete situation in the world of work. You may also find other applications of these principles, both at home and on the job. Do not overlook them.

Good luck!

I The Big Picture

Part I contains five chapters designed to introduce you to the supervisor's special place in management and the essentials that all managers have in common. Chapter 1 focuses on the unique problems of being a supervisor in any kind of organization. The special skills, responsibilities, roles, and attributes required of supervisors are examined in detail.

Chapter 2 concerns you and your future. Where you will be next year and five years from now is largely for you to determine. What you must have are goals, a plan for your advancement, the necessary resources the plan calls for, and the commitment to translate your dreams into action. Personal growth through educational programs and on-the-job experiences must be considered as part of your planning strategy. This chapter will help you to assess your strengths and weaknesses and to plan the evolution of your career.

Chapter 3 defines management as both an activity and a team of people. The concepts of authority, power, responsibility, and accountability are defined and illustrated, along with the three levels of management. The basic steps for making effective decisions and managing time are examined.

Chapter 4 covers the essential management functions of planning, organizing, leading, and controlling as they relate to all levels of management and to the supervisor in particular. The basic principles and tools that apply to each function are examined along with the ways in which supervisors can put them to use.

The unit concludes with an overview and a discussion of the specifics of communicating—the art of getting your ideas into the minds of others. Communicating is at the heart of all your efforts and activities. It is the most basic process performed by every manager in every organization, and it is governed by principles and procedures—the most essential of which are explored in this chapter. Chapter 5 also includes an analysis of the common barriers that prevent you from getting your messages across, tips for more successful spoken and written communication, and a discussion of how supervisors can cope with the grapevine, or informal communications network, that exists in every working environment.

1

The Supervisor's Special Role

Outline

Objectives

After reading and discussing this chapter, you should be able to do the following:

1 Define this chapter's key terms.

2 List and define the three management skills every supervisor must possess and apply.

3 List the three groups to whom the supervisor is responsible and what those responsibilities are.

4 Explain the concepts of effectiveness and efficiency as they apply to a supervisor's performance.

5 List the rewards for successful supervision that a supervisor has the right to expect.

Key Terms

foreman

linking pin

management skills

peer

role ambiguity

role conflict

role prescription

sanction

supervisor

team adviser

Introduction

Supervisor
One who oversees the work of non-management people (workers)

Foreman
A supervisor of workers in manufacturing

A **supervisor** is a manager whose subordinates are nonmanagement employees (called *workers*). The term **foreman** may be used interchangeably with the word *supervisor*. In common usage, the word *foreman* usually refers to a supervisor of workers who perform manufacturing activities.

Being a first-level supervisor is one of the most difficult, demanding, and challenging jobs in any organization. Buried in an organizational web, this person must be adroit at administering a unit and at perceiving which, among all the daily tasks delegated downward, are the most important to accomplish. Through such administrative competence, he or she must be able to link the unit's accomplishments to the functioning of other organizational subunits.[1]

The supervisor is the person in the middle, caught between the workers and higher-level managers. Both groups differ in their attitudes, values, and priorities and in the demands they make on the supervisor. Demands from workers and other managers create conflicts in both emotions and loyalties. The supervisor must work to maintain a balance between these two groups and to gain a sense of job satisfaction and identity in the process. To a great extent, the goals of the organization and its subunits will be reached or missed as a direct result of how well the supervisors are managing and relating to their subordinates.

Professors Sasser and Leonard from the Harvard Business School specialize in business administration and the roles of supervisors. Here is their definition: "A supervisor not only commands, directs, controls, and inspects, but also takes responsibility for, leads, shepherds, administers, guides, consults, and cares for."[2]

Our final definition of a supervisor comes from two federal laws. The Taft-Hartley Act of 1947 says that any person in authority who can hire, suspend, transfer, lay off, recall, promote, discharge, assign, reward, or discipline other employees while using independent judgment is a supervisor. The Fair Labor Standards Act of 1938 states that supervisors may not use more than 20 percent of their time performing the same kind of work that their subordinates perform and that they must be paid other than an hourly wage.

Today, the operating or supervisory level of management is probably receiving greater attention and emphasis throughout industry than ever before. This is due primarily to a wealth of research and information published in recent years that points out the unique impact of supervisors on productivity and profitability. We shall examine some of this research and information in this chapter and in the ones that follow.

Three Types of Management Skills

Management skills
Categories of capabilities needed by all managers at every level in an organization

No matter how supervisors are defined, they routinely must apply basic skills. According to Robert L. Katz, a college professor of business administration, corporate director, and management consultant, the basic **management skills** required of all managers at every level in an organization can be grouped under three headings: human, technical, and conceptual. Managers at different levels in an organization will use one or another of these skills to a greater or lesser degree, depending upon the managers' positions in the organization and the particular demands of the circumstances they find themselves in at any given time. See Exhibit 1.1.

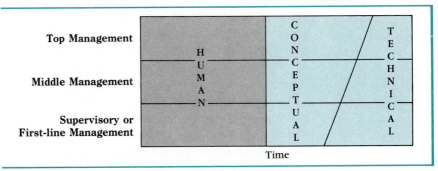

Exhibit 1.1   **The proportions of management skills needed at the three levels of management.**

Human Skills

Human skills can be subdivided into two parts: (1) leadership ability within a manager's own unit and (2) skill in intergroup relationships. Human skills determine the manager's ability to work effectively as a group member and to build cooperative effort within the group he or she leads and between that group and all the other groups with which it comes into contact.[3]

Supervisors who have developed human skills know themselves well; are tolerant and understanding of the viewpoints, attitudes, perceptions, and beliefs of others; and are skillful communicators. People with human skills are honest and open. They create an atmosphere in which others feel free to express their ideas, and they make every effort to determine how intended actions will affect others in the organization. Supervisors who once held their subordinates' jobs have empathy for them—the ability to relate to what they are experiencing and feeling.

Managers at every level need human skills, but such skills are particularly important to supervisors because they must create harmony within and among the heterogeneous mixture of people so often found in worker groups. Many supervisors are experiencing the influx of minorities, women, and younger workers for the first time. Our more highly mobile work force, our higher retirement ages, and our rapidly changing society have all placed new strains and demands on managers at every level.

The following quotation from an upper-level manager summed up the way twenty-five managers of supervisors felt in a recent study: "Being able to work with people is the most important characteristic a first-level supervisor can have. I can buy technological expertise, but it's hard to find someone with good, basic communication skills."[4]

Human skills are your most important set of skills, regardless of how high you climb up an organization's management ladder. Your job as a manager at any level is to get work done with and through others. If you cannot relate to individuals, if you cannot see or have time for their personal points of view, you will have trouble getting them to cooperate.

Practicing human skills means taking time to listen to your subordinates, your boss, and others with whom you must deal. Assigning work to your people with a request rather than a direct order not only will be an exercise in good manners but also will encourage them to be polite. When you show respect for others and their feelings, you get it in return. Such an approach invites questions that can only help to clarify some aspect of your instructions or of their duties that they find difficult to understand or execute. More will be said about the specifics of putting your human skills to work in chapters 5 and 8.

Technical Skills

Managers with technical skills understand and are proficient in specific kinds of activity. Their expertise may be in computer programming or repair, in utilizing precision equipment and tools, or in design and drafting. Any technical skill requires its practitioner to know procedures, processes, and methods. "Technical skill involves specialized knowledge, analytical ability within that specialty, and facility in the use of the tools and techniques of the specific discipline."[5] Technical skills are the primary concern of training in industry and in vocational education programs.

Technical skills are essential to supervisors for several reasons. Supervisors' influence over subordinates comes to them in part because of their technical competence. They must be able to do the work that they supervise, and they must be able to train others to do it. Without an understanding of their unit's machinery, equipment, procedures, and practices, they cannot adequately maintain it or evaluate their subordinates' performances properly. As with human skills, technological skills can be learned and developed.

Practicing technical skills requires that you first possess them at a level sufficient to apply them and to pass them along to others. Many supervisors are promoted from a highly skilled job and then must turn around and supervise others who apply those same skills. If you are such a person, you have sound experience in skill applications. Such experience will prove quite useful to you when directing others who use those skills. But you will no longer have to execute your skills on the job, as you did as a worker. Your task is to get those you supervise to be as proficient as they can be in the execution of their skills. You, as a supervisor, should not do the work that your subordinates do. You are being paid to see to it that *they* do *their* jobs, with any assistance they may require from you.

Some supervisors are appointed or brought in from jobs that did not give them first-hand experience with the application of the skills their subordinates must exercise. If this is your situation, lacking first-hand experience will mean that you must gain sufficient knowledge to understand the skills required and how they are to be applied. Company training programs, outside classes, reading, and discussions with others who possess the skills can help to fill the gap. Workers who lack sufficient skills can learn through much the same methods. When training cannot be undertaken by a company, extra care must be taken to hire only those who have the necessary skills. But before hiring such people, the person or persons responsible for hiring them should possess an in-depth knowledge of the position or positions that are to be filled.

Conceptual Skills

Supervisors with conceptual skills are able to view their organizations as a whole with many parts, all of which are interrelated and interdependent. Executives must be able to perceive their company as a part of its industry, its community, and the nation's economy.[6] Supervisors must be able to perceive their sections as part of, and contributors to, other sections and the entire organization. Every decision made by every manager has the potential of creating a ripple effect that may influence others outside the particular decision maker's control.

Consider this example from a supervisor in a plastics molding plant. Charlie noticed a malfunction in one of his injection molding machines. Upon inspection he found that the machine had not been maintained properly. He immediately stopped the production line, called a meeting of his production people, and proceeded to berate them for failing to maintain their equipment. His shouting lasted over thirty minutes, causing his people to miss about ten minutes of their lunch break and making Charlie late by about twenty minutes for a meeting with his boss.

The temptation is great for most supervisors to take the first course of action that appears to be valid, when attempting to solve problems or make decisions. This quick-fix approach, more often than not, leads to difficulties later. Any ripple effect that results from this approach is likely to be negative in its impact on others in the organization, as long as there is an absence of concern about how the solution will affect them.

Acquiring a conceptual point of view becomes increasingly important as you climb higher on the management ladder. An employer must provide means for you as a supervisor to know what is happening in other parts of the company than just your own and must do so before changes are implemented. Memos, reports, committee meetings, supervisory workshops, and regular meetings with your boss will keep you informed as to how the output from your sector affects and will affect other supervisors' sectors and the company as a whole. Keep in touch with fellow supervisors, and read the official correspondence that flows across your desk. Doing so will make you a team player and will help you avoid surprises that are unpleasant for both you and your boss.

The Supervisor's Responsibilities

Supervisors have responsibilities to three primary groups: (1) their subordinates: (2) their peers in management; and 3) their superiors in management. They must work in harmony with all three groups, if they are to be effective supervisors.

Relations with Subordinates

The responsibilities supervisors have to their subordinates are many and varied. To begin with, supervisors *must* get to know their subordinates as individual human beings. Each subordinate, like his or her supervisor, has specific needs and wants. Each of us has certain expectations from work, certain goals we wish to achieve through work, and fundamental attitudes and aptitudes that influence our performances at work. When supervisors get to know each subordinate as an individual, they are able to approach each person in a specific, careful way.

One of the first principles of good communications (see chapter 5) is to keep your audience in mind when you attempt to communicate. If you are to be effective in your dealing with another person, you should know as much about that person as you can *before* attempting to communicate any message.

Subordinates want to know that their supervisors care about them and are prepared to do something about their problems. A sure sign that supervisors care about their subordinates is common courtesy—using a person's name, a respectful tone of voice, personalized greetings, and sincere inquiries about the subordinate's health and well-being.

Getting to know subordinates well can be difficult. Some people are easy to know, while others are not. In addition, you can never really know your subordinates thoroughly for long because most people develop and change with the passage of time and with new experiences in life and on the job. These obstacles, however, should not be used as excuses to avoid trying to know your subordinates. Rather, such difficulties should be viewed as barriers that can be overcome through a sincere effort and openness on your part.

You will get to know your subordinates well only if you spend time with them and become familiar with their problems. Study each subordinate's personnel file. Talk to each person whenever you get a chance. If contacts with your people are informal, use the time for some casual conversation about them and what is going on in their lives. A sincere interest on your part usually results in open responses from them. If contacts are formal, start out with a personal greeting, get through the formal communications of orders or instructions, and then end on a friendly note. For example, you might say, ''Well, I've had my say; is there anything you want to talk about?'' Only after you have a good understanding of each subordinate can you expect to be successful in your dealings with them.

Additional responsibilities supervisors have to their subordinates include the following:

- Tailoring jobs to fit the job holder or finding people who are well equipped to handle their duties
- Standing behind your people when they act under your orders or with your permission
- Providing them with constructive criticism and adequate instruction, training, and evaluation
- Handling their complaints and problems in a fair and just way
- Safeguarding their health and welfare while they are on the job
- Providing an example of what good behavior on the job should be like
- Praising them for work well done

These are just a few of the many responsibilities supervisors have to their subordinates. If such obligations are carried out well, the supervisors will be looked upon by their subordinates as leaders. Such supervisors gain the respect of their subordinates, and this is the key to effective supervision and personal achievement. Your subordinates represent the most important group to whom and for whom you are responsible.

Relations with Peers

All managers at the same level of management, with similar levels of authority and status, are **peers.** As a supervisor, your peers are your fellow supervisors throughout the company. They are the individuals with whom you must cooperate and coordinate if your department and theirs are to operate in harmony. Your peers directly or indirectly affect the outcome of your own operations. The reverse is true as well. Be on the lookout for ways to cement good working relationships with them and to

Peer
Person on the same organizational level as you are; one who possesses a similar level of status and authority

lend a hand to them when you can. In turn, you can expect assistance from them when you need it.

Your peers normally constitute the bulk of your friends and associates at work. If they do not, you should suspect that something is wrong with your relationships with them, and you should take steps to correct the situation. Your peers represent an enormous pool of talent and experience that will be yours to tap and to contribute to, if they view you in a favorable way. For this reason alone, it is to your advantage to cultivate their friendship both on and off the job. Your peers can teach you a great deal about the company, and they are often a fine source of advice on how to handle difficult situations that may arise. They can do more to keep you out of trouble than any other group in the company. In so many ways you need each other, and both you and they stand to benefit from a partnership or alliance based on mutual respect and the need to resolve common problems.

Your responsibilities to your peers include the following:

- Knowing and understanding each of them as individuals
- Approaching and cooperating with each of them as individuals
- Providing what help you can to enable them to achieve the measure of satisfaction they desire from their jobs
- Fostering a spirit of cooperation and teamwork between yourself and all your peers

Your success as a supervisor is linked to your peers and to what they think of you as a person and a supervisor. Your personal and professional reputation with them is important. If they think highly of you, they will be drawn to you and be willing to associate with you. They will give freely of their time and energy on your behalf.

If you are off in your own little world or are unwilling to share your knowledge and know-how, you deny yourself the growth and experience that your peers stand ready to offer. As a result, you may be labeled as uncooperative or antisocial and destined, at best, for a career as just a supervisor. People in higher positions in business as a rule have no need for withdrawn or isolated managers. You will discover (if you have not already done so) that, the more you give of what you have, the more you will receive from others.

Relations with Superiors

Your responsibilities to your superiors, both line and staff, can be summarized as follows:

- Transmitting information about problems, along with recommendations for solving them
- Operating within your budget and respecting company policy
- Promoting the company's goals
- Striving for efficiency whenever and wherever possible
- Preparing records and reports on time and in the proper form
- Using the company's resources effectively
- Scheduling work so as to meet deadlines
- Showing respect and cooperation

If you are a supervisor, your boss or supervisor is a middle manager who is accountable for your actions. Your boss is similar to you in being both a follower and a staff or line manager. He or she executes all the functions of management and is evaluated on the basis of his or her subordinates' performances. Like you, your boss must develop and maintain sound working relationships with his or her subordinates, peers, and superiors. Moreover, your boss has probably served an apprenticeship as a supervisor, so you can probably count on his or her understanding of your own situation.

Your superiors should be consulted, and their advice should be followed. To your boss, you owe allegiance and respect. You must be a loyal follower if you intend to be a successful leader. To the company's team of staff specialists, you are like a laboratory through which their ideas and recommendations are implemented. Chapter 8 has more to say about how you can get along with and cooperate with your peers and superiors in management.

Being Effective and Efficient

Managers at every level are expected to practice the skills outlined above effectively and efficiently. *Effectiveness* is defined by noted management author and consultant Peter Drucker as "doing the right thing."[7] Doing the right thing means not spending time and energy on tasks that can wait until later while avoiding tasks that must be done now. It also means (for a supervisor) selecting the right goal and the appropriate means to achieve that goal. Doing the right thing demands that managers at every level plan their work, set priorities, stick to their plans, and execute their duties in a timely manner. An *ineffective* manager gets work done late, is not where he or she should be, and receives poor performance ratings from superiors.

Efficiency is defined as doing things right. The efficient supervisor gets the task done with a minimal expense of time, money, and other resources. The efficient supervisor avoids waste of all kinds. The *inefficient* supervisor spends too much of one thing or several things in executing tasks. The inefficient supervisor also receives poor performance ratings and places future operations in jeopardy because the needed resources may not be available—having been consumed excessively to complete earlier operations.

Clearly, a supervisor must be both effective and efficient. Effectiveness is probably the more important of the two, because essential tasks will get done. Effectiveness with inefficiency can often be tolerated by organizations, at least in the short run. But efficiency without effectiveness is not tolerable, even in the short run: essentials remain undone, and vital work is left incomplete.

Supervisory Roles

Like actors who have to learn their parts well, all supervisors are expected to learn and play specific parts or roles in order to execute their duties successfully. The precise role of each supervisor depends on his or her understanding of the job he or she holds, as well as on the pressures, rewards, and guidelines brought to bear on him or her from inside and outside the organization. What follows is a brief but important discussion of the ways in which roles are assigned to, designed for, and perceived by each supervisor in a business enterprise. The author is indebted to Robert L. Kahn and his associates[8] and to Professor John B. Miner[9] for much of this discussion.

Role Prescriptions

Role prescription
The collection of expectations and demands from superiors, subordinates, and others that shapes a manager's job description and perception of his or her job

The subordinates, peers, friends, family, and superiors of supervisors help shape and define the kind of roles the supervisors play and the way in which they play them. Demands made on the supervisors by these groups and by the business organization in which the supervisors work prescribe the roles (or write out **role prescriptions**) for them to follow as they define and play out their roles at work. Through the expectations and demands placed on the supervisors, people help shape each supervisor's perception of his or her job. Organizational influences—such as policies, procedures, job descriptions, and the union contract—also exert influence on the roles of each supervisor. Of course, the demands of different people and of the organization itself can and do create conflicts in the minds of supervisors as to just what their roles should be and how precisely they should play them.

Professor and researcher Henry Mintzberg describes all management behavior with ten roles (see Exhibit 1.2). The ten roles were developed through close observations of five chief executives for a two-week period. Mintzberg found that different managers emphasized different roles and spent varying amounts of time on each, depending on their personalities, on the job at hand, and on the situation. All supervisors play these roles to greater or lesser degrees as they interact with others, inform their subordinates and bosses, and make decisions.

Role Conflict

Role conflict
A situation that occurs when contradictory or opposing demands are made on a manager

When conflicting and contradictory demands are made on supervisors, they find themselves in awkward or difficult positions. How they react to such pressures and what precisely they do to cope with such conflicts depend on their own values and perceptions and on the circumstances of the **role conflicts**. Consider the following incident that happened in a suburb north of Chicago. Two paramedics discovered a conflict between the instructions in their medical manual and the provisions of Illinois law about the proper method of treatment for heart-attack victims. If the paramedics followed their manual, they believed they would be in violation of state law. If they followed the law, however, they believed they would be giving incorrect or outmoded treatment to their patients. Perplexed, they asked their hospital administrator for clarification of the treatment procedures. To their surprise, they received in reply a letter that called them incompetent and suspended them from their duties as paramedics! This example highlights a common job situation, in which an employee's training in organizational procedures contradicts the demands of the immediate boss. Role conflicts can and do occur, and when they do, they create tensions and job dissatisfaction for the employees.

Role Ambiguity

Role ambiguity
The situation that occurs whenever a manager is uncertain about the role that he or she is expected to play

Whenever a supervisor is not sure of the role he or she is expected to play in a given situation or how to play it, he or she is a victim of **role ambiguity.** Role conflict results from clearly contradictory demands. Role ambiguity results from unclear or nonexistent job descriptions, orders, rules, policies, or procedures. Where role ambiguity exists, supervisors may do things they should not do, may fail to do things they should do, and may find it hard to distinguish where one manager's job begins and another's ends.

Role	Description	Identifiable Activities from Study of Chief Executives
Interpersonal		
Figurehead	Symbolic head; obliged to perform a number of routine duties of legal or social nature	Ceremony, status, requests, solicitations
Leader	Responsible for the motivation and activation of subordinates; responsible for staffing, training, and associated duties	Virtually all managerial activities involving subordinates
Liaison	Maintains self-developed network of outside contacts and informers who provide favors and information	Acknowledgements of mail, external board work, other activities involving outsiders
Informational		
Monitor	Seeks and receives wide variety of special information to develop thorough understanding of the organization and environment; emerges as nerve center of internal and external information of the organization	Handling all mail and contacts concerned primarily with receiving information
Disseminator	Transmits information received from outsiders or from subordinates to members of the organization; some information factual, some involving interpretation and integration	Forwarding mail into organization for informational purposes, verbal contacts involving information flow to subordinates

Exhibit 1.2   **Mintzberg's ten management roles.** (*Source:* Chart from *The Nature of Managerial Work* by Henry Mintzberg. Copyright © 1973 by Henry Mintzberg. Reprinted by permission of HarperCollins Publishers.)

Role Performance

Even if there is no role conflict or role ambiguity, supervisors may still fail to meet the demands of their role prescriptions for one or more of the following reasons:

Role	Description	Identifiable Activities from Study of Chief Executives
Informational		
Spokesman	Transmits information to outsiders on organization's plans, policies, actions, results, and so forth; serves as expert on organization's industry	Board meetings, handling mail and contacts involving transmission of information to outsiders
Decisional		
Entrepreneur	Searches organization and its environment for opportunities, and initiates projects to bring about change	Strategy and review sessions involving initiation or design of improvement projects
Disturbance Handler	Responsible for corrective action when organization faces important, unexpected disturbances	Strategy and review involving disturbances and crises
Resource Allocator	Responsible for the allocation of organizational resources of all kinds—in effect the making or approving of all significant organizational decisions	Scheduling, requests for authorization, any activity involving budgeting and the programming of subordinates' work
Negotiator	Responsible for representing the organization at major negotiations	Negotiation

Exhibit 1.2   *(cont.)*

1. Supervisors may not perceive their jobs in the way specified by the role prescriptions.
2. Supervisors may not want to behave in the way specified by the role prescriptions.
3. Supervisors may not have the knowledge, mental ability, or physical skills needed to behave in the way specified by the role prescriptions.[10]

Role Sanctions

To encourage supervisors at all levels to play their roles in accord with the role prescriptions established by their superiors, business organizations often make use of positive incentives or rewards. If the rewards for proper role playing prove to be ineffective, the superiors may use negative means to secure conformity. Such means, which may include threats or actual punishments, are known as **sanctions.** If a business organization does not provide adequate sanctions, the roles played by various supervisors and the ways in which they understand them may deviate widely from their superiors' role prescriptions. Unless people want to play their roles as prescribed or feel that they have no real alternatives to doing so, they will usually tailor the roles they play to suit themselves.

> Where role behavior deviates from role prescriptions because of faulty role perceptions or insufficient role capacity, the usual solution is either to provide more information or to alter the individual's role prescriptions so that he [or she] can meet them. Where motivation is lacking or inappropriate, it is typical to manipulate sanctions with a view to inducing a greater desire to act in accord with role requirements.[11]

Sanction
Negative means, such as threats or punishments, used by superiors or the organization to encourage subordinates to play their roles as prescribed by superiors or the organization

Supervisors as Linking Pins

Because human beings are social animals, you need to consider some recent theories about how people interact in a social organization such as a business enterprise and how the role of individual supervisors is shaped and influenced by other managers. These theories will add greatly to your understanding of the behavior of people on the job.

Most business organizations contain many people who interact with one another on a regular basis, both individually and in groups. The typical organizational chart shows a division of labor among individuals employed by the organization to accomplish its tasks. It also shows certain key individuals who head up and link the independent groups within the organization. These key individuals are often called **linking pins** because, as members of two or more groups, they link or lock these groups together.[12] Consider the following situation. A supervisor is the organizational leader of a working section but is also the subordinate of a middle manager. Each supervisor, therefore, is a member of at least two groups: a working section or department, and a group of fellow supervisors (peers) who report to the same middle manager. In turn, the middle manager is in charge of a group of supervisors, and he or she is also a member of a group of middle management peers who report to a member of the top management of the company.

As Exhibit 1.3 shows, Supervisor C is a member of three groups: (1) Middle Manager B's department; (2) the group of B's subordinate supervi-

Linking pin
Key individual who is a member of two or more formal groups in an organization, thus linking or connecting the groups

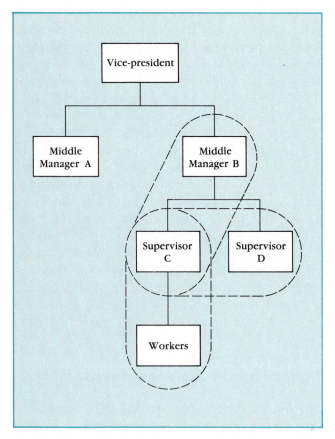

Exhibit 1.3 Use of an organization chart to identify linking pins—where the circles linking group members overlap, you have a linking pin.

sors, who are Supervisor C's peers; and (3) Supervisor C's own working section. The circles that overlap Supervisor C in the figure reveal that he or she is a linking pin—that is, a manager who joins together three groups and who can serve as a communications link and coordinator between and among them.

Supervisors as Team Advisers

The strong trend of the 1990s has been in the direction of letting workers participate in the planning and execution of their tasks. Supervisors in every industry are increasingly called upon to share their management authority with their subordinates. What has emerged is the "team management'' concept, which, simply put, creates a team out of workers and their supervisor and allows for joint decision making, problem identification, and problem solving. The supervisor becomes a **team adviser**, sharing responsibility with the team for ''cost, quality, and on-time delivery of the product. So [supervisors] must train their teams to manage the production process, including work assignments, and to solve the problems that crop up along the way, rather than provide solutions themselves.''[13]

Team adviser
Supervisor managing a team of people who share his or her formal authority and who jointly run their operations in terms of decision making and problem solving

Team advisers become facilitators—making certain that the team has the resources it needs when they are needed, arranging the meetings where information is passed along and ideas put to use, representing the team's views and concerns to others, and helping to settle disputes. To be an effective team adviser, you must be skilled at presenting your ideas in a group setting, at running different kinds of meetings, at sharing your skills and knowledge willingly and freely, at turning decision making into a learning experience for all team members, and at taking control in a crisis.[14] Chapter 9 has more to say about team management and about what is involved in being a successful team adviser and coach.

Current Trends Affecting Supervisors

One thing is certain: the demands being made on today's supervisors are growing in complexity. Great changes are taking place in both our work force and our places of work. A brief look at some major trends will indicate a few of the problems and opportunities they represent for all of us.

Information and Technology

Our economy is experiencing dramatic and fundamental changes in the ways in which business is conducted and in the ways in which people are employed. The vast majority of working Americans now earn their living by creating, processing, and distributing information. Innovations in communications and computer technology have displaced thousands of workers and opened thousands of opportunities to them. Today our homes, automobiles, offices, and factories depend on electronics and computer chips to perform their most basic functions. The power of computers is now at the fingertips of the majority of working people.

Portable laptop computers, cellular telephones, laser printers, and fax machines are the hallmarks of a modern office. Automobiles come equipped with voice-activated telephones, computers, printers, and fax machines. Their portability frees managers from their desks and allows them to take their technology with them. Meetings are being held by cable television, eliminating many business trips and their corresponding expenses. Electronic mail links people within a building and their counterparts in different states and countries. In 1990, Wal-Mart Stores Inc., the giant discount chain, informed its suppliers that it was adopting electronic data interchange (EDI) and if they desired to continue selling their goods to Wal-Mart, they would have to adopt it too.[15] EDI allows for instantaneous transfer of electronic data between points, eliminating communication delays between suppliers and purchasers, engineers and product design teams, and professionals and clients.

The most competitive manufacturers have put the power of computers to use through *CAD/CAM* (computer-aided design/computer-aided manufacturing), which offers their best hope for future increases in quality, competitiveness, productivity, and profits. CAD allows draftspeople and engineers to design, analyze, and test products entirely by means of computers and their video displays. Without putting pencil to paper, researchers can put new products through the rigors of testing, thus saving great amounts of time and dollars that would otherwise be invested in building and testing a prototype. CAM has come to mean computer control of production tools and machines. Both can be programmed and reprogrammed to work at a variety of tasks, providing users with dependable, predictable output at speeds no skilled person can match.

Robots are CAM machines that are capable of working every hour of every day with great speed and reliability. They have been used for work that is toxic, dangerous, repetitive, boring, or extremely precise. Robots have made it possible for very small businesses to enter highly competitive and labor-intensive industries with confidence. They have become our nation's ''steel collar'' workers, demanding sophisticated supervision by a new breed of managers with the latest in high-tech education.

Workers and Work Schedules

According to the U.S. Bureau of Labor Statistics, about 75 percent of all jobs in the United States are in the service sector, such as managerial and professional positions and jobs in sales, administrative support, repair, security, hospitality, and finance. About 6 percent of working men and women hold more than one job. By the year 2000, women will account for over 50 percent of the work force. African Americans, Hispanics, and Asians will account for over one-fourth of employed Americans by that year. Today's work force is mobile, middle-aged, and increasingly made up of other than full-time workers. About 20 percent of our nation's work force consists of part-time employees. Several trends are in evidence: job sharing, job splitting, permanent part-time jobs, and flextime.

Flextime allows people to work a core of hours but vary their starting

NEWS
You Can Use
The Bechtel Group, a construction and engineering firm, has 27,800 employees worldwide. In 1990 it created a flexible schedule for its employees in Houston, Texas. Under the plan, employees work nine-hour days, Monday through Thursday each week. Each Friday, about half the employees work eight hours, and the other half have the day off. All employees work eighty hours in nine days. Management initially feared that longer work days would mean lower productivity, but productivity has improved. Employees seemed to be scheduling more of their personal business for their off time. Absenteeism decreased, and worker responses to the new schedule seem to be most positive. How would you like to work under this schedule?

and ending times. A company may require all employees to be on the job from 10:00 A.M. until 1:00 P.M., but some may start at 6:00 A.M., 7:00 A.M., 8:00 A.M., or as late as 10:00 A.M. Some may go home as early as 1:00 P.M. Flexible scheduling appeals most to working women with families that include school-age children and to a growing number of self-managing information workers. But such work schedules make it difficult for one supervisor to manage people who work over a span of ten or more hours. As a result, supervisors have opted for flextime too. Such work schedules make weeks of four ten-hour days possible for many Americans.

Job sharing allows two or more people to work at one full-time job. Businesses have used job sharing with both management and worker positions. A growing number of people want to work part-time, while a growing number of businesses want more part-time employees. The employer benefits in several ways. It gets double the creativity for each shared job. It cuts payroll costs and pension expenses. People come to work refreshed and eager to perform. Workers experience less fatigue and stress. Boring jobs can become more attractive when performed for fewer than 40 hours each week.

Job splitting takes a job and cuts it in half. One part-time worker does one-half, and another part-time worker does the other half. There is no overlapping of duties. In supermarkets one person, usually of high-school age, is hired to stock shelves in the morning, and another is hired to stock in the evening. The two stock different merchandise in different aisles. Another approach involves one worker who replaces stock and another who prices it. All work less than forty hours each week.

Permanent part-time workers usually work for small companies that do not have enough work for a full-timer to perform. Part-time work may be for any number of hours and days per week, up to thirty-five hours or as many as four and a half days. In 1991, over one million jobs were filled each day in America by temporaries—people employed by a temporary help service, which assigns its people to work part-time for its clients who need temporary help. Most come well trained to their jobs and work in skilled areas such as computer services, secretarial, and accounting. Permanent part-time work appeals to older workers, women with families, and people working two jobs.

Education

According to the U.S. Census Bureau, about 75 percent of Americans over twenty-five years of age have currently completed high school, and about 25 percent of these have completed four or more years of college. About 18 million American households are headed by college graduates. Of these, 40 percent include a working wife. Today, over 50 percent of all college students are women.

The growing educational level of America's work force has brought brighter, more demanding employees to the ranks of both workers and management. Increasingly, people want a voice in planning and executing their work. They bring competence and skills to the workplace, and they desire growth through challenging work and meaningful tasks. They want to be listened to and to be respected as individuals with their own specific needs and goals.

Increasingly, we are becoming a lifetime-learning society. No longer can any of us rely on one employer or one career during our working lives. People can expect to make an average of ten to fifteen job changes and three to five career changes within their lifetimes. Each of us must be committed to programs that extend our skills and employment opportunities to make us truly ready for our next decade at work.

The Successful Supervisor

When executives are polled for the reasons that have led to their success, they list many things. Many surveys of executives have been made over the years, and they all seem to point to several factors that account for a successful management career: hard work, intelligence, communications skills, experience, integrity, concern for getting results, and a desire to achieve and to take responsibility. In the end, if you want to succeed in a career, you must be willing to commit the resources of time, money, and effort. You have to learn by doing and from your mistakes and those of others. Exhibit 1.4 describes the road to success in another way. It talks about the specific errors any manager can commit when attempting to supervise his or her subordinates. By being aware of the pitfalls identified in the exhibit, you can try to avoid them. Simply put them into positive, reverse statements to see what you should do.

Rewards for Successful Supervision

This chapter puts forth the basic concepts that you must know and apply to your work if you are to be a successful supervisor. Exercising the various sets of skills, carrying out your responsibilities to various groups, and exercising your many and varied roles will lead to success, and that success can bring you several rewards.

Pride

Personal awareness that you know your job, are doing it to the best of your abilities, and are working to improve comes to you in several ways. First, you know intuitively whether your work is good or not. It is either something you are proud of or something less. The various ways in which your subordinates respond to you—to your directions, to your help, to you as an individual—tell you whether in their eyes you are a success in human relations or you are not. Their openness or lack thereof will let you know to whom you appear as a good boss. Your boss in turn, if he or she is doing his or her job, will let you know informally each day and formally several times a year just how well you are doing. The pride that is essential to keep you growing and happy in your work comes from your subordinates and boss in the forms of cooperation and support. Your pride will affect your future work as well as the work of those around you. We all want to work for and with a person who has our respect and the respect of others that only comes from being both effective and efficient—in other words, a success.

Pay

Your formal appraisals from your boss spell out what you are doing well and what needs improvement. Your appraisals are the base needed for pay increases. Success in most organizations is linked to pay. If it is not

1. Try to be liked rather than respected.
2. Don't ask your subordinates for their advice and help.
3. Don't develop a sense of responsibility in your subordinates, and don't expect it from your peers.
4. Emphasize rules rather than skills among your employees, and thwart personal talent.
5. Don't keep criticism constructive.
6. Ignore employee complaints.
7. Keep people uninformed—not respecting their right to know.

Exhibit 1.4   **Seven deadly sins of supervision.** (*Source:* Reprinted with permission from *Success* magazine. Copyright 1987 by Hal Holdings Corporation.)

where you work, consider a change. Nothing is more harmful to a person's self-image than to see mediocre performers get the same pay increases as superior performers. However, with pay increases may come additional duties—duties that were formerly your boss's but that now become part of your routine. Welcome such increases, as they are the expression of your boss's confidence in you and are paving the way for future advancement.

Reputation

Your success on the job will enhance your reputation in the eyes of your subordinates, your boss, and your peers and in your own eyes as well. You will be known as a person who delivers the goods and who has the job well in hand. You will become a source of support and help in the eyes of others. You will have their trust and loyalty, provided that you do not let your success go to your head. Most people want to associate with a winner. Winners tend to move up, making room for those below them. True winners earn their rewards with a combination of hard work and the efforts of others. They do not forget to be grateful and to give credit where it is due.

Your good reputation can lead to bigger things with your present employer or with other employers. If you decide to seek employment elsewhere, your reputation will be the single most important recommendation you will have. If your former employer is sorry to lose you because you were a successful performer, your new employer will be anxious to get you.

Sources of Supervisory Personnel

Most employers look for supervisory personnel from one of two sources: existing employees or a list of outside applicants. Most companies would prefer a person with experience, because most are not able to spend the time and money required to train someone to be a supervisor. This means that in most companies the person who aspires to become a supervisor—to move from worker to management—must take on the responsibility of preparing himself or herself for such a promotion. This preparation involves finding out what you have already of what you will need and acquiring the rest through your own efforts. Exhibit 1.5 lists the ten attributes that companies look for in applicants for management jobs at all levels. Take a few minutes to study it. Consider it a checklist, and be honest as you decide whether you possess a given attribute or not, and, if you do possess it, whether you need to improve on it. Schools can help, and research on your own also is useful. A job change may be the best step you can take to obtain further experience that could be useful in improving a skill or gaining an attribute.

Many employers prefer to hire some or all of their supervisory personnel from the ranks of junior or senior college graduates. After some preliminary training and understudy, these people are installed as functioning supervisors. The practice of hiring all or some of a firm's new supervisors from outside the company takes its toll on the morale of the employees. Personal incentive and the competition for supervisory positions are enhanced, however, since fewer positions are available to be filled by advancing workers. As a result, some workers may begin to pursue a college education, while others may be encouraged to complete the advanced training they began years ago. The practice of hiring supervisors from outside the company may also prevent excessive inbreeding and infuse new ideas and approaches into the organization.

A major disadvantage of the practice of going outside the organization for new supervisors fresh from college is that they may lack the first-hand experiences and technical skills needed to supervise the company's workers. They may also fail to understand the attitudes of the workers and their interactions among themselves. The new supervisors may be young, and as a result they may experience a built-in resistance to their supervision from older, more experienced members of the department.

Many workers do not wish to be promoted to the ranks of management. Some are reluctant to give up the security that goes with knowing their job and doing it well. Others may be convinced that the extra prestige is not worth the extra time, problems, and responsibilities that go

1. Oral communication skill—effective expression in individual or group situations (includes gestures and nonverbal communications).

2. Oral presentation skill—effective expression when presenting ideas or tasks to an individual or to a group when given time for presentation (includes gestures and nonverbal communication).

3. Written communication skill—clear expression of ideas in writing and in good grammatical form.

4. Job motivation—the extent to which activities and responsibilities available in the job overlap with activities and responsibilities that result in personal satisfaction.

5. Initiative—active attempts to influence events to achieve goals; self-starting rather than passive acceptance; taking action to achieve goals beyond those called for; originating action.

6. Leadership—utilizing appropriate interpersonal styles and methods in guiding individuals (subordinates, peers, superiors) or groups toward task accomplishment.

7. Planning and organization—establishing a course of action for self and/or others to accomplish a specific goal; planning proper assignments of personnel and appropriate allocation of resources.

8. Analysis—relating and comparing data from different sources, identifying issues, securing relevant information, and identifying relationships.

9. Judgment—developing alternative courses of action and making decisions that are based on logical assumptions and reflect factual information.

10. Management control—establishing procedures to monitor and/or regulate processes, tasks, or the jobs and responsibilities of subordinates; taking action to monitor the results of delegated assignments or projects.

Exhibit 1.5   **Ten attributes that organizations look for in applicants for management positions.** (*Source:* Reprinted with permission from *HRMagazine* (formerly *Personnel Administrator*) published by the Society for Human Resource Management, Alexandria, Virginia.)

along with a management position. In some cases a worker may be asked to take a pay cut if he or she accepts a promotion to supervisor. This is due to the loss of hourly pay status, annual pay increases, and overtime pay. Although the cut may only be temporary, it is still a lot to ask of a worker.

In addition, the attitude of the company toward supervisors may make many workers shy away from a supervisory role. In far too many companies, supervisors are given lip service as managers but are not treated with the respect other managers are entitled to and receive.

1. The supervisor is the only manager whose subordinates are non-management employees called *workers*.

2. The three most important types of skills for any manager to possess are human, technical, and conceptual. All are required for success, but different levels of management need them to different degrees.

3. Supervisors are responsible to three groups: their peers, their subordinates, and their superiors. Each group represents a source of support, demands on the supervisor's time, and potential problems or challenges for the supervisor.

4. Each organization attempts to define a supervisor's role through the creation of a job description and through the demands that various groups and individuals place on the supervisor. Problems can result from role conflict and role ambiguity.

5. Supervisors, as well as other managers, represent linking pins, tying two or more organizational groups or units together by their memberships in each.

6. Educational levels of workers are rising, women's roles are changing, and the types of jobs that supervisors must manage are undergoing alterations. Flextime, shared jobs, and temporary workers offer new challenges to supervisors today.

7. The rewards for successful supervision include pride in oneself, pride in one's performance, pay increases, promotion, and career growth opportunities through the formation of a reputation for getting a job done effectively and efficiently.

Glossary **Foreman** traditional term for a supervisor engaged in managing production or workers engaged in manufacturing.

Linking pin key individual who is a member of two or more formal groups in a business organization, thus linking or connecting the groups.

Management skills categories of basic abilities required of all managers at every level of the organization.

Peer person at the same level of the organization as you are, in terms of formal authority and status in the organization.

Role ambiguity a situation that occurs whenever a manager is not certain of the role he or she is expected to play at work.

Role conflict a situation that occurs when contradictory or opposing demands are made on a manager.

Role prescription   the collection of expectations and demands from superiors, subordinates, and others that shapes a manager's job description and perception of his or her job.

Sanction   negative means, such as threats or punishments, used by superiors or the organization to encourage subordinates to play their roles as prescribed by superiors or the organization.

Supervisor   the only manager whose subordinates are nonmanagement employees called *workers*.

Team adviser   supervisor managing a team of people who share his or her authority and who jointly run their operations in terms of decision making and problem solving.

Questions for Class Discussion

1. Can you define this chapter's key terms?

2. What are the three essential management skill areas that supervisors must have and apply? Give an example illustrating the application of each skill area.

3. What are the three groups to whom supervisors have responsibilities? Give an example of a responsibility to each group.

4. How do the concepts of effectiveness and efficiency apply to a supervisor's performance?

5. What rewards can a supervisor expect to receive for being judged successful?

Incident

Purpose   To discover the world of business publications and to learn how to use your library's many references.

Your Task   Choose a topic of interest to you from among the following listed areas for research. Then find three business journals from the last twelve months that have articles on your topic. Write a one-page (100–150 words) summary of each article, being sure to name the article, its date, author(s), page numbers in the publication, and the title of the publication. Choose your journals from the list below.

Topics
team management
worker teams
flextime
part-time employment services
information technology
electronic mail
teleconferencing
the portable office
the importance of first-line management
the changing role of today's supervisor

Journals

BusinessWeek
Fortune
Nation's Business
Harvard Business Review
Sloan Management Review
Forbes
The Wall Street Journal
Entrepreneur
Inc.
Business Horizons
Personnel Journal
Supervisory Management
Supervisor's Bulletin

Case Problem 1.1   The Cajun Dog

The Cajun Dog is a fast-food restaurant owned by Jim Foster and specializing in unique and traditional treatments of that old American favorite, the hot dog. Jim started his restaurant about four months ago, and it has become a neighborhood favorite. He employs four high-school students, each of whom works no more than four hours each day, Monday through Saturday. Three come in about 4:00 P.M., and one works from about 7:00 or 8:00 P.M. until closing. The workers are high-school seniors; after they graduate, Jim wants to offer one of them a full-time position, so he can work fewer hours. Decision time is about two months away, so Jim will have about six months of experience with each of them. He plans to pick the one who demonstrates the best overall performance.

Jim has worked in the fast-food business for about three years and has solid experience in food preparation and counter service with two of the largest chains. He saved his money and at age 26 bought his business from a husband-and-wife team that wanted to retire. Before he took over, however, he worked with them for about one month to get the feel of the business. Although Jim had never been a supervisor of others, he felt his experiences had taught him all he needed to know.

Although Jim pays above minimum wages to his part-timers, he has not seen the enthusiasm he had expected from them. They sit idle during slow periods, and he has to hound them to keep them busy. When one or more of them show up late, it usually means a tough time for Jim, and it overburdens the ones who do come in on time. Jim finds it hard to understand why they do not have the same drive he had when he worked in their jobs. In his words, "If I don't stand over them all the time, they let me down. They bring their friends in, but their friends just want to sit around and gab."

When he hired his people Jim spent about three hours with each of them, patiently showing them what he wanted them to do. All of his help have been trained in waiting on customers and preparing the shakes and soft drinks. None of them prepares the food. Jim has reserved this task for himself, although two of his people have expressed a strong interest in food preparation.

Jim's management philosophy is simple. He has learned that people should do as they are taught and not deviate from "*the* method." As Jim puts it, "There is no room for creative counter people and Pepsi preparers. All I ask from my help is that they do what they are told, when they are told, and in the exact manner in which the task was taught. I don't want any back talk. Do it my way or get out.'' When Jim corrects a person, he usually does it in a personal way, attacking the individual as ''lazy'' or ''stupid.'' When Ellen, an employee, offered a suggestion for speeding up the flow, Jim blew his stack.

One employee, Ben, is really upset and thinking about leaving. Last week Jim added two new hot dog specialties to the menu. Unfortunately, he forgot to tell Ben and the others. They only found out about the new items through the customers, who seemed pretty irate when Ben told them that the items did not exist.

Questions

1. Using Exhibit 1.4 which of the ''seven deadly sins'' has Jim fallen victim to? Give examples from the case to support your choices.
2. Do you think Jim's workers are unique because they work part-time? Why or why not?
3. Do you think Jim's background has equipped him to be a successful supervisor? Why or why not?

Case Problem 1.2 The College Graduate

The Excelsior Company is in the process of reorganizing its operating level of management. Many departments have grown rapidly over the last year because of the company's fine line of packaging materials and aggressive salesmanship. As a result, several departments are to be split, creating the need for additional supervisory personnel. Excelsior has no formal training program and little time to prepare one. The personnel manager decided, therefore, to obtain candidates among recent college graduates. Six people were selected after extensive interviewing. After serving a three-month period as assistant supervisors, they were placed in charge of their own groups.

Sam Jordan is one of these graduates. He has finished four years of college with a bachelor's degree in management. He served his apprenticeship under Alan Johnson, an old-timer in charge of the shipping and receiving department. Half of Alan's subordinates are now Sam's.

Alan is not a college graduate but has enrolled at the local junior college as a night student in business. He is a popular supervisor and gets along well with his people, all of whom are high-school graduates. He consults them frequently and is quick to adopt an idea that he thinks has merit. He often told Jordan, ''Put the workers first, and they will take care of the rest.''

On Thursday morning of his second week as supervisor, Sam was approached by his chief clerk, Phil Watson.

''Sam, I wonder if I could leave a little early tomorrow. It's the wife's birthday, and I want to pick up a nice plant for her at the florist shop. They close at 5 P.M. and I want to be able to get there before then.''

''Sure,'' said Sam.

On Friday Sam ran into Alan at lunch.

''Say, Sam, you sure got me and some of the boys in a bind today. I must have had two requests this morning to leave early. Seems the men got wind of your letting Watson go early today.''

''He only wanted to get a plant for his wife, and the shop closes before he can get there.''

''Don't you know company policy about letting people go early? It's O.K. in an emergency but not for personal convenience.''

''Gee, I'm sorry, Alan, I didn't know the policy. It never came up before, and I felt I had to give him an answer.''

Questions

1. What do you think of Excelsior's decision to hire college graduates instead of promoting workers from within?
2. Do you think Sam was following Alan's suggestion about putting the worker first?

3. Do you think Watson knew about the company policy? If so, why did he ask for time off?
4. What responsibilities of a supervisor did Sam ignore in this case?

5. Why do you think he ignored these responsibilities?
6. How could this situation have been avoided?

Notes

1. W. Earl Sasser, Jr., and Frank S. Leonard, ''Let First-Level Supervisors Do Their Job,'' *Harvard Business Review* (March–April 1980): 113.
2. Ibid., 115.
3. Robert L. Katz, ''Skills of an Effective Administrator,'' in *Business Classics: Fifteen Key Concepts for Managerial Success* (*Harvard Business Review,* 1975), 23–35.
4. Thomas De Long, ''What Do Middle Managers Really Want from First-Line Supervisors?'' *Supervisory Management* (September 1977): 8.
5. Katz, ''Skills of an Effective Administrator,'' 24.
6. Ibid., 26.
7. Peter Drucker, *Managing for Results* (New York: Harper & Row, 1964), 5.
8. R. L. Kahn, D. M. Wolfe, P. R. Quinn, J. D. Snoek, and R. A. Rosenthal, *Organizational Stress: Studies in Role Conflict and Ambiguity* (New York: John Wiley & Sons, 1964).
9. John B. Miner, *Management Theory* (New York: Macmillan, 1971), 39–48.
10. Ibid., 44–46.
11. Ibid., 45–46.
12. Rensis Likert, *New Patterns of Management* (New York: McGraw-Hill, 1961), 61.
13. Janice A. Klein and Pamela A. Posey, ''Good Supervisors Are Good Supervisors—Anywhere,'' *Harvard Business Review* (November–December 1986): 126.
14. Ibid.
15. Jon Van, ''Laptop Leads Cast of Office Offerings but Bosses Must Filter What's Needed from What's New,'' *Chicago Tribune,* sect. 20 (March 17, 1991): 7.

Suggested Readings

Belker, Loren B. *The First-Time Manager: A Practical Guide to the Management of People.* 2d ed. New York: AMACOM, 1986.

Fierman, Jaclyn. ''Do Women Manage Differently?'' *Fortune* (December 17, 1990): 115–116, 118.

Kotite, Erika. ''Can You Read This?'' *Entrepreneur* (September 1990): 93–98.

Kotter, John P. ''What Leaders Really Do.'' *Harvard Business Review* (May–June 1990): 103–111.

Loden, Marilyn, and Rosener, Judy B. *Workforce America.* Homewood, Ill.: Business One Irwin, 1991.

Nuventures Consultants, Inc. *America's Changing Workforce—About You, Your Job and Your Changing Work Environment.* LaJolla, Calif.: Nuventures Publishing, 1990.

Stayer, Ralph. ''How I Learned to Let My Workers Lead.'' *Harvard Business Review* (November–December 1990): 66–69, 72, 74, 76, 80.

Stone, Florence M., ed. *The AMA Handbook of Supervisory Management.* New York: AMACOM, 1989.

2 You and Your Future

Outline

Objectives

After reading and discussing this chapter, you should be able to do the following:

1 Define this chapter's key terms.
2 Explain how managers can avoid personal obsolescence.
3 List the six steps involved in preparing oneself for advancement.
4 List the five steps involved in planning a career.
5 Explain the importance of a personal code of ethics.

Key Terms

career   networking
career path   obsolescence
ethics   résumé

Introduction

In 1991, the U.S. Census Bureau reported that computers were in 15 percent of U.S. households. In households where annual income was more than $50,000, about 40 percent had home computers. By the time most young people reach junior high school, they have been exposed to computers and know the fundamentals connected with their programming and use. Today, most jobs call for familiarity with computers (computer literacy), and more will require it each day.

Our offices and factories are routinely equipped with integrated and multifunction workstations, voice and electronic mail, and robotics. Cable television hookups enable businesses to hold meetings without the need to travel. Businesses exist in an information age with a tremendous reliance upon electronics for the performance of nearly every kind of task. Pressures from foreign competition require an ability to respond to challenges quickly and to plan for the future with greater speed than ever before.

Work in America is shifting from manufacturing to the service sector at an increasing rate. According to the U.S. Department of Labor, service-related jobs will grow three times as fast as manufacturing jobs in our economy from now through 1995. The nature of work is shifting from the routine, the fatiguing, and the monotonous to the intriguing, the exciting, and the challenging, thanks primarily to the growth in computer literacy and the nationwide push for more cost-efficient output. As John Naisbitt puts it in his book, *Megatrends,* we are moving from an industrial society to an information society.[1]

All of these changes and challenges mean that you are now in or will soon be entering a world of work that is more demanding and stressful than it has ever been before. But your future is still in your hands. What you are willing to invest in your future today will determine where it takes you tomorrow. None of us can count on our jobs existing in the future, so we need to stay current, to keep growing and learning, and to master the new technologies as they come along, in order to be ready for future job security. This chapter is concerned with your future—with your need to avoid personal obsolescence by planning for your own advancement.

Obsolescence

Obsolescence
A state or condition that exists when a person or machine is no longer able to perform to standards or to management's expectations

Obsolescence exists when a person or machine is no longer capable of performing up to standards or to management's expectations. What choices does management have when confronted with an obsolete person or machine? Exhibit 2.1 spells out these alternatives.

You can see from this analogy between person and machine that the best you can hope for from your company are training and some incentives for self-development. In theory, every employee is eligible for training, but in practice not everyone is qualified for it. Since it is your future we are discussing, you are the one who should be most concerned with it. Do not wait for your company to make the first move. You must take and maintain the initiative. Your boss is waiting for you to do so. Let your company know you are ready for and worthy of additional investments of its efforts and resources.

Personal obsolescence can happen quite suddenly. Overnight changes can render an individual's performance inadequate. Computers have had this impact on workers as well as on managers. When one company buys or merges with another, changes take place in a rapid and unpredictable manner. New skills and knowledge are necessary for the changes in personnel and job descriptions that will take place. Those who possess the potential and have prepared themselves for bigger things will be playing

Person	Machine
Invest in the person through training and development, and offer incentives for efforts at self-improvement.	Keep the machine and modify it, when economically feasible to do so, to improve its efficiency and longevity.
Tolerate the person and his or her limitations and inefficiencies.	Keep the machine and live with its limitations and inefficiencies.
Tolerate the person, but reduce his or her role in the organization by deletion of duties or demotion.	Keep the machine but reduce its role in production, relegating it to backup or temporary use.
Discharge the person and replace him or her with a better-qualified individual.	Scrap the machine and replace it with a more up-to-date model.

Exhibit 2.1   Alternative ways of dealing with obsolescence in a person or machine.

more important roles when the dust settles. Those who have not will be looking for new positions outside the company.

According to the findings of a 1990 poll of business executives taken by the National Alliance of Business, 64 percent of major U.S. companies are not happy with the reading and writing scores of the high-school graduates entering the work force. Only a small majority possess minimum competencies in reading, writing, and computing (minimum competencies are defined by the National Alliance as being able to read beyond the seventh grade level and to compute at higher than a fifth grade level). Alliance president, William Kolberg, says that by the year 2000, between 5 and 15 million jobs will require skills other than those needed today and that an equal number of service jobs will be obsolete. Minimum competencies mean entry into jobs with minimum pay and limited opportunities.[2]

Coauthors Gail Garfield Schwartz and William Neikirk in their book, *The Work Revolution,* assert that flexibility is the key to employability.[3] To avoid becoming superfluous, individuals need to become computer literate. They must prepare themselves for the "smart jobs"—the ones that computers and robots cannot do. These include working with people; providing care, advice, and information; and working with sophisticated machines. "Others involve gathering information and building and repairing everything from highways to helicopters."[4]

A person can become obsolete in attitudes, knowledge, skills, and abilities. Obsolescence in any of these areas marks a person as a potential candidate for the scrap heap. He or she may become too costly to keep or maintain (see Exhibit 2.2).

Ask yourself the following questions to determine your degree of personal obsolescence.*

Attitudes

1. Is my mind free from anxiety over personal matters while I work?
2. Do I believe in myself—my knowledge, skills, and abilities—and in my associates?
3. Am I open and receptive to advice and suggestions, regardless of their sources?
4. Do I look for the pluses before looking for the minuses?
5. Am I more concerned with the cause of management's action than with its effect?

Knowledge

1. Am I curious—do I still seek the *why* behind actions and events?
2. Do I read something and learn something new every day?
3. Do I question the old and the routine?
4. Do I converse regularly with my subordinates, peers, and superiors?
5. Have I a definite program for increasing my knowledge?

Skills

1. Is what I am able to do still needed?
2. In light of recent trends and developments in my company and industry, will my skills be required one year from now?
3. Do I practice my skills regularly?
4. Do I regularly observe how others perform their skills?
5. Have I a concrete program for acquiring new skills?

Abilities

1. Do my subordinates, peers, and superiors consider me competent?
2. Do I consistently look for a better way of doing things?
3. Am I willing to take calculated risks?
4. Do I keep morally and physically fit?
5. Have I a specific program for improving my performance?

Exhibit 2.2   **Twenty questions to help you assess your degree of personal obsolescence.** *Note that these questions put the burden to avoid obsolescence on you. For every "no" response, you highlight an area where you need a change in behavior. Your "yes" responses pinpoint areas that are keeping you current and growing.

The Importance of Education

Your best defense against personal obsolescence is an investment in education, both in and out of classrooms. U.S. government reports regularly confirm that the more education a person has the more income and job security he or she achieves. A look at Exhibit 2.3 will show you that the median income (the figure at which there are as many people above the number as there are below it) for American households varies dramatically as the educational attainment of the heads of these households increases. The exhibit also shows starting salaries for recent college graduates.

Education is achieved through various sources: community colleges, colleges and universities, professional associations, on-the-job training, and many others. In addition to helping you acquire bachelor's, master's, and doctorate degrees, the courses you can take in individual industries are quite valuable and will improve your chances for raises and promotions. By joining certain professions and professional associations, you become eligible for their various training programs. Two organizations that are designed for supervisors are the International Management Council and the National Management Association. Together they have formed the Institute of Certified Professional Managers, which offers certification testing in several skills areas. For more information on how they can help you and for information about home study, write to the following addresses:

American Society for Training and Development
600 Maryland Avenue, S.W.
Washington, D.C. 20024

International Management Council
2250 East Devon Avenue
Des Plaines, IL 60018

National Management Association
Dayton, Ohio 45439

Institute of Certified Professional Managers
P.O. Box 386
Dayton, Ohio 45409

According to a recent survey by Robert Half International, a New York–based executive-recruiting firm, 61 percent of 100 corporate executives believed that the most vital ingredient a person can have in his or her inventory to make it to the top of an organization is competence.[5] Competence comes from learning both on and off the job and through persistent effort to make oneself better. The Japanese have a word for this commitment: *kaizen.* According to *kaizen,* everyone in a company has two basic obligations: to maintain standards and to seek to improve them. Each person employed has to seek gradual improvement in his or her personal and working life.[6] Each of us needs to make a commitment to continue our educations and to work toward steadily improving ourselves and our situations.

Median income comparisons of year-round workers by educational attainment 1987 (persons 25 years and over). Figures in $1,000.

Years of school completed	Median Income		Income gap in dollars	Women's income as a percent of men's	Percent men's income exceeded women's
	Women	Men			
Elementary school:					
Less than 8 years	$ 9,927	$14,903	$ 4,976	66	50
8 years	12,174	18,939	6,765	64	55
High School:					
1 to 3 years	12,940	21,269	8,329	61	64
4 years	16,461	25,394	8,933	65	54
College:					
1 to 3 years	$19,843	$29,536	9,693	67	49
4 years or more	22,554	34,380	11,826	66	52

(Source: Department of Commerce, Bureau of the Census. NOTE: Data are latest available.)

Average Starting Salaries in Thousands of Dollars for College Graduates.

		1990	1991
Bachelor's Degrees	Engineering	$32.9	$34.3
	Accounting	27.5	28.4
	Sales-marketing	25.1	26.9
	Business administration	25.4	26.2
	Liberal arts	25.3	26.1
	Computer	30.3	31.9
	Chemistry	29.9	31.1
	Mathematics or statistics	29.7	29.9
	Economics or finance	26.6	27.6
		1990	1991
Master's Degrees	Engineering	$37.8	$39.4
	Other technical fields	36.8	38.0
	MBA with technical BS	41.2	42.1
	MBA with nontechnical BA	43.6	44.3
	Accounting	33.1	33.8

(Source: 1991 Northwestern University Endicott-Lindquist Report, as quoted in the *Chicago Tribune,* December 14, 1990, sect. 1, p. 1.)

Exhibit 2.3   The relationship between education and income.

Planning for Advancement

Your future must be planned if you wish to control it. You start by knowing where you have been and where you are now. Then decide where it is that you want to go. The six steps in planning for advancement are as follows:

1. Take a personal inventory.
2. Analyze your present situation.
3. Set your objectives for self-improvement.
4. Develop a program.
5. Set your program in motion.
6. Evaluate your progress periodically.

Taking a Personal Inventory

Take a good, honest look at yourself. Try to see yourself as others see you. Your boss's appraisals will help. So too will the honest assessments of friends and family members. You must know your strengths and weaknesses. Label your successes and failures, what you do well and what you cannot do. Make a list of personal commitments to insiders and outsiders that affect your role at work. From this effort will emerge a list of what is in stock and what must be procured.

Exhibit 2.4 shows a checklist that will help you to label your likes and dislikes (your *interests*) and what you believe to be important (your *values*). After you have checked the statements that fit, list the five things that you do best and the five things that are most important to you. Note the areas that have no checkmarks, and ask yourself if they should be checked and if they represent areas that need more effort on your part.

Along with your interests and values, you should assess your *aptitudes*—your ability, talent, or capacity to perform certain mental and physical processes. The aptitudes most frequently measured by employers and used to match applicants to jobs are:

1. *Abstract reasoning*—the ability to think logically without using numbers or words. Skilled craftspersons, technicians, engineers, scientists, and computer programmers must have this ability.
2. *Verbal reasoning*—the ability to think, comprehend, and communicate effectively through the use of words. Authors, teachers, administrators, salespeople, and secretaries must have this ability.
3. *Mechanical reasoning*—the ability to recognize the mechanical prin-

What I do well. Check the items that apply to you:

☐ Organizing	☐ Innovating
☐ Handling details	☐ Making decisions
☐ Making things	☐ Teaching others
☐ Researching	☐ Supervising
☐ Creating	☐ Dressing well
☐ Reasoning/logic	☐ Persuading
☐ Writing	☐ Communicating
☐ Drawing/painting	☐ Dealing with criticism
☐ Computing/mathematics	☐ Coordinating activities
☐ Dealing with others	☐ Developing new skills
☐ Other (specify)	

My 5 most important abilities are: _____

_____

What is important to me. Check the items that apply to you:

☐ Helping others	☐ Fast pace
☐ Working alone	☐ Gaining knowledge
☐ Working with others	☐ Creativity
☐ Making decisions	☐ Change and variety
☐ Chance for advancement	☐ Security
☐ Monetary reward	☐ Recognition
☐ Physical challenge	☐ Excitement
☐ Power and authority	☐ Independence
☐ Improving society	☐ Responsibility
☐ Competition	☐ Intellectual challenge
☐ Other (specify)	

My 5 most important concerns are: _____

_____

Exhibit 2.4 **Assessment checklist.** [*Source:* Adapted from Chris Bardwell, ''A Career-Seeker's Q & A,'' *Key: A Guide to College and Careers* (Liberty, Mo.: Key Publications, 1987), 36–37.]

ciples that govern the use of machines and tools. Draftsmen, repairmen, engineers, mechanics, and skilled craftspersons must have this ability.

4. *Numerical ability*—the ability to solve mathematical problems and to think in numbers. Bank tellers, economists, accountants, designers, and technicians must feel comfortable with numerical reasoning.

5. *Spatial relationships*—the ability to make things three-dimensional and to imagine the shapes and sizes of things. Depth perception and the ability to estimate distances are also part of this aptitude. Drivers, assemblers, draftspersons, scientists, and technicians share this aptitude.

6. *Manual dexterity*—the ability to move the hands skillfully and easily. Nearly every assembly operator, craftsperson, and technician needs to have this aptitude. So do artists and musicians.

By taking a battery of aptitude tests through your college's counseling office, you will discover which aptitudes you have and what kinds of jobs you would be most capable of handling. Nearly every job demands one or more of these aptitudes from the jobholder. Through proper interpretation of the test results, you will learn what kinds of jobs you are best suited for. Failure to assess your aptitudes accurately will prevent you from finding out any false perceptions you may have of your own abilities. Exhibit 2.5 shows how certain aptitudes relate to some specific occupations.

This first step is designed to give you a realistic understanding of your interests, values, and aptitudes. Once you know your strengths and weaknesses, you know what you have going for you and what you need to acquire. You can then set about the task of planning to get what you need.

Analyzing Your Present Situation

Your present situation consists of the resources you have available to spend in acquiring what you need and the view you have toward your present state in life. How much money and time have you available to help you get what you want and lack? How strong is your commitment to improve on what you have? What roadblocks may stand in your way? How happy are you with your present income, job, education, and quality of life? The more you desire to change, the easier it will be to do so. Consider also the supports you have that will aid your efforts to improve yourself and your life. Family, friends, your boss, peers, programs at work, and the schools and professional associations in your community are but a few resources available to help you.

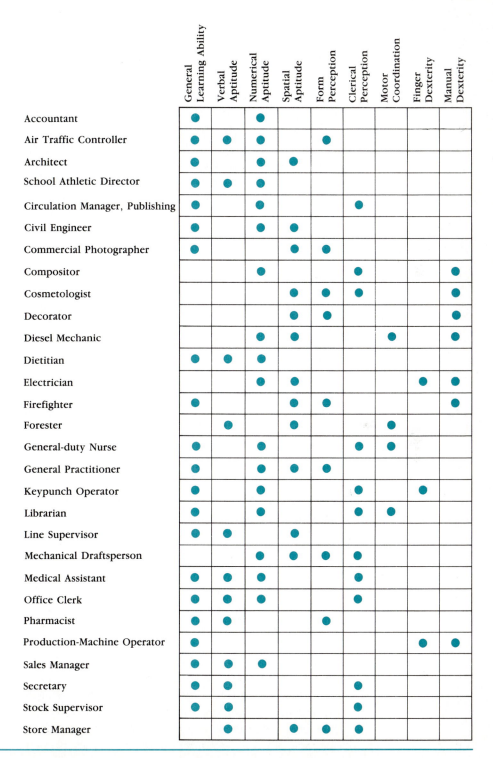

	General Learning Ability	Verbal Aptitude	Numerical Aptitude	Spatial Aptitude	Form Perception	Clerical Perception	Motor Coordination	Finger Dexterity	Manual Dexterity
Accountant	●		●						
Air Traffic Controller	●	●	●		●				
Architect	●		●	●					
School Athletic Director	●	●	●						
Circulation Manager, Publishing	●		●			●			
Civil Engineer	●		●	●					
Commercial Photographer	●			●	●				
Compositor			●			●			●
Cosmetologist				●	●	●			●
Decorator				●	●				●
Diesel Mechanic			●	●			●		●
Dietitian	●	●	●						
Electrician			●	●				●	●
Firefighter	●			●	●				●
Forester		●		●			●		
General-duty Nurse	●		●			●	●		
General Practitioner	●		●	●	●				
Keypunch Operator	●		●			●		●	
Librarian	●		●			●	●		
Line Supervisor	●	●		●					
Mechanical Draftsperson			●	●	●	●			
Medical Assistant	●	●	●			●			
Office Clerk	●	●	●			●			
Pharmacist	●	●			●				
Production-Machine Operator	●							●	●
Sales Manager	●	●	●						
Secretary	●	●				●			
Stock Supervisor	●	●				●			
Store Manager		●		●	●	●			

Exhibit 2.5 Aptitudes and their relationships to several kinds of jobs.

Setting Your Objectives for Self-Improvement

As clearly and precisely as you can, put the qualities you wish to obtain and the skills and abilities you wish to develop into writing. Be specific. Determine which of these you need most urgently, and make them objectives for the short run. Set a time limit by which each is to be procured, then stick to it as well as you can. Set the remainder of your needs as long-term goals—goals to be achieved within a year or two. Finally, consider the means you wish to use to reach each goal. Be realistic and a little conservative. Do not take on too much at once, or you will only be setting yourself up for a letdown and frustration. Start with the goals you need most urgently, and select the one that appears easiest to achieve. As with a diet, early success is important to both commitment and continuation.

Developing Your Program

The program you formulate should contain the answers to *who, what, when, where, why, how,* and *how much.* Break it down into phases, each with specific goals and time limits. Keep it in writing and in front of you so that you constantly remind yourself of the targets you wish to hit. Share its contents with your loved ones: they can boost your willpower. Exhibit 2.6 can help you get started. Complete it and check on your progress regularly. When you reach one goal, add another.

Setting Your Program in Motion

Begin your execution of the program as soon as it is formulated. If you meet heavy resistance in one or another of its phases, leave that phase and divert your attention and efforts to another. Then come back to that phase and try again.

Evaluating Your Progress Periodically

If certain goals you have stated appear to be impossible, you may have to abandon them. With each goal you abandon or achieve, establish another in its place. Remember that the program is a continuing effort at improvement and personal growth. Check your progress against the time limits you established. Were you realistic? Are you on course? Share your successes and setbacks with your husband or wife, or with a good friend. Seek counsel from the sources that you feel are best qualified to help. But keep working at your program!

The results of my aptitude, abilities, and skills inventories show the following:

MY FIVE GREATEST WEAKNESSES   date: _____   19 ___

1. *Not being up-to-date enough in my chosen field.*
2. *Poor at speaking to groups on my feet.*
3. *Being unsure of my abilities to use my personal computer to its full potential.*
4. _____
5. _____

What I Want Within 1 Year	**How I Intend to Get It**	**Cost**
1. *Keep up-to-date.*	*Read the journals in my field regularly, and subscribe to the most appropriate one.*	*$25*
2. _____		
3. *Build my computer*	*Enroll in a night course next semester at Wright College.*	*$115*
4. *skills.*		
5. _____		

What I Want Within 2 Years	**How I Intend to Get It**	**Cost**
1. *Improve my public speaking.*	*Enroll in Toastmasters in Town.*	*$?*
2. _____		
3. _____		
4. _____		
5. _____		

Exhibit 2.6   Sample self-development program in written-out form.

Most companies offer their managers many opportunities for growth and development. Programs range from reading materials to college degrees underwritten by company funds. Find out what options are available to you and what the requirements are for taking advantage of each of them. Pick the ones that you and your boss feel will be most beneficial to you. Be selective and do not overcommit yourself. It is better to do one or two things splendidly than to do several only adequately.

Planning Your Career

You have planned to improve your skills and attitudes and to develop your aptitudes. In like fashion, you must plan the evolution of your career. Such planning is not entirely within your control, however, as employers have plans of their own for you and for the kinds of jobs and career paths they think most beneficial to them.

Career
A sequence of jobs that takes people to higher levels of pay and responsibility

A **career** consists of a sequence of jobs that takes people to higher levels of pay and responsibility. As a career progresses, it leads a person to positions that require different skills, competencies, and areas of specialization. This series of jobs that constitutes a career is often called a **career path**. *Career pathing* (routing an employee through a series of related horizontal and vertical moves to jobs with ever-increasing responsibilities) for managers is now common to most large companies, but it may be sadly lacking in other, smaller firms. If you are in a job at present, find out what career paths it can lead to. If you find that no clearly defined path has been designated by your employer, the burden will be yours to determine a path with your current employer or with another. You may find that a career path has been set up for you but that it is not to your liking. Again, planning will be up to you.

Career path
A route chosen by an employer or employee through a series of related horizontal and vertical moves to jobs of ever-increasing responsibilities

Like your future, your career must be planned if you are to control it. You are now (or can become) qualified for more than one career. Many skills, aptitudes, and interests are common to more than one career field. Five recommended steps for you to take in planning your career are as follows:

1. Determine your career objectives.
2. Investigate jobs and career paths.
3. Label likely employers.

4. Seek employment.

5. Assess your situation periodically.

Determining Your Career Objectives

Start by putting your career goals in writing. State as clearly as you can just what you want from work and what kind of work you want to specialize in over the next three to five years. Your work with Exhibits 2.4 and 2.5 can help with this step. Now state job responsibilities—what you want to achieve—over the next few years. You will then have in front of you your career goals. Keep in mind that you can always change your objectives and plans. Most of us work many jobs and more than one career in our lifetimes. As you grow in experience and pass through several jobs, you will change and may decide that the path you are on is not for you.

Investigating Jobs and Career Paths

You may wish to begin this step by looking at the jobs that best match up with your interests and aptitudes. The *Dictionary of Occupational Titles,* published by the U.S. Department of Labor, lists hundreds of jobs and describes what they require in the way of tasks and responsibilities. A second publication from the same source, the *Occupational Outlook Quarterly,* speaks to the futures forecast for hundreds of jobs and career fields. These, along with many privately published reports and periodicals, can help you assess the jobs and career fields that will be in demand in the long term. Check with your college's placement office and with local librarians for a list of useful sources of information.

Various on-campus clubs offer help with investigations. They often feature guest speakers from occupations that are related to the clubs' activities and may sponsor field trips to visit several major employers' facilities. Another good source is campus recruiters, who represent many different employers and who interview applicants and share information about what it is like to work in different areas. Your professors can help, too.

There is no substitute for talking in-depth with someone who does the kind of work you wish to do. Schools can often put you in touch with experienced people in various areas through their alumni offices. Family and friends can do the same. Private and public employment services can also help by exposing you to the specifics of various jobs and by helping you to assess your suitability for certain types of employment. Finally,

Many corporations and small businesses are offering a growing number of women (working mothers) alternative work schedules and distinct career paths tailored to their needs for time to raise and nurture their children. Although some women are fearful that these "mommy tracks," as they have become known, will sidetrack their careers, others are most appreciative of the willingness of their employers to accommodate their temporary situations. Is a separate career track for women just another example of discrimination on the basis of sex? What about a male single parent? Should companies offer similar accommodations to their male single-parent employees? Women already earn only about 65 percent as much as men do on average. Won't "mommy tracks" keep this difference in force?

there are lectures, professional conferences, and professional associations in your community that stand ready to help you research a specific career opportunity.

Labeling Likely Employers

Once you have a specific kind of work and job in mind, you are ready to begin labeling likely employers. What you want to do here is find the specific job that you would like to get with a specific employer. One way to start is to determine if the area you are in is right for you. Is it growing in population, especially in terms of new businesses and job opportunities? Is the area you are in right for you in terms of its climate and the quality of life that it offers? It may be that you should begin researching jobs in another city or state. It makes the most sense to start your search in a place where you want to live and where the opportunities are most numerous.

Exhibit 2.7 shows you the projected growth for the fifty states in terms of new jobs added and the occupational growth expected for selected jobs through the year 2000. Keep in mind that about half of all working Americans work for companies with less than 500 employees. Small businesses are excellent places to get a career started and to begin adding skills and experiences to your inventory.

Sources to help you determine where the jobs are that fit your needs include help-wanted ads, private and public employment services, local colleges' placement offices, friends, family, and contacts employed in various companies. Using this last source is often called **networking.** Begin by talking to your closest friends and relatives—people who know you well and have your best interests at heart. Let them know your career ob-

Networking
Using one's friends, family, and work-related contacts to help find employment or to advance one's career

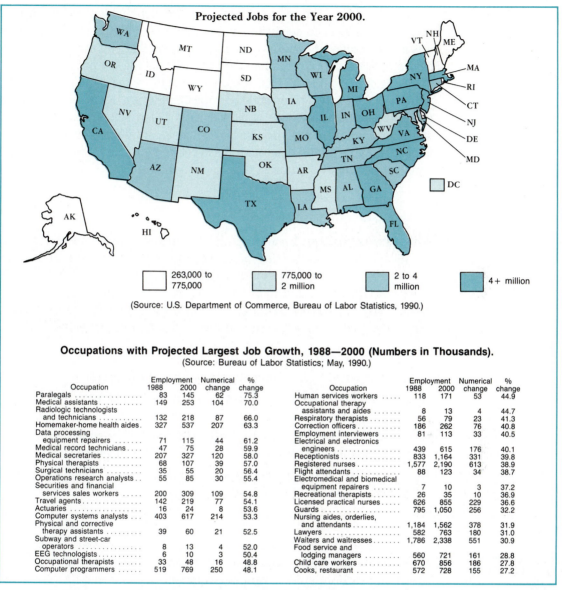

Projected Jobs for the Year 2000.

| | 263,000 to 775,000 | | 775,000 to 2 million | | 2 to 4 million | | 4+ million |

(Source: U.S. Department of Commerce, Bureau of Labor Statistics, 1990.)

Occupations with Projected Largest Job Growth, 1988—2000 (Numbers in Thousands).
(Source: Bureau of Labor Statistics; May, 1990.)

Occupation	Employment 1988	Employment 2000	Numerical change	% change
Paralegals	83	145	62	75.3
Medical assistants	149	253	104	70.0
Radiologic technologists and technicians	132	218	87	66.0
Homemaker-home health aides	327	537	207	63.3
Data processing equipment repairers	71	115	44	61.2
Medical record technicians	47	75	28	59.9
Medical secretaries	207	327	120	58.0
Physical therapists	68	107	39	57.0
Surgical technicians	35	55	20	56.4
Operations research analysts	55	85	30	55.4
Securities and financial services sales workers	200	309	109	54.8
Travel agents	142	219	77	54.1
Actuaries	16	24	8	53.6
Computer systems analysts	403	617	214	53.3
Physical and corrective therapy assistants	39	60	21	52.5
Subway and street-car operators	8	13	4	52.0
EEG technologists	6	10	3	50.4
Occupational therapists	33	48	16	48.8
Computer programmers	519	769	250	48.1

Occupation	Employment 1988	Employment 2000	Numerical change	% change
Human services workers	118	171	53	44.9
Occupational therapy assistants and aides	8	13	4	44.7
Respiratory therapists	56	79	23	41.3
Correction officers	186	262	76	40.8
Employment interviewers	81	113	33	40.5
Electrical and electronics engineers	439	615	176	40.1
Receptionists	833	1,164	331	39.8
Registered nurses	1,577	2,190	613	38.9
Flight attendants	88	123	34	38.7
Electromedical and biomedical equipment repairers	7	10	3	37.2
Recreational therapists	26	35	10	36.9
Licensed practical nurses	626	855	229	36.6
Guards	795	1,050	256	32.2
Nursing aides, orderlies, and attendants	1,184	1,562	378	31.9
Lawyers	582	763	180	31.0
Waiters and waitresses	1,786	2,338	551	30.9
Food service and lodging managers	560	721	161	28.8
Child care workers	670	856	186	27.8
Cooks, restaurant	572	728	155	27.2

Exhibit 2.7 Growing Occupational Opportunities.

jectives, and ask them for help in identifying possible sources of employment. Some companies pay a "finder's fee" for each new hire recommended by a current employee. You can also network by attending professional meetings and conferences; there you can meet people from different areas and employers and let them know, once they know you, that you are in the job market.

Once you have information about a specific job that looks good, investigate the employer to determine what kind of an environment it offers. If it is a corporation, it may have an annual report that you can read. A visit to the local chamber of commerce can tell you the company's employment history. A scan of local newspapers can reveal specific stories in which the company's plans and accomplishments are discussed. You want to know as much about an employer as you can before you attempt to apply for employment. Every employer has a community history and an image, and you should determine these before you attempt to give a company a voice in your future.

Seeking Employment

With your research in hand, you are now ready to make contact with a specific employer. Use a *letter of application* (see Exhibit 2.8), and make certain that it is addressed to a specific person. Your letter should request a personal interview, and it should be used when (1) the employer is in another city, (2) you are sending a résumé, and (3) you are answering a help-wanted ad. Your letter should meet the following guidelines:

1. It should be typed neatly; should use proper grammar, spelling, and sentence construction; and should be signed (by hand).
2. It should be on clean bond paper of standard letter size (8½″ × 11″).
3. It should be addressed to a specific individual (if possible), and its envelope should be marked "Personal" or "Confidential."
4. It should be clear and brief, and it should state the position you are seeking.
5. A résumé should be enclosed.

Résumé
An employment-related document submitted by the applicant and containing vital data such as the person's name, address, employment goals, and work-related education and experiences

Your **résumé** should contain your personal data—name, address, and phone number(s) (age is optional)—your employment goal, relevant education information, and relevant job experiences: those that in some measure have helped to prepare you for the job you now seek. Try to keep your résumé to one page, as shown in the sample in Exhibit 2.9. Including references is optional. Some applicants simply state that they will be happy to supply them "upon request." A good résumé is short, neat, carefully done, and typed on standard bond paper.

The Job Interview   Your employment interview is your chance to sell yourself and the employer's chance to sell you on a job and an environment. You can prepare for the interview by (1) going over your research,

539 Tenth Avenue
Chicago, Illinois 60600
(Date)

Mr. William R. Johnson,
Personnel Director
J & M Electronics
3872 South Wabash
Chicago, Illinois 60615

Dear Mr. Johnson:

Recently I learned, through the Wright College Placement
Office, of the expansion of your company's sales operations
and your intention to hire several managers for outside
salespeople. If a position is currently available, I would
appreciate your considering me for it.

I have had progressively more responsible and diverse
experience in selling and customer services. I have sold your
company's fine products at the retail level and currently
manage a salesforce of 6 people.

For your review I am enclosing my resume. I would
appreciate a personal interview with you, at your earliest
convenience, in order to discuss my application further.

Very truly yours

John D. Jones

Enclosure [Your résumé]

Exhibit 2.8 Letter of application to accompany the résumé shown in Exhibit 2.9.

(2) dressing appropriately, and (3) rehearsing your answers to these most
often asked questions:

1. Why have you picked our company?
2. Why did you leave your last job?
3. What are your career expectations?
4. What salary do you require?

```
                          John D. Jones
                        539 Tenth Avenue
                     Chicago, Illinois 60600
                         (312) 555-1345


Job Objective:      To manage salespeople in the electronics
                    field at the wholesale level.

Education:          Two-year degree in marketing from Wright
                    College, City Colleges of Chicago, 1991.

Work Experience:    Retail sales in consumer electronics, Sears,
                    Golf Mill store, 1989-1990.

                    Manager, retail sales staff, Electronics
                    Venture, Northbrook store, 1990 to present.

Accomplishments:    Won ''Best Salesperson'' award for my
                    department 1989, 1990 at Sears, Golf Mill.

                    Employee of the Month at Electronics
                    Venture, May of 1991.

                    Youngest supervisor of retail sales
                    department in Electronics Venture's history.

Skills:             Fluent in Spanish.

References:         Furnished on request.
```

Exhibit 2.9   **A personal résumé**.

5. What are your personal goals for the next year? Three years? Five years?

6. How do you react to criticism?

7. What are your strongest points?

8. What are your weaknesses?

9. What do you want out of work?

10. Would you object to moving if your job were to require it?

You should have clearly-thought-out answers to these questions before you take the interview. When you are stating a weakness, let the interviewer know what you are doing about it. When you are asked for dollar figures, ask the employer what the job pays. Emphasize that you are interested in other things besides money, such as satisfaction and a chance to get your start in a promising career with a fine company.

You in turn need to find out as much about the job and the employer as you can during your interview. Before you can say "yes" or "no" to any job offer you should have the answers to the following questions:

1. What has been the company's recent growth record?
2. What is its reputation as an employer locally, with the people in its community?
3. Does it offer career tracks or promote from within?
4. What are its major products and markets and long-term plans for growth in the future?
5. What have been its greatest successes recently?
6. What is your boss-to-be like as a person?
7. What, specifically, will your working conditions be in the job being offered?

You may be asked to interview more than one person, and you may be the participant in a group interview with two or more persons asking you questions. If you are applying for a supervisory job, you may be given problems that typically are faced by supervisors and asked to deal with them quickly. Expect "open" questions that call for you to explain your thinking and to give details. You should find yourself doing most of the talking. Be certain to get the information you need to make a decision before you answer the employer.

Take all the things you need to the interview if they are not already in the interviewer's hands. Such items may include the following:

Social security card, and all necessary licenses

Résumé

Transcript of grades

Pen and pencil

A list of people who have agreed to act as personal references for you

Names and addresses of previous employers and the dates you worked for them

A few words of caution from recent research are in order. An Accountemps poll of 1,000 executives indicates that job candidates who smoke during interviews may be hurting their chances to be hired: 73 percent of the executives polled said that smoking would reduce an interviewee's chances of being hired.[7] A Robert Half International survey of 1,000 personnel executives labels the most common mistakes made by job candidates in interviews as follows:

- Failing to research the company (24 percent)
- Being unprepared for the interview (23 percent)
- Failing to project strengths and skills (12 percent)
- Failing to state accomplishments (8 percent)
- Having a poor personal appearance (8 percent)
- Being too aggressive (7 percent)
- Exaggerating qualifications (7 percent)[8]

Finally, Al Sussman, vice-president of Dunhill Personnel Systems, tells us that eight out of ten college graduates recruited into white-collar jobs suffer some kind of ''reality shock.'' By this he means that they find out soon after reporting to work that their jobs are not what they thought they would be.[9] Either the job was oversold and misrepresented or the candidate did not get the information and facts he or she should have during the interview.

Evaluating Your Job Offer If you get a job offer at the employment interview, be prepared to say ''no,'' ''yes,'' or ''can I get back to you?'' You can turn an offer down if it does not fit your expectations and needs. There is little hope of success for anyone who takes a job just to get one. If the job meets your approval in the following areas, you should probably grab it:

- Does the company think as you do (are they your kind of people)?
- Do you like the people you have met and what you have seen of the work environment?
- Is the job high-profile (one where you will be noticed)?
- Would you be willing to stay for at least four or five years?
- Are the pay and benefits what you want?[10]

Assessing Your Situation Periodically

Every few months, look closely at your job situation. Ask yourself the following questions: Have my expectations become reality? Is this the job I thought it would be? Am I getting from it what I expected to get? Do I know where I am on a career path? Are the promises made to me being kept? Are the promises I made being kept?

After your first two performance appraisals you should know how your boss thinks and what he or she is looking for in your performance. Whatever your situation, commit yourself to your job for a minimum of one full year. This commitment gives you time to earn many benefits and to see a full-year cycle of events occur. It also offers the employer a return on the investment made in you.

There may come a time when you feel the need to change jobs. Before leaving your present employer, make certain that there are no other positions in the company for which you qualify. Your experience is usually worth more to your present employer than it is to another. You know it is time to move on when doors are closed to you, you hate going to work each day, and your best efforts go unrewarded. But do not quit your job until you find another. It is better to bargain from a position of employment with another company than from a position of unemployment.

Career Stages

Most of us find ourselves making two or more career changes before we settle into a true career path. We usually pass through four distinct stages once we have settled on a career. Exhibit 2.10 summarizes these four stages and the emotional needs they help to satisfy.

The trial stage includes the planning for self-improvement and career planning phases we have just examined. It includes the experimentation and self-exploration that allow us to decide on goals and a path to achieve them. The second stage, establishment and advancement, allows us to make a commitment to our chosen field. It gives us a sense of competence and confidence. It is a time of growing responsibilities on the job and in our family lives. The midcareer stage establishes our places in our organization and allows us to share what we have mastered with younger and newer members of the company. New and different goals and priorities emerge, along with new jobs and their challenges. By late career, we are more concerned with grooming our successors and with planning for our retirement than in any other stage.

Professional Ethics

Ethics
A field of philosophy dealing with the rightness of human conduct in society

Ethics is a field of philosophy dealing with the rightness of human conduct in society. It is of concern to most people who are contemplating any action that will affect others. Before taking an action, the ethical person

Stage	Task Needs	Emotional Needs
Trial	1. Varied job activities 2. Self-exploration	1. Make preliminary job choices 2. Settling down
Establishment and advancement	1. Job challenge 2. Develop competence in a specialty area 3. Develop creativity and innovation 4. Rotate into new area after 3–5 years	1. Deal with rivalry and competition; face failures 2. Deal with work/family conflicts 3. Support 4. Autonomy
Midcareer	1. Technical updating 2. Develop skills in training and coaching others (younger employees) 3. Rotation into new job requiring new skills 4. Develop broader view of work and own role in organization	1. Express feelings about midlife 2. Reorganize thinking about self in relation to work, family, and community 3. Reduce self-indulgence and competitiveness
Late career	1. Plan for retirement 2. Shift from power role to one of consultation and guidance 3. Identify and develop successors 4. Begin activities outside the organization	1. Support and counseling to see one's work as a platform for others 2. Develop sense of identity in extraorganizational activities

Exhibit 2.10   **The four stages most careers pass through.** [*Source:* D. T. Hall and M. A. Morgan, "Career Development and Planning." *Contemporary Problems in Personnel*, rev. ed., eds. W. C. Hamner and Frank L. Schmidt (Chicago: St. Clair Press © 1977). Reprinted by permission of John Wiley & Sons, Inc., New York.]

will think about the circumstances surrounding the intended action and its possible consequences. Our moral and ethical thinking is affected by our religious values and by our experiences in similar situations and circumstances. The ethical person will do his or her best to refrain from taking any action that will be harmful to others. Personal beliefs such as "the greatest good for the greatest number" also act as guides for judging the effects of intended actions. Ethics helps individuals and groups determine what actions are the most beneficial and the least harmful, for at times we must take actions that harm some but help others. When a government taxes one group to help another, some people are harmed while others are helped. When an employer decides to stop manufacturing one item in favor of manufacturing another, more profitable one, some employees and suppliers may be hurt while others are helped.

Many professionals—including lawyers, doctors, and accountants—and many corporations have stated codes of ethics that they are expected to live up to or incur some penalty. All of us have a conscience that helps us to know when we are acting properly and when we are not. For most people, no guilt means that they believe they have acted properly and ethically. The decisions that supervisors must make each day have to be considered in terms of some kind of ethical test or code. If they are not, serious personal and legal problems can and will arise for both the supervisor and the employer.

Certain kinds of jobs carry rather specific ethical prescriptions. Purchasing agents, salespeople, and health service professionals have clearly defined do's and dont's—a code of conduct designed to keep them from compromising their employers, their patients, their customers, or themselves. But for most management positions, there are no clearly defined and published codes of conduct. Consequently, supervisors who have no well-formed conscience or who lack good common sense are liable to make unethical decisions that will have serious negative consequences for themselves and their employers.

As a supervisor, you have not only ethical concerns but legal ones as well. You are charged to act both ethically and within the law. Just refraining from doing things that are illegal is not enough for a person who has authority over others and the resources of a company. It may be legal to fire a person you do not like for that reason alone, but is it ethical to do so? What may be the consequences to you, to your subordinate, and to your company if you do so?

Your reputation is far too precious a thing to waste on hasty, ill-thought-out decisions that fail to consider both the law and ethics. Times will come when you are asked to act in a way that you believe is immoral or unethical. What will you say to a boss who makes such a request of you? Are you prepared to cover up for a derelict employee? Once you are caught in a lie, your integrity is gone, and it is almost impossible to retrieve. Without personal codes of conduct and values we will fight to defend, our integrity will be compromised by our own actions and the actions of others. It is better to leave an environment that is unethical than to remain and become so ourselves.

Causes of Supervisory Success and Failure

Opinion Research Corporation, a management consulting firm in Princeton, New Jersey, has found that in well-managed companies, supervisors ''are perceived to be more knowledgeable about their jobs, more accessible'' than they are in companies that are judged by their people to be poorly managed. Opinion Research also found that the supervisors in well-managed companies ''provide better performance feedback and treat subordinates with more respect.''[11]

Burke Marketing Research, Inc., surveyed the vice-presidents and personnel directors of 100 of our nation's largest corporations, with this question: ''What employee behavior disturbs you the most?'' The offensive traits and attitudes uncovered were as follows (and in this order): dishonesty, attending to personal business on company time, arrogance, a complaining attitude, absenteeism and tardiness, not following company policy, a lack of enthusiasm and dedication, pettiness, disrespect, displays of anger, inability to get along with others, and taking credit for the work of others.[12] These traits and behaviors can be avoided by making a concerted effort to do so. Keep in mind that they irritate others, especially higher-level managers, and thus can and do affect performance ratings and promotion possibilities.

In addition to irritating traits and behaviors, habits can be irritating. Padgett-Thompson surveyed 529 managers and supervisors to determine what employee habits irritate them most. The following list was compiled: smoking (over 40 percent rated this as most irritating); wardrobe and grooming problems (18 percent); chewing gum/eating on the job (18 percent); talking too much or too loudly (16 percent); poor personal hygiene (13 percent); and making personal phone calls (11 percent).[13] Again, these annoying habits can be dispensed with easily and will help to improve a person's image at work.

On January 16, 1985, a video version of the best-selling book *In Search of Excellence* was aired on public broadcasting stations nationwide. It summarized the basic lessons for managers contained in the book by Thomas J. Peters and Robert H. Waterman, Jr. Through eight case studies of such companies as IBM, Walt Disney Enterprises, Apple Computer, and North American Tool & Die, the ninety-minute broadcast let viewers hear and see what works well for various successful managers. The managers in the film are successful because they are cheerleaders, facilitators, and nurturers of champions. These companies have created environments in which people do not fear failure, company goals are clearly defined and communicated to all employees, company efforts are focused on the customer, and employees trust their managers and feel that they are part of a team.

Instant Replay

1. A supervisor, like a machine or a method, can become obsolete in skills and abilities in the absence of a continuing program for his or her future development.

2. Education, both in and outside college classrooms, is a supervisor's best defense against obsolescence.

3. The higher a person goes in formal education, the greater his or her job security, promotability, and earnings become (on average).

4. Planning for personal advancement includes efforts aimed at determining strengths and weaknesses and at building a program for removing weaknesses.

5. Your career is largely in your hands and must be planned for.

6. A supervisor needs a personal code of ethics in order to survive, with integrity, in any career.

Glossary

Career a sequence of jobs leading to higher levels of pay and responsibility. These jobs require differing skills, competencies, and areas of specialization.

Career path a route chosen by an employer or employee through a series of related horizontal and vertical moves to jobs of ever-increasing responsibilities.

Ethics a field of philosophy dealing with the rightness of human conduct in society.

Networking using one's friends, family, and work-related contacts to help find employment or advance in one's career.

Obsolescence the state that exists when a person or machine is no longer capable of performing up to standards or management's expectations.

Résumé an employment-related document submitted by the applicant and containing vital data such as the person's name, address, employment goals, and work-related education and experience.

Questions for Class Discussion

1. Can you define this chapter's key terms?

2. How can you avoid personal obsolescence?

3. What are the six steps this text recommends to help you plan for your own advancement?

4. What happens in each step?

5. What are the five steps this text recommends to help you plan your career?

6. What happens in each step?

7. Why do you think it is important for each person to have a personal code of ethics?

Incident

Purpose To get you thinking about and planning for an entry into a new job or a new career.

Your Task To complete the following questionnaire as completely as possible and to note the areas in which you are having trouble with completion. You should discover a few facts about yourself and your outlook on life. You will discover what you know and how completely you know it.

Your Goals

1. What, specifically, do you want from a job? (Consider the psychological rewards available through work such as pride, a sense of accomplishment, a chance to learn new skills, a chance for advancement, and a sense of challenge.)

   _____

   _____

   _____

2. What environmental conditions are important to you at work? Consider the kind of boss you would like to have, the type of coworkers, the kinds of hazards you would be able to tolerate, the levels of different kinds of stress you can handle, and the status symbols that are important to you.

   _____

   _____

   _____

3. What pay and benefits are needed now? Consider take-home pay that would be the minimum required to live adequately and the type of fringe benefits (insurance, paid holidays, vacation time, and so on) that you consider minimal.

   My pay would have to be $_____ per week to survive.

   My benefits would have to include, as a minimum, _____

   _____

   _____

   _____

4. The kind of job I would most prefer at this point in my life would have the following duties/responsibilities:

_____

_____

_____

5. The job described above would be in the following industry or industries: manufacturing, transportation, retail, services.

_____

6. The area in which I would like to make my career is (Northeast, East, Southeast, Midwest, South, Southwest, West, Northwest, I'm not sure, It does not matter)

_____

7. The state I would most want to work in among the fifty is

_____

8. The size of the company I would most want to work in is (less than 100; less than 500 but more than 100; a major corporation)

_____

Personal Strengths

1. The personal strengths I now possess are (consider reading, writing, computing, computer skills, reasoning abilities, formal education completed, and foreign language abilities)

_____

_____

_____

2. The personal, work-related experiences I have had are (consider job experiences, hobbies, organizations you belong to, group-interaction experiences)

_____

_____

_____

Personal Weaknesses

1. The major weaknesses I now possess are (consider the same areas mentioned in numbers 1 and 2 above)

_____

_____

_____

2. I intend to overcome the weaknesses listed above by the following specific courses of action:

_____

_____

_____

Personal Barriers

1. The following things and conditions stand in my way right now to overcome my weaknesses (consider attitudes, money, time, human relationships, family ties, and anything else that can stop your progress):

_____

_____

_____

2. I intend to do the following specific things to overcome the barriers that I have identified above:

_____

_____

_____

Case Problem 2.1   Indecision

Juan Gonzales has been working as a bank teller in a small neighborhood bank since he graduated from high school about four years ago. Today he has just learned that the promotion he was hoping for has fallen through. He lost out to a teller with higher seniority. Since Juan is planning to marry in a few months, he was counting heavily on a promotion and is very disappointed. "It was my chance to get away from customers," thought Juan, "to get away from the routine and to get into management." Juan thought back on the last four years. He has had nearly perfect performance appraisals and has been complimented by his boss on numerous occasions. He decided to have a talk with his boss, Mary.

Mary was pleased to explain the promotion decision to Juan. She told him that the woman who won the promotion had one year more service and excellent evaluations. But more important, she had completed two correspondence courses offered through the company's training department and had enrolled in a third. The courses gave her an edge and much needed understanding about the things she would be doing in her new job. "With that kind of commitment to progress," said Mary, "the bank had to promote Susan. To do otherwise would be saying that additional education doesn't count for anything."

After work, Juan discussed his unhappiness with his friend, Pete. Although Juan and Pete are about the same age, Pete is already a supervisor of six people in a large savings and loan office two blocks away from Juan's bank.

"What's your secret, Pete? How come you

got to management with only a high-school education in the same time on the job that I have?"

"It's no secret, Juan. My office employs about twice as many people as your bank and my office is just one of three in town. People move up faster in bigger organizations, and there are more jobs to bid for. I had my ears and eyes open, and when a promotion came along I bid for it. It took two tries, but I was in the right place at the right time."

"I think my best move would be to get a job at a bigger business and get out of banking. I haven't learned anything new in three years, and I'm getting to the point where I don't want to go to work in the morning."

"Before you make a move, Juan, make sure you know what you want. Remember, your experience is of more value to your present employer than to any other. It has an investment in you."

"All I know is that I don't want to be a teller the rest of my life. I need a change to a job that pays more money—and fast. I'm getting married soon, and my woman makes more than I do."

"You know, Juan, you aren't getting any younger. One difference between us is that I have found my interest. I love accounting and finance, and I'm getting a lot of good training. Next month I'm enrolling in a night course for my first real look at college-level accounting. The company is paying my tuition and will pick up the tab for an entire college education if I can get that far."

Juan left the conversation with a sinking feeling in his stomach. He began to feel that he was going nowhere fast. On his way home, he stopped at the drug store to pick up a paper. "Maybe there are some jobs in town that pay more," he thought. "I'll start looking around tomorrow."

Questions

1. What career stage is Juan in now?
2. Do you think Juan is ready for a job change? Why or why not?
3. What advice do you have for Juan?
4. What differences exist between Juan and Pete?
5. Is Juan in danger of becoming obsolete? Why or why not?

Case Problem 2.2 The Exit Interview

Ms. Campbell, the assistant personnel manager of the Harlequin Stores, had just conducted an exit interview with Sherman Wu and had recorded his candid comments. (See Figure A.) She was sorry to see Sherman leave after only four months on the job. When she recruited Sherman, she had been impressed by his personality and eagerness to succeed. His hiring helped the company's affirmative action program, which called for more minorities in management positions. Ms. Campbell still did not understand well why Sherman had decided to leave.

As she reviewed her notes in preparation for her formal report to her boss, Ms. Camp-

bell went back in her mind to the week when she had first welcomed Sherman and other management trainees to the company. They had all been anxious and nervous. They were a good mix, she recalled thinking at the time, all of them young and fresh out of college. They represented a fine blend of ethnic and academic backgrounds. Three had been business majors while three others were from the liberal arts. All showed above-average results on the tests they had taken and on their college transcripts.

Ms. Campbell remembered how the recruits had been officially greeted by the president of the Harlequin Stores, and they had all

```
           EXIT INTERVIEW
           ─────────────

NAME:       Sherman Wu

AGE:        23

INITIAL ASSIGNMENT:  Management Trainee

DURATION OF TRAINING:  2 months

PLACEMENT FOLLOWING TRAINING:  Retail sales -- Men and Boys Wear, 2nd Floor,
          Main Street Store

REASONS FOR LEAVING:

  1. Training program was too high-level for job assignment. Trainee
     claims he was groomed for top management position and given a clerk's
     job.
  2. Failure to get along with coworkers. None of his peers were his
     equals educationally. Found them somewhat hostile.
  3. During first two months on job, trainee had no formal contact with
     fellow trainees and few encounters with management.
  4. Trainee was groomed for a job requiring innovative and creative
     thinking and sound decision making in line with his liberal arts
     training in college, but was given a job requiring none of these
     characteristics.
  5. Found no one in management willing to listen to complaints.
     Department supervisor generally unavailable and somewhat hostile.
     Trainee felt he could not serve his remaining four months under Mr.
     Wiley's supervision.

REMARKS:

  1. Pay and benefits received were adequate from trainee's point of view
     (placed on salary that was higher than the average clerk's salary
     plus commission).
  2. Has no immediate job to go to and has no definite career goals. Wants
     to travel for awhile before returning to work. Says he knows what he
     doesn't want but uncertain what he does want.
  3. Mr. Wiley rates Mr. Wu as a below-average performer and a loner.
```

Exhibit A   **Exit interview comments.**

received a royal treatment during their first two months on the job. For a moment she thought Sherman must be ungrateful and impetuous. She reconsidered that judgment, however, because Sherman had shown none of those traits while a trainee or a sales clerk.

Perhaps the real reason for Sherman's departure had not yet appeared in Ms. Campbell's notes. Sherman had known that he would be a sales clerk in at least three depart-

ments for six months after his initial training. After that "ground-floor" experience, however, he would be an assistant supervisor and have his own department within two years from the date he finished his training—earlier perhaps if those new stores on the drawing boards opened up on schedule. Sherman knew all this and had known it when he accepted the trainee's position. If Sherman had stayed a few more months, he surely would have earned a responsible job in the future, especially in view of his minority status.

Ms. Campbell began to feel somewhat annoyed again. That kid had cost the company a lot of money to train, she concluded, and we didn't get half of it back. He took a valuable seat in an expensive training program that could have been offered to another individual who might have stayed on and been more grateful. She picked up her pen and added these final words to her notes:

Like most minority members this interviewer has dealt with, Mr. Wu has a chip on his shoulder and wants instant success without having to earn it. Would not rehire.

Questions

1. Why did Sherman decide to leave?
2. What, if anything, would you do to change the training program?
3. What accounts for Ms. Campbell's change in her attitudes toward Sherman? Do you agree with her diagnosis of him? Why or why not?
4. What lessons are there in this case for a college graduate about to start a career in business?

Notes

1. John Naisbitt, *Megatrends* (New York: Warner Books, 1984), 1.
2. "Employees give job seekers a poor grade," *Chicago Tribune,* sect. 1 (July 16, 1990): 3.
3. Gail Garfield Schwartz and William Neikirk, *The Work Revolution.*
4. "Flexibility: Key to Future Jobs," *Chicago Tribune* (April 1984): 5.
5. "Inside Track," *Success!* (March 1987): 28.
6. For a more detailed treatment see Masaaki Imai, *Kaizen: The Key to Japan's Competitive Success* (New York: Random House, 1987).
7. "USA Snapshots," *USA Today* (March 10, 1987): 1A.
8. "USA Snapshots," *USA Today* (April 30, 1985): 1B.
9. "Reality Shock a Common Ailment," *USA Today* (October 29, 1986): 5B.
10. Jim Spenser, "Analyzing a Job," *Chicago Tribune* 5 (March 18, 1987): 2.
11. "Workers Take Dim View of Bosses, Study Finds," *Chicago Tribune* 2 (July 2, 1984): 3.
12. "What Employers Dislike the Most," *Chicago Tribune* 8 (January 20, 1985): 1.
13. "What Gets Under the Boss's Skin," *USA Today* (January 16, 1985): 1B.

Suggested Readings

"Best Jobs for the Future." *US News & World Report* (September 17, 1990): 55–99.

Brown, Paul. "Report on the States." *Inc.* (August 1989): 85–87.

Case, John. "Where the Growth Is." *Inc.* (August 1989): 25–26.

Freeman, Sue J. M. *Managing Lives: Corporate Women and Social Change.* Massachusetts: University of Massachusetts Press, 1990.

Kanter, Rosabeth Moss. "The New Managerial Work." *Harvard Business Review* 6 (November–December 1989): 85–92.

Kirkpatrick, David. "Is Your Career on Track?" *Fortune* (July 2, 1990): 38–48.

Labich, Kenneth. "Breaking Away to Go On Your Own." *Fortune* (December 17, 1990): 40–44.

Nuventures Consultants, Inc. *America's Changing Workforce.* California: Nuventures Publishing, 1990.

Rehfeld, John E. "What Working for a Japanese Company Taught Me." *Harvard Business Review* (November–December 1990): 167–176.

Sato, Gayle. "Who's the Boss?" *Entrepreneur* (September 1990): 87–91.

3 Management Concepts

Objectives

After reading and discussing this chapter, you should be able to do the following:

1 Define this chapter's key terms.
2 List and define the four essential elements of any formal organization.
3 List and explain the four steps involved in delegating.
4 Identify the three levels in the management hierarchy, and describe the activities of each.
5 Identify the four major functions performed by all managers.
6 List and explain the six steps in this chapter's decision-making model.
7 Specify the kinds of decisions that require your group's involvement.
8 Explain the value of a daily planner and a time log to supervisors.

Key Terms

accountability

authority

delegation

formal organization

functional authority

hierarchy

line manager

management

manager

middle management

operating management

power

responsibility

staff manager

supervisor

top management

worker

Introduction

Everyone needs to be able to take charge of his or her own life. Each of us must be able to plan our daily activities, control our use of resources, interact with others to get jobs done, and accumulate the resources necessary to accomplish tasks and to reach our goals. Management (defined below) is both an art and the application of known, proven principles to all of the above. Through the practice of management we become better people. All that we share together in this book will help to make you a better manager of your finances, social relationships, family, and career and will promote your advancement in life.

Defining Management

Management
The process of planning, organizing, leading, and controlling human and material resources for the purposes of setting and achieving stated goals. Also, a team of people making up an organization's hierarchy

Manager
A member of an organization's hierarchy who is paid to make decisions. One who gets things done, with and through others, through the execution of the basic management functions

Formal Organization
An enterprise that has clearly stated goals, a division of labor among specialists, a rational design, and a hierarchy of authority and accountability

Management is an activity that uses the functions of planning, organizing, leading, and controlling human and material resources for the purposes of setting and achieving stated goals. Management is also a team of people that oversees the activities of an enterprise in order to get its tasks and goals accomplished with and through others.

A **manager** is a member of a team of decision makers that gets things done with and through others by carrying out the four management functions or activities. Managers occupy positions of trust and power in a formal organization such as a business.

The term **formal organization** is used here to distinguish our concern from other types of organizations—for example, social or informal organizations. A formal organization is one put together by design and rational plan, such as a business or industrial union. A formal organization is basically the coming together of several people for the accomplishment of stated purposes. The necessary tasks to be performed are identified and divided among the participants. A framework for decisions and control is established.

The four essential elements of any formal organization are as follows:

1. A clear understanding about stated purposes and goals
2. A division of labor among specialists
3. A rational organization or design
4. A hierarchy of authority and accountability

Each of these elements is related to the others. We shall look at each of them separately, in order to understand all of them better.

Stated Purposes and Goals

Every business enterprise is established so that its owners and managers can make a profit. How they intend to make this profit is summed up in very clear statements as to what kind of business they wish to engage in (for example, manufacturing or retailing) and exactly what aims or objectives they are trying to attain.

Managers of each department establish for themselves both short- and long-range goals. The goals the managers set for themselves and for their staffs and departments are influenced directly by the organization's goals established by the top management. These goals are targets to be reached within certain periods of time, as a result of certain limited expenditures of company resources, through the exercise of management functions.

A Division of Labor Among Specialists

We live in a world of specialists. In teaching, medicine, law, and business, men and women are asked to choose areas in which to specialize so that they can concentrate their energies and efforts on the gathering of knowledge, skills, and proficiencies in order to become masters of their fields.

Any formal organization is set up to make good use of the special talents and abilities of its people. Each person is assigned tasks that he or she is best qualified to complete through the application of his or her specialized knowledge. Through the coordination of these specialists—each of whom contributes a part to the whole job—the entire work of the organization is planned and then carried out.

A Rational Organization or Design

Formal business organizations must have order and planning within their operations if they are to be successful. There must be established policies, programs, and procedures, as well as an uninterrupted flow of information and work from the start to the finish of each project.

Before a building can be constructed, many specialists must be called upon to assist in its planning. Architects, engineers, and draftspeople must determine its size and shape in line with the functional demands placed upon the structure. Then more specialists are needed to clear the land, lay the foundation, construct the walls and roof, and finish the interior. Only with precision, planning, and timing can the design become a building.

Hierarchy
The group of people picked to staff an organization's positions of formal authority—its management positions

A Hierarchy of Authority and Accountability

The term **hierarchy** refers to a group of people (managers) who are picked to staff an organization and make all the necessary plans and decisions that allow it to function. Men and women with specialized abilities are installed at different levels of authority and accountability throughout the organization. These people make up management and fill all formal positions of power. From the chief executive to the supervisors, these managers must plan, organize, direct, and control the many activities that have to take place if the organization's goals are to be reached.

Authority

Authority is the right to give orders and instructions to others. Every manager needs authority in order to mobilize the resources that are required to get tasks done. Authority is the right to make a decision or to perform a specific action that will affect the employer. All managers have the authority of their offices or positions. This kind of authority is often called *positional* or *formal* authority because it resides in a job or position and is there to be used by the person who holds that job or position.

Formal or positional authority is usually described in a formal written document called a *job description,* which outlines the specific duties that the position holder is expected to execute. Managers' job descriptions usually give them the right to assign work to subordinates, to oversee the execution of that work, to utilize various kinds of capital equipment, and to spend specific amounts of budgeted funds. As a supervisor, you must be careful to act within the scope of your prescribed duties in order to avoid interfering with the authority of other managers.

As a supervisor, you have the right and duty to act within the scope of your job description. But giving orders and instructions and having them carried out in a satisfactory way are two different things. Have you ever wondered why two managers with the same job descriptions often get very different results? Managers must have the ability and the capacity to enforce their orders and instructions. The essential differences between managers often are in their unique talents, skills, experiences, and abilities to influence others.

Power

Power is the ability to influence others so that they will respond favorably to the orders and instructions that they receive. Two managers may have the same authority but not the same power over others. One may be

Power
The ability to influence others so that they respond favorably to orders and instructions

effective, while the other is ineffective. Power is the ability to command—to get others to do what you want them to do, when you want them to do it, and in the manner you prescribe.

Power can come to a manager in different ways: from the position held and from the individual manager's personality and bank of experience. Power that flows to a manager from the position held is called *legitimate* or *position* power. It consists of the right to punish and reward.

Power can also come to you because of how your subordinates perceive you. If they believe that you are well respected by more senior managers, you will have influence over them and more influence with your people.

Another source to power is your personality—your sense of humor, integrity, openness, and sincere concern for your subordinates and others. Your personality helps attract others to you, because others wish to associate and to identify with you.

Finally, your power over others is directly related to your level of competence—to how well you execute your job, to your willingness to help others in theirs, and to your demonstrated capabilities. Your subordinates view you as a person who can and will help them. Your boss views you as someone who can get the job done.

All sources of power are important to you if you desire to be a truly effective manager. Authority alone is not enough. You must be the kind of person others respect and want to follow. Authority and power make a manager a leader—a person others willingly follow.

Responsibility

Responsibility
The obligation each person with authority has to execute his or her duties to the best of his or her abilities

Responsibility is the name given to each employee's obligation to execute all duties to the best of his or her ability. Because we all, as employees, have the authority of our job descriptions, we all have responsibility. The concept of responsibility tells us not only that we must perform our duties but also that we must do so in line with the instructions we receive from above. Failure to do our best may bring punishment or denial of rewards.

Accountability

Accountability
Having to answer to someone for your performances or failure to perform to standards

Accountability is having to answer to someone for your actions. Authority outlines our duties. Responsibility tells us to execute those duties. Accountability makes us answer to superiors for the ways in which we perform our duties and the end products of our decisions. It asks us to give an account of how responsible we are or have been.

Suppose you have a job description that assigns you the duty to prepare a monthly report on the output of your department. Administrative routine dictates that this report be delivered to your boss on the first day of each month. Your authority is your job description. Your task is the report. Your responsibility is to do the report properly to the best of your ability and to deliver it to your boss by the start of each month. You begin the report but fail to finish it by the due date. You will now have to answer for that failure to your boss. You will have to give an accounting of your progress and accept the credit or the blame. All employees of any organization who are assigned duties have authority, responsibility, and accountability.

Delegation

Delegation is the act of passing one's authority, in part or in total, to another. Only managers can delegate. When you accept a duty through delegation from your boss, you accept new authority and the responsibility for it, and you agree to be held accountable for your performance of the new duty. When you as a supervisor delegate authority, you agree to be held accountable for your decision to delegate (the way you have chosen to handle your responsibility) and for the execution of the delegated duty by your subordinate. The act of delegation, therefore, creates a duality of both responsibility and accountability related to the same task or duty and its execution. If this were not so, any manager could pass a tough job to a subordinate and escape from it entirely, with no adverse consequences. But the concept of accountability tells us that giving a task away is a way in which a manager has chosen to execute a task—the way the manager has chosen to handle responsibility for the task. That decision must be answered for.

Again, an example is in order. Suppose you are going away from your job on Tuesday for personal business. You have one task that must be executed during your absence, and you decide to delegate it to a subordinate. You take your day off. When you return, you discover that the task was not performed. Your boss will want to know why, and you will be asked to answer for the failure to execute the task. You, in turn, will want to know what went wrong and why. Both you and your subordinate are accountable for the ways in which you chose to handle responsibility for the same task. But you, as supervisor, shoulder the primary burden of accountability in the eyes of your boss.

Why You Must Delegate

Delegation is a tool that allows you to train subordinates. By introducing your most capable subordinates to bits and pieces of your job, you get them ready to advance. Unless you have a trained successor to fill your shoes, it will be very hard for you to get promoted. Your boss will not want to create a "hole" in the operations by letting you move up if it means leaving behind a leaderless group.

Second, by delegating you can free yourself from time-consuming routines that might be better performed by subordinates. Until you create some free time for yourself, you will not be able to accept delegation from your boss. Like yourself, your boss wants to meet your need to grow by letting you experience greater responsibilities, thus getting you ready to move up.

Some managers fear the delegation process because they do not want to give up any of their authority. They fear that a subordinate cannot do the job as well as they can or that they will lose control over the execution of their authority once it is in the hands of another. They may fear that, once subordinates knows their bosses' jobs, they will be a threat to their job security. But fearing the act of delegation is no excuse for not doing it. You must recognize that you will have no other choice. Your boss expects it, subordinates may demand it, and you will be away from your job at times because of illness and vacations. Keep in mind that delegation frees you from any task that your subordinates can do, helps you identify the subordinates that you can depend on, and lets you spend more of your time on things that only you can do or that you do best.

How to Delegate

Four basic steps are involved in the decision to pass some of your authority to another person:

1. Decide on the task(s), limits, and supports.
2. Choose the subordinate.
3. Give the assignment.
4. Stay in touch.

1. *Decide on the Task(s), Limits, and Supports* Spell out in as much detail as you think necessary exactly what you want the subordinate to do, the limits you are placing on the execution, and the supports you have to offer. (You want Sally to collate a report, but you do not want her to staple the pages together or to deliver them to anyone but yourself. You want the collating done by the close of business today. You will be available in your office if she needs any help.)

2. *Choose the Subordinate* The person you choose may be one in need of the experience, one who is capable of doing the job already, or one who wants exposure to the task. You may want to choose

more than one person so that several people get the training or exposure. This will give your people more flexibility and will allow you to be less dependent on any one person.

3. *Give the Assignment* Let the person know what you want done, the limits, and the supports. You may want to put everything in writing. This is a good idea if you will be away while the person must accomplish the task. It is also recommended that you tell the person why he or she was picked to do the job. Be honest. Explain why the task is necessary and the kind of results you expect. Ask the subordinate for feedback. Find out if there are any misunderstandings. When the subordinate can restate the assignment and limits accurately and knows how to perform the task(s), you are ready for step four.

4. *Stay in Touch* Even so-called "simple" tasks are not so simple when an inexperienced person has to perform them. Keep track of the person's progress by checking with him or her periodically. You may ask for periodic reports of progress if the task is to stretch over several days or weeks.

When the task is accomplished, let the subordinate know how you evaluate his or her efforts. You may want to reward the person with praise and point out what went well and what could be improved.

What You Do Not Want to Delegate

In general, you should *not* delegate a task that you do not understand or know how to perform. If you do, you will be unable to offer any support when trouble arises, and you may not be able to evaluate the results fairly. As a supervisor, you should not delegate the authority to punish or reward. People work to please those who have this authority. Delegation should never strip you of these rights and duties. Finally, if you have no one who is capable of taking on the task, you must either get someone ready to take it or keep the task for yourself.

The Management Hierarchy

We have concluded that, among other things, managers make up a team of decision makers charged with operating the formal organization of a business. You will recall that one of the characteristics of a formal organization is that it has a hierarchy of authority and accountability. We shall now examine this hierarchy.

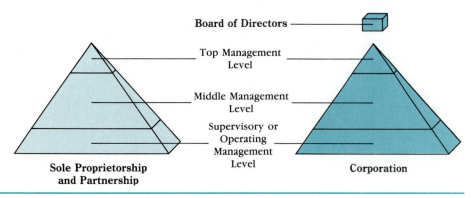

Board of Directors

Top Management Level

Middle Management Level

Supervisory or Operating Management Level

Sole Proprietorship and Partnership

Corporation

Exhibit 3.1   The pyramid of the management hierarchy.

The simple pyramid shown in Exhibit 3.1 is our symbol for the management hierarchy. This pyramid is divided into three levels: the top management, the middle management, and the supervisory or operating level of management. As depicted in the exhibit, both the top and bottom levels are rather thin in comparison with the middle level. This pyramid is typical of a medium-sized (500–1,000 employees) or larger business. A smaller enterprise might well have an even distribution at each level or only one manager performing all the activities at each level. The point is that, whether the roles for each level are played by many people or by a few, these roles must be played.

Many sole proprietorships and partnerships have only one or a few managers who must, out of necessity, direct more than one specialized area. Most sole proprietorships and partnerships are extremely small in terms of both the number of people they employ and the dollars they earn and spend. They cannot afford, nor are their operations complex enough, to demand more than one or two levels of management. In many small businesses, managers have themselves as subordinates. They must perform the functions of managers and then execute their own plans and direct their own efforts in the process.

The examination that follows uses a business corporation as its model. Much of the discussion applies to sole proprietorships and partnerships. One exception: a corporation is the only type of business organization to have a board of directors and to include a secretary (a corporate officer) as a member of its top management.

The Board of Directors

Outside and above the corporate management pyramid is the *board of directors,* which is represented graphically in the second pyramid in Exhibit 3.1. The board members, who are elected by the stockholders or owners of the corporation, elect their own chairperson. The directors exercise jurisdiction over the actions of the chief executive of the corporation. They review the major decisions of the chief executive. The board decides what the company's business is and should be. It formulates company *policy*—general guidelines for management action at every level when dealing with recurring situations—picks the chief executive, and diagnoses and recommends treatment for business ills in the absence of recommendations from the chief executive. In short, the board of directors is a watchdog for the owners' interests and a tough court of review before which the chief executive's case is tried. The majority of a board's members are full-time executives working for other companies or corporations. They are usually specialists, such as lawyers and bankers.

Only in a crisis does the board depart from its role of judge and adopt an executive approach. It may give orders to remove or replace the chief executive, in order to bring the firm through a period of difficulties. Only at such rare times can the board function as the top management of the corporation. When the crisis ends, the board quickly returns to its judicial role.

The Top Management Level

Top management
The uppermost part of the management hierarchy, containing the positions of the chief executive and his or her immediate subordinates

Occupying only the small topmost portion of the pyramid, the **top management** level is the location of the chief executive (president) and his or her immediate subordinates (vice-presidents or their equivalents). In a sole proprietorship, the owner is usually the chief executive. In a partnership, the role of the chief executive is usually shared between or among the partners, each of whom concentrates on his or her specialties.

In a corporation the top management is composed of the officers of the company: a president, one or more vice-presidents, a treasurer, and a secretary. Any two (or more) offices may be held by the same person, except the offices of secretary and president.

The Chief Executive's Role   The chief executive must play at least two roles: he or she must be a person capable of both careful analysis and effective action. He or she must develop and establish the major objectives for the business and make the major decisions necessary to attain them. The chief executive is the one manager who must be able to observe and comprehend the entire operation. Like the captain of a ship, the chief executive is responsible for his or her own decisions and is accountable for those of all the other managers. He or she must be able to plan, control, organize, and direct the work of subordinates in order to attain the stated objectives of the company.

The Vice-President's Role   Vice-presidents are the immediate subordinates of the chief executive. They are charged with the overall operation of the company's functional areas:

Marketing—sales and all sales-connected activities

Production—manufacturing and procurement of raw materials

Finance—managing the company's funds and credit through accounting

Personnel—recruitment of employees and managers and administration of employee benefits

Other business activities, such as engineering, research and development, and purchasing may fall under one or another of these headings, or they may be led by their own specialized members of top management.

The vice-presidents must plan, organize, direct, and control the general operation of their departments so as to achieve their departments' (as well as their company's) stated objectives. Their subordinates are the middle managers.

The Secretary's Role   The corporate secretary has the following duties: (1) to keep the minutes of the meetings of the stockholders and the board of directors; (2) to keep all stock ownership records; and (3) to act as the custodian of the corporate records and of the corporate seal, which is affixed to all corporate shares and documents as a proof that they are official acts of the company. He or she may also serve the company in another capacity, such as finance manager, personnel manager, or some other executive position. The job of corporate secretary is seldom a full-time position.

The Treasurer's Role   The treasurer has the following duties: (1) to accept charge of, custody of, and responsibility for all funds and securities of the corporation, receiving and depositing all moneys due and payable to the corporation; (2) to control all disbursements of company funds; and (3) to prepare all financial statements, such as the balance sheet and the profit-and-loss statement. The treasurer is either the chief financial officer of a corporation or a member of that staff.

The Middle Management Level

Middle management
The members of the hierarchy below the rank of top management but above the rank of supervisor

Occupying the middle area of the pyramid, the **middle management** level is the location of all managers below the rank of vice-president and above the operating level. Each functional area has many specific tasks to be performed. Exhibit 3.2 illustrates the hierarchy of a retailer with branch

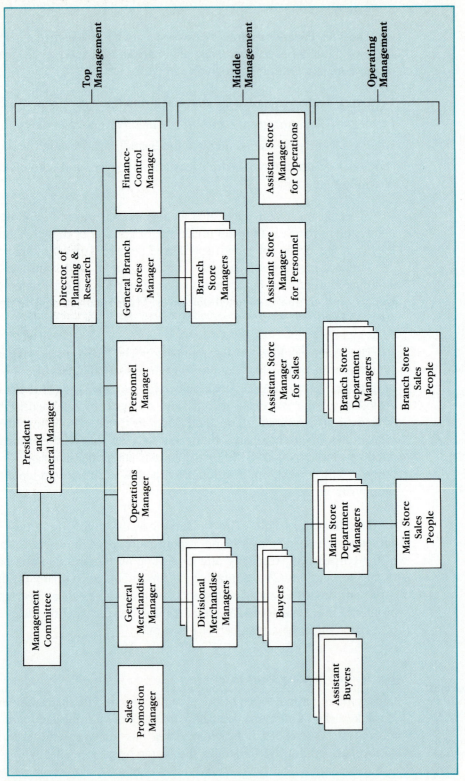

Exhibit 3.2   A retail business organization showing the three levels of management. One approach to the organization of a retailer whose central management oversees the operation of three branch stores. (*Note:* Only the merchandise manager's and the branch store manager's subordinates are shown.) (*Source:* Courtesy of the National Retail Merchants Association, New York, N.Y.)

stores. The store's divisional merchandise and branch store managers are not specialists, but all their subordinate managers are. Each one must carry out the operation of a specific part of the store's activities. Like those of all managers, the middle manager's functions are to plan, direct, control, and organize.

The Operating Management Level

Operating management
The level of the hierarchy that oversees the work of nonmanagement people (workers)

Shown at the bottom of the management pyramid, the **operating management** level is the place where supervisors and foremen are found. A **supervisor** is a manager whose subordinates are nonmanagement employees (**workers**). If a manager directs the work of other managers, he or she does not belong on this level.

It is important to note here that the supervisory level of management is changing in many companies today. The supervisor is evolving into a "team leader," who facilitates the efforts of the group he or she heads. Typically, team leaders train, encourage, and support in any ways necessary the efforts of the team members. The position of team leader may even rotate on a monthly basis, allowing each member of the team who wants to gain experience as a manager to get it. More will be said about the team leader position throughout this text.

Supervisor
A member of the operating level of management's hierarchy who directs the work of nonmanagement employees (workers)

It should be remembered that Exhibit 3.1 depicts only the management team. The majority of workers in an organization form the base of the pyramid, the group of people upon which managers depend to execute plans and to achieve goals. Exhibit 3.3 shows the complete picture of a typical business corporation.

Worker
Any employee who is not a member of the management hierarchy

Line and Staff Authority

Line Managers

The formal authority that flows from the top of an organization to all its management positions is also termed *line authority*. From the top to the bottom of any formal organization, formal authority flows from superiors to subordinates in a continuous line. The management positions connected by this line authority make up the organization's hierarchy.

Line authority allows its holder—a manager—to exercise direct supervision over his or her subordinates. Managers who have line authority can give direct orders to, appraise, and discipline those who receive their orders.

The managers in the organization hierarchy who manage activities or

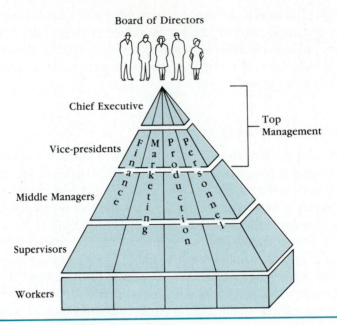

Board of Directors

Chief Executive

Top
Management

Vice-presidents

Finance Marketing Production Personnel

Middle Managers

Supervisors

Workers

Exhibit 3.3   A corporation's management pyramid showing the functional areas and the base of workers.

departments that directly influence the success (profitability) of a business are called **line managers.** Their departments make direct contributions toward achieving the company's goals.

Line manager
A member of the organization's hierarchy who oversees a department or activity that directly affects the organization's success—the vital functions

Since line activities are identified in terms of the company's goals, the activities classified as line will differ with each organization. For example, a manufacturing company may limit line functions to production and sales, while a department store, in which buying is a key element, will include the purchasing department and the sales department in its line activities.[1]

When an organization is small, all positions may be line roles; staff roles are added as the organization grows and as it becomes useful to devote specialists' time to assist the line members in doing their primary jobs.[2]

Staff Managers

Staff manager
A member of the organization's hierarchy who renders advice and service in his or her areas of expertise to anyone who needs them

Staff authority, like line authority, is a kind of formal authority. It is distributed throughout the organization to various managers at any level who advise and assist other managers. **Staff managers** are specialists who supervise activities or departments that do not directly contribute to achieving the company's major goals. The staff managers' primary mission is to help all other managers who need their specialized knowledge.

The concept of *staff* is only relevant as applied to the relationships between and among managers. A manager is a staff manager if his or her job is to advise, counsel, assist, or provide service to another manager. You can tell if managers are staff or line managers by observing what their relationships are to the other managers.

Since staff managers are linked to the top of an organization, they receive line authority also. If they have subordinates, they direct, appraise, and discipline those subordinates, just as any line manager does with his or her subordinates. It is safe to say that when a staff manager directs the work of subordinates, he or she is acting as a line manager. But when the staff manager gives advice or assistance to another manager, he or she is acting exclusively as a staff manager.

Exhibit 3.4 is an abbreviated organization chart of a management hierarchy that shows both line and staff positions, as well as the relationships of authority. Note that staff and line managers appear at both the top and the middle of the hierarchy.

Organization charts are just one of several tools used to show the part that each person or section plays in the entire enterprise. They should show the following things:

- Who reports to whom
- The flow of authority and accountability
- Formal positions of authority and their titles
- Lines of communication
- Lines of promotion

Functional Authority

Functional authority
The right that a manager of a staff department has to make decisions and to give orders that affect the way things are done in another department

Functional authority is the right given to a manager of a department (usually a staff department) to make decisions that govern the operation of another department. Exhibit 3.5 illustrates the flow of functional authority from the staff managers to the other managers in an organization. The lines of functional authority indicate a measure of control by a staff manager over a line manager and his or her people and their activities.

The normal practice (where functional authority is not used) is for a line manager to have complete control over his or her area of responsibility and relative freedom to make his or her own decisions. Staff managers have been installed to help the line as well as other staff managers but usually only when called upon to do so. It is as though the line managers are saying, "Don't call us, we'll call you." Under this arrangement, a staff

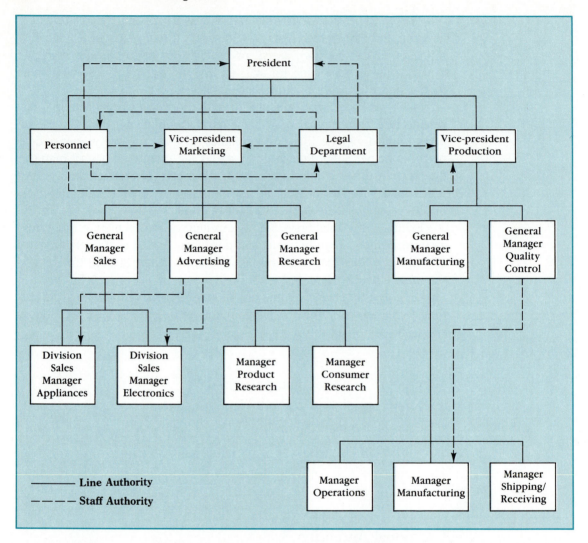

Exhibit 3.4 **Organization chart showing four staff positions and the flow of both line and staff authority.**

manager may never be consulted. Line managers must take full responsibility for their actions when acting on staff advice. After all, they could have ignored the advice of the staff manager.

For this and other reasons, many companies make use of the concept of functional authority. This concept holds that, if a staff manager makes a decision about his or her area that has application to the area of another manager, the manager of that other area is bound by the staff manager's decision. For example, the payroll department issues a directive stating that henceforth all payroll data from each department must

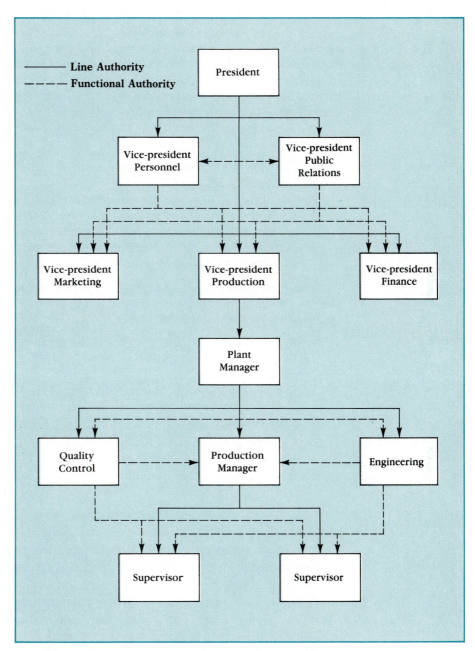

Exhibit 3.5 The flow of functional staff and line authority in a manufacturing business.

According to professor of management science Elliott Jaques, every manager needs to be held accountable for adding value to his or her work, for the work of subordinates, for sustaining a team of subordinates capable of doing their work, and for setting directions and persuading subordinates to follow willingly and enthusiastically. "In brief, every manager is accountable for work and leadership."

Professor Jaques believes that to do the job, managers need the following:

1. The right to say "no" to any applicant who falls below minimum standards of ability
2. The authority to give work assignments
3. The authority to give performance appraisals to subordinates and the authority to make decisions about raises and rewards
4. The authority to initiate removal from the manager's team anyone who is incapable of doing the work

Finally, Professor Jaques believes that a management hierarchy is the best way to get things done in a business organization. Through it the organization can meet four essential needs:

1. To add value to work as it moves through the organization
2. To provide accountability at each level of the value-adding process
3. To place competent people at each level of the hierarchy
4. To build a common consensus and acceptance of the management structure that achieves the above

Adapted from: Elliott Jaques, "In Praise of Hierarchy," *Harvard Business Review* (January–February 1990): 127–133.

be submitted on a specific form, in a specified way, and by a certain date. If the managers throughout the business wish to get themselves and their people paid on time and in the correct amounts, they had better follow the directive.

Functional authority seems to give a manager many bosses. But does it? Isn't a company merely removing many important, but not essential, areas from a manager's concern in order to promote uniformity and efficiency? When many routine decisions about problem areas are made outside the department, each manager is freed of the responsibility to consider these matters. As a result, the manager has more time to devote to his or her specialized, essential tasks. What is lost in autonomy is more than compensated for by an increase in efficiency and economy in the overall operation of the business.

The Manager's Functions

We shall now briefly explore the four major functions of management. By *major functions* we mean the most important and time-consuming activities common to all managers. These functions consists of *planning, organizing, leading,* and *controlling.* Planning and organizing are the preparatory phases for management action. Leading is the actuating phase. Leading is supervising, which means literally to *oversee* the work or performance of another. Leading, more than any of the other functions, is our prime concern throughout this text. Controlling is the follow-up phase that attempts to guarantee the successful execution of the other functions.

Planning

Planning is the first and most basic of the management functions. Through planning, managers attempt to prepare for and forecast future events. Planning involves the construction of programs for action designed to achieve stated goals through the use of people and other resources. Planning is also a part of the other functions of management: organizing, leading, and controlling. It is the first thing you must do before executing any of these functions.

Organizing

The organizing function determines the tasks to be performed, the jobs or positions required to execute tasks, and the resources needed to accomplish the tasks and to reach the organization's goals. Organizing is directly related to and dependent on planning.

Leading

The leading function includes the activities of overseeing, training, evaluating, disciplining, rewarding, and staffing. Staffing is concerned with adding new talent to an organization, promoting or transferring people to new jobs and responsibilities, and terminating people from the organization.

Controlling

The controlling function is concerned with preventing, identifying, and correcting deficiencies in all phases of an organization's operations.

Through controlling, standards of performance are established, communicated to those affected by them, and used to measure the operations and performances of individuals and the entire organization.

These four functions apply to all managers, but each level of management spends different amounts of time performing each (see Exhibit 3.6). While top management spends most of its time on planning, supervisors (operating management) spend most of their time on leading. Chapter 4 explores these functions in more detail from the supervisor's perspective.

Related to the four major management functions are two other sets of activities that are part of each. It would be impossible to speak of planning or any other function without recognizing the need to communicate. Communicating (the subject of chapter 5) is the ability to get your ideas across to others by means of the spoken or written word. It is impossible to carry out your management duties without interacting with others. You need the input from others, and others need yours. The second set of activities has to do with coordinating what you do with others in your organization. By coordinating their efforts, supervisors attempt to prevent people and units from interfering with each other. Before, during, and after taking action, you need to promote harmony and mutual cooperation in order to keep your human relationships in good order and to prevent the waste of resources. By keeping in regular communication with subordinates, peers, and superiors, you aid your efforts at coordination. Chapter 4 examines the coordinating function in more detail.

Decision Making

You have been making decisions all your life. You have made many already today. As a supervisor, you are paid to make them to the best of your ability. As we have already seen, you have a responsibility to make them and are accountable for the results. A *decision* in its most essential form is a conclusion that you reach by making judgments. A decision usually begins in the mind in the form of a question such as "What will I have for lunch?" This question leads to others such as "What am I in the mood for?" Past experiences and desires come to mind. Different foods are considered, along with certain restraints that may exist such as the amount of money and time we have available for lunch and the kinds of restaurants we desire. Our minds deal quickly with such variables and restraints, and we reach a decision quite easily. In fact, such a decision may already be made for us because some of us are creatures of habit and routine: we eat at the same place so regularly that we don't give it much thought; we just find ourselves at the same place each lunchtime.

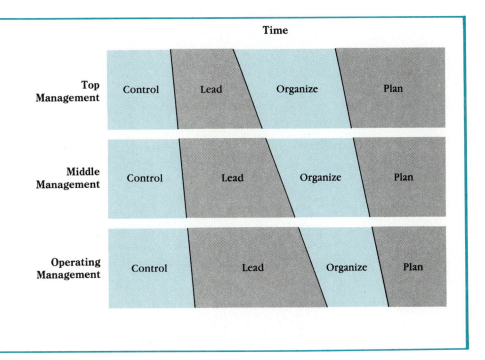

Exhibit 3.6 The proportions of time spent on the management functions by the three management levels.

What goes on in our minds in deciding where to eat and what to eat for lunch leads us to a process for making decisions. Most of us have a process, but we may never have put it in writing. It's simply there in our minds and serves us each time we try to answer questions and make a decision. What follows is one approach that can help you make difficult decisions rationally. This approach will remove a great deal of uncertainty and will give you a method for problem solving that will help you avoid making many bad or mediocre decisions.

A Rational Model

The rational model in Exhibit 3.7 has six steps. None of them is really new to you, but all are essential and basically easy to take. They simply put what you have been doing all your life into a systematic framework that will help you make better decisions. We shall work through the steps by using an example.

1. *Define the Problem* A problem exists when what you are facing is not as you wish it to be or as it should be. Symptoms are usually

1. Define the problem. (The effort here is to define the difference between what is and what should be. Avoid the pitfall of defining symptoms and go beyond them to their causes.)

2. Identify your restraints. (Your restraints are such resources as time, money, and talent. Anything that limits your abilities to solve a problem as you would like is a restraint.)

3. List your alternatives. (Alternatives are possible solutions. List as many as you can without regard for their good and bad points. Involve the ideas of others if they can be of assistance.)

4. Evaluate your alternatives. (Go back to step 2 and consider each alternative with your restraints in mind. List the advantages and disadvantages for each course of action.)

5. Decide on the best alternative(s). (Pick one or a combination of two or more that have the least serious disadvantages and the most important advantages.)

6. Implement the decision and follow up. (This is the action step that tries out your solution. Learn from the application, and be prepared to fall back to another solution if the one you have chosen does not give positive results.)

Exhibit 3.7   Steps in the rational decision-making process.

the first signs of a problem's existence. For example, your toaster won't toast, or your television's channels are all snowy.

Ed, the supervisor of data control, has noticed several computer operators sitting idle and the central computer out of operation. All should be operating. What is the problem? Lazy workers? Broken machines? Without further investigation, Ed will not be certain. He first talks with the operators to discover the source of their idleness. His investigation tells him that a necessary set of figures from the accounting department has not arrived on schedule and that work on the report can progress no further without the figures. What is the problem now? Missing data from accounting? Ed calls the accounting supervisor and discovers that the data were sent over two hours ago. Ed conducts a search and discovers the data on his desk, buried under items that arrived later.

Ed started with symptoms and moved to an investigation that led him to the discovery that vital information was getting lost in his own department on his own desk. This discovery tells Ed that his problem is related to the way in which information from outside his office is received and filed. Ed now frames the problem as a question: ''How can information flowing to us from the outside be properly handled to avoid losing it?'' Having defined his problem, Ed is now ready to proceed to step 2.

2. *Identify Your Restraints* Restraints are limiting factors that affect your efforts to make a decision. Restraints generally fall under several headings such as who, what, when, and where. Who will be involved in the decision-making process? Is it a decision that needs the group's support and input? If so, the group must be involved in the process. ''Who'' also asks us to consider who is affected by the problem and whether or not the affected people have a role to play in solving it. What is involved? What resources may be affected and may have to be committed in order to make and implement the decision? Money, time, and other resources will surely be involved in some way. When must a solution be delivered? By what date must a decision be made? Finally, where is the solution needed and best implemented?

Ed has decided that he must make the decision and that the others will simply be informed about it and their parts in it after they give him their ideas about handling the problem. Ed has further decided that few resources will be needed. Time is the primary resource he and others must expend to make a decision. Ed thinks that the ''when'' is best answered with ''as soon as possible'' and assigns the highest priority to dealing with the problem. Ed believes the ''where'' is his office, with its routines and paperwork flow. Ed is now ready for step 3.

3. *List Your Alternatives* Alternatives are the courses of action that you believe will solve your problem. Alternatives should be developed without criticism, as they are offered and listed. Their merits and drawbacks can be dealt with in step 4. In developing your list, be as creative as you can, and seek counsel wherever you think an idea might reside. All of your alternatives should represent possible ways to correct the difficulties you are experiencing.

Ed consulted his work force and over a period of several hours put together a list of four solutions:

a. Do nothing, as this is the first time the problem has occurred. Ed should merely check his desk more often.
b. Have all incoming work delivered directly to Ed.
c. In Ed's absence, have all work delivered to his secretary.
d. Set up a special location for incoming work at the entrance to the office, with a clearly labeled sign informing delivery persons to deposit their items at the designated location.

Ed is now ready to evaluate his alternatives.

4. *Evaluate Your Alternatives* This step asks you to look critically at your listed alternatives and to focus on their relative merits and disadvantages. In doing so, you must consider the restraints you have labeled in step 2. For some merits and disadvantages, you may wish to assign a relative point value to give either a higher or lower importance to each.

   Ed evaluates his first alternative as follows: The problem is new but could recur. It resulted from the fact that, through habit, people have always delivered their items to Ed's desk, not to Ed. Ed checks his desk regularly, but there are blocks of time when he finds it impossible even to get back to his office. For this reason, alternative a is rejected.

   Ed realizes that the remaining three alternatives require cooperation from the delivery person in other departments if they are to work. All three would prevent the problem from recurring. Alternative d is advantageous in that no person from his department need be present for the system to work. However, its major disadvantage is that all personnel in Ed's section, Ed himself, or Ed's secretary would have to check the new location regularly for their work instead of getting it directly from Ed as in the past. The major disadvantage to alternatives b and c is that a person must be present. If Ed and his secretary were absent, work would be dropped on a desk, as in the past. The current problem might then recur. Ed is now ready to move to step 5.

5. *Decide on the Best Alternative(s)* At this step, the best alternative or combination of alternatives is chosen. The relative merits and disadvantages of each are considered, and the alternative offering the least serious disadvantages and the most merits is chosen. Keep in mind that, after deciding and implementing, you may find that the problem still persists or that a new problem has arisen. Your efforts will then have to be reexamined and other methods tried. For this reason, you may want to set up an alternate plan and be ready to implement it when necessary.

   Ed has decided to go with his fourth alternative. It overcomes what Ed feels is the biggest disadvantage of the other two alternatives: the physical presence of either himself or his secretary is required for them to work. Even though he will have to get outsiders broken in to the new routine, Ed feels that they will cooperate with little opposition. It will take a visit or two from each of them to get them used to the new routine.

6. *Implement the Decision and Follow Up* Without implementation, a decision just sits there and helps no one. Everyone involved in the decision must be informed in advance as to their individual roles

and responsibilities. They must know what is expected of them, what is new and different, and when things are to change. In addition, they must be committed to their roles in the solution if it is to reap the best results. After the decision is enacted, the results must be monitored.

Ed has contacted the heads of the various departments that supply his work and has been assured that the new procedure will be made known to delivery persons. Ed has instructed his people to accept no work personally but to direct the delivery to the specially marked area and its receptacles. Both Ed and his secretary will make it a habit to check the delivery area regularly and to distribute the work found there to the proper persons. Ed sets the time when the new procedure will be implemented and arranges to monitor the results.

Common Elements in Decision Making

Most supervisors are new to formal decision making. Before becoming a member of management's team, you have specific goals and orders, resources provided by your boss, and a problem solver represented by the boss. You may or may not have been consulted when decisions had to be made. But once you become a manager, you soon realize the need to consult with others before, during, and after the period when a decision is made.

Most decisions share the following common elements:

- A situation that demands action
- Time pressures created by things getting steadily worse
- A lack of all the information you would like to have before deciding
- Some uncertainties that force you to take some risk
- The likelihood of costly consequences if your decision is wrong
- The likelihood of benefits for effective decision
- The existence of at least two alternatives[3]

Given these elements, you have to gather what input you can from whatever sources are available in the time allotted for your decision. Keep in mind that others may have been down the path you face before you. Your boss, your peers, and your subordinates may have the experience and ideas that you lack. Use whatever help you can to avoid as many traps as possible. Your aim is to make the best decision you can, given the resources and restraints that exist.

1. If time permits discussion and analysis; that is, if you don't have to have the decision immediately.
2. If the decision affects the personal or business lives of the employee(s); at least their input and feedback will help you make a mutually acceptable decision.
3. If the problem you have stems from the behavior of another person, and only that person's corrective action will solve your problem.
4. If you accept final responsibility for a decision that has been given to you and not to the others, but collective discussion would yield a better solution than simply mulling it over on your own.
5. If responsibility for the decision can be shared by the group with no one person's being held liable if a decision that seems right turns out not to work after all.
6. If data available to others are not available to you, or if their expertise will help you solve the problem.
7. If implementation requires group commitment and effort.

Exhibit 3.8   **When to involve others in decisions that you have to make.**
[*Source:* Reprinted by permission of the publisher from *How to Be a Successful Manager*, by Donald Weiss, copyright 1986 by AMACOM, a division of American Management Association, New York. All rights reserved]

Sharing Decisions

You should involve members of your work group in a decision if they have valuable input to give, if they are going to have to implement it, and if their commitment to the decision is essential to make it work. The decisions you can make alone or without the approval of members of your work group are ones that you can implement alone with satisfactory results. Exhibit 3.8 offers some additional insights about when to involve others in your decisions. Chapter 9 looks at decision making with groups in detail.

Managing Your Time

We all have the same amount of time in each day. The differences between us are in how we use that time. Studies have indicated that most of us waste time on the job through a variety of means. We may make or accept personal phone calls. We may stretch breaks by several minutes on a regular basis. We may fail to plan our work, instead reacting to things as they come, without giving the work to be done a timetable or priorities. People who use time well have time for their tasks. They complete work on schedule. They have time to train others. They have time to take on additional tasks that groom them for higher responsibilities. Using time well gives us a sense of pride, while wasting it gives us a sense of guilt and frustration.

A good way to improve your use of time is to start keeping records of how you use your time at present. Keep a record of your use of time at work by stopping each hour (or after each task is completed) to record how much time you have spent and what you have spent it on. This tactic will let you know very quickly at the end of each day where you wasted time and where you used it productively.

Time Logs

Exhibit 3.9 is one example of a *daily time log*. It provides an easy way for you to list the activities you perform each day, to record the time each activity took, and to classify each activity as a regular, recurring one or as one that is unexpected and unusual. The recurring activities routinely make up a part of each working day: evaluating subordinates, planning your work schedule, attending planned-for meetings, and preparing regular reports. The unexpected activities include unexpected visitors (drop-ins), unexpected telephone calls, and crises—problems that have arisen but could not have been foreseen. After a few days, some interesting patterns will emerge. You will have a clear understanding of how you are using time, and you will then be ready to start planning in a realistic way for using it more efficiently.

Getting Rid of Interruptions

Your time log will list the unnecessary interruptions that have taken place. The next step is to consider what to do about them. For most supervisors, unexpected phone calls are among the most frequent sources of interruption, second only to unplanned-for visitors who drop by to "shoot the breeze" or get your opinions. If you have a secretary, have him or her screen the calls. Calls can be classified as "deal with now," "I'll get back to you," or "leave your message." Asking people to write brief memos instead of using the telephone can help, too. Drop-ins can be asked, courteously, to book an appointment so that you will have enough time to deal with them properly. Social visits can wait for breaks and lunch.

Daily Planners

Exhibit 3.10 is an example of a *daily planner* that you can use to start getting your use of time at work under control. Before your workday

REGULAR ACTIVITIES

Time Spent with Others

	Mon	Tue	Wed	Thur	Fri	Sat	Sun	TOTALS
1. Evaluating/praising/disciplining								
2. Attending scheduled meetings								
3. Training/coaching								
4. Making telephone calls								
5. Meals and breaks								
6. Other (specify) _____								
_____								

Time Spent Alone

	Mon	Tue	Wed	Thur	Fri	Sat	Sun	TOTALS
1. Reading memos, letters, reports								
2. Preparing reports and correspondence								
3. Planning and scheduling work								
4. Efforts at self-development								
5. Travel time to and from scheduled events								
6. Other (specify) _____								
_____								

UNEXPECTED ACTIVITIES

	Mon	Tue	Wed	Thur	Fri	Sat	Sun	TOTALS
1. Receiving telephone calls								
2. Communicating with drop-ins								
3. Attending last-minute meetings								
4. Dealing with unexpected problems								
5. Other (specify) _____								
Totals								

Exhibit 3.9   **Daily time log.** (Use this log to keep track of how you spend your time at work, away from work, or both. Use multiples of 5-minute intervals and keep track in minutes.)

begins, list your objectives—the specific goals or results you hope to have achieved by the end of the day. List them in the order in which you hope to accomplish them. It is a good idea to start with the results you *must* have, moving then to other results. In the "Activities" section, list the specific tasks, people, places, and other essentials required to reach each of your goals. Consider your planner a "living" document. You can add to or change your objectives and activities throughout the day, as time and circumstances dictate.

By keeping your planners and reviewing them each day, you will learn how realistic your planning of time and activities has been and can make it more accurate in the future. When reviewing your daily planner, ask yourself the following questions:

- Did I accomplish all that I expected to? If not, why not?
- Were my time estimates realistic? If not, why not?
- What did I learn about time planning that I can use tomorrow?

It won't be too long before you are blocking out time in your head, as well as on paper, and making better use of it. Then you can eliminate the log and become a regular user of the standard desktop calendar.

Using "Spare" Time

Use your previously unproductive time productively. Time spent traveling to and from work in your car or on a train can be used to catch up on essential, work-related tapes or reading. You can make notes with a note-pad and pen or on a portable tape recorder. Good ideas can be captured and remembered as they occur. Time spent in an office waiting room can be used productively by simply taking work with you. By doing these things, you will get more accomplished and will look good to others—and to yourself.

How Supervisors Spend Their Time

Many studies have been done on how supervisors spend their time. Surprisingly, the studies show many similarities, although in specific details there are wide differences among supervisors. Exhibit 3.11 is a composite constructed from several studies including some done by the author. It is intended merely as a guide for comparison when you examine your own use of time. Once you know how you spend your time, use Exhibit 3.11 to note any major differences. Spending too much time on one activity may mean not having enough time available for others.

MY OBJECTIVES FOR TODAY: Date: _____ 19 ____

1. _____

2. _____

3. _____

4. _____

5. _____

ACTIVITIES (who, what, when, where, how)	Start Time	Ending Time
1. _____		
_____		
2. _____		
_____		
3. _____		
_____		
4. _____		
_____		

Exhibit 3.10   **Daily planner.** (Start by listing your major objectives for the day, in the order in which you wish to accomplish them. Under the ''Activities'' section, list the specific tasks you need to perform to reach your objectives and the estimated starting and ending times for each. Complete the ''Results'' portion at the end of the day.)

Three Categories

By dividing your work into categories, you can more effectively execute tasks and assign priorities to them. For example, consider the pile of work on your desk each morning. There is work left over from preceding days, the mail, memos and work generated by others, and various notes that

5. _____

   _____

6. _____

   _____

7. _____

   _____

8. _____

   _____

9. _____

   _____

10. _____

   _____

RESULTS: _____

_____

What to Carry over to Tomorrow:

_____

_____

_____

you have left for yourself. Divide this work into three categories: "read and discard," "to be delegated," and "must do." The material, when first read, will fall into one of these categories. Memos sent to keep you informed fall into the first. Work you want others to act on falls into the second. Work only you can do falls into the third. Take the work to be assigned to others, and determine a due date for it based on when it must be completed. Assess your third category from two points of view: how

Supervisor's Activity	Approximate Portion of 8-hour Day	Approximate Number of Minutes
Production supervision	25%	120
Personnel administration and grievances	20%	96
Meetings and conferences	15%	72
Appraising worker performance	10%	48
Concern for machines, materials, and equipment	10%	48
Planning and scheduling work	8%	38
Other activities	12%	58
	100%	480 minutes

Exhibit 3.11   Typical distribution of a supervisor's time.

much time each task will take and by what date it must be completed. Then block out the time you will need on your calendar, working ahead as time allows and planning early completions where possible.

Instant Replay

1. Management is an activity that uses the functions of planning, organizing, leading, and controlling human and material resources for the purpose of achieving stated goals.

2. Management is a team of people that rationally oversees the activities of an enterprise and attempts to get its tasks and goals accomplished with and through others.

3. A manager is a member of a team of paid decision makers who gets things done with and through others by executing the four management functions. Managers occupy positions of formal authority in an organization.

4. Managers work for formal organizations that have clearly stated purposes and goals, a division of labor among specialists, a rational organization or design, and a clearly defined hierarchy of authority and accountability.

5. A person's job description outlines the authority he or she possesses to mobilize the organization's resources.

6. Power flows to a person from two sources: the job he or she holds and the skills, experience, and personality he or she possesses.

7. Authority can be delegated. Responsibility and accountability cannot be.

8. Your decisions should be made with the aid of a rationally prepared decision-making model so that you can consider your alternatives carefully and avoid problems.

9. The management hierarchy consists of three levels inherent in most businesses: top, middle, and supervisory or operating.

10. In order to be most effective, staff managers may exercise functional authority over many other managers.

11. Managing time is as important as managing a career to a supervisor. Time, like other resources, must be used effectively and efficiently.

Glossary   **Accountability**   having to answer to someone for your actions. It makes us answer to our superiors for the quality of our performance and for the ways in which we choose to perform our duties.

Authority   a person's right to give orders and instructions to others as a result of the position he or she occupies. Authority is also called *formal authority*.

Delegation   the act of passing one's authority, in part or in total, to another. Only managers can delegate, and only authority is delegated.

Formal organization   an enterprise that has clearly stated purposes and goals, a division of labor among specialists, a rational design or organization, and a hierarchy of authority and accountability (management).

Functional authority   the right that a manager of one department (usually a staff department) has to make decisions and to give orders that affect another department. For example, the personnel department can dictate hiring practices to all other departments.

Hierarchy   the group of people picked to staff an organization's positions of formal authority—its management positions. Members of the hierarchy oversee all the people and activities of the organization.

Line manager   a member of the organization's hierarchy who oversees a department or activity that directly affects an organization's success (profitability), such as production, finance, or marketing activities.

Management   (1) an activity that uses the functions of planning, organizing, leading, and controlling human and material resources for the purpose of achieving stated goals; (2) a team of people (the hierarchy) that oversees the activities of an enterprise in order to get its tasks and goals accomplished with and through others.

Manager a member of an organization's hierarchy who is paid to get things done with and through others by executing the four management functions. Managers always have formal authority, but to be effective they should also possess power (informal authority).

Middle management members of the hierarchy below the rank of top management but above the supervisory level. Their subordinates are other managers.

Operating management the level of the hierarchy that oversees the work of nonmanagement personnel (workers).

Power the ability to influence others so that they respond favorably to orders and instructions. Power comes to people through their personalities and jobs. It is often called *informal authority,* and it cannot be delegated.

Responsibility the obligation each person with authority has to execute all duties to the best of his or her ability.

Staff manager a member of the organization's hierarchy who renders advice and assistance to all other managers or departments in his or her area of expertise.

Supervisor a member of the operating level of the management hierarchy who directs the activities of nonmanagement employees (workers).

Top management the level of the hierarchy that includes the chief executive and his or her subordinates.

Worker any employee who is not a member of the management hierarchy.

Questions for Class Discussion

1. Can you define this chapter's key terms?
2. What are the four essential elements of any formal organization and the definitions of each?
3. What are the four steps you should take when using delegation?
4. What are the three levels of the management hierarchy and the activities performed by each?
5. What are the major functions performed by all managers?
6. What are the six steps in this chapter's decision-making model, and what happens in each?
7. In general, what kinds of decisions require the involvement of your subordinates?
8. How can you use a time log and a daily planner to help you to improve your use of time?

Incident   **Purpose** To give you experience with the rational decision-making model as a guide to your decision making and problem solving.

Your Task You walk to your car, get in, and insert the key to start it, and nothing happens. Nothing but a click is heard. You have thirty minutes to get to work, about the exact time it takes to drive your normal route. You must go to work today and would prefer to arrive on time. At this point you have at least two problems: the car that won't start and the need to get to work on time, if possible. Using the steps in Exhibit 3.7, work your way through the problem of getting to work as quickly as possible.

1.   What is your problem?

_____

_____

_____

2.   What are your restraints?

_____

_____

_____

3.   What are your alternatives?

_____

_____

_____

4.   What are the pluses and minuses for each of your alternatives?

_____

_____

_____

5.   Which alternative has the least serious defects and the best chance for working?

_____

_____

_____

6.   What do you think will happen when you try your alternative? What have you learned by this experience about decision making? About planning?

_____

_____

_____

Case Problem 3.1   Who's Responsible?

Ms. Charles, president of SeraRamics, Inc., picked up her phone and dialed 74. Sam Deadwood, vice-president of product development, answered.

"Deadwood here."

"Sam," said Charles, "I have to give a status report to the board of directors in ten days on our new line of housewares. Can you prepare a report filling me in on the details as to when we intend to test-market it and where?"

"You bet, Ms. Charles, I'll put my best man on it right away. You should have the report by the eighteenth, the day before the meeting with the board."

Deadwood pressed his intercom switch.

"Ellsworth here," it crackled.

"Bill, Charles just called and wants a status report on our new line of housewares. She needs the details of the test-market plans. Put together all the details in a report and give it to my secretary, Betty, to type. Charles needs it by the eighteenth."

"Can do, Mr. Deadwood," Bill Ellsworth walked over to Al Farley's desk. He explained the project to Farley and told him to get the report to Betty by the seventeenth for final typing.

Farley prepared all the data, laid it out in rough form, and took the report to Betty's desk on the morning of the seventeenth. Betty was not there so he left it in her in-basket.

On the morning of the nineteenth, Charles called Deadwood. "Sam, where is that report you promised me on the housewares line? I'm due at the board meeting in an hour."

"I gave the assignment to Ellsworth, Ms. Charles. I'll check it out right away."

After some hasty phone conversations and checking, the report was discovered on Betty's desk, still untyped. Ms. Charles had to give her report to the board from the rough draft.

Betty had taken a three-day leave of absence on the sixteenth for a family emergency. She was not due back until the next day.

Questions

1. Who is responsible?
2. Who is accountable?
3. How could this situation have been avoided?

Case Problem 3.2   Who's in Charge?

Last year the board of directors of the Castlewood Company formulated a maintenance policy based on the suggestions of the vice-president of production and the president. Under this policy the chief engineer was to be responsible for scheduling major maintenance (overhauls, major modifications, and parts replacement), and the scheduling of routine maintenance was left to the plant supervisors in charge of the equipment.

As a result of this policy, Chief Engineer Ted Bates required each supervisor to file a report each week with his office, noting the hours each machine had logged during the week. Ted used this information for determining major maintenance scheduling. Figure A shows the organization of the production department.

Supervisor Mark Edison was responsible for three milling machines. These machines had a history of minor mechanical failures, and it seemed that one or another of them was always in need of attention. Ted's workers were almost "regulars" in Mark's department.

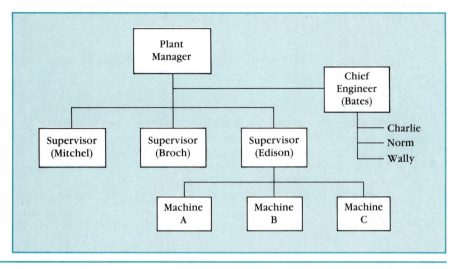

Exhibit A   **Production department organization.**

Monday was a bad day for Mark. All last week he had been pushing his workers and equipment to finish several rush jobs. Several of his better workers had worked overtime on the milling operations, and still there was a backlog. As his shift started work, machine A quit altogether and machine B was in need of routine department maintenance, which was scheduled for that morning. Mark quickly cancelled the routine maintenance and transferred the work from machine A to B.

By the middle of the afternoon, machine B ground to a halt. This left the department with only one milling machine in operation. Mark picked up his phone and called maintenance.

"Ted, this is Mark, I have two machines out and a pile of work to do. Can you get someone up here right away?"

"It will be a few minutes. I'm shorthanded now, but Charlie is due back shortly. I'll send him up as soon as he gets here."

Twenty minutes later Charlie arrived and looked at machine A. "She's in bad shape—needs parts we don't stock. I'll order them, but it will take a week or more."

Charlie moved to machine B. The transmission shaft was frozen, and the grease reservoir was dry. "You burned a bearing. It will take

awhile, but I can get her going by tomorrow."

The facts were: milling machines were normally operated thirty hours per week. Based on hours of operation, machine A should have been scheduled for an overhaul thirty-four hours ago. If it had been, it is likely that the parts would not now be needed, and the failure could have been prevented. Moreover, Mark had stopped submitting maintenance reports to Ted for several weeks because in his words, "You fellows are here so often you should have known it needed an overhaul and done it." The routine maintenance scheduled for machine B included greasing and had already been postponed twice.

Questions

1. Discuss how the concept of functional authority is used in this case.
2. What do you think of Mark's reason for not filing maintenance reports?
3. Are any changes in the maintenance procedures or program needed? What would you recommend?
4. What is wrong with the company's maintenance policy?
5. If you were the plant manager in this case, what action would you take?

Notes

1. James A. F. Stoner, *Management,* 2d ed. (Englewood Cliffs, N.J.: Prentice-Hall, 1982), 310.
2. Ibid.
3. Auren Uris, *The Executive Deskbook,* 2d ed. (New York: Van Nostrand Reinhold, 1976), 66.

Suggested Readings

Ashkenas, Ronald N., and Schaffer, Robert H. ''Managers Can Avoid Wasting Time.'' *Harvard Business Review* (May–June 1982): 98–104.

Bliss, Edwin C. *Doing It Now.* New York: Bantam Books, 1986.

Clemens, John K., and F. Mayer, Douglas. *The Classic Touch.* New York: Dow Jones Irwin, 1987.

Horton, Thomas. *What Works for Me.* New York: Random House, 1986.

Huber, G. P. *Managerial Decision Making.* Glenview, Ill.: Scott, Foresman, 1980.

Mintzberg, Henry. *The Nature of Managerial Work.* Englewood Cliffs, N.J.: Prentice-Hall, 1980.

Peters, Tom. Thriving on Chaos. New York: Alfred A. Knopf, 1987.

Plunkett, Warren R., and Attner, Raymond F. *Introduction to Management.* Boston: PWS-Kent, 1992.

Sellers, Patricia. ''Does the CEO Really Matter?'' *Fortune* (April 22, 1991): 80–82, 86, 90, 94.

Semler, Ricardo. ''Managing Without Managers.'' *Harvard Business Review* (September–October 1989): 76–84.

Senge, Peter M. ''The Leader's New Work: Building Learning Organizations.'' *Sloan Management Review* (Fall 1990): 7–23.

Weiss, W. H. *Decision Making for First-Time Managers.* New York: AMACOM, 1985.

4 Management Functions

Outline

Objectives

After reading and discussing this chapter, you should be able to do the following:

1 Define this chapter's key terms.

2 List and briefly explain the five steps in the planning process.

3 List and briefly describe the five principles of organizing.

4 List and briefly explain the five steps in the organizing process.

5 List and briefly explain the specific activities that make up the leading function.

6 List and briefly explain the five essential steps in the control process.

7 List and briefly describe the three kinds of controls used by managers.

8 Describe five ways in which a supervisor can coordinate his or her operations.

Key Terms

controlling

goal

leading

management by exception

management by objectives

management by wandering around (MBWA)

mission statement

organizing

planning

policy

procedure

program

rule

standard

Introduction

As was stated in chapter 3, the four major functions of a manager are planning, organizing, leading, and controlling. These represent the most time-consuming activities performed by all managers. In this chapter we examine all of these functions briefly, with a focus on how you, as supervisor, can execute them. Planning and organizing, which are the preparatory phases for management action, are examined first. Both are efforts to predict and prepare for the future; consequently they will help you prevent problems and will provide the structure and resources through which your decisions can be made and carried out. Leading and controlling put resources and decisions into action and monitor processes and results.

Chapter 3 also mentioned two other sets of activities—communicating and coordinating—that are part of every supervisor's day. While chapter 5 looks at communicating, coordinating is dealt with at the end of this chapter. Both of these sets of activities are part of the four major functions. You must do them both, simultaneously, as you perform your planning, organizing, leading, and controlling activities.

Although our analysis treats each function separately, keep in mind that all of the functions are interrelated and interdependent. For example, planning is at the heart of the other functions. You must think ahead, have objectives in mind before attempting to act, and decide what actions are most appropriate. The organization within which you implement your decisions as a supervisor is largely fixed and not open to a large amount of manipulation on your part. The planning done at higher levels has set the structure of your section or department, and higher management's organizing efforts have determined the number and kind of human resources you will be asked to utilize and oversee.

Planning

Planning

The management function through which managers decide what they want to achieve and how they are going to do the achieving

You must first decide where you want to go and what you want to achieve, before you commit any of your resources to the journey or the quest. **Planning** is the management activity through which managers decide what they want to or must achieve and how they are going to do the achieving. Planning sets goals and constructs a program of action to achieve them. The goals to be achieved may be set by individual supervisors, or they may be set for them by higher-level managers. The programs supervisors use are usually theirs to construct, but they must conform to guidelines that are established by top management. Exhibit 4.1 outlines the flow and parts of planning in a formal organization. We shall examine each of these parts next.

Philosophy of Management

The way in which the management of a company looks at all the people and events that have an impact on the business is known as the *philosophy of management*. It is the result of the principles, attitudes, and thought processes possessed by all managers. It results in general and

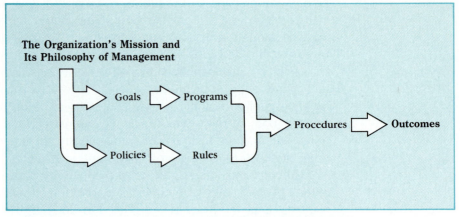

The Organization's Mission and Its Philosophy of Management

Goals ⇒ Programs

Policies ⇒ Rules

⇒ Procedures ⇒ **Outcomes**

Exhibit 4.1   The flow and parts of planning in a formal organization.

usually predictable approaches to setting goals, solving problems, and establishing plans.

As a supervisor, you have a personal philosophy of management. You have, through your experiences, developed predictable patterns of behavior that are based on your attitudes toward people, your job, your company environment, and your perception of your role in your company. Your individual ways of approaching people, problems, and events make you unique as a person and as a manager. Your philosophy colors all your judgments and, therefore, your decisions and their results.

Mission Statement

Mission statement
The central purpose behind the existence of a formal organization—its reason for being

Every organization needs a **mission statement:** the formal statement about the central purpose behind its existence—its reason for being.[1] "Simply put, a mission statement is a proclamation of corporate purpose: What is this company supposed to do? What is its single driving force?"[2]

Mission statements usually contain only a few words. Consider, for example, the mission statement of the California-based computer software maker The Computer-Aided Design Group: "The mission of [CADG] is to profitably provide quality facility-management software, products, and services, which meet Customer needs."[3]

Once a mission statement has been constructed, all the people in the organization must know about it and subscribe to it. Keep your organization's mission in front of you and your people. Before you engage in any management activities, make certain that what you plan to do conforms with that mission and will help the company fulfill its mission. The mission statement should be your vision as a member of management. Keep focused on it, and stay committed to it.

Goals

Goal
The objective, target, or end result expected from the execution of programs, tasks, and activities

The objectives that managers decide to work to achieve are known as their **goals.** Typical goals for a company might be to reduce expenses by 10 percent or to increase efficiency by 5 percent. These company-wide goals must be translated into divisional and departmental goals by managers at various levels. As goals are being formulated, the resources that may be needed to achieve them should be considered. There is little point in setting goals that are beyond the capabilities of a company, manager, or work force to achieve.

As a supervisor, you will find that many of your goals are extensions of the goals set by higher levels of management and reflect how those goals are to be achieved in your specific area of responsibility. Your goals dictate the part you and your people will play in achieving those higher goals. In addition, your goals, which usually require your boss's approval, must be coordinated with goals in other areas of the company to avoid duplication of effort. Once your goals have been decided on, they must be put in writing and described as precisely and specifically as possible.

Policies

Policy
A broad guideline constructed by top management to influence managers' approaches to solving problems and dealing with recurring situations

The broad guidelines for management action that have been formulated by members of the top management are known as **policies.** They are an attempt to coordinate and promote uniformity in the conduct of the business and in the behavior of managers. In a corporation the board of directors usually formulates the policies, which are basically plans for ensuring smooth and harmonious operations of the company. Policies tell managers what top management wants done or what it hopes to work toward achieving.

Policies affect your role as a supervisor because you must act within their limits when carrying out your duties. For instance, if a policy on hiring for your department says that the company will not discriminate for or against any applicant because of his or her age, sex, race, color, creed, or marital status, you had better consider all applicants equally and seek a variety of applicants before you decide to hire. Exhibit 4.2 gives an example of a clear policy that bans discrimination.

Rules

Rule
A regulation on human conduct at work

Inflexible guides for the behavior of employees while at work are known as the company **rules.** They are specific directions that govern the way people should act. Many are prohibitions, such as "no smoking" while on the job or in certain locations; others are simply instructions, such as "turn lights off when they are not in use." Rules promote safety and

> It is the policy of the City Colleges of Chicago that no citizen of the United States or any other person within the jurisdiction thereof shall, on the grounds of race, color, national origin, religion, sex, age, or handicap, be excluded from participation in, or be denied the benefits of, or be subjected to discrimination in employment or under any educational program or activity of the City Colleges of Chicago.

Exhibit 4.2   **An antidiscrimination policy.**

security; they attempt to conserve resources and to prevent problems from arising during the course of the company's operations.

Most rules that govern your area of operations may be up to you (as a supervisor) and your people to set. If you have a mix of smokers and nonsmokers, you may experience the need to provide separate working environments for each group. Many companies are now deciding this issue for you by banning smoking in certain areas or by providing specific areas in which smoking can take place without harming others. If you have a union to work with, specific work rules will come from the labor agreement. Examples of such rules include break schedules, the wearing of safety equipment, and specific offenses for which punishment may be given.

Programs

Program
A plan listing goals and containing the answers to the who, what, when, where, how, and how much of the plan

Plans for each department or division and for the entire company must be developed after goals are set, in order to achieve those goals. A **program** is such a plan. It starts with the goal to be achieved (the "what" of the plan), identifies the tasks required, and details the who, when, where, how, and how much that are needed. The people needed, their specific roles, the other resources required, the time allowed for goal achievement, the methods to be employed (procedures), and the dollars that are allotted to the effort are all pieces of a program. Most programs are single-use plans; programs to acquire new equipment are examples. They are created and operate until the goals they seek are reached. Other programs are ongoing. They deal with continuing situations such as hiring, paying personnel, and billing customers. These are periodically examined and improved as necessary.

Procedures

Procedure
A general routine or method for executing day-to-day operations

Procedures are the "how" in programs. They are the ways or methods chosen to carry out the tasks that a person or group must perform to reach a goal. Like programs, some procedures are single-use, while others are ongoing. New programs may call for the creation of new procedures. Such is the case when a committee is set up to solve a new problem that affects its members and is then dissolved when the problem is solved. Procedures within your department are probably yours to create and change as your situation and tasks dictate. But before you change a procedure, consider who is and will be affected, and consult with them before you make the change. The people closest to a task or problem are often the best source of information about how to improve it. Keep in mind, too, that people hate surprises when it comes to their work routines.

Outcomes

The main reason for establishing procedures, programs, rules, and policies is to reach goals in a satisfactory way. The results of efforts to achieve goals and execute programs are called *outcomes.* In large measure, managers are judged on how effectively they achieve outcomes and on the outcomes themselves. Since most outcomes you are expected to achieve result directly from your subordinates' efforts, their performances are critical factors in determining your rating as a supervisor. This is just one more reason why you need both the authority and the power of your office, along with the power that comes from personal skills and a likeable personality. Good human relations with your subordinates and boss are essential for achieving satisfactory outcomes.

Steps in Planning

Every manager has an approach to planning that has been developed over time and refined by experience. But just about everyone can improve his or her planning efforts. The five steps shown in Exhibit 4.3 can help you to become a better planner. As you read about each in the subsections that follow, consider how they are related to the steps in decision making discussed in chapter 3. After all, planning involves a series of decisions, as do the other management functions. Step 1 sets your destination. Steps 2, 3, and 4 develop your program. Step 5 keeps track of your progress and evaluates your outcomes. All are related and should be taken in the se-

Step 1: **Setting Objectives (Goals)**
Establishing targets for both the short and the long term.

Step 2: **Determining Your Alternatives and Restraints**
Building a list of possible courses of action that can lead you to your goals, and the limits you must live within.

Step 3: **Evaluating Your Alternatives**
Measuring each alternative's advantages and disadvantages in order to choose the alternative with the least-serious defects.

Step 4: **Implementing Your Course or Courses of Action**
Placing your plan in the hands of those who will carry it to completion.

Step 5: **Following Up**
Monitoring the progress, or lack thereof, of your efforts and your subordinates' efforts to achieve the goal.

Exhibit 4.3   **Steps in constructing and implementing plans (the planning process).**

quence shown. Each may be affected by people and events outside your jurisdiction and ability to control.

Step 1: Setting Objectives

Your objectives or goals dictate your purposes and direction. They require a commitment of resources to achieve. Each goal you set must be clearly stated, specific, achievable with available resources, measurable, and not in conflict with your other goals and the goals of others.

Some of your goals are set for you through the planning of others. Your boss may instruct you to reduce your operation costs by 10 percent by next month. How you do it may be left entirely up to you to decide. However, most of your goals will require consultation and cooperation with others, such as the union steward, fellow supervisors, or a staff manager.

Step 2: Determining Your Alternatives and Restraints

Your alternatives are the various courses of action (sets of tasks) that are feasible and available to you to enable you to reach your goals. As with your goals, external factors can limit and influence the courses of action available to you. One course of action may be in violation of the union agreement or may exceed your budgeted funds. Company policies and your subordinates' capabilities can also restrict your choices.

When you know your limits and the restraints placed on you by others and by your situation, you are ready to make a list of possible courses of action. As you construct your list, do not worry about the specifics of each. Make your list as complete as your time and circumstances allow. Do not be afraid to ask others for their suggestions. Your peers may have faced similar situations in the past, and you can benefit from their experiences. An excellent way to put human skill to work is to consult with peers and with your subordinates, who will have to execute your plans.

Step 3: Evaluating Your Alternatives

Create a list of advantages and disadvantages for each of your alternatives. Consider what each alternative calls for in resources such as time, labor, and materials. Consider combinations of alternatives. If no one best alternative emerges from your analysis, consult with your boss. That is one reason you have a boss.

Finally, using your conceptual skill, consider the impact of your alternatives on your group, on other sections that affect your operations or that your operations affect, and on your company as a whole. You will have to work with and through those other people and sections in the future, so avoid any loss of their goodwill. You do not want to incur any negative side effects that you can avoid. Keep your company's mission statement in mind.

Step 4: Implementing Your Course or Courses of Action

You have weighed the relative merits and demerits of each of your alternatives and have chosen the one or the combination of two or more that has the fewest serious problems connected with it. You are now ready to move from the thinking phase into the action phase of planning.

Meet with those who will share responsibility for executing your choice of alternatives. Explain your course of action in detail, emphasizing the limits and means available. Set completion dates for various operations and essential parts. Explain to your people that you are available and stand ready to assist them in times of difficulty and that you want to be kept informed of their progress.

Step 5: Following Up

You chose the goal and the courses of action to reach it, so you bear the primary responsibility for reaching the goal. Do not rely on your subordinates to come to you with problems. Check with them periodically, allowing yourself and them time to make adjustments and to avoid surprises. You may find that progress is ahead of schedule and that new target dates can be established.

Be sure to practice your human-relations skills by recognizing good performance and by demonstrating sincere concern for problems. Keep in mind that delegation transfers authority but leaves you with accountability. Your reputation and success depend on your subordinates' efforts, and you will be needing them to execute your future plans. We are now ready to examine the organizing function.

Organizing

Organizing
The management function that requires tasks to be determined, a creation of a hierarchy, assignment of work to people, and allocation of resources needed to accomplish tasks

Organizing consists of three primary tasks.

1. Determine the tasks to be performed.

2. Establish a framework of authority and accountability among the people who will accomplish them.

3. Allocate appropriate resources to accomplish the tasks and reach the objectives.

Organizing is directly related to and interdependent with planning. These two preparatory functions must be considered together.

At the top management level, concern should be for the entire operation. What is the best way to organize the overall operation so as to perform our tasks with a minimum amount of conflict? The answer may result in a division of labor along functional lines (marketing, production, and so on), along product lines, or according to a geographical division. Whatever the method chosen, it must effectively involve the necessary people and resources in a cooperative effort to complete the assigned tasks.

As a supervisor, you will focus your organizing efforts primarily on the best ways to distribute your unit's work among the people available to do it. Limits on your abilities to assign work or tasks include the following:

- Existing job descriptions, rendered in writing (which list the duties of people, and upon which their current levels of pay are based)
- Your skills and your subordinates' technical and human skills levels
- The willingness of your people to accept challenges and new tasks
- The union–management collective bargaining agreement

Organizing Principles

You should keep in mind five widely recognized *organizing principles* as you plan an organization, evaluate one, or attempt to redesign one: unity of command, span of control, delegation of authority, homogeneous assignment, and flexibility. Each of these principles will help prevent the designer of any business organization from falling victim to the most common pitfalls of organizing.

Unity of Command   Unity of command requires that there be only one individual responsible for each part of an organization. In each organization, each element of the organization should be under one chief. No person should have more than one person to whom he or she is accountable. Each individual throughout an organization should have only one boss. This principle helps prevent conflicting orders and instructions and makes control of people easier.

Span of Control   Span of control is a principle based on recognition of the fact that there is a limit to the number of individuals a supervisor can manage effectively. Many variables can influence the span of control. Two of these variables are the kind and complexity of the tasks performed by your subordinates, and the degree of experience and expertise your subordinates possess. In general, the higher one goes in the management hierarchy, the smaller becomes the number of subordinates each manager has to supervise.

Delegation of Authority   Delegation of authority means that individuals are given enough authority to carry out their duties. In addition, each manager should delegate routine or repetitive tasks to subordinates, in order to concentrate his or her own efforts on the most important duties and to gain time to handle new duties received from his or her boss. Through delegation you train your subordinates to handle aspects of your job while you learn aspects of your boss's job. You groom others for promotion while you groom yourself for promotion.

Homogeneous Assignment   Homogeneous assignment is the predominating principle by which functions are grouped. Similar or related functions give rise to similar problems and require individuals with similar levels of intelligence, experience, and training to deal with them.

Flexibility   Flexibility means that an organization must have the capability of reacting to changing conditions even as it carries out its current assigned tasks. Once any organization is set up, changes begin to take place. Managers must periodically review the organization's relevance and adaptability to new situations. The manager must balance what is with what should have been. Attention should be given to the subtle changes worked out by an organization's individual members. Often they incorporate changes that will lend greater efficiency and effectiveness to the operation as a whole.

Steps in Organizing

The organizing process involves a knowledge of many factors, including the skills, knowledge, and abilities possessed by individuals available to perform work; the nature of the tasks to be performed and the best ways to perform them; the principles of organizing; and the five steps shown in Exhibit 4.4.

Step 1: Determining the Tasks to Be Accomplished

The *tasks* (collections of activities) to be accomplished in your unit will be, in large measure, dictated by past responsibilities, traditional roles played by your unit, and the job design decisions that come to you and your people through the efforts of staff specialists and upper-management decisions. The goals of the organization will require that goals be set at every level of the hierarchy in order to reach the organizational goals. The part that your unit must play in achieving organizational goals will be dictated in part to you by decisions at higher levels. Your unit's goals will then dictate the tasks your unit must execute.

Step 1 illustrates the link between planning and organizing. Planning sets goals and determines the tasks to be executed to reach those goals. Programs are constructed at various levels of the hierarchy. They set forth what is to be done and by whom, and determine what resources are to be expended. Tasks must then be broken down into the specific activities required.

Step 2: Subdividing Major Tasks into Individual Activities

Staff specialists can help individual unit supervisors break unit tasks down into specific activities. Existing and familiar tasks usually present no particular problem. Units and unit personnel are already equipped to deal with them. When new tasks are assigned or created, however, an analysis must be done to determine what each will require in the way of personal skills, knowledge, and abilities.

Step 1: **Determining the Tasks to Be Accomplished to Reach Planned Goals**

Tasks are identified and included in programs, which then become the specific responsibilities of organizational units to accomplish.

Step 2: **Subdividing the Major Tasks into Activities to Be Performed by Individuals**

Through analysis, tasks are broken down into specific activities, which can then be assigned in part or in total to individuals who possess the needed skills, knowledge, and abilities.

Step 3: **Assigning Specific Activities to Individuals**

The skills, knowledge, and abilities needed to execute specific activities are identified, and individuals who possess them are assigned activities. Where existing personnel cannot adequately handle the activities, training, new people, or outside assistance may be required.

Step 4: **Providing the Necessary Resources to Accomplish Activities**

In order to accomplish their assignments, individuals and units may need additional people, authority, training, time, money, or materials.

Step 5: **Designing the Organizational Relationships Needed to Facilitate the Execution of Tasks**

A hierarchy must be designed, or the existing one adapted, to provide the necessary arrangement of authority and responsibility needed to oversee the execution and completion of assignments. The principles of organizing must be adhered to.

Exhibit 4.4   **The steps in constructing an organization (the organizing process).**

Step 3: Assigning Specific Activities to Individuals

The specific skills needed to perform specific worker activities can generally be broken down as follows:

Data processing skills—the abilities to analyze, compile, interpret, synthesize, and compare data or information

Human skill—the abilities to communicate, instruct, direct, persuade, negotiate, and help people

Technical skill—the abilities to manipulate, operate, set up, guide, and follow procedures throughout the exercise of one's area of expertise

Once these skills are identified as being a part of an activity, individuals who possess the degrees of the skills required can be assigned to execute the activity. Workers are matched by their particular skill levels to the activities that must be executed. Conceptual skills are generally not needed by nonsupervisory personnel.

American automotive manufacturers have forged several partnerships with Japanese and European auto makers. Combined engineering, market research, and manufacturing knowhow have led to the Mazda-Ford Probe, the Chrysler-Mitsubishi Stealth, and the Chevrolet-Toyota Geo. Through such partnerships, all have gained knowledge and experience and have become better for the experiences. General Motors has borrowed Japanese participative management techniques learned from its partnership with Toyota and applied the concepts to most of its domestic operations. Mazda was so impressed with the Ford Explorer that it worked out a deal to sell it under its name as the Navajo. This represents the first time that a U.S. car maker has given its model to a Japanese firm. Can you think of any other partnerships that have led to a common product line offered by U.S. and foreign producers outside of the auto industry? What do you think are the advantages and disadvantages of such partnerships for both sides?

Step 4: Providing the Necessary Resources

Additional demands on people and their time may tax them beyond their capabilities. If the activities cannot be absorbed by the existing work force, new people may have to be obtained, or the work may have to be transferred to an outside source. Where existing people do not have the expertise or levels of skills required, additional training may be needed to bring them up to the levels needed. Talent from other areas may be temporarily assigned to assist with the execution of specific activities. Additional funds and authority may be needed to accomplish all the tasks given to a particular individual or unit.

Step 5: Designing the Organizational Relationships Needed

The existing hierarchy of management positions may be adequately set up to oversee the execution of the tasks. When it is not, a new design—temporary or permanent—may have to be established. Enough authority and responsibility needs to be in the hands of those designated to execute the various tasks or to oversee that execution. Everyone involved must have clear knowledge of who is to do what, by what time, and to what standards. The principles of organizing will help you design the hierarchy so that it can function properly. The end result can be shown in graphic form as an organization chart.

Leading

Leading may be briefly defined as supervising or directing. As a function of management, leading includes the specific activities of staffing, training, offering incentives and examples, evaluating performances, and disciplining. The supervisor leads by setting examples for subordinates and fellow team members to follow. Leaders act to remove any obstacles that may stand in the way of individual and group performances. Leaders are directors in the sense that they must act to bring out the best that their subordinates have to give. Leaders are helpers, enablers, coaches, and cheerleaders.

Leading means coupling the formal authority of your position in management with the ingredients that bring you power. The powers of your job description, your personality, and your abilities draw others to you. These combine to give you real influence over others, but such influence must be based on mutual trust and integrity. Chapter 10 is devoted entirely to leadership concepts and practices.

To lead your subordinates properly, you as a supervisor must gain their respect, confidence, and willing cooperation. Each supervisor must strive to build an effective organizational unit—one in which the company can achieve its goals—and an efficient organizational unit—one in which the members can find the means to achieve their personal goals.

The leadership provided to subordinates is by far the most demanding and time consuming of all supervisory functions. If it is done well, your success is practically guaranteed. If it is done poorly, personal and organizational failure usually result. Your reputation as a supervisor depends on the efforts of your subordinates. Their response to your efforts to direct them will either promote your own advancement or retard it. These are the primary reasons why directing subordinates has been chosen as the focal point of this book.

Staffing

Staffing involves adding new people to the organization, promoting people to higher levels of responsibility, transferring people to different jobs, and terminating people from their employment. It is based on human resource planning—the analysis of the organization and its present and future needs for people with particular talents. An inventory of existing personnel is taken to determine who is now at work, what their skill levels are, how long they are likely to remain in the organization, and who among them is qualified for larger responsibilities. Existing personnel are matched to the organization's present and future needs, in order to determine what will be needed in the future. Through staffing, the organization attempts to provide itself with the proper human talent to fill its jobs and execute its tasks. Specific staffing activities are defined as follows:

1. *Recruiting* is the search for talented people who are or might be interested in doing the jobs that the organization has available. It often occurs inside as well as outside the organization. Announcements about job opportunities may be posted on bulletin boards and/or placed in newspapers or trade journals. Everyone who responds is considered a potential employee until the decision to hire is made. Chapter 11 has more to say about the supervisor's role in recruiting.

2. *Selecting* screens the potential employees and job applicants to determine who among them is most qualified. Tests, interviews, physical examinations, and records checks are used to eliminate the less qualified. The applicants are narrowed down to the one or more who are most qualified, and eventually a decision to hire one or more people is made. Selection is often considered a negative process because every applicant has flaws, faults, or deficiencies. The people hired have the least-serious or fewest deficiencies for the job opening. Chapter 11 discusses the supervisor's role in selection.

3. *Placement* follows as soon as the person is hired. It involves introducing the new employee to the company—its people, the jobs, and the working environment. The new employee is given the proper instructions and equipment needed to execute the job for which he or she has been hired. Once work rules are explained and co-workers are introduced, the break-in period begins. Chapter 11 has more to say about the supervisor's role in placing and introducing a new person to the job.

4. *Promoting* involves moving people from one job in the organization to another that offers higher levels of pay and responsibility. Promotions usually require approval by two levels of management and the assistance of the personnel department, where one exists. As a supervisor, your continual concern should be to qualify yourself for promotion and to get one or more of your subordinates ready to take your job.

5. *Transferring* moves people from one job to another on either a temporary or a permanent basis. A transfer does not usually carry with it an increase in pay or responsibilities. Most transfers are lateral moves, and many are done for training purposes.

6. *Terminating* people from their employment can be done on a voluntary or an involuntary basis. Voluntary terminations include quits

and retirements. Involuntary terminations include firings (termination due to disciplinary actions) and indefinite layoffs (terminations due to reductions in forces, economic slowdowns, and company reorganizations).

Training

Training teaches skills, knowledge, and attitudes to both new and existing employees. It can be provided through classroom instruction, laboratory experiences, and on-the-job instruction. While the supervisor of each trainee has the primary duty to train, the actual instruction may be done by any person who is qualified to train. Often the personnel department assists supervisors in training by providing training materials or by teaching them how to train their subordinates. In some cases, supervisors delegate the authority to train to an experienced subordinate, while retaining accountability for the training. Chapter 12 explores the supervisor's training duties in more detail.

Offering Incentives

Incentives are things or states of being that the company hopes will have a strong appeal to their employees. Those who desire one or more of the incentives offered by their employer will be encouraged to give a better-than-average performance in their jobs in order to earn the incentives.

Incentives offered to employees vary from one business to another and from one department within a business to another. They all are offered with the intention of helping managers build an effective and efficient organization. Most companies attempt to offer a wide variety of incentives, in the hope that they will have something for everyone. The idea is that what may not appeal to one employee as desirable and worth having will appeal to another.

The kinds of incentives most businesses offer include raises, bonuses, promotions, better working conditions, greater challenges and responsibilities, and symbols of status in the organization. Status symbols can be as small as a phone on the desk, as large as an executive suite, or anything in between. Which one, if any, appeals to a given employee at a given time depends on the individual—his or her current level of job satisfaction and financial condition. Chapter 7 looks at human motivation in more detail.

Evaluating

Evaluating requires each supervisor to make periodic appraisals of each subordinate's on-the-job performance. To do this adequately, each supervisor must have precise guidelines and standards to follow. People are rated on the basis of what they were expected to do and how well they did it.

Evaluating employees is done informally each day through routine, regular observations of their work by their supervisors. Formal appraisals are usually done once or twice each year. Supervisors who are not with their people regularly usually find it difficult to rate them properly. Supervisors who do not know themselves well—their own biases and prejudices—often make employee appraisals that are something less than objective or honest. Supervisors who do not know their subordinates and their work well find it impossible to make honest and fair appraisals.

The aim of employee evaluations is to help people improve their performance on the job and, therefore, their usefulness to their employer and their pride in themselves. Chapter 13 explores the appraisal process in more detail.

Disciplining

Disciplining requires supervisors to act on the knowledge they have about their subordinates' mistakes and shortcomings on the job. *Positive discipline* demands that employees be informed about and understand the rules that govern their behavior, the standards that govern their output, and the expectations their bosses have of them. The emphasis is on preventing trouble through the creation of an educated, self-disciplined subordinate. *Negative discipline* is concerned with handling infractions, usually through reprimands or more severe penalties. Chapter 14 deals with the supervisor's duties in this vital area.

Management by Wandering Around (MBWA)

Management by wandering around
A leadership principle that encourages supervisors to get out of their offices regularly so that they can touch bases with those who affect their operations and those whom their operations affect

Management by wandering around (MBWA) is a principle of management that encourages managers to get out of their offices regularly so that they can touch bases with customers, suppliers, and others in their own organizations. MBWA encourages managers to listen, empathize, and stay in touch with people who are important to their operations and their mission.[4]

For most supervisors, MBWA can be practiced each time they meet another person at work or make contact with outsiders during the course of their business activities. When you meet customers, interact with them to find out how they like your products and services. If you uncover any complaints or criticisms, take them to the people who should know and who can do something about them. According to a 1986 Gallup survey of 698 senior executives, top management relies more on customer complaints to judge the quality of its products and services than it does on its own quality-control experts.[5]

MBWA with suppliers is especially important if your people are receiving unacceptable levels of quality in the resources those suppliers provide. Before most companies' purchasing agents decide on a supplier, they visit various suppliers' facilities and talk with those who will be responsible for creating what they need. If suppliers are making your life and the lives of your subordinates more difficult, practice a little MBWA with them.

Your most frequent use of MBWA will be with your subordinates. Casual and informal meetings, as well as formal encounters, create lots of opportunities to interact with them. You and they can then catch up on what is happening in your lives. You get a chance to see them in action: to watch and to listen. When people have the opportunity to see first-hand what someone is working on with enthusiasm, that enthusiasm spreads. There is probably no better way to spend most of your time at work than with your people—those who make or break your own reputation and on whom you depend for the execution of your plans and instructions. Most of the activities we examine in later chapters depend on your practice of MBWA.

Controlling

Controlling
The management function that sets standards that are applied to performances. Controls attempt to prevent, identify, and correct deviations from standards

Controlling involves the ability to prevent, identify, and correct deficiencies in all phases of business operations. It is an integral part of all the other functions of a supervisor, and it must be designed into them as each of them is carried out.

When managers control, they attempt to determine whether their plans are being observed and what progress is being made toward their objectives. The essence of control consists of three components: (1) establishing standards; (2) measuring the results of activities against these standards; and (3) taking necessary corrective actions when deviations from the standards occur.[6]

Standards

Standard
A device for measuring or monitoring the performances of people, machines, or processes

A **standard** is a device for measuring or monitoring the behavior of people (management standards) or processes (technical standards). Management standards include policies, rules, procedures, and performance appraisals. They are used to prevent, identify, and correct deviations in key performance areas. Technical standards include devices to control what people do and how they are to do it, in regard to the application of their various technical skills.[7]

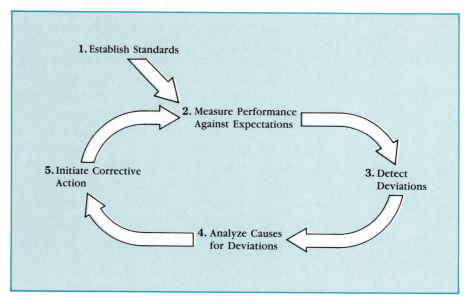

Exhibit 4.5   **The control process in a formal organization.**

The Control Process

Exhibit 4.5 summarizes the control process in any formal organization. Any collection or system of controls should establish standards, measure the performance of managers and workers against those standards, detect deviations from those standards, analyze causes for the deviations (using the problem-solving or decision-making process), and initiate action to correct deviations from standards.

1. *Establishing standards.* Standards answer the questions *who?, when?, why?, what?,* and *how?* with regard to employees' performance at work. Qualitative and quantitative standards need to be established wherever key activities (those directly affecting goal achievement) are to take place. People must know their limits and what is expected of them in the performance of their duties.

2. *Measuring performance against expectations.* If managers are going to prevent, identify, and correct deviations from standards or norms, they must be able to compare performance to established standards. It is only through comparisons that *good* or *bad, hot* or *cold* take on meaning. For example, the comparison of planned production levels to actual levels of production output will let a manager know if the actual is in line with the desirable.

3. *Detecting deviations.* As a result of comparisons, deviations are detected and noted. For example, a worker was supposed to generate fifteen parts per hour for each of the last four hours. The supervi-

sor compares output to this standard and discovers that the worker is five parts short of the goal. In order to do this, a supervisor needs accurate and timely information about each worker's production output. Both the worker and the supervisor need to know the standard output and how that standard is applied.

4. *Analyzing causes for deviations.* The supervisor has noted the deviation, in the form of a lack of sufficient quantity of productive output. An investigation needs to be conducted to determine why the deviation has taken place. Who or what is at fault or not functioning as planned? The decision-making process (chapter 3) is applied, and possible remedies are determined.

5. *Initiating corrective action.* Additional training or more explicit instructions and supervision may be called for. Problems with machines, equipment, supplies, or raw materials may call for changes in maintenance procedures, work flow, sources of materials, and more. The objective is to get things back to normal—to turn what is into what should be.

The control process may tell managers or an organization that its standards are inappropriate—either too loose or too strict. Also, the need for additional standards may be uncovered when a supervisor investigates the causes of deviations. New controls may be required to monitor other operations. Recently, a midwestern university discovered that one of its trusted financial officers had spent over $600,000 for his personal needs and pleasures over a four and a half year period. These funds had been drawn from three special accounts over which the officer had *complete* control. When he took a leave of absence for an illness, the theft was uncovered. Such a misappropriation of funds could have been prevented with routine financial controls such as annual audits and the requirement of two signatures to authorize all expenditures.

Types of Controls

Preventive controls are familiar to all of us. Safety devices on a machine or firearm to avoid unintentional operation and accidents, a lock on a door to prevent unauthorized entry, safety locks on medicine containers to keep children from opening them, and the various checklists throughout this text are all examples of preventive controls.

It is usually better to prevent trouble than to have to deal with it. If all our problems could be foreseen, we would need no other types of controls.

Diagnostic controls attempt to identify trouble when it occurs. Ideally, they should do so immediately. Just as a physician cannot prescribe a treatment for an illness until its cause is identified, a manager needs to know why something has gone wrong in his or her department before corrective measures can be taken.

Some familiar examples of diagnostic controls are warning lights, meters, and gauges. Personal observation and the detection of abnormal sounds and sights are daily routines that managers use to detect trouble. Once you detect problems, you must identify their causes and deal with them efficiently.

Therapeutic controls are usually automatic in their operation. They are designed to deal with and correct deficiencies once the causes are known. Thermostats that regulate the operation of heating and cooling systems are a good example. A safety valve that opens to release excess steam when the pressure reaches a certain level is another example.

All of these controls are necessary to most operations and should form an integrated approach to controlling. No one type is completely adequate. It is only through their combined use that a manager can effectively control resources and activities.

A budget and the budgeting process will help illustrate effectively the three types of controls. A budget is both a plan and a control. It plans for the expenditure of money that is expected to be available over a fixed period of time. The people who will be spending the money usually participate in its preparation. They are also bound to follow the budget or money plan once it is approved.

A budget is a preventive control because it prevents (or helps prevent) unauthorized expenditures of funds. It is a diagnostic control because it helps monitor the funds being spent as they are spent and matches actual expenditures against planned expenditures. Where the actual expenditures significantly differ from what was planned, an investigation should be made to determine why. If the budgeting process is at fault, changes can be introduced to make it more realistic. Budgets have a built-in therapeutic control. When more money is requested than has been authorized, it cannot be spent without higher approval.

Control Characteristics

Controls may have one or more of the following characteristics:

1. *Acceptance by members of the organization who must enforce them and over whom they are enforced.* Consultation with and the consent of the governed are hallmarks of effective controls.
2. *Focus on critical points that affect individuals' and the organization's abilities to achieve goals.* Critical points include essential areas of marketing, financial, production, and personnel activities.

3. *Economic feasibility.* Controls must be cost efficient—the benefit they give has to be worth their costs of installation and operation. Too much control can be worse than too little. Appropriateness is the key.

4. *Accuracy.* Controls must provide information about operations and people in sufficient quantity and quality to enable managers to make meaningful comparisons to standards. Too much information can be worse than too little.

5. *Timeliness.* Information needed for comparisons has to be in a manager's hands in time for him or her to take effective action. Delays in preparing, gathering, or disseminating information can prolong the occurrence of deviations.

6. *Clarity.* Controls and their applicability to specific situations must be communicated clearly to those responsible for implementing controls and to those who will be controlled by them.[8]

All of these characteristics are important, but a control need not have all of them to do the job for which it is designed.

To illustrate these characteristics, we shall look at a toolroom situation. Supervisor Fred wants to control the use of his department's tools. He starts by locking them up in a toolroom. Next he assigns to one person the task of issuing and accounting for each tool. Then he issues an I.D. card to each subordinate and sets up a procedure whereby tools are exchanged for these cards. Finally, he establishes records of the condition the tools are in and fixes responsibility for changes in their condition.

This may or may not be a good control system, depending on the circumstances. It may be too expensive, depending on the value of the tools he is safeguarding. It may be inadequate and impractical if, in the absence of the toolroom supervisor, no one can get a tool. It may be inappropriate if only one or two workers ever need the tools. In short, all of the six control characteristics may be necessary; if any one of them is missing, the controls may accomplish something less than is desired.

Controls used in offices should have needed control characteristics. Controls used to prevent problems include company policy, procedures manuals, periodic status reports of work in process, follow-up visits and memos, periodic staff meetings, and routine observations by office supervisory personnel.

Management by exception
A control principle asserting that managers should spend their time on those matters that require their particular expertise

Management by Exception

The recognized principle of **management by exception** applies most directly to controlling. A manager should spend his or her time only on areas that demand personal attention. The routine should be delegated to

Task	Keep	Delegate	Other Action
Appraisals of subordinates	✔		
Interviewing applicants for job vacancies	✔		
Handling regular reports to higher-ups		✔	Read before sending
Answering correspondence	Those only supervisors can answer	Those others can do well or better	Read before sending
Attending meetings and conferences	When your expertise is needed	When your input is not required	Have substitute brief you

Exhibit 4.6   **Management by exception in the execution of supervisory tasks.**

others, and procedures should be established to deal with it. When exceptions occur, they are usually situations for which there are no precedents. Then the manager's attention is warranted. Where controls reveal exceptions for which there is no prescribed cure, the manager must take action.

The theory underlying management by exception is illustrated in Exhibit 4.6, which identifies a few of the everyday demands on a supervisor's time and tells how the supervisor should handle each of them. Whenever possible, supervisors should delegate routine tasks to their subordinates, to free themselves for additional tasks they may receive through delegation from their superiors and to enable them to spend more time on their most essential and important tasks—those that demand their personal attention and expertise. Competent subordinates usually appreciate management by exception because it suggests that the manager has confidence in them.

Management by Objectives

Management by objectives
A control principle that encourages subordinates to set goals for their performances that are in line with their unit's and organization's goals and that are approved by their supervisors

Objectives are goals or targets to be achieved or reached within some specific time. **Management by objectives** (MBO) requires each manager (and sometimes each worker) to sit down periodically with his or her boss and work out goals that can be mutually agreed upon. These goals will, when achieved, result in a more efficient and economical operation for a section or department. Such goals can be set only after a clear understanding is reached about what a department's weaknesses are and what its capabilities seem to be. Goals set by any manager must be in line with—

not contradictory to—those of his or her superiors and those of departments with whom the manager must coordinate.

If MBO is to work efficiently, those participating in it must set clear, specific, and realistic goals for both the short and long run. Once goals are set, progress (or lack of it) in reaching each goal is monitored by both the person who set the goal and his or her superior. The goal-setter's reputation and performance appraisals will be based in large measure upon his or her efforts and success in reaching the established goals.

MBO reduces the need for close supervision, by involving subordinates in setting their own sights on specific targets and then having them work out the methods by which each goal is to be reached. In such a system, results are what really matter. In setting goals, each subordinate and his or her superior get to know more about themselves, their individual capabilities, their current operations, and their personal commitments to achieve. Chapter 13 includes further discussion of MBO.

Coordinating

Coordinating is the managerial task of making sure that the various parts of your organization all operate in harmony with each other. It involves integrating all the details necessary for reaching your goals. Each activity must be executed without interference with or from other activities, in order to have a unified effort in both the planning and the execution phases of every operation.

The coordinating function should happen simultaneously with all the others. Through it, you attempt to foresee potential conflicts or to deal with existing ones. The organization may have to be redesigned for better efficiency, or plans may have to be modified to include a better mix or balance between people and events. Controls may be so rigid that they restrict completion of the work. The direction of subordinates may be so poor that they rebel and resist instructions or work against organizational objectives. Lack of coordination means chaos.

Kinds of Coordination

Basically, there are two kinds of coordinating: *coordination of thought* and *coordination of action*. You coordinate thought by making certain, through effective communication, that all parties involved in planning an operation have the same concepts, objectives, and overall understanding. You coordinate action by including in your plans for a project the steps to be taken in its execution, the sequence of those steps, the roles that each person must play, and how all the persons involved are to cooperate. As these definitions suggest, coordinating is both an aid to planning and an objective to be realized through planning.

Coordination of thought and coordination of action are best provided for by fixing responsibilities. Each person should have an up-to-date, clear definition of his or her duties in general, as well as of the particular role for each project in which he or she becomes involved. In this way, the efforts of everyone are directed toward common purposes with as little wasted effort and overlap as possible. Coordination is the thread that binds an entire operation together. It must be practiced by all managers at every level, both horizontally and vertically.

Coordination Techniques

Organizational units can coordinate their operations in three basic ways: by plans, through feedback,[9] and through lateral interaction.[10] Plans help in coordination by establishing programs, procedures, and schedules. Methods and timetables are established, and frequent checks are made by those in charge to determine if each person or group is avoiding interference with or from others. Feedback consists of the regular interchanges of information between superiors and subordinates. It takes place during the issuance of orders and instructions and during follow-ups by superiors. Lateral coordination requires individuals and groups from different departments to touch bases with each other at regular intervals. The larger the organization, the greater the need for these three efforts at coordination. Chapter 5 will relate them to organizational communications.

As a supervisor, you can adopt the following measures in your efforts to coordinate your operations:

- Enforcement of company policies
- Enforcement of departmental procedures
- Regular meetings with people who share responsibilities for projects
- Practice of *management by wandering around*—communicating regularly with those who feed you work, those who do your department's tasks, and those to whom you feed work or output
- Use of the organization's established lines of authority and channels of communications
- Sharing information with those who need it through regular routing of bulletins, newsletters, memos, and copies of pertinent documents

Yes	No	
☐	☐	1. Are intelligent cooperation and mutual understanding exhibited throughout my organization?
☐	☐	2. Are my people cross-trained to keep them aware of the overall operation and the need to cooperate?
☐	☐	3. Are operating procedures in writing, understood by those who must follow them, and accessible to those people?
☐	☐	4. Are vertical as well as horizontal communications channels extant, open, and used?
☐	☐	5. Are external activities monitored, interpreted, and integrated, where appropriate, to our operations?
☐	☐	6. Is someone available at all times to execute my role in the event of my absence?

Corrective actions for all "no" responses:

_____

_____

_____

_____

Exhibit 4.7   **A checklist to help you coordinate your activities.**

- Being available to those who need you, letting people know where you are and how they can reach you both on and off the job
- Rotation of responsibilities, in order to cross-train your people
- Playing your management roles of liaison, monitor, disseminator, spokesperson, disturbance handler, and negotiator
- Constantly refocusing yourself and others on the mission

Exhibit 4.7 contains a checklist to help you coordinate your operations and people.

1. Planning is often called the first management function because it is a part of every other function.

2. The planning process require five sequential steps that set goals, construct a program to reach those goals, and monitor the progress and results of that program.

3. Organizing requires managers to determine tasks, break them into activities, identify the skills needed to perform them, and assign them to qualified people.

4. The organizing process requires five specific steps that must be taken sequentially and in line with the basic principles that affect organizing.

5. Leading requires managers to staff their operations and to train, offer incentives to, evaluate, and discipline their subordinates.

6. Staffing is concerned with meeting an organization's needs for qualified human resources. It involves human resource planning and development—recruiting, selecting, placing, promoting, transferring, and terminating people.

7. Controlling establishes standards to govern people's conduct and output at work, measures performance and conduct against those standards, detects deviations, finds the causes for the deviations, and implements appropriate remedies.

8. Controls may be preventive, diagnostic, or therapeutic. Plans can set forth objectives, programs, and methods to prevent problems. Diagnostic controls sense deviations and communicate the fact that they are occurring. Therapeutic controls deal with deviations as they occur.

9. Controls should be accepted by those who must use them and should be focused on critical points in vital operations; they must also be economically feasible, accurate, timely, clear, and easily understood.

10. The principle of management by exception tells a manager to spend time on only those matters that demand the manager's personal attention and expertise. Other matters can be delegated or reduced to routines.

11. Management by objectives requires bosses and subordinates to set goals that will become the standards by which their performances are measured. Each employee sets performance goals with which the employee's boss can concur. Timetables are established for reaching each goal, and performances are moni-

tored. Periodic adjustments may be made to the goals or to the methods of achieving them.

12. Supervisors must take measures to coordinate the thoughts and actions of those that affect their operations, to avoid confusion, waste, and duplication of effort.

Glossary

Controlling the management function that sets standards—both managerial and technical—that are then used to evaluate and monitor the performances of people and processes in order to prevent, identify, and correct deviations from standards.

Goal the objective, target, or end result expected from the execution of specific programs, tasks, and activities.

Leading the management function involving the specific activities of staffing, training, offering incentives, evaluating, and disciplining.

Management by exception a control principle asserting that managers should spend their time on only matters that require their particular expertise.

Management by objectives (MBO) a control principle that encourages subordinates to set goals for their performances that are in line with unit and organizational goals and are approved by their supervisors. These mutually agreed-upon goals become the standards by which the subordinates' performances are evaluated.

Management by wandering around (MBWA) a principle of management that tells supervisors to get out of their offices regularly so that they can communicate with customers, suppliers, subordinates, and others who affect their operations and whose operations they affect.

Mission statement the formal statement of the central purpose behind the existence of an organization—its reason for being.

Organizing the management function that requires (1) determination of tasks to be accomplished, (2) establishment of a framework of authority and accountability (hierarchy) among the people who will do and oversee the tasks, and (3) allocation of resources needed to accomplish the tasks.

Planning the management function that attempts to prepare for and predict the future. Plans construct goals, programs, policies, rules, and procedures.

Policy a broad guideline constructed by top management and intended to influence managers' approaches to solving problems and dealing with recurring situations.

Procedure a general routine or method for executing the day-to-day operations of a unit or organization.

Program   a plan developed at every level of the management hierarchy that lists goals and the methods for achieving them. Programs usually contain the answers to *who, what, when, where, how,* and *how much.*

Rule   a regulation or limit placed on the conduct of people at work. Rules specify what is or is not to be tolerated in people's behavior.

Standard   a device for measuring or monitoring the behavior of people (management standard) or processes (technical standard).

Questions for Class Discussion

1. Can you define this chapter's key terms?
2. What are the five steps in the planning process, and what happens in each?
3. What are the five principles that govern the organizing function, and what does each mean?
4. What are the five steps in the organizing process, and what happens in each?
5. What activities belong to the leading function, and what is involved in each?
6. What are the five steps in the control process, and what happens in each?
7. What are the three kinds of controls, and how does each function?
8. What are the major ways in which supervisors can coordinate their actions and operations within and outside their work units?

Incident

Purpose   To allow you to apply your experiences in living to the concepts discussed in this chapter.

Your Task   After each of the following situations, decide if it is a planning, organizing, leading, or controlling problem or a combination of these. Then explain what advice you would give to each person involved.

Situation 1   Charlie is puzzled. He has been told that he is not very good at setting goals. His boss has indicated through his evaluations that Charlie spends too much time fighting fires and not enough time in trying to prevent them.

Charlie's problem is basically one of _____.

What would you recommend that Charlie do?

Situation 2   Beverly has just been given two major tasks to perform that will enlarge her group's responsibilities. Beginning next Monday, her department will be responsible for preparing its annual budget, a task that she has not had to perform before. Second, her department must take over the payroll function now being performed by the accounts department. The two payroll clerks from accounts will be transferred to Beverly's control next payroll period.

Beverly's problems are _____.

What would you recommend that Beverly do?

Situation 3 Terry is having trouble using the word-processing program on his computer terminal. He has run into difficulties in preparing the reports in the ways in which Chris has requested. Terry has never had to prepare reports and has no experience with the basic uses for letters and memos.

As Terry's boss, what is the problem? _____

As Terry's boss, with the knowledge he lacks, what should you do?

Situation 4 You are going on your annual two-week vacation beginning in one week. Most of your normal duties have to be farmed out to either your boss or your subordinates. A few can wait until you return.

Your basic problem here is _____.

What duties of the following would you delegate to (1) your boss and (2) your subordinates? (Assume that they are duties your subordinates know how to handle.) a. supervising your subordinates. b. working with other department heads in coordination of your efforts. c. inspecting the output of individual subordinates. d. disciplining subordinates who break the rules.

Case Problem 4.1   Remember the Mission

"Another twenty-seven units returned this morning? That makes over four hundred rejects this month. What's the reason for the returns?. . . Yeah. I could have guessed. That damn plastic gear just isn't strong enough. You know, Grace, at this rate we'll eat the whole two thousand 720s by next month. . . . O.K., I'll be in touch." Phil, the supervisor of the loading dock, hung up his phone in disgust. He began to think about where he was going to put these new returns. He was running out of space and wasn't prepared for the additional workload they represented. "I bet those boys in the plant are shaking now," thought Phil.

The gear problem could be traced to a decision made about four months ago when the model 720 was undergoing design and testing. The computer built the model and printed out the results, and the number crunchers went to work on costing the parts and manufacturing. The numbers were just too high, and a meeting was called to bring them down. All the managers who had anything to do with the 720's design and manufacture were brought together and addressed by the president. She ended her remarks as follows:

> There you have it. We need everyone's input on getting these costs in line. Until we shave another $9.50 per model off the 720, we can't make the kind of profit we need.
>
> I want all of you to give me any idea

that will save us money. Remember our mission: we want the most cost-effective products we can produce. We are in business to make profits. That's the bottom line. That's what we are all here to do. Now get cracking, and give me your ideas by next Monday.

After the president left, the managers agreed to attack the biggest cost items first. Within minutes they focused on the take-up gear—a precision part requiring two separate machining operations. After much debate and without any testing, a decision was made to go with a molded gear in plastic. The savings would be just over $10 per unit. Delighted, they stopped their search. The president approved the change, and the piece was contracted to a regular supplier without any competitive bidding. The supplier was chosen because it had a good track record for on-time delivery and could tool up in two weeks. As time was running short for start up on the new 720, there was little else the production people could do and still be able to meet their commitments to their dealers.

Just one week after the first of the new 720s were shipped to dealers, complaints and returns began. Several defects were responsible for customer returns, but the biggest problem was the plastic gear. It accounted for 92 percent of the returns received by the company to date. When the earliest returns were pulled apart and examined, the gear's teeth were found on the bottom of the casing. Evi-

dently, if an operator pressed the number key while the machine was still moving in forward mode, the gear would lose some teeth. As designed, the gear was simply not molded in the correct thickness to stand up to the stress. When contacted, the supplier reported that it could not mold the gear any thicker without new equipment.

Another management meeting was called. After considering the options, the president decided to reprint the instruction manual given to operators of the 720s and to replace the broken gears with plastic gears of the existing design. All new machines would be shipped with the new operator's manual, which would call attention to the procedure that broke the gears. Operators were warned as follows:

> CAUTION: Using the number key while the machine is in forward mode will cause serious damage to the machine.

Questions

1. What do you think about this company's mission statement?
2. How was the decision to cut costs made, and how should it have been made?
3. What do you think of the plan to keep the thin gear and to solve the problem by changing the manual?
4. How could this problem have been avoided in the design phase by using MBWA?

Case Problem 4.2 One Man, One Boss?

Philip Turnbull, age 25, was recently appointed to the temporary position of assistant to the director of personnel, in order to train for a new position to which he will be assigned at some future date: director of recruitment for corporate personnel. Philip has a bachelor's degree in business administration and two years' experience as a personnel interviewer with his present employer. He liked

the work, was considered a bright up-and-comer, and had been good at his old, nonsupervisory job.

What he had been doing was performing the final or selection interview with applicants for supervisory positions. He interviewed both current employees who were being considered for promotion and outsiders who were applying for available positions. As

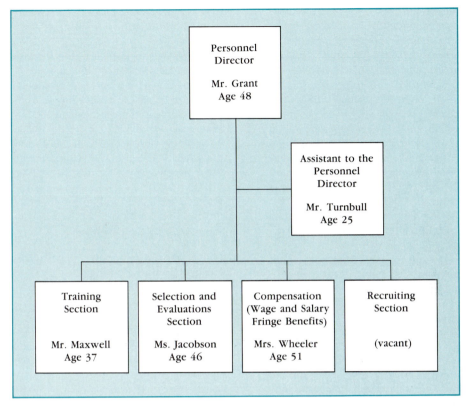

Personnel
Director

Mr. Grant
Age 48

Assistant to the
Personnel
Director

Mr. Turnbull
Age 25

Training Section	Selection and Evaluations Section	Compensation (Wage and Salary Fringe Benefits)	Recruiting Section
Mr. Maxwell Age 37	Ms. Jacobson Age 46	Mrs. Wheeler Age 51	(vacant)

Exhibit A

director of recruitment, he would be involved with interviewing graduates of junior and senior colleges and supervising two college recruiters whom he would have to hire.

As assistant to the personnel director, Philip had to perform many routine duties that his boss normally would have handled. In addition, he was to learn the company's personnel policies, programs, and procedures thoroughly so that, when he moved to the director's job, he would follow them in his recruitments. As an understudy to the various section supervisors (see Exhibit A), Philip was to study how each of them operated and evaluate their operations in a formal report, which was due on Mr. Grant's desk in two weeks. His report was to consist of three parts: (1) present operations—programs and procedures; (2) effectiveness of existing personnel programs and procedures; (3) recommended changes in existing programs and procedures.

Philip soon found out that, although he had responsibilities, he had no real authority to carry them out. He met with strong resistance and what he considered to be delaying tactics on the part of the supervisors of nearly every section. When he requested an interview with a supervisor, he would find that the interview either had to be rescheduled or had to be cut short because the supervisor was involved with "more important" business. As Mr. Maxwell put it:

Look here, Turnbull, I haven't time for you now. I have four subordinates out there who need my time and direction. We have work to do that directly affects this company's work force. The information you need will take time to dig up. Just give me a list of what the old man wants to know about my operations, and I'll see that he gets it.

Philip also found that two of the section supervisors were under the impression that he was to assist them with their routine work. Ms. Jacobson wanted him to do a statistical analysis of the reliability and effectiveness of several tests she used to help predict success on the job. Mrs. Wheeler wanted him to conduct an informal wage survey in the community to see if the company's wages were in line with those of other local employers. When Philip tried to explain that he was supposed to serve only Mr. Grant, both supervisors pointed out that he was their understudy and was charged with evaluating their operations. What they wanted him to do for their sections was clearly in line with his duties, as the two supervisors understood them.

Frustrated and fearful that his report would be inadequate and late, Philip decided to have a conference with Mr. Grant. After patiently listening to Philip's description of his problem in carrying out his assigned tasks, Mr. Grant gave the following monologue:

Philip, I cannot understand why you have been unable to progress any further than you have. You are a disappointment to me at this point and raise serious doubts in my mind as to your ability to handle the new director's job.

Mrs. Wheeler and Ms. Jacobson are both highly qualified professionals. You are their understudy while you are working under my supervision, and the work they have requested you to do will help you evaluate

their operations and make recommendations to me about how to change things for the better.

Mr. Maxwell is also correct in his assertion that his people need his time more than you do. He has two new people who have to be broken in and twenty new workers to help train throughout the company.

Now what I propose is this. Take care of the Wheeler and Jacobson studies first. Then give Maxwell a list, and he will have the answers for you. He's a good man. I'll give you one more week to get your report finished, but it has to be in my hands in three weeks to the day. Agreed?

Philip moved uneasily in his chair. "Agreed," he said with a sigh.

"Fine. Now how are those routine matters we discussed on Monday coming along?"

Questions

1. What are the major planning problems in this case? What would you do to solve each of them?
2. What organizing principles have been violated? How has each of them been violated?
3. Evaluate Mr. Grant's monologue in light of your answers to questions 1 and 2.
4. If you where Philip, what would you do? Why?
5. Do you see any problems in the way the personnel department is organized? if so, how would you reorganize it?

Notes

1. Warren R. Plunkett and Raymond F. Attner, *Introduction to Management* (Boston: Kent Publishing, 1986), 107.
2. Mark B. Roman, "The Mission: Setting Your Vision in Words Is the Crucial Executive Act," *Success!* (June 1987): 54.
3. Ibid., 54–55.
4. For an in-depth treatment of MBWA, see Thomas J. Peters and Robert H. Waterman, *In Search of Excellence* (New York: Harper & Row, 1982), chapter 5, and Tom Peters and Nancy Austin, *A Passion for Excellence* (New York: Warner Books, 1985), chapter 2.
5. "Money Line," *USA Today* (October 14, 1986): 1B.
6. Edgar F. Huse, *The Modern Manager* (St. Paul, Minn.: West Publishing, 1979), 186.
7. Vincent G. Reuter, "A Trio of Management Tools Increases Productivity and Reduces Costs," *Arizona Business* 24, no. 2 (February 1977): 12–17.

8. Peter F. Drucker, *Management Tasks, Responsibilities, Practices* (New York: Harper & Row, 1974), 489–504.

9. J. March and H. Simon, *Organizations* (New York: John Wiley & Sons, 1958).

10. R. C. Huseman and Archie B. Carroll, *Readings in Organizational Behavior: Dimensions of Management Action* (Boston: Allyn & Bacon, 1979).

Suggested Readings

Brown, W. Steven. *13 Fatal Errors Managers Make and How You Can Avoid Them*. New York: Berkley Books, 1985.

Fierman, Jaclyn. "Do Women Manage Differently?" *Fortune* (December 17, 1990): 115–116, 118.

Howard, Robert. "Values Make the Company: An Interview with Robert Haas." *Harvard Business Review* (September–October 1990): 132–144.

Kanter, Rosabeth Moss. "The New Managerial Work." *Harvard Business Review* (November–December 1989): 85–92.

Kotter, John P. "What Leaders Really Do." *Harvard Business Review* (May–June 1990): 103–111.

Mintzberg, Henry. "The Effective Organization: Forces and Forms." *Sloan Management Review* (Winter 1991): 54–67.

Pearson, Andrall E. "Six Basics for General Managers." *Harvard Business Review* (July–August 1989): 94–101.

Rodgers, T. J. "No Excuses Management." *Harvard Business Review* (July–August 1990): 84–98.

Rosener, Judy B. "Ways Women Lead." *Harvard Business Review* (November–December 1990): 119–125.

Uyterhoeven, Hugo. "General Managers in the Middle." *Harvard Business Review* (September–October 1989): 136–145.

5 Communications

Outline

Objectives

After reading and discussing this chapter, you should be able to do the following:

1 Define the key terms.

2 List the four major goals of communication.

3 Describe the purposes of a management information system (MIS).

4 List the basic components in the communication process.

5 Outline the steps one should take in planning a communication.

6 List and explain six barriers that can inhibit your efforts to communicate at work.

7 Explain four ways of improving your listening skills.

Key Terms

communication

direction

feedback

grapevine

information

medium

message

receiver

transmitter

Introduction

Communication
The transmission of information and common understanding from one person or group to another through the use of common symbols

Information
Any facts, figures, or data that are in a form or format that makes them usable to a person who possesses them

The importance of communications to you as a supervisor cannot be overstated. You must routinely give orders and instructions and relay information and ideas to and from your subordinates, superiors, and peers. Your plans can come to fruition only through effective communications.

Communication is the transmission of information and understanding from one person or group to another through the use of common symbols. **Information** can be facts, figures, or data that are in a usable form or format. Information is usable if it conveys meaning or knowledge. The understanding that you should seek when receiving a communication is the exact perception of what the other person or group is trying to convey or transmit to you. You, in turn, should attempt to give the other person your exact perception and meaning. Communicating requires a two-way effort. Both parties to the process must be active participants. Finally, the common symbols used can be verbal and nonverbal. Language—written or spoken—can be used, along with colors, pictures, objects, facial expressions, gestures, and actions.

Communications can flow downward (vertically or diagonally), upward (vertically or diagonally), or horizontally (left or right). Recalling our previous discussions in this text with regard to organization charts, you will remember that the lines connecting the various blocks of the management hierarchy are, among other things, lines for formal and routine business communications. They are to be used when one manager wishes to share information and understanding with other managers. By using them, managers are helping to plan, organize, lead, control, and coordinate their operations.

Goals of Communication

All of your communications have as their objective or goal the production of one or more of the following responses:

- To be understood—to get something across to someone so that he or she knows exactly what you mean
- To understand others—to get to know their exact meanings and intentions
- To gain acceptance for yourself and/or for your ideas
- To produce action or change—to get the other person or group to understand what is expected, when it is needed, why it is necessary, and how to do it

All of these goals point out the two-way nature of communications: communications take place between one person or group and another person or group. There must be a *common* understanding; that is, each person must know the other's meaning and intent. In order to gain an exact perception of another person's meaning and intent, **feedback** efforts may be required. One or both parties may have to ask questions to determine exactly what the other person means. The person who initiates the communication may ask the other person to respond to it in a way that will indicate that a common understanding has taken place. Whether you are the initiator of or the target for a communication, you have the duty to seek common understanding—to be understood and to understand.

Feedback efforts include listening to and restating ideas. Before you

Feedback
Any effort made by parties to a communication to ensure that they have a common understanding of each other's meaning and intent

can listen attentively to another person, the area surrounding you must be free of distractions. Both parties must concentrate on the ideas and offerings under discussion, clearing their minds of anything that could interfere with the exchange. After a person speaks to you, try rephrasing what the person has said. Put what you think the person said into your own words, and ask if that is an accurate restatement. Rephrasing is important because it forces you to listen for meaning as well as words. You may restate a person's words verbatim and still not understand their underlying meaning. Once the words are understood, try next to understand what the other person means by using them. Techniques of effective listening are examined later in this chapter.

Planning Communications

No matter to whom or why you feel the need to communicate your ideas, planning must precede the act of communication. The following checklist will serve you well as a sequential list of questions to answer as you prepare to communicate.

1. *Is this communication really necessary?* Will whatever I want to communicate improve the present situation? If you have no clear answer to these questions, proceed no further until you do.

2. *What are the objectives I wish to achieve by communicating?* Do I want action? understanding? acceptance?

3. *What are the essential facts?* Do I know them, and (more important) am I able to express them properly?

4. *Are my thoughts outlined?* Whether your outline is mental or in writing, keep it brief and to the point.

5. *Have I considered my receivers?* What are their needs, and how can I sell my message to them? Do I know their backgrounds and frames of reference for this message? What about our relationship? Have I included the *why* in the message?

6. *Have I chosen the right symbols?* Whether words, pictures, or some other symbols, are they correct for this communication? Remember that words take on meaning both from the context in which they appear and in the minds of the people involved in the communication process.

7. *How should I communicate this message?* Face to face? in writing? If

in writing, should I use a memo? a letter? Have I time for formal channels, or should I go directly to my intended receivers?

8. *When should I communicate?* Am I aware of the time element and the receptiveness of my receivers? When will the environment be most free from anticipated disturbances?

9. *Have I provided for feedback?* Will I be able to judge my receivers' reactions, and will they be able to seek further information from me if they want to? How will I be sure my message has been received and properly interpreted?

The Communication Process

There are five major components or variables in the communication process: the **message,** the **transmitter** (sender), the **direction** (flow) of the message, the **medium** (message carrier), and the **receiver.** The interaction and mix of these can cause effective or ineffective communications to take place. In a communication, an incorrect choice in any of the five components can mean something less than the transmission of information and understanding.

The Message

Message
The ideas, information, and feelings that you wish to communicate to a receiver

Your message consists of the ideas, information, and feelings that you wish to communicate. You and your choices of a receiver, a medium, and a direction all influence what you wish to say or write. In turn, what you wish to say or communicate may dictate some of your choices.

The first question to ask yourself is why you want to communicate. What do you hope to accomplish—what is your goal—through communicating? When you know why, you are ready to outline your thoughts. Your choice of words will be influenced in part by your intended receiver and her, his, or their points of view with regard to the subject matter of your message. How much you have to include, as well as how you will phrase your message, depends on what your receiver already knows about the subject. Abbreviations and slang may be acceptable *if* your receiver knows what you mean when you use them. References to past communications with the receiver can eliminate the necessity to include their contents in your present message.

The Transmitter

Your message is also influenced by your knowledge and attitudes about its subject matter. Where you lack the depth necessary to communicate, re-

Transmitter

The person or group that sends a message to a receiver

search and analysis may be needed to avoid future complications and misunderstandings. Your attitudes reflect your predispositions toward a subject and will affect the tone that your message takes. Receivers will know by listening to or reading your words how you feel about their content. A sense of importance will come through (or not), depending on your feelings about the information.

The Direction

Direction

In communication, the flow or path a message takes in order to reach a receiver

As a supervisor, you will most frequently send your communications in an upward or downward direction. You will be communicating most often with subordinates or with your boss. Both directions carry with them inherent problems. The major problem is that the content of your message will be filtered through and possibly distorted by each person or level that it passes through.[1] People will often assume that they know what is meant and will rephrase the message in their own words as they pass it along to others. Lack of first-hand knowledge or experience with the subject can also cause trouble. The necessary background information may be missing on the higher or lower levels.

Two solutions exist for these problems. Require feedback from your receivers so that you can check on their understanding of your message. Use more than one medium to carry your message. If you sent your message by voice, follow up with a memo or later conversation. If you received the message by voice, follow up with a memo of understanding.

As a supervisor, you use diagonal communication to communicate with staff specialists. You use horizontal communications to coordinate with peers and when attempting to resolve mutual problems or conflicts. Diagonal communication can occur outside formal channels, leaving your boss out of the flow. This is often the case when staff managers possess functional authority. It is wise, therefore, to keep records of all such correspondence and to check with your boss before answering or reacting to staff orders or requests. A simple memo can keep your boss informed of actions that you eventually take. When contacted by staff specialists who do not have functional authority, ask them to clear their requests through your boss.

The Medium

Medium

A channel or means used to carry a message in the communication process

Your choice of a medium may be dictated by your choice of a receiver. If the receiver is a subordinate, oral conversations in person or by telephone are usually adequate. Your boss, however, may require written correspondence most often, especially when asking for updates on your unit's progress. Important matters should be handled in writing. This will provide specific evidence at a later date as to just what was communicated, when, and to whom. Complicated messages are best transmitted in writing, too, especially when information is best presented in tables, charts, graphs, or pictures. Such visual media can communicate at a glance what would otherwise take many paragraphs to get across.

Different media have different impacts on receivers. Most people are used to seeing company bulletins, memos, and newsletters because they are routinely used to carry information. As a result, these media lose their ability to capture people's attention and gain their interest. They are read casually, if at all, and may be set aside during busy times to be read at a later date. Overuse or improper use of such markings as *urgent* or *for your immediate attention* can cause them to become routine and worthy of no great concern. Unusual media should be used to carry only unusual messages.

The Receiver

Receiver
The person or group intended by transmitters to receive their messages

Just as you must know yourself—your feelings and attitudes about your subject—so, too, should you know your receiver's inclinations. Your own experience tells you that some subjects are received with more enthusiasm and interest than others. Some subjects touch off emotional responses and can inhibit reason and understanding. Try to determine your receiver's prior knowledge and predisposition toward the subject about which you wish to communicate, before you attempt to do so. Delicate subjects, such as those requiring reprimands or punitive measures, are best handled in person, one on one, and in private. By knowing your receivers well and anticipating how they are likely to view your message, you can tailor your message's words, tone, and method of delivery to fit the circumstances.

Communications Barriers

The essential ingredients in the communications recipe are the message, the message sender (transmitter), the message carrier (medium), and the receiver. If any of these ingredients is defective in any way, clarity of meaning and understanding will be lacking. *Communications barriers* can arise that will spoil these ingredients and the communications process. There are six major barriers to successful communications, each of which we will consider in turn.

Uncommon Symbols

Words take on meaning only in the context of the message they compose. Facial expressions can be misinterpreted. Gestures viewed out of context can take on entirely different meanings than were intended. Every child knows the blank expression that his or her slang expressions can evoke in the face of a parent. Every employee knows the worry that accompanies the boss's departure from his or her normal and predictable patterns of behavior.

Example   Sally, the supervisor of a data-processing section, has an established pattern of communications. Each morning upon entering her section, she makes it her duty to greet each of her seven subordinates warmly and to inquire about their well-being and work. Today she entered the office and went straight to her desk, ignoring her subordinates. As a result, what do you think might happen in the minds of her subordinates? What might the impact of her change in behavior be on today's work output?

Improper Timing

Unless the receiver is in the right frame of mind and tuned in on the proper channel, he or she will not hear your message. The sender can be upset, agitated, or improperly prepared to communicate. Sometimes the need for the message is too far removed from its transmission, or the message gets delayed in transmission and arrives too late to be effective. We all know the regrets that go with speaking in haste while we are in the heat of emotion or not thinking clearly. When we are distracted, we may hear words but not their intended meanings.

Example   Charlie is upset because of a personal problem with his wife. He has been thinking about it on and off since his arrival at work two hours ago. His supervisor approaches him and begins a detailed explanation of a task he wants Charlie to perform before leaving today. Although Charlie is clearly distracted, he nods assent throughout his boss's instructions. What might happen? What should the boss have done that he did not do?

Atmospheric Disturbances

The atmosphere or environment of your communications should be as free as possible from noise, interruptions, and physical discomfort for both you and your receiver. You have certainly felt the frustration of trying to be heard above the din of machines or the confusion of others talking simultaneously. Remember the *what?* that you received so frequently? Wouldn't it have been better to have changed your environment before you tried to communicate?

Example   A supervisor had no sooner begun to interview a job applicant in her office when the phone rang. After handling the call, she resumed the interview. Five minutes later a change in shift occurred, creating noise and confusion outside her office. How successful do you think this interview was for both people?

Improper Attitudes

Unfavorable predispositions toward the subject, the sender, or the receiver will interfere with understanding. In fact, they may provoke emotional and harmful responses in place of the desired ones. A poor attitude in the sender or the receiver will confuse rather than clarify.

Example   One of your subordinates, Shirley, comes to ask you again today if she has gotten the pay raise you recommended for her two weeks ago. She has been asking you about it for the past five days, and you have told her that, as soon as you know, you will tell her. Since you have not heard anything yet, you answer her tersely, ''No! Now don't bother me!'' Have you created problems for yourself by such a response? How do you think Shirley will react?

Background Differences

A lack of similar backgrounds in the sender and the receiver with respect to education, previous experiences, or present environment may hinder receptiveness to a message and prevent a proper reaction to it. The newcomer attempts to give advice to the old-timer without success. The grade school graduate attempts to gain acceptance from the college graduate and fails. These and many similar situations arise every day at work, preventing a mutual understanding. One person has made improper assumptions about the other, and a barrier has been erected.

Example   Allen, age 25, is being broken in by Arthur, who is about to retire. Arthur is teaching Allen his job. While certain established procedures are being discussed, Allen recommends a change he feels will speed things up. Instead of evaluating Allen's proposal, Arthur shuts him off by stating, ''Who's the expert here, you or me? This is the way I have always done it, and it works.'' What do you think will be Allen's reaction?

Sender/Receiver Relationships

Potentially conflicting functional relationships, such as between line manager and staff manager or between engineer and accountant, can hinder communications. Suspicion on the part of one about the other's intentions or doubt about his or her ability to communicate about the other's specialty can block the transmission of information. Unequal positional or status relationships, such as between supervisor and subordinate or between skilled worker and apprentice, can cause one to tune out the other.

Example A production manager is told by a personnel manager (who has the functional authority over hiring) that the production section will receive a qualified minority worker—the first for the production manager's section. Since the production manager resents being told whom to hire, he or she begins to plot the newcomer's failure for the sole purpose of embarrassing the personnel manager. What are the possible consequences of such an action? How could they have been prevented?

Regardless of the type of barrier encountered, it will have an equivalent effect on communications: something less than a proper understanding will result. Knowing that these barriers exist is half the battle. The other half is working to tear them down or to minimize their effects.

Management and Information

All managers are paid decision makers. To make their decisions, they need a steady flow of timely, up-to-date information. That information must be gathered, analyzed, interpreted, generated, and delivered to the managers who need it. Specialized departments and activities have been created in most larger organizations to create and control the flow of information. Data processing, word processing, and corporate planning departments are just three examples.

Management Information Systems

In most large businesses, a systems approach is needed to manage the inflow, processing, and outflow of information. Managers need to be protected from receiving unnecessary information. A *management information system* (MIS) is a formal method for making accurate and timely information available to management to aid in the decision-making process and to provide for effective execution of the management's and the organization's functions.[2] An organization's MIS should provide usable and needed information to the right people, at the right time, in the right amount, and at the right place. It may or may not use computers.

Designing an MIS begins with conducting a study or survey to determine who needs what kind of information, when, and in what quality and form. Information users help determine how the system will operate and what it will generate. Both users and information processors must cooperate to ensure that the system produces only what is needed—no more and no less. It must do this in a timely and efficient manner, at a reasonable cost.

One example of an MIS that uses computers is found in many supermarket chain stores. Their checkout lanes are equipped with cash registers and electronic sensing equipment that are linked directly to a central computer. Most items in these stores' inventories have data stored in the *universal product codes* (UPCs)—the panels on the packages that contain solid black lines and numbers below them. The UPCs are sensed at the checkout counter, and the data they contain are sent directly to a computer. Exhibit 5.1 summarizes such a checkout system. It is only one part of the chain's MIS—but a vital one. It provides data needed to supply immediate information to the checker, the customer, and the store's and the chain's managers. The UPC data are needed to keep track of the store's inventory and sales, to assist in consolidated purchasing by the chain, and to carry out the routine accounting activities for both the store's and the chain's managers.

The Supervisor and the MIS

As a supervisor, you are part of your organization's MIS. Whether it is a formal, planned system using sophisticated electronics or not, you get information from others and provide it to others. In one way or another, you execute the several steps that exist in a MIS: you must determine your need for information, by deciding what you need to do your job; you must determine the sources of the information you need and must arrange some method of gathering what you need; you must organize what you receive in a way that makes it most useful to you; you must interpret and process the data you receive, or you must generate it and determine who should receive it; you must transmit information to those who need it; and you must examine all of the above steps periodically in order to determine how to make it more efficient and to adjust it to new demands as things change.

Are you receiving too much information, information in the wrong form, outdated information, or not enough information? If so, take action now to improve your situation. Stop the flow of unneeded information. Tune yourself in to the necessary channels to receive the information that you lack. Let those who generate your information know what you need, when, and in what form. You will be saving time for yourself and others

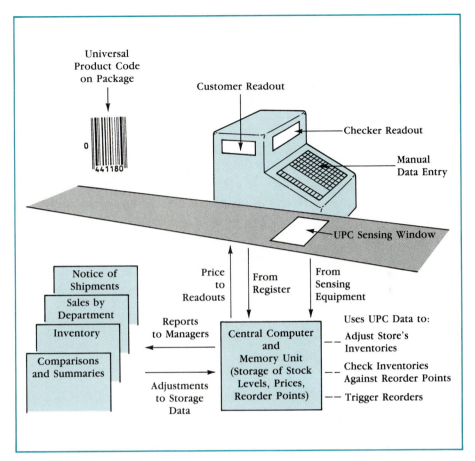

Exhibit 5.1   The part of a chain store's MIS that uses electronic sensing and computerized data processing to assist in checkout, inventory control, and accounting procedures.

and helping your employer use resources more efficiently. If your organization lacks an adequate MIS, investigate what you and your fellow supervisors can do to create one.

A recent Louis Harris and Associates poll of office workers, design professionals, and managers discovered that "free information flow between employees and management and the opportunity to contribute significantly to their companies" was rated as very important by 74 percent of the people surveyed.[3] As a supervisor, you communicate to three groups on a regular basis: subordinates, peers, and other managers (superiors and staff). They all desire a free flow of information on a variety of subjects for a variety of reasons.

Communicating with Subordinates You communicate with subordinates most often and for many reasons. Your people want to know what you expect from them. They expect and need information from you on their progress, successes, and shortcomings. You should pass memos, bulletins, and reports from others to them on an ''as needed'' basis. Your practice of management by wandering around (MBWA) allows you ample opportunity to find out what is on their minds, what they are feeling and thinking about, and how you should rate them and their performances. Their activities and goals must be coordinated with those of your other subordinates.

Communicating with Peers Your peers consist of all managers who are on the same level of the company's hierarchy as you are. Touching bases with peers regularly allows you to build friendships, share information, coordinate operations, and teach as well as learn. Open and honest communication with peers builds the type of teamwork and mutual commitment to values, goals, and strategies so essential to good working relationships.

Communicating with Others Others you must communicate with regularly include your boss, staff managers, and outsiders such as customers and suppliers. The boss wants to be kept up to date on your progress and on that of your section, without having to ask for updates. He or she wants to know what your goals are and what information and help you need. Staff people want to be consulted so that they can share their expertise. They need to know your progress on problems they have been asked to help you solve. They want to find you receptive to their suggestions and assistance.

In all of your communications, you should recognize two principles: (1) that you have the right to be heard and understood and (2) that you must respect the same right for others. Self-esteem and respect for others are the two most essential attitudes of supervision and leadership.[4]

Computers and Communications

Two-thirds of today's office workers and about 45 percent of top executives use a personal computer or a computer terminal.[5] Nearly all of the top 500 corporations in America use electronic mail: messages sent from computer to computer are stored until read or no longer needed. Elec-

NEWS
You Can Use
America's largest and most successful retailer is Wal-Mart, which also includes Sam's wholesale outlets. Sam Walton, CEO, has seen to it that his stores and managers are connected to his companies' suppliers. Through interfacing computer networks, store managers track sales by inventory item, rarely run out of stock, keep in touch with suppliers, keep tabs on the progress of orders, and allow suppliers to tap in to their computer memories. Such instant communication and monitoring allows the organization to respond to any trends and changes in consumer preferences within a few hours. Stores can communicate with the home office, each other, and their suppliers with the touch of a few keys on their computer keyboards. Vendors stay in touch to stay on top of the trends that may be developing and are able to respond to the buyer's needs within hours. What uses have you found at work for your computers besides turning out letters and reports? Are you able to communicate to outsiders by using your computers at work? Should you be?

tronic mail has gone a long way toward eliminating memos and telephone calls, and the user can access them at his or her convenience. The sender can even tell if the message has been received (read).

IBM has some unique applications for the computers it uses. An IBM computer can dial a repair office when it is in need of fixing. Its electronic bulletin board connects computer dealers across the United States so that they can find out about price changes and other news. All 20,000 IBM repair people carry hand-held computers to send messages to and from the home office through a network of 1,000 radio towers across the nation. By networking its computers, IBM gives its people everywhere access to data stored at many locations.[6]

Computers can make work faster and more efficient. They can eliminate paperwork, make information flow more freely, put information into more useful forms, and reduce costs. Unfortunately, they can also create more stress and strain for the people who use them. As with so many other things, the manner in which computers are used can mean either that work will be more efficient or that it will be more tedious. If people are not taught how to use their computer technology properly, they will fear and misuse it. If people see computers as another way that management can keep track of them and monitor their work, they may resent management.

What is developing in many companies is a managerial workstation—one equipped with several systems that can increase the efficiency and productivity of managers at every level. See if any of these modern systems is a part of your job or that of other managers in your company:

- Word processors for preparing memos, letters, and reports
- Computer terminals for sending and receiving electronic messages, accessing data stored elsewhere, creating computer graphics, performing calculations, and handling various design activities (CAD/CAM)
- Letter-quality printers for desktop publishing of letters, memos, and reports and for obtaining hard copies of items in electronic storage[7]

If this equipment looks and sounds strange to you, it won't for long. Do what you can now to become familiar with how you and your company can put computers and terminals to use in managing your tasks, people, and information more effectively. Exhibit 5.2 looks at the office of the future—what it has and will have soon in the way of communications technology.

Spoken Communications

All successful managers have two basic qualities in common: the ability to think logically, and the ability to communicate effectively. The most frequently used form of communication for a supervisor is oral. The ability to express yourself effectively through the use of spoken words is the most important tool at your disposal.

Effective speaking is much more than knowing correct grammar. You must have a clear purpose in mind, know your audience, and be certain of the type of response you wish to receive. Your way of talking to Bill is probably different from your way of talking to Sue, even though your subject is the same. Bill may require a slower rate of speech, while Sue may respond best to a soft delivery.

As you speak, watch your listeners' facial expressions. Give your listeners time to ask questions. If they do not, ask some of your own, in order to check their understanding and keep their attention. Saying things twice in different ways lends emphasis and clarification, so do not be afraid of repetition.

Tailor your message to your audience. Choose your words carefully. Use the minimum number of words possible to get your point across. Be honest and open, and your message will be welcomed. Stick to the facts and leave out the personal opinions. If your listeners desire more information than you have, do not bluff. Tell them you will get it and give it to them as soon as you can; be sure to do so.

Exhibit 5.2   **A look inside the ultimate office.** (*Source:* Copyright 1987, *USA Today.* Reprinted with permission.)

Basic Ingredients

An effective oral presentation to individuals or to groups usually contains three stages or parts: the *introduction,* the *explanation,* and the *summary.* All three parts have a definite purpose and specific ingredients. Our primary focus here is on communications between individuals alone or in groups.

The Introduction   The introduction or beginning of your oral presentation should attempt to do three things: (1) get the listener's attention; (2) arouse interest; and (3) introduce the subject matter and purpose of the communication.

The introduction can enable you to gain the listener's attention through a number of devices: a statement designed to startle or amaze, a quotation from a famous source, an anecdote or story with a moral or lesson, or a question that will be answered later in the oral communication (see Exhibit 5.3). To convey the subject matter and the purpose of the communication, you as speaker can simply state what you intend to talk about, why the communication is necessary, and what goals and responses you have in mind. To obtain and keep the listener's interest, you need to say why the communication is necessary and how the message will affect your listener. An effort should be made to relate the oral presentation and the words you choose to your listener's past experience, job, or special interests.

The Explanation   The explanation follows the introduction and should also be well organized. It will be well organized if it flows logically from one key point to another. To make sure that it does, you must identify the key points or ideas; you must group them in a sequence that makes sense; and then you must present them in that sequence to your listener. Transitions from one point to another should be thought out, and they should carry your listener logically from one point or idea to the next.

Emphasis should be used to help your listener define in his or her own mind what the key points are and why they are worth knowing and remembering. Some devices for adding emphasis include repetition, voice tone and inflection, specific wording such as ''this is really important,'' visual aids, and specific questions. As the speaker, you can use such devices to fix important points or ideas in your listeners' minds.

The Summary   A summary may occur at any stage in an oral presentation where it might be helpful to restate important points you have been making. Frequent summaries aid the memory and add emphasis. Any oral communication should be concluded with a comprehensive summary of all the key ideas, as well as of the responses expected from your listener. This final summary is your opportunity to reemphasize major points, to clarify the message through questions, and to leave a lasting impression with your listener. It may list rewards to be received by the listener who reacts favorably to your message and a statement of penalties that may result from unfavorable or negative responses. It should restate the goals and actions expected as a result of the communication, in line with the way they were first stated in your introduction.

The Informational Meeting

An informational meeting is used to disseminate various kinds of information to all of your people or to certain groups of them. Usually you

Guide to Planning an Oral Presentation

Introduction

- Gain the listener's attention.

- Arouse the listener's interest.

- Introduce yourself.

- Introduce your purpose.

- Introduce your idea.

Explanation

- Develop your idea with logic and examples.

- Link your idea to the listener's interests.

- Use language your listener will understand.

- Keep it brief and on track.

- Use illustrations and graphics whenever possible.

- Invite questions when and where appropriate.

Summary

- Restate your idea and its advantages to your listener.

- Call for questions and be prepared to ask some of your own to check on the listener's understanding of the topic.

- State the specific actions you desire and are calling for.

Exhibit 5.3   Guide to planning your oral presentation.

will use the lecture format, with yourself on the speaker's platform communicating information about such topics as status reports on work, new projects or programs in progress, or the interpretation of changes taking place elsewhere in the company that will affect your department and its members.

Many supervisors hold such meetings on a fairly regular basis, as they feel it offers them an excellent opportunity to relate to their people and communicate with them efficiently with relatively little time and effort. It is easier to say things once to all those affected than to try to reach each individually. In addition, items of interest that accumulate daily can be assembled and dispensed with before they become dated or too numerous to handle efficiently in a single informational session.

Informational meetings promote cooperation among group members by fostering individual growth, by keeping people informed, and by giving people the reasons behind changes that will be necessary in the future. Informational meetings work best when they permit the supervisor and group members to accomplish the following purposes:

1. Keep informed about what is going on in all areas of the company and in their division, department, or section.

2. Obtain observations and information from people outside their group—for example, from higher management authorities, guest lecturers, or consultants.

3. Report on decisions and changes that have been made or will be handed down from a higher level of the hierarchy.

Employees benefit greatly from such meetings. Their time is efficiently utilized, they get a chance to relate to one another, and they understand more fully how each part contributes to the whole. They are reminded that they are members of a team and are kept informed and up to date on individual and group progress (or the lack of such progress). Although the format is usually a lecture, time should be set aside for questions, so misunderstandings can be cleared up at the earliest possible time or be entirely avoided. Exhibit 5.4 points out a number of things to think about before you decide to hold such a meeting.

Using the Telephone

One of the greatest business machines is the telephone, but probably no other machine is misused so often by so many people at work. How many times have you called and been answered by a simple "Hello?" The lack of identification of a person or a place forces you to ask for that information and wastes time. There is a proper phone etiquette for both the caller and the receiver. While specifics vary from one company to another, a uniform way to make and to answer a call should be followed by all of a company's personnel. If you have no prescribed procedures, the following tips should prove useful.

When calling, identify yourself and determine who the person is that you are speaking to. Keep a pencil and paper handy to jot down names, numbers, and other bits of information as you receive them. If the first person contacted is the one you want, state your purpose and inquire if your call is being received at a convenient time. If it is not, set a time with him or her for a return call, and determine who will make it. If the time is right, make your call as brief as possible, and close the call with a sincere statement of thanks. Remember that phone calls usually represent an interruption in someone's day and, as such, can catch him or her unprepared or in an awkward moment. Keep in mind that your voice represents yourself and your company to others. Business calls are no place for emotional and uncourteous remarks.

When you receive a call, identify yourself and your position in the company, and make certain that the caller does the same. Determine the

- Be certain that one is absolutely necessary.
- Forewarn all who must attend well in advance; have those who cannot attend send a substitute.
- Notify all who are invited, in advance, about the meeting's purpose, starting time, ending time, and place.
- Reserve required facilities and equipment; arrange for qualified movers and operators to be on hand as needed.
- Prepare notes for the meeting, and rehearse your presentation.
- Prepare and distribute the written outline of the meeting's proceedings (agenda).
- Start the meeting on time.
- End the meeting once the purpose is achieved or at the scheduled ending time (even if purpose is not achieved).
- Gather input from all people in attendance.
- Keep the meeting on its agenda.
- Record significant contributions.
- Summarize the meeting's results before and after adjournment.
- Make certain that all participants know their new roles or the changes that arise from the meeting.
- Follow up on the results of the meeting.

Exhibit 5.4   **Guide to planning your meetings.**

caller's purpose and decide if you are the best person to handle the call. If the time is not convenient, arrange for a callback, including who will do it and when. Keep a pencil and paper handy for taking notes.

Listening

Nearly one-half of your working day as a supervisor and about 90 percent of your class time as a student are spent in listening.[8] Most of what you know and believe, you have learned by listening to others. Your business and academic success depends as much on listening as it does on writing, speaking, or reading. Listening attentively will allow you to respond intelligently to what you hear, but this requires a conscious effort on your part.

The speaker's goal is to be understood. The listener's goal is to understand and to listen with understanding. This means that, as a listener, you should attempt to see the expressed idea and attitude from the other person's point of view—to sense how it feels to the speaker, and to achieve the speaker's frame of reference in relation to the speaker's subject.[9] Few people can do this well, and that is why so few people are good listeners.

Studies done at Columbia University and at the University of Minnesota have proved that we operate at a 25 percent level of efficiency when listening to a ten-minute talk.[10] Pidgeon Savage Lewis, Inc., of Minneapolis conducted a study of the communicative efficiency of 100 business and industrial managements and found that 37 percent of information passed from the board of directors to vice-presidents was lost. By the time the information had been relayed to foremen and supervisors, 70 percent had been lost. Workers ultimately got 20 percent of what had been initiated by the board.[11]

Most of us speak at from 100 to 125 words per minute, but most of us can think at between 400 and 500 words per minute. This difference allows us time to criticize and to let our minds wander off on tangents while listening.[12] Our criticisms can be of the speaker, the delivery, or the content. Being critical, judgmental, approving, or disapproving of a speaker's message takes us away from our primary goals: to perceive the other person's point of view, to know how that person feels, and to understand what the frame of reference is. Wandering off on mental trips during listening shuts down our hearing and perceptions.

Barriers to Effective Listening   Many things (including our own attitudes) stand in our way when we attempt to listen to another person. Here are the major barriers to effective listening:

- Wanting to talk more than we want to listen
- Not being in the right (rested and alert) frame of mind
- Prejudging what the speaker is going to say, based on what we know about the speaker's knowledge of the subject, experience, and point of view; that is, failing to keep an open mind
- Letting the speaker's less-than-perfect delivery turn us off to the ideas and words
- Taking exception to a speaker's remarks as they are made and thus not listening to what follows those remarks
- Allowing events and those around us to distract our attention from the speaker
- Labeling the speaker or the subject dull or boring
- Dealing only with the speaker's facts and not listening for the speaker's emotional content
- Tuning out the speaker because he or she disagrees with what we ''know'' is right

Directions: Read the questions below and rate yourself according to the following:

Always .... 3 points
Usually .... 2 points
Rarely .... 1 point

	Choices
1. Do I let speakers send their messages without interrupting them?	3 2 1
2. Do I take notes, recording the most important points made by a speaker?	3 2 1
3. Do I try to connect the speaker's points with my past experiences to help me remember them?	3 2 1
4. Do I try to restate the speaker's points to make certain that I understand them?	3 2 1
5. Do I give the speaker my undivided attention, blocking out any noise or distractions?	3 2 1
6. Do I keep my emotional reactions to the speaker in check, not allowing them to distract me?	3 2 1
7. Do I keep my emotional reactions to the speaker's message in check, not allowing them to distract me?	3 2 1
8. Do I keep listening even if the message is boring or uninteresting to me?	3 2 1
9. Do I try to get at the speaker's intended meaning by listening "between the lines" of the speaker's words?	3 2 1
10. Do I formulate questions to ask the speaker that will clear up any unclear messages in the speaker's words?	3 2 1

Exhibit 5.5 **Measuring your listening skills**.

Exhibit 5.5 is a short quiz to help you determine how effective your listening efforts are. In addition to taking this quiz yourself, you should encourage your subordinates or team members to take it also. Your maximum score is 30. A rating of 24 or more indicates that you are an above-average listener. A score of 18 to 23 is average. Below 18, your listening skills need improvement.

Active Listening Active listening is "listening and responding in a way that makes it clear that the listener appreciates both the meaning and the feelings behind what is said."[13] Here are two examples of the process.[14]

EMPLOYEE: Don't you think my performance has improved since the last review?

SUPERVISOR: It sounds as if you think your work has picked up over these last few months?

and

EMPLOYEE: Just who is responsible for getting this job done?

SUPERVISOR: Do you think you don't have enough authority?

Active listeners leave a door open for a person to continue to tell what is on his or her mind. In the two instances just presented, the supervisor answered the employee's question with a question to draw the employee out and to get a deeper insight into the problem or at least the employee's perception of it. Active listeners follow the following guidelines:

They think with people and respond to their needs.

They avoid passing judgment, either positive or negative.

They listen for total meaning—both for content and for feelings.

They respond to what a person is really saying. For example, if a subordinate came to you and said, "I've finished your assignment," your response should be different than if the statement was, "Well, I've finally finished your damn assignment!"[15]

Keep in mind that listening is not a passive activity. It requires mental alertness and manipulations. Use every opportunity to seek clarification of the speaker's subject, feelings, and frame of reference. Questions are the key. Of course, when you have the information and understanding you need, questions are no longer needed.

Written Communications

Probably the most difficult form of communication is the written form. Yet nothing will mark you more clearly as a poor manager than your inability to write your thoughts effectively and correctly. Your written communications may be around a long time and will put you on record for future reference. A badly written, poorly constructed piece of writing can discredit you as nothing else can.

Just what is good writing? It is writing that transmits an idea or information clearly to the intended reader in accordance with the rules of grammar and proper sentence construction. Before you put your thoughts into writing, you should satisfy four criteria: (1) have something specific that must be communicated; (2) have something that is best stated in writing; (3) have command of language fundamentals, such as proper punctuation and spelling; and (4) have a specific reader in mind.

Effective writing, like effective oral presentations, must accomplish several things. It should especially be gauged to accomplish the following purposes:

- Command the reader's attention. Something in your writing or its appearance has to get the reader to read.

- Arouse interest. The writing's appeal must be aimed at the reader's specific interests. The "what's in this for you" should be up front. A benefit can be promised or a potential loss or cost can be cited. Tailor your message to a specific reader or reader interest.

- Specify the action called for. The basic purpose of most business correspondence is to get a favorable response or an acceptance from the reader.

Written summaries and reminders make effective follow-ups to oral communications. The combinations of the two forms of communications help to add importance and emphasis to key points, prevent misunderstandings, and provide evidence that communication about a subject has taken place. If you are a regular computer user, use your word-processing software to help you prepare professional written messages. If you are not, learn about the many uses of word processing and how it can help your written communications.

Effective writing amounts to "talking on paper." Effective writers make their points clearly, using ordinary language that is familiar to the people they are trying to reach. Your writing should read well—sound good to the ear when read aloud. As you write say what you are writing to yourself. When polishing your writing, read it aloud to catch any awkward phrases or sentences, any disconnected or unclear thoughts. When you write, you have complete control over the message. Consequently, if your communication is less than effective, you have only yourself to blame.[16]

Mechanics

Writing effectively is not easy. But you can make it a lot less difficult for yourself if you lay a proper foundation before you try to write. First, you should have a specific objective in mind. Next, you should gather your facts (this may involve searching your files or consulting with others). Then, you should make an outline—that is, a simple breakdown of your major points. Expand each major point by writing underneath it the minor ones that you wish to use to support it. You can use a sequence of numbers, letters, or both to identify major and minor points. Use whatever system is comfortable for you. Then arrange your points in the order best suited for a logical presentation.

Although much of your writing will be done with little or no research, it may sometimes be necessary for you to research a problem before you write about it. When you have to do research, remember the sources of information available to you: your own files, library indexes, individuals in your own section or unit, and higher authorities. You may want to use $3'' \times 5''$ cards to record information. When you decide that your research is complete, test the results by drawing conclusions from what you have learned and recorded. You should be able to prepare an outline from these conclusions while the details of what you have learned are still fresh in your mind.

Practice using simple, familiar, and concrete words. In reviewing your writing, be sure that *you* clearly understand the words you have used. Then ask yourself the following questions: "Will my readers understand my words? Will they get the same meaning that I do from them?" With some words, there is little danger of any misunderstanding. For example, the word *book* means much the same thing to all of us. Other words, however, may have wide differences in meaning for various people. Consider, for example, the term *implement*. A farmer would probably think you meant a plow, but in business memos, the word means to carry out a policy or a plan. If you have any doubt about a word, find another word that you are sure will be understood to carry the meaning you intend. If your readers must continually stop to ponder the meaning of your words, they will lose track of what you are telling them.

If you want your written communications to have impact, use short sentences. Professional writers know that writing is easier to read and remember if most of the sentences and paragraphs are brief. You should not use short sentences all the time, however, because such writing tends to strike readers as choppy and monotonous. Try to alternate a long sentence with one or two short ones, and try to keep sentences to fifteen or twenty words.

In preparing your paragraphs try to limit each of them to a single topic. As a rule, start each paragraph with a topic sentence that tells what the paragraph is about. Use transitional devices to tie both your sentences and your paragraphs together. The final sentence in a paragraph can either emphasize the points you wish to get across or lead the reader to your next subject.

The introductory paragraphs tell what the writing is about. The paragraphs that make up the body of a communication state the writer's case

Memo A

April 24, 1991

TO: ALL SECTION SUPERVISORS

The newly designed personal data sheet--Form 14A--has a necessary,
essential, and vital purpose in our organization. It provides the
necessary and statistically significant personal data required by the
personnel department to be kept on file for future references regarding
promotions, transfers, layoffs, and more.

During our recent relocation efforts from the rented facilities at Broad
Street to our present location here at Cauley Boulevard, files were lost,
damaged, or misplaced, necessitating the current request for
replacement of vital personal data on each and every manager in this
department. It is also the company's policy to periodically update
personal data on file through periodic, personal perusal of one's own
records--updating and adding new information as required and deleting
obsolete or outdated personal data on file.

Therefore, please complete the attached personal data sheet at your
earliest possible convenience but no later than Thursday, May 14, and
return it to me by the close of the business day on the 14th.

Jane Barton

Memo B

April 24, 1991

TO: ALL SECTION SUPERVISORS

Attached is our company's revised edition of the personal data sheet.
Please fill it out completely and return to me no later than the close of
business on Thursday, May 14. Thank you.

Jane Barton

Exhibit 5.6   **Two memos compared: Memo A, the original memo; and Memo B, an improved revision.**

(facts, figures, and so on). The closing paragraph or paragraphs recommend an action and/or summarize the important points of the paper. Once you are convinced that you have said what you want to say in the way you want to say it, stop writing.

Exhibit 5.6 shows an actual memo (memo A) sent by Jane, a middle manager, to her subordinate managers. Read it first, and then read memo B, which is a suggested improvement. Do you believe that memo B carries the basic message intended by the author of memo A? Which memo would you prefer to receive if you were one of Jane's subordinates?

Writing Letters

Unlike memos and reports, letters are sent to outsiders. Like phone calls, they represent you and your company to customers, vendors, government officials, and others. Before you write the letter, consider the following:

Can I identify my reader and his or her interests?

Have I a central purpose clearly in mind?

Is a letter the best way to communicate?

What style, of the approved styles I have to work with, is best?

As you write the letter, consider the following:

What is the person's name, its correct spelling, his or her job title, and his or her current address?

How can I say what I must in as brief and clear a way as possible?

Have I outlined my thoughts to flow smoothly and logically?

Have I linked my ideas to my reader's interests?

Have I been courteous?

Have I checked the spelling and grammar I have questions about?

When you are satisfied that it represents your best effort (others you trust may help you make this decision), send the letter. If it called for a response within a certain time and that time is past, follow up on your correspondence in the most appropriate way.

Getting Help

If you need help in the area of communications, get it. A course at your local college can improve your spoken and written communications. The results will be well worth your investment of time and money, as you will harvest the benefits for the rest of your life.

There is an old saying: "Nothing is ever written, only rewritten." From the time you pen the first few words of your message, you will probably want to revise or rewrite your thoughts. From the rough draft to the finished communication, you will be polishing, tightening up, and filling in. Keep a dictionary handy. Do not be afraid to refer to a basic grammar text either. Remember that your words carry your reputation.

The Grapevine

Grapevine
The transmission of information and/or misinformation through the use of informal channels at work

Transmission media or channels of communication can be formal or informal. Formal channels are those specifically set up for the transmission of normal business information, instructions, orders, and reports. The organization chart of a business outlines formal channels. Informal channels—the **grapevine**—are not specifically designated for use in the dissemination of information, but they are used for this purpose by nearly every employee. See Exhibit 5.7.

Informal channels exist because of the natural desire of employees to be in the know and to satisfy their curiosity. Because employees mix and socialize frequently during and outside their normal working relationships, they speculate and invent "information." The less they know about something, the more they invent. At coffee breaks, during lunch, or at social events, people often "pass the poop," even though they may not have all the facts.

The grapevine will often give managers a clue as to what is bothering their people and where the need for immediate or future action lies. Although it is generally a means by which gossip and rumors about the company are spread, managers should be tuned in to it. Do not, however, use the grapevine for disseminating orders or instructions to your people. It is no substitute for formal channels.

Gossip can sometimes serve you in your role as a supervisor by acting as an early warning system. When you hear a rumor, ask yourself what you would do if it were true. Gossip also alerts you as to where the leaks are and who may be letting unauthorized communications get into circulation.

To prevent the grapevine from yielding a crop of sour grapes, satisfy your people's need to know what is happening in their department, by applying the following rules to your daily situation:

1. Tune in on their informal communications.
2. Combat rumors and gossip with the facts.
3. Discredit people who willfully spread improper information.
4. Be available and honest with your people.
5. Know when to remain silent.

By applying these rules, you create in your subordinates a feeling of confidence about what is true and what is not true. You also strengthen your personal reputation as a source of sound information, and you foster better morale and cooperation. As a result, resistance to change can be lessened, and its impact can be softened.

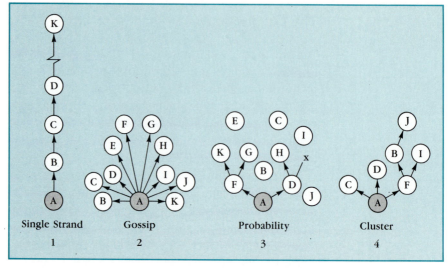

Exhibit 5.7   The four basic types of organizational grapevines. 1. *The single-strand grapevine:* A tells B, who tells C, who tells D, and so on. This type of grapevine tends to distort messages more than any other. 2. *The gossip grapevine:* A informs everyone else on the grapevine. 3. *The probability grapevine:* A communicates randomly, for example, to F and D. F and D then continue to inform other grapevine members in the same way. 4. *The cluster grapevine:* A selects and tells C, D, and F. F selects and tells I and B, and B selects and tells J. Information in this grapevine travels only to selected individuals. (*Source:* Samuel C. Certo, *Principles of Modern Management,* 4th ed. Mass.: Allyn & Bacon, 1989, p. 337.)

Instant Replay

1. Communication is the transmission of information and a common understanding from one person or group to another, through the use of common symbols.

2. A common understanding is achieved when both the sender and the receiver know each other's ideas, attitudes about the ideas, and frames of reference.

3. The major goals of the communication process are to be understood, to gain understanding, to gain acceptance for yourself or for your ideas, and to produce action or change.

4. A management information system (MIS) is a formal method for making accurate and timely information available to management to aid the decision-making process and to aid in the execution of

management and organization functions. Computers are making all kinds of communications more effective and efficient.

5. The major components or variables in the communication process are the message, the transmitter, the direction, the medium, and the receiver.

6. Communication barriers act to interrupt the flow of information and understanding and/or to inhibit it from taking place. Communications efforts should be planned with the barriers in mind, in order to eliminate them or to minimize their effects.

7. Delivering a speech or a lecture usually involves the use of an introduction, an explanation, and a summary. .

8. Listening takes up nearly one-half of our days. It is a skill that can be learned and improved by anticipating a speaker's next point, by identifying the speaker's supporting elements, by making mental summaries, and by adopting a tailored approach to note taking.

9. The grapevine consists of the transmission of information or misinformation through informal channels in the working environment.

Glossary   **Communication**   the transmission of information and common understanding from one person or group to another through the use of common symbols.

Direction   in communication, the flow or path a message will take in order to reach a receiver. The four directions are upward, downward, diagonal, and horizontal.

Feedback   any effort made by parties to a communication to ensure that they have a common understanding of each other's meaning and intent.

Grapevine   the transmission of information and/or misinformation through the use of informal channels at work.

Information   any facts, figures, or data that are in a form or format that makes them usable to the person who possesses them.

Medium   a channel or means used to carry a message in the communication process.   .

Message   the transmitter's ideas and feelings that form the content to be transmitted to a receiver.

Receiver   the person or group intended by transmitters to receive their messages.

Transmitter   the person or group that transmits or sends a message to a receiver.

Questions for Class Discussion

1. Can you define this chapter's key terms?

2. What are the four major goals behind the effort to communicate? Which do you think are part of every effort to communicate?

3. What does a management information system do for (a) managers, and (b) the organization?

4. What are the basic components of the communication process? How might the choice in one category influence the choices in others?

5. You are getting ready to communicate to your subordinates about a change in a safety procedure. What should you do before you attempt to relay your message?

6. What are five barriers to effective communication? Can you give an example of each from your experience?

7. How can you improve your listening skills and your ability to retain more of what you hear?

Incident

Purpose To evaluate your ability to get specific concepts across to others through the use of the spoken word.

Your Task Using only words (no gestures, hand signals, or visuals), get your audience to reproduce the following geometric forms in the center of an 8½" by 11" piece of paper. (You may want to photocopy the drawing below to hand out to your audience to check your success.) Encourage your audience to ask any questions they think are necessary. Suggested time: five minutes. Suggested tools for participants: one 12"-ruler and a penny.

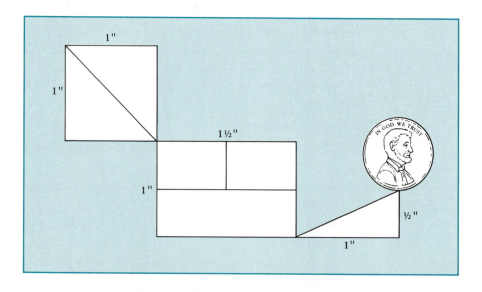

Case Problem 5.1   MIS or Mess?

"Have a seat," said Linda Presley, the management information center director.

Patty Hutton pulled a chair close to Linda's desk.

"We have a problem. The shop supervisors are complaining that they are not getting the production information they need on time. Wesley stopped by this morning to let me know that their daily status reports arrive from three to four hours after the start of each shift. What she and the other supervisors need is a report within the first hour."

"Look, Miss Presley, we can only give them data that comes from their data. They don't send the information my people need until well after each shift ends. Then we have to process it through the central computer and print it."

"Patty, I don't want to hear any excuses. You have been warned before about this, and you promised that you would cure the problem. Why haven't you?"

"Miss Presley, I investigated the matter and sent a standard interoffice memo to all the supervisors. I told them that if I was to help them, they would have to help me. I detailed what I needed and when. So far, only two of the six supervisors have responded with any change in their behavior. Some of the reports I get are almost illegible. When my people have to waste time trying to unscramble their scribblings, it affects the time it takes to generate their reports."

"Well, the matter has come to the attention of Briggs, the plant superintendent, and he has spoken to me about this on more than one occasion. I don't want to have to explain your failures to him again. Do you understand me?"

"What do you suggest I do, Miss Presley?"

"Get Briggs and those supervisors off my telephone and out of my office. I'm getting a little tired of taking heat for your failures. If you can't resolve this simple situation, maybe someone else can."

Patty got up from her chair, visibly upset. She turned and walked to the office door.

"I resent your personal attack on me and my people. We work hard and have managed to satisfy every other demand that management has thrown our way. I'm getting frustrated, along with my people, at the failure of so-called management people like those supervisors to follow simple instructions. We have far more important people to serve and much more important data to generate."

Before Linda could speak, Patty Hutton was out the door and slamming it.

"I'll fix her," said Linda to herself. She picked up her pen and began to write a memo to the personnel director. She also wrote a record of the encounter in the form of a "memo to file."

"I've got to start building my case," thought Linda.

Questions

1. What barriers to effective communication do you see from Patty's position?
2. What are the goals of this communication?
3. Why have the four supervisors failed to respond to Patty's requests?
4. What were the problems that the meeting was intended to deal with? What are the problems at the end of the case?
5. How could Linda have handled the meeting better?

Case Problem 5.2   On Your Guard

On your desk this morning was the memo shown in Exhibit A. It is from the personnel department and contains a few instructions, fancy words, and spelling and grammar mistakes. As Mr. Johnson's assistant, you are to correct its errors, eliminate the fancy words where possible, and make the memo shorter before it is distributed to your fellow supervisors.

Your Tasks

1. Photocopy Exhibit A and correct its spelling and grammatical errors on your copy
2. Rewrite the memo making it as clear, brief, and correct as you can.

MEMO

To: all supervisor in personnel   May 3, 19
From: Mr. A. J. Johnson, Personnel director
Subject: vacation and leave scheduling

Last year at this time we all had the pleasant or unpleasant chore of scheduling our vacations. To avoid disfunctioning and organizational chaos that resulted from unsynchronized and incompatible procedures, the following new procedure is to be implimented posthaste. (1) the scenario for choosing vacation bloks commences with the most senior supervisory person and ends with the least senior. (2)Times available are on the department bullitin board. (3) supervisors place their names next to the two week blok they require (no two supervisors can pick the same bloc.) (4) The finished list will then be ''carved in stone'' and followed religiously with no exceptions.

Exhibit A

Notes

1. R. C. Huseman and E. R. Alexander, III, "Communication and the Managerial Function: A Contingency Approach," in *Readings in Management,* ed. Max D. Richards (Cincinnati: South-Western Publishing, 1982), 103.
2. James A. F. Stoner, *Management,* 2d ed. (Englewood Cliffs, N.J.: Prentice-Hall, 1982), 645.
3. "Office Line," *USA Today* (June 8, 1987): 8E.
4. Donald Weiss, *How to Be a Successful Manager* (New York: AMACOM, 1986), 33.
5. Leslie Braunstein, "Move It! Computers Put on the Pressure," *USA Today* (June 8, 1987): 11E.
6. Mark Lewin, "IBM: There's Message in High-tech Madness," *USA Today* (June 8, 1987): 10E.
7. Henry C. Lucas, Jr., "Utilizing Information Technology: Guidelines for Managers," *Sloan Management Review* (Fall 1986): 41.
8. Ralph G. Nichols, "Listening Is Good Business," in *Readings in Management,* ed. Max D. Richards (Cincinnati: South-Western Publishing, 1982), 109–24.
9. C. R. Rogers and F. J. Roethlisberger, "Barriers and Gateways to Communication,"

in *Business Classics: Fifteen Key Concepts for Managerial Success* (Cambridge, Mass.: Harvard Business Review, 1975), 45.

10. Nichols, "Listening Is Good Business," 111.
11. Ibid., 112.
12. Ibid., 122.
13. C. R. Rogers and R. E. Farson, "The Meaning of Active Listening," in *Active Listening* (Chicago: Industrial Relations Center of the University of Chicago), 3.
14. Ibid., 6.
15. Carl R. Anderson, *Management Skills, Functions, and Organization Performance* (Dubuque, Iowa: Wm. C. Brown, 1984), 202.
16. Donald Weiss, *How to Write Easily and Effectively* (New York: AMACOM, 1986), 49–50.

Suggested Readings

Culligan, M. J.; Deakins, C. S.; and Young, A. H. *Back to Basics Management.* New York: Facts on File, 1983.

Gootnick, David E., and Gootnick, Margaret M., eds. *The Standard Handbook of Business Communication.* New York: The Free Press, 1984.

Kaumeyer, Richard A., Jr. *How to Write and Speak in Business.* New York: Van Nostrand Reinhold, 1985.

Konsynski, Benn R., and McFarlan, F. Warren. "Information Partnerships—Shared Data, Shared Scale." *Harvard Business Review* (September–October 1990): 114–120.

Lucas, Henry C. "Utilizing Information Technology: Guidelines for Managers." *Sloan Management Review* (Fall 1986): 39–47.

Neuman, A. *Principles of Information Systems for Management.* Dubuque, Iowa: Wm. C. Brown, 1982.

Roddick, Ellen. *Writing That Means Business: A Manager's Guide.* New York: Macmillan, 1984.

Weiss, Donald H. *How to Make an Effective Speech or Presentation.* New York: AMACOM, 1987.

Weiss, Donald. *How to Write Easily and Effectively.* New York: AMACOM, 1986.

II You and Your People

Part II contains five chapters about topics that influence or bear directly on the routine interactions between supervisors and their subordinates. Chapter 6 defines attitudes—how they form, how they influence those who have them, and how they can be changed. As our innermost perceptions of the world around us, attitudes determine how we approach problems, situations, and other people. As a manager, your attitudes and those of your subordinates will directly affect the success of your operations and department. Additionally, the causes and methods for coping with stress are examined in Chapter 6.

Chapter 7 examines the most important theories and models dealing with human behavior: Why do people do what they do? What is behind our everyday and extraordinary actions and interactions? Chapter 7 presents the needs all humans have in common, important theories about motivation, and what individual supervisors can do to stimulate themselves and their subordinates to improve their work performances.

The daily interaction between and among supervisors, peers, and subordinates as individuals is the topic of chapter 8. Its focus is on the four basic roles that every manager must play when relating to others at work. The role of educator involves teaching and training. The role of counselor involves listening, offering advice, and making meaningful responses to the person in need. The role of judge requires equity and justice in rewarding, punishing, and settling disputes. The role of spokesperson requires sharing credit and blame and fighting for just causes.

Chapter 9 focuses on the interaction between a manager and groups of his or her subordinates. In addition, formal and informal groups are examined, along with how they form and affect their members. The benefits and the detrimental effects of competition between an organization's groups are also explored. Some very useful tips are given to help supervisors cope with their subordinates' informal groups.

Chapter 10 covers the various theories and principles that govern the complexities of leading and being perceived as a leader. It details basic leadership and management styles and offers advice on when and how to use each of them. The choice of a style may be dictated by the kind of subordinate you are dealing with, as well as the forces at work in your organizational environment. Once you gain the status of a leader in the minds of your subordinates, your job and theirs will become more pleasant and productive.

6 Managing Change and Stress

Outline

Objectives

After reading and discussing this chapter, you should be able to do the following:

1 Define the key terms.

2 Explain how people form their attitudes.

3 List and briefly explain the four basic steps you can take to change a person's attitude.

4 List and briefly explain six techniques available to change people's attitudes.

5 List six causes of stress on the job.

6 List six ways of coping with work-related stress.

Key Terms

attitude

belief

force-field analysis

opinion

organization development

stress

Theory X

Theory Y

Theory Z

value

work ethic

Introduction

The United States is presently engaged in an economic battle for the survival of its major industries and for the preservation of their market shares in major markets at home and abroad. We are facing major competitive threats from all our trading partners and from the developing nations, where labor is relatively cheap. Markets that we used to call our own are being taken by foreign competition that delivers better, cheaper, higher-quality goods and services. U.S. makers of steel, automobiles, leather and textiles, computers, consumer electronics, and more have lost their reputations for reliable and desirable products. Even banking has yielded to foreign competitors offering better service and lower loan rates.

Many American industries are responding to the challenges of foreign producers by:

- Increasing their use of automation and computer-driven machines and processes

- Redesigning jobs to put more decisions into the hands of those who know the work best, creating teams and hands-on managers

- Reducing the ranks of middle managers and cutting back on jobs that do not contribute directly to profits and production

- Introducing new and renewed efforts at controlling costs and improving quality

- Setting up shop outside the United States to take advantage of lower costs and less government regulation

The results have been a mixture of success and failure. Managers are discovering that there is no "quick fix" on the road back to competitiveness. Efforts at improving quality must start with the commitment of top management in each business and spread to every employee. "Engineers, designers, marketers, administrators, and the production workers on the line have to work together to ensure quality, and they all have to know that they are critical to the process."[1]

People are the key to better quality in both goods and services. People are the most valuable resource in the effort to survive, grow, and prosper. The attitudes, values, and beliefs that people bring to work and that are formed at work influence them either in a positive way or in a negative one. Without the commitment of each person to produce to the best of his or her abilities, a company's efforts will yield less-than-satisfactory results.

Attitudes, Beliefs, and Values

This chapter looks at attitudes, beliefs, and values that influence a company's output and rewards. It examines how they form and how they influence individuals in the workplace. It discusses how you as a supervisor can influence individuals to become or to remain good producers. Finally, it offers advice on how you can manage change and stress in yourself and in others.

Attitudes

Attitude
A person's manner of thinking, feeling, or acting toward specific stimuli

An **attitude** is a person's manner of thinking, feeling, or acting toward specific stimuli. Attitudes—the feelings people have toward things and other people—determine people's readiness to respond favorably or unfavorably to other people and to events. Two fundamental attitudes you should have as a supervisor are respect for yourself and respect for others. Without belief in yourself and in the value of others, you cannot create or maintain a positive, productive environment in which people, including yourself, can give their best and feel a true commitment to quality work.[2]

"A dynamic relationship exists between behavior and attitudes. Generally, people try to keep them consistent with each other, so that if an attitude is changed, behavior will also alter to correspond. It also turns out that changing behavior can influence a change in attitude."[3] If you hold the attitude that sharing decisions is a good thing, you will share decisions when you can. But a supervisor who thinks that sharing decisions with subordinates is a foolish idea will resist pressures to share decisions until he or she changes that attitude.

Our experiences have, to a great extent, made us what we are today. Our experiences, coupled with those of others, have taught us lessons that have helped to shape our personalities and to give us the attitudes we now possess. The Center for Creative Leadership, a nonprofit management training and research organization in North Carolina, asked seventy-nine executives to describe the experiences that led to lasting changes in them. Their responses were grouped into sixteen categories and thirty-one types of lessons. Overall, their responses indicated that, from their past challenges and assignments, they gained confidence, independence, knowledge, and toughness. From exposure to others, the good and the bad, these executives "learned to balance their toughness with a fundamental sensitivity to and respect for human beings. And from hardships endured, they balanced their confidence and independence with a recognition of their own limits and a better sense of themselves."[4]

Beliefs

Belief
A perception based on a conviction that certain things are true or probable in one's own mind (opinion)

Opinion
A belief based on a perception of what seems to be true or probable in one's own mind

Their work experiences and the people they worked with created changes in these executives at various stages in their lives. So it is with all of us. Our experiences have taught us our individual sets of beliefs. A **belief** is a conception based on a conviction that certain things are true *or* are based on what seems to be true or probable in one's own mind. This latter kind of belief is called an **opinion.** Beliefs shape our attitudes, and our attitudes, when made known to others, display our beliefs. Let us consider an example to cement these ideas together.

Your boss has, over a period of several weeks, lied to you twice, failed to back you up when you executed his order, and told a lie about you to your fellow supervisors. These experiences have helped you to form beliefs about your boss. You now believe that your boss lacks integrity and cannot be trusted. These beliefs help to form a negative attitude in your mind toward your boss. This negative attitude now causes you to doubt your boss when he speaks to you, to question his orders and not execute them carefully, and to avoid giving him your trust and confidences. Your beliefs have formed an attitude that will affect your future feelings, thoughts, and actions with regard to your boss.

When you are confronted with people or concepts not already part of your experience, you are usually not predisposed in any specific way toward them. You lack definite attitudes, opinions, and beliefs about them. It is at this point that you are most open and impressionable about the new contacts. Initially, you try to make your own observations, gain some insights, and draw your own conclusions. This is the normal process by which we form new attitudes. Friends or associates can influence us to some degree, depending on how true and useful we feel their attitudes are. Your attitude toward a source of information determines whether you accept that source's conclusions, wholly or in part, or reject them. In forming new attitudes, we make reference to our existing attitudes.

Think back to the time when you were seeking employment with your present employer. Why did you decide to apply to that company rather than to other companies? If you had no prior experience with your present company, you probably relied on its reputation, as relayed to you by others whose beliefs and opinions you respected. A friend may have suggested that you apply because he or she worked there and liked the company. You were willing to put your future in the hands of an employer on the basis of another's attitude and your attitude toward that person. As a new applicant, you made your own observations during the selection process and got answers to specific questions. Your beliefs toward your new employer were taking shape, and when you accepted the job, you had probably formed a positive set of attitudes toward both your employer and your new job. Your attitudes, therefore, had a definite influence on your behavior. They will continue to do so.

According to a study conducted by the Work in America Institute, a nonprofit research firm in New York, the way that employees view top management affects their work attitudes more than any other single variable in the workplace.[5] The study focused on unionized assembly-line workers and how they formed their attitudes toward work. Group interviews and questionnaires were used in ten automobile assembly plants of one U.S. auto maker. The study showed that an employee's perceptions of top management had a stronger direct influence on job satisfaction than any other variable studied, including such factors as salary, fringe benefits, job training, coworker relationships, company policies and procedures, and the employee's relationship with his or her supervisor. Remarkably similar findings have been uncovered by American Telephone & Telegraph Company in its ongoing study of its employees. Factors that create a favorable view of top management among employees include:

- Keeping people informed—letting people know both the good and the bad and what changes are coming and why
- Treating employees with respect and honesty
- Listening to and using employees' suggestions
- Giving supervisors and team leaders the authority and support they need to get the job done well
- Emphasizing quality over quantity

Values

Value
An activity, condition, or object that we feel has merit or worth in our lives

One set of beliefs that we all have are our **values**—activities, conditions, and objects that we feel have merit or value in our lives. Values include judgments about what is right and what is wrong. Values are often expressed as wants and as things worth working hard for both to keep and to obtain. Having a high-paying job and working for an employer whom you admire and respect are examples of values. Like attitudes, values are learned throughout life and are usually more difficult to change than attitudes are.

Exhibit 6.1 is a quick way to assess your attitudes and values. Check the listings to determine which are of most importance to you at this time in your life. Keep the most important ones in mind when attempting to change your job or career.

People's Attitudes About Work

A recent poll by Robert Half International surveyed vice-presidents and personnel directors of 100 of the 1,000 largest corporations in the United States and concluded that about 23 percent of our nation's 113 million employed persons were not happy with or successful in their jobs.[6] Just think for a minute what these people must live with each day and what kind of an effort they must give to their jobs—jobs they dislike.

Another recent poll by Louis Harris and Associates discovered that 42 percent of the 1,250 adult employees polled were "very satisfied" with their jobs and that the same percentage felt "somewhat satisfied." This leaves 16 percent who did not find satisfaction in their work.[7] How well a job and its environmental conditions match up with an individual's strongest attitudes, values, and beliefs determines to a great extent what kind of satisfaction the job will give to the job holder.

After each of the listings below, indicate which is most important, somewhat important, or of no importance in your life at present.

	Most Important	Somewhat Important	Not Important
1. Having a challenging job—one that taxes your abilities and forces you to grow.	___	___	___
2. Having a chance to make a signifi-cant contribution—having the feel-ing and belief that your work is really important.	___	___	___
3. Having a boss that you can respect —one who is honest, open, and a real source for help when it is needed.	___	___	___
4. Having the pay and benefits that are competitive and fair.	___	___	___
5. Having control over your work—being able to set your own pace and to inspect the quality of your output.	___	___	___
6. Working for a company that recog-nizes that it is a citizen of a com-munity outside of itself and acts in a socially responsible manner.	___	___	___
7. Working for a company that really cares about its employees' needs, both those that are and those that are not job related.	___	___	___
8. Working in a career field that is admired and respected by those whose opinions matter most to you.	___	___	___
9. Having coworkers or peers whom you can relate to and respect.	___	___	___

Exhibit 6.1   Assessing your attitudes and values.

The Work Ethic

Work ethic
People's attitudes
about the importance
of working, the kind
of work they choose
or are required to do,
and the quality of
their efforts while
performing work

People's attitudes about work—their **work ethics**—can be grouped into
three areas: the importance of working, the kind of work a person
chooses or is required to perform, and the quality of the person's individual efforts while performing work. Your attitudes in each of these areas
will affect the attitudes you hold in the other areas. Your attitudes may
change or be reinforced, depending on the experiences you have had and
will have in seeking employment, in carrying out your work, and in

receiving rewards from working. As a supervisor, you can influence the experiences of your subordinates and, therefore, help to shape their attitudes about work and their individual work ethics.

Author/professor David J. Cherrington in his book, *The Work Ethic: Working Values and Values That Work,* has discovered that significant differences exist between and among different age groups and between men and women with regard to their work ethics. Older workers tend to have more positive attitudes toward their work and quality of performance than do younger workers. More men than women work primarily for money, while the reverse is true when it comes to seeking personal satisfaction from work. There are exceptions of course, but as a supervisor you need to recognize your own work ethic and the work ethic of each of your subordinates so that you can work to improve the negatives and to take advantage of the positives. You need to know why people are working for you and your company, what they think of their work, and the quality of their performances. Only then can you understand them as individual workers. Generally speaking, the more positive a person's work ethic, the more valuable that person is as an employee and as your subordinate.

Theories X and Y

A professor of management at Massachusetts Institute of Technology, Douglas McGregor, constructed two theories that attempt to summarize the two prevalent yet opposing sets of attitudes adopted by managers today with regard to human nature and motivation.[8] **Theory X** portrays a somewhat traditional view that unfortunately all too often underlies managers' behavior:

Theory X
A set of attitudes traditionally held by managers that assumes the worst with regard to the average worker's initiative and creativity

1. The average person has a natural dislike for work and will try to avoid it.
2. The average person has to be threatened, controlled, coerced, and punished to give a fair day's work.
3. The average person avoids responsibility, lacks ambition, and needs constant direction.

The real tragedy of Theory X is that it is a self-fulfilling prophecy about people. If a manager really believes what this theory holds about subordinates, he or she will treat them in an authoritarian and suspicious manner, threatening them and looking down on them. The new employee who has a different makeup from the boss's will soon learn that his or her ideas, initiative, and drive are not respected or rewarded. He or she will learn to behave in the way the boss expects him or her to behave. Soon the employee will adopt the ''what's the use'' attitude that this boss assumed existed from the beginning. Then the boss can smile and say, ''See, I told you so.''

What Theory X does not say, but assumes, is that a small minority of people are exceptions to the theory and that they are destined to rule others.

Theory Y
A set of attitudes held by today's generation of managers that assumes the best about the average worker's initiative and creativity

Theory Y, on the other hand, is an attempt to apply what is now known about the majority of people in light of recent research on human behavior and motivation. Theory Y states the following propositions about the average person:

1. The average person desires work as naturally as he or she does play or rest.
2. The average person is capable of controlling and directing himself or herself if committed to achieving a goal.
3. The average person is committed to a goal on the basis of the rewards associated with it and its achievement.
4. The average person desires responsibility and accepts it willingly.
5. The average person possesses imagination, ingenuity, and initiative.
6. The average person is intellectually underutilized in the average industrial setting.

A manager who adopts this set of beliefs about his or her subordinates will take an entirely different approach in relationships with them than would a manager who adheres to Theory X. The Theory Y manager will assume the best and expect no less from each individual, while also demanding the best from himself or herself. Look around you at work. You will probably find many examples of men and women, both in and out of management, who are putting forth a mediocre effort. This often is the result of their managers' expecting nothing more from them. Subordinates learn to give what is expected. A mediocre subordinate is usually the reflection of a mediocre manager.

Theory Z

The early 1980s brought a sharp focus on management practices and techniques as exhibited by Japanese managers. Aside from Japan's unique culture and relatively homogeneous population, several major differences

Table 6.2

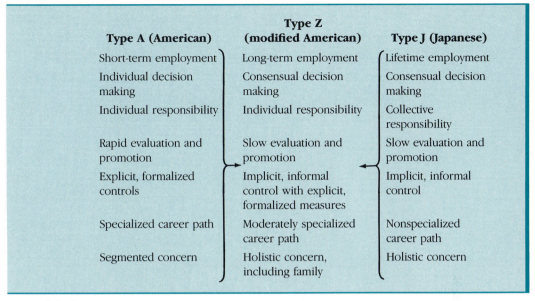

	Type Z	
Type A (American)	**(modified American)**	**Type J (Japanese)**
Short-term employment	Long-term employment	Lifetime employment
Individual decision making	Consensual decision making	Consensual decision making
Individual responsibility	Individual responsibility	Collective responsibility
Rapid evaluation and promotion	Slow evaluation and promotion	Slow evaluation and promotion
Explicit, formalized controls	Implicit, informal control with explicit, formalized measures	Implicit, informal control
Specialized career path	Moderately specialized career path	Nonspecialized career path
Segmented concern	Holistic concern, including family	Holistic concern

Exhibit 6.2   **Characteristics of three types of organizations.** (*Source:* W. G. Ouchi and A. M. Jaeger, "Type Z Organization: Stability in the Midst of Mobility," *Academy of Management Review,* vol. 3, no. 2 (April 1978): 305–14.)

Theory Z
A set of approaches to managing people based on the attitudes of Japanese managers about the importance of the individual and of team effort to the organization

exist in the attitudes held by American and Japanese managements. In Japan, input from workers and managers at every level is sought before decisions are made. Supervisors are taught to seek input from their subordinates before deciding an issue. Middle managers seek the input of their subordinates before deciding issues. Japanese workers generally feel more loyalty to their employers than do their American counterparts. These attitudes of loyalty are built, in large measure, on a set of factors shown in Exhibit 6.2. **Theory Z** is a blend of the factors listed under the Type J organizations. This theory is characterized by high motivation and productivity from workers and is the result of high levels of trust and commitment to workers on the part of their managements.[9] We have benefited from the Japanese approach to industrial management and have borrowed many of its concepts.

The Supervisor's Attitudes

Exhibit 6.3 illustrates the attitude situation for workers and for management. Depending on your attitudes, you fit into one of three locations in the diagram. Before and during the initial stages of training of workers to

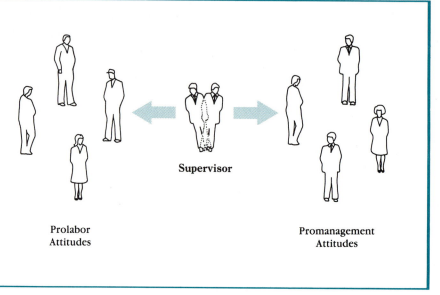

Supervisor

Prolabor
Attitudes

Promanagement
Attitudes

Exhibit 6.3   The positions of workers and managers in relation to their attitudes.

become supervisors, the workers' attitudes place them to the left of center, in the prolabor area. The major job of supervisory training programs is to change the trainees' attitudes toward and their conceptions of management. If the program is successful, it will lead to a shift in the trainees' attitudes toward the center line—the fence between prolabor and promanagement attitudes.

The center line or fence is the awkward yet mandatory position for most operating managers because of their unique roles as spokespersons for both labor and management. They are concerned most directly about the welfare of their subordinates and at the same time must protect and fortify management's position. Needless to say, this fence straddling can be uncomfortable and demanding at times, but it is necessary nonetheless. Truly, supervisors are the people in the middle, caught between the needs of their subordinates and the needs of their superiors.

As a manager, your attitudes should be in harmony with your company's policies and your understanding of sound management principles and practices. You should be willing to question your own attitudes whenever you observe contrary ones in either a peer or a superior. Try to be objective in determining which are the better attitudes to hold. Maintaining an open mind and being receptive to the new and different will stimulate your growth and improve your knowledge and understanding of yourself and your position.

Beware of accepting the attitudes or opinions of others as your own. We all have a tendency to fill a void in our knowledge by the quickest means available, but this can be a dangerous practice. When you first became a supervisor, you may have heard from your boss or predecessor, "Watch out for Al; he's a sneak." Or, "You sure are lucky to have Agnes; she's a peach." Dismiss these "insights" and wait to form your own attitudes and opinions through your personal observations. What subordinates or superiors were like with your predecessor and what they will be like with you are almost always two different things.

If you believe in yourself and set your standards above the average, your results will, in time, match those standards. So should it be with your subordinates. Believe in your people, assume the best about each one of them, and do all in your power to help them realize the inherent potential you know they possess.

The Pygmalion Effect

George Bernard Shaw's play about an English flower girl in the slums who is groomed to become a lady of English society was called *Pygmalion*. The Broadway musical *My Fair Lady,* later made into a film, was based upon Shaw's play. From these we have deduced what has become known as the *Pygmalion effect:* assuming the best about people will often result in their giving their best; assuming less will often yield less in their performances. In short, people learn to give what they are expected to give. Students and trainees often learn in accordance with what their teachers and trainers expect of them.

Research done by J. Sterling Livingston and others has given us the following insights about the supervisor's impact on subordinates, with regard to the Pygmalion effect:

1. What a manager expects of subordinates and how he or she treats them largely determine their performance and career progress.

2. A unique characteristic of superior managers is their ability to create high performance expectations that subordinates fulfill.

3. Less effective managers fail to develop similar expectations, and the productivity of their subordinates suffers as a result.

4. Subordinates, more often than not, appear to do what they believe they are expected to do.[10]

You should have little doubt that you, as a supervisor, can help or hinder a new person's ability to adjust and to succeed in your company's environment. Your attitudes will soon shape those of your subordinates.

They will look to you for respect, guidance, and example. What you expect from them and what you exemplify each day to them will determine their attitudes and reactions toward you and toward their own work.

Allow me to share with you an experience I had with a student one evening following class. The student—let's call him Greg—asked me how to make a résumé. He explained that he wanted to seek a new job. Greg related how he had been in contention for his boss's job in middle management but had been frustrated when the president of the company brought in his brother from outside to fill the vacancy. Greg, who had had over fourteen years with the company, went on to state that the new man had no experience, did not know the business, and did not know the jobs of his subordinate supervisors. Greg was really depressed and understandably so.

I asked Greg two questions: (1) How long did he think the president's brother would occupy a low-level middle-management position? (2) Wasn't it true that the president's brother was totally dependent on Greg and his fellow supervisors both for learning his job and for gaining a successful reputation?

Greg thought for a moment and began to smile. He reasoned that the answer to question 1 was *not very long* and that the answer to question 2 was *yes*. When our conversation was over, he was dedicated to helping that new man become the best middle manager possible. After all, it does not hurt to have a future executive in high places who respects your abilities and is indebted to you, in part, for his success.

Problem Supervisors

Without realizing it, some supervisors may be the primary cause of an employee's difficulties. Through their actions or lack of action, supervisors can and often do influence their subordinates' behavior. Supervisors have the ability to aggravate their subordinates' difficulties and to put them off balance. A supervisor can confront subordinates who are on the edge of trouble and either help them steer clear of it or push them into it. Like a parent or older brother or sister, the boss should be someone to look up to for a good example and good advice. Your people are very conscious of your behavior and read into it guidelines for their own behavior.

A few thoughts about perception are needed here. One person's perception of another person is a unique thing. Perceptions of people come from several sources, including what we see them do or hear them say, what we learn about them from others, and what we think about them based on our past experiences and our beliefs.

How your people perceive you—what they think of you as a person and as a boss—is very important to you. You need to recognize that, although you are one person, you are seen and heard by many others. Your observers are all unique individuals with different attitudes, values, and experiences. Each will observe you at different times and under different circumstances. Therefore, each person's perception of you will be unique and unlike any other. Consider the checklist in Exhibit 6.4. If some of the questions "sting" you a bit, you could be a cause for unhappy and poor performing subordinates. With every "yes" response to the items, you are sowing seeds for trouble in your relationships with subordinates. Without positive perceptions of you, your subordinates will not have the trust and respect for you that they should. You will lack power to influence them by means other than threats and punishment. In short, you will lack leadership ability.

Your Subordinates' Attitudes

Your people have attitudes about their work, the company, and you as their boss. When you first take office in your new job as a supervisor, your people will adopt a wait-and-see attitude about you and your abilities. They are, for the most part, open and objective, waiting for evidence

Questions	Yes	No
1. Do I like to control my people with threats?	——	——
2. Do I like to keep them a little off balance and insecure?	——	——
3. Am I unpredictable in my behaviors and dealings with them?	——	——
4. Do I make promises that I do not or cannot keep?	——	——
5. Do I betray confidences?	——	——
6. Do I issue conflicting orders and instructions?	——	——
7. Do I forget to compliment them for work well done?	——	——
8. Do I discipline them in public?	——	——
9. Do I carry a grudge?	——	——
10. Do I play favorites?	——	——
11. Do I take my subordinates for granted?	——	——

Exhibit 6.4 **What you are doing that influences your subordinates' perceptions of you.**

on which to base their opinions. The attitudes they will eventually adopt about you are almost entirely within your power to mold. The attitudes they already possess toward other things are hidden from view and will take some time to uncover. These were formed in an environment and through experiences of which you were not a part. Nevertheless, their attitudes will surely influence their performances, their output, and the reputation of the department. Your success and theirs are linked directly to attitudes—both yours and theirs.

One of the most important tasks for managers (and particularly for supervisors) is to identify improper or unacceptable attitudes—attitudes held by subordinates that interfere with their rendering better-than-average or average performances. Once these attitudes are uncovered, managers must begin the demanding task of changing them in order to bring their people to a greater realization of their potential and their departments to a higher state of effectiveness.

Good Attitudes Versus Bad Attitudes

We all have a tendency to label things as *good* or *bad.* Such a label is based on our own individual points of view. With regard to labeling our own attitudes as *good* or *bad,* good ones serve us well, while bad ones cause us trouble. Once we recognize an attitude as the source of problems, we are encouraged to change it. We consider our good attitudes to be proper, while we consider our bad attitudes to be improper. But problems arise when we attempt to label other people's attitudes. First, we attempt to determine the other person's attitudes through observations of the person's actions or words. Second, we may be quick to label another person's attitude *bad* or *improper* simply because it differs from ours.

As a supervisor, you need to determine your attitudes and those of your subordinates, and you need to discover why you and they have these attitudes. Labels are not important. The key questions are: Do I know what attitude that person has? Do I know why the person has it? Is the attitude a source of problems to me as a supervisor or to the person as an employee? The attitudes you must attempt to change in yourself and in your subordinates are those that are a source of problems.

Suppose, for example, that as a supervisor in a machine shop you observe a subordinate named Joe not wearing his safety goggles while operating a grinding wheel. Safety regulations tell him to wear safety goggles while grinding. You remind him to wear them, and he agrees to do so. Ten minutes later you pass the same workman again; he is again not wearing his safety goggles. At this point you may ask yourself why. The question should have been asked earlier. If it had been, the second infraction of the rules might have been prevented. The answer to the question lies in the worker's attitude toward wearing safety goggles. He believes that his attitude is a proper one, or he would not behave in this manner. As his supervisor you do not hold the same attitude because you believe his behavior is improper. Your tendency is to label his attitude *bad* or *improper.* At this point the dialogue might go as follows.

SUPERVISOR: "Joe, you know we have a shop rule about wearing safety goggles, don't you?"

JOE: "Yeah, I know the rule."

SUPERVISOR: "Do you want to lose an eye?"

JOE: "Nope."

SUPERVISOR: "Didn't I tell you a few minutes ago to wear your goggles?"

JOE: "Yep."

SUPERVISOR: "Well, why don't you wear them then?"

JOE: "The strap's too tight. It gives me a headache."

The lesson should be obvious. Whatever attitudes people reflect by their behavior are viewed by them to be adequate. Until they see a need for change or can be shown an alternative that gives them better results, they have no incentive to change. Joe was willing to take a risk to his eye in order to avoid a headache. Why he did not complain without being asked is another problem. If he has to buy goggles out of his own money, he may be reluctant to buy another pair. If the company furnishes them, the storeroom may be out of Joe's size. There could be a dozen reasons. The point is, what is the person's attitude, and why does the person have it? When you know the answers to these questions, you can begin to change the attitudes that are the sources of the problems.

Uncooperative Attitudes: Why People Resist Change

Cooperation means working together to reach common objectives or goals. If you are the kind of supervisor this book is trying to develop, you will have minimized your problems and found little resistance to overcome. The primary barrier to cooperation, therefore, is yourself—your weaknesses, inadequacies, and failure to offer a good example. Look first at yourself and your practices of management before you accuse others of wrongdoing. If you can honestly say that the barrier to cooperation lies outside yourself, then the remainder of this chapter should prove helpful to you.

At the core of a person's noncooperation is his or her lack of motivation to cooperate. This means that the person has no desire at present to do so. It falls to you, therefore, to attempt to provide the climate and incentives that will foster a spirit of cooperation in each of your people. As a rule, people are unwilling to cooperate for either of two kinds of reasons: personal or social.

Personal Reasons

Individuals may be unwilling to cooperate with you or their fellow workers because they see no personal advantage in doing so. They may not understand the changes you propose in your operations, and they may fear the implications of such changes to them in their jobs, status, pay, or future. How well people accept changes may be contingent upon how well changes have been introduced in the past. They can remember what happened at that time, and they will assume that similar results will occur this time. If a change was handled well in the past, the gate remains open for new changes. If not, you can anticipate resistance or opposition to the change.

On the other hand, people may resist changes because of the personal advantages they can keep if the changes are thwarted. For example, if people know their jobs well and are successful at them, they have job security. They are using tried and proved methods, and feel no need to make an effort to learn something new. Thus they have no need to alter their present routines.

Most of us have a built-in fear of change. This fear seems to grow as we advance in years and experience. Nearly all such fear is based on ignorance—not knowing what the changes might mean to us and to our position. We have seen people displaced through advances in technology. We have seen old and traditional skills and crafts eliminated. A change in methods may be viewed as a criticism of our present performance, especially when the change is enforced from outside our department.

The supervisor is an initiator, translator, and implementer of change. As such, he or she must plan for change, communicate its need effectively, and show subordinates the advantages that will accrue to them as a result of adopting the change. In short, the supervisor must point out the need for and advantages of cooperation and must remove any attitudes that stand in its way.

Social Reasons

As you are well aware, most people in a business do not work by themselves. They are probably members of both informal and formal groups.

Changes proposed or suspected may give rise to a fear that the worker's social relationships may be upset, either by the loss of his or her present associates or by the need to find new ones.

An individual may be in favor of a change because he or she can see personal advantages in the new development. The group to which he or she belongs, however, may be against the change. What then can the individual member of a group do? He or she can either adopt the group's viewpoint about the change and risk difficulties with the supervisor or favor the change and risk expulsion from the group.

Changing the Attitudes of Subordinates

A supervisor can bring about a change in a subordinate's improper attitude or behavior through a four-step process. After you have observed improper behavior on the part of a subordinate, or after you have heard an improper attitude expressed by a subordinate, you should take the following steps:

1. Identify the improper attitude or behavior.
2. Determine what supports it—opinions and beliefs (root causes).
3. Weaken or change whatever supports it (root causes).
4. Offer a substitute for the improper attitude or behavior.

Consider the following example, contributed by one of my students: Mike was a supervisor of thirty assemblers in an electronics plant in Chicago. It was his practice to turn each new employee over to an experienced worker for training until the new person adjusted to the job and became capable of meeting both quality and quantity standards on his or her own. One day Mike hired a young, recent immigrant from India named Ehri. Ehri was placed under the direction of Dave, an experienced and willing worker-trainer. Once on his own, however, Ehri's production was marked by an unacceptable level of rejects.

Step 1: Identifying the Improper Attitude or Behavior

When you determine that a subordinate's behavior is improper, you must look for the attitude behind it and state it in precise terms.

Mike went to Ehri and observed him at work. Ehri was working at an almost frantic pace. Mike assumed that this was the reason for the large number of rejects and asked Ehri to slow his pace and concentrate on quality, not quantity.

Often, just by investigating the action, showing concern, and giving corrective instructions, you will be able to solve the problem. The worker may realize at that point that his or her behavior is unacceptable and change it to meet the demands of the supervisor. This did not happen with Ehri.

Mike had failed to identify the attitude that supported the fast pace of work. Instead, he simply identified an action, which he attempted to stop with orders and instructions. He had dealt with the symptom of an attitude, not with the opinions or beliefs that were causing the problem.

Step 2: Determining the Root Causes

On the basis of your investigation and analysis, see if you can spot the roots of the attitude—the primary beliefs that both support and feed the attitude in the employee's mind. The best way to do this is to get the employee talking about his or her true feelings.

Some frequent root causes that support and nurture incorrect attitudes including the following:

- Group pressures
- Faulty logic
- Misunderstood standards
- Previous supportive experiences

Mike thought the problem had been ended. After all, when a supervisor lays down the law, especially to a new worker, the subordinate should respond. Ehri's production, however, continued to yield an unacceptable number of rejects. Next, Mike and his boss both talked with Ehri. They again emphasized quality and included an implied threat that unless the situation reversed itself, Ehri's job was in jeopardy. But still the problem persisted.

Mike had not uncovered the root cause. Even though he was armed with the additional authority of his boss, Mike was still treating a symptom of the attitude. He had not yet uncovered the attitude and its root causes.

Finally it occurred to Mike that the problem may have originated in Ehri's training. He approached Dave and related the problem of too much quantity and too little quality. After stating that Ehri's job was at stake, he asked if Dave knew how this situation might have evolved. Dave became somewhat embarrassed and, upon further questioning, Mike discovered that Dave had told Ehri that quantity was all management really cared about, regardless of what they said to the contrary. Mike had finally struck pay dirt. He now knew what Ehri's attitude was and the root cause for it—misunderstood standards.

Step 3: Weakening the Root Causes

Once the root causes are known, they can be analyzed and their vulnerabilities noted. A program of action can then be constructed to change beliefs systematically through the use of reason. One way is to point out flaws in the employee's assumptions or changes that have taken place to weaken those assumptions since they were formed.

Mike instructed Dave to go to Ehri and explain that he had been misinformed. Dave apologized to Ehri and made it clear that he had only been kidding about quantity over quality.

Dave had the reputation of being a practical joker, and he really had meant no harm by what he did. He was only taking advantage of a novice who was naive to the ways of a skilled worker like Dave. Ehri had a language difficulty with English and tended to take things literally. Thus he had been easy prey for a joker. Dave felt certain that once Mike talked to Ehri, Ehri would realize that he had been had. When Dave understood that Ehri had not responded to Mike's talk, he was most eager to help correct the problem.

Step 4: Offering a Substitute

Dave had no trouble persuading Ehri to change his thinking because Ehri had received quite a bit of pressure by that time. Once Ehri realized (as a result of the statements of both Dave and Mike) that his attitude was based on misinformation, he became a superior worker.

You may be able to change behavior by constant harping and criticism, but, like the action of water in wearing away a rock, it may take too long a time and leave some noticeable scars. In general, people will change only if they see that the attitudes they hold are no longer worth keeping. Threats and orders usually only suppress a natural and observable behavior and drive it underground. The person becomes sneaky and does what you say only when you are there to police your order. When you are absent, his or her old behavior pattern resurfaces. The fact that you do not agree with or accept this behavior is usually not enough. You must identify the attitude, find its roots, and get the individual to question his or her own position. Only then will you be able to initiate a permanent change in that person's behavior.

Techniques for Changing Attitudes and Introducing Change

Fortunately, there are many tried and proven methods for changing attitudes, reducing resistance to change, and instilling a desire to cooperate. These methods depend on your understanding of the previous chapters and your ability to apply the knowledge they contain. There are six basic techniques at your disposal for introducing changes and resolving conflicts.

- Force-field analysis
- Effective communications
- Persuasion techniques
- Participation techniques
- Training programs
- Organization development activities

Force-Field Analysis

Force-field analysis
A method for visualizing the driving and restraining forces at work within an individual so as to assess what is needed to make a change in a person's attitudes

Kurt Lewin, a social psychologist, has given us the research in human relations upon which **force-field analysis** is built. It is a useful device for visualizing the situation you face when you attempt to overcome resistance to change in your subordinates.

There are two types of forces within individuals with regard to any issue affecting them at any given time: driving forces, and restraining forces. Driving forces encourage us to change, while restraining forces encourage us to resist change. Whether we are predisposed toward a change in a negative way or in a positive way depends on the nature and quantity of these forces. If there is a balance between them, we are in a state of inertia. If a change is to take place, driving forces must outweigh the restraining ones, the restraining ones must be reduced, or a combination of these must take place. Exhibit 6.5 illustrates this concept.

In order to understand more clearly this type of analysis, let us consider an example. Assume that you want one of your workers, Barbara Adams, to work over a coming holiday. Since overtime is a voluntary situation in your shop, Barbara has a choice. Let us assume that you have asked her, and she has refused. The situation might appear as follows.

Driving Forces	Restraining Forces
1. She will receive additional pay at overtime scale.	1. She has no immediate need for extra pay.

Supervisor's
Attitudes, Words, and Actions

Subordinate's
Attitudes

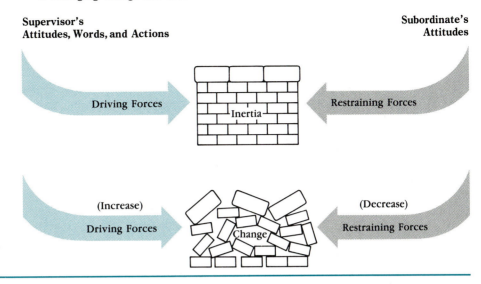

Exhibit 6.5 Representation of a force field: above, the situation before desired changes occur; below, the situation after resistance to change is overcome.

Driving Forces	Restraining Forces
2. If she works, she will please you.	**2.** She has a desire to be with her family.
3. Working over the holiday is better than being idle.	**3.** She has a preference for time off over extra pay.

At this point, there appears to be a standoff. You cannot order her to work, so you must try to weaken her restraining forces and/or add to the driving forces. Before attempting to do either, be sure that you see the situation as she does. Assuming that the forces listed above represent a true picture of her conception of the situation, and that she understands the driving forces that are present, let us see what you can do to change her mind.

In view of the restraining forces, the easiest step is to increase the driving forces. You might be able to get her best friend at work to come in over the holiday. Once Barbara knows that someone she respects and admires has agreed to help out, she may too. In addition, you could let her know that the reason you have asked her is that you really need her and her abilities. If she is the best person for the work to be done, let her know you feel that way. You can also appeal to her group loyalties, by explaining that the team needs her for a successful performance rating and that without her it stands a good chance of falling below expectations. In other words, the reputation of her group, either formal or informal, will be tarnished without her unique contributions.

If you are a leader in Barbara's eyes, you may get her to work overtime by putting your request on a personal basis such as, "Barbara, can you work overtime this Monday? I really need you." But not all managers are leaders, nor are all of them leaders to all of their subordinates. You should not try these steps unless you are sincere. We are not talking here about playing games with people or their feelings.

You can change a person's mind and his or her prior attitude toward an idea or a suggestion, if you manage to change his or her perception of a situation. This means that you must attempt to perceive the situation as the other person does and then go to work on the forces. You will not always succeed, but the effort is worth making if the change you are trying to make is important to your department.

Effective Communications

Chapter 5 dealt with the fundamentals of successful communications in general. Everything contained in that chapter is essential to every manager. Unless you have open channels with your people, peers, and outside specialists, you will have no real chance of winning their cooperation. To overcome fears, attitudes, and the lack of motivation to change, you must employ effective communication techniques. Regardless of the form of communication you use, you must lay the groundwork for change and get its advantages across to your people before you can expect them to go along with you. Remember that your goal is to get your particular understanding of a situation into their minds. To do this, you must listen to and observe them.

Persuasion Techniques

Each of the following persuasion techniques works well in certain situations. Which one you choose depends on your understanding of the people and events involved in the particular situation you face. Become familiar with all of them so that you will always carry with you one or more techniques that can be applied to any set of circumstances.

1. *Give your subordinates the reason behind the proposal.* Let your people know why the change is necessary. Put it in their terms, and tailor your message to each individual.
2. *Show them how.* Explain how the change will affect them, how it will help them, and how it will be implemented. Appeal to their individual needs.

3. *Tell them the truth.* If the change will be painful, let them know it. If Joe is to be displaced, assure him that the company will either relocate him or retrain him for a new position if this be the case. Do not lie to them or kid them. They will respect your integrity and remember it in the future.

4. *Try a compromise.* It is not always possible to give a little or meet them halfway, but when you can, do so. You may not have foreseen all the possibilities, and maybe they have some good points on their side. Often the method is not as important as the results you expect of them.

5. *Give them an example of a past accomplishment.* Tell them about similar situations and the positive results that were obtained. Explain how each person benefited as a result of the change.

6. *Plant a seed.* Give them an idea and let it germinate. In advance of the change, converse with them about "How nice it would be if . . ." or "Have you guys thought about . . ." Then nurture that idea with the proper care and feeding. Your subordinates may come to you with the very suggestion you anticipated. Even better, they may think it is their own idea.

7. *Ask them questions.* Ask your subordinates the kinds of questions that, if they are honest with themselves, will yield support for a change or remove the cause of a possible conflict. Properly presented, these leading questions will lead them to the proper predisposition.

8. *Offer them a choice.* The choice you present is not whether to do something or reject it but rather when or how or by whom it will get done.

9. *Offer them a challenge.* Put the idea as a goal to be reached or a standard to be surpassed. Present the change as a test of their team's abilities and skills. Turn the event into a game or contest— a way of probing their potentials.

10. *Make them a promise.* If possible, give them your promise that, if the idea is not successful or does not yield the desired results (given an honest effort), you will retreat from your position and withdraw the directive.

11. *Try making a request.* Instead of ordering compliance and being autocratic, ask them to cooperate. You will be amazed at what a difference requests make in a person's attitudes. This technique especially appeals to the individual who feels insulted by demands but who bends over backward to meet an appeal for help.

12. *Give them a demonstration.* Show them by your own performance what the new system calls for, how it will work, and how it will benefit the group or individual. Introduce the change with a planned and carefully executed tryout, and the doubts will fade in the light of reason. Seeing is believing.

13. *Involve them in the decision.* Using a problem-solving session, get them into the problem with both feet. State the dimensions of the problem, and then lead them in reaching a consensus.

Before you decide on any one of these suggestions, put yourself in your subordinates' shoes. Identify with their attitudes and set your course to meet their restraints and increase their drives. By finding the supports for their resistance and weakening those supports through logic and facts, you will pave the way for their acceptance of a substitute.

None of these persuasion devices, however, is a substitute for proper management or leadership. In fact, their success or usefulness depends on your being the best person and the best manager you can be. Only then can the potential of your people be released and fully utilized.

Participation Techniques

As we have seen throughout this chapter, people have a need to be in the know about the things that affect them. Managers must utilize various means to involve their people in decision making and to allow them to participate more fully in the work of the department.

The first device for employee participation open to managers is their formal authority. Be delegating it to the more responsible members of their groups, they go a long way toward exposing their subordinates to the complexities of their jobs and toward developing them and their potential. How much a manager gives away depends on many things. Is he or she allowed to delegate by the boss? Does the manager have subordinates who are responsible enough and good enough at their jobs to handle new responsibilities? Has the manager paved the way for delegation through proper training, appraisals, and human relations? All of these are essential questions that must be answered before managers can give away any of their duties.

Another device is the problem-solving session, which is discussed in chapter 9. It is a most demanding kind of effort at participation and involves subordinates directly in management decisions. It requires a good deal of patience and preparation, as it is much more difficult than making the decisions yourself. The value of such meetings is immeasurable, however; they are perhaps the most effective way to explain the facts behind the decisions and to promote understanding and cooperation. We all react more favorably to and promote much harder ideas we gain on our own and as a result of our own efforts. When we see we are in the minority on an issue, we are strongly inclined to go along with the majority.

The third method of enlisting participation depends on the style of supervision you adopt toward your subordinates. The democratic and spectator styles promote a feeling of shared responsibility and a voice in what affects people. Each of these styles places a solid trust in the workers and makes the supervisor more dependent on them. The workers know this and usually act accordingly. No one wants to betray the trust of another unless he or she is emotionally ill. For the most part, people want to live up to the expectations others have of them, provided that they have the abilities and skills to do so. (Chapter 10 explores in some detail different styles of management, their advantages, and their disadvantages.)

All these methods are effective if the necessary prerequisites exist. They give workers a much-desired voice in the decision-making process. If these tools are utilized properly, a manager cannot help but succeed in winning support from the majority of his or her subordinates.

Training Programs

Training programs are formal ways in which you and your organization can teach employees skills, knowledge, and attitudes that they need to perform their present tasks. When teaching one of your subordinates how to operate a piece of machinery, you impart the information needed to understand the machine's performance capabilities. Through practice, the operator gradually gains the manual dexterity required for efficient operation of the machine. Finally, the proper attitudes are imparted with regard to safe operation, proper operating procedures, and appropriate maintenance by the operator. All are taught simultaneously and with equal emphasis. Chapter 12 covers training in greater detail.

Organization Development

Organization development
A planned, managed, systematic process used to change a culture, system, and behavior of an organization to improve its effectiveness in solving problems and achieving goals.

Organization development (OD) has been defined by the Conference Board, a nonprofit research group, as "a planned, managed, systematic process [used] to change the culture, systems and behavior of an organization in order to improve the organization's effectiveness in solving problems and achieving its objectives." This process involves efforts in education and training that eventually affect everyone in an organization.

Organization development requires an organization to identify its strengths and weaknesses, define its objectives, identify its problem areas, establish OD goals, set up programs for achieving its OD goals, and evaluate the progress made toward improvement. Outside consultants and experts are usually used to conduct research into the organization's operations and to recommend and to teach the implementation of OD programs for change. If OD efforts are to succeed, the commitment of top management to them is essential. Organizational changes, if they are to be lasting, must begin at the top.

OD Goals   Organizations that adopt organization development programs must set specific goals for their entire operation and its various divisions and subunits. The total organization may have the following goals: (1) to improve the overall performance of the organization's productivity, profitability, and human resources; and (2) to improve the organization's efforts at communicating, promoting intergroup cooperation, and preparing for and coping with change.

As a supervisor, your goals will be influenced by those of your boss and your unit or division. One goal might be to reduce waste and scrap by 10 percent. Another might be to improve the communication skills of the personnel in your department. Specific programs can then be designed to accomplish your goals.

OD Programs   OD programs include those designed to assess employee attitudes, to improve employee cooperation, and to build team spirit. A few commonly used programs are quality circles, joint labor/management committees, and training programs of various kinds. *Quality circles* are groups of workers or managers who come together regularly on a voluntary basis to discuss mutual problems and possible solutions to them. Labor and management committees work to reduce conflict and to promote common interests in such areas as reduction of waste, removal of health and safety hazards, and reduction of employee turnover. Chapter 9 examines working with these groups and others in more detail. Training programs can be designed to improve skills, communications, teamwork, and just about anything else the company wants to improve. OD programs and activities may be designed and conducted by the company or by outside agencies.

OD activities need your commitment if they are to succeed. You, like all the managers above you, must be committed to them, and you must be willing and able to sell them to subordinates who will or must participate in them. Remember that OD is an organization-wide effort to control and to introduce change. Change can mean security for those who know it is coming and are prepared for it. It can mean insecurity for those who do not. You can do a great deal to reduce insecurity and stress among your people if you and your subordinates are willing participants in your organization's efforts to control its evolution.

So you think your job is stressful. Well, many Japanese employees believe that their job can kill them. *Karoshi*—fear of death from overwork—plagues nearly one-half of salaried employees according to several surveys done in Japan in the 1990s. That country's work force is short of labor and pushing ever harder for improvements in everything people do at work. Overtime is expected, and most employees do not take their vacations out of both loyalty to their employers and fear of losing respect of bosses and coworkers alike. Cases of sudden death at work are rising, and fatigue is a normal daily symptom exhibited by many salaried employees. As their stress levels rise, workers begin to fear their jobs. Stressed-out workers are not able to give their best or exercise real creativity. As a result, relieving stress has become a primary focus for individuals and businesses. Books with self-help approaches are selling well, and several large Japanese companies have paid the survivors of those who have died at work substantial settlements. Like the alcoholic, the workaholic can die from the addiction.

Stress

Stress
Worry, anxiety, or tension that accompanies situations and problems we face and makes us uncertain about the ways in which we should resolve them

Changes, the passage of time, and rumors sent over the grapevine can cause stress among organizational members. **Stress**—tension, anxiety, worry—occurs in people when they face situations and problems but are uncertain about what they should do to resolve them.[11] All of us experience stress on and off the job. When we attempt to learn new skills, when we meet new people, when we have to chair a committee or run a meeting, we are usually a little uncertain about exactly what we should do and what the outcomes of our efforts will be. When we face a series of stress-inducing activities or situations, such as role conflict or role ambiguity, our peace of mind and our health can suffer. Among the most serious health threats associated with stress are peptic ulcers, high blood pressure, and heart trouble.[12] People who face continual stress, such as air-traffic controllers, physicians, and surgeons, can become victims of chronic depression that sometimes leads to dependence on drugs.

A 1987 *USA Today* nationwide poll found that 80 percent of the (more than 800) adult workers polled said their jobs were stressful. The major causes for stress on the job and their rankings were:

- Daily demands of the job (64 percent)
- Lack of communication (50 percent)

- Understaffing (46 percent)
- Too many demands (44 percent)
- Not being able to leave one's work at the office (38 percent)
- Incompetent supervisors (32 percent)
- Difficult coworkers (32 percent)
- Too many work hours (31 percent)[13]

A stress test appears at the end of this chapter in the "Incident" feature. Take it to determine the level of stress in your life.

Coping with Stress

Some stress is healthful. It gets us motivated and raises our energy levels. But excessive stress has to be recognized and the causes eliminated or brought under control.

Both organizations and individuals recognize the need to manage the stress in their environments and lives. Stress can and does cause both physical and psychological harm. Courts and juries are awarding significant damages to employees who suffer both kinds of harm due to stress. The workers' compensation boards of many states will let workers recover damages for psychological injuries arising out of physical ones. Managers at every level of an organization have a legal duty to identify causes of stress, to work to reduce their impacts on employees, and to identify and try to help employees who have trouble handling their stress.

If you have a subordinate or team member who is having difficulty handling the stress on the job, meet with that person to construct a stress-coping and stress-reduction program of action. If the cause seems to be lack of ability to perform duties, training may be the cure. If the stress comes from other sources, your company may have in place an employee assistance program (EAP) that can help. Many organizations have the following types of EAPs to assist their employees:

- Facilities for exercise such as health club memberships, jogging tracks, exercise instruction, and weight-training rooms
- Courses to teach people how to handle stress through such means as meditation, proper nutrition, time management, and communications workshops
- On- or off-site confidential counseling opportunities to explore such stressors as financial, drug, marriage, and psychological problems

Clay Sherman, president of Management Hours, Inc., a Chicago-based consulting firm, has these recommendations for people under stress:

1. Try a physical escape—go somewhere else and work or exercise.
2. Daydream for awhile—get your mind on pleasant things.
3. Take a recreation break and play a game.
4. Socialize—talk about your problem with friends.
5. Vent—cry, yell, get it out of your system.
6. Problem-solve—attack your work, confront your problem head-on.[14]

In addition to taking these steps, try getting the proper amount of rest, and eat a proper diet to build up your resistance and stamina. Try to play as hard as you work, and separate your work from your family and social life. Getting a better handle or control over your use of time can create free time where you had none before. Improving your skills at good communication can prevent problems and make up for others' lack of these skills. Management by wandering around puts you in regular touch with others who may have good advice and experiences that you lack.

Technostress

With today's highly technical society, a new kind of stress is emerging called *technostress*. The introduction of new machines and technology often brings new stress to an organization and its people. Managers need to plan for the selection of, introduction of, and adaptation to new machines and equipment to reduce the stress on employees as much as possible. People need to be consulted and trained in advance of introducing any new equipment. With new technology come new demands on both workers and supervisors. Workers fear new, higher quotas and being asked to learn new skills. Supervisors fear underutilization of equipment and morale problems that can result from the improper introduction of equipment.

The new technology brings the need for changes in routines, procedures, output quotas, and even break schedules. Worker/operators are usually better judges of the individual kinds of stress and its levels than are supervisors. Craig Brod, an industrial psychologist and management consultant, calls for company policies that will let supervisors and middle managers trust their employees' own perceptions of what they can and cannot accomplish with new technology. He calls for matching jobs to people rather than the other way around. He cautions against overspecialization of jobs into what many have called ''stupid work''—highly specialized, machine-operator tasks that require only information processing skills.[15] While right for a small number of people, such jobs quickly lead to boredom and fatigue in many. Most of us need variety and challenges that will allow us to use our creative energies.

Coping with Technostress

Technology in the office has brought about a number of stressful conditions. Many high-tech machines make noises that, over time, can become extremely annoying. Copiers, printers, video display terminals, and desktop computers are but a few examples. Improper training in how to use such equipment puts people under stress as well. Improper arrangements of office equipment and workstations adds to discomfort and emotional distress.

For help with office and workstation arrangements, consider the services of an architectural interior designer. Pay attention to the complaints of people who must use the equipment and spaces. Interior office design professionals are practitioners of *ergonomics:* the successful blending of people, equipment, and machines.

For people who spend most of their hours in front of word processors and video display terminals, eye strain, muscle fatigue, and mental fatigue are common complaints. Advice from experts in coping with these problems include the following:

- Positioning screens and operators to avoid glare from windows and overhead lights
- Using screens with adjustable contrast and color shades
- Using adjustable screens and chairs to accommodate each operator
- Instituting breaks in place, where the operator refocuses his or her eyes for a minute or two, every half hour or so
- Instituting five-minute stretch breaks that allow operators to move away from their workstations every hour[16]

Several cities have passed or are considering legislation that implements most if not all of the above. The city of San Francisco adopted an ordinance in December of 1990 regulating the use of video display terminals in the workplace. It mandates the following for all employers of fifteen or more employees:

- Special lighting, antiglare computer screens, and adjustable computer furniture
- Fifteen-minute break or transfer to another task after working at a computer terminal for two hours

The law took effect in 1991, and all its provisions will be phased in over a four-year period. It has been estimated that the law will affect over 50,000 employees and cost between $31.5 and $76.5 million to area employers from 1991 to 1995.[17]

If you and your employees face continual stress, your attitudes about work, your employer, and your coworkers are bound to be affected. Since stress is the result of uncertainties, you can usually do various things to give your people more certainty. Training is one way to give people the level of skills and the knowledge of procedures that are lacking and may be causing their stress. Hopelessly unqualified individuals may be transferred to jobs that they can handle. Professional help may be available through your company's personnel office, or fringe benefits such as trained counselors, psychiatrists, and drug-addiction programs may be available. These can help people cope with their stress and the results of it more effectively.

Instant Replay

1. Our experiences help shape our individual beliefs.
2. Our beliefs help shape our attitudes.
3. When supervisors observe improper attitudes or conduct in subordinates—attitudes or conduct that prevents average or above-average performances—they must act to change them.
4. Changing attitudes requires us to (a) identify the attitude that needs changing, (b) determine the supports for it, (c) weaken those supports, and (d) offer a substitute and sell it.
5. Techniques for changing attitudes include force-field analysis, effective communications, persuasion techniques, participation techniques, training programs, and organization development activities.
6. Stress is worry, anxiety, or tension that accompanies situations and problems we face and causes uncertainty about the ways in which we should resolve them. Stress can distract us from our work, adversely affect our attitudes, and injure our health, unless we learn to cope with it or to remove it.

Glossary **Attitude** a person's manner of thinking, feeling, or acting toward specific stimuli.

Belief a perception based on a conviction that certain things are true, or based on what seems to be true or probable in one's own mind (opinion).

Force-field analysis a method for visualizing the driving and restraining forces at work within an individual so as to assess more accurately what is needed to make a change in his or her attitudes.

Opinion a belief based on a perception of what seems to be true or probable in one's own mind.

Organization development a planned, managed, systematic process used to change the culture, systems, and behavior of an organization to improve its effectiveness in solving problems and achieving goals.

Stress worry, anxiety, or tension that accompanies situations and problems we face and makes us uncertain about the ways in which we should resolve them.

Theory X a set of attitudes traditionally held by managers that assumes the worst with regard to the average worker's initiative and creativity.

Theory Y a set of attitudes held by today's generation of managers that assumes the best about the average worker's initiative and creativity.

Theory Z a set of approaches to managing people based on the attitudes of Japanese managers about the importance of the individual and of team effort to the organization.

Value an activity, condition, or object that we feel has merit or worth in our lives.

Work ethic people's attitudes about the importance of working, the kind of work they choose or are required to perform, and the quality of their efforts while performing work.

Questions for Class Discussion

1. Can you define this chapter's key terms?
2. How do you form an attitude about a person, place, or thing?
3. What kinds of attitudes held by workers need changing? How would you go about changing a subordinate's attitude?
4. What are the six techniques or tools described in this chapter that can help you to change your own or other people's attitudes?
5. What are six major causes of stress in the workplace?
6. What are six ways in which a person can cope with work-related stress?

Incident

Stress on the job? Ask yourself*

How to take this quiz This quiz will help you recognize your level of stress on the job. Take the test, figure your score and then see if your stress level is normal, beginning to be a problem, or dangerous. Answer the following statements by putting a number in front of each:

1—seldom true
2—sometimes true
3—mostly true

_____ 1. Even over minor problems, I lose my temper and do embarrassing things, like yell or kick a garbage can.

_____ 2. I hear every piece of information or question as criticism of my work.

_____ 3. If someone criticizes my work, I take it as a personal attack.

_____ 4. My emotions seem flat whether I'm told good news or bad news about my performance.

_____ 5. Sunday nights are the worst time of the week.

_____ 6. To avoid going to work, I'd even call in sick when I'm feeling fine.

_____ 7. I feel powerless to lighten my work load or schedule, even though I've always got far too much to do.

_____ 8. I respond irritably to any request from co-workers.

_____ 9. On the job and off, I get highly emotional over minor accidents, like typos, spilt coffee.

_____ 10. I tell people about sports or hobbies that I'd like to do, but say I never have time because of the hours I spend at work.

_____ 11. I work overtime consistently, yet never feel caught up.

_____ 12. My health is running down; I often have headaches, backaches, stomachaches.

_____ 13. If I even eat lunch, I do it at my desk while working.

_____ 14. I see time as my enemy.

_____ 15. I can't tell the difference between work and play; it all feels like one more thing to be done.

_____ 16. Everything I do feels like a drain on my energy.

_____ 17. I feel like I want to pull the covers over my head and hide.

_____ 18. I seem off center, distracted—I do things like walk into mirrored pillars in department stores and excuse myself.

_____ 19. I blame my family—because of them, I have to stay in this job and location.

_____ 20. I have ruined my relationship with co-workers whom I feel I compete against.

Scoring:

20–29—You have normal amounts of stress.

30–49—Stress is becoming a problem. You should try to identify its source and manage it.

50–60—Stress is at dangerous levels. Seek help or it could result in worse symptoms, such as alcoholism or illness.

*Stress test: just how stressed are you at work? (Source: Copyright 1987, *USA Today.* Reprinted with permission.)

Case Problem 6.1   Burdens

As Peter approached Patricia he noticed that she was deep in thought. "Mind if I take a few minutes?" asked Peter.

"Oh, sorry, I was a million miles away. Pull up a chair."

"I won't take much time, Pat. I just need your help. The Townsend report is going to be late this week because I can't get the figures I need from production control. I have asked those people for the numbers about six times, and they keep assuring me they will send them. Can you put a bug in their ears to hurry the data along?"

"I'll call them today and see what I can do." Just then Pat's phone rang, and she picked it up. After a few minutes of mostly listening, Pat hung up and turned to Peter with a worried look on her face. "Pete, I know you are swamped with work now that your department has been reduced by three people, but Sarah needs your help. You are the only person left who understands the computer program for inventory control. She inherited the job that Walters vacated and can't seem to get the program to operate properly. If you could get her started and go over things with her, I think that she will be able to carry on. She learns fast and . . ."

Pete interrupted Pat. "If you want me to help another department, I will; but you had better give me more time for my regular work. Since last month's cutback, my people have been experiencing about a 20 percent increase in their workloads. Al is threatening to quit, what with all these new demands on him. By the way, rumor has it that more cuts are due.

Will my department get any? I'm down to muscle now. Any more cuts will take out bones."

Patricia assured Peter that no more cuts were coming and watched as he shuffled off to Sarah's office. She looked at the pile of papers on her desk and sighed. Another week of twelve-hour days lay ahead for her, with no relief in sight. She thought back over the last few weeks, mentally listing her problems. After last month's cutbacks, her department had been merged with two others, and she had become a middle manager. Her staff was now about 80 percent of what it had been, and her workload had more than doubled. The new computers were more of a problem than a blessing for her at present. The only people who really understood how to use them effectively were either laid off or moved to other areas. Peter was one of two people she had had to promote to head the new departmental structure, and she had not trained them to become supervisors. They were both in trouble now, and she had to do much of what they should be doing. She picked up her phone and canceled her lunch date. "Looks like another lunch of coffee at my desk," she thought.

Questions

1. What sources of stress is Patricia experiencing?
2. What sources of stress is Peter probably experiencing?
3. What would you recommend to them as ways of coping with their stress?

Case Problem 6.2   Section C

Jim Daly had been expecting a promotion for almost a month. He figured there was no way he would not get it. He had two years' experi-

ence on the job, and was regarded as the best worker in Section C. Of course, he realized that a coworker, Marge Madison, had been in the section longer than himself, but their boss, Hazel Sam, had given him every indication that he was first in line to replace Hazel when she moved up to a middle management position.

No wonder then that Jim was so shocked and upset when Hazel called the section together last week to announce that Marge would be her replacement. Jim had great difficulty keeping his emotions under control at that meeting. In fact, he could not bring himself to congratulate Marge on her new responsibilities.

Since that time, the best worker in Section C had become its least enthusiastic and least productive member. Jim was rapidly becoming a negative influence among his four coworkers—so much so that two of them were beginning to shun him.

Marge was aware of the whole situation and knew that she would have to act quickly. She had been upset when Jim did not congratulate her on winning the promotion. She realized, too, that his resentment of her was bound to enter any conversation she might have with him. On the other hand, doing nothing was bound to make things worse. Although she knew that some action was called for, she could not decide what steps to take. That's when she decided to have a talk with Hazel. Their conversation yielded the following information:

1. Hazel admitted that she had wanted to give the promotion to Jim but had been overruled by the personnel department because more women were needed as supervisors to meet the company's affirmative action quota for promoting females.

2. Hazel also admitted that she had assured Jim that he would be the next supervisor of Section C.

3. Hazel stated that she had not spoken to Jim since the meeting of a week ago when Marge was given the promotion.

4. Hazel was unsympathetic to Marge's request for help. Her only advice was as follows:

   "Well, Marge, how did you expect the man to react? He was the better choice—he knew it, personnel knew it, and I knew it. You're the problem, not Jim."

Questions

1. Do you agree that Marge is the "problem," not Jim? Why?
2. Why have two members of Section C begun to shun Jim?
3. What do you think of Hazel's attitudes toward the promotion and toward her subordinate manager, Marge?
4. What should Marge do now?

Notes

1. Karen Pennar, "America's Quest Can't Be Half-Hearted," *Business Week* (June 8, 1987): 136.
2. Donald Weiss, *How to Be a Successful Manager* (New York: AMACOM, 1986), 8–9.
3. Lester R. Bittel and Jackson E. Ramsey, eds., *Handbook for Professional Managers* (New York: McGraw-Hill, 1985), 421.
4. "What's New in Management," *New York Times* (April 1, 1984): F15.
5. "Good Boss Is Top Job Factor: Study," *Chicago Tribune* (April 5, 1981).
6. "Monday Ticker," *Chicago Tribune* (May 25, 1987): 4.1
7. Mark Mammott, "Office Line," *USA Today* (June 8, 1987): 8E.
8. Douglas M. McGregor, "The Human Side of Enterprise," in *Classics in Management,* ed. Harwood F. Merrill (New York: American Management Association, 1970), 461–75.
9. W. G. Ouchi, *Theory Z: How American Business Can Meet the Japanese Challenge* (Reading, Mass.: Addison-Wesley, 1981); and R. T. Pascale and A. G. Athos, *The Art of Japanese Management* (New York: Simon & Schuster, 1981).

10. J. Sterling Livingston, "Pygmalion in Management," in *Harvard Business Review on Human Relations* (New York: Harper & Row, 1979), 181.

11. Randall S. Schuler, "Definition and Conceptualization of Stress in Organizations," *Organizational Behavior and Human Performance* (April 1980): 184–215.

12. M. Moser, "Hypertension: A Major Controllable Public Health Problem: Industry Can Help," *Occupational Health Nursing* (August 1977): 19.

13. *USA Today* (June 16, 1987): 7B.

14. Ibid.

15. Craig Brod, *Technostress: The Human Cost of the Computer Revolution* (Reading, Mass.: Addison-Wesley, 1984).

16. *USA Today* (June 8, 1987): 3E.

17. "S.F. mayor signs first VDT law," *Chicago Tribune* sect. 4 (December 28, 1990): 1.

Suggested Readings

Beer, Michael; Eisenstat, R. A.; and Spector, Bert. "Why Change Programs Don't Produce Change." *Harvard Business Review* (November–December 1990): 158–166.

Brod, Craig. *Technostress: The Human Cost of the Computer Revolution.* Reading, Mass.: Addison-Wesley, 1984.

Davidson, W. L. *How to Develop and Conduct Successful Employee Attitude Surveys.* Chicago: Dartnell, 1979.

Grothe, Mary, and Wylie, Peter. *Problem Bosses.* New York: Facts on File, 1987.

Janis, Irving. *Stress, Attitudes, and Decisions.* New York: Praeger, 1982.

McGregor, D. *The Human Side of Enterprise.* New York: McGraw-Hill, 1960.

Ouchi, W. G. *Theory Z: How American Business Can Meet the Japanese Challenge.* Reading, Mass.: Addison-Wesley, 1981.

Pascale, R. T., and Athos, A. G. *The Art of Japanese Management.* New York: Simon & Schuster, 1981.

"Special Report: The Push for Quality." *Business Week* (June 8, 1987): 130–44.

Taguchi, Genichi, and Clausing, Don. "Robust Quality." *Harvard Business Review* (January–February 1990): 65–75.

Walton, Richard E., and Susman, Gerald I. "People Policies for the New Machines." *Harvard Business Review* 2 (March–April 1987): 98–106.

7 Human Motivation

Outline

Key Terms

human needs

job enlargement

job enrichment

job rotation

maintenance factor

motivation

motivation factor

productivity

quality

quality of work life

Introduction

People are the most complex, difficult-to-manage resource that any business has. All of us are constantly changing and growing. Each day we are a little different from the way we were the day before. We bring our hopes and ambitions to work, along with our problems and defects. Most of us want our jobs and careers to provide us with many things. Some of us view our jobs as a source for the money we need in order to live the kind of life we feel is important. Some of us want a challenge, work that we can take pride in, and a sense of progress and accomplishment.

Most employers recognize that their employees are complex creatures who expect more than a paycheck from their employment. Employers know that dissatisfied, unhappy workers are generally poor performers. They know that satisfied workers often produce above the standards set for their jobs. Knowledgeable employers recognize, therefore, that it is in their best interests to attempt to provide their employees with the kinds of satisfaction they seek on the job.

This chapter explores the common human needs we all share and their relationship to our behavior. It introduces you to popular theories on human motivation and describes what you and employers can do to help others get more from their jobs than simply a paycheck. Finally, it links motivation with the all-important concepts of productivity and quality.

Motivation Defined

Motivation
The drive within a person to achieve some goal

Motivation is the drive within a person to achieve a personal goal. There are several theories about how individual motivation operates. All attempt to explain why people behave as they do. The five models we examine in this chapter build on one another. All are useful to you because they will help you visualize and interpret the causes behind your own and your subordinates' behaviors. The more you know about such behaviors, the easier it will be for you to influence the behaviors of others. As a supervisor, your primary responsibility is to influence behaviors in order to create more effective and efficient operations and employees.

Human Needs

When people work for subsistence-level wages, as most Americans did until the late 1940s, they concentrate on surviving. Their primary concern is for employment that will give them the necessary money to furnish themselves and their families with the necessities of life—food, clothing, and shelter. They live in fear of losing their jobs and, therefore, tolerate nearly any kind of working conditions and environment. People who observed the industrial economy of the United States in the early years of the twentieth century found little joy in its workers' hearts. Many companies and their managers believed that people worked primarily for money, and they were partially correct in those beliefs. Theory X (chapter 6) had many disciples.

The Hawthorne Studies

Since the 1920s, businesses have studied their employees in efforts to find out more about them—why some work well and others do not, why some last only a short time on the job and others stay for many years. Most of the ideas you read earlier and will read in this chapter have come from studies made by businesses and social scientists. Probably the single most important study—one that launched intense interest about and research into employee behavior and motivations—was the Western Electric Company's study in the 1920s. In 1927, engineers at the Hawthorne Plant of the Western Electric Company near Chicago conducted an experiment with several groups of workers to determine the effect of illumination on production. When illumination was increased in stages, the engineers found that production did increase. To verify their findings, they reduced illumination to its previous level—and, again, production increased! Perplexed, they called in Elton Mayo and his colleagues from Harvard to investigate.

The First Study   The Harvard researchers selected several experienced women assemblers for an experiment. With the permission of these workers and the records of their past production, management removed the women from their formal group of assemblers and isolated them in a room. The women were compensated on the basis of the output of their group. Next followed a series of environmental changes, each discussed with the women in advance of its implementation. For example, breaks were introduced and light refreshments were served; the women received no direct supervision as they had before, only indirect supervision from several researchers in charge of the experiment; the normal six-day week was reduced to five days, and the workday was cut by one hour. Each of these changes was accompanied by an increase in the group's output.[1]

To verify the assumptions that the researchers made, the women returned to their original working conditions: breaks were eliminated, the six-day week was restored, and all other conditions that had prevailed before the women were isolated were reinstated. The results were that production again increased!

In the extensive interviewing that followed, Mayo and his group concluded that a team spirit had been created, quite by accident, when management singled out these women to be the study group and then consulted with them before making each change. The women felt that they were something very special, both individually and collectively. Their isolation as a group and their close proximity at work provided an environment for the development of close personal relationships. The formal group had been transformed into an informal one—a *clique.*

The Second Study   To test the researchers' findings, a new group of workers was selected and isolated. This time the researchers chose a group of men. Several of them were involved in wiring equipment, while others soldered the wired connections. Two inspectors were part of the group and approved the finished jobs. An observer was on hand throughout the working day to record the men's work and reactions.

Several important events happened in this formal group. The men eventually split into two separate informal cliques. The basis for the split was that one group felt its work was more difficult than the other's. Its members adopted a superior attitude. This left the remainder of the workers to form another clique. Both cliques included wirers, solderers, and an inspector. Each group also engaged in setting standards of output and conduct. The members of the group that considered itself superior mutually agreed on production quotas. Neither too little nor too much production was permitted, and peers exerted pressure to keep fellow group members in line. As intergroup rivalry developed, the output of the other group began to decline. The superior group became superior in output also, which caused additional condescending behavior and a still greater decrease in morale and output in the other group. The workers who produced the most in each group were excluded from their group if they did not conform. Even though each man was to share in a bonus based on the formal group's total output, informal group conflict resulted in a decline in production.

These two experiments revealed that people work for a variety of reasons—not just for money and subsistence. They seek satisfaction for more than their physical needs at work and from coworkers. For the first time in our industrial history, clear evidence was gathered to support people's social and esteem needs.

A Hierarchy of Needs

Human needs
Physiological and psychological requirements that all humans share and that act as motives for behavior

The Hawthorne studies and many more that followed have given us a much wider view of why people work and what they expect from work. A well-known psychologist, Abraham H. Maslow, has identified five universal **human needs** that act as fuel for our internal drives to change or achieve. Exhibit 7.1 shows this *hierarchy of needs* as levels or steps in an upward progression from the most basic to the highest psychological need.[2]

The Needs-Goal Model of Motivation

Human needs provide the basis for our first theory of motivation. Our definition of *motivation*—the drive within a person to achieve a personal goal—tells us that motivation is an internal process. It is something we do within ourselves, not something we do to others. The term *drive* in our

Self-realization Needs	Job-related Satisfiers
Reaching Your Potential	Involvement in Planning Your Work
Independence	Freedom to Make Decisions Affecting Work
Creativity	Creative Work to Perform
Self-expression	Opportunities for Growth and Development

Esteem Needs	Job-related Satisfiers
Responsibility	Status Symbols
Self-respect	Money—as a Measure, for Some, of Self-esteem
Recognition	Merit Awards
Sense of Accomplishment	Challenging Work
Sense of Competence	Sharing in Decisions
Sense of Equity	Opportunity for Advancement

Social Needs	Job-related Satisfiers
Companionship	Opportunities for Interaction with Others
Acceptance	Team Spirit
Love and Affection	Friendly Co-workers
Group Membership	

Safety Needs	Job-related Satisfiers
Security for Self and Possessions	Safe Working Conditions
Avoidance of Risks	Seniority
Avoidance of Harm	Fringe Benefits
Avoidance of Pain	Proper Supervision
	Sound Company Policies, Programs, and Practices

Physical Needs	Job-related Satisfiers
Food	Pleasant Working Conditions
Clothing	Adequate Wage or Salary
Shelter	Rest Periods
Comfort	Labor-saving Devices
Self-preservation	Efficient Work Methods

Exhibit 7.1   A. H. Maslow's hierarchy of human needs, shown with job-related satisfiers that companies can provide to meet each need. (*Source:* Maslow's ''Hierarchy of Needs'' from *Motivation and Personality,* by Abraham Maslow. Copyright © 1954 by Harper & Row Publishers, Inc. Copyright © 1970 by Abraham H. Maslow. Reprinted by permission of HarperCollins Publishers.)

definition denotes a force that is fueled by human needs common to all of us. These needs, both physical and psychological, provide motives for our actions and behavior. In order to achieve our goals, we must take actions. Our actions toward achievement are efforts, both mental and physical, that we feel are necessary to attain our goals.

Our goals may be tangible or intangible. We may desire or want a new car or a job with higher status. The specific forms our goals take are a result of our personal makeup and desires at given moments in time and are shaped in part by our past experiences, our individual perceptions, and our current environments.

According to the needs-goal theory of motivation, a person who is motivated is in a state of unrest because he or she feels or believes that something is lacking—the goal. It is the unfulfilled need that creates the state of unrest. And since our needs can never fully be satisfied, we are continually setting goals. It is in our nature to want more—to continually strive to progress, to improve our conditions, and to acquire something new.

Exhibit 7.2 illustrates the needs-goal motivation process. As you study the figure, keep in mind the following assertions about human needs and motivation:

- The unsatisfied need is the strongest motivator.

- People can be influenced by more than one unsatisfied need at any given time.

- Needs can never be fully satisfied. They may cease to motivate behavior for a time, but they can and will return to act once again as motivators.

- People who seek satisfaction in one need area and do not find it will experience frustration and may try to compensate by overemphasizing another need.

- The perception of what we need at any given time is shaped in part by our past experiences, by external influences on us, and by our capabilities to change our situations.

We shall now look at each of the human needs.

Physiological Needs

Physiological or bodily *needs* are at the base of the needs hierarchy. These are the needs for adequate food, clothing, and shelter and the instinct for survival. Unsatisfied physiological needs can influence behavior, whereas satisfied physiological needs are not motivators. For example, when we

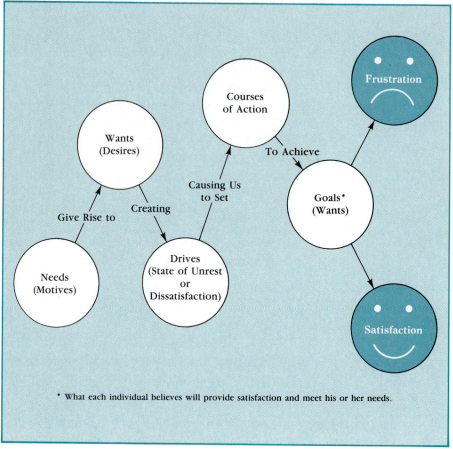

* What each individual believes will provide satisfaction and meet his or her needs.

Exhibit 7.2   The motivation process in which needs act as motives for human behavior.

are hungry, we desire food of a type and in a quantity necessary to satisfy our hunger. Once we have eaten our fill, our hunger dissipates and no longer motivates our actions. New needs surface and take over as motives for our actions. But, as we all know, hunger will return.

Safety Needs

The second level of human needs—*safety needs* or physical security—is our next concern. Having satisfied our physiological needs for the moment, we are concerned about providing for their satisfaction in the future. Once we have achieved an economic position that provides the means necessary to secure our physical maintenance, we desire to protect this condition. A person who gets a job is anxious to keep it. He or she is concerned with preventing its loss and the accompanying loss of the ability to provide for physical needs. The person may, as a result, join a union to gain this kind of security. He or she may take out insurance as protection against economic losses from illness or accident. Like his or her physical needs, the person's need for security will weaken as a motive for actions once the individual reaches an adequate degree of satisfaction. But if his or her job is threatened, the need for security may once again become an active motivating force.

Social Needs

With the satisfaction of safety or security needs can come the desire to satisfy *social needs.* These needs include a desire for human companionship, for affiliation with people and groups, for love and affection, and for a sense of belonging. Once we have achieved a measure of satisfaction that we feel is adequate, our social needs begin to wane, and the fourth level of need stimulates our behavior.

Esteem Needs

The *need for esteem* is two-sided. First, we have a desire to be appreciated for what we are and for what we have to contribute—to be respected by others. Second, we need to have a feeling of self-esteem—to know we are worth something to ourselves and to others. We need a positive self-image. From this need comes the desire for praise and for symbols that reflect our self-approval and others' appreciation of our efforts. We seek prestige and status positions among our peers. We behave in ways that are pleasing and acceptable to others whose opinions we value. We wish to master the tasks given us, thus becoming competent performers. We want fair and equitable treatment from others.

Self-Actualization Needs

Finally, our *need for self-actualization* takes over when we achieve some measure of satisfaction in the previous four levels. We begin to experience a need to fulfill our potential and to be creative. To some, this means striving for higher levels in company management and obtaining the added power and prestige that such positions represent. To others, it means being the best machinist or supervisor or teacher or biologist that they have the potential to become. The need for self-actualization causes a person to pursue interests and knowledge for their own sake and for the joy of the pursuit. The necessary prerequisite for this need is some satisfactory level of achievement in each of the other four need categories. Clearly, a hungry person struggling for survival will not be motivated by self-actualization needs until some time after the person achieves a satisfactory subsistence level.

All these needs are common in all of us to some degree. At any given moment, one or more of them are active, while the others lie dormant. When we search for satisfaction in one or more areas and find it to a degree that we feel is adequate, the need will cease for a time to be an active motive for our behavior. What is enough satisfaction for some, however, may be too little or too much for others. In general, no need is ever completely satisfied, and none can ever cease completely to be a motivator. It is the unfulfilled need that is the strongest motive for human behavior.

Supervisors and Human Needs

What does all this mean to you as a supervisor? You have learned that people's jobs can be a source of satisfaction or of dissatisfaction to them in their search for self-improvement and self-development. You know that our common needs provide the motives for human behavior, and that each person is a unique individual with personal goals that may be quite different from those of his or her peers. As a supervisor, you are in a unique position to assist your subordinates and to provide them with some of the satisfactions they are seeking. You can be most helpful with regard to their safety, social, and esteem needs, as we shall now see.

With regard to your subordinates' needs for safety and security, you are probably the one who initially provided them with their training. When your subordinates joined your department, chances are that you received and welcomed them. You assessed their strengths and weaknesses and got to know as much about them and their abilities as possible. Then you determined their specific needs for training so that they might improve their performances and skills. What you were doing was providing them with the knowledge, skills, and attitudes they would need to keep their jobs. You were increasing their sense of security and helping them remove some of their initial fears. You taught and enforced safety on the job. Your actions helped them achieve a measure of satisfaction for both their physical and safety needs.

You helped your subordinates with their need for affiliation when you introduced them to their new jobs and work groups when they first arrived. Your effort to know them has made you aware of their individual needs for affiliation and has enabled you to identify workers who are satisfied and those who are frustrated with regard to their social needs. If you were doing your job, you went to work on the problem of those who needed more social contacts and were not experiencing them; you did all you could to help the isolated individuals gain acceptance, by fostering a team spirit among your subordinates and by making them all feel part of a larger group. If you have not been doing these things, begin doing them right now. You have been missing some great opportunities to be of service to your people and to promote greater efficiency. It is your job as their supervisor to do so.

In regard to your subordinates' esteem needs, you have several key roles to play. In your appraisals, you are providing your people with the raw material they need to help them know themselves and to improve. You are also giving them an accurate assessment of how they rate with you and with the company. You can pass out praise if they deserve it and note the specific areas they must work on to gain your continued praise and acceptance. You also have authority that, if delegated, can enrich their feelings of importance and give them a way to learn certain aspects of your job. They know that this is an important sign of your faith and confidence in their abilities. You know that, if you are to advance, you must know your boss's job, and if they are to advance, they must know your job. Each day you may receive suggestions from your people. If they are good, use them and give the credit to the source of each suggestion. If they are not suited to the operation, tell the subordinate the reason. These are but a few ways to help your people and your operation to improve.

A major difficulty may arise if you attempt to discover which of the five need levels is a conscious concern to each individual subordinate at any given time. This is difficult knowledge to gain because, when you observe your people, you do so in a fragmented way. You see them at work under the influence of many forces from within and outside the company. Even if you know each of your people well, you can be fooled by your observations. In observing the actions of others, we seldom see the motives for them. You, like your subordinates, tend to play roles at work that mask or hide your true feelings and motives. Yet every supervisor concerned about his or her job and subordinates must attempt to determine what needs are most important to those subordinates. This knowledge will allow you to provide some incentives that could trigger a greater effort or contribution by subordinates. They, your department, and your reputation will benefit by their improved performance. The remainder of this chapter explores four additional motivation theories and what companies and managers can do to stimulate motivation.

Maintenance and Motivation

As a further help in understanding motivation, let us examine the contributions of Dr. Frederick Herzberg and his associates, whose work on motivation in business has demonstrated some applications of Maslow's hierarchy of human needs.[3] They have found that two sets of factors must be provided in the working environment to promote motivation.

Maintenance or Hygiene Factors

Maintenance factor
According to Herzberg, a factor that can be provided by an employer in order to prevent job dissatisfaction

First, there is a set of factors they label **maintenance** or *hygiene* **factors.** These items will not cause employee motivation in the great majority of people, but a lack of them will cause dissatisfaction. Provided in the right mix, they can prevent such dissatisfaction. The best a business can hope for by providing these factors is that the average employee will put forth an average commitment in time and effort at his or her job.

Herzberg identifies five maintenance factors:

1. *Economic*—wages, salaries, fringe benefits, and the like
2. *Security*—grievance procedures, seniority privileges, fair work rules, and company policy and discipline
3. *Social*—opportunities to mix with one's peers under company sponsorship at parties, outings, breaks, and the like
4. *Working conditions*—adequate heat, light, ventilation, and hours of work
5. *Status*—privileges, job titles, and other symbols of rank and position

If these maintenance factors are absent or inadequate, employees will become dissatisfied. If they are provided in adequate quantity and quality (from the individual's point of view), they can merely prevent dissatisfaction. The best a business can hope for is a fair day's work for a fair day's pay. In the absence of a proper mix of these factors, employees will withhold some of their average contributions to the company's goals.

Motivation Factors

Motivation factor
According to Herzberg, a factor that has the potential to stimulate internal motivation to provide a better-than-average performance and commitment from those to whom it appeals

The second set of factors is called **motivation factors.** They furnish the working environment with the conditions necessary to spark a better-than-average commitment from the great majority of employees and provide the means by which individuals can achieve greater satisfaction of needs through their jobs. Motivation factors, if provided in the proper quantity and quality, have the potential to satisfy the employees' needs and cause an increased commitment of time and energy by the employees. Herzberg identifies seven motivation factors:

1. *Challenging work:* The average person wants to view his or her job as offering an avenue for self-expression and growth. Each person needs something to tax his or her abilities.

2. *Feelings of personal accomplishment:* The average employee gets a sense of achievement and a feeling of contributing something of value when presented with a challenge that he or she can meet.

3. *Recognition for achievement:* The average employee wants to feel that his or her contributions have been worth the effort and that the effort has been noted and appreciated. Money awards, for some, help here.

4. *Achievement of increasing responsibility:* The typical employee desires to acquire new duties and responsibilities, either through the expansion of his or her job or by delegation from the supervisor.

5. *A sense of individual importance to the organization:* Employees want to feel that their personal presence is needed and that their individual contributions are necessary. Higher-than-average compensation can help here for some people.

6. *Access to information:* Employees want to know about the things that affect them and their jobs; they want to be kept in the know.

7. *Involvement in decision making:* Today's employees desire a voice in the matters that affect them and a chance to decide some things for themselves. They need freedom to exercise initiative and creativity.

These factors, unlike the common human needs they help satisfy, need to be designed into the structure and operations of a business. Some employees do not desire all or even a few of these factors and the opportunities they represent. This may be true because, for the moment at least, they lack ambition and do not feel the need to change. Still others, because of mental or emotional limitations, may lack the potential to take advantage of these factors and to master higher job responsibilities. For those who, in the manager's opinion, can take advantage of these factors but for the present do not do so, some standards and goals must be set to prod them to keep growing. The manager should make it clear to these employees that more is expected of them and that more rewards can be received in return for an increased effort. In short, the boss must try to get such employees oriented toward making progress, both for themselves and for the company.

For subordinates who have the potential and the drive to achieve something greater, supervisors have a duty to provide an environment that contains the motivation factors. If they are made available like different kinds of fine foods on a buffet, the motivated people in a group will pick and choose among them to satisfy their appetites for growth.

Exhibit 7.3 integrates Maslow's and Herzberg's needs theories. Hygiene factors generally help us satisfy our physical, safety, and social needs. Motivation factors generally help us satisfy our esteem and self-realization needs. In some cases and for some individuals, a hygiene factor can help satisfy esteem needs. A reserved parking place close to the company entrance is a status symbol and a condition of employment. It reinforces one's feeling of importance and one's image in the eyes of coworkers.

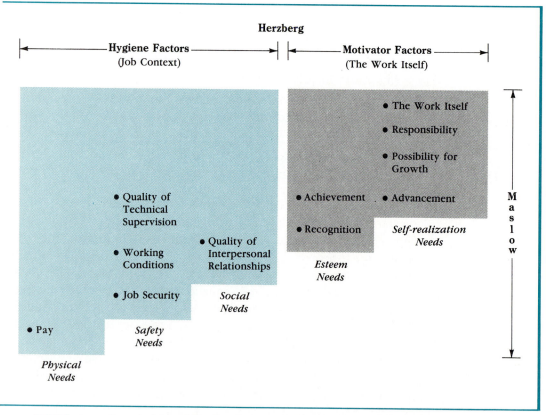

Exhibit 7.3 **Integration of Maslow's needs hierarchy with Herzberg's maintenance/motivation theory.** [*Source:* Warren F. R. Plunkett and Raymond Attner, *Introduction to Management,* 3rd ed. (PWS-Kent Publishing Company, 1989), p. 306]

The Contingency Theory

John J. Morse and Jay W. Lorsch have built upon Douglas McGregor's Theory Y and Herzberg's motivation and maintenance factors with their theory of motivation called the *contingency theory.* Morse and Lorsch conducted research to determine how the fit between an organization's characteristics and its tasks relates to individuals' motivations. They found that an organization–task fit affects and is affected by the quality of task performance and by individuals' feelings of competence.[4]

The contingency theory has four basic components:

1. Among people's needs is a central need to achieve a sense of competence.

2. The ways in which people fulfill this need vary from person to person, depending on how the need interacts with other needs and on the strengths of those other needs.

3. Competence motivation is most likely to be fulfilled when there is a fit between task and organization.

4. A sense of competence continues to motivate people even after competence is achieved.

All of us desire to possess a sense of competence—to be thought of as competent and to perceive ourselves that way. According to Morse and Lorsch, people performing highly structured and organized tasks perform better in organizations that use formal procedures and employ managers who adopt McGregor's Theory X approach. People performing unstructured and uncertain tasks perform better in organizations that exercise less formal control over workers and employ managers who adopt McGregor's Theory Y approach. Our need for a sense of competence is never completely satisfied because new challenges and tasks eventually face us and must be mastered. Real satisfaction comes from producing a continuing series of achievements, each reinforcing our sense of competence.[5]

The contingency theory tells managers to tailor jobs to fit people or to give people the skills, knowledge, and attitudes they will need to become competent in the jobs they are to be given. Both tasks and people must be analyzed before appropriate fits can be made. Controls on workers and their managers' approaches to them must be appropriate for the tasks being executed and for the psychological needs of the employees.

As a supervisor, you can use the contingency theory when you are seeking new people, looking for someone who is right for a new task, or delegating your formal authority. But you must know your people well—their needs, strengths, and goals—if you want to make the proper

Does money have the power to motivate? Is the desire for money sufficiently strong to cause us to become stimulated to action and to set goals? Herzberg and his researchers report that money is not seen as a motivation factor—one that will trigger in individuals at work a better-than-average commitment and performance. If a person hates a job, offering that person more money will in no significant way change the nature of the duties he or she faces for each work shift. Money cannot offer people intrinsic satisfaction. It can offer people the means to achieve some of their goals. Money can offer a measure of security and comfort. It can be used to meet most of the demands of daily living. In some measure, it gives people a measure of status in their own minds and the minds of others.

The quest for money is often a mask hiding a quest for what the money, once obtained, can buy. We work to support ourselves and our families. We need money to purchase many things it takes to live. But we also work to achieve psychological rewards that come from others like praise for a job well done and a chance to grow and to meet new challenges. Money will not help us in our search for these satisfactions. Ask yourself, "What is the role of money in my life? What do I use it for?" The answers will probably astound you.

decisions in assigning work. You need to know what kinds of reward go with each task. Then you are ready to match people to work that they are capable of doing, thus giving them (or reinforcing in them) a sense of competence. You can tailor your supervisory approach to fit the needs of each person, watching and controlling some more than others. You can provide the instructions and training they need to become or to remain competent.

Maslow's needs, Herzberg's sets of factors, and the contingency model can help us understand how individuals' needs affect their motivation. We are now ready to examine two additional theories that relate to the modification of human behavior at work. The theories that follow help explain what you and your organization can do to "engineer" subordinates' behavior, by identifying why people choose their behaviors. Both theories help explain how individuals' perceptions, influenced in large measure by external stimuli, lead them to select a course of action aimed at achieving a personal and/or a company goal.

The Expectancy Theory

The *expectancy theory* of motivation is related to all the other theories discussed in this chapter. It focuses largely on the individual perceptions of people in an organization that wishes to use the theory. Simply stated, the expectancy theory holds that people will do what their supervisors want them to do if all of the following conditions exist:

1. People know, as precisely as possible, what performance or behavior they are being asked to give (how they will be graded).
2. They perceive themselves as being capable of giving the performance or behavior.
3. They strongly desire the reward that is being offered by their supervisor or organization.
4. They perceive that the performance or behavior, once given at the specified level of quality, will bring the desired reward to them fairly quickly.[6]

As a supervisor, you can influence conditions 1, 2, and 4 most directly. Condition 3—the individual's perception of the desirability of the reward—is largely beyond your ability to influence in any meaningful way. We look next at the ways in which you can influence employee perceptions (see Exhibit 7.4).

The Performance

You must spell out in as much detail as possible what you want people to do. Your subordinates must have a clear understanding about the task, the standards that will be used to grade their performances, and the level of quality you as their supervisor expect. In most cases where this theory is applied, the performance or behavior should be an unusual one—something above and beyond the normal performances and behaviors that are routinely demanded or expected.

As an example, suppose you have a project that you wish to delegate to a subordinate. According to the expectancy theory, you must communicate to your subordinate exactly what you want done, how you want it done (the standards you will apply to determine completeness), when you want it done, and what limits (if any) may affect the subordinate's performance. Then, and only then, can the person know what he or she is being asked to do.

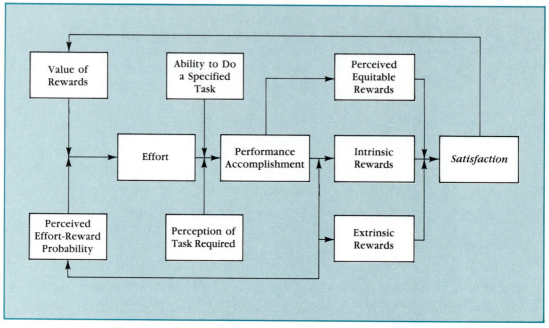

Exhibit 7.4   The Porter-Lawler motivation model, illustrating the expectancy theory of motivation. (*Source:* From L. Porter and E. Lawler, III, *Managerial Attitudes and Performance,* © 1968, p. 165, Richard D. Irwin, Inc., Homewood, Ill. Reprinted by permission.)

Capabilities

Your subordinate knows what is expected. If he or she perceives himself or herself to be capable of giving the performance—completing the delegated assignment at the level of quality specified—the subordinate may or may not want to give the performance. But what happens when the person feels *incapable* of giving the performance? In this case, he or she will most likely turn down or at least resist the assignment. Here are some ways of influencing your subordinate's perception about his or her capability to perform:

- During the hiring process, try to match the person you hire as closely as you can to the demands that the job will make. This means that you must know in detail the tasks that must be performed and the training, experience, and skill levels that the job holder must have.

- With an existing employee or new hire, try to provide, through training, the skill levels needed for a task *before* assigning or asking the person to perform it.

- Try to redesign the job your subordinate has so that he or she will be asked to perform only those tasks that the person feels capable of performing. This may require you to increase or decrease tasks and responsibilities for a subordinate. Only when a person has self-confidence and a feeling of competence is he or she willing to tackle bigger and more demanding tasks.

- When job redesign is not possible or not appropriate, a transfer or promotion may be called for. People who have mastered their jobs and are becoming bored with them cannot be expected to give high-quality performances until their jobs make greater demands on them or offer them greater rewards.

When you have a subordinate who knows what is being asked of him or her, feels capable of performing to the level expected, strongly desires the reward being offered, and is assured that delivering the performance will elicit the reward, you will have a motivated, willing employee.

Rewards

A few words are in order here about what rewards you or your organization can offer and how to link them to performances. The usual rewards are increases in pay, increases in authority and responsibility, and praise. Intrinsic rewards—those noted in Exhibit 7.3 and called *motivators* by Herzberg—can be offered to employees through delegation, transfers, and promotions. Just be certain that rewards are given to high performers and not to employees who deliver less. If a person works hard, delivers what is called for, and gets no significantly greater reward than that received by mediocre performers, you will have one unhappy, soon-to-lose-motivation employee on your hands.

Second, make sure that the performance being rewarded is under the complete control of the employee and not dependent on some factor over which the person has no control. If this is the situation, and if the person believes that the way in which he or she is being evaluated is fair, rewards can stir people out of complacency and into a motivated state.

A few words of caution are in order. Keep in mind that people, jobs, and the organizations in which they exist keep changing. So too will the perceptions that people have about everything and everyone around them. Today's motivated employee may be lazy next week. People who showed no interest in new challenges and growth last month may suddenly become motivated by the desire for these rewards. Finally, while you may think a subordinate is perfectly capable of giving a high-quality performance, your perception is not what really matters; it is the perception of the person whom you want to help motivate that counts.

The Reinforcement Theory

The reinforcement theory has its foundation in B. F. Skinner's behavior modification theories.[7] This theory encourages appropriate behaviors by focusing on the consequences of those behaviors. Simply stated, behavior that is to be repeated should be rewarded, while behavior that is not to be repeated should be punished. If a manager or a company desires to modify employee behavior, appropriate consequences should result from that modified behavior.

Reinforcement for behaviors can be positive or negative. *Positive* reinforcement should occur as soon as possible after the desired behavior has occurred. Good performances can be rewarded (positively reinforced) through praise, pay increases, promotions, and special favors within a manager's power to dispense. Through the practice of positive reinforcement, rewarded behaviors tend to be repeated. *Negative* reinforcement attempts to discourage repeat performances through punishments. In this regard, people learn what not to do but not what they should do. Negative reinforcements may include denial of privileges, reprimands, and loss of pay or of opportunities. As with positive reinforcement, the closer the reinforcement is to the time of the behavior, the greater will be its impact. See Exhibit 7.5.

Certain performances need no reinforcement. Actions that are undesirable but have small (if any) consequences may often be ignored. Tempo-

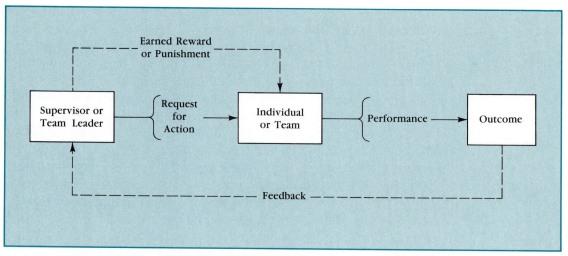

Exhibit 7.5   The reinforcement theory in action.

rary, nonserious misbehavior may simply be noted and go unpunished. Supervisors are often required to make a judgment as to the cause of the behavior and to the intent behind it. Most people lose their tempers now and then, and all of us make minor mistakes fairly regularly. Save your punishment for serious offenses, and punish people in private. Pass out your rewards publicly and as often as you can.

As a supervisor using this theory, keep the following points in mind:

1. People learn what is expected of them through advance warnings and trial and error. Keep your people aware of what is expected and of the consequences for failing to meet expectations.
2. Rewards and punishments must be tailored to the behaviors they are intended to reward or punish. Consider the consequences, intent, and seriousness of the results of the punishments or rewards.
3. Don't reward mediocre or poor performances.
4. Don't punish inconsequential instances of misbehavior.
5. Don't fail to reward behavior you want repeated.
6. Don't fail to punish behavior you want eliminated.

Managing Motivation

In chapter 6 we discussed the importance of employees' beliefs, attitudes, and values. These affect how they perceive their world and the demands that are made upon them. What all of us look for in a job is a "fit" between what we want from work and what our organizations want from us. The closer the fit, the more likely it is that we will find job satisfaction and the means to achieve our personal and professional goals. As Herzberg's theory tells us, job satisfaction comes from the work itself, not from things external to it. Without job satisfaction we will find it difficult if not impossible to become or to stay motivated—to give our best effort to our performances at work.

Employees become dissatisfied for a variety of reasons. They may enter a job expecting too much. Often employers are not as honest as they should be about what a worker will find in the way of satisfactions once he or she is on the job. They often oversell a job and its potential benefits. People are sometimes hired for jobs that are too difficult or too easy. Applicants for employment are often desperate and take the first job offer that comes their way because they need money. Once on the job, people find boredom, unsafe conditions, inadequate training, and uncooperative coworkers. All of these situations add up to problems for the new employees and their employers. Most job dissatisfaction can be prevented, but both employees and employers have to work at prevention.

Job Dissatisfaction and Productivity

Productivity
The measurement of the amount of input needed to generate any given amount of output

Productivity is the measurement of how much input is needed to produce an amount of output. It is usually expressed as a ratio between these two variables, yielding a productivity index (PI). By dividing units of input into units of output, a PI can be calculated for most clerical or manufacturing activities. Inputs may be tons of materials, hours of machine time, dollars of invested capital, or hours of labor invested to produce an output. Outputs are the units realized through the investment or application of inputs. To illustrate, assume that you invested three hours of hard labor into the production of six reports to your boss. Your productivity index would be 6 divided by 3, or a PI of 2. By continually calculating a PI a person or an organization can arrive at several numbers (PIs) and compare them to note improvements or setbacks.

Productivity can be improved by producing the same number of outputs for less inputs or by increasing the outputs with the use of the same or reduced amounts of inputs. Either way, the costs connected with the production effort should fall, yielding a more efficient and effective use of resources. People are a main ingredient to the constant search for improvements in productivity. The more motivated and satisfied the individuals, the more productive they are likely to be. On the other hand, people suffering from job stress and job dissatisfaction tend to produce less than their opposites.

A look at the typical symptoms exhibited by dissatisfied workers and managers should tell you how they affect productivity in a negative way. The typical symptoms are tardiness, absenteeism, delayed work, shoddy work, lost time to gripes and complaints about their stations in life, and actual efforts at theft or sabotage to destroy company property or to simply vent their frustrations on their employer's assets. Over time, dissatisfied employees tend to become emotionally and physically ill, further reducing their productive capacities. If they decide to leave their source of dissatisfaction, they will cost their employers the funds needed to find and train replacements. Time will be lost to production through turnover, and those who remain will probably be overburdened with the work left undone by the departing employee.

Productivity and Quality

Quality
The totality of features and characteristics of a product or service that bear on its ability to satisfy stated or implied goals

The American Society for Quality Control defines **quality** as the totality of features and characteristics of a product or service that bear on its ability to satisfy stated or implied goals.[8] Quality and productivity are two fingers on the same hand. Improvements that lead to increased productivity must also lead to increased or sustained high levels of quality in both products and services. Exhibit 7.6 highlights the eight dimensions of quality.

Although General Motors suffered a decline in sales through 1991, its Buick division did not. Among all the cars produced at GM, only the Buick models placed among the top ten cars as rated for quality by their owners in the J. D. Powers and Associates annual polls. It seems as though the people in the Buick division have convinced the consumers that its products have quality. Complaints from consumers are dealt with swiftly and directly by dealers and factory personnel alike. A "hotline" puts the service departments of Buick dealerships in direct contact with factory personnel who can diagnose and prescribe cures for most problems encountered by dealers and owners.

At Buick and at the Japanese counterparts, every effort is made to promote quality, from product design to distribution and servicing. Mazda's Miata sports car has a tuned exhaust to give a throaty sound, a stiff gear shift to denote precision, and a fit and polish inside and out that sets its image as one of a quality product.

High-quality products and services are created by providers who are in close touch with what their consumers want. These producers design the quality into their end products and set precise performance standards for all their component parts. From the product design teams to the engineering and production teams, concern for quality dominates the efforts of all concerned. Once the suppliers are chosen (in part for their reputations for

1. **Performance Characteristics.** A product's operating features and the final outcomes that they produce.
2. **Users' Perceptions.** The ways in which a product feels, looks, and performs—its fit and finish.
3. **Useful Life.** The length of time that the product can be expected to deliver performances that are in line with user expectations.
4. **Serviceability.** The manufacturer's willingness and ability to furnish quick and reliable repairs—how well the producer backs up the product and its users in their time of need.

Exhibit 7.6 Dimensions of quality.

quality production), contracts are let and close contact is maintained to assure that all the parts meet the standards set in design.

Improvements to both quality and productivity begin with a personal commitment from everyone involved with the product or service. Top management must commit the dollars and hours necessary to plan for and to produce quality products. People must be given the necessary training and incentives to become and stay motivated and committed to quality performances. Managers and workers must adopt the philosophy that the best is yet to come—that no matter how good we are, we can be better. The Japanese have a word for this continual search for a better way, for better and more rewarding improvements: *kaizen.* Try to adopt this simple philosophy for yourself, and try to instill it in your subordinates or team members. After all, dollars conserved through improvements made will be there to ensure a better future for the employees and the organization. It is only through improvements in productivity and quality that an organization can ensure that it will have a future.

Quality of Work Life

Quality of work life
A general label given to various programs and projects designed to help employees satisfy their needs and expectations from work

Quality of work life (QWL) has been defined by the American Center for the Quality of Working Life as "any activity which takes place at every level of an organization which seeks greater organizational effectiveness through the enhancement of human dignity and growth."[9] The two major goals of QWL—making working life better for individuals and making the company more effective—are accomplished through a variety of programs in most major companies. Each organization needs to define what it means by QWL and to decide which of the available programs it wants to use throughout its levels.

Typical QWL programs include employee counseling services, performance appraisal systems, training programs, problem-solving sessions, labor/management committees, job improvement methods, employee surveys, and any other attempt by a company to give more employees more of a voice in what affects them at work.[10] If these programs are to work, every level of management and participating workers must be committed to their success. The programs must be carefully planned, with specific goals and methods decided on for each. All those affected should have some input and should be forewarned about specific efforts at implementation.

Worker Participation Techniques

Many organizations have discovered that the best way to improve operations is to consult those who are closest to the work that needs improvement. Companies have involved workers in their own quality-control operations by letting those who produce a product inspect it and certify its performance capabilities. Time is set aside in many plants for general gripe sessions and for dealing with problems that affect everyone at work. Supervisors may or may not participate in these sessions.

Quality circles are an excellent way to get the work force involved in a cooperative effort to improve working life as well as product quality. Although quality circles originated in Japan, over 850 American companies use them regularly to cut costs and to improve methods. In most companies, quality circles operate at the supervisory management level and are staffed with volunteers. Meetings are held regularly and focus on one or two problems that are the most important at the time. Priorities are often assigned to problems by the supervisors in charge of the section affected. Supervisors may or may not attend the sessions, depending on how the company has decided the circles should function. The results of each session are made known to participants and nonparticipants alike. Progress is noted and credit given to those responsible for it.

Recent research from eight American manufacturing plants belonging to four multinational corporations has discovered that supervisors affected by employee involvement programs have varying degrees of appreciation and commitment to them.[11] While 72 percent of the supervisors view such programs as beneficial to their companies, less than one-third see them as good for employees and as beneficial to themselves. The reasons given by the supervisors may sound familiar to you and should serve as warnings to you and to others. They were not involved in planning some programs and, consequently, felt no real commitment to them. Some supervisors were afraid that their power was being eroded and so resisted. Others felt that the programs were a passing fancy of top management that would disappear in time. The key lesson from this research is this: ''The support of first-line supervisors is essential if meaningful changes in the workplace are to take root. But if supervisors view programs that increase employee involvement as detrimental to themselves, they will withhold their support, potentially dooming the initiative.''[12]

Job rotation
Movement of people to different jobs, usually for a temporary period, in order to inform, train, or stimulate cooperation and understanding between and among them

Job Rotation **Job rotation** moves people to different jobs, usually on a temporary basis, to give them additional experience, understanding, and challenges. It is most frequently used to cross-train people and to give them a better appreciation for the importance of jobs and their interrelationships. Employees who experience job rotation are usually more valuable to themselves and to their employers because they can perform in more than one job competently. From this, supervisors gain more flexibility and can deal with absences more effectively.

Job rotation helps get people ready for promotions or transfers. It may mean that the worker gets more pay for the time that a different job is occupied, and it usually means that time will be lost to production while the person is learning the new job. It is a useful tool for improving the morale of some people but not for all. To some, job rotation may represent a threat to their sense of security and competence.

Job Enlargement **Job enlargement** increases the number of tasks a job includes or the amount of output expected from the job holder. It does not increase the number of responsibilities or the level of personal involvement experienced by the job holder. It usually requires people to do more of the kind of tasks they are already doing regularly. It is most useful for people who are suffering from having too little to do. Since job enlargement can add challenges for some, it can aid in motivation and a renewed interest and enthusiasm for work. And for some, a sense of competence can arise from being able to produce more, both in quantity and quality.

Job enlargement
Increasing the number of tasks or the quantity of output required in a job

Job Enrichment Today, many highly specialized, hazardous, and routinized assembly-type tasks are being turned over to robots by manufacturers. For human workers, the emphasis now is strongly on **job enrichment**—enriching a job by providing the job holder with variety, deeper personal interest and involvement, greater autonomy, and an increased amount of responsibility and challenge.

Job enrichment
Providing variety, deeper personal interest and involvement, greater autonomy and challenge, or increased amounts of responsibility on the job

Maytag, the home appliance manufacturer, has worked wonders on employee efficiency with numerous experiments in job enrichment. Some workers assemble entire components that were previously designed to be a team effort. Volvo, the Swedish car manufacturer, has small teams of workers who assemble entire automobiles. Texas Instruments, a precision scientific instruments company, has involved its workers not only in additional duties, such as testing and inspecting their output, but also in planning their work by setting their own quality and quantity goals. General Motors, in the construction of its new Saturn Division, makes extensive use of both robots and job enrichment techniques. Workers work in teams, master and perform several jobs, and assemble entire components.

In general, the opportunity for enrichment presents itself on nearly every highly refined and routinized job. The question then becomes, "Do the people working these jobs desire enrichment?" For many, the answer is a surprising *no*. A large number of production-line workers prefer their repetitive, specialized tasks. Their reasons are many. Some do not want a challenge and the additional effort it represents. Others are working to their capacities with their jobs the way they are and could not adjust to more duties. Still others do not like the new responsibilities, or the way in which their jobs were, are being, or will be enriched. A number of companies that embarked on job enrichment as the best answer to the blue-collar blues found that many more difficulties were created than eliminated. Consequently, they have dropped their wholesale attempts and have become much more selective in their approaches. Job enrichment is not the ultimate solution to job dissatisfaction, sagging production, employee absenteeism, and employee turnover. David Sirota, a professor of management and a management consultant, has listed a few problems that *cannot* be solved through job enrichment.

- Dissatisfaction with pay and fringe benefits
- Employee insecurity
- Technical incompetence
- Obstacles to getting the work done, such as poor administrative support and inferior tools and materials[13]

What Employees Can Do About Job Dissatisfaction

Preventing job dissatisfaction is not entirely in an employer's hands. Employees can do a few things for themselves. At the time employees are hired, their first job is to make their employer aware of them and their abilities, interests, and skill levels. Employees should not oversell themselves; they should be honest about what they have done and can do. This will help prevent them from getting into a job or situation for which they are not ready.

Before you go job hunting, you should be sure that you know what you want and are qualified to do. If what you want does not match up with your present skills and abilities, an employer may be willing to provide what you need or to underwrite your efforts. Tuition refund plans are quite common and can help you work for yourself while you work for an employer.

If you are currently working and are dissatisfied, find the true source of your unhappiness. Is it the job, the job's environment, or you? If it is the job, find out what changes would make you happy. If your boss can arrange the changes, let him or her know of your dissatisfaction. Always take your complaints and requests to the person who has the authority to deal with them. It may be that your problems will disappear with a transfer or a promotion. Work toward that end. If the true source of dissatisfaction rests in you, you may find that a personal change (or changes) is called for. Only you and your own efforts can bring about change in yourself.

Finally, you can avoid a common pitfall and source of dissatisfaction—becoming too specialized. Having a specialty is great, but it can lead to dead-end jobs and jobs that may evaporate in the future. You need to keep expanding your interests and skills. If you are to be ready to take advantage of new opportunities, you must keep growing intellectually. Keep current in your field and in all aspects of your chosen career. Create your own opportunities by getting ready and staying ready for the future.

Instant Replay

1. Industrial studies have shown that people are stimulated to action by five basic human needs and rewards, outcomes, or incentives offered by their employers.

2. The Hawthorne studies of the 1920s demonstrated the social and esteem needs that people have and the natural tendencies of workers to form their own groups or cliques.

3. Abraham Maslow has ranked human needs in a hierarchy that progresses from physical needs through four psychological needs. Each has the power to act as a motive for human behavior.

4. Managers and their organizations have the power to assist employees in their search for satisfaction in every need category.

5. Frederick Herzberg has identified two sets of factors that can either prevent dissatisfaction or promote motivation in employees. These are called, respectively, *maintenance* and *motivation factors*.

6. The contingency theory of motivation holds that all of us desire a sense of competence. That desire can be met by organizations and managers who tailor jobs, job assignments, and supervisory approaches to fit individuals' needs and capabilities.

7. The expectancy theory of motivation holds that people will work to exhibit the behaviors an employer or boss expects if they know what the rewards will be, are certain that the reward is forthcoming, desire to possess the reward, and have or per-

ceive that they have the capabilities required to exhibit the behaviors required.

8. The reinforcement theory states that behavior that is desirable will be repeated if rewarded and that undesirable behavior can be discouraged by providing punishment for it.

9. Productivity and quality go together. Efforts to improve one must also act to improve the other. Efforts to improve both must never end.

10. Quality of work life (QWL) involves programs and projects to help employees satisfy their needs and fulfill their expectations about work. It is part of organization development and uses such approaches as job rotation, job enrichment, and training programs.

Glossary

Human needs physiological and psychological requirements that all humans share and that act as motives for human behavior.

Job enlargement increasing the number of tasks or the quantity of output required in a job.

Job enrichment providing variety, deeper personal interest and involvement, greater autonomy and challenge, or increased amounts of responsibility in a job.

Job rotation movement of people to different jobs, usually for a temporary period, in order to inform, train, or stimulate cooperation and understanding between and among them.

Maintenance factor according to Herzberg, a factor that can be provided by an employer in order to prevent job dissatisfaction.

Motivation the drive within a person to achieve some goal. Human wants and needs fuel our drives.

Motivation factor according to Herzberg, a factor that has the potential to stimulate internal motivation to provide a better-than-average performance and commitment from those to whom it appeals.

Productivity the measurement of the amount of input needed to generate any given amount of output. A basic measurement of the efficiency of a business.

Quality the totality of features and characteristics of a product or service that bear on its ability to satisfy stated or implied goals.

Quality of work life a general label given to various programs and projects designed to help employees satisfy their needs and expectations from work.

Questions for
Class Discussion

1. Can you define this chapter's key terms?

2. What are the five needs we humans have in common? What are some examples of satisfactions that are available to us through our work?

3. What are the motivation factors identified by Professor Herzberg? What is their purpose in an organization?

4. What are the maintenance factors identified by Professor Herzberg? What is their purpose in an organization?

5. What is the contingency theory of motivation? Does it apply to your life?

6. What is the expectancy theory of motivation? How has it been demonstrated in your own experience?

7. What is the reinforcement theory of motivation? How has it worked in your own experience?

Incident

Purpose To assess the motivational climate at work for both you and your subordinates.

Your Task Take the quiz below. Tally your responses as follows: for each "usually" response, 2 points; for each "sometimes" response, 1 point. A score of 28 or higher indicates that you work in a highly motivating job. Let your subordinates or team members take this quiz. The results may help you create more stimulating environments and jobs for subordinates.

	Usually	Sometimes
1. I have regular duties that are interesting to perform.	_____	_____
2. I look forward to going to work each day.	_____	_____
3. My duties force me to keep growing intellectually.	_____	_____
4. I have enough authority to get my work done.	_____	_____
5. I have the kind of control over my work and pace of work that is satisfying to me.	_____	_____
6. I am proud of my work and look forward to my boss's reaction to it.	_____	_____
7. I receive the kind of recognition I need for my performances at work.	_____	_____
8. I know how my work connects to that of those who feed me work and to those to whom my work goes.	_____	_____
9. I feel that my work is very important to me.	_____	_____
10. I feel that my work is essential to the success of my company.	_____	_____

11. I receive adequate rewards for my performances. _____ _____

12. I know my boss personally, and he or she treats me as an individual. _____ _____

13. I know where my job will take me in my company and what future job prospects are ahead for me. _____ _____

14. The punishments or reprimands that I have received were earned and expected. _____ _____

15. I refrain from doing personal business on company time. _____ _____

16. I respect my company's property and do not waste my resources. _____ _____

17. My boss asks for my opinion and suggestions. _____ _____

18. I feel secure in my job and not threatened by loss of it. _____ _____

19. I feel that my pay (salary or wage and benefits) is fair and equitable. _____ _____

20. The challenges I have faced were within my powers to conquer. _____ _____

Case Problem 7.1   Julio's Place

Since his promotion to supervisor of menswear at his uncle's store, Julio has been puzzled by the shifts in performances by his two salespeople. Chester has dropped to second place after nearly one year as the best salesperson. Since Chester's fall, Roger has become the top salesperson, but his sales volume has yet to reach the average sales that Chester used to generate when he was on top.

Before his promotion four months ago, Julio worked side by side with Chester and Roger. All were supervised by Julio's uncle, Pedro. Over the two years Julio was a salesperson he had never earned the top spot. Although he liked selling, he liked handling stock and creating displays better. Julio now performs these duties, and he assumed that Chester and Roger would continue to perform as they had when he worked with them. He is at a loss to understand why Chester has seemingly lost his ability to sell.

Chester is 30, four years older than Julio and two years younger than Roger. He has worked for Pedro for five years, and for the last two years, Chester has been pursuing a two-year college degree in marketing. He married last year, and his wife works as a bookkeeper. She is now earning, for the first time, more than Chester. Until about three months ago, Chester was a ball of fire. He was the first person to report to work, opening the store on many mornings and full of enthusiasm for his work. He was a never-ending source of ideas about how to stimulate sales. He was aggressive, practically ''attacking'' customers and always eager to help. Pedro used to call him ''a tiger waiting for his prey.'' But all this has changed. Julio practically had to force

Chester to wait on two customers yesterday.

Roger has worked for Pedro for about ten months. He has a dream of owning his own clothing store one day. He wants to get all the selling experience he can and is saving his money like a miser. Since Chester and Roger earn over half their income with commissions on sales, Julio has worked out a system whereby they share customers who do not request either Chester or Roger. When a new customer enters the store, the two salespeople take turns waiting on them. But Chester now seems content to let Roger wait on every customer who enters. Thus Roger's earnings have increased at the expense of Chester's.

Pedro has expressed his unhappiness with the decline in sales and with the decline in Chester's performances. He has asked Julio to "do something quick." Julio is worried because he is not certain what to do. His talks with Chester have been disappointing, to say the least. Julio finds Chester unwilling to discuss any problems. He is evasive and gets angry when the subject of his decline is mentioned. In his discussion with his uncle

this morning, Julio said the following: "I don't know what else I can do with Chester except fire him. I want to get rid of the problem, too, but I'm not able to motivate him. You promoted me knowing that I'd make a better manager than I make a salesman."

Pedro answered Julio as follows: "You are the manager now and you must deal with this problem. You cannot fire Chester. He has a loyal following of scores of customers. We may lose them if we lose him. Now deal with this problem. Use your experience and college training in business. I want results. If you expect to run this business when I retire you better learn how to deal with poor performers."

Questions

1. What does Chester's decline tell you about human motivation?
2. What theory of motivation seems to fit Roger best? Why?
3. If you were in Julio's position, what would you do?

Case Problem 7.2   The Sleepy Hollow Motel

For five years Lillian Porter has been the receptionist at the Sleepy Hollow Motel. Her main duties include operating the switchboard, booking reservations, registering guests, and sorting the mail. In addition to her duties at the motel, Lill is the mother of three youngsters who live at home with her. In addition, she has two grandchildren.

Lill is not a perfectionist but close to it. She demands the best she can give of herself and performs her duties consistently well. She is intolerant of errors that anyone makes and was recently heard reprimanding a guest who had filled out the reservation card improperly. On that occasion she showed extreme annoyance with the same guest who was slightly intoxicated; as a result, the guest decided to seek other accommodations. Lill rarely smiles, and

she has a rather stern matronly appearance as a result of her facial expression and way of dressing. She is rather fond, it seems, of two "basic black" dresses, both of which are out of style and unflattering to her figure. Lill hates to arrive late or to be asked to stay late. To date she has flatly refused to work even a minute overtime.

Lill's work area is well equipped, since the motel is only five years old. She receives above average pay for her job. She works pretty much alone and on her own and likes it that way.

Her boss, Ben Sanderson, has often stated that he would be lost without Lillian. In Ben's words, "She seems to be able to handle six things at once."

"Everything about her is just great," said

Ben in a conversation with his night manager, Angelo Fortini. "The only problem I have is with the four housekeepers. They always seem to be behind schedule. Nearly every day Lill sees one of them goofing off, and she is quick to point this out to them. When they fail to respond to her corrections, she is forced to come to me."

"Are you letting Lill supervise the housekeepers, too?" asked Angelo.

"No, it's just that Lill is the one who seems to catch them all the time. I have never seen any of them goof off."

"Ben, you know that Lill's husband was killed in a car accident a year ago."

"Yes, I know that."

"Do you remember how it happened?"

"Yes, it was a head-on collision at Route 41 and Ventura about 9 P.M. Why do you ask?"

"Well, did you know that it was a carload of migrant workers that ran the stoplight and killed Mr. Porter? The driver was drunk, and he escaped the crash with only a few scratches."

"So, what are you getting at?"

"Just this. What ethnic background are our housekeepers? Spanish, right?"

"Mexican, but they are legal residents. I don't follow you . . . Oh, now I see what you are getting at."

Questions

1. Which of the human needs seem most important to Lill?
2. Which maintenance and motivation factors is Lill receiving at work?
3. How can you explain Lill's lack of a pleasing disposition or personality?
4. Assuming that the motel's housekeepers are goofing off, how do you explain Ben's behavior?
5. What seems to be Lill's attitudes toward her work, coworkers, and liquor?

Notes

1. Elton Mayo, *The Social Problems of an Industrial Civilization* (Boston: Division of Research, Graduate School of Business Administration, Harvard University, 1945), 68–86.
2. Abraham H. Maslow, *Motivation and Personality,* 2d ed. (New York: Harper & Row, 1970).
3. Frederick Herzberg, "One More Time: How Do You Motivate Employees?" in *Business Classics: Fifteen Key Concepts for Managerial Success* (Harvard Business Review, 1975), 13–22.
4. John J. Morse and Jay W. Lorsch, "Beyond Theory Y," in *Harvard Business Review on Management* (New York: Harper & Row, 1975), 377–78.
5. Ibid., 387.
6. Lester R. Bittel and Jackson E. Ramsey, eds., *Handbook for Professional Managers* (New York: McGraw-Hill, 1986), 586–89.
7. B. F. Skinner, *Contingencies of Reinforcement* (New York: Appleton-Century-Crofts, 1969).
8. Ross Johnson and William O. Winchell, *Management and Quality* (Milwaukee, Wis.: American Society for Quality Control, 1989).
9. "Quality of Work Life: How to Do It and How Not to Do It," *The Wharton Annual* 8 (1983): 152.
10. "Quality of Work Life Becomes a Movement of the '80s," *Chicago Tribune,* 30 (November 1981).
11. "Why Supervisors Resist Employee Involvement," *Harvard Business Review* (September–October 1984): 87–95.
12. Ibid., 88.
13. "How Industry Is Dealing with People Problems on the Line," *American Machinist* 12 (November 1973): 86.

Suggested Readings

Adler, Paul S.; Riggs, Henry E; and Wheelwright, Steven C. "Product Development Know-How: Trading Tactics for Strategy." *Sloan Management Review* (Fall 1989): 7–17.

Belcher, John G., Jr. *Productivity Plus: How Today's Best Run Companies Are Gaining the Competitive Edge.* Houston: Gulf Publishing Co., 1987.

Berry, Leonard L."Five Imperatives for Improving Service Quality." *Sloan Management Review* (Summer 1990): 29–38.

Burt, David N. "Managing Suppliers Up to Speed." *Harvard Business Review* (July–August 1989): 127–135.

Dyer, William G. *Team Building: Issues and Alternatives.* Reading, Mass.: Addison-Wesley Publishing Co., 1987.

Juran, J. M. *Juran on Planning for Quality.* New York: The Free Press, 1988.

Pinder, Craig C. *Work Motivation: Theory, Issues, and Applications.* Glenview, Ill.: Scott, Foresman and Co., 1984.

Reichheld, Frederick F. "Zero Defections: Quality Comes to Services." *Harvard Business Review* (September–October 1990): 105–111.

Semler, Ricardo. "Managing Without Managers." *Harvard Business Review* (September–October 1989): 76–84.

Walton, Mary. *Deming Management at Work.* New York: G. P. Putnam's Sons, 1990.

8 Building Relationships with Individuals

245

Objectives

After reading and discussing this chapter, you should be able to do the following:

1 Define the key terms.

2 List and briefly explain the five purposes of human relations.

3 Describe the application of each of the four human relations roles to the relationship between a supervisor and his or her subordinates and peers.

4 Describe how a middle manager's job is different from a supervisor's job.

5 Describe how a supervisor can create and maintain good human relations with his or her boss.

Key Terms

counselor

educator

human relations

judge

peer

spokesperson

Introduction

This chapter explores how you as a supervisor can build good working relationships with each individual with whom you must work. Relating successfully to others is the key to your growth and advancement. From solid individual relationships will come the cooperation and assistance you and others at work need to reach your goals.

Human relations
The development and maintenance of sound on-the-job relationships with subordinates, peers, and superiors

The development and maintenance of sound on-the-job relationships with subordinates, peers, and superiors is usually referred to as **human relations.** From the moment you first meet another person at work, a relationship begins. How you relate to each person with whom you must work is largely up to you to determine. The quality of your interpersonal relationships, however, will determine just how effective and efficient you will be. None of us work in a vacuum. We all must depend to some extent on others.

Much of what this chapter examines is related to the contents of chapters 1, 5, and 7. It will carry over to all the remaining chapters in this text, as well, for sound working relationships are at the heart of building teams, leading, staffing, training, appraising, and disciplining.

Goals of Human Relations

Managers should have the following goals in mind in their approach to human relations:

1. To know and understand each individual as an individual

2. To approach and supervise each subordinate as an individual

3. To provide what help you can to enable each individual to achieve the measure of satisfaction he or she wishes to achieve on the job

4. To increase each individual's (a) contribution of intellectual effort, (b) commitment to the company and to his or her job, and (c) quantity and quality of output

5. To foster a spirit of cooperation between yourself and your subordinates and peers and between yourself and your boss

These are worthy but difficult goals for any manager, but they are especially difficult for supervisors. The chief reasons for this difficulty are the wide diversity of ages, the differing backgrounds, and the lack of similar experiences so often found among workers. The heterogeneous mixture of people among the workers contrasts sharply to the homogeneous mixture so often found in the ranks of management. Workers have always made the execution of the leading function much more difficult for supervisors than managers do for each other. What we are about to explore is not easy, but it is absolutely necessary if you are to prevent the most common cause of failure in supervisory personnel: failure caused by faulty human relations.

Communicating Supportively

All of your efforts at developing sound human relations involve communicating with your subordinates and with others outside your immediate sphere of influence. The ways in which you communicate (your behavior and approaches toward others) can cause others to be open and honest or closed and defensive. If your approaches and behavior show that you are supportive of the feelings and efforts of others, you encourage open and honest two-way communications. This two-way communications process should firmly bridge your relationships with your subordinates, your peers, and your superiors.

In chapter 5, you discovered that active listening requires, among other things, that you avoid passing judgment on another's ideas until you fully understand them and can restate them to that person accurately. After the other person finishes, simply state your views and ideas and tell

		Usually	Rarely
1.	I make time to listen to my people's problems.	——	——
2.	I greet my people warmly and sincerely express my interest in their well-being.	——	——
3.	I give my people the information they need to perform effectively.	——	——
4.	I encourage my people to come to me with their ideas and suggestions.	——	——
5.	I am slow to criticize any idea given to me and try to look for its good points first.	——	——
6.	I use humor when it is appropriate in my chances to communicate.	——	——
7.	I share any praise I receive when part of it is due to the efforts of my subordinates or team members.	——	——
8.	I take the chance, whenever possible, to talk with my people, one on one.	——	——
9.	I express sincere interest in my people's families, inquiring as to their health and well-being.	——	——
10.	I consider my people's feelings and circumstances before attempting to judge or criticize their actions.	——	——
11.	I take every opportunity to compliment people for any job that is well done.	——	——
12.	I give quick feedback to my people on all matters that are of importance to them.	——	——
13.	I try not to keep those waiting to see me waiting too long.	——	——
14.	I offer explanations for my actions and decisions.	——	——

Exhibit 8.1   A short quiz to measure how supportive you are when communicating to subordinates or team members.

how they differ from his or hers. Criticizing other people's ideas puts them on the defensive. Try to empathize—putting yourself in the other person's position—and avoid emotional responses. Try to remain objective. Keep your encounters with others problem oriented and directed toward finding mutually beneficial solutions. Avoid "playing games" and simply be yourself, honestly and sincerely. Finally, avoid a know-it-all attitude. You will learn from the other person just as you hope he or she will learn from you. Keep these ideas in mind as you read about and execute the human relations roles that follow. Take the short quiz in Exhibit 8.1. Any "rarely" responses indicate a need to improve your communications efforts.

Developing Sound Working Relationships with Subordinates

As was stated in earlier chapters, your success as a manager is directly related to and dependent on the performance of your subordinates. Your reputation is in their hands, since it is a product of their efforts. Your future therefore depends in large measure on how well you are able to relate to them and to promote in them a desire to excel. With this recognition should come a personal commitment on your part to guide all your people toward a more complete realization of their own potential.

The ideal on-the-job relationship between yourself and your subordinates will be the end result of your understanding, mastering, and executing the four fundamental roles of the supervisor, listed in Exhibit 8.2. These roles are related to and depend on one another. It is the supervisor's duty to initiate and maintain these relationships. Specifically, the four relationships are defined in the following ways:

1. *Educator*—a builder of skills and developer of potentials
2. *Counselor*—an adviser, director, cheerleader, and coach
3. *Judge*—an appraiser and dispenser of justice
4. *Spokesperson*—a disseminator of timely and accurate information

Your Role as Educator

Educator
The human relations role in which the supervisor is a builder of skills and a developer of potentials in subordinates

Your role as an **educator** is usually the first one you play in relation to a new subordinate. When new people first arrive, they usually are introduced to their coworkers, are shown the facilities and workstations, and have their duties and responsibilities explained by their supervisors. If the supervisor played a part in the hiring, he or she has already begun to assess the individual's strengths and weaknesses. If not, the supervisor must begin to do so promptly. With this assessment comes a determination about the type of training, if any, needed to bring the new employee up to par. This initial training is vitally important, as it sets standards and communicates skills, knowledge, and attitudes that have a lasting effect on the individual and his or her department. Training, when properly planned and executed, does much to remove the initial fears we all have as we begin something new. It convinces the new people of our interest in and concern for their getting off on the right foot. They should emerge from it with a clear understanding of what is expected of them and how they are supposed to achieve it. By doing this, the supervisor has demonstrated his or her commitment to helping the new person toward self-realization and a successful performance.

Educator

Judge

Counselor

Spokesperson

Exhibit 8.2   The four human relations roles played by supervisors.

There is a second phase to your role as an educator. You will recall from chapter 4 that we included in our definition of leading the element of educating. We stated there that to educate meant to foster subordinates' intellectual development. By this we meant making new skills and knowledge available to subordinates and establishing proper attitudes; we also meant promoting an individual's own efforts to achieve these things. Your example in seeking further personal growth through formal education exemplifies your commitment to your company's emphasis on education. This just might be the incentive a subordinate needs to continue formal education on his or her own or to take advantage of company-sponsored programs that aid in self-development.

By understanding your role as an educator, mastering the knowledge and skills you wish to teach others, and executing this role in accordance with established training principles and procedures (chapter 12), you are well on your way toward promoting your own success by fostering success in others.

Your Role as Counselor

Think back to encounters with school counselors that you have had throughout your formal education. What was it they were trying to do for you? Why did the school feel they were necessary? Their advice was usually related to school and general growth-and-development problems common to most students. If the counselors were doing their jobs, they wanted what was best *for you*. They tried to get to know you and your individual needs, aspirations, and desires. They listened to you and, in turn, hoped you would listen to them—to their advice as to what was realistic thinking on your part and what was not. Sometimes they suggested solutions to your problems. If they were wise, they did not suggest solutions to personal or emotional problems, but they may have instead suggested that you talk with a specialist—an authority better equipped than they were to help you in that particular area.

In case you have not guessed, this is also a description of how you should execute your role as a **counselor** to your subordinates.

Counselor
The human relations role in which a supervisor is an adviser and director to subordinates

Mr. A. A. Imberman, a management consultant, states that there are two tests that employees use to judge their supervisors:

1. Is the supervisor aware of me? Can I turn to him or her for friendly help? Will he or she listen to me?

2. Will he or she do something about my problem?[1]

If the answers to these two questions are *yes,* the workers view their boss as a good one. By the first question, the employees really want to know if the supervisor knows them personally. Does the supervisor know about their ambitions and their family and individual needs? By the second question, they ask if the supervisor is willing to do something about a problem. Notice that the workers are not asking for the boss to come up with a solution every time they present him or her with a problem. They only want the boss to try. Doing something can be as simple as being available to listen to them. We all know the release that accompanies our talking out a problem with a sympathetic listener. We often reach our own solution after or during such an experience. Sometimes we are not really looking for a solution because we know that only we ourselves or time can provide it, as in the case of a family argument or illness. Of course, job-related problems are something else. If it is within your power to solve the problems or recommend solutions, do so. If the problems must be resolved at a higher level, see that they are referred there, and that the disposition or decision is relayed to your subordinate. Even if the results do not satisfy the individual, you have tried to help. You have done the best you could, and a subordinate will know it. You will have passed a major test.

Staying Aware In order to get to know your people in depth, you should meet with each of them informally, face to face, at least once a month for twenty to thirty minutes. These counseling or coaching sessions allow you to accomplish several things:

1. Get to know each person as an individual
2. Periodically update your knowledge about each of your subordinates
3. Pinpoint personal and business-related problems that you may be able to help resolve
4. Find out how each subordinate is doing on the job
5. Show your concern for each subordinate's growth and improvement

Many supervisors ignore counseling until a problem arises. Then they call a hasty conference and belittle, berate, or chew out the subordinate who is in trouble. Very soon subordinates get the message that the only time they see or hear from the boss is when he or she is unhappy or upset about their performance. Some supervisors claim that they do not have the time or that the time spent on counseling could be better spent on other things. The plain fact is that if supervisors do not counsel their people, they will have plenty of fires to put out and very little time for counseling. But if they invest the time necessary to touch base with each person periodically, they will be able to spot trouble coming and thus prevent many problems that later on might require corrective measures or hastily called sessions to deal with the difficulty.

"Doing Something" If you are going to "do something" about a subordinate's problem, a formal interview should be conducted. The four basic principles that apply to a problem-centered coaching interview are described in the following extract:

> The *first principle* of successful coaching is to get your subordinate involved. The more active a part the subordinate can take in appraising the problem for himself, and in outlining possible courses of action, *the more committed he will be* to the solution. And, the more enthusiastically he will work for its success.
>
> The *second principle* is that you encourage him to participate actively in the interview. Your role in the coaching interview is not to *tell* your subordinate what to do or how to do it, but rather to *help him develop for himself* a plan of action for dealing with the problem at hand. You can raise key questions which will help him find a solution, but don't lead him by the hand unless it is absolutely necessary.
>
> The *third principle* is to make sure you both understand the meaning of what is being discussed and said. The only sure way of doing this is to get your subordinate to express his views in his own words. You should restate those views, in different words, to see if you can reach agreement. Otherwise, the two of you could come away from the coaching conference with entirely different ideas of the issues discussed and decisions made.
>
> Finally, the *fourth principle* is to force yourself to *do more listening than talking*. Even if you say relatively little during your meeting, the interview can prove of considerable value—provided you listen. If he is upset, you give your subordinate a chance to let off steam. You also give him an opening to try out his ideas on you for a change.[2]

An analogy can be drawn between the supervisor's role in the motivation of subordinates and the director's role in bringing out the best in actors. A director knows that, like a supervisor, he or she cannot motivate an actor to put on a superior performance. The director realizes that motivation comes from within, and that certain limitations exist in and around every actor that can interfere with a superior effort. But the director knows that he or she can do much to provide the climate and incentives for the actor that can spark an inner drive to excel. He or she may remove distractions that might interfere with an actor's concentration. He or she can make certain that the actor has done the necessary homework and learned the lines. The director can confer with the actor to find out how the actor perceives the role. The director is able to set the stage with props and lighting that will allow the actor to perform to the best of his or her ability. Lastly, throughout the rehearsals and the performances, the director offers advice and criticism. This coaching and sincere concern are often the spark the actor needs to give a superior performance. By sensing the actor's needs, strengths, and weaknesses, the director can tailor advice and direction to bring about a commitment to excel within the actor.

Supervisors must get to know themselves well, and they must get to know their subordinates in depth. Having committed themselves to these tasks, they will find that they are able to build sound human and working relationships with their subordinates. Supervisors should be able to tailor their approaches with an eye to the needs and responses of each subordinate.

Your Role as Judge

Judge
The human relations role in which the supervisor enforces company policies, rules, procedures; evaluates subordinates' performances; settles disputes; and dispenses justice

Playing **judge** successfully involves being proficient at four important tasks:

1. Enforcing company policies and regulations, as well as your department's procedures and rules
2. Evaluating your subordinates' performances
3. Settling disputes among your people or between your people and yourself
4. Dispensing justice

Enforcement   In order to enforce company policies and regulations, you must first become aware of them. You have to know what they say, as well as their proper interpretation. Then you must see to it that they are followed by both your subordinates and yourself. Finally, you must be certain that they are not violated by your section's procedures, practices, and rules. Consistency of enforcement is the key to gaining acceptance of company policies and management decisions.

You must follow a similar procedure with regard to your department's procedures and practices. Do people know about them? Do they understand them? Are they following them? All these questions are usually answered through various controls you design into your operation. Proper induction and training should go a long way toward ensuring that the department's procedures and practices are properly interpreted and utilized.

Evaluation   Evaluating subordinate is one of your most important and time-consuming tasks as a supervisor. Appraising your people involves making judgments about their performances and their attitudes. Using established standards for each job, you must make an objective and honest evaluation of each person's output and individual contribution to the department. Is he or she meeting production standards? Is he or she correcting or trying to correct deficiencies noted in previous appraisals? Are his or her attitudes proper, or are they interfering with his or her efforts and those of other workers in the department?

Appraisals take place daily. In routine visits with your people, you have an excellent opportunity to note their successes and question their deficiencies. This will allow you to catch an error when it first appears and take corrective action to prevent its recurrence. At the same time, you are letting your people know regularly how they stand with you. Your being with them routinely gives them the opportunity to ask questions and to clear up misunderstandings. When the time finally rolls around for the formal semiannual or annual review, there should be no surprises. You have kept your people informed on a daily basis.

With regard to attitudes, your appraisals each day blend nicely with your role as a counselor. Much of appraising has to do with counseling. When your observations tell you that a worker's attitude causes a deficiency in his or her output or conduct, try to find out why he or she harbors it. Chapter 6 contains much helpful information on attitudes and how to change them. You will recall that it is only when people see their attitude as improper that they are willing to reject it. Chapter 13 probes more deeply into the specifics of the appraisal process.

Settling Disputes Part of your role as a judge is to act as a peace-maker. People problems are the most persistent and frequent problems you have to deal with each day. Inevitably, two or more individuals or groups of subordinates will do battle with each other. It would be best if these battles could be prevented, but that is not always possible. Sometimes the causes are hidden from your view and only surface under stress with an open display of hostility.

When you witness such disturbances, begin an investigation to uncover the causes on both sides. Analyze your evidence and make a decision. Try to avoid treating the symptoms, but concentrate your energies on the disease. When you have reached a conclusion as to the merits on both sides, confront the participants with your findings. Work toward a reconciliation that will not leave any scars as lasting reminders of the battle. Avoid any emphasis on who was at fault (chances are, both sides share the blame), but point out why the problem got started and how it can be avoided in the future.

Once a student of mine who was a production foreman in the construction industry told me about one of his peers who, whenever they were together on breaks, would emphasize his own achievements on the job, while criticizing and playing down those of my student. This had been going on for nearly a year. My student finally decided to avoid the other foreman for a while to relieve his feelings of frustration and to remove their cause. Within a month the two men were reconciled. His peer began to miss my student's companionship on the job and realized why he had been avoided. When the other foreman dropped his critical attitude (he saw that keeping it would deprive him of needed companionship), they were able to build a new and better relationship.

Dispensing Justice   *Justice,* in this connection, means seeing to it that each of your subordinates gets what he or she deserves. When they are doing a good job, they deserve your praise. When they break a rule or violate a procedure, they must be shown the error of their ways. Rest assured that people desire to know the bounds that limit them and their activity. Once these limits are explained, people expect them to be enforced and usually anticipate some admonishment for each of their infractions. This admonishment may simply be a verbal warning, but in the case of repeated offenses, it may take the form of some other disciplinary action.

Improper or unacceptable conduct on the job cannot be tolerated. To prevent it, your company installs you as its chief enforcement officer in your department and gives you power to discipline violators. It provides you with policies and regulations, while you provide your department with procedures and rules. When these preventive devices fail, corrective measures must take over.

To many, discipline means simply punishment. This is the negative side of a much broader concept. The positive side is the one that emphasizes informing organization members ahead of time as to the limits that surround acceptable conduct. It places the emphasis on self-control and mutual trust. When new employees are hired, you should inform them of the rules on the very first day, and you should make it clear to them what constitutes acceptable behavior and performance and what does not. When you take over a section as its supervisor, promptly inform the members of the standards you will enforce and the expectations you will have of each member. When infractions occur, take action. To do otherwise would ultimately undermine your formal authority and your integrity. You will find that it is much better to start out tough than to try to become so later. It is an unpleasant and difficult duty to discipline people for infractions of a rule that you failed to make clear to them.

When punishment is necessary, you must be certain that it fits the offense. Quite often, when dealing with unionized workers, the manager's disciplinary powers are limited by the union contract. Be certain that you have the power to take a specific action before you do so. And keep in mind that subordinates expect you to act equitably—to be impartial and fair. Chapter 14 deals in more detail with the tasks to be encountered in disciplining.

Your Role as Spokesperson

Your superiors expect you to represent management's point of view adequately to your subordinates. You are the only manager who can translate management's plans into action. Your boss, in particular, is counting on you to defend and to reinforce management's position. But you must be a **spokesperson** for your work group as well.

Spokesperson
The human relations role through which a supervisor represents management's views to workers and workers' views to management

You must realize that you are (or should be) a fountainhead of timely and accurate information to your people. They look to you for an interpretation of the events they witness. They expect you to help them separate fact from fiction and truth from rumor. Their need to be kept "informed" demands that you prepare them in advance for changes. They look to you as *their* spokesperson—backing them up either when they are right or when they are wrong because they executed your orders. If they believe that a policy or regulation is unfair, relay their feelings to those in a position to change it. You can do much to protect your people from harassment and from getting shortchanged. Just as you hope for their loyalty, they need yours.

What has just been said once again emphasizes that the supervisor is the person in the middle, caught between two different groups with individual demands that, at times, are opposed to one another. The supervisor is the manager straddling the fence between the demands of management and those of labor. Both sides expect the supervisor to be their representative to the other. But take heart. This is a necessary and totally logical evolutionary step in your movement through the ranks of management. Such experiences will serve you well for the rest of your career.

You must respect the confidences of both your superiors and your subordinates. Just because your people request an answer to a question, and you know the answer, is no reason you should give it. Information given to you in private with a request for your silence must be respected. If you betray a confidence, you will soon find yourself on the outside of the group, looking in.

There are times when your employees seem to know more about future events than you do. This is natural, and this situation may be explained in part by the grapevine. If they ask for a clarification or verification and you cannot give it, do not bluff. Admit your lack of accurate information, and assure them that you will try to get it. Then be sure to deliver.

If you properly execute your role as spokesperson, your superiors and your subordinates will learn to trust you and to rely upon you more in the future. This will strengthen your relationships with them and will promote harmony and cooperation in your department. Take the quiz in Exhibit 8.3 to help you to assess how well you are playing your four human relations roles with subordinates.

	Usually	Rarely*

Educator Role

1. I make certain that my actions do not contradict my words and instructions.   ____   ____

2. I carefully construct a program for training my people, being certain to set specific objectives.   ____   ____

3. I make certain that my people have the information and resources they need to do first-class work.   ____   ____

4. I assign work to people based upon their willingness and their abilities to perform it.   ____   ____

5. When I find an attitude in a subordinate that is interfering with the performance, I work on changing it.   ____   ____

Counselor Role

1. I make time for anyone who wishes to see me about a personal or work-related problem.   ____   ____

2. I make certain that any counseling I do is in private and free from interruptions.   ____   ____

3. I give the person seeking my help my undivided, sincere attention.   ____   ____

4. I recognize that I cannot solve every problem and should not try to give people all the answers.   ____   ____

5. When I cannot help someone solve a problem, I will try to refer them to another person with more expertise.   ____   ____

*Each "rarely" response indicates that you need to improve on your conduct.

Exhibit 8.3   A short quiz to help you assess how well you are playing your human relations roles with subordinates.

Maintaining Your Relationships with Subordinates

So far we have discussed how to build a sound relationship with your individual subordinates. How can you preserve it once you have established it? The answer lies in persistence. When we talked about personality formation, we agreed that it was a continuous process. So it is with on-the-job relationships. Like any other living thing, human relations need constant attention. Each day brings about changes in the parties involved so that what worked well yesterday may not today. Recognition of this dynamic aspect of people and their relationships dictates the need for maintenance.

	Usually	Rarely*

Judge Role

1. I look for causes behind any failures by my people to meet the standards set for their performances. ⎯⎯ ⎯⎯

2. I withhold any criticism until I have all the facts and am aware of all the circumstances surrounding an issue. ⎯⎯ ⎯⎯

3. I try to discipline without emotion. ⎯⎯ ⎯⎯

4. I recognize that circumstances should temper any approach to discipline. ⎯⎯ ⎯⎯

5. I know that it is better to forewarn and to forearm subordinates about the expectations I or the organization has for them than it is to have to punish people for failing to meet standards.

Spokesperson Role

1. I take every complaint or gripe I hear from subordinates seriously. ⎯⎯ ⎯⎯

2. I listen carefully to subordinates' suggestions and ideas and try to use them. ⎯⎯ ⎯⎯

3. Any problem my people give me that I cannot solve will be taken to a higher authority for resolution. ⎯⎯ ⎯⎯

4. When my people experience successes, I make certain others higher up hear about it. ⎯⎯ ⎯⎯

5. I try my best to accurately reflect management's points of view, defending them and enforcing its decisions. ⎯⎯ ⎯⎯

Maintenance of your relationships with subordinates can be compared to the situation of gardeners who wish to keep their gardens in a healthful and beautiful condition. They have plans for the care and development of the gardens. There are schedules for feeding, for pruning, and for preventive measures such as spraying and weeding. Their daily observations tell them about the gardens' state of repair and keep them in touch with each plant and its present state of health. What precedes all this is a genuine love for gardening and a commitment to a program for maintaining the gardens. So it must be with your human relations efforts. Establishing a sound relationship with each person is only a beginning. If the relationship is to grow and be mutually beneficial, maintenance must be scheduled and performed.

Desert Storm, Desert Shield, 541,000 U.S. military personnel from all branches of the armed forces active and reserve. These people under the able leadership of literally thousands of noncommissioned and commissioned officers achieved a stunning victory against the Iraqi forces in the field. When many of these people returned to civilian life they had a job waiting. Others began the search for a life outside the military. Executive recruiters have found good-paying, career-oriented jobs for these returning veterans in the ranks of management.

The Military Recruiting Institute is just one of many firms that specializes in recruiting military officers for civilian employers. It has some very large multinational companies as clients. What attracts corporate clients to junior-grade military officers is their training and experience in leading people. Today's brand of leadership in the military is linked to the application of popular motivational theories. It stresses the need to help people to become motivated and to stay that way. It emphasizes the need to communicate effectively, one on one and in groups. Junior-grade officers (second lieutenants, first lieutenants, and captains) lead by molding teams whose members are very dependent on one another to get the job done. They practice the four human relations roles regularly on a wide variety of people with very different cultural and ethnic backgrounds. It is hard to imagine a more effective training grounds for turning out qualified leaders than the U.S. military. Training is their only business when they are not fighting to preserve freedom. The chances are good that your boss has some military training. Ask him or her how valuable that training has been in the practice of supervision.

Friendship

There is a distinct difference between the relationship between supervisor and subordinate that this chapter advocates and the relationship between two people called *friendship*. At the base of sound human relations are common interests (effective and efficient operation of the department, for example), mutual respect, and a concern for the other person's welfare. This is or should be true about your relationships with your friends, as well. But you should try to prevent a true friendship from emerging out of sound human relations with your subordinates.

If you allow a friendship to form between yourself and a subordinate, you do so at your own expense. How easy is it to give orders to a friend? Do you appraise your friend's performance and freely offer criticism to him or her? How about the times when you have to pass out an occasional dirty job? Would you consider your friend objectively as a candidate for it? You cannot form a friendship with all your subordinates, so aren't you opening yourself to criticism about playing favorites?

Your honest answers to these questions should alert you to the inherent dangers of friendship with subordinates. The subordinate you befriend is open to criticism, too, and his or her relationships with his or her peers may be in jeopardy. Your friends at work should be other supervisors.

Getting Along with Staff Specialists

Probably dozens of times each week you come across the effects of staff specialists on your department. A good percentage of the forms and reports you generate are destined for their desks. The advice and service you receive at the press of a button or the twist of a dial can save you hours of agony and independent research. These people form an invaluable group of counselors on professional matters. Do everything you can to take advantage of their labors and to foster a cooperative and receptive atmosphere. At times they may appear to you as prying eyes or fifth wheels. But over the long run, your success as a supervisor—as well as that of all other managers—depends on your seeking and utilizing their advice. And as the concept of functional authority suggests, you may have no choice.

Developing Sound Human Relationships with Peers

Peer
A person with the same level of formal authority and status in the organizational hierarchy as you have

Your **peers** are all the other managers who are on the same level of the management hierarchy as you are. You work more closely with some than with others, but situations can change rapidly in business. The most important reasons for establishing good human relations with your peers are these:

1. To know and understand all of them as individuals
2. To approach and cooperate with all of them as individuals
3. To provide what help you can to enable all of them to achieve the measure of satisfaction they desire from their jobs
4. To foster a spirit of cooperation and teamwork among your peers
5. To tap their funds of knowledge, skills, and experience

Your success as a manager is linked to your peers and what they think of you as a person and as a supervisor. Your personal and professional reputation with them is important for a number of reasons. If they think highly of you, they will be drawn to you and be willing to associate with you. They will freely expend their time and energy on your behalf and help you with advice. How you measure up with them and how they react when your name is mentioned are factors that may influence your boss, as well. When your boss looks at his or her subordinates—you and your peers—for someone to delegate responsibility to or to train for a higher position, he or she cannot help but compare you to them. If you cannot get along with or are avoided by your peers, your boss will know it.

Your peers represent an enormous pool of talent and experience that is yours to tap and contribute to if they view you in a favorable way. For this reason, if no other, it is to your advantage to cultivate their friendship both on and off the job. In many ways you need each other, and all of you stand to benefit from a partnership or alliance based on mutual respect and the need to resolve common problems.

If you are off in your own little world and are unwilling to share your knowledge and know-how, you deny yourself the advice and experience they stand ready to give. You may be branded as uncooperative or antisocial and destined, at best, for a career as a supervisor. Higher positions have no need for isolates. You will find, if you have not already done so, that the more you give of what you have, the more you will receive from others.

Your Role as Educator

The two-way nature of your role as educator includes assisting your fellow supervisors in their growth and development, as well as enlisting their help on your own behalf.

You have a great deal to give your peers. You have talents and skills that may be developed to a greater degree in you than in some of them. You have knowledge about human nature, your job, and management in general that can be beneficial to others. You have attitudes and a personality that can be the basis for friendship and that can sustain a fellow supervisor when he or she needs it most.

Most people have experienced the joy that comes with sharing what they have with others. Parents know the pleasure they receive when they give of themselves to their children. They have seen the delight when they show their children how to do things and when they help their children develop their skills and increase their knowledge. Do you remember the fun you had when you took a friend for a ride in your new car? Can you recall the enjoyment you felt when you helped younger, less experienced people solve a problem that was so difficult for them and yet so easy for you?

Besides the momentary joy you feel when you share your knowledge and your tricks of the trade, you also get something much more lasting: a good reputation. Psychologically, all of your peers who profit through your efforts on their behalf are in your debt. They may not always show overt appreciation (and you should not always expect it), but they will find it hard not to reciprocate, to share what they have with you. When you need a favor, a bit of advice, or a helping hand, your colleagues will respond when and if they are able to do so.

Your peers' advice and know-how cannot be found in books. In a relatively short span of time, you will receive (if you are wise enough to ask) what might take you years to discover on your own. Which is easier and more fun: reading about how to do something difficult or having someone who knows how to do it show you how it is done? Your peers probably feel the same way about this as you do.

If you know yourself well, you know your strengths and weaknesses. Where you are weak, a peer may be strong, and vice versa. The more peers you know well, the greater the quantity of help available to you. Give what you have, and take advantage of what others have to give. Do not bury your talents, and do not let them bury theirs.

Your Role as Counselor

Counsel is a *mutual* exchange of ideas and opinions. Counselors are people to whom you go for advice and to try out your ideas. They provide you with guidance and a plan in the absence of one of your own. The key to counseling your peers is empathy—the intellectual and imaginative understanding of another's feelings and state of mind. From this develops a mutual respect and appreciation.

As with subordinates, just being available and favorably predisposed toward your peers may give them what they need at precisely the moment they need it—a sympathetic ear. By listening to others who have difficulties, you provide emotional first aid. By responding when asked and when qualified to do so, you may give people the support they need to resolve their difficulties.

When a friend asks you for advice and you have empathy for that person, speak your mind freely. Without empathy (which usually means without friendship), you should confine your guidance to work-related matters. Steer clear of personal advice unless you know the person well.

A few words of caution are in order. It is one thing to be asked for your opinion and quite another to give it without being asked. You do not want a reputation as a "buttinski," so avoid any counsel unless it is solicited.

We all have known the value of being on the receiving end of good counsel. An interested, sympathetic adviser and friend not only can temper our views, he or she may resolve our difficulties as well. When we consult a friend, we are either looking for answers we think he or she possesses or seeking a shoulder to lean on. The value of either cannot be measured, but it is tremendously helpful, nevertheless. Our counselor brings a certain neutrality and objectivity to bear on the issue that we are powerless to muster on our own.

In order for the give and take of counseling between friends and associates to work, we must have communications channels open to the left and to the right. Do your best to avoid arguments and displays of temper with your associates. Do not burn any bridges so that you cannot return to a pleasant relationship once a momentary storm passes. If for a time you alienate a peer, stand ready to apologize when you have been in the wrong. Be quick to forgive a colleague who has injured you. You do not have to call all of your peers your friends, but you should not call any of them enemies. By sharing the successes of others, you enrich the returns to them. By sharing the sorrows of others, you capture their friendship. So it is also when they reciprocate.

Your Role as Judge

Closely allied with the counseling role in human relations with your peers is the role of judge. You have three specific duties to attend to: enforcement, settling disputes, and evaluating.

Enforcement   The duty you have to enforce company policies and regulations affects your peers as well. There is an urgent need for all supervisors to be uniform both in the interpretation and in the application of these policies and regulations. You probably have experienced the unhappy situation that results when one supervisor is lenient and another is severe. Imagine a situation in which you are trying to get your workers to arrive and leave on schedule, while the supervisor in the adjacent department allows his or her people to come and go as they please. How much more difficult has this supervisor made your job? Where two managers interpret or enforce the same regulation or policy in different and conflicting ways, a wedge is driven between them. This wedge acts as a barrier to both communication and cooperation. Managers at every level must agree with and work parallel to each other if they are to act in a united and effective way.

Settling Disputes Where you find yourself at odds with a peer over an interpretation of policy or of how to enforce a rule, get together with that individual and work it out between you. Quite often, your duties overlap those of another supervisor. A meeting and a polite discussion are all that are usually required to resolve the difficulty. If you two cannot work the matter out, get together with your boss and his or hers. Do not let the conflict continue any longer than necessary. Take action as soon as you are aware that a problem exists.

Periodically you may be called upon by circumstances to serve as a peacemaker. For example, two of your associates are engaged in an argument and their emotions have taken over. As a witness to the dispute, you may be able to intervene with a calmness and logic that the others lack. Do so when you find yourself in such a situation. It does managers no good to squabble, especially in public. Workers read all kinds of things into such events. You may save a friend or associate from the embarrassment of making a fool of himself or herself.

Evaluation Study your peers for an understanding of their management techniques. All of them have their unique characteristics and methods. Hold your standards up to theirs, and see how they compare. Where you discover significant differences, make every effort to determine which is the better set to follow. In the final analysis, both your and their techniques may prove to be inferior to yet another set of standards.

Your peers make excellent working models to observe and evaluate. Try out your theories and applications on your associates, and get their reactions to them. Watch how they handle themselves in difficult as well as routine matters. Test your attitudes against theirs, and see if you can refine your viewpoints and pick up some of their methods.

Criticism When you observe a peer engaged in improper or forbidden conduct, you owe him or her a bit of friendly correction. You and your fellow supervisors are a team of managers who must not work at cross-purposes if you are to succeed. When one of your number engages in unauthorized and harmful activities, he or she hurts all other supervisors. Others, especially workers, who observe a supervisor's improprieties, draw conclusions that inevitably harm his or her reputation and yours. You are all in this together.

When a peer's actions and objectives are contrary to yours, you must confront him or her with your observations. Let him or her know, in a tactful and sincere manner, what you know. After all, if you know what he or she is up to, it is quite likely that others—including the boss—do, too. Of course, you must still discuss the matter in private. You may find more often than not that a peer is unaware that he or she is doing anything wrong and will appreciate your drawing attention to the matter.

You, in turn, must stand ready for constructive criticism yourself. We all need it occasionally and, in fact, stop growing without it. Contentment and smugness creep in, and a false sense of security takes over. We begin to believe that we are consistently right and gradually close our minds to the new and different.

The strongest kind of friendly correction you can exert is your own good example. By promoting the things in which you believe and by opposing the things you believe to be wrong, you take a stand and exhibit principles for others to see and admire.

Do not go looking for the problems and failings of others. But when you discover them, you have a duty to alert the other person. A friendly warning or a few words of counsel to let the manager know that he or she may be on thin ice are all that is called for.

We all have a tendency to cover for a friend or peer in trouble. If you do, you may gain a few temporary benefits. But in the long run, you stand to lose far more than you could ever gain. You will identify yourself as an ally of improper conduct and demonstrate wholly unacceptable attitudes for any manager to hold. You do not hold a position of power and trust in order to shield your friends from earned discipline. That would constitute an inexcusable abuse of your position. Nor should you punish; that is a superior's duty. You need not inform on a peer, since, in time, things have a way of surfacing and getting to those who should know. But do not compromise your own position of trust and personal integrity to help anyone. You will only be hurting yourself. You have too much to lose for too long.

Your Role as Spokesperson

You owe loyalty to your peers but only when they are in the right. Allegiance to someone is a precious gift, not to be given lightly. It must be earned as well as respected. Loyalty implies mutual trust and confidence. When not mutual, they cannot persist.

You should never spread a rumor about anyone. But when you hear one, it is your job as a spokesperson to refute it if you can. If you cannot, ask the other person to substantiate his or her statement. Inquire as to the source. The person will know what you are thinking—that he or she is spreading gossip. When this bit of gossip relates to a peer, let that individual know its content and its source.

When an untrue rumor pertains to you, and you view its content as serious (all attacks on your character are), defend yourself. Trace it to its originator and confront that individual with your knowledge. Control your temper, but make your point as forcefully as you feel is necessary. Then bury the incident and try not to carry a grudge. If a rumor is minor and not related to your character, let it go. You do not have the time to track down all rumors, nor should you try to do so.

Respect legitimate demands for your silence, as is the case when conversing about personal matters with a friend. Information revealed to you by a peer that pertains to him or her alone should not be a topic of conversation with others. If you reveal a secret or break a confidence, your peer is sure to find out about it. What will happen to your reputation then?

The role of spokesperson also pertains to spreading good news or praising the ideas, contributions, and accomplishments of your peers. Giving credit where it is due and expressing your appreciation for benefits received, especially in public, is a pleasant duty one manager or friend owes another.

When you receive information from a peer, such as orders or instructions, be sure that you verify its content. If you act upon it without doing so, you may be in for a shock. He or she may be passing along second-hand data and much accuracy can be lost in handling and translation. Be certain when you relay information from the boss to a peer that you preserve its original form and intent. If what you received was written, pass it along in the same format.

Finally, remember that you are also a spokesperson for your subordinates. When another supervisor interferes with them or their work, make it clear to the other person that you resent the interference. Such an action challenges your authority. You must shield your subordinates and yourself from outside interference and conflicting orders or instructions.

Competition with Your Peers

Keep in mind that, although you should maintain good relations with your peers and develop cooperation with them (as suggested in chapter 6), you are still in competition with them. In much the same manner as a professional athlete, you have to maintain a balance between individual displays of talent and ability and the need for team play. All great athletes achieve their greatness in this way. You must be willing to take a back seat now and then and let another manager's talents come through. If you hog the ball, you do so at the expense of team play, and eventually you will find that the ball stops coming your way.

Just remember that your reputation and performance evaluation are primarily in your subordinates' hands. Only secondarily do your peers play a part. If you are wise, that part is yours to write, produce, and direct. You have the ability to influence it through your human relations efforts and through interactions with your peers.

The best way to maintain good human relations is to develop yourself into the best person and manager you have the potential to become. You will gain both rational and charismatic power in so doing, which will draw people to you. In giving what you have and drawing upon what others have to give, you will build bonds of friendship and strengthen your reputation with your peers.

Use the checklist shown in Exhibit 8.4 as a guide to evaluate your human relations efforts in dealing with your peers. Any *rarely* responses indicate a need to make an adjustment.

Getting Along with Your Boss

Before we get into specifics about your relations with your boss, a few words are in order about your boss: how your boss's job resembles yours, and how it differs from yours.

Since you are a supervisor, your boss is a middle manager. He or she is accountable for your actions. Your boss is similar to you in that he or she is both a follower and a staff or line manager. He or she executes all the functions of management and is evaluated on the basis of his or her subordinates' performances. Your boss, like yourself, must develop sound working relationships with subordinates, peers, and superiors. He or she probably served an apprenticeship as a supervisor, so you can probably count on him or her to understand your situation.

When compared to a supervisor, however, a middle manager has more differences than similarities. As the following list shows, your boss has a number of duties and interests that are unlike yours:

1. Directs the work of other managers
2. Exhibits strongly promanagement attitudes
3. Spends more time on planning than on any other function
4. Spends less time with subordinates
5. Spends more time with peers and superiors
6. Is more of an adviser than a director
7. Has more freedom of action and flexibility
8. Has more information and a broader perspective

	Usually	Rarely*
1. I carry my own weight.	——	——
2. I lend a hand when and where needed.	——	——
3. I have the best interests of my peers in mind.	——	——
4. I am loyal to my peers.	——	——
5. I respect the privacy of things told to me in confidence.	——	——
6. I refrain from engaging in negative gossip.	——	——
7. I share my expertise and experiences with peers.	——	——
8. I have earned the respect of peers.	——	——
9. I show my peers common courtesies and respect.	——	——
10. I share information with peers.	——	——
11. I avoid passing the buck.	——	——
12. I am a team player.	——	——
13. I defend my peers' actions in their absence.	——	——
14. I do not bear any grudges.	——	——
15. I try to avoid making any enemies.	——	——

Exhibit 8.4   A short quiz to help you evaluate how well you are playing your human relations roles with peers.

*Any "rarely" responses indicate a need to improve.

9. Is less concerned with procedures and practices (tactics) and more concerned with planning and programs (strategy)

10. Is more concerned with tomorrow than with today

11. Is more concerned with the causes of management actions than with their effects

As to the last item on this list, a supervisor and his or her subordinates often evaluate a management decision on the basis of its effect or impact on them. This is quite natural and to be expected: what affects your people adversely or is the cause of gripes or worse is always of great concern to you. But the way you react to management decisions reflects upon you and your potential to take the duties of a high position.

Suppose that higher management has recently reduced the plant budget for overtime. This decision is translated at your level into less overtime for the department and less income for the workers. Your people see this decision as it affects them—as a reduction in their potential earnings. If you and they have grown dependent on overtime or see it as necessary to current operations, your section may be in for some trouble. Your boss was in on the initial decision. He or she knows the reasons for it and the management objectives it was designed to achieve. For instance, a decision to reduce overtime expenses may conserve income, allow your company to price its line more competitively, and reduce overall expenses. Your boss is concerned with these matters because they affect him or her more directly than your problems do. The boss sees all of these objectives as being logical and sound and supports them. Once the reasons behind a decision are known to you, you should support the decision as strongly as your boss does. Give what facts you can to your subordinates to soften the blow. Emphasize that the conservation of income may prevent layoffs and save jobs. You must be flexible enough to meet rapidly changing situations such as this. Add to this flexibility a readiness to adjust to situations as they are, not as you would like them to be.

Your Boss's Expectations

Primarily, most middle managers expect their subordinate managers to be loyal followers. Your boss, like yourself, needs the respect and support of subordinates. He or she must be able to count on your willingness and ability to enforce company policies and standards. He or she is relying on you to carry out decisions with the proper attitude. You must not let him or her down. In the eyes of your subordinates, the boss's reputation is as important to them as your own. They have a right to believe that they have good leadership—that you and your boss consistently exercise good judgment. Do not let any action or innuendo on your part jeopardize your boss's reputation. Take the short quiz in Exhibit 8.5 to assess your attitudes toward management. If you can honestly answer *yes* to each question, your attitudes are strongly promanagement, as they should be. When you are promoted to supervisor, you join management's team.

Your boss expects you to get along well with your peers and with the company's various staff specialists as well as with your subordinates. If you are able to resolve your disputes on your own, without arguments and displays of temper, you are demonstrating resourcefulness. By developing and maintaining a cooperative spirit, you open the channels through which aid and advice will flow.

Initiative is an extremely important characteristic for any manager to possess. Are you the kind of manager who waits for orders or instructions before acting? Do you need something to be in writing before you implement a change? If you do, you lack this essential quality. We are not talking here about assuming anything: that is always a dangerous practice. But when you have the authority to act in a situation and you know what must be done, you must not be afraid to respond. Unless you are completely at a loss as to what you should do, you should act. You will not always be right or pick the best method, but you will not appear

Questions	**Yes**	**No**
1. In a labor dispute, do I take management's side?	___	___
2. Do I believe in my company, its policies, programs, and products?	___	___
3. When I disagree with a decision from higher management, do I implement it, hide my feelings from my subordinates, and relay my displeasure to those who can change things?	___	___
4. Do I defend management and managers when they are unjustly attacked?	___	___
5. Do I accept accountability for the actions of my subordinates?	___	___
6. Do I avoid attempts to cover up or shield my subordinates or peers from discipline they have earned?	___	___
7. Do I consider myself a contributing member of management's team?	___	___
8. Do I routinely exhibit respect and loyalty to my superiors?	___	___
9. Do I demand and encourage the best from my people?	___	___
10. Do I evaluate my subordinates fairly and objectively?	___	___

Exhibit 8.5 **A short quiz to assess whether your attitudes are strongly pro-management or not.**

paralyzed either. If you wish to make progress, you must be able to perceive what is needed and, when you have the power, see that the need is satisfied. Don't forget that, besides your boss, your peers and the company's staff specialists stand ready to help.

Finally, your boss expects you to keep him or her informed. Share your knowledge about essential operations with your boss. Nothing can injure you quite as effectively as for the boss to be surprised—to find out about something secondhand. The boss hates surprises where you and your people are concerned. You can make your boss look awfully stupid if you fail in your duty to keep him or her abreast of developments. Share what information you have with the boss, without betraying any confidences.

Winning Your Boss's Confidence

If you meet your superior's expectations, you are well on your way toward gaining his or her confidence. In addition, try to learn from your mistakes. Each error you make has a lesson or two for you. Study your errors to avoid repeating them. Whatever else you do that demonstrates an effort at self-development should be brought to your boss's attention. The courses you take in school and recent articles or books you have read that have been helpful in your work are all worthy topics of conversation with your boss.

Consider the following five courses of action. See if you agree with the thousands before you who have tried them and found them to be of great benefit.

Finding a Better Way

Long ago, as an undergraduate student in management, I learned four magic words on methods improvement that have served me and my students well:

combine

eliminate

rearrange

simplify

When you look at a plan, program, procedure, or practice with these words in mind, you have an essential tool for evaluating them. Nothing is as valuable on your personnel record as the initiation and discovery of a better way to do something. The time, effort, and money that can be saved are important, but the effect on your reputation and career is even more important. Just be certain that the idea is yours before you take credit for it. Where help was received, credit should be given to that individual.

As a manager, you should give methods improvement a high priority. No matter how smoothly an operation is running, there is usually room for improvement. Turn your attention to the most costly operations first. That is where you stand to realize the greatest savings. Then systematically work your way through the rest of your operations. Do not keep your successes to yourself. Share them with your peers and superiors. Others can profit from your innovations.

Keeping Your Promises

A "can do" attitude is great if you really can do what you promise. Before making a promise, be as certain as possible of the resources at your disposal and the limits on your operations. If, in your best judgment, you have what it will take to get the job done, commit yourself and your people to the endeavor. It is better to be a little bold than to be too cautious. If circumstances change dramatically for reasons beyond your ability to foresee, let your boss know. He or she will understand, and adjustments can be made. If you should have known about or suspected the changes, your reputation will suffer. Try to avoid going out on a limb that is too weak to support you.

Speaking Positively or Not at All

Whatever the topic of conversation and wherever it takes place, be sure that what you say is positive. There is a temptation to engage in gripe sessions and to put the other person down. Such displays are clearly negative and completely without redeeming qualities. If your gripe is justified, reveal it to those who can act upon it. If the person you wish to criticize is a subordinate, approach him or her in private and keep it constructive. No one, especially not a boss, benefits from associating with a person who is always negative. Few activities are as futile as gripe sessions. Names are dropped and things are said that all too often you later wish you could retract or forget. If you have nothing of a positive nature to say, you are better off saying nothing.

Constructive criticism, whether of an individual or of an idea, is not negative, and you are perfectly right to engage in it as long as the environment is correct. When an argument is put forth that favors a course of action and you see a disadvantage to it, you must air that point if the advocate of the proposal fails to do so. When the boss or anyone else puts forth a proposal in your presence, he or she wants your honest reactions. Loyalty demands that you do your best to prevent a person from making a mistake or suffering some humiliation, when and where you can. Do not refuse a subordinate, a peer, or a superior such aid when you have it to give.

Taking a Position

You are a thinking human being and a member of management's team. But you must be a contributing member—one who carries his or her own weight and stands ready to help teammates. If you want the respect of others, you must have convictions. These convictions or beliefs tell others what you are and where you stand. Your character and principles are demonstrated when you take a stand on an issue. Before you do, however, make sure that you think it through and anticipate the possible drawbacks, as well as your supportive arguments. Then prepare your defense.

When you take your stand and find it untenable, do not be reluctant to yield to superior forces. Bullheadedness is not a quality that endears you to anyone. Be reasonable. You want to be thought of as a person of principle—as a man or woman who thinks things through and fights for what he or she believes in. The corollary to this is equally important: you must oppose things you believe to be improper or wrong.

Involving Your Boss in Major Decisions

Just as you stand ready to help a subordinate or peer with a problem, your boss stands ready to help you. The boss's time is too valuable to be expended on trivial matters, so reserve your requests for assistance to the critical items.

Most middle managers have regular meetings for both individual and group discussions. Others maintain an open-door policy, relying upon their subordinates to bring in their problems. You should know and adjust to your boss's approach.

When you have a problem with which you have wrestled but to which you have no certain solution, set up a meeting with your boss, explaining in advance what you wish to discuss. Assemble your research and facts. Construct a list of alternatives you have considered. Then be sure to report to the meeting on time.

During the meeting, follow the advice of the catchword KISS (*Keep it Short and Simple*). You want the maximum benefits from the shortest possible time. What the boss wants most is to see that you have considered the matter and given it your best effort. He or she will not make your decisions for you, except when you have reached an impasse. Even then, most bosses only offer suggestions and direct your attention to additional items you may have overlooked. That method may be a little frustrating, but the learning experience is invaluable to you.

Each contact you have with your boss should be as professional as you can make it. Be yourself, but be prepared.

Obtaining Some of Your Boss's Authority

It is your job to know yourself well and to seek self-improvement. It is your task through human relations to know and approach your subordinates, peers, and superiors as individuals. Fundamental to your relationship with your boss is getting to know him or her well—his or her needs and ambitions, strengths and weaknesses. You can learn from a strong boss. You may be able to help a weak one.

The boss, like you, is probably looking for subordinates who can assume time-consuming details and routine tasks. By delegating them, the boss creates time for more important tasks—the ones he or she alone must tackle. Your boss is also gaining time to devote to taking on a larger portion of his or her boss's duties, thus training for advancement. So it goes from supervisor to chief executive. Through delegation, each trains another. While providing for a subordinate's growth and progress, the boss helps to ensure his or her own advancement. A manager who has not trained a subordinate to move up may be unable to move up. The manager who will not grow or help others grow is generally not a manager for long. His or her lack of mobility acts as a ceiling on those with ambition and ability below. A manager's failure to grow may mean the loss by the company of promising young talent.

When you have proved to your boss that you are worthy of his or her respect and confidence, the delegation of duties to you will begin. You will get details and routine tasks at first. If you handle them well, you can look forward to increased responsibilities, with the challenges they represent. The increased duties may become yours permanently, enlarging your job description and serving as justification for increases in pay and status, and a possible change in title.

If your boss is reluctant to delegate, you should urge him or her to do so. First you must free yourself from your details and routines, in order to make time available. Then go to your boss with time on your hands and a plea for additional duties. If you have your eye on specifics, let the boss know what they are and why you feel qualified to take them. Here again, take a stand; then sell it and defend it. You may not be successful at first; old habits die slowly. But you have planted a seed, and a good manager will not let it die. Your boss will be disturbed by your idleness and impressed by your initiative. If you persist, the boss will respond.

Do not assume any of your boss's duties or anyone else's without consultation. There is a tendency for a bright and eager young supervisor to spot something that needs doing and do it. This is fine as long as you have jurisdiction over the matter. But when the duty you perform belongs to another, you are guilty of grabbing power from that person. This will be interpreted to your disadvantage. After all, how would you react if a peer or subordinate took on your responsibilities without first consulting you?

Do not get yourself into a position where your boss becomes too dependent on you. If the boss views you as indispensable, he or she may consciously or unconsciously restrict your chances for advancement. He or she will fear your loss, through promotion or transfer, and the corresponding upsetting of the status quo this may represent. Your best defense is to train a successor. When the opportunity arises and the time is right, you can then point to a subordinate with pride and confidence as your logical and well-trained successor.

Your Expectations of Your Boss

Besides respect and loyalty—which are essential prerequisites for a working relationship—your boss should provide you with the following:

- Constructive criticism
- Fair evaluations
- Essential guidance
- A constant flow of necessary information
- Recognition for jobs well done
- An appropriate management style
- Training for growth and development
- A good example

Where one or more of these items is lacking, look first at yourself for the cause. Something in you or your performance may be missing. If you do not give respect or loyalty, you have none coming. If you do not respond well to criticism, you may not receive it. If you do not think your boss's evaluations of your performance are fair, why did you accept them without protest? You may not be receiving guidance because you have not asked for any. Is the guidance you seek really essential? If you do not get information, maybe it is because you cannot keep a secret or have no need to know. If no recognition is due you, you will not receive any. Do not expect recognition for simply doing your job. If your boss's management style with you is not to your liking, have you discussed it with him or her? If your boss will not delegate, have you enough time to take on the additional duties? Have you asked your boss for more things to do?

You may find, as many management students do, that the more you learn about management principles and practices, the more critical of people in authority you become. If this is happening to you, do not be alarmed. You are experiencing what all children growing up experience: the realization that the adult who occupies a position of trust and authority is really just a human being. As children realize this, they must search for a new understanding and relationship with their parents. No longer are children content with blind obedience; no longer can they accept instructions or orders without knowing the why behind them. They are becoming critical and questioning and are now armed with standards on which to base their questions and criticism.

The beauty of all this is that you will now know when something goes wrong and why. How you react to your new knowledge and act upon it determines whether you remain always a freshman or become a senior and graduate. Knowledge is power, and power needs controls on its use. As you are maturing, you will discover flaws where you saw none before. An inadequate manager often provides a better learning situation than a real professional does. When things run smoothly, you often do not know why they do. But when things go sour, you have a chance to ask and determine why. That goes for your mistakes as well as for those of the boss. It is through your analysis of your boss's shortcomings that you can prevent them from plaguing your own efforts. Most of the cases in this book (and in every other management text) portray managers with flaws and inadequacies for just this reason.

According to a recent study by professors and psychologists Robert Hogan and John Morrison of the University of Tulsa, the average subordinate thinks that managers he or she works with are competent between 60 and 75 percent of the time. In another study done by

---

1. I think my boss really cares about me and my progress because:

   _____

   _____

   _____

2. I think my boss is (pick one or more)

   a. hardworking ____ b. compassionate ____ c. a good role model ____
   d. a good decision maker ____ e. a good planner ____ f. fair ____
   g. a team player ____ h. competent ____ i. enthusiastic ____
   j. other (please specify) _____

3. The thing that really "bugs" me about my boss is:

   _____

   _____

4. The one thing I need from my boss and am *not* getting is:

   _____

5. If I were in my boss's job, I would do the following things differently:

   _____

   _____

6. The lessons I have learned by studying my boss are:

   _____

   _____

   _____

   _____

Now, what are you going to do about all this?

Exhibit 8.6   **Rate your boss. Photocopy this evaluation form and see how you feel toward your present boss.**

Personnel Decisions Inc. of Minneapolis, a human resource consulting firm, 56 percent of the 800 people surveyed thought their bosses were "top-notch," while only 8 percent thought that their bosses treated them unfairly.[3]

Exhibit 8.6 is a short evaluation form you can use to rate your boss. Only you can decide if you want to keep the results of your rating confidential.

Instant Replay

1. Human relations involves the development and maintenance of sound on-the-job relationships with subordinates, peers, and superiors.

2. Building sound human relationships with subordinates and peers requires you to play four fundamental roles: educator, counselor, judge, and spokesperson.

3. As an educator, you share your knowledge, skills, and experiences with others.

4. As a counselor, you provide advice, service, and a sympathetic and empathetic ear.

5. As a judge, you evaluate performances of subordinates, enforce company and departmental rules and standards, settle disputes, and dispense justice.

6. You win your boss's respect and confidence by meeting his or her expectations of you and by playing your role as it has been prescribed.

7. You learn your boss's job by creating time in which to execute the boss's tasks. Just as you train your replacement through delegation of your formal authority, so too does your boss train his or her replacement.

Glossary

Counselor   the human relations role in which a supervisor is an adviser and director to subordinates.

Educator   the human relations role in which the supervisor is a builder of skills and a developer of potentials in subordinates.

Human relations   the development and maintenance of sound on-the-job relationships (educator, counselor, judge, spokesperson) with subordinates, peers, and superiors.

Judge   the human relations role in which the supervisor enforces company policies and departmental rules and procedures, evaluates subordinates' performances, settles disputes, and dispenses justice.

Peer a person with the same level of formal authority and status in the organizational hierarchy as you.

Spokesperson the human relations role through which a supervisor represents management's views to workers and subordinates' views to management.

Questions for Class Discussion

1. Can you define this chapter's key terms?
2. What are the five major purposes of human relations?
3. How should a supervisor play the four basic human relations roles with subordinates? With peers?
4. How is a middle manager's job different from a supervisor's?
5. What is involved in creating and maintaining a good working relationship with one's boss?

Incident

Purpose To familiarize you with how counseling interviews are conducted by the trained, professional counselors at your school or institution.

Your Task Make an appointment with a professional counselor at your school or institution. The subject for discussion and investigation may be anything you wish it to be (what courses to take next, what career opportunities exist in your chosen specialty, where to transfer your credits, and so on). Evaluate the interview using the following criteria, and report your experiences to your class in writing or in person, as you or your instructor decides.

Criteria

1. The interview started on time.

   _____

   _____

   _____

2. There were no serious interruptions or distractions.

   _____

   _____

   _____

3. You had the counselor's undivided attention.

   _____

_____

_____

4. The counselor seemed to have your best interests at heart.

_____

_____

_____

5. The interview was conducted in private, out of earshot of outsiders.

_____

_____

_____

6. The counselor made you feel relaxed and at ease.

_____

_____

_____

7. The counselor did not tell you what to do but suggested courses of action.

_____

_____

_____

8. The counselor did not interrupt you when you were speaking.

_____

_____

_____

9. The counselor treated you with respect and common courtesies.

_____

_____

_____

10. The counselor made a written record of the session with notes and other records.

_____

_____

_____

11. You left the interview with more information and ideas than when you entered it.

12. You definitely feel that the counselor knew what he or she was talking about.

13. You definitely feel that the interview was constructive and helpful to you.

Case Problem 8.1 Looking Ahead

As the last of his subordinates said goodnight, Mike took pencil in hand and began to think about next week. He started with a mental review of the completed projects and then turned his attention to the unfinished ones. Starting with Monday's column, he began to block out time for unfinished business. After about thirty minutes of intense thought and a careful review of his notes, Mike grabbed his coat, turned off the shop lights, and left for the day. Here is what his notes showed for Monday (all first names mentioned belong to Mike's subordinates; all surnames belong to other managers):

Monday:

1. Work on Henry's personal problem—see at 8 A.M.
2. Check on Suzie's progress with the backlog of shipments. 8:30 to 9:00 A.M.
3. Talk with the old man about late data—got to get the info from him faster to meet reporting deadlines. 9:30 to 9:45 A.M.
4. Meet with Wilson to coordinate enforcement of safety procedures—he isn't enforcing—setting a bad example. 10 to 11 A.M.
5. Meet Harry for six-month review—notes in file. 11 to 11:30 A.M.
6. Lunch with Perkins from Personnel—new job description for machinist 2 classification. 11:45 to 12:30 P.M.
7. Update shipping reports 12:30 to 1:30 P.M.
8. Introduce Billy to new maintenance procedures on no. 14—maintenance due by Tuesday P.M. 1:45 to 2:15 P.M.
9. Check with payroll about Friday overtime. 2:15 to 3:00 P.M.
10. Place orders for restocking—do with Al and Bert so they know procedures. Pick one for the task next week. 3:00 to 5:00 P.M.

Questions

1. Which of the items on Mike's list affect his relations with subordinates? Which role will he likely play with each subordinate?
2. Which of the items on Mike's list affect relations with peers? Which human relations role will he likely play with each peer mentioned?
3. Which of the items relate to staff specialists?
4. Which of the items relate to Mike's relations with his boss?

Case Problem 8.2   Just Friends

The Small Cleaners on Oak Street is one of three family-owned outlets in Mayfield, a town of thirty thousand people. Sylvia Halpern, age thirty-eight, has recently been promoted to supervise the operations of the third and newest branch outlet. Although she has received no formal academic or on-the-job training as a supervisor, she has been working in a Small Cleaners branch for nearly four years and has had a good boss, Mary Ritchards, as a model.

Since her promotion four weeks ago, Sylvia has had little difficulty with paperwork or customer relations. She has gone out of her way to be friendly to the customers and to her three subordinates. Al, the pressman, Cindy, and Beverly are all good people who know their jobs. In fact, the owner, Mr. Small, assembled the work force for the third branch outlet by taking the best people he had in the other two branches.

Sylvia has invited her subordinates to a small cocktail party at her home, has taken them to lunch on two occasions, and is trying to stimulate interest among them to compete in bowling matches with the other two outlets. So far, however, her subordinates have shown little interest in such a team. Sylvia wants desperately to be more than a boss to her subordinates—she wants to be their friend as well.

Two weeks ago Al declined to join Sylvia, Cindy and Beverly for lunch. Since then, Sylvia has noticed that Al, who was formerly a gregarious, cheerful guy, has become withdrawn. He rarely smiles and now speaks only when he is spoken to. He no longer joins in the friendly banter that has been a part of the Oak Street store from the first day it opened. Al is married, twenty-five years old, and the father of two children. Beverly is a good-natured soul with lots of interests outside the business. She and Sylvia were best friends when they worked together in the Fairfax Street store, and they have kept their friendship alive. Since neither Sylvia nor Beverly is married, they have time to share. Both like many of the same things, and their favorite activity is to go out to dinner and a show. Sylvia would like to model her relationship with Cindy after her relationship with Beverly.

Cindy, age twenty-two, is currently enrolled in a community college, where she is taking business courses. She is not quite certain what major she wants to pursue, but she seems to favor accounting. Cindy gets along with Beverly and Sylvia but cannot stand Al. It seems that every time they are together, they exchange some unpleasant words.

Cindy also has trouble relating to the customers. On the few occasions when she has filled in for Beverly, she has been awkward with people and less than cordial. She has trouble operating the new electronic cash register and, although Sylvia has tried to explain its operation, Cindy has managed to misring sales more often than not. She hates making out a separate receipt for customers. As she has stated more than once, "Why can't they be satisfied with a cash register receipt? It carries the same information."

Sylvia's old boss, Mary Ritchards, has been

a good friend and a source of counsel to her. She had a basic maxim that she has followed in all her relations with her subordinates: "Treat them like good friends, and everything else will take care of itself!" It certainly seemed to be good advice; Sylvia, who idolized Mary, was certain that her friendship with Mary didn't hurt her when Mr. Small was looking around for a supervisor for the Oak Street store. Sylvia has tried very hard to gain the friendship of her subordinates but so far has been unable to do so with Cindy and Al. Perhaps, she thinks, they just need more time to adjust to the new situation. After all, they have only been working together as a team for a month.

Questions

1. What human-relations roles does Sylvia need to carry out with Al? With Cindy? With Beverly? How should each be executed?
2. Do you think friendship with subordinates is an ideal to be sought by a supervisor? Why?
3. Would Sylvia's old boss approve of what she is trying to do? Why?
4. Is it possible to be a friend with every subordinate you supervise? Why or why not?
5. What barriers exist that seem to prohibit friendship from forming between Sylvia and Al? Between Sylvia and Cindy?

Notes   1. A. A. Imberman, "Why Are Most Foreman Training Courses a Failure?" *Bedding* 96 #6 (July 1969): 40–41.
2. *Training and Coaching Techniques* (East Lansing, Mich.: Educational Institute of the American Hotel & Motel Association, 1976), 75.
3. L. A. Winokur, "Well, They Say There Are Lies, Damn Lies, Statistics and Bosses," *The Wall Street Journal* (January 10, 1991): B1.

Suggested Readings

Apgar, Toni, ed. *Mastering Office Politics*. New York: National Institute of Business Management, Inc., 1988.

DuBrin, Andrew. *Winning Office Politics*. Englewood Cliffs, N.J.: Prentice-Hall, 1990.

Fader, Shirley Sloan. "What Your Boss Wants You to Know." *Business Week Careers* (October 1985): 43–45.

Josefowitz, Natasha. *You're the Boss!* New York: Warner Books, 1985.

Kennedy, Marilyn Moats. "How to Manage Your New Boss." *Business Week Careers* (April 1987): 93–95.

Quick, Thomas L. *Inspiring People at Work*. New York: Executive Enterprises, 1986.

Robbins, Stephen P. *Training in Interpersonal Skills*. Englewood Cliffs, N.J.: Prentice Hall, 1989.

Schaffer, Robert H. "Demand Better Results—and Get Them." *Harvard Business Review* (March–April 1991): 142–149.

9 Supervising Groups

Outline

Objectives

After reading and discussing this chapter, you should be able to do the following:

1 Define this chapter's key terms.
2 List and briefly explain the forces that shape a group's personality.
3 Describe the duties of a meeting's chairperson before, during, and after a group problem-solving session.
4 Describe the duties of a group's members before, during, and after a group problem-solving session.
5 List and briefly describe the group-serving and self-serving roles played by members of a group problem-solving session.
6 List the three types of cliques, and give an example of each.
7 Describe how group behavior can be affected by internal group competition—what happens to the winning side and what happens to the losing side.

Key Terms

clique	problem-solving meeting
formal group	synergy
group	syntality
informal group	

Introduction

Group
Two or more people who are consciously aware of one another, who consider themselves to be a functioning unit, and who share in a quest for common goals or benefits

Each individual has a personality that undergoes constant change through exposure to his or her environment and to new experiences. When two or more dynamic people interact with one another, the process of change in each of them is accelerated. The coming together of two or more people for the purpose of achieving or obtaining some mutual goal or benefit is the basis for the formation of what we shall call a *group*.

More specifically, a **group** is two or more people who are consciously aware of one another, who consider themselves to be a functioning unit, and who share in a quest to achieve one or more goals or obtain some common benefit. When we say that the members are "aware" of each other, we mean that they know something about each other, are clear about why they are together, and recognize the need to cooperate.

Two basic kinds of groups exist in organizations: the formal group that is created by management and the informal group created by the members of the organization. This latter type of group is formed primarily for social purposes and allows its members to congregate with others who share their values and interests. As a supervisor, you must learn to work with both kinds of groups.

Throughout American factories and offices, self-managing work teams have been created and are having a tremendous impact on the quality and productivity of their organizations' output. The value of such teams is flexibility for management and job enrichment and motivation to excel for team members. The role of the supervisor is changing because of the team structure. Supervisors may be elected members of such teams, serving on a rotating basis, or they may become more of a coach than a traditional manager. This chapter focuses on how groups form and how you can effectively manage and get along with groups at work.

Collective Entrepreneurship

Modern companies that have been able to compete successfully in today's economic environment both at home and abroad have one major thing in common: they have managed to create a team spirit in their employees that translates into high levels of innovation, adaptability, and financial success. Employees at all levels come to believe in common goals and in united efforts to achieve them. Talent and energy then are pooled into what author Robert Reich has labeled *collective entrepreneurship*.[1]

The term *collective entrepreneurship* is derived from the fact that the companies using it no longer focus on one person—the founder or the top executive—as a guiding light. Employees feel a real partnership and commitment to the company's future because they feel that they are the company. Rewards and praise flow to teams of employees, not to individuals. When hard times arrive, burdens are shared by all the employees, and great efforts are made to keep employees on, not to lay them off. Technology is looked upon as a means to aid workers and managers, to cut routine, and to give them more opportunities to use their imaginations and insights for their company.[2]

For workers, collective entrepreneurship means "accepting flexible job classifications and work rules; agreeing to wage rates linked to profits and productivity improvements; and generally taking greater responsibility for the soundness and efficiency of the enterprise."[3] For managers, collective entrepreneurship means "continually retraining workers for more complex tasks; automating in ways that cut routine tasks and enhance worker flexibility and creativity; diffusing responsibility for innovation; taking seriously labor's concern for job security; and giving workers a stake in improved productivity through profit linked bonuses and stock plans."[4]

Collective entrepreneurship relies heavily on integrating individual skills into groups:

> Over time, as group members work through various problems and approaches, they learn about each others' abilities. They learn how they can help one another perform better, what each can contribute to a particular project, how they can best take advantage of one another's experience. . . . Coordination and communication replace command and control. Consequently, there are few middle-level managers and only modest differences in status and income of senior managers and junior employees.[5]

The Personality of Groups

A group, like the people who compose it, has a personality as unique and subject to change as any individual's. The group's personality is partially a composite of the personalities of its members. We say "partially" because a group is always something more than the sum of its parts. That something more comes about because of the interaction of group members, which creates energy and qualities that may not be possessed by any of the group members or by a majority of them. An example would be a basic training group in the military. Individually, its members may not have the desire or the will to excel and may not know their capabilities. But in group situations, the pressure to conform and the feeling that, "If they can do it, so can I" will dominate. If twenty men were dispatched on a twenty-mile hike, one at a time at intervals of ten minutes, very few (if any) would complete the march. When all twenty men embark on the hike together, all the men will finish, even if their buddies have to carry some of them. Men in combat units often exhibit tremendous courage that none of them would exhibit without the support of and the commitment to their comrades.

There is a term for this two-plus-two-equals-five-or-more quality that many groups seem to possess: **synergy** (pronounced *sin-er-jee*). Common table salt is a chemical combination of two poisons—sodium and chlo-

Synergy
Cooperative action or force of two or more elements pulling together that yields a result greater than the sum of the results that could be achieved separately by the elements

rine. Alone they are dangerous; together they are beneficial and take on beneficial properties that neither has alone. It has been common knowledge for about a century that two horses can pull more than the combined loads each is capable of pulling alone. A team of twelve horses can pull more than twice the load that a team of eight can pull.

The term *synergy* applies to any combined operation or action; thus it can be either positive or negative. Satisfied groups or group members can exhibit greater positive action or forces for change than the individuals within the group could do on their own.

Syntality

Syntality
A group's "personality"—what makes it unique

Syntality is used by social scientists to mean "for a group what personality does for the individual."[6] Groups develop a syntality through their exposure to the interactions of their members, through the pressures exerted on them, through their experiences, through their successes and failures, and through their commitments to causes or goals. Groups, like people, can be lazy, hostile, or enthusiastic. As a group leader you need to assess your group's syntality, in order to determine its strengths and weaknesses; then you must provide the kind of leadership it needs at any given time.

One question you can use to assess your group's syntality is: "To what extent does the group work with me to achieve objectives?" A hostile group is one that actively or passively opposes your efforts to achieve group goals. "A lazy group is one with insufficient motivation and lack of drive in assisting you to reach designated goals. An enthusiastic group is one that shares your interest in achieving group goals."[7]

If your group is not enthusiastic, ask yourself what it needs (lacks). What is causing it to be lazy or hostile? Possible answers include the following:

- *Inexperience*—the group is too new, the members unfamiliar with procedures and with each other
- *Lack of training*—individuals lack the individual expertise and skill levels required for solid performances
- *Lack of discipline*—you lack the power or authority to keep them on target or in line
- *Lack of proper guidelines*—the goals are unclear, and the authority limits are not understood
- *Existence of a problem member*—one or more persons in the group tend to be disruptive, uncooperative, at odds with the others
- *Existence of a problem team leader*—the leader seems to be reluc-

tant to let the team perform, lacks skills needed to guide the team, or feels uncomfortable in the role of coach and facilitator of the team

Once you have identified what is missing, you can begin to supply the deficiencies. Keep in mind that people who are being asked to work in groups for the first time will have the most difficulties—supervisors included. Moreover, "the behavior of individuals is affected by the character of the group to which they belong."[8]

Some groups are quite strong and forceful, achieving what they set out to get. Other groups may be weak, lacking the leadership or the will to achieve. The syntality the group exhibits is most directly influenced by the personalities of the stronger members. The strongest member will usually emerge as the leader of the group, or at least as its spokesperson. The strength we mention here is primarily intellectual, and the force is primarily that of each person's will and drive.

It is just as difficult to comprehend a group's syntality as it is to understand an individual's personality. Since we all work in groups of one kind or another, we need to study the behavior of people in groups and the effects of group membership on both ourselves and those we supervise. Attempting to observe and analyze these effects is quite properly a manager's job. You must begin to see your people as individuals who are also group members and therefore subjected to forces that accelerate change in them. This makes your task of knowing each one a little more difficult.

As you might imagine, there are countless groups of many different sizes and descriptions. For our purpose, however, we shall classify groups as either *formal* or *informal*.

Defining Formal Groups

Formal group
Two or more people who come together by management decision to achieve specific goals

A **formal group** may be defined as two or more people who come together by management decision to achieve specific goals. All formal groups are results of the organizing function, through which people are assigned to different tasks and task units. In most cases we are placed in formal groups by some higher authority outside or at the head of the group. Your company, your department, your shift, and the various management committees are but a few of the many formal groups you encounter each day.

Any individual, especially a manager, may belong to more than one formal group simultaneously. For instance, you are an employee of a com-

NEWS
You Can Use

On Friday, March 8, 1991, General H. Norman Schwarzkopf bid farewell to departing troops in Saudi Arabia. What follows are excerpts from that event in the general's own words.

"It's a great day to be a soldier! Big Red One, First Team, Old Iron Sides, Spear Head, Hell on Wheels Platoon, Jay Hawk Patrol: Today you're going home. You're going home to Ft. Riley, Kan., you're going home to Ft. Hood, Texas, you're going home to locations all over Germany. Your country, your countrymen, your wives, your children and your loved ones are all there waiting for you.

"You're all going home as part of the symbolic force of all the soldiers, of all sailors, of all the airmen, all the Marines, all the Coast Guard, all the National Guard, all the reserves, all who took part in Operation Desert Shield and Desert Storm. And your comrades in arms will be following you. . . .

"I can hear the war stories now. Over Lone Star beer, over Colorado Kool-Aid, over some great German beer, a bottle of wine or two and what you drink the most: that Diet Pepsi and Coca-Cola. I know what those war stories are going to be, what glorious stories they are going to be.

"Valiant charges by courageous men over 250 kilometers of enemy territory, along with a force of over 1,500 tanks, almost 250 attack helicopters, over 48,500 pieces of military equipment, moving around, behind and into the enemy and totally breaking his back and defeating him in 100 hours. It's a war story worth telling, and every one of you deserve to tell it.

"I ask all of you when you tell that story, don't forget to tell the whole story. Don't forget to mention the great Air Force that prepared the way for you and was overhead the entire time you fought. Don't forget the great Navy pilots that were there, and the great ships that were

pany, working in a particular functional division and within a specific department. You are a member, therefore, of three formal groups at least. If you serve on a committee, you belong to a fourth formal group.

Formal groups may be temporary or permanent in nature. An ad hoc committee—one set up to solve a particular problem and dissolved when the solution is determined—is an example of a temporary formal group. Most formal groups in your company are permanent, although even whole divisions can be dissolved or merged into others on occasion, as the needs of the business may dictate.

Every formal group has a leader. The heads of most formal groups are managers who have been installed for just that purpose. The leader of a committee may be elected or appointed. Either way, the formal leader has the formal authority of the position at his or her disposal.

at sea that embargoed and kept the ammunition out of the hands of the enemy.

"And don't ever forget to say that the First Tank Division of the United Kingdom was protecting your right flank. And don't ever forget to say there was an Egyptian corps protecting their right flank and there was an Arab task force of Saudi Arabians protecting their right flank. And two divisions of Marines out there making a hard push into Kuwait City with a fine Saudi Arabian force protecting their flank.

"And don't ever forget to say in your story there were Kuwaitis, Omanis, French Foreign Legion protecting our right flank, with Egyptian forces involved, because you were part of the great coalition—the great coalition of forces determined not to let a petty dictator, no matter what size his army, no matter how many tanks he had, no matter how many men he had armed—despite the fact you were badly outnumbered, you were determined to show a petty dictator that they just can't get away with bullying his neighbors and taking what they want because they think they are so tough. . . .

"So hopefully you'll tell that war story with a lot of pride in yourselves, but don't forget to make sure that everyone understands that we did it as part of a team. We did it as part of a joint team, as part of an international team. We all did it together, we all paid the price, we all shared in the victory. . . .

"It's hard for me to put into words how proud I am of you, how proud I have been to be the commander of this war. I'm proud of you, your country's proud of you, and the world's proud of you.

"God bless you, and Godspeed for your trip home, and God bless America!"

(Source: "Schwarzkopf Offers a Few Things to Remember," *Chicago Tribune,* March 10, 1991, sect. 4, pp. 1, 4.)

Management Teams

Teams of managers may be permanent or temporary. They usually

> make decisions by consensus in areas affecting the entire operation—resource allocation, funds distribution, facility design, budgeting, hiring—subject to the approval of top management. . . . [A] team effort yields better decisions, protects . . . from arbitrary or careless actions, and, above all, strengthens team-members' commitment to [the company's] goals. . . . [A] boss cannot obtain by decree the creativity, initiative, and dedication needed to do a job properly; such allegiance can come freely only from people who have a sense of "ownership" [entrepreneurship] of the organization's goals.[9]

As a manager, you will serve on many teams. The fact that you are a manager makes you a member of management, which is a team of decision makers. As a supervisor, you head a formal unit within a formal organization—your work group. When you serve on a committee or advise your boss on your progress, you act as a linking pin, connecting the unit you head with other units. You should benefit from such connections by gaining a better understanding of others in your organization and by sharing in their experiences.

The automotive parts supplier A. O. Smith Corporation has created teams that give its seven unions a voice in planning and decision making. It has problem-solving committees on the shop floor, plant-wide advisory committees with union representatives, and union officials on the top management strategic planning committee.[10] Most major corporations have product design teams that include engineers, market researchers, production managers, and representatives from regular suppliers to ensure from the very beginning that a product is created that the consumer wants and that can be built efficiently and with quality. Another kind of management team is the crisis team—a group of managers from various departments that can act swiftly in the face of any crisis the company may face. When not actually dealing with a crisis, it is planning to do so.

Worker Teams

Ideally, you should be concerned with molding your people into a team or group of teams that feels an owner's concern for the organization and its goals. If you have the permission or the order of higher authority to create and manage work teams, you will need a few personal characteristics and skills. A true team leader or adviser is much more than the head of a group of workers.

Team leaders must have personalities that are both mature and secure. Maturity is required so that emotions can be controlled and responses given by an adult to those who may be less mature. Security is required so that the leader does not fear sharing management authority with others and does not fear being challenged, maybe for the first time. Managers who are new to team management have much teaching and learning to do. They must master a participative style of supervision, be willing to teach problem solving and decision making to team members, and be able to take the time necessary to deal with time delays and possible waste of resources that group approaches often involve. The qualities of patience, tact, and enthusiasm for the process are essential.

Team advisers must be good at communicating, problem solving, decision making, running group meetings, and coordinating group and intergroup activities. As a team leader, you must learn that your major tasks are to act as a facilitator—one who defines the goals, sets the limits for the team, arranges for the resources the team requires, and molds a cooperative and committed spirit. You need to create an environment in which team members grow and develop by actively participating in the execution of essential tasks. In addition to working out the internal dynamics of your team, you must also manage relations between your team and other company units.[11]

Johnsonville Foods, Inc. of Wisconsin has created worker teams that make a variety of their own decisions and that have eliminated the need for three layers of management. Worker teams inspect their output, program their production, set their improvement goals, and hire and reward their members.[12]

McGuffey's Restaurants, Inc. of North Carolina decided to turn its Asheville restaurant into a self-managing store. Employees are given specific financial goals. If they beat them, they split half the difference in cash. The employees choose their uniforms, have a say in hiring, handle the scheduling, and serve on committees after hours to plan on improvements. The dining room staff voted to give the lunch crew a raise to compensate them for their typically lower tips.[13]

At Toyota's Georgetown, Kentucky, plant, teamwork is the watch word. "Everything we do here is geared to the team environment—from the way we produce top quality Camrys to the way we solve problems. We do everything together and everybody participates," says Alex Warren, senior vice-president. Everyone is expected to reach out and to take responsibility for whatever has to be done. Everyone is accessible to everyone. No walls, no barriers.[14]

Measuring Group Effectiveness

Recent research has identified three variables that can be used to determine a group's effectiveness: task interdependence, outcome interdependence, and potency. These three "influence group performance and can be influenced by members and supervisors of groups."[15]

Task interdependence relates to the degree to which a group member is concerned with or involved in the work of other group members. Should the group members be involved with each other as partners or as competitors? Will they have the opportunity to interact infrequently or on a regular basis? Will they feed each other work, or will they work parallel to one

1. The "atmosphere" tends to be informal, comfortable, relaxed. There are no obvious tensions. It is a working atmosphere in which people are involved and interested. There are no signs of boredom.

2. There is a lot of discussion in which virtually everyone participates, but it remains pertinent to the task of the group. If the discussion gets off the subject, someone will bring it back in short order.

3. The task or the objective of the group is well understood and accepted by the members. There will have been free discussion of the objective at some point, until it was formulated in such a way that the members of the group could commit themselves to it.

4. The members listen to each other! The discussion does not have the quality of jumping from one idea to another unrelated one. Every idea is given a hearing. People do not appear to be afraid of being foolish by putting forth a creative thought even if it seems fairly extreme.

5. There is disagreement. The group is comfortable with this and shows no signs of having to avoid conflict or to keep everything on the plane of sweetness and light. Disagreements are not suppressed or overridden by premature group action. The reasons are carefully examined, and the group seeks to resolve them rather than to dominate the dissenter.

On the other hand, there is no "tyranny of the minority." Individuals who disagree do not appear to be trying to dominate the group or to express hostility. Their disagreement is an expression of a genuine difference of opinion, and they expect a hearing in order that a solution may be found.

Sometimes there are basic disagreements which cannot be resolved. The group finds it possible to live with them, accepting them but not permitting them to block its efforts. Under some conditions, action will be deferred to permit further study of an issue between the members. On other occasions, where the disagreement cannot be resolved and action is necessary, it will be taken but

Exhibit 9.1   **Douglas McGregor's eleven characteristics of a work team.** (*Source:* Douglas McGregor, *The Human Side of Enterprise*, pp. 232–235. Copyright © 1960 by McGraw-Hill Book Company. Used with permission of McGraw-Hill Book Company.)

another? Quality circles have a high degree of task interdependence, while scientists engaged in basic research and development often have a low degree of it.[16]

Outcome interdependence exists when task accomplishment by a group yields consequences that are important to and shared by some or all group members—for example, pay, time off, and recognition. The "outcomes" are bestowed by people other than group members, usually a supervisor or senior manager. They may be rewards or punishments; they may include pay, promotion, skill acquisition, exposure, or survival . . . [and] do *not* include any benefits derived from within the group, such as social interaction. . . .

with open caution and recognition that the action may be subject to later reconsideration.

6. Most decisions are reached by a kind of consensus in which it is clear that everybody is in general agreement and willing to go along. However, there is little tendency for individuals who oppose the action to keep their opposition private and thus let an apparent consensus mask real disagreement. Formal voting is at a minimum; the group does not accept a simple majority as a proper basis for action.

7. Criticism is frequent, frank, and relatively comfortable. There is little evidence of personal attack, either openly or in a hidden fashion. The criticism has a constructive flavor in that it is oriented toward removing an obstacle that faces the group and prevents it from getting the job done.

8. People are free in expressing their feelings as well as their ideas both on the problem and on the group's operation. There is little pussyfooting, there are few "hidden agendas." Everybody appears to know quite well how everybody else feels about any matter under discussion.

9. When action is taken, clear assignments are made and accepted.

10. The chairman of the group does not dominate it, nor on the contrary, does the group defer unduly to him or her. In fact, as one observes the activity, it is clear that the leadership shifts from time to time, depending on the circumstances. Different members, because of their knowledge or experience, are in a position at various times to act as "resources" for the group. The members utilize them in this fashion and they occupy leadership roles while they are thus being used. There is little evidence of a struggle for power as the group operates. The issue is not who controls, but how to get the job done.

11. The group is self-conscious about its own operations. Frequently, it will stop to examine how well it is doing or what may be interfering with its operation. The problem may be a matter of procedure, or it may be an individual whose behavior is interfering with the accomplishment of the group's objectives. Whatever it is, it gets open discussion until a solution is found.

Potency is the collective belief of group members that the group can be effective. This belief depends on group members' sense that they have what they need to succeed—for example, training, skills, talented members, money, time, access to key organization members, and feedback about group performance. Potency tends to be closely linked to performance. . . . Additionally, task interdependence and potency are linked.[17]

For groups to succeed and be effective, they need outcome interdependence, a minimal belief in their own effectiveness (potency), and a degree of interaction that is right for the task (enough opportunities for interaction must be provided). The more successes the group has, the greater its sense of potency. The more meaningful the rewards and the more equally they are distributed, the greater the group's effectiveness.[18] Exhibit 9.1 shows you the hallmarks of effective groups in detail. Use it to evaluate the groups to which you belong.

As a group's supervisor, you need to be a facilitator. You must clearly define the group's goals, listing the essential tasks and the degree of quality you wish to see in their performance. You need to determine what resources will be required, and you need to provide them. You must structure the group, providing enough chances for interaction among and between group members. You must monitor the group and be willing to intervene, when necessary, to offer leadership and coaching. Finally, you must be certain that group perceptions hold that important group outcomes depend on group performance, both individually and collectively.[19]

Building a team requires that you give the intended members a "common approach and a common language for addressing management concerns. . . . The best method for coordinating the inputs of managers and employees with different functional skills is to provide simple, common, sensible guidelines and procedures. These guidelines should be used jointly to carry out responsibilities without inhibiting individual contributions."[20] One common way to begin is to teach a common approach to solving problems and making decisions. Once the individuals participate in group training sessions and begin to focus on common objectives, they get to know one another, they see the value of many minds concentrating on a common problem, and they see the value of compromise and cooperation.

Group Decision Techniques

Two general categories of groups exist to help you research and determine solutions. The *interacting group* allows its members to meet face to face and gives them the opportunity to make suggestions, react to each other's suggestions, and synthesize the results. Such meetings are best for evaluating ideas and for arriving at a group solution, but they are not best for formulating ideas.[21] Two other kinds of group decision approaches are best for generating new ideas: the brainstorming session and the round-robin method. These two are not interacting approaches because they do not allow for criticism of group members' offerings. After a brief look at the latter two types of meetings, we will examine the interacting group.

Brainstorming

In brainstorming sessions, individuals are given a statement of a problem or issue that requires their input. Members are asked to offer suggestions in the form of ideas or potential approaches that they think will be useful.

Quantities of "wild" or unusual ideas are sought, as they tend to open new directions of thought and to bring forth more new ideas. The group leader discourages criticisms of the offerings but allows modifications or combinations and lists them as they are put forth. Each person is encouraged to speak out on each item put forth by the group leader. Members are chosen for their ability to offer constructive and meaningful contributions. This technique is used to create advertising slogans, new uses for existing products, new products, and new approaches to existing procedures; it is also used to spark creative thinking and creative thinkers.

Round Robins

A variation of the brainstorming, noncritical group session is the round-robin approach. In it, people are invited to list, in writing, their contributions on a variety of subjects. The group leader directs the flow of topics and background information and asks each individual to list his or her ideas. All members are exposed to the same input but not to one another's contributions.

The brainstorming and round-robin sessions work best in creating lists of possible solutions for group evaluation from which a final decision is made. The interacting group approach is best used to evaluate alternatives and to obtain a group solution in the form of a consensus of opinions.[22] The most common kind of interacting group is the problem-solving meeting.

The Problem-Solving Meeting

Problem-solving meeting
Gathering to reach a group consensus or solution to a problem affecting the group

The **problem-solving meeting** is usually set up and conducted in order to reach a group consensus or a solution to a problem affecting the group. It works best when it utilizes the discussion format, which allows the members to participate actively under the skillful direction of the chairperson. All of the people who are affected by or have information about the problem should be included. Their first-hand knowledge and experience can be of value in both the discussion of the problem—its causes and effects—and the listing and analysis of possible solutions.

One, a few, or all of the following steps for solving problems may be the focus of your problem-solving sessions:

1. Identify and define the problem(s).
2. List possible solutions.
3. Evaluate the positive and negative features of each solution.
4. Choose a solution or solutions.
5. Assign responsibility and authority for implementing the solution(s).

If it is to be successful, the problem-solving session requires a great deal of thought and preparation on the part of the supervisor. By using this type of meeting, you are involving your people in the formal decision-making process of your office. This is not without its hazards.

If you have never included your subordinates in your decision-making process in the past, they may be suspicious of your attempt to do so. Furthermore, each subordinate brings to the meeting his or her particular interests and attitudes, and each is influenced by his or her informal group. (Informal groups are discussed later in this chapter.) The informal group leader will be part of the meeting too, so his or her ideas and attitudes may well affect the quality and quantity of ideas of his or her followers. He or she can inhibit or promote open participation. The meeting, in other words, might be dominated by the informal leader. In a case where two or more informal leaders are present, the meeting might degenerate into a contest of strength. As the formal group leader, you may have your ideas and attitudes challenged openly for the first time. You may be subjected to group criticism for the first time, and you may find yourself pitted against the informal leader or leaders.

All of these problems and more can be prevented or minimized by proper planning. The first question you must answer is whether your boss will allow you to share your decision-making authority with your subordinates. If he or she agrees, you must answer another question: "What kinds of problems are my people best equipped to solve?" The answer lies in part in distinguishing among different categories of problems, as is done in the following list:

- Problems involving the reduction of waste or scrap
- Problems relating to health and safety
- Problems relating to housekeeping
- Problems about methods improvement

These problems relate to entire departments, sections, or shifts. By soliciting concrete suggestions and taking advantage of your subordinates' involvement in these problem areas, you will be sharing your authority and enlarging your perspective.

Once you have received permission to involve your people and have determined the kind of problems they are best able to solve, you are ready to embark upon a truly difficult but rewarding effort to win and utilize group participation. Through it, you stand a good chance of changing group behavior by changing the individual and group attitudes of your subordinates.

Dr. Thomas Gordon, a psychologist and management consultant, offers the following observations for group leaders.[23]

1. Once a leader becomes like another member of the group, any tendency for him or her to participate too frequently can be dealt with by the group much more easily than when he or she is perceived as *the* leader. People feel free to exert some control over the participation of members but are afraid to curb the participation of the leader.

2. The more dependent the group is on its leader, the more his or her contribution will inhibit the participation of other members.

3. A leader's awareness of the potentially inhibiting effect of his or her participation on the participation of the members helps control his or her participation. This awareness encourages the leader to be more alert for subtle signs indicating that group members are inhibited.

Ground Rules for Meetings

If the problem-solving session is to accomplish meaningful results, certain rules and procedures must be established and agreed upon in advance by all concerned. Imagine playing a sport in which each participant had his or her own set of rules. Chaos would be a certainty. In like fashion, most sports need an umpire or referee whose job it is to enforce the rules and prevent infractions. This role is yours to play as the supervisor.

Several essential rules are listed in the subsections that follow. Using this listing as a guide while planning and conducting your meetings should prevent most hazards from occurring—or at least prevent any serious conflicts.

Before the Meeting

When you have a specific problem to be solved, communicate it to the group members in advance of the meeting. Be as clear as you can be in defining the problem to be attacked and in specifying the goals you want the meeting to achieve.

Be certain that limits such as time, company policy, and the amount of authority the group will have are clear to the group. Are they empowered only to recommend solutions or actually to choose them? In the latter case, you must delegate some of your formal authority to the group. If you alone have the power to decide, tell them so.

Give your members all the relevant data you have accumulated, to assist them in adopting a realistic point of view. Share your ideas and those of others in management that bear on the problem. Make your members aware of any precedents.

Let them know where, when, what, how, and in what order (the agenda) the group will consider the issues.

Reserve the space or room you will need to meet in, gather the aids necessary for conducting the meeting (chalk, flip charts, pencils, paper), and get there a little early to make certain that things are in order. Set specific starting and ending times. Assign seats and prepare name tags when you think it necessary.

Before each meeting, all who have been chosen to attend should be made aware of their responsibilities to prepare for the meeting. Specifically each member should make the following preparations:

1. Read the agenda and prepare a list of questions that he or she should answer before facing the group.

2. Gather the information, materials, visuals, and so on that he or she will be responsible for presenting or disseminating to the group.

3. Arrange his or her schedule to avoid being late for the meeting or having to leave early.

4. If a group member should be unable to attend the meeting for any legitimate reason, relay the input expected from that group member to the chairperson.

During the Meeting

Start the meeting promptly, direct the discussion, stick to the agenda and time limits, draw out each member, list the alternatives, and summarize frequently. Maintain order and keep the meeting on the subject.

During each meeting, the group members have specific responsibilities that should be communicated to them in advance and briefly repeated to them at the start of each session. If the meeting is to be beneficial to all concerned, each member should be prepared to do the following:

1. Be an active participant by listening attentively, taking notes, following the discussions, seeking clarification when confused, and adding input if the group member has the expertise or experience to do so.

2. Promote discussion and input from all members by respecting their right to their opinions and attitudes and by avoiding discourteous or disruptive behavior (the chairperson should not hesitate to call on quiet members, using specific questions and asking for opinions).

3. Practice group-serving roles (described in the next section).

From the alternatives listed and analyzed, bring the group to one mind as to the best alternative or combination of alternatives to endorse. If the solution is to work, the majority must be behind it. Be ready to compromise in order to break any impasse.

Assign tasks to those affected, if need be, and put the solution into operation as quickly as possible. At the close of each meeting, the participants should be made aware of any specific duties or assignments they will have as a result of the meeting. The chairperson should not allow the members to leave until each of them is clear about his or her new tasks. In addition to the specific duties each person may receive, all participants have the following general obligations:

1. Keep the results and contents of the meeting confidential, by not sharing them with anyone or any group that does not have a need to know.
2. Relay decisions and changes to those for whom the group member may be responsible and who will be affected by them.
3. Carry out promises made and assignments received as quickly as possible.

After the Meeting

After a problem-solving meeting, check on the results and on the group reactions. Follow up on individual assignments.

Group Member Roles

At a meeting, members of the group may play several different roles; some of these will be helpful to the attainment of the meeting's goals, while others may hinder the group's attempts to achieve success. Two categories of roles—self-serving and group-serving—are available to all members of a group, and the chances are that many different roles will be exhibited at each meeting. Exhibit 9.2 summarizes these roles.

Self-Serving Roles

Self-serving roles can have either positive or negative effects on the meeting and on group members. For example, suppose that, as a group leader, you block another participant by not recognizing his or her raised hand. If

Self-serving Roles	Group-serving Roles
Attention-getting	Coordinating
Blocking	Fortifying
Criticizing	Initiating
Dominating	Orienting
Withdrawing	Researching

Exhibit 9.2   Roles played by group members.

you do so in order to get another person to speak who until then has been withdrawn, you have a positive motive and effect on the group. But if you do so in order to promote your own ideas at the expense of others' (a selfish motive), the action can have a negative effect on the group.

As chairperson, you may decide that it is best to withdraw—that is, become an observer—when one of the members begins to criticize another's suggestions. In this way, a participant may be forced to justify his or her proposal, new information may emerge, and others may be persuaded as to the validity of an idea more readily. Why not let a participant tell his or her peers what you want said? Attention getting is the role whereby a member focuses attention on himself or herself. He or she may be attempting to get the floor in order to add information or to redirect the discussion to the central point.

Dominating involves pushing a special interest; it may involve blocking by continuing to talk and not allowing another to get into the conversation. Whether these roles go unchecked and exhibit a positive or negative influence is up to the chairperson to determine. Use your good sense and listen intently. Try to get at the motive behind the role a member is playing. If, in your judgment, the motive is positive, let him or her continue. If not, take action.

Group-Serving Roles

Group-serving roles are almost always positive in their effects. No matter who practices them, they attempt to draw members together and shed light where there was darkness. They all promote unity and harmony, and each is essential in order to reach a consensus. They tend to keep a meeting on track, while systematically separating the unimportant from the relevant.

Fortifying is the process by which a member adds encouragement and insights to already aired ideas. It helps elaborate and interpret what has been said. Initiating introduces ideas and major points in order to get the reactions and contributions of group members. Orienting tells the membership where they have been and where they are at present. It may serve to add emphasis or to clarify ideas, and it keeps people from traveling again over the same ground or going around in circles. Researching involves fact-finding and introducing background material pertinent to the discussion, so as to remove smoke from people's eyes and substitute facts for fiction.

Observe and label these activities in your group encounters from now on. You will see various positive and negative applications of all these roles in your classes at school, as well as in meetings at work. Study your instructor and the various roles he or she plays. You will pick up some valuable examples of each of these roles, most of which you will be able to use at work when you find yourself a group leader or participant.

Pitfalls

Problem-solving sessions may result in problems if poor leadership results in a violation of the ground rules listed in the preceding section. In addition, several other major pitfalls or traps exist that can cause a meeting to be a sheer waste of time.

The Hidden Agenda

A member's hidden agenda consists of his or her personal feelings toward the subject discussed, the group itself, and the individuals who make up the group. We all have such an agenda whenever we attend a group session, whether with our formal or informal group. If a proposal or an action is put forth that conflicts with our pet beliefs, we can only try to pick it apart or live with it. People tend to promote (or not oppose) ideas that they feel they can live with and to resist (or offer alternatives to) ideas they feel will mean conflicts, problems, or more effort for them or for those they represent. Often critical remarks toward group members or their ideas are motivated by a dislike or distrust of those persons and their intentions—not their ideas. You must recognize that, as a chairperson, you have the duty to see behind the words and get to the motives. Often you can nullify the hidden agenda's effect simply by explaining that another person or department does not necessarily have to gain at someone else's expense. What is good for the gander can be, and often is, good for the goose.

An Improper Setting

How many meetings have you attended that were complete disasters because of poor ventilation, bad lighting, or too much background noise? Maybe the facilities were okay when they were reserved, but the timing was wrong for their use. Possibly the room was selected without regard for the number of people who would attend, so many people had to stand or could not even enter the room. I am reminded of a meeting I attended in an industrial firm, where the central feature was to have been a film. After the projector was started, we soon realized that the lamp had burned out. So much for that meeting and its organizer.

A Competitive Spirit

Many sessions start out as and continue to be a stage for the display of one member's accomplishments over the others' or of one group's achievements over another's. Competition is fine on the athletic field, but it has no real purpose among members of the team. Watch for the remark that attempts to build one person's reputation at the expense of another's. Nothing can ruffle feathers so quickly or create defensive reactions more effectively. A quick review of the second Hawthorne study should refresh your memory about intergroup competition and its dangers.

Chapter 7 discussed the now-famous experimental studies conducted in the late 1920s at Western Electric's Hawthorne plant. The second study uncovered the formation of two informal cliques—one quite strong and the other somewhat weak. Both influenced their members in significant ways. They offered proof that workers' cliques can be positive or negative factors with respect to company standards, policy, and regulations. If they view management in a favorable way, they are capable of achieving standards of output even higher than management may expect. If they feel negative toward management, the informal group will generate much less production than expected. How workers, individually or in groups, relate to management is largely a result of their supervisor's approach. If he or she practices sound human relations and relates positively to his or her group of subordinates, the supervisor can and does influence the behavior and productivity of the subordinates.

Talkative Members

Have you ever tried to carry on a conversation with someone who only stopped talking to think about what to say next? It is quite a frustrating

1. Try a one-on-one meeting. Schedule a meeting for just the two of you. Confront the person with your observations about how the person is disrupting the group's efforts. Listen for all the reasons and perceptions that unfold. See if you can turn disruptive behaviors around with force-field analysis in the meeting or afterward.

2. Let the group confront the individual. Let the individual face the group members directly. Let the members air their grievances about the problem member's behaviors. Talk about what effects those behaviors are having on the group. Avoid personal attacks. Describe the behaviors that have negative consequences.

3. Place limits on the problem member's participation. Let the group leader prescribe the level of participation allowed. For example, the leader may want to deal directly with the individual after each meeting, not during it. Or the leader may not allow the problem member to participate in group discussions when signs of disruptive behaviors occur.

4. Separate the problem member from the group meetings. Let the individual contribute but on an individual basis, away from the other group members. Assign work that will help the team indirectly.

Exhibit 9.3   **Some tips for dealing with problem group members.**

experience. Your voice only fills the gaps between his or her remarks. Listening is not one of that person's virtues. Members in meetings can quickly fall in love with their own voices and viewpoints. It is the chairperson's job to prevent this. Make sure that everyone has a say and that each person's views are duly noted. Blocking, however, can serve a useful purpose with a talkative member.

Sabotage

Group members who carry on their own conversations while another is speaking, people who attempt to sidetrack the issues, hidden decisions that are made without group consultation: these and similar factors represent efforts to render a meeting useless. The subversive's motivation may be that no decision will enhance the status quo. Disruptive behavior will sour the group and tear down its will to reach a decision or continue the meeting: interest wanes and attention slips away. The chairperson must assess the motives and effects of conscious or accidental sabotage and must act to block it or to confront the saboteur directly. The meeting must be pulled back to its proper focus. Exhibit 9.3 gives you some interesting alternatives for dealing with a disruptive group member.

Informal Groups

Two or more people who come together by choice to satisfy mutual needs or to share common interests are considered an **informal group.** The distinguishing feature between formal and informal groups is the matter of choice. Informal groups are formed because of the mutual social needs of people and because the environment at work favors or at least does not prohibit their formation. Formal groups can also be informal groups, provided that all members freely choose to associate with one another on and off the job.

There are three primary types of informal groups: *horizontal, vertical,* and *random* (sometimes called *mixed*).[24] These types of informal groups are often referred to as **cliques.** Exhibit 9.4 is an organization chart we shall refer to in discussing the three different types of cliques.

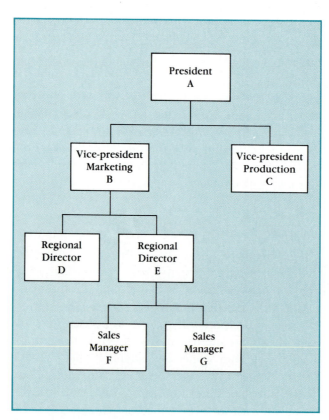

Exhibit 9.4   **An organization chart.**

Horizontal Cliques

A horizontal clique consists of two or more people from the same functional area and on the same level of the hierarchy. In Exhibit 9.4, F and G constitute a horizontal clique, provided that they have chosen one another's company voluntarily on social occasions. D and E would also form a horizontal clique, under the same conditions. B and C would *not* form a horizontal clique, as they represent two different functional areas (marketing and production).

Vertical Cliques

A vertical clique consists of two or more people from the same functional area but *different levels of the hierarchy.* In Exhibit 9.4, F and E would be an example, as would D, E, and B. If all members of the marketing department formed an informal group, they would also constitute a vertical clique. Vertical cliques involve friendships between a boss and one or more subordinates. Review the cautions in chapter 8 here.

Random Cliques

A random clique is composed of two or more people from two or more functional areas. In Exhibit 9.4, B and C would be a good example of this. E, B, and C would also form a random or mixed clique. Whether the members of a random or mixed clique are from the same level of the hierarchy or not makes no difference. If A, the president, is a part of any clique, that clique automatically would be a random one. The reason is that the president is the only manager who oversees all the functional areas of the business. Therefore, he or she does not belong to any one of them but stands alone at that level of the hierarchy.

Your subordinates will usually constitute one or more horizontal or (on occasion) random cliques. Seldom will you find them belonging to a vertical clique. Your analysis of your subordinates' group memberships can help you in your attempts to understand them as individuals and to develop your relationships with their groups.

Let us assume that you have recently become the operating supervisor of the Health Insurance Systems Group, illustrated in Exhibit 9.5. You have observed your people and their interactions and have drawn the connecting rings as shown, creating what is usually called a *sociogram*. Since your subordinates work in close proximity to workers in the Life Insurance Systems Group, it would seem natural for members of the two groups to mix informally on social occasions such as coffee breaks and lunch periods.

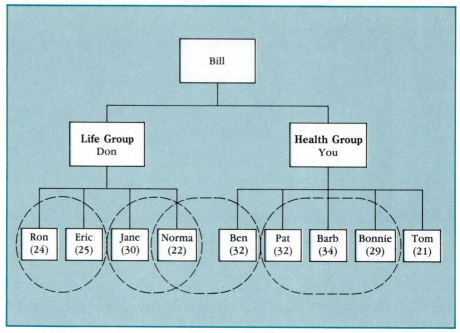

Exhibit 9.5 A sociogram showing the informal groupings of members in formal groups.

The rings you have drawn encircle the members of the informal groups who most frequently interact at work with one another socially. The numbers in parentheses represent their ages. All of the groups represented are horizontal cliques. Even though Ben and Norma are from two different work groups, they are in the same functional area called *systems*.

Now let us see what you have discovered. Pat, Barb, and Bonnie are a clique and prefer each other's company over that of others when they have a choice. This may be due in part to the fact that they are the only women in the health systems area. It may also be due to the close proximity of their ages. More knowledge is needed for a really thorough analysis. You should know their marital status, their individual interests, their backgrounds, and more before you can make any hard and fast conclusions as to the nature of their clique.

Ben has chosen Norma's company and vice versa. This is interesting because he has gone outside his section for companionship. Norma is part of two informal cliques. Norma may be an informal leader to either Ben or Jane or both. But again more information would be needed before you could decide for sure. For example, Ben may be romantically inclined toward Norma.

Tom is another situation. He is the youngest member and as such may have little in common with the others. He might be an *isolate*—a person who wants to belong to one or another of the cliques but is rejected or denied membership for some reason. His age, his personality, his education, or some other factor may be keeping him on the outside. If he is a new employee, he has not had enough time to become accepted or to choose a group to which he might want to belong. He might be a *deviate*—a person who does not aspire to join or belong to a group. Quite often an isolate will evolve into a deviate if he or she is kept out long enough.

What we have just done in a small way is to observe the social interaction of subordinates and attempt to analyze our findings. If these observations were pursued in greater depth and detail, a better understanding might emerge of why these groups have formed, what keeps them together, and what they mean to you as a supervisor. Such a process will aid you by giving you more direct information about the forces at work on your people and the group influences on their attitudes and performance at work.

Every informal group has a leader. Unlike his or her counterpart in the formal group, the informal leader derives power through the informal means discussed in chapter 3. The clique members subordinate their wills to one of their number because he or she is a great person to be with or because of the knowledge, skills, and abilities he or she possesses. It is seldom the case that the formal leader of the formal group is an informal leader with a clique of his or her subordinates. This is as it should be. As was pointed out in chapter 8, a manager's friends should be his or her peers.

Joining a Clique

Once a new employee is hired, he or she is placed in a specific job, which makes him or her automatically a member of several formal groups that constitute the business enterprise. If the design of work and the working relationships permit them, informal groups or cliques will have been formed as well. The newcomer, like those who have preceded him or her, will naturally desire the companionship of one or more coworkers on a more or less regular basis, both during working hours and while on his or her own time.

The problem confronting the new arrival is that he or she is initially on the outside of the existing informal groups and, although he or she desires membership in one of them, is not certain about which one to choose. He or she needs time to assess the values, attitudes, and reputation of each group. The groups in turn are going to be evaluating the person for prospective membership. In this sense, the new employee is similar to a person seeking admission to a fraternity or sorority. He or she has to look at what it stands for and get to know its members, while in turn its members look the applicant over.

You as a supervisor can do a great deal for the new employee. If you know your people well and understand their groups, you can do all in your power to help him or her gain admittance to a group of subordinates that constitutes a positive force and will exert a constructive influence on the newcomer. You hope that all of the informal cliques in your section are working with management and not against it. But if one or another is not, do your best to steer the new arrival away from that clique and into more beneficial surroundings. This topic is covered further in chapter 11.

Stages of Induction

Before the individual on the outside of a clique can truly become a participating member of the clique, he or she must go through three separate but related stages of induction: (1) observation, (2) transformation, and (3) confirmation.

Stage 1: Observation   Observation is the initial stage we all find ourselves in as newcomers. By necessity, we must remain neutral toward all the informal groups we encounter, until we have time to know them. As time goes on, neutrality becomes increasingly difficult to maintain, as we feel pressure from within and from without to make a decision or choice. We may begin a kind of trial membership period, wherein we are invited to participate with a group by one or more of its members. While meeting with each clique, we are somewhat passive and open to group members' opinions and attitudes, preferring to listen rather than to speak our mind.

Stage 2: Transformation   The next step is for us to decide which group we like best. If the group honors our choice, we begin to confine our socializing almost exclusively to the new group. We mask any personal opinions that are contradictory to those the group holds as essential, and we begin to mouth agreement to these essential attitudes. Like a parrot, we begin to remember and repeat the sacred beliefs, even though we may not agree with them. Without this stage, we can never really become an accepted member in a strong, informal group.

Stage 3: Confirmation   The confirmation stage is complete when we actually abandon attitudes we once held that were in direct opposition to those of the group and adopt the group's values as our own. We give up our individuality while with the group, although we may retain it on our own. The group has changed us and our attitudes in much the same way as was discussed in chapter 6. The difference is that several people may have been at work on us here, instead of only one.

From this point on, the group has more influence over our behavior than any other force at work. We now weigh the relative merits of proposals against the group's willingness to accept them. If the group vetoes the action, each member feels bound to support that veto.

Not long ago a student involved me in the following story. At the start of the business day one Friday, two of George's more able workers presented him with a petition signed by all twenty-six of his subordinates. It requested that the workday begin and end one-half hour earlier. George was quite concerned, as such a request was not in his power to grant, and he felt that the plant manager would not buy the suggestion. Wisely, he refrained from giving an immediate answer but assured the workers that he would consider the matter carefully.

The following week George and I discussed the problem. I asked if he was sure that all the workers really wanted the change. He reiterated that they had all signed the petition. But as we all know, people will sign almost anything—for a variety of reasons. So George decided to interview each worker separately over the next two weeks to determine just how committed each of them was to the proposed change. The results were amazing. Two men were solidly in favor of the change—the same two who had confronted George with the petition and had initiated it. Eight workers were neutral but willing to go along with the others. The remaining sixteen were clearly against it. After George announced his findings, the demand was dropped, and only two people were really unhappy with the decision.

What made the twenty-four other workers sign? The two men were strong personalities, and one was an informal leader of a large clique. Beginning with his clique members, starting with the weakest, the informal leader got one signature after another until nearly two-thirds of the workers had signed. The others fell into line when confronted with the sheer weight of numbers. Not wishing to obstruct the will of the majority, the few remaining holdouts also signed up.

Group Competition

We have seen that intergroup competition at Hawthorne caused ill will and declining productivity within the formal group. Edgar H. Schein of the Massachusetts Institute of Technology has added much to our understanding of what happens within and between competing groups.[25]

Whether we are dealing with formal or informal groups, the following situation would apply.

What happens *within* competing groups? Each group exhibits the following behavior:

- Exhibits greater togetherness and cohesion
- Becomes more organized and highly structured
- Expects greater loyalty and conformity from its members
- Willingly accepts autocratic supervision
- Becomes more task-oriented and less concerned with the needs of individual members

All of these results, at first glance, may appear to be desirable. But as we consider what happens *between* competing groups, the picture becomes less attractive. In Schein's words:

1. Each group begins to see the other group as the enemy, rather than merely a neutral object.

2. Each group begins to experience distortions of perception—it tends to perceive only the best parts of itself, denying its weaknesses, and tends to perceive only the worst parts of the other group, denying its strengths; each group is likely to develop a negative stereotype of the other. ("They don't play fair like we do.")

3. Hostility toward the other group increases while interaction and communication with the other group decreases; thus it becomes easier to maintain negative stereotypes and more difficult to correct perceptual distortions.

4. If the groups are forced into interaction—for example, if they are forced to listen to representatives plead their own and the others' cause in reference to some task—each group is likely to listen more closely to their own representative and not to listen to the representative of the other group, except to find fault with his presentation: in other words group members tend to listen only for that which supports their own position and stereotype.[26]

If this intergroup competition—whether between informal or formal groups—results in one group's emerging as the victor and the other as vanquished, the problems are compounded dramatically. To paraphrase Professor Schein, the winning group behaves in the following way:

- Keeps its cohesiveness
- Tends to become self-satisfied

- Loses its task orientation and reemphasizes individual needs
- Becomes reassured that its self-image must be a correct one and loses the incentive to question its perceptions

On the other hand, the losing group behaves in the following way:

- Becomes initially unrealistic as to its perception of why it lost, tending to transfer blame to some external cause
- Tends to lose its cohesiveness
- Becomes more dedicated to tasks and winning
- Experiences less intragroup cooperation and less concern for individual needs
- Eventually reexamines its beliefs and self-image and becomes more realistic in its perceptions

It should be clear to you that intergroup competition has more disadvantages than advantages. The loser may improve, while the winner declines. This is not to say that competition is wrong—only that competition between groups within a company is dangerous. Competition can be a powerful tool to muster greater output and cohesiveness among your department's members if the "enemy" is not a group of coworkers but rather some outside force or group. If the thing to be beaten is a standard or a past record of output, the group can muster its forces in a cooperative spirit to excel and exceed its previous record. Like a long-distance runner out to beat the best recorded time for his or her event or to surpass his or her previous best time, groups at work can try and succeed or they can fail with no lasting detrimental effects. To the contrary, they will most likely redouble their efforts and reexamine their operations, and they may seek outside help in the process—a desirable outcome.

Outsiders and Insiders

You are affected each day at your workplace by many factors, some of which are outside your company and some of which are inside it. The same is true for your subordinates.

Outside Factors

When was the last time you went to work with a personal family problem so much on your mind that your performance suffered? Your family is but one of many outside groups that can and do influence your efficiency. Your academic classes in management may be another example. We all hope that you will obtain from your instructor and classmates the means to achieve a more successful performance. But sometimes what you learn will bring you into conflict with your traditional beliefs or with those of your boss, putting you at odds with him or her when you attempt to act upon your new knowledge. You may find that you know more about a particular task and the best methods for dealing with it than your boss does. The problem will then be one of your selling your idea to your boss and getting permission to implement it.

Customers and competitors can place demands on the business, in turn directly affecting your operations. Their requests, threats, and innovations may be translated into new products, service methods, or procedures for your department. New schedules of production may be the result, with added pressures, and tensions for you and those under you.

Inside Factors

The groups within the company that directly or indirectly affect your performance are your superiors, your peers, and your subordinates. Superiors construct the programs, policies, and regulations that you must enforce and translate to action. Your peers place demands on you for conformity, cooperation, and uniform approaches to problems. They form the nucleus of your friendships and place demands on your time and talents. Your subordinates, as members of your formal groups and as members of their own informal cliques, ask a great deal from you. How you cope with these groups and their demands directly relates to how well you can adjust to tension and frustration. Numerous times you will be faced with conflicts between what you think you should do and what others are asking you to do. Often you must yield completely to the demands of others. On occasion you must work out compromises. In all cases, however, you are being tested. How strong is your company loyalty? How strong is your friendship? How sincere are you in your commitment to your people? How much do your children really mean to you? Whoever said that life or holding a job was easy?

You and Your Informal Group

The informal group that you choose or that chooses you will have a dramatic and lasting impact on your reputation and your future. Choose any informal group with the same caution you would exercise when choosing a friend. Pick out the ones that will have the greatest positive effect on your growth and the ones that have the most to offer. As a result, some of their luster and brilliance will rub off on you. You are judged in part by the company you keep. Why open yourself to criticism or end up having to defend your companions or yourself? You do not have to alienate those bent on self-destruction. Simply avoid any permanent bonds or relationships with them. Remain civil but apart.

One of the hazards inherent in membership in an informal group is the restrictions it places on your contacts with others. Once you have reached either the transformation or confirmation stage of induction, you probably have begun to confine your socializing at work to a specific few. In time, you may become rather narrow and cut off from differing opinions. You may be denying yourself the valuable companionship and variety that others have to offer. Do not take yourself out of circulation. Break your routine on occasion and mix and maintain contacts with others of similar rank. It is foolish to restrict your explorations to the same mountain. After a while, there is nothing left to explore.

Coping with Subordinates' Cliques

There are seven main principles you should follow in order to minimize group conflicts and tensions and to maximize group cooperation and contribution:

1. *Accept your subordinates' cliques as a fact of life.* Just as you belong to one or more, so it is with them. Consider their informal groups as allies and additional forces to be won over and brought to bear on mutual problems. The trick is to learn to work with them—not to fight them or try to eliminate them.

2. *Identify and enlist the cooperation of the informal leaders.* They represent a force to be reckoned with. Many of them have the potential to be tomorrow's managers. The informal power they have over others can work for you both. Practice sound human relations with them as you would with anyone in your charge. Share with the best of them (whenever you can) some of your formal authority through delegation. They are usually perfect candidates for leadership roles. They are also ambitious people who recognize the advantages that management has to offer.

   Informal leaders are not hard to spot. They are the ones that others like to be with. They are influential with their followers and with other informal groups and their leaders. Informal leaders know the opinions and attitudes of their groups' members and often act as spokespersons for their groups to management. Note who sits with whom at lunch and on breaks. Then note how these people interact—who seems to dominate discussions and settle arguments.

3. *Prevent intergroup competition and the occurrence of a win-lose situation.* As stated earlier, groups in conflict have a tendency to tear at each other and to reduce the organization's overall effectiveness. The loser will profit, while the winner suffers. Hold out standards to be achieved and surpassed. Use past performance records as targets to hit and scores to beat. These abstract enemies are harder to visualize but easier to beat.

4. *Do not force your people to choose between you and their group.* If you put it to them on an either/or basis, they will usually pick their group. Their loyalty to and membership in a clique does not have to be at your expense. They can serve both company and group demands. They can be loyal and unopposed to you if you are predictable and loyal to them.

5. *Adopt a coach's attitude toward your group(s).* Foster a team spirit, and nurture the comradeship that cliques promote. Play fair and demand that your subordinates do the same. Team players know the value of rules and team play. Enlist their participation as a group and protect their self-image.

6. *Appeal to each group member and to each group's sense of competence.* We all have the urge to be good at what we do and to know that others think we are. Give your people a series of challenges that, when met, will give them a sense of accomplishment and pride.

7. *Use the traditional and the not-so-traditional levers available to you.* Levers are tools that can be used to influence people in specific situations. None is suitable to every situation. Levers such as job assignments, overtime, disciplinary actions, and deserved praise may or may not be within your control, but most of the levers in Exhibit 9.6 will be yours to use. The effectiveness of most of them has to do with your competence in interpersonal and intergroup relations.[27] Most are effective when they are used by a person who commands the respect of the people they are used with. This respect comes from the user's skills, knowledge, and demonstrated concern for the group and its members.

By setting goals and helping your subordinates set their own, you will be providing incentives for them to excel and ways for them to build self-respect and confidence. Point out how a poor performance hurts others and makes their jobs more difficult.

- Use positive reinforcement in the form of incentive schemes, job redesign, and awareness of psychological needs, including peer group acceptance and pride.

- Try negative reinforcement—both the traditional type (write up, fire, suspend) and more indirect means (job reassignment, job redesign, forced overtime).

- Appeal to workers for support on the basis of having gone out on a limb for them or having given over some prerogative to them in the past.

- Appeal to workers on the basis of understanding their position, since first-level supervisors once stood in their shoes.

- Appeal to workers on the basis of previously agreed-on goals and plans for achieving them.

Exhibit 9.6   **Supervisors' levers for gaining group cooperation and compliance.** (*Source:* W. Earl Sasser, Jr., and Frank S. Leonard. "Let First-Level Supervisors Do Their Job." *Harvard Business Review* (March–April 1980): 119–20.)

One example of this point involved assembly-line workers on a Corvette assembly operation. They were installing fiberglass parts provided by an outside supplier. These parts had rough edges in their openings that were designed to take dashboard instruments. The rough edges had to be filed clean before the instruments could be inserted. This should have been done by the supplier, not by the assembly-line workers.

To deal with the growing sense of frustration and irritation among their assembly workers, General Motors' supervisors arranged a meeting with the supplier's workers at the GM plant. The workers responsible for the rough-edged moldings witnessed first-hand how their sloppy work affected their counterparts. Moldings quickly began to arrive with smooth openings. All now knew why their work was necessary and what would happen at the other end when it was not done properly.

Instant Replay

1. A group is two or more people who are aware of one another, who consider themselves to be a functioning unit, and who share a quest for a common goal or benefit.

2. Problem-solving meetings may or may not allow for interaction between and among group members. Interaction allows individual group members to react to input from other members.

3. The interacting group works best to evaluate possible alternatives and to obtain a group solution in the form of a consensus of opinions.

4. Brainstorming and round-robin sessions work best to construct a list of potential solutions or ideas that bear on the subject under discussion.

5. The roles that group members play may affect the group either positively or negatively, depending on what motivates each group member in the use of each role.

6. Various pitfalls can undermine group meetings and their results. Being aware of them and acting to render them negligible is the job of every group leader or chairperson.

7. Groups that compete experience both positive and negative changes. The most negative feature of intergroup competition is what happens between competing groups: hostility, lack of cooperation, and outright sabotage can result, eventually bringing both groups down.

8. Supervisors must recognize that informal groups exist and can wield positive or negative powers. Their leaders possess strong personalities and are potential management material.

Glossary

Clique   an informal group of two or more people who come together by choice to satisfy mutual interests or to pursue common goals. Cliques can be vertical, horizontal, or mixed.

Formal group   two or more people who come together by management decision to achieve specific goals.

Group   two or more people who are consciously aware of one another, who consider themselves to be a functioning unit, and who share in a quest to achieve one or more goals or some common benefit.

Informal group   two or more people who come together by choice to satisfy mutual needs or to share common interests (a clique).

Problem-solving meeting   meeting conducted in order to reach a group consensus or solution to a problem affecting the group. It uses the discussion format, which allows members to participate actively under the direction of a chairperson.

Synergy   cooperative action or force of two or more elements pulling together that yields a result greater than the sum of the results that could be achieved separately by the elements.

Syntality   a group's ''personality''—its collection of traits, strengths, and weaknesses that make it unique.

1. Can you define this chapter's key terms?

2. What are the forces that help shape a group's syntality?

3. As a problem-solving group's chairperson, what should you do before, during, and after a session?

4. As a participating member of a problem-solving session, what should you do before, during, and after the session?

5. What are the group-serving and the self-serving roles played by group members in meetings?

6. What are the three types of informal groups described in this chapter? Can you give an example of each from your own experiences?

7. What happens to the winning group in intergroup competition? to the losing group? between the groups?

Incident   Many people work outside the office and factory. Some, such as outside sales people, must be with clients and customers on a regular basis. Others work at home, linked to their boss and coworkers by electronic devices such as a telephone hookup to the company's computer or a fax machine for receiving and sending work, and by telephone for voice-to-voice contacts. The advantages are many to both employee and employer. The employee can stay at home with children in need of day care and avoid the time and expense of commuting to work. The company can operate in smaller spaces, providing less in the way of office furniture and equipment. But what about a team spirit linking the telecommuter to his or her coworkers and others at work?

Your Task List as many ways as you can for attempting to include the home-working employees in a group's efforts and activities at work. What would you do to instill the absent employees with a real spirit of team work?

Case Problem 9.1   Barbara's Brainstorm*

Barbara Leyton was excited about the recent seminar the company had sponsored on gaining group participation in improving quality. She was particularly interested in trying the brainstorming session with her people. The director of the seminar had encouraged all the managers in attendance to experiment, and the company's chief executive officer had given the contents of the seminar his full support.

Armed with her notes and her superior's approval, Barbara reserved the conference room, set a date, and sent a memo to her seven subordinate managers and their sixteen subordinates, inviting them to attend "a most exciting exercise in improving our quality of service to our customers." By the time of the meeting, all but two had agreed to participate.

Barbara opened the meeting with a brief statement of its purpose. She told the group that they were to feel free to offer any ideas they had on improving services to customers. She promised that all ideas would receive equal treatment and that any ideas adopted would be credited to their proper sources. Barbara stated that the more ideas that were generated, the better for all concerned. Barbara began by turning on her tape recorder and offering two quick ideas. Her ideas were quickly endorsed by two others, and another idea was offered by one of Barbara's subordinates. This idea generated a great deal of controversy between two participants. One saw it as an underhanded criticism of his operations. The other saw it as stupid and immature.

Several more ideas were offered with no criticism from the group. Within a few minutes many ideas about improving nearly every aspect of the company's operations began to flow freely. Critical comments were offered on nearly all recently adopted procedural changes. After about one hour, the ideas stopped and Barbara terminated the meeting.

During her lunch hour, Barbara replayed the tape of the morning's meeting. As she sat with pen in hand, recording the thoughts that were on the tape, she began to realize several important facts. First, the group had offered only three concrete ideas about customer service improvements. Many of the other ideas had no bearing on the subject of the meeting. Second, Barbara recognized that three voices were dominant throughout the meeting. All were her immediate subordinates. Third, some highly critical remarks were made about the company's top management and the ways in which changes were being made. More than five voices talked about the lack of consultation with people before changes were made, or as one voice put it, "announced on high."

Questions

1. Evaluate the effectiveness of the meeting, using the text's description of how brainstorming sessions should be conducted.
2. What other techniques could Barbara use to explore ways to improve customer service?

(*Source: Warren R. Plunkett and Raymond F. Attner, *Introduction to Management,* 3rd ed. (PWS-Kent Publishing Company, 1989), pp. 155–156.)

Case Problem 9.2   Claims and Counterclaims

Lee Cannoli joined the Claims Processing Department of the Thomas Paine Insurance Company three weeks ago, and today marked his first full week on the job. Lee is one of fourteen full-time clerks who initially screen customer claims before routing them to an adjuster for final processing. During his first two weeks he attended a claims-training course and underwent the usual company orientation. For the past five days Lee has averaged thirty-two claims a day and is quite proud of his progress. His supervisor, Lois Clements, complimented him on several occasions for his output and the quality of his work. Although there is no hard and fast rule about output, Lois made it clear that most new employees were expected to do between twenty and twenty-four claims a day for their first month or so.

Henry Pullman, a fellow claims clerk, approached Lee that afternoon.

"Hi," said Henry.

"Hello."

"I'm Hank Pullman. You're Lee, aren't you?"

"Yes. We met on Tuesday when Ms. Clements introduced me to the other workers. I've been so busy that I really haven't had much time to visit."

"Yeah, I noticed. How many claims do you get through a day, anyway?"

"Well, so far I have been doing between thirty and thirty-two."

Hank winced. "Most of the guys do twenty to twenty-five each day. Looks like you're going to set a record. You make some of us old-timers look pretty slow."

"The claims I'm getting are pretty simple. I've only had a few that took a lot of time."

"But, Lee, if you do thirty or more a day, you are putting the other guys and gals in a bind. Lois will think we are doggin' it. You wouldn't want that to happen now, would you?"

"Gee, I didn't realize I was causing any problems."

"Well, Lee, the other workers are doing the more advanced ones, and they can't work quite as fast on them. You'll find out soon enough when you graduate to the big leagues."

"I don't want to hurt anyone," Lee replied.

"I knew you would understand. Say, some of us are putting together a softball team from the department to compete with the other company teams. Do you play?"

"Heck, I haven't played ball for a couple of years."

"Don't worry about that. It would be a great chance to get to know the kingpins around here. All the best are in on it. Our first practice is tomorrow at Langly Park, just around the corner on Fifth and Greenleaf. About 9:00 A.M. Can we count on you?"

"I'd like that very much. Say, Hank, what does Ms. Clements say about our output? I mean, doesn't she have a quota for us?"

"Claims people are hard to find today. If she gets tough she knows the workers will leave. Anyway, her boss leaves her alone, and she leaves us alone. Come on, Lee, let's have a cup of coffee. I'll fill you in on this place and who really runs it."

As the two men walked to the cafeteria, Lee thought to himself, "I sure don't want to hurt the other workers. . . . What the heck, I'll have a little more time to socialize like the others. Hank has been around a long time . . . he ought to know."

Questions

1. What accounts for Lee's switch from diligent worker to acceptance of a slower pace?
2. Has Lois Clements failed in any way? Is she responsible for what is happening to Lee?
3. Comment on Hank's statement, "I'll fill you in on this place and who really runs it."
4. Which of the three stages of induction into a clique is Lee in at present?

Notes

1. Robert B. Reich, "Entrepreneurship Reconsidered: The Team as Hero," *Harvard Business Review* (May–June 1987): 77.
2. Ibid., 82–83.
3. Ibid., 83.
4. Ibid.
5. Ibid., 81.
6. Auren Uris, *Techniques of Leadership* (New York: McGraw-Hill, 1964), 58.
7. Ibid., 61–62.
8. Ibid., 56.
9. Tolly Kizilos and Roger P. Heinisch, "How a Management Team Selects Managers," *Harvard Business Review* (September–October 1986): 6.
10. John Hoerr, "The Cultural Revolution at A. O. Smith," *Business Week* (May 29, 1989): 66, 68.
11. Janice A. Klein and Pamela A. Posey, "Good Supervisors Are Good Supervisors Anywhere," *Harvard Business Review* (November–December 1986): 125–28.

12. Ralph Stayer, "How I Learned to Let My Workers Lead," *Harvard Business Review* (November–December 1990): 72–76.

13. Joshua Hyatt, "The Odyssey of an 'Excellent' Man," *Inc.* (February 1989): 63–66.

14. "Teamwork Is the Key," *Toyota Today* (Fall 1988): 4.

15. Gregory P. Shea and Richard A. Guzzo, "Group Effectiveness: What Really Matters," *Sloan Management Review* 28 #3 (Spring 1987): 25–26.

16. Ibid.

17. Ibid., 26.

18. Ibid.

19. Ibid., 27–28.

20. Lester R. Bittel and Jackson E. Ramsey, eds., *Handbook for Professional Managers* (New York: McGraw-Hill, 1985), 218.

21. A. H. Van de Ven and A. L. Delbecq, "The Effectiveness of Nominal, Delphi, and Interacting Group Decision-Making Processes," *Academy of Management Journal* 17 (1974): 605–21.

22. A. H. Van de Ven and A. L. Delbecq, "Nominal Versus Interacting Group Processes for Committee Decision-Making Effectiveness," *Academy of Management Journal* 14 (1971): 203–12. See also F. C. Miner, "A Comparative Analysis of Three Diverse Group Decision-Making Approaches," *Academy of Management Journal* 22 (1979): 81–93.

23. Thomas Gordon, *Leader Effectiveness Training: L. E. T.* (New York: Wyden Books, 1977), 141–42.

24. Melville Dalton, *Men Who Manage: Fusions of Feelings and Theory in Administration* (New York: John Wiley & Sons, 1959).

25. Edgar H. Schein, *Organizational Psychology,* 2d ed. (Englewood Cliffs, N.J.: Prentice-Hall, 1970).

26. Ibid., 97.

27. W. Earl Sasser, Jr. and Frank S. Leonard, "Let First-Level Supervisors Do Their Job," *Harvard Business Review* (March–April 1980): 119–20.

Suggested Readings

Aquayo, Rafael. *Dr. Deming: The American Who Taught the Japanese About Quality.* New York: Carol Publishing Group, 1990.

Boudette, Neal E. "Give Me a 'T!' Give Me an 'E!' " . . . *Industry Week* (January 8, 1990): 62–63, 65, 67.

Bylinsky, Gene. "Turning R&D into Real Products." *Fortune* (July 2, 1990): 72–74, 76–77.

Delbecq, A.; Van de Ven, A. H.; and Gustafson, D. H. *Group Techniques for Program Planning.* Glenview, Ill.: Scott, Foresman, 1975.

Deutsch, Claudia. "Business Meetings by Keyboard." *The Wall Street Journal* (October 21, 1990): 25, sect. F.

Dyer, William G. *Team Building: Issues and Alternatives,* 2d ed. Reading, Mass.: Addison-Wesley Publishing Co., 1987.

Mosvick, Robert K., and Nelson, Robert B. *We've Got to Start Meeting Like This!* Glenview, Ill.: Scott, Foresman, 1987.

3M Meeting Management Team. *How to Run Better Business Meetings.* New York: McGraw-Hill, 1987.

Stayer, Ralph. "How I Learned to Let My Workers Lead." *Harvard Business Review* (November–December 1990): 73–76.

10 Leadership and Management Styles

Objectives

After reading and discussing this chapter, you should be able to do the following:

1   Define this chapter's key terms.
2   List and give examples of this chapter's eleven principles of leadership.
3   Briefly define the contingency model of leadership.
4   Briefly explain the managerial GRID concept of blending concern for production with concern for people.
5   List and give situations in which each of the four management styles would be appropriate.
6   List and briefly explain four leadership indicators.

Key Terms

autocratic style   leadership

bureaucratic style   spectator style

democratic style

Introduction

In chapter 3 we defined *authority* as the right to give orders and instructions. *Power* was defined as the ability to influence others—to get them to subject their wills to yours. In this chapter we will see that leadership rests in the use of both power and authority but depends most heavily upon power. While all managers need authority—the ability to punish and to reward that rests in their formal positions—manager-leaders need both power and authority. It is possible to be a manager and yet not be a leader.

Power is the ability to influence. It flows from one's person and work position. "The people you're trying to motivate have to believe that you have more leverage in the company than they have. They have to accept you as an authority figure whose influence can help or hurt them . . . but they must respect you for your integrity and your ability, and that doesn't come with a title—it has to be earned."[1] If your people see you as a person who can "get things done"—one who will deliver as promised, who can be trusted, and who can be relied on to help them—you are a leader in their eyes and according to their perceptions.

Chapter 3 pointed out that power comes from one's position. As a manager, you have the right to punish and reward. Power also comes from your personality, your abilities, and your reputation at work. People look up to authorities who have the expertise they lack. People respect others who are fair and honest. People want to be with and work for others whom they can trust. But trust must be mutual. If you don't trust them, they will find it difficult to trust you. Trust in your people comes from knowing them well—their abilities, goals, and values. You demonstrate it in what you say and do each day. Your behavior at work either earns respect and trust for you or it does not. The example you give sets the tone for your interrelationships and encourages others to use it as an acceptable model for their own behaviors.

Leadership

Leadership
The ability to get work done with and through others while winning their respect, confidence, loyalty, and willing cooperation

Leadership is the ability to get work done with and through others, while simultaneously winning their respect, confidence, loyalty, and willing cooperation. The first part of our definition is true of *management* as well. It is the second half of the definition that distinguishes a leader from a nonleader. It is likely that, while you may be a leader to some of your subordinates, you may not be to others. The goal of a leader is to be one to all of his or her subordinates. Leadership is an art that can be acquired and developed by anyone with the motivation to do so.

All leaders have three limiting factors to contend with. First, they are limited by themselves—by their knowledge, skills, attitudes, and abilities, as well as by their weaknesses and inadequacies in the exercise of their roles. Second, they are limited by the groups over which they have authority—by the level of experience, the skills, the proficiencies, and the attitudes of their subordinates, as individuals and as a group. The ways in which subordinates perceive and interact with their bosses, their jobs, and each other are factors affecting both the quality and the quantity of their output. Finally, leaders are limited by their environment—by the resources and conditions available to them in their efforts to accomplish the assigned tasks and reach the established goals. All these factors undergo

Traits	Skills
Adaptable to situations	Clever (intelligent)
Alert to social environment	Conceptually skilled
Ambitious and achievement-oriented	Creative
Assertive	Diplomatic and tactful
Cooperative	Fluent in speaking
Decisive	Knowledgeable about group task
Dependable	Organized (administrative ability)
Dominant (desire to influence others)	Persuasive
Energetic (high activity level)	Socially skilled
Persistent	
Self-confident	
Tolerant of stress	
Willing to assume responsibility	

Exhibit 10.1   **Traits and skills commonly associated with leader effectiveness.** (*Source:* Gary A. Yukl. *Leadership in Organizations,* © 1981, pp. 70. Adapted by permission of Prentice-Hall, Inc., Englewood Cliffs, N.J.)

almost constant change, which requires the leaders to reassess these factors continually in determining the difficulties to be confronted.

Leadership Traits

Since the early 1900s, attempts have been made to discover a list of traits that would guarantee leadership status to their possessor. The United States Army surveyed all levels of soldiers exiting the service in the late 1940s to determine what traits were possessed by the commanders who were perceived to be effective leaders. Although a list of fourteen traits emerged from the survey, no commander had all the traits listed, and many famous commanders lacked several.

A list of leadership traits appears in Exhibit 10.1. As in the case of the Army's survey, quite a few traits are listed. It is unlikely, therefore, that any manager-leader would possess all of them. Research has failed to give us a final list of traits that guarantee leadership status to those who possess them. But the absence of some or all of the traits listed can keep you from becoming a successful leader and can interfere with your career advancement.

Employers watch for individual leadership traits in their employees and in prospective employees when they screen them for particular jobs

1. Be technically proficient.
2. Know yourself and seek self-improvement.
3. Know your people and look out for their welfare.
4. Keep your people informed.
5. Set the example.
6. Ensure that each task is understood, supervised, and accomplished.
7. Train your people to work as a team.
8. Make sound and timely decisions.
9. Develop a sense of responsibility in your subordinates.
10. Employ your resources in accordance with their capabilities.
11. Seek responsibilities and accept accountability for your actions.

Exhibit 10.2   **Principles of leadership.** (*Source:* U.S. Army.)

and training programs. Various psychological tests can be used to construct a personality profile of a person. Jobs are often assigned to people who possess leadership traits related to the particular job. Your eligibility for a management job or training program may rest on your employer's assessment of your traits of initiative, decisiveness, judgment, and loyalty.

Besides psychological tests, your routine performance appraisals, filled out by your boss, often call for the evaluation of specific traits that you may or may not possess. Certain traits may be considered indispensable, while others may be a plus but not essential. All the traits listed in Exhibit 10.1 can be developed and perfected through a commitment to programs designed to do so. Education, training, and experiences can help you acquire various traits. Endurance can be increased through a better diet, sufficient exercise, and enough sleep. Decisiveness and judgment can be improved with a structured decision-making approach to problems and practice at solving them.

Leadership Principles

What follows are established principles or guidelines that should govern the exercise of your informal and formal authority. These principles, along with a concerted effort on your part to acquire and develop leadership traits, practically guarantee your attainment of leadership status in the eyes of your peers and subordinates. These traits and principles are mutually supporting: the exercise of the principles helps develop the traits, while a person possessing the traits of a leader is inclined to follow the principles. Exhibit 10.2 lists eleven principles of leadership.

Each of these principles holds sound advice for you in any leadership position. They serve as concise reminders and as a checklist to which you should make frequent reference. They constitute a handy guide to help you assess your practice of management and the exercise of your authority over others. If you understand their meaning and make an honest effort to act in accordance with their wisdom, you can avoid numerous errors and problems.

You should note a similarity between the leadership skills identified here and the management skills discussed in chapter 1: technical, conceptual, and human. Principles 1, 6, and 10 relate to your development and use of technical skills. Principles 3, 4, 5, and 6 relate to your human skills. Principles 7, 9, and 10 relate to conceptual skills. All of the traits mentioned earlier relate in some way to each of the principles.

Seven Characteristics of an Ideal Leader

Francis G. ''Buck'' Rodgers, the former vice-president of marketing for IBM, lists seven characteristics of ideal leaders:

1. They never separate the word *accountability* from the word *responsibility.*
2. They always seek advice and criticism to gain new insights into their performance and into the goals they set.
3. They recognize situations where a little extra effort is required.
4. They maintain their enthusiasm in any circumstances.
5. They have the foresight to plan continually and to think ahead.
6. They understand how to prioritize amid a wide variety of daily choices.
7. They love to win but, at the same time, accept the risks involved in losing.[2]

After examining several important theories about leadership, we will discuss Buck Rodgers's basic steps for becoming a leader, at the end of this chapter.

The Contingency Model of Leadership

Fred E. Fiedler and others have speculated that the effectiveness of a group or organization depends on two main factors: the leader, and the situation the leader and group find themselves in. The leader's authority and power will place limits on his or her ability to get things done through others. Leaders tend to be either task-oriented or relationship-oriented. Fiedler's situational factors include leader-member relations, task structure, and the leader's positional authority to punish or to reward.[3]

Leadership Personalities

According to Fiedler's contingency model (sometimes called *situational leadership*), leaders are primarily motivated by their tasks or their interpersonal relationships with their followers. Whether one or the other is an appropriate focus depends upon the leader's situation. Task-oriented leaders seek accomplishments that fortify their sense of self-esteem and competence. Relationship-oriented leaders seek the admiration and respect of their followers to fortify their social and esteem needs. Both types of leaders need to be able to play both kinds of roles. The task-oriented leader may, as the need arises, adopt the relationship orientation. A relationship-oriented leader may focus on getting the job done when a crisis arises and time is short. But each will then return to his or her former orientation. This flexibility marks a true leader who is destined to achieve higher authority. Not all people have this flexibility.[4]

The Leadership Situation

According to Fiedler's contingency model, a leader's situation has three variables: the degree to which the leader is or feels accepted by followers; the degree to which the task to be accomplished is structured or defined; and the extent of the leader's powers to punish or reward. The greater the leader's powers and acceptance by followers, and the more highly structured the task, the easier it is for the leader to control the situation.[5]

The interaction of these variables is shown in Exhibit 10.3. On the bottom of the figure are eight combinations of the three variables, each describing a possible work situation. In position III, for example, the manager enjoys good member relations, the tasks of the subordinates are unstructured, and the leader possesses a strong organizational power base.

On the upper half of the figure are the two orientation styles: employee orientation and task orientation. In position I, the manager could employ a task-oriented approach. In position IV, where the leader-member relations are good, the task is unstructured, and the leader position power is weak, an employee-oriented behavior would be more appropriate.

Research into the contingency model shows that task-oriented leaders

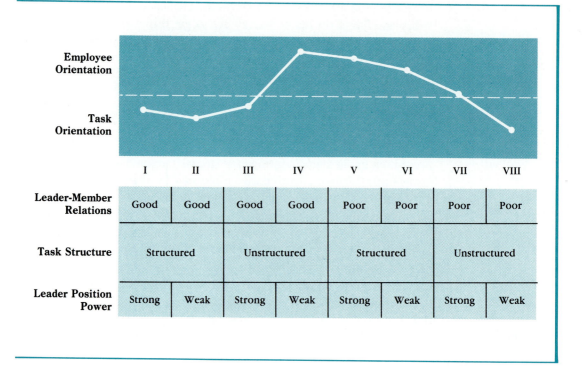

Exhibit 10.3   **How the style of effective leadership varies with the situation.** *(Source:* Reprinted by permission of *Harvard Business Review.* An exhibit from "Engineer the Job to Fit the Manager" by Fred E. Fiedler (September-October 1965). Copyright © by the President and Fellows of Harvard College. All rights reserved.)

perform best when they have either high or low concentrations of power, control, and influence over their situations. Relationship-oriented leaders perform best with moderate power, control, and influence. Leaders should be matched to the situation that calls for their favored approach or orientation. Instead, organizations often require managers to adjust to a variety of situations calling for different approaches by managers.

The Managerial GRID®

Many studies show that a leader's concern for or focus on his or her subordinates should be balanced against a concern for production or results. In the short run, managers who bow to organizational pressures

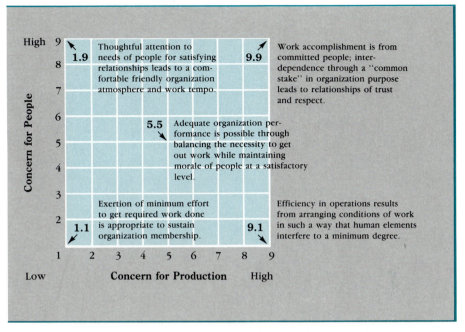

Exhibit 10.4 **The managerial GRID.** (*Source:* Adapted and reprinted by permission of *Harvard Business Review.* An exhibit from "Breakthrough in Organization Development" by Robert R. Blake, Jane S. Mouton, Louis B. Barnes, and Larry E. Greiner (November/December 1964). Copyright © 1964 by the President and Fellows of Harvard College. All rights reserved.)

to get results often achieve the greatest success by focusing on production and ignoring the needs of their subordinates. This kind of crisis management works best to put out fires, when time is short. It almost always utilizes the autocratic style of leadership, which is described later in this chapter.

Research tells us that, in the long run, however, the best leadership style is one that attempts to maintain a balance between the needs of subordinates and the demands of the organization for results. Exhibit 10.4 shows the managerial GRID concept developed by Robert Blake and his associates.

Position 1.9 on the GRID may be described as one in which thoughtful attention to the needs of people for satisfying relationships leads to a comfortable, friendly organizational atmosphere and work tempo. Position 1.1 allows for the exertion of minimum effort to get the required work done and to hold on to the organization's members. Position 5.5 represents a balancing between the need to get work accomplished and the need to maintain adequate morale levels. Position 9.1 represent a maximum focus on getting work out and arranging conditions of work so that human elements interfere to a minimum degree. Position 9.9 allows for work to be accomplished by committed people, for an interdependence of workers and management through a common stake in the organization, and for a relationship between leaders and followers that is based on trust and respect.[6]

Where the leader fits on the GRID at any given time is not entirely for him or her to decide. The leader's personality and management orientation, the company environment, and the competence of the followers all influence placement. Leaders should strive for the 9.9 position but remain flexible enough to adapt to the needs of the followers and the situation. As Professors Tannenbaum and Schmidt have pointed out in their excellent article on choosing a leadership pattern, a successful leader knows the forces that influence his or her behavior at any given time and accurately understands himself or herself, the individuals and group he or she is dealing with, and the broader social environment in which he or she operates. The leader can then determine the most appropriate orientation to take, and behave accordingly.[7]

The appropriate position for a manager to take at any given time may be dictated by the people and circumstances involved. When time is short and deadlines are fast approaching, a shift to position 9.1 may be called for. With new and inexperienced people who are undergoing training, position 9.1 may again be called for. The key idea under both sets of circumstances is to get work out or get people productive as soon as possible. As time progresses and pressures subside, the manager has time to focus on subordinates as individuals and begins to move toward a 5.5 position. With highly competent, experienced people, a manager can move to a 9.9 position—one in which teams are molded and individuals pool their skills to focus on a goal common to all team members.

As a manager, you will not be in any one position on the GRID with all of your people. Some may call for a 1.9 or a 9.1 position today and later may require a 9.9 or a 5.5 position. The real value of the GRID is to help you decide, at any given time, what position you are in with regard to an individual or to your entire group of subordinates. Then you must ask yourself if you should be in the position you are in. The theories that follow will help you pick a proper GRID position.

The Leadership Continuum

Exhibit 10.5 shows the continuum of choices a manager may face with regard to sharing decisions with subordinates. At the left the manager holds the authority to make all decisions, avoiding all delegation and

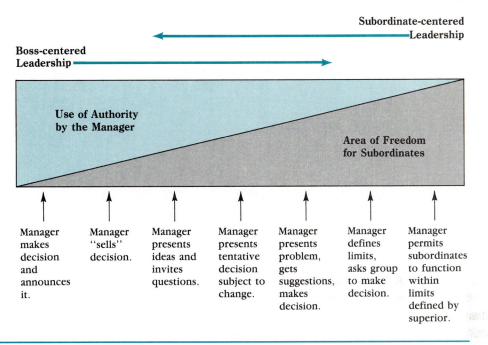

Subordinate-centered
Leadership

Boss-centered
Leadership

Use of Authority
by the Manager

Area of Freedom
for Subordinates

| Manager makes decision and announces it. | Manager "sells" decision. | Manager presents ideas and invites questions. | Manager presents tentative decision subject to change. | Manager presents problem, gets suggestions, makes decision. | Manager defines limits, asks group to make decision. | Manager permits subordinates to function within limits defined by superior. |

Exhibit 10.5   **The continuum of leadership behavior.** (*Source:* Reprinted by permission of *Harvard Business Review*. An exhibit from ''How to Choose a Leadership Pattern'' by Robert Tannenbaum and Warren H. Schmidt (May–June 1973). Copyright © 1973 by the President and Fellows of Harvard College. All rights reserved.)

power sharing. On the right of the continuum, the manager allows subordinates a great deal of freedom of action and shares many of the decisions that must be made. The amount of the formal (position) authority that you decide to share with your subordinates will determine your management or leadership style. But the decision to share authority is not entirely your own to make. Your boss will have some influence, as will your experience and confidence and those of your subordinates in sharing decisions.

Leadership Behaviors

Gary Yukl and his colleagues have conducted research to develop ''meaningful and measurable categories of leader behavior.''[8] They have given us nineteen categories of leader behavior, along with definitions and examples (see Exhibit 10.6). These categories clearly label just what leaders do and help us to recognize these behaviors in our own daily lives. Since

1. *Performance Emphasis:* The extent to which a leader emphasizes the importance of subordinate performance, tries to improve productivity and efficiency, tries to keep subordinates working up to their capacity, and checks on their performance.

    EXAMPLE: My supervisor urged us to be careful not to let orders go out with defective components.

2. *Consideration:* The extent to which a leader is friendly, supportive, and considerate in his or her behavior toward subordinates and tries to be fair and objective.

    EXAMPLE: When a subordinate was upset about something, the supervisor was very sympathetic and tried to console him.

3. *Inspiration:* The extent to which a leader stimulates enthusiasm among subordinates for the work of the group and says things to build subordinates' confidence in their ability to perform assignments successfully and attain group objectives.

    EXAMPLE: My boss told us we were the best design group he had ever worked with, and he was sure that this new product was going to break every sales record in the company.

4. *Praise-Recognition:* The extent to which a leader provides praise and recognition to subordinates with effective performance, shows appreciation for their special efforts and contributions, and makes sure they get credit for their helpful ideas and suggestions.

    EXAMPLE: In a meeting, the supervisor told us she is very satisfied with our work and said she appreciated the extra effort we made this month.

5. *Structuring Reward Contingencies:* The extent to which a leader rewards effective subordinate performance with tangible benefits, such as a pay increase, promotion, more desirable assignments, a better work schedule, and more time off.

    EXAMPLE: My supervisor established a new policy that any subordinate who brought in a new client would earn 10 percent of the contracted fee.

6. *Decision Participation:* The extent to which a leader consults with subordinates and otherwise allows them to influence his or her decisions.

    EXAMPLE: My supervisor asked me to attend a meeting with him and his boss to develop a new production schedule, and he was very receptive to my ideas on the subject.

7. *Autonomy-Delegation:* The extent to which a leader delegates authority and responsibility to subordinates and allows them to determine how to do their work.

    EXAMPLE: My boss gave me a new project and encouraged me to handle it any way I think is best.

Exhibit 10.6   **Yukl's nineteen categories of leader behavior.** (*Source:* Gary A. Yukl, *Leadership in Organizations,* © 1981, pp. 121–25. Adapted by permission of Prentice-Hall, Inc., Englewood Cliffs, N.J.)

8. *Role Clarification:* The extent to which a leader informs subordinates about their duties and responsibilities, specifies the rules and policies that must be observed and lets subordinates know what is expected of them.

   EXAMPLE: My boss called me in to inform me about a rush project that must be given top priority, and she gave me some specific assignments related to this project.

9. *Goal Setting:* The extent to which a leader emphasizes the importance of setting specific performance goals for each important aspect of a subordinate's job, measures progress toward the goals, and provides concrete feedback.

   EXAMPLE: The supervisor held a meeting to discuss the sales quota for next month.

10. *Training-Coaching:* The extent to which a leader determines training needs for subordinates and provides any necessary training and coaching.

    EXAMPLE: My boss asked me to attend an outside course at the company's expense and said I could leave early on the days it was to be held.

11. *Information Dissemination:* The extent to which a leader keeps subordinates informed about developments that affect their work, including events in other work units or outside the organization, decisions made by higher management, and progress in meetings with superiors or outsiders.

    EXAMPLE: The supervisor briefed us about some high-level changes in policy.

12. *Problem Solving:* The extent to which a leader takes the initiative in proposing solutions to serious work-related problems and acts decisively to deal with such problems when a prompt solution is needed.

    EXAMPLE: The unit was short-handed due to illness, and we had an important deadline to meet; my supervisor arranged to borrow two people from other units, so we could finish the job today.

13. *Planning:* The extent to which a leader plans how to efficiently organize and schedule the work in advance, plans how to attain work unit objectives, and makes contingency plans for potential problems.

    EXAMPLE: My supervisor devised a shortcut that allows us to prepare our financial statements in three days instead of the four days it used to take.

14. *Coordinating:* The extent to which a leader coordinates the work of subordinates, emphasizes the importance of coordination, and encourages subordinates to coordinate their activities.

    EXAMPLE: My supervisor had subordinates who were ahead in their work help those who were behind so that the different parts of the project would be ready at the same time.

Exhibit 10.6   *(cont.)*

15. *Work Facilitation:* The extent to which a leader obtains for subordinates any necessary supplies, equipment, support services, or other resources; eliminates problems in the work environment; and removes other obstacles that interfere with the work.

> EXAMPLE: I asked my boss to order some supplies, and he arranged to get them right away.

16. *Representation:* The extent to which a leader establishes contacts with other groups and important people in the organization, persuades them to appreciate and support his or her work unit, and uses his or her influence with superiors and outsiders to promote and defend the interests of the work unit.

> EXAMPLE: My supervisor met with the data processing manager to get some revisions made in the computer programs, so they will be better suited to our needs.

17. *Interaction Facilitation:* The extent to which a leader tries to get subordinates to be friendly with each other, cooperate, share information and ideas, and help each other.

> EXAMPLE: The sales manager took the group out to lunch to give everybody a chance to get to know the new sales representative.

18. *Conflict Management:* The extent to which a leader restrains subordinates from fighting and arguing, encourages them to resolve conflicts in a constructive manner, and helps settle conflicts and disagreements between subordinates.

> EXAMPLE: Two members of the department who were working together on a project were having a dispute about it: the manager met with them to help resolve the matter.

19 *Criticism-Discipline:* The extent to which a leader criticizes or disciplines a subordinate who shows consistently poor performance, violates a rule, or disobeys an order; disciplinary actions include an official warning, reprimand, suspension, or dismissal.

> EXAMPLE: The supervisor was annoyed that a subordinate kept making the same kinds of errors and warned him to make a more concerted effort.

Exhibit 10.6   *(cont.)*

these behaviors are quite specific, they can help you identify what you are doing—or are not doing but could do—to perform your job effectively.

As you study the nineteen categories, rate yourself on how many of them you put to use regularly. Try to link each behavior to the skills and traits in Exhibit 10.1. Then try to relate each one to your knowledge of

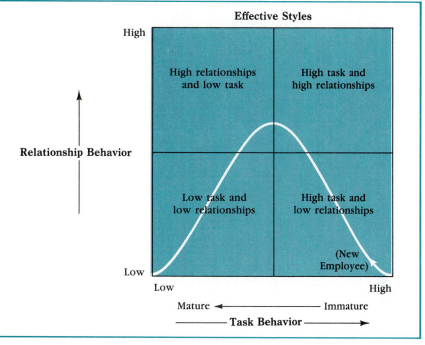

Exhibit 10.7   Adaptation of Hersey and Blanchard's life-cycle theory of leadership.
(*Source:* Paul Hersey and Kenneth H. Blanchard, *Management of Organizational Behavior,* 4th ed. 1982, pp. 89–90).

human motivation and to the various theories we examined in chapter 7. Finally, consider how each ties in with your roles of educator, counselor, judge, and spokesperson.

The Life-Cycle Theory

People need different styles of supervision and leadership at different times. Paul Hersey and Kenneth Blanchard have given us a theory of the general evolution in the leadership approaches to employees as their tenure and experiences grow. The *life-cycle theory,* detailed in Exhibit 10.7, shows that the new employee (block 1) needs a high-task focus. As the employee takes on new knowledge and skills and demonstrates competence, he or she requires a high-employee/high-task focus (block 2). With employees who have matured in both tenure and capabilities, the supervisor can move from a high-direction to a low-direction focus, as required (block 4—the experienced, secure employee).[9]

Management Styles

What all these theories have been leading up to is exemplified in the styles of management that follow. These boil down to how much authority you will share with subordinates and how you will focus on tasks or people.

There are four main styles of management available to you: autocratic, bureaucratic, democratic, and spectator. All but the bureaucratic style are also leadership styles. At the left extremity in Exhibit 10.5 is the autocratic leader or manager. In the middle is the democratic leader or manager. At the far right is the spectator leader or manager. The bureaucratic manager is not shown in Exhibit 10.5 because he or she is not considered a leader.

Each of the four styles can have either positive or negative effects on your subordinates, depending on the characteristics of the people who are subjected to them and on the circumstances of their use. Like a firearm, they can be an instrument for winning prizes or a means of inflicting injury.

The Autocratic Style

Autocratic style
A management and leadership style characterized by the retention of all authority for decision making by the leader

Leaders of the **autocratic style** keep power to themselves and do not delegate to their subordinates. The making of a final decision is reserved for the leaders alone. They keep their subordinates dependent on them for instructions, and they allow their subordinates to act only under their direct supervision.

Prerequisites The necessary prerequisites for using the autocratic style are the following:

1. You must be an expert in the practice of management, as well as in the handling of your subordinates' jobs.
2. Your subordinates must be in need of this approach.
3. You must wish to communicate primarily by means of orders and detailed instructions.

Limitations on the Autocratic Style In general, you should restrict your use of this style to the following situations:

- When you are dealing with new employees who are unfamiliar with the tasks and methods they are expected to perform

- When time is short or when there is an emergency situation that does not allow you to explain the reasons for your orders
- When you are directing a stubborn or difficult subordinate who does not respond favorably to requests or to your use of the other three styles of supervision
- When your authority is directly challenged (by putting your wishes in the form of orders, you thereby place your subordinate in the position of either following the orders or being guilty of insubordination)

You should restrict your use of this style of supervision to the situations outlined above. If you lack the necessary prerequisites, you cannot use it effectively. As soon as the situation changes, you should shift to another leadership style. Keep in mind that the autocratic style is both a management style and a leadership style.

Employee Reactions People subjected to the autocratic style will generally be high-quantity producers but only for the short run. They will tend to be tense and somewhat fearful of you. If the style is used on a person too long—that is, after the need for it has ceased—he or she will become resentful and withhold his or her normal contributions to the job. It is not a style that builds team players or encourages strong ties among the workers. It causes subordinates to become dependent on their leaders.

The Bureaucratic Style

Bureaucratic style
A management style characterized by the manager's reliance on rules, regulations, policies, and procedures to direct subordinates

The **bureaucratic style** is typified by the manager's reliance on rules, regulations, policy, and procedures. They represent to him or her authority and certainty. It is management by the book. Through the exercise of this style, the manager adopts the posture of a police officer religiously enforcing rules and depending on superiors to resolve problems not covered in the manual.

Unlike the other three styles of supervision, the bureaucratic style cannot really be a leadership style, because managers who practice it are not really directing their people in a personal way. Instead, they are directing them through regulations, procedures, and policies.

Prerequisites There are three major prerequisites for the use of the bureaucratic style:

1. All the other styles must be inappropriate for use.

2. Subordinates subjected to this style must be in need of it.

3. Latitude in decision making and deviations from procedures must be forbidden to the manager and subordinates.

Limitations on the Bureaucratic Style   This style is appropriate for governmental bodies, military services, and nonprofit enterprises such as public hospitals and charities. It has a very small place in businesses, and its use there should be limited to the following situations:

- During the installation of new equipment and operations, when the people in charge of an operation are specialists

- In doing research or conducting analytical studies

- In training recordkeeping, filing, and other clerical personnel, where faithful adherence to set procedures is essential for the success of the job

- In enforcing safety or carrying out strictly routine, highly repetitive operations

If utilized properly, the bureaucratic approach can be an effective style that has positive effects on people. If used improperly, it can be devastating to anyone subjected to it who has ambition and creativity.

Employee Reactions   This style does little to build motivation in subordinates. It promotes the formulation of strong work habits that, after a time, become very difficult to change in even the smallest way without strong employee resistance. Employees tend to adopt an indifferent attitude toward their peers and their work. The supervisor becomes rather unimportant to the subordinates and is perceived by them as a watchdog rather than a manager. Workers generally do what is expected of them but little more. There are a number of people, however—both in and out of management—for whom this style represents security, and they respond well to this style for that reason. For most people, however, it is only of value in the special situations listed previously.

Democratic style
A management and leadership style characterized by a sharing of decision-making authority with subordinates by the leader

The Democratic Style

Managers of the **democratic style** adopt a "we" approach to their work and to their subordinates. They play the role of coaches, drilling their teams on fundamentals and sharing decision-making authority with them. They make frequent use of problem-solving meetings, as outlined in chapter 9. They delegate freely to subordinates who have earned their confidence, as well as to members of the group in general. They attempt to build a strong team spirit and to foster mutual respect and interdependence between themselves as coaches and the members of the team, as well as among the team members and their peers.

This style of supervision often goes by other names, such as the consultative, general, or participative style. It is a leadership style very much in use today.

Prerequisites   The following conditions are needed in advance of implementing the democratic style:

1. You should have your superior's permission to use it.
2. You should be willing to accept a certain number of mistakes and delays in the early stages of its implementation.
3. You should have a personal commitment to this style and a strong belief in its ability to motivate people; once you extend this style to your subordinates, you will find it difficult to shift to a different style.
4. You should have carefully prepared your subordinates by means of initial delegations of some of your authority, and you should be willing to continue to consult with your subordinates on small matters during the early stages of the new style's use.
5. You should have a high degree of patience and the time required for group meetings on decision making and other topics.

Some supervisors may feel threatened by this style. If so, they should not attempt to use it or be asked to use it until they have been prepared through training to do so. A worker who has never in the past been asked for the time of day, let alone an opinion on new procedures, might become quite suspicious at sudden attempts to obtain his or her participation in matters affecting the department.

Limitations on the Democratic Style   This style is best used in the following situations:

- When your workers are highly skilled and/or highly experienced at their jobs
- Where time is sufficient to permit participation by your subordinates as individuals or as a group

- When preparing groups or individuals for changes
- When attempting to solve problems common to the group, such as an improvement in methods, in safety, or in environmental conditions
- When attempting to air gripes or otherwise relieve workers' tensions.

Employee Reactions   The great majority of today's workers are educated enough for the democratic style of leadership. Through it they can achieve and sustain a high quality and quantity of output for extended periods. The supervisor who uses this approach is employee-centered rather than work-centered, and his or her people know it. They appreciate the trust and freedom that the supervisor expresses in them through the use of the democratic style. Cooperation and group spirit are strongly promoted, and a corresponding boost is given to morale. Under the democratic style, workers tend to understand the contributions of their peers to a greater degree, and they get to know each other better than under any of the other styles.

The Spectator Style

Spectator style
A management and leadership style characterized by a strong reliance of the leader on the skills, knowledge, and initiative of subordinates

The **spectator style** is characterized by treating everyone as an individual. The team concept is either played down or nonexistent. Subordinates perceive themselves as and are treated as professionals—that is, experts in their fields.

The manager makes himself or herself available for consultations in accordance with a strong open-door policy, but he or she is generally physically removed from direct and frequent contact with subordinates. If the workers need help, they know where to go to find it. If they do not need assistance, the boss will tell them so. This style is not a cop-out on the part of the supervisor who adopts it. Even though the boss is remote from his or her subordinates, he or she remains in touch with them and their work through conferences, reports, and records of output.

Prerequisites   The prerequisites of the spectator style of leadership are as follows:

1. Since the workers are treated as experts under this style, they should really be highly skilled at their crafts.

2. Controls other than direct and frequent observations must be established to monitor the workers' performance.

3. The workers must possess pride in their work, as well as endurance and initiative.

Limitations on the Spectator Style   The use of the spectator style should be restricted, as a rule, to the folowing groups or situations:

■   When you have in your department highly skilled, experienced, and educated personnel

■   When you are using outside experts, such as staff specialists, consultants, or temporary skilled help

■   When you as the boss are new at your job or lack previous personal experience in the work being performed by your subordinates.

Employee Reactions   Workers who work under the spectator style perceive themselves as being in business for themselves; that is, they adopt a somewhat independent air and see their boss as a kind of staff assistant who stands ready to help them if they need him or her. This style generally promotes high levels of individual output for indefinite periods of time. It fosters pride and morale better than the other styles do. But if the boss becomes too remote or inaccessible, insecurity may set in, along with resulting fears and frustrations. All the workers are pretty much on their own and strongly feel the need to prove themselves to their boss and their peers. Consequently, people working under this style need constant reassurance that they are performing up to standard and that they are appreciated.

As a supervisor at any level, you must be familiar with all four of the management styles. You will be faced with subordinates and situations at one time or another that will call upon you to use each of these styles.

During the training of a new employee, you should probably rely on the autocratic style, the bureaucratic style, or a blend of the two. Once the newcomer has been placed in his or her job and is performing up to standard, you should switch to one of the other styles of leadership. If you do not, your worker may rebel, and you will have gone a long way toward helping to bring about his or her termination.

If you try to use a style that is wrong for a specific subordinate, he or she will probably let you know it. Changes in a subordinate's attitudes and behavior are the first sign that you may be using an improper style of

A recent study of 456 executives (355 women and 101 men) reveals some interesting differences between the ways in which both sexes approach the leadership role. Women respondents tend to be "interactive"—encouraging others' participation, making people feel part of the organization, and making them feel good about themselves and their contributions. The women made frequent references to their efforts to include others by sharing power and information. Interactive leaders "try to instill . . . group identity in a variety of ways, including encouraging others to have a say in almost every aspect of work, from setting performance goals to determining strategy. To facilitate inclusion, they create mechanisms to get people to participate and they use a conversational style that sends signals inviting people to get involved."

The men in the survey described their styles as being a set of "transactions with subordinates—exchanging rewards for services rendered or punishment for inadequate performance. The men are also more likely to use power that comes from their organizational position and formal authority." Both the men and the women claimed to have an equal mix of traits considered to be "feminine" (understanding, compassionate, sensitive, dependent), "masculine" (dominant, tough, assertive, competitive), and "gender-neutral" (adaptive, tactful, sincere, efficient, and reliable).

Some men are leading with participation and inclusion while some women lead with the emphasis on exercising their formal authority. Both styles of leading can be effective, depending upon the circumstances. ". . . what is a disadvantage under one set of circumstances is an advantage under another. The 'best' leadership style depends on the organizational context." Both have much to learn from each other's styles.

(Sources: Judy B. Rosener, "Ways Women Lead," *Harvard Business Review* (November–December 1990): 119–125. Sharon Nelton, "Men, Women and Leadership," *Nation's Business* (May, 1991) pp. 16–22.)

leadership. Selecting the proper style for individual workers is easy, once you acquire some experience as a supervisor, but it may involve a bit of trial and error on your part. Do not hesitate to switch if the style you are presently using fails to get the desired results. And don't forget that a lot of help is available to you through the advice and counsel of your peers and your superiors.

You may not be entirely free to select your own styles of leadership. Your boss may frown upon the use of one or another of them. You may feel inadequate in your understanding of how to implement one or more of the styles. Your tendency might be to use the one you feel most at home with on all your people. This is almost always a mistake. A subordinate who has worked well under a spectator style may, because of changes in his or her job, require an autocratic or democratic style of direction to get him or her through a period of transition to a new assignment. You should stand ready to offer the style each subordinate needs. It is only by practice and study that you can feel confident enough to use all four styles successfully.

The Basic Steps to Being a Leader

After many years in the marketing management of IBM, Buck Rodgers, retired vice-president of marketing, reports that there are nine basic steps, as he sees it, to becoming an influential manager-leader:

1. Establish who's in charge. Each person in a unit within an organization must be clear about his or her authority, responsibility, and accountability.
2. Know what you want to accomplish. Define your goals, short- and long-term. Map out your priorities for each day. Monitor your use of time, and check on your progress regularly.
3. Know what you want each person you manage to accomplish. Set specific goals for a person to achieve, and let that person know the quality of performance expected. Judge performance on achievements, not on style.
4. Let the person know what you expect. Don't let people guess at what you want from them or about how they are doing. Communicate regularly with each individual about what you expect and about what will happen when those expectations are met, exceeded, or not met.
5. Find out what your employee wants for himself or herself. Insist that each subordinate spell out goals, aspirations, and expectations.
6. Find out what your employee expects of you. What is expected in terms of help—more frequent or less frequent contact with you? more responsibility?
7. Take being a role model seriously. Subordinates do as you do more often than they do as you say they should do. Your example provides the psychological and performance models for your group.

8. Expect others to be self-motivated, but don't count on it. People have their peaks and valleys. You may need to intercede on occasion, helping subordinates to improve, grow, and prosper.

9. Understand that the quality of your leadership is determined by the methods you use to motivate others. What you use and apply to others will be used and applied to you. Open, honest, and sensitive communication builds mutual trust and respect.[10]

Assessing Your Leadership Ability

You can rely on four major indicators as you attempt to determine the effectiveness of your leadership with your people: (1) morale; (2) group spirit; (3) proficiency; and (4) self-discipline. Each of these in turn can be evaluated to help measure the impact you and your methods are having on your formal-group members, individually and collectively.

Morale

People's attitudes toward all of the individuals, things, and events that affect them at work constitute their morale. *Morale* can be defined as an individual's state of mind with regard to his or her job, supervisor, peers, and company. It reflects a person's level of involvement in work and appreciation of the people and conditions that he or she must relate to every day. Through the actions and statements of people, you can effectively measure their morale. If your subordinates are positive individuals who take pride in their work, they reflect favorably on you and your group. If they are absent frequently, fail to attend to their duties, or dwell on negative factors, you can assume that you strike them as less than a leader.

Group Spirit

What are the major attitudes reflected by the members of your formal group and any informal groups associated with it? Are they positive and supportive, fostering teamwork and harmony, or are they negative and destructive? Both individual and group attitudes are shaped in large measure by your human relations efforts. If your group is without team spirit, have you recently voiced your appreciation for its achievements? Are you trying to work with its members and to utilize their talents? Do you know their needs and values? Do you know your group members as individuals?

Proficiency

How good are you at your job? How good are your subordinates? Are you making an effort to improve both your own level of competence and theirs? Are you aware of any efforts on their part to seek a higher level of competence? Are you fostering their growth and development? This indicator is tied directly to morale and group spirit. If these are low or negative, your subordinates' demonstrated proficiency levels will be, too.

Self-Discipline

Can your shop or office function in your absence? Do your people respond promptly and in a positive way to your instructions? Do they accept honest criticism well? Have you had to reprimand more often than praise? Do your people know the why behind what they are expected to do? Can they be trusted? If not, what are you doing about these problems?

You can rate yourself by using these indicators at any time. Chances are that your boss is doing so regularly. If you are placing the kind of emphasis that you should on your human relations, you should experience little difficulty in these general areas.

Instant Replay

1. Leadership is based on a person's skills, knowledge, and formal authority.

2. Not all leaders are managers, and not all managers are leaders. People who can get work done through willing followers who respect them in the process are leaders.

3. Various leaders have various different traits, such as enthusiasm, tact, and endurance. No one set of traits is common to all leaders.

4. Leadership principles offer advice on how a person who wants to be a leader should behave. They are illustrations of the three skills of a manager studied in chapter 1.

5. The contingency model of leadership holds that the effectiveness of a group or organization depends on the leader and the leader's situation.

6. Basic leader orientations are task- or relationship-oriented. Most leaders focus on one or the other, as the circumstances dictate.

7. The management GRID system represents the possible positions managers may take with respect to their focus on and blending of their two primary orientations—people and tasks.

8. The leadership continuum illustrates the positions a leader can take with regard to sharing authority with subordinates.

9. The four basic management styles are autocratic, democratic, spectator, and bureaucratic. Only the last is not a leadership style.

Glossary **Autocratic style** a management and leadership style characterized by the retention of all authority by the leader, who keeps subordinates dependent on the leader for instructions and guidance.

Bureaucratic style a management style characterized by the manager's reliance on rules, regulations, policies, and procedures to direct subordinates.

Democratic style a management and leadership style characterized by the sharing of authority and decision making with subordinates through problem-solving sessions, delegation, and the development of a team spirit.

Leadership the ability to get work done through others while winning their respect, confidence, loyalty, and willing cooperation.

Spectator style a management and leadership style characterized by a strong reliance of the supervisor on the skills, knowledge, and initiative of subordinates, with the corresponding development of a high level of independence and pride among the subordinates.

Questions for Class Discussion

1. Can you define this chapter's key terms?

2. What are this chapter's eleven principles of leadership? Can you give an example of each from your own experience?

3. What is the contingency model of leadership's basic parts?

4. What does the managerial GRID system attempt to show with regard to leaders?

5. What are the four basic management styles? Which is not a leadership style, and why isn't it?

6. What style of supervision would you use in each of the following situations, and why would you use it?

   a. A new employee with two years' experience in a similar job

   b. An old-timer who appears to be an informal leader of one of the cliques in your department

   c. A neurotic employee with a good deal of experience, whose neurosis is interfering with his or her job performance

   d. An employee with many more years' experience than you have, who resents you personally and your authority

7. What are four indicators of how well a person is leading?

Incident   **Purpose** To identify the leadership ability and potential you currently possess.

Your Task Take the quiz shown, marking whether you "agree" or "disagree" with each of the statements. Do not look at the scoring key that follows the quiz until you have thought about each statement and marked your choices.

	Agree	Disagree
1. I usually give my people clear and concise answers, instructions, and assignments.	_____	_____
2. My people respect me for my abilities.	_____	_____
3. My people see me as a source of help when they encounter difficulties with assignments.	_____	_____
4. I believe that leaders can be created, that leadership is an art that can be learned.	_____	_____
5. I think that people must be popular and well liked in order to lead effectively.	_____	_____
6. Effective leaders always explain the "why" behind their orders and requests.	_____	_____
7. Followers should be able to adjust to a leader's style, not the other way around.	_____	_____
8. Without me, my people and my department would be in serious trouble.	_____	_____
9. I should be the only person to perform the most vital tasks for which my group is responsible.	_____	_____
10. When making decisions that rely on the group for implementation, I seek input from the group.	_____	_____

11. To be truly successful, all the manager's decisions must be supported by the group.   _____   _____

12. I am ultimately accountable for my group's and individual group members' performances.   _____   _____

13. I think that it is important to have the symbols of status that separate a leader from followers.   _____   _____

14. I know who I am and what my values are, and I have priorities in my life and at work.   _____   _____

Key

The following answers earn you 1 point each. A score of 10 or more means that you are or have the potential to be an excellent leader. Discuss with friends and classmates why the scoring key is what it is.

1. agree; 2. agree; 3. agree; 4. agree; 5. disagree; 6. disagree; 7. disagree; 8. disagree; 9. disagree; 10. agree; 11. disagree; 12. agree; 13. disagree; 14. agree.

Case Problem 10.1   Conflicts

Peggy Simmons has just been appointed supervisor of the shipping operations at Fantasy Products, a Midwest mail-order operation specializing in unusual consumer products. She has worked for the company in several capacities, but this is her first supervisory position. She is now responsible for five women, three of whom she has worked with as a coworker in the past. Her section packs and ships orders as they are received from the order-processing department.

Peggy has a reputation with three of her subordinates as a "fun person." Betty, Susan, and Ellen have all worked with Peggy in the past and know her to be full of life and a joy to be with. Peggy knows a great many jokes and shares them whenever she can. She "joked" her way through many of the rush days from November through December. Although she has been known to come late and to leave early on occasion, she worked hard and carefully when she was on the job.

During her first week as supervisor, Peggy tried to remain her old self. But problems began to appear. With the Christmas season just

two weeks away, Peggy knew that things had to get better soon if orders were to be processed quickly enough. She sensed a carefree and leisurely atmosphere, which already had caused a backlog of several days' orders. No one seemed to take Peggy seriously.

When Peggy tried to change her approach from "they know what to do, let them do it" to "from now on, it's by the book," Betty was the first to react. In discussions during breaks, Betty made it clear to her coworkers that she felt Peggy was letting power go to her head. Ellen agreed and added that she and the others probably knew what to do better than Peggy did. Susan believed that in a few weeks all the fun would be out of their work if Peggy persisted in rigid work routines and shipping schedules. All three had influence over the other two women because they had been around a long time and had worked with Peggy for several years.

By the end of Peggy's third week, it was clear that a revolt was in the making. Her subordinates seemed to be ignoring her quotas for the day and just smiled at her when she tried to get them to pick up the pace. Breaks seemed to be stretching from fifteen minutes to thirty. When Peggy called Susan aside to talk with her about the problems, Susan was openly hostile and told her that Betty and Ellen were on her side and doing what she was doing, too. Susan demanded to know why she was being singled out for criticism. One day Peggy was absent and returned to find that the shop had fallen nearly two days behind. It was clear to her that the five subordinates had sat on their hands in her absence.

Questions

1. Assess Peggy's leadership using the four measures at the end of this chapter.
2. What leadership traits does Peggy seem to lack? What leadership skills does she lack? (Use Exhibit 10.1 in your answer.)
3. What could Fantasy Products have done to prevent Peggy's current situation?
4. What style of management did Peggy begin with? What style is she attempting to use at the end of the case?

Case Problem 10.2   Let George Do It

George McArthur is Computer Services Director of the First Guaranty Trust and Savings Bank of Pepperton, Ohio. He was financial assistant to the vice-president, Mr. B. J. Sloan, for three years prior to being promoted to his present job. George has three supervisors reporting to him, and they in turn direct a staff of twenty-one employees—fourteen on the first shift and seven on the second.

George's promotion took him from a staff position where he had no subordinates and worked almost entirely on his own. He was promoted, when the previous middle manager left, because he had designed most of the present office and accounting systems now in use and because of a superior performance in his past position.

Since taking over his new post eight months ago, all three of the original supervisors have left the bank. One asked for and received a transfer; one quit to work for a savings and loan; the third was fired by George for "failure to follow instructions and an insubordinate attitude."

In addition to the personnel turnover, much of the routine work is not getting out on schedule, and the computer room has become somewhat disorderly. An unusual number of complaints have been recorded by the departments and customers served by George's section, and two of the operators on the first shift have threatened to quit.

George is a demanding and formal person of impeccable dress. He insists that everyone call him "Mister McArthur" and has a very low tolerance for failures. He seems to be "all business" in the words of his boss. He has never been known to compliment his subordinates but makes them quite aware of their mistakes.

On several occasions the two supervisors on the first shift (the only one he is physically present to supervise) have complained to George about his habit of going directly to operators to order changes in procedure or production schedules. This has disrupted services and the regular production of reports and data to such a point that a growing backlog of work has been created which is overtaxing the second shift. One of the first-shift supervisors, Douglas Waltham, has openly talked of leaving if "McArthur doesn't get off my back."

In McArthur's last seven years with the bank, he has been complimented numerous times by his superiors. He rose from a teller to loan officer and then to assistant to the vice-president. In none of these previous positions did he directly supervise employees.

Questions

1. What style(s) of supervision is George using and what, if anything, is wrong with it or them?

2. What clues do you have that George might not have been the best choice for Computer Services Director?

3. What leadership traits is George lacking?

4. Cite a violation of leadership principles committed by George.

5. If you were George's boss, what would you do?

Notes

1. Buck Rodgers, with Irv Levey, *Getting the Most Out of Yourself and Others* (New York: Harper & Row, 1987), 122.
2. "Buck Rodgers's Kind of Leader," *Success!* (March 1987): 30.
3. Fred E. Fiedler, "The Contingency Model—New Directions for Leadership Utilization," *Journal of Contemporary Business* 3 #4 (Autumn 1974): 65–80.
4. Ibid.
5. Ibid.
6. R. R. Blake and J. S. Mouton, "Breakthrough in Organization Development," in *Business Classics: Fifteen Key Concepts for Managerial Success* (Cambridge, Mass.: Harvard Business Review, 1975), 162.
7. Robert Tannenbaum and Warren H. Schmidt, "How to Choose a Leadership Pattern," *Harvard Business Review* (May–June 1973): 162–164, 168, 170, 173, 175, 178–180.
8. Gary A. Yukl, *Leadership in Organizations* (Englewood Cliffs, N.J.: Prentice-Hall, 1981), 121.
9. Paul Hersey and Kenneth H. Blanchard, *Management of Organizational Behavior: Utilizing Human Resources,* 4th ed. (Englewood Cliffs, N.J.: Prentice-Hall, 1982), 88–91.
10. Rodgers, note 1, 122–29.

Suggested Readings

Bennis, Warren, and Nanus, Burt. *Leaders: The Strategies for Taking Charge.* New York: Harper & Row, 1985.

Fiedler, Fred, and Chemers, Martin. *Leadership and Effective Management.* Chicago: Scott, Foresman, 1974.

Fiedler, Fred; Chemers, Martin; and Mahar, L. *Improving Leadership Effectiveness: The Leader Match Concept.* New York: John Wiley & Sons, 1976.

Huey, John. "Secrets of Great Second Bananas." *Fortune* (May 6, 1991): 64–65, 70, 72, 76.

Kotter, John P. "What Leaders Really Do." *Harvard Business Review* (May–June 1990): 103–111.

Rodgers, Buck, with Levey, Irv. *Getting the Most Out of Yourself and Others.* New York: Harper & Row, 1987.

Rosener, Judy B. "Ways Women Lead." *Harvard Business Review* (November–December 1990): 119–125.

Schaffer, Robert H. ''Demand Better Results—And Get Them.'' *Harvard Business Review* (March–April 1991): 142–149.

Sellers, Patricia. ''Does the CEO Really Matter?'' *Fortune* (April 22, 1991): 80–82, 86, 90, 94.

Stewart, Thomas A. ''Do You Push Your People Too Hard?'' *Fortune* (October 22, 1990): 121, 124, 128.

Nelton, Sharon. ''Men, Women and Leadership.'' *Nation's Business* (May 1991): 16–22.

Yukl, Gary A. *Leadership in Organizations.* Englewood Cliffs, N.J.: Prentice-Hall, 1981.

III Shaping Your Environment

Part III includes four chapters directly concerned with how well you, as a supervisor, will be able to influence the productivity of your subordinates. This section deals specifically with the proper ways to bring in new people, get them ready to perform to standards, appraise their results, and correct their deficiencies. Through the successful application of the principles in these chapters, you will exercise proper leadership to influence the performances of your subordinates directly.

Chapter 11 explains the difficult but regularly needed processes of selection and introduction of new employees. The primary emphasis is on the supervisor's role in hiring and welcoming new people into work groups. Legal restraints and pitfalls are discussed, to give you the knowledge you need to get the best people and to get them off on the right foot. You will learn what to do, how to do it, and what not to do while executing these two vital activities.

Chapter 12 explores the ways in which you can impart new knowledge, skills, and attitudes to workers. Through training, you give each worker what is needed to perform to standards, to excel, and to stay out of trouble. You enhance workers' chances for advancement and for increased earnings by training them in accordance with certain all-important principles. Along with the principles, the various training methods are discussed, in order to help you to pick the one that is most appropriate for your training programs.

In Chapter 13, we explore the leader's role as judge—the process through which you evaluate your subordinates' performances. Appraisals help you to determine the effectiveness of your training efforts and give you the backup you need to reward and punish.

Chapter 14 examines both positive and negative aspects of discipline. If you are to discipline effectively, you must stress prevention along with efforts to correct individuals. The principles and pitfalls of disciplining subordinates are explored in detail.

11 Selection and Orientation

Outline

Objectives

After reading and discussing this chapter, you should be able to do the following:

1 Define the key terms.

2 Describe the role of a supervisor in the selection process.

3 Describe the assistance normally rendered in the selection process by a personnel or human resource department.

4 List and briefly describe four selection devices.

5 Describe what a supervisor should do to prepare for a selection interview.

6 List and briefly explain four pitfalls of the selection process.

7 List the basic goals of an orientation program.

8 List the basic goals of an induction program.

9 Describe what takes place during a new employee's socialization process.

10 State the five basic questions new employees want answered.

Key Terms

directive interview

disparate impact

induction

interview

job description

job specification

minority

nondirective interview

orientation

psychological contract

selection

socialization

validity

Introduction

Selection
The personnel or human resource management function that determines who is and is not hired

Selection is the personnel or human resource management function that determines who is hired by a business firm and who is not. It is the process by which applicants are evaluated so as to determine their suitability for employment. The basic aim of the selection process is to find the number and kind of employees required by a company to meet its needs for personnel at a minimum cost to that company. Selection begins with a definition of the kind of person needed to fill a vacancy and ends with the decision to hire a person. When a company is looking for nonmanagement personnel, the person who would supervise the prospective employee should be involved in that person's selection.

Catherine D. Bower, spokesperson for the American Society of Personnel Administration, says that replacement costs for an hourly paid employee average about two months' pay; for a salaried employee, they average about three months' pay; for management employees, they average about six months' pay. Clearly selection is an important and costly process that, if done badly, can add significantly to a company's inefficiency. She also notes that it is becoming increasingly difficult to terminate employees because of various state, local, and federal laws that guarantee employment and civil rights. This means that it is even more important to hire right the first time.[1]

After a new employee has been recruited, interviewed, tested, and hired, you must begin to prepare for his or her arrival and initiation. Some groundwork for this procedure is laid in the course of the selection process. The applicant is informed as to the nature of the job, the company's operations in general, and the wage and fringe benefits that go with the job. What remains to be done is the careful planning for and execution of the new employee's formal introduction to the company, the job, the supervisor, and the working environment in depth.

This chapter looks at these extremely important functions from a supervisor's viewpoint. In some companies, the supervisors have nothing much to say about hiring new workers. They are told that new people have been assigned to their departments, and they must accept that decision. This is not as it should be. Therefore, we shall turn our attention to the kind of selection process in which supervisors play a significant role.

Advantages of Supervisor Involvement

If adequate selection is to take place in a business, the decision to hire a new worker should be made by the person who will become his or her boss. This is because the manager has first-hand knowledge about his or her department, the work force, and the job that must be filled. He or she is best equipped to assess each applicant's suitability and potential both for performing the duties he or she will inherit and for getting along with the existing work force. It makes a great deal of sense, therefore, to involve supervisors in the selection process and, in particular, to give them the power to make the final decision to hire a new employee.

If a new person is dropped into your lap or shoved down your throat, your receptiveness and interest in his or her ultimate success on the job is somewhat less than it would be if you had had a say in the hiring.

When you know that your decision is the final and binding one, you are putting your reputation on the line. Before you pick a person for your department, you will probably look over all the applicants carefully in order to select the best from among the many individuals you interview. Since the person hired is someone you have chosen, you will feel a personal commitment to him or her that otherwise would be missing. You will want him or her to make it because, if this does not happen, it will adversely affect you as well as the new employee. Part of your success and that of your department will be riding on your choice. If you are the department head, you should have a voice in adding new people to it.

If new employees stumble a bit or have troubles of one kind or another, you as supervisor are likely to be more concerned with helping them through their difficulties if you yourself hired them. When you are responsible for selecting your department's new employees, their chances for success are much greater.

The Selection Process

Exhibit 11.1 outlines the selection process as it occurs when both a supervisor and the company's personnel or human resources department work together. In most medium- to large-size firms, the supervisor places a request for a new worker with the personnel department as soon as the need for such a person arises. Enough time must be allowed, when possible, to search for, select, and hire a person before the absence of his or her predecessor can create serious problems.

To ensure that both the supervisor and the personnel department know what kind of person they will be looking for, an up-to-date description of the job and its duties must be prepared or kept on hand, along with a detailed listing of the personal skills and abilities required of the job holder. These two documents are called the *job description* and the *job specification,* respectively.

Job Description

Job description
A formal listing of the duties that make up a formal position in the organization

A **job description** is a listing of the duties (tasks and activities) and responsibilities of a job or formal position in an organization. All jobs you supervise should have such a listing. Reference to this document proves

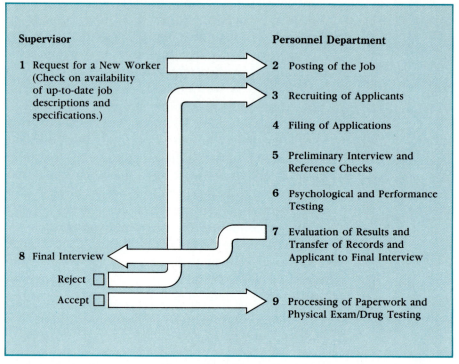

Supervisor   **Personnel Department**

1 Request for a New Worker   2 Posting of the Job
(Check on availability
of up-to-date job   3 Recruiting of Applicants
descriptions and
specifications.)   4 Filing of Applications

                                        5 Preliminary Interview and
                                          Reference Checks

                                        6 Psychological and Performance
                                          Testing

                                        7 Evaluation of Results and
8 Final Interview   Transfer of Records and
                                          Applicant to Final Interview
    Reject ☐

    Accept ☐   9 Processing of Paperwork and
                                          Physical Exam/Drug Testing

Exhibit 11.1   A typical selection process involving a personnel or human resource
management department and the supervisor of a new hire.

helpful in assigning work, settling disagreements, appraising subordinates, and filling vacancies. Exhibit 11.2 consists of a job description for
a secretarial position. You will note that nothing on it deals with the
personal characteristics desirable in the job holder. These are detailed in
the job specification.

Job Specification

Job specification
The personal charac-
teristics and skill
levels that are re-
quired of an individ-
ual to execute a job

Exhibit 11.3 shows the **job specification** — a listing of the personal characteristics and skill levels a person must have in order to fill the secretarial
position described in Exhibit 11.2. Such factors as typing speed, clerical
and secretarial experiences, and formal education are listed. Knowledge of
these data is extremely important in selecting someone to fill a job, in
assigning work, and in determining promotions.

   As time passes jobs change. So, too, must their descriptions and specifications. It is standard practice to review and update these documents at
least once every two years. If you have them and they are up to date, use
them. If this is not the case, you should set about the task of constructing
them or bringing them up to date.

Title: Secretary   Job No. C-10   Grade 4
Effective Date   1-92

General	Performs clerical and secretarial duties involving typing, dictation, correspondence and report preparation, filing, maintaining records, scheduling appointments, distributing mail. Handles confidential information regularly.
Specific Duties	Take dictation in shorthand and transcribe. Compose and type routine memos and business correspondence. Compile and type routine reports. Sort and distribute mail daily. Maintain and set up files of memos, letters, and reports. Obtain data and information by telephone or personal contact on behalf of supervisor. Receive visitors. Schedule supervisor's appointments. Answer phone and take messages. Handle confidential files.
Equipment	Electric typewriter, dictation machine, photocopier, desk top computer, and printer.

Analysis by: _____ Approved by: _____

Exhibit 11.2   **Job description for personal secretary.**

Steps 2 through 7 in the selection process (as illustrated in Exhibit 11.1) are usually performed for you by your company's personnel department. Posting the job so that all present employees are aware of it may be required by union contract. Posting allows existing employees to apply for the vacancy and can result in promotions and transfers that will create new vacancies. Recruiting applicants from outside can be done in several ways and usually must include sincere efforts to attract minority and female applicants.

After receiving and processing the paperwork that results from steps 4 through 7, personnel will usually send you two or more applicants for a final employment interview. As a rule, personnel will only send you applicants who qualify for and have the potential to succeed on the job you want to fill. You must pick the person you believe to be the best qualified of the applicants you interview. Then you turn the applicant over to the personnel department for final processing.

Exhibit 11.4 lists and briefly describes the federal restrictions placed on the selection process. In the discussions that follow, the impacts of these federal laws are examined as they relate to each of the selection steps or devices. They may be summarized briefly as follows:

Title: Secretary   Job No. C-10   Grade 4
Effective Date   1-92

Factor	Explanation
Education	High-school graduate or equivalent.
Experience	Secretarial, including stenographic duties and word processing.
Training Period	1 month.
Dexterity	Precise movement of hand and fingers required to operate keyboard at no less than 60 words per minute and take shorthand at 90 words per minute.
Adaptability	Must be able to adjust to frequent changes in duties, such as typing, filing, composing letters, handling telephone.
Judgment	Must be able to follow existing procedures and establish new practices where necessary. Must be able to compose business letters, establish filing systems, and receive visitors.
Responsibility for Losses to Company	Maximum loss possible: $200, due to clerical errors.
Contact with Others	Frequent contacts with visitors, vendors, and company managers.
Physical Demands	Lifting requirements: under 10 pounds.

Analysis by: ——————— Approved by: ———————

Exhibit 11.3   **Job specification for the secretarial position shown in Exhibit 11.2.**

1. It is unlawful for an employer to fail or refuse to hire or to discharge an individual because of race, color, religion, sex, age, national origin, or handicap.

2. It is unlawful for an employer to limit, segregate, or classify an employee or applicant for employment in any way that would tend to deprive the individual of employment opportunities because of race, color, religion, sex, age, national origin, or handicap.[2]

Recruiting

A good source for potential new employees is your present work force. People currently employed at your company have friends, neighbors, and relatives that might make good employees who are compatible with cur-

Law	Type of Employment Discrimination Prohibited	Employers Covered
U.S. Constitution First Amendment	Religious discrimination	Federal government
U.S. Constitution Fifth Amendment	Deprivation of employment rights without due process of law	Federal government
U.S. Constitution Fourteenth Amendment	Deprivation of employment rights without due process	State and local governments
Civil Rights Acts of 1866 and 1870 (based on 13th Amendment)	Race discrimination in hiring, placement, and continuation of employment	Private employers, unions, employment agencies
Civil Rights Act of 1871 (based on 14th Amendment)	Deprivation of equal employment rights under cover of state law	State and local governments (private employers if conspiracy is involved)
National Labor Relations Act of 1935	Unfair representation by unions, or interference with employee rights, that discriminates on the basis of race, color, religion, sex, or national origin	Private employers and unions
Equal Pay Act of 1963	Sex differences in pay for substantially equal work	All employers & labor organizations
Executive Order 11141	Age discrimination	Federal contractors & subcontractors
Title VI, 1964 Civil Rights Act	Discrimination based on race, color, religion, sex, or national origin	Employers receiving federal financial assistance
Title VII, 1964 Civil Rights Act (as amended in subsequent years)	Discrimination based on race, color, religion, sex, or national origin	Private employers with 15 or more employees, governments, unions, employment agencies
Executive Orders 11246 & 11375 (1965)	Discrimination based on race, color, religion, sex, or national origin	Federal contractors & subcontractors

(continues)

Exhibit 11.4 **Federal antidiscrimination laws.** (*Source:* James Ledvinka and Vida G. Scarpello, *Federal Regulation of Personnel and Human Resource Management.* Boston: Kent Publishing Co., 1991, 30–32. Copyright by Wadsworth, Inc. Reprinted by permission of PWS-Kent Publishing Co., a division of Wadsworth, Inc.)

Age Discrimination in Employment Act of 1967 (as amended in 1978 and in subsequent years)	Age discrimination against those over 40 years of age	Private employers with 20 or more employees, unions with 25 or more members, employment agencies
Title I, 1968 Civil Rights Act	Interference with a person's rights due to race, religion, color, or national origin	Persons generally
Executive Order 11478 (1969)	Discrimination based on race, color, religion, sex, national origin, political affiliation, marital status, or physical handicap	Federal government
Title IX, Education Amendments of 1972	Sex discrimination	Educational institutions receiving federal financial assistance
Vietnam Era Veteran's Readjustment Act of 1974, Executive Order 11701 (1973)	Discrimination against disabled veterans and Vietnam-era veterans (affirmative action required)	Federal contractors, federal government
Rehabilitation Act of 1973; Executive Order 11914	Discrimination based on physical or mental handicap (affirmative action required)	Federal contractors, federal government
Americans with Disabilities Act of 1990	Discrimination based on physical or mental handicap (affirmative action required)	Employers generally
Civil Service Reform Act of 1978	Specifically incorporates Title VII, 1964 Civil Rights Act; mandates federal government as "workplace reflective of the nation's diversity"	Federal government
Federal Employees Part-Time Career Employment Act of 1975	Requires increased part-time career employment opportunities	Federal government
Immigration and Reform Control Act of 1986	Discrimination based on citizenship or national origin	Employers generally
Civil Rights Restoration Act of 1987	Discrimination based on race, color, religion, sex, national origin, age, and handicap	Educational institutions receiving federal financial assistance

Exhibit 11.4   *(continued)*

1. Hispanics: Spanish-surnamed Americans
2. Asians or people from the Pacific islands: Oriental Americans
3. Blacks not of Hispanic origin: Negroes, African Americans
4. American Indians: Natives of North America
5. Alaskan natives: Eskimos

Exhibit 11.5   **Minorities as defined by federal laws and EEOC guidelines.**

Note: Women, handicapped Americans, and ethnic whites are also protected by law from discrimination in employment, but are not considered to be minorities.

rent employees. But herein lies a problem: like recommends like. If there is a need to expand the work force to include more women, minorities, and handicapped people, you will need to look beyond your present work force for new employees. Also, you may be required by management policy or union contract to post the job, letting others who are currently employed apply for your job vacancy.

EEO Policy and Recruiting

Minority
According to the EEOC, a member of the following groups: Hispanics, Native Americans, blacks, Asians or Pacific Islanders, Alaskan natives

Many companies today have an Equal Employment Opportunity (EEO) policy that states the employer's intent to recruit, hire, train, and promote people in all job categories without regard to race, color, creed, sex, age, country of origin, or handicap. From this policy come the guidelines for specifically recruiting representative numbers of **minority** members and women. Minorities include the groups described in Exhibit 11.5.

Ethnic Whites Now Protected Under EEO

In two May 18, 1987, cases, the Supreme Court expanded civil rights protection to Jews, Arabs, and all other ethnic and religious groups by its interpretation of an 1866 federal law. According to Justice Byron White, author of the Court's majority opinion, "Congress intended to protect from discrimination identifiable classes of persons who are subjected to intentional discrimination solely because of their ancestry or ethnic characteristics." Justice White explained that, when the law was passed, Congress followed common usage and treated Jews, Arabs, Germans, English people, and others as belonging to separate races rather than as being members of the Caucasian race.[3]

Title VII of the 1964 Civil Rights Act requires parties who file discrimination complaints to do so within 180 days of the alleged violation. It provides two basic remedies when discrimination is proved: reinstatement, and recovery of lost pay. The 1866 law permits jury trials, punitive damages, and an average of two years to file actions (this average is based on state laws for personal injury suits).[4]

Affirmative Action Programs

When companies have been found guilty of discriminatory practices in the past, or when they admit that they need to improve their employment record with regard to women and minorities, they develop or are required to develop an *affirmative action program (AAP)*. One important part of an AAP is a stated goal and timetable for achieving the goal of hiring the missing women or minorities. As a supervisor, you may be allowed to hire only women or minorities until the stated goal for your area is reached.

The Supreme Court's Consensus on Affirmative Action

On March 25, 1987, the Supreme Court strongly endorsed the affirmative action concept and, according to several Court-watching experts, has now reached a consensus on how affirmative action plans should work. In a 6–3 decision, the Court approved a Santa Clara County (California) Transportation Agency plan that gave a dispatcher's job to a woman even though six men were more experienced. The woman and the men were all qualified for the promotion, but the dispatcher job lacked women job holders. The following seems clear at this writing. For promotions and hiring, affirmative action can be used if:

- It avoids specific numbers of openings for women and minorities
- It avoids hiring or promoting an unqualified woman or minority member over a qualified candidate
- A "conspicuous imbalance" in the representation of women and minorities exists in a job category (or the work force as a whole).[5]

Reverse Discrimination

The now famous *Bakke* v. *Regents of the University of California* case of 1978 dealt with the issue of reverse discrimination. In its review of this case, the Supreme Court of the United States held that race could be used as a criterion in selection decisions, but it could not be the only criterion. Affirmative action programs are permissible when a case of prior discrimination has been established and when an employer has a significant underrepresentation of minority and female employees (considering the makeup of the labor force the employer has to draw from).

Recruiting Women

Under current federal and state laws, few jobs can be denied to women. Companies are under an obligation to redesign jobs, where necessary, to allow women access to them. Job specifications can be changed to allow women to hold a job. Schools that train professionals and either receive federal grants or use federal scholarship funds are actively recruiting female applicants. As a result, more and more qualified women are entering what were once male-dominated professions. Companies have even hired unqualified women and minorities and paid for their education and training to meet their affirmative action and equal employment goals. As a supervisor in charge of hiring new workers, you must consider women and seek them from whatever sources you can. It's the law.

Recruiting and the Handicapped

The handicapped in America are those individuals who:

- Have a physical or mental impairment that substantially limits one or more major life activities
- Have a record of such an impairment
- Are regarded as having such an impairment

Two major laws govern the protection of people with such disabilities: the Rehabilitation Act of 1973 (covering firms doing business with the federal government) and the Americans with Disabilities Act of 1990 (covering nearly every firm with fifteen or more employees). Protection is extended to people with current or past physical and mental conditions. Examples of those protected are people with dependency on legal drugs whose dependency does not impair work performance; people with a history of cancer, heart trouble, or a contagious disease, providing that their conditions do not pose a significant risk to coworkers or render them unable to perform their work; and people who have undergone or who now are undergoing rehabilitation for their drug dependencies.

Under both laws, employers must make reasonable accommodations for the handicapped. Jobs may have to be redefined, removing those tasks that the handicapped person cannot perform. Prerequisites such as passing a physical exam may have to be waived when parts of that exam are not job related. Physical facilities may have to be altered to accommodate access by the physically handicapped. Signs in braille and wheelchair ramps are but two examples. For private businesses not engaged in doing business with the federal government, affirmative action to hire the handicapped is not required. Both laws give employers some flexibility in that they do not require toleration of lower performance levels from handi-capped employees and they do not force employment of handicapped persons who would pose a significant threat to the health and safety of others at work.

Recruiting Minorities

Recruiting minorities usually involves seeking them where they live—in their neighborhoods—if enough likely prospects are to be found to form a pool of applicants. Neighborhood associations, churches, community action groups, state employment offices, ethnic newspapers, and current minority employees should be contacted. And before minorities are introduced to a work force, the existing workers must be encouraged to cooperate with the company's affirmative action efforts. As with all new employees, every effort must be made to find the best-qualified and to ensure their early success on the job. As a person involved in hiring, you may have to get rid of many of your preconceived notions about minority groups and commit yourself to their successful assimilation and retention.

The Supervisor's Role in Minority Hiring

After extensive interviewing of managers and employees in forty-three companies representing retailing, service, and industrial areas, Professor Lawrence A. Johnson of the University of Massachusetts found that the supervisor is a major key to the minority worker's success or failure.[6] In companies committed to employing members of minority groups, coaching the minority newcomer's supervisor is as important as training the worker. If the program is to be a success the supervisors must succeed in the following tasks:

1. Learn to listen to and understand the minority worker's point of view.
2. Communicate effectively.
3. Expect considerable testing and probing from the minority worker as to the company's standards and the supervisor's attitudes and sincerity.
4. Be made aware beforehand of their own possible reactions to probable situations in their relationships with minority workers.

With the increased emphasis on recruiting and hiring minority members today, you are more likely now than ever before to encounter minority employees in every department of your company. They, like everyone else, expect an even chance for success. They may need extra training to fill the gaps left in their formal education and previous employment experiences. They want and need to be respected and appreciated for their good points and potentials. They want to carry their own weight.

You must realize that a minority worker may arrive expecting the worst: resentment, rejection, hostility, and isolation. He or she may tend to read into your actions and words or those of peers more than is in them. He or she may seem hypersensitive. In a way, he or she may be looking for signs of discrimination, as well. What a nonminority worker might brush aside, a minority member may consider an insult or personal attack. Until all of your subordinates feel that they are being treated as individuals, you can expect a measure of discontent.

All of the roles that you must play in order to achieve the sound human relations described in chapter 8 are even more necessary when you deal with minorities, who may demand additional effort and diligence on your part in order to relate successfully to each of them. This is particularly true when such a person first joins your department.

There are always a few workers, however, who will try to take advantage of the situation. Some workers will be looking for special privileges. They may want to use the fact that they are women or members of minorities as a lever in attempts to gain favored treatment. This inequity, although clearly understandable, must be prevented. Your success and that of your workers will be hampered if you do not prevent such inequities. You will suffer most of all through alienation of your other subordinates and their accusation that you are playing favorites.

Enforce your department's standards of performance and conduct impartially. Let all of your workers know their rights and the avenues open to them when they feel that they have been treated unjustly.

Applicant Screening Procedures

According to Victor R. Lindquist, director of placement at Northwestern University and author of the recent Northwestern Endicott-Lindquist survey of 230 major U.S. firms, more firms are beginning to take precautions to protect themselves against the costs of hiring unsuitable workers. According to the report, verifying education claims of applicants is the most

Age? Date of Birth? Since state and federal laws prohibit discrimination, do not use the answer to this question illegally. Requesting the applicant's age is generally permissible as long as the information is not used for a discriminatory purpose.

Arrests? Since an arrest is no indication of guilt and minorities are arrested more proportionately than other segments of the population, this question should be avoided because it is discriminatory. Such an inquiry is prohibited by the Illinois Department of Human Rights.

Convictions (other than traffic violations)? This question is not advisable on a general basis, but it may be appropriate for screening candidates who have been convicted of certain offenses and are under consideration for certain kinds of jobs. The same applies to less than honorable military discharges. If this information is necessary, exercise care in how these records are used in order to avoid possible discrimination.

Available for Saturday or Sunday Work? While employee work scheduling is an important factor, this question may discourage applications from members of certain religious groups. If this question is necessary because of business requirements, indicate that an effort will be made to accommodate the religious needs of employees.

Age and Number of Children? Arrangements for Care? While the intent of these questions is to explore a source of absenteeism or tardiness, the effect is potentially discriminatory against women.

Citizenship? Unless required by national security, this question should be avoided because it creates a potential for discrimination on the basis of national origin.

Credit Record? Own a Car? Own Home? Unless required because of business, these questions should be avoided because of potential adverse effects on minorities or women.

Eyes? Hair Color? Eye and hair color are not related to job performance and may serve to indicate an applicant's race or national origin.

Exhibit 11.6   Inquiries on application forms that may be potentially discriminatory.
(Source: Illinois Department of Employment Security.)

frequently used screening procedure, followed by verification of the applicant's past employment. "The cost of verifying applicants' backgrounds, giving physical examinations and testing for drugs is tremendously expensive, but companies cannot afford not to conduct extensive screening because it will cost them more in the long run. . . . The cost of hiring a drug user (whose drug use impairs on-the-job performance) is estimated to be $7,000."[7]

Steps 4 through 8 listed in Exhibit 11.1 deal with several selection tools or screening devices: the application, the preliminary interview, various kinds of tests, and the final interview. These devices, like recruiting, are governed in some ways by federal antidiscrimination legislation.

Fidelity Bond? Since a bond may have been denied for an arbitrary or discriminatory reason, use other screening considerations. A federal program administered through the Illinois Job Service will bond most workers if commercial bonding is not available.

Friends or Relatives? This question implies a preference for friends or relatives of employees and is potentially discriminatory because such a preference is likely to reflect the demography of the company's work force.

Garnishment Record? Federal courts have held that wage garnishments do not normally affect a worker's ability to perform effectively on the job.

Height? Weight? Unless height or weight is directly related to a job requirement, this question should not be listed on the application form.

Maiden Name? Prior Married Name? Widowed, Divorced, Separated? These questions are not related to job performance and may be an indication of religion or national origin. These inquiries may be appropriate if required for identification purposes in pre-employment investigations or security checks.

Marital Status? A federal court has held that refusal to employ a married woman when married men occupy similar jobs is unlawful sex discrimination.

Sex. State and federal laws prohibit discrimination on the basis of sex except where sex is a "bona fide occupational qualification" necessary to the normal operation of business.

NOTE: If certain information is needed for postemployment purposes, such as Affirmative Action plans, it can be obtained *after* the applicant has been hired. Maintain this data apart from information that is used in the hiring decision process.

The best general guideline to follow on employment application forms is to ensure that the information elicited is related to qualifications for effective performance on the job.

The Application

Applications are your primary method for obtaining the key facts about an individual candidate for a job. What it contains and how it is prepared by an applicant can help you weed out unqualified people, thus avoiding the need and time it takes to interview applicants. An application "should state that your company is an Equal Employment Opportunity Employer and that you do not discriminate on the basis of race, color, religion, national origin, age, sex, marital status, or handicap," and the application should also make it clear that your company hires "at will."[8] This last statement indicates that the person is not guaranteed any specific period of employment.

Examine your employer's application form. If it contains any of the inquiries discussed in Exhibit 11.6, your guard should go up. Evaluate the need for each question and eliminate those that are not closely related to job performance or to predicting success on the job for which the applicant will be considered.

Interviews

An **interview** can be defined as a conversation between two or more parties that is under the control of one of the parties and that tries to accomplish a special objective. A conversation is a two-way verbal interchange of ideas and information. Thus an interview is a verbal interchange between two or more persons, and the employment interview is an exchange between you (as a representative of your company) and the applicant. It must be carefully planned and skillfully executed if its special objective is to be achieved.

As a supervisor you will be using interviews to help instruct your people, to evaluate them and share their evaluations with them, to screen and hire new employees, to solve problems, to gather information, and to sell your subordinates on the need for changes. Interviews demand a quiet environment, a clear understanding by the parties of the special purpose of the interview, and extensive use of open and closed questions (see Exhibit 11.7).

The major purpose of an interview is to get the interviewee talking freely and frankly about all matters that are relevant to the accomplishment of the interview's purpose. The interviewer listens attentively, never interrupts, and usually refrains from expressing opinions or making snap judgments. The interviewee should do most of the talking.

As an interviewer, you must be certain that you and the person being interviewed are of one mind, that your understanding and his or hers are the same with regard to the purpose of the interview and to what each person means by his or her contribution. While you encourage a free flow of information, you must keep the interview on track, avoiding time-consuming and wasteful meanderings by all parties.

The employment interview has two primary purposes: to evaluate the qualifications and suitability of the applicant to fill the job opening and to give the applicant the information needed to make an intelligent decision about accepting an offer of employment, should it be given. Be honest about the working conditions, the chances for advancement, and the type of duties you will expect the new employee to perform. Review the job description and the job specification for the job before you conduct the interview, and have them handy for reference during the interview.

Avoid asking questions that could open you and your employer to accusations of employment discrimination. Exhibit 11.8 gives you precautions to follow when conducting the interview. In addition to these, conduct all your interviews in the same manner, using the same format,

Open questions usually begin with:	Closed questions usually begin with:
What	Can
When	Is
Where	Do (Does)
Which	Have (Has)
Who	Shall (Will)
How	

NOTE: A closed question can be answered with *yes* or *no*; an open question cannot be. The opening word in a question determines whether it will be open or closed.

Exhibit 11.7   **Open and closed question starters.**

questions, and environment. Some supervisors tape record their interviews so that every word is a matter of record for future reference.

There are two basic kinds of interviews and approaches to interviewing: the directive and the nondirective. The directive interview is planned and controlled by the interviewer. The nondirective interview is planned by the interviewer but controlled by the interviewee.

Directive interview
An interview planned and totally controlled by the interviewer

Directive Interviews   The **directive interview** is based on a format of specific questions set down in advance and followed exactly. The questions should ask for the information the interviewer considers most essential. Here are some examples: "What did you do between your job with the ABC Company and your employment at XYZ, Incorporated?" "Why did you leave the ABC Company?" These questions generally ask for facts and leave little room for opinions on the part of the candidate. The only opinions you should look for are those that directly affect how the person views the job and type of working conditions that he or she will experience if hired.

Generally, the interviewer will ask the set of questions (questions he or she has written down in advance) in the order in which they are listed. Feel free to record the applicant's responses as they are given. Certain questions may be more important than others, as they may reveal more valuable information. These questions should be marked in some way to highlight them so that you make certain not to forget to ask them. You will probably do as much talking as the applicant does, as you must both ask questions and supply information. Make sure that the applicant knows the nature of the job for which he or she is being interviewed and that he or she has an opportunity to ask questions too.

This type of interview works best when you are dealing with applicants for routine production or clerical positions. It allows you to obtain the maximum amount of job- or performance-related information in the minimum amount of time.

- Do ask questions that are job-related or necessary for determining an applicant's qualifications for employment.

- Do question candidates in a consistent and uniform manner, regardless of race, sex, national origin, age or handicap.

- Do evaluate applicants on job-related criteria in accord with the actual requirements for successful performance of the job.

- Do select the best-qualified individual for the job. If the position is "underrepresented" with minority group or female applicants, maintain a record of good-faith attempts to recruit and consider minorities and/or females for the position.

- Do accord special consideration to the disabled and handicapped and Vietnam era veterans. If feasible, consider whatever minor adjustments or accommodations can be made to enable the handicapped to perform the job successfully.

- Do make reasonable accommodations to the religious observance obligations of employees.

- Do not ask any questions of a female applicant that would not be asked of a male candidate (i.e., inquiries pertaining to child care, marital status, birth control methods or hindrances to travel or working weekends).

- Do not ask questions of one race that would not be asked of another (i.e., questioning one's ability to work in a location with members of another racial group).

- Do not establish a negative tone in the interview in an effort to discourage any applicant from seeking the position.

- Do not give undue emphasis to the hazardous or tedious aspects of a job, especially if they occur on an infrequent basis.

- Do not inform an applicant that the position is "reserved" or must be filled by a female or minority group applicant because of Equal Employment Opportunity

Exhibit 11.8 Major "do" and "don't" guidelines for conducting an employment interview. (*Source:* Illinois Department of Employment Security.)

Nondirective interview

An interview planned by the interviewer but controlled by the interviewee

Nondirective Interviews   The **nondirective interview** is also planned in advance but it is generally less structured and more flexible. Questions are written down, but they are designed to be open or loose, in order to allow applicants more freedom in their responses so as to reveal the attitudes behind their words. Typical questions that might be asked include the following: "Why did you apply for this job?" "Which job have you held that you liked best (least) and why?" The object of these open questions is to let the applicants talk so that their aspirations, goals, and preferences can come out.

The interviewer is not bound to a rigid format with this indirect approach. One question can lead to others, with the applicant's responses determining the direction and flow of the interview. Quite often you will find out a great deal more from an applicant's detailed explanations and will uncover much more than you would in a direct interview. People left to talk on their own will say more than they normally would because they are not sure how much you want to know. They will seize the or Affirmative Action obligations or regulations. Affirmative Action is not a license to discriminate against anyone in an effort to compensate for past hiring inequities. A possible exception to this suggestion may occur when a court or regulatory agency has made a finding of discrimination and directs remedial action in the form of specific hiring goals.

- Do not impose additional "desirable" qualifications beyond the actual requirements of your job opening.
- Do not devise additional testing requirements as part of a pre-employment screening procedure unless the testing is job-related and properly validated.
- Do not ask the birth place of an applicant nor require that the applicant submit proof of birth. Since birthplace may indicate a person of foreign origin, it is better to avoid this question than to risk a discrimination charge on this basis.
- Do not ask the citizenship of an applicant. Ask whether the person is a citizen or has a visa authorizing full-time permanent employment.
- Do not ask questions that tend to identify the age of the applicant when age is not related to successful job performance.
- Do not ask a person's religious affiliations.
- Do not ask about an applicant's type of military discharge from general military service. You may ask about job-related experience in the U.S. Armed Forces.
- Do not ask if the applicant has ever been arrested. You may ask if the person has ever been convicted.
- Do not ask questions on the general physical or mental condition of an applicant. You may ask if the applicant has any physical or mental condition that may limit his/her ability to do the job.

opportunity to speak their minds if they are relaxed and encouraged to speak up.

Either type of interview may include an on-the-job performance test if you think it necessary. Such a test is designed to let the applicants demonstrate their ability to run a machine, meet close tolerances, file correspondence, type correct copy, and the like. If this type of test has not already been done by the personnel department, you have an excellent opportunity to do it during or after your interview.

Preparing to Interview Like any other type of interview—whether for counseling, for sharing your evaluations, or for interrogation and fact finding for disciplinary actions—the employment interview should be held in private and in an environment as free from interruptions as you can make it. Since you usually know well in advance when an applicant is due to report, set aside enough time to do the kind of interview you desire and do your homework in advance of the meeting. Read the candidate's

The Applicant	Present Situation	The Job
Bearing	Maturity	Skills required
Dress	Health	Working conditions
Speech	Sincerity	Hours
Experience	Social adjustment	Duties
Strengths	Why is he/she here?	Tools/equipment
Weaknesses	Present wage	Special demands/hazards
Hobbies	Education earned	
Limits/handicap		
	Personal Goals	
Previous Employment	Aims and objectives	
Reasons for taking	Wage requirements	
Reasons for leaving	Education desired	
Work liked best		
Work liked least		
Relations with supervisor		
Relations with peers		

Exhibit 11.9   A checklist to help you formulate your interview questions.

application form thoroughly and consult the comments, if any, from the personnel interviewer. Look over the candidate's test scores and make a list of any deficiencies that you feel will interfere with his or her successful performance. Prepare a brief checklist of the essentials you wish to cover so that you do not waste time or overlook an important area. Exhibit 11.9 is such a list.

Conducting the Interview   No matter what type of interview you choose, you should observe the following basic procedure:

1. *Put the applicant at ease.* Keep in mind that the applicant will probably be a bit nervous, so do what you can to eliminate this barrier to successful communications by planning to make him or her comfortable as soon as you meet. A comfortable chair, a quiet room, good ventilation, a cup of coffee, an ash tray close by, and a smile along with your handshake will go a long way toward relieving his or her tension.

2. *Stick with your schedule.* If you have planned your questions and prepared an outline to follow, stay with them. Watch the time so that you cover what you must before your time runs out. There may be a temptation on both your parts to wander from essential areas and talk randomly about whatever arises. You have several point to cover, and you do not usually have the luxury of unlimited

time. If you do not get what you are there to get, you will have to make a decision on the basis of less-than-complete knowledge about the applicant.

3. *Listen.* By now you are probably sick of reading about listening, but it is of the greatest importance to the communications process— especially when you are engaged in a discussion. If you do all the talking, you will learn nothing. If you use the time between your questions simply to plan for what you will cover next, you will miss the applicant's answers. If you are not attentive to the applicant, you will shut him or her off. Summarize your thoughts about the applicant periodically, in writing, as time and discussion lags permit.

4. *Remain neutral.* Retain your impressions and opinions until the end of the interview. Mask your reactions, whether favorable or unfavorable. If the applicant senses your feelings one way or the other, he or she will begin to tailor responses to your reactions. You will receive what you have indicated you want to hear, not what the applicant wants to say. When you disagree with a response, ask the applicant for his or her reasons. Try to uncover his or her way of looking at things. You will gain a perspective on the individual and his or her attitudes that otherwise would be denied to you. As with appraisals, you should not concern yourself with an applicant's opinions that are not related to the nature of the job, to working, or to the working environment. If an applicant's attitudes or feelings are contrary to yours, simply ask yourself if it really matters. Will those opinions keep the applicant from a successful job performance? If not, forget them.

   Avoid asking leading questions. Questions formulated to lead a person to the answer you want to hear will do just that. An example is, "You got along with your boss, didn't you?" If a person answers *no,* he or she is pretty stupid. These questions simply waste time. They tell an applicant where your values are, but you will not learn the applicant's values.

5. *Give the applicant your decision.* If you have decided that a person is not right for the job, let him or her know it. It is not fair to keep people hanging or to put them off when you have definitely ruled them out. They have other plans to make and need to know where they stand as soon as possible. If you like a candidate but wish to interview one or two others before you decide, let the applicant know that, as well. He or she may be interviewing several employers and may not be ready to give you a decision either. But give a specific time by which he or she will have your final decision. Then

stick to that time limit as best you can. If you delay your decision too long, you may lose your prospect. If you know this person to be the best you have seen thus far and totally qualified for the position you have vacant, offer him or her the job. You have what you need. Further searching may be expensive and may yield no one better. You may be surprised to hear the applicant tell you that he or she is not sure and wishes to examine other opportunities. If you really want that person, set a time by which he or she should give you a definite answer.

During the interview, all you can hope to do is to assess what the person has done and what you believe him or her to be capable of doing. You cannot assess what an applicant will do; you can only gauge his or her potential based on past performances. You should concern yourself most with the person's ability to handle the duties of the job in question. This is the most important consideration.

Tests

Under federal guidelines, *tests* are any criterion or paper-and-pencil or performance measure used as a basis for any employment decision, including selection and hiring. Such measures include interviews, application blanks, psychological and performance exams, physical requirements for a job, and any other device that is scored or used as a basis for selecting an applicant.[9] All types of tests you use should attempt to measure only the performance capabilities that can be proved to be essential for success in the job to be filled.

Disparate Impact   Federal guidelines say that selection devices must have no **disparate impact**. Disparate impact exists when a significantly different selection rate exists for women and/or minorities than for other groups. For example, if an employer hires 60 percent of white males who apply but less than 80 percent of that figure (less than 48 percent overall) of women and minorities, the employer may be open to charges of disparate impact. In order to avoid such accusations, employers need to recruit large numbers of applicants for each employment vacancy to ensure that enough women and minorities are included in the screening process. Accurate records of all those interviewed and hired must be kept. All applicants whether hired or not must be classified as to sex, race, and ethnic group, including whites.

Disparate impact
The existence of a significantly different selection rate between women and/or minorities and nonprotected groups

Some screening devices that may lead to disparate impact are educational requirements, height and weight requirements, preference of employer for relatives of existing employees, promotions restricted to current employees, and reference checks. Unless a screening device can be shown to be job related, it should not be used. A few selection devices have been accepted in most cases. These include state-mandated licensing requirements, language abilities, and apprenticeship training for skilled craft positions.

Validity
The degree to which a selection device measures what it is supposed to measure or is predictive of a person's performance on a job

Validity   **Validity** is the degree to which a selection criterion or device measures what it is supposed to measure. With respect to testing for employee selection, the term often refers to evidence that the device is job related—that the device is a valid predictor of future performance on a job. The two kinds of validity in testing are criterion validity and content validity.

Criterion validity basically involves the demonstration that those who perform well on the test will perform well on the job. Conversely, those who do not perform well on the test will not perform well on the job. *Content validity* means that the test is a fair sample of the content of the job. Content validity is built into a test by carefully studying the behaviors that are called for on a job and then building ways to test for an ability to perform those behaviors.

An example of validity follows. A state decided to construct a physical exam for the selection of highway patrol persons. It decided to use a standard test given to military recruits. After using the test for a period of months, it went back to see how well the troopers were doing in relation to their test scores. They found little relationship between how well the troopers did on the test and their performance ratings on the job. The test was thrown out as invalid.

To construct a valid physical test, the state decided to study the physical demands made on troopers during the execution of their daily duties. A short run with full weight of equipment was created. A drag-and-carry test simulating the extraction of accident victims was fabricated. The test was given to recruits but was not used to hire them. After the recruits were selected and had their job performances rated by their superiors, the test results were compared to their ratings. A good relationship was found, and the test was then considered a valid selection device. It simulated with accuracy what physical demands were made on troopers, and the test included major examples of their daily requirements.

Drug Testing

Although nearly all large companies have had some experience with drug-addicted employees, less than half of our nation's largest companies have drug policies. Drug-addicted workers can and do cause injuries to themselves and to others and damage to property. But the problem of testing all applicants for jobs is a large and difficult one. The expense related to drug testing can run as much as several hundred dollars. Reliable labs must be found to do the testing. There is the problem of taking the samples: some hold that it is an invasion of privacy; the process requires someone to monitor the taking of samples. There is the additional concern for privacy of the results and what to do with a "positive" result. Many experts agree that common over-the-counter drugs can lead to a positive test result. Blood and urine samplings together tend to yield the best, most reliable results.

As a supervisor, the extent of your involvement in drug testing will probably be limited to getting the results after the offer of employment has been made and the test(s) given. Offers of employment are usually conditional on successful completion of physical exams and drug tests.

AIDS and Hiring

Acquired immune deficiency syndrome (AIDS) describes a physical condition in which a virus has crippled a person's immune system. The infected person falls victim to a host of "opportunistic" diseases and infections, which eventually cause death. Since 1981, when the disorder was first diagnosed, over 100,000 Americans have died from AIDS. While there is no known cure for AIDS at present, the disease is not casually contagious.

Fear of AIDS is a reality in the workplace. But some states and cities have passed laws or are considering passing laws that protect people with AIDS and those who test positive to the virus. Find out if your state, city, or town has any laws relating to hiring and AIDS, and find out what those laws permit. More and more companies are formulating policy on this issue, and your company may need to do so. It is likely that, sooner or later, an AIDS victim or a person who has been exposed to the AIDS virus will apply for work or show up as an employee on the payroll.

On March 3, 1987, the Supreme Court held in a 7–2 decision that simple fear of contagion by any virus—without any medical assessment that the fear is well founded—cannot justify firing a worker with any contagious disease. Through this decision, AIDS victims (along with others who suffer from contagious diseases) have been placed under the protection of the 1973 Vocational Rehabilitation Act, which prevents discrimination against the handicapped by schools, governments, and any business doing business with the federal government.

Screening by Polygraph

The polygraph, sometimes called a *lie detector,* was used by 10 percent of U.S. companies to screen job applicants before being banned by a federal law effective December 27, 1988. The Employee Polygraph Protection Act

NEWS
You Can Use

Applicant Screening: An Example

Thomas Melohn, president of North American Tool & Die, Inc. (a California company featured in the book *In Search of Excellence*), believes in passing applicants through screens with progressively smaller holes. At North American, the hiring process begins as early as possible—at least one month before a new person will be needed. North American's source of applicants are referrals from existing employees (about 20 percent of new hires) and people who respond to the company's carefully worded local newspaper ads. Local ads are used because they reach people who will have a short commute to work. Melohn does not like to hire anyone who must drive or ride for more than 45 minutes to work each day. The ads are run for ten consecutive days, in the hope of attracting as many qualified people as possible.[10]

After the pool of applicants forms, Melohn uses five screens:

- A thorough review of each application
- In-depth interviews by Melohn and other managers
- A reference check with the applicant's previous supervisors
- A half-day trial period where the applicant actually works for half a day on the job
- A one-month "engagement party" or probationary period[11]

Melohn says that 90 percent of applicants are eliminated by a careful review of applications. Since North American is looking for people with highly technical skills, Melohn looks for evidence of precision in the applicant's effort to fill out the application. Poor spelling and grammar are tolerated if English is not the applicant's native language. Evidence of job tenure is scrutinized (Melohn is reluctant to interview anyone who has spent less than one year on any one job), along with the applicant's outside interests. Melohn looks for evidence that the person is interested in helping others and is outgoing.[12]

During his interviews, Melohn allows about thirty minutes, to encourage candidates to speak frankly. He notes what he is looking for and makes certain that the interviewee is comfortable and learns as much about North American as Melohn learns about him or her. When he learns about the applicant's preferences (early shift versus late shift, and so on), he makes every effort to accommodate them.[13]

When talking to the applicant's previous supervisors, Melohn asks whether they would hire the applicant again, what the applicant's greatest strength and weakness are, and how they would rate the applicant on a scale of 1 to 10.[14]

North American's half-day trial usually involves a few of the best applicants spending half a day on the job so that they can get to know what the job requires and so that the coworkers can get to know them. Melohn looks for such traits as enthusiasm for the work, curiosity about the company, willingness to be a team player, and performance capabilities.[15]

(continued)

Finally, workers are hired with a clear understanding that the first month is one in which both parties get to know one another. Weekly reviews are given by the new hire's supervisor, and the company reaffirms its commitment to helping the new person succeed. By the end of the thirty days, the new person knows whether North American Tool & Die is right for him or her. With new hires, Melohn repeatedly stresses the values that he sees as crucial for his company's success and eventually starts them on job rotation to build flexibility and to help them find the jobs they like best.[16]

states that private employers may not require, request, or suggest that employees or prospective employees take lie detector (polygraph) tests, except when conducting in-house investigations. Employers may then request employees to take lie detector tests under strict conditions.

Several companies are marketing honesty tests, which are written and graded by the vendor. The use of such tests is suspect, as many have yet to be determined to be valid and reliable. Many states have passed laws to restrict their use.

The Immigration Reform and Control Act

The Immigration Reform and Control Act of 1986 requires most employers to hire only American citizens and aliens who are authorized to work in the United States. When you hire, you must verify the employment eligibility and identity of each employee and complete and retain the one-page federal form, I-9 (see Exhibit 11.10). The documents authorized to prove employment eligibility, identity, or both are listed in Exhibit 11.11. In general, you must complete Form I-9 for persons employed for three days or more (except for employees of temporary employment services and contractors' employees), by the end of the third business day following the hire. For persons employed for less than three days, you must complete the form by the end of the first day of employment.

All new hires must provide a document or documents from the lists in Exhibit 11.11. If an employee provides a document from List A, only that document is required. Otherwise a document from List B and another from List C must be provided. Proof that a document has been applied for is acceptable at time of hire, but the document itself must be furnished within twenty-one days of hiring and recorded on Form I-9.

Once Form I-9 is completed by the employer and the new hire, the documents or document used to verify identity and employability should be photocopied and kept on file with the Form I-9 for three years after the date of hiring, or for one year after the date the employment is terminated—whichever is later.

For specific details about this law and about your responsibilities as an employer, write to Immigration and Naturalization Service, 425 I Street, Washington, D.C. 20536, and ask for their *Handbook for Employers, M-274.*

Pitfalls

In employee selection, as in most of your duties, a number of pitfalls may snare you if you are not aware of them. Since there is a strong similarity between appraisals of subordinates and appraisals of applicants, some of the same pitfalls discussed in chapter 14 apply here as well.

1. *The halo effect.* This occurs when you let one outstanding good or bad characteristic in an applicant influence your overall assessment of him or her.

2. *The rush job.* If you are inadequately prepared for an interview, how can you find out all you need to know about an applicant?

3. *Comparisons.* It is not fair to compare, for example, an applicant to someone who has had years of experience on the job. You should ask yourself if the applicant can meet the standards set by the job description. (For example, you have no reason to expect that the new person can replace right away all the skills of a retiring worker who has had thirty years' experience on the job.)

4. *Failure to follow the principles of sound interviewing.* After you have completed this chapter, you should have a good grasp of what these principles are.

5. *Overselling your company or the job.* By overstatements, puffed-up generalizations, and inaccurate or untruthful information, you might be sowing the seeds that eventually frustrate the new person and lead him or her to quit. The person may be taking the job with false hopes and on the basis of your inaccurate promises. He or she will soon discover that his or her mental images do not coincide with the hard realities encountered on the job. Selection is an expensive process. If the person you select only stays a short time, you will have to repeat the whole process all over again. You will

SECTION 1: TO BE COMPLETED BY THE EMPLOYEE

STEP 1
Fill in the personal information.

STEP 2
Check the box for work eligibility. Give other information where needed.

STEP 3
Read, sign, and date.

STEP 4
(Preparer/Translator only)
Read, fill in information, and sign.

EMPLOYMENT ELIGIBILITY VERIFICATION (Form I-9)

1 EMPLOYEE INFORMATION AND VERIFICATION: (To be completed and signed by employee.)

Name: (Print or Type) Last	First	Middle	Birth Name
Smith	Mary	Eileen	Adams

Address: Street Name and Number	City	State	ZIP Code
4502 Birch Ln.	Danville,	TN	37832

Date of Birth (Month/Day/Year)	Social Security Number
6/26/53	408-08-4505

I attest, under penalty of perjury, that I am (check a box):

☒ 1. A citizen or national of the United States.
☐ 2. An alien lawfully admitted for permanent residence (Alien Number A _____).
☐ 3. An alien authorized by the Immigration and Naturalization Service to work in the United States (Alien Number A _____ or Admission Number _____, expiration of employment authorization, if any _____).

I attest, under penalty of perjury, the documents that I have presented as evidence of identity and employment eligibility are genuine and relate to me. I am aware that federal law provides for imprisonment and/or fine for any false statements or use of false documents in connection with this certificate.

Signature	Date (Month/Day/Year)
Mary Ellen Smith	6/20/87

PREPARER/TRANSLATOR CERTIFICATION (To be completed if prepared by person other than the employee). I attest, under penalty of perjury, that the above was prepared by me at the request of the named individual and is based on all information of which I have any knowledge.

Signature	Name (Print or Type)		

Address (Street Name and Number)	City	State	Zip Code

SECTION 2: TO BE COMPLETED BY THE **EMPLOYER**

2 **EMPLOYER REVIEW AND VERIFICATION:** (To be completed and signed by employer.)

Instructions:

Examine one document from List A and check the appropriate box, **OR** examine one document from List B **and** one from List C and check the appropriate boxes. Provide the **Document Identification Number** and **Expiration Date** for the document checked.

List A Documents that Establish Identity and Employment Eligibility		List B Documents that Establish Identity		List C Documents that Establish Employment Eligibility

STEP 5

Examine the document and check the box that corresponds to the document. Fill in document number and expiration date.

5 ▶

List A — Documents that Establish Identity and Employment Eligibility

☒ 1. United States Passport

☐ 2. Certificate of United States Citizenship

☐ 3. Certificate of Naturalization

☐ 4. Unexpired foreign passport with attached Employment Authorization

☐ 5. Alien Registration Card with photograph

Document Identification

_YO16534_

Expiration Date (if any)

Oct. 21, 1991

and

List B — Documents that Establish Identity

☐ 1. A State-issued driver's license or a State-issued I.D. card with a photograph, or information, including name, sex, date of birth, height, weight, and color of eyes.

(Specify State)

☐ 2. U.S. Military Card

☐ 3. Other (Specify document and issuing authority)

Document Identification

#

Expiration Date (if any)

List C — Documents that Establish Employment Eligibility

☐ 1. Original Social Security Number Card (other than a card stating it is not valid for employment)

☐ 2. A birth certificate issued by State, county, or municipal authority bearing a seal or other certification

☐ 3. Unexpired INS Employment Authorization Specify form

#

Document Identification

#

Expiration Date (if any)

STEP 6

Read, fill in information, and sign.

6 ▶

CERTIFICATION: I attest, under penalty of perjury, that I have examined the documents presented by the above individual, that they appear to be genuine and to relate to the individual named, and that the individual, to the best of my knowledge, is eligible to work in the United States.

Signature	Name (Print or Type)	Title
J. D. Walsh	_JOSEPH J. WALSH_	_PRESIDENT_
Employer Name	Address	Date
JOSEPH WALSH, INC.	_807 N. MAIN ST., DANVILLE, TN_	_6/25/87_

Form I-9 (05/07/87)
OMB No. 1115-0136

U.S. Department of Justice
Immigration and Naturalization Service

Exhibit 11.10 Portions of Form I-9 to be completed by the employee and the employer.
(*Source:* U.S. Immigration and Naturalization Service. *Handbook for Employers*, 1987, p. 3.)

LIST A

Documents That Establish Identity and Employment Eligibility

- United States Passport
- Certificate of United States Citizenship (INS Form N-560 or N-561)
- Certificate of Naturalization (INS Form N-550 or N-570)
- Unexpired foreign passport that

  —Contains an unexpired stamp that reads "Processed for I-551. Temporary Evidence of Lawful Admission for permanent residence. Valid until _____ Employment authorized."

  or

  —Has attached thereto a Form I-94 bearing the same name as the passport and contains an employment authorization stamp, so long as the period of endorsement has not yet expired and the proposed employment is not in conflict with any restrictions or limitations identified on the Form I-94
- Alien Registration Receipt Card (INS Form I-151) or Resident Alien Card (INS Form I-551), provided that it contains a photograph of the bearer
- Temporary Resident Card (INS Form I-688)
- Employment Authorization Card (INS Form I-688A)

LIST B

Documents That Establish Identity

For individuals 16 years of age or older:

- State-issued driver's license or state-issued identification card containing a photograph. If the driver's license or identification card does not contain a photograph, identifying information should be included, such as name, date of birth, sex, height, color of eyes, and address.
- School identification card with a photograph.
- Voter's registration card
- United States Military card or draft record
- Identification card issued by federal, state or local government agencies

Exhibit 11.11 **Documents that establish identity, employment eligibility, or both.**
(*Source:* U.S. Immigration and Naturalization Service, *Handbook for Employers,* 1987, 11.)

have been unfair to both your company and the employee. You will probably be worse off than you were before because of the further disruption to your work force and production schedules. Your subordinates may begin to suspect that your judgment is not what it should be.

6. *Omitting pertinent information.* If you leave out some vital facts with regard to the applicant's duties or working conditions, he or

- Military dependent's identification card
- Native American tribal documents
- United States Coast Guard Merchant Mariner Card
- Driver's license issued by a Canadian government authority

For individuals under age 16 who are unable to produce one of the documents listed above:

- School record or report card
- Clinic doctor or hospital record
- Daycare or nursery school record

LIST C

Documents That Establish Employment Eligibility

- Social Security number card, other than one which has printed on its face "not valid for employment purposes."
  NOTE: This must be a card issued by the Social Security Administration; a facsimile (such as a metal or plastic reproduction that people can buy) is not acceptable.
- An original or certified copy of a birth certificate issued by a state, county, or municipal authority bearing an official seal
- Unexpired INS employment authorization
- Unexpired re-entry permit (INS Form I-327)
- Unexpired Refugee Travel Document (INS Form I-571)
- Certification of Birth issued by the Department of State (Form FS-545)
- Certification of Birth Abroad issued by the Department of State (Form DS-1350)
- United States Citizen Identification Card (INS Form I-197)
- Native American tribal document
- Identification Card for use of Resident Citizen in the United States (INS Form I-179)

she will be forced to make a decision on the basis of incomplete information. If the applicant had known all the facts, he or she might not have accepted the position. Therefore, once they become known, the applicant may decide that you have misled him or her and quit. You may experience a tendency to leave out the unpleasant aspects of the job or to skip over them lightly. This can only lead a person to think badly of you and may give rise later to gripes and frustration. Give the facts as clearly as you can, leave out the sugar coating, and be complete in your description of the job.

7. *Neglecting sound public relations.* By either overselling or omissions you may be paving the way for a later termination. Moreover, if your decision at the close of your interview is a negative one, and you have not left the person with a good impression about your company and its people, you will be promoting unfavorable public opinion about your organization that could cause a decline in job applicants and even in sales. Treat the applicant as you would a guest in your home. You want to make an honest but favorable impression so that, no matter what happens, when the visit is over both parties will leave with positive impressions.

8. *Asking questions of a discriminatory nature.* Companies can get into major difficulties with federal and state governments if they seek information of a discriminatory nature on application forms and during interviews. Antidiscrimination laws and the Equal Employment Opportunity Commission (EEOC) guidelines must be obeyed; failure to do so exposes you and your employer to legal actions, fines, and bad public relations that will make it more difficult to conduct business in the future.

9. *Hiring friends and relatives who don't qualify.* This error can result from putting emotions ahead of logic. Pressures from these two groups can be tremendous and must be overcome so that members of these groups are subjected to the same screening devices and procedures that apply to all other candidates. If you feel that you cannot be objective in hiring, you may have to let other, more objective people make the decision to hire.

Planning the Newcomer's First Day

Assuming that you have offered the job and the applicant has accepted, you must now begin your planning to welcome the new arrival. During the interview and after it, you should have a fairly good idea as to the need for training that exists. If you know that some training will be needed, begin to map out your plans and get the program organized in a way that allows you to begin as soon as possible. Prepare your people for the new person by communicating everything you know that is positive and not confidential. Get the work area ready, the passes (if any) on hand, and all the items prepared that he or she will need to get right to work. In short, plan to make that first day a truly positive experience—one that will tell the applicant that his or her decision to work for you was correct.

Orientation

Orientation includes the planning and conduct of a program to introduce the new employee to the company, including all policies, practices, rules, and regulations that will affect the employee immediately. Orientation programs are usually conducted by members of the personnel or human resource management department and usually occur within the first few days after the new person arrives. The programs may last for a few hours or for a few days, depending on the size of the company, the content of the program, and the number of new employees to be oriented.

Recent research tells us that about 85 percent of most businesses provide some kind of formal or informal orientation program for their new employees. Approaches range from company-wide meetings and small group conferences to the use of printed materials, such as manuals and handbooks, on company policies and procedures.[17] Most orientation programs give employees a broad overview of the entire organization, with a special emphasis on how and where the new person(s) fits in.

As a supervisor, you may or may not play an active role in your company's orientation program. But you must know the specific contents of the program so that you can reinforce its major messages and build on them with your own efforts during induction. You don't want to contradict any of the key points of information given to new employees. If you are in charge of orientation, you will find Exhibit 11.12 helpful, as it provides a checklist of the major ingredients in most orientation programs.

Orientation Program Goals

The goals of an orientation program usually include the following:

- To instill a favorable first impression with regard to the company, its products, its leadership, and its methods of operation
- To familiarize the new people with the policies, procedures, rules, and benefits that are initially most important
- To outline in detail the specific expectations that the company has for its employees with regard to on-the-job behavior

- Employee assistance programs (EAPs)
- Company history, products, and organization
- Pay and benefits (paydays, vacations, holidays, and insurance)
- Work rules (policies and rules governing all employees while on the job and dictating their conduct)
- Disciplinary procedures
- Grievance procedures (union contract if applicable)
- Safety procedures and responsibilities
- Health facilities (what and where located)
- Opportunities for advancement and training
- Social functions and facilities
- Quality-of-work-life programs

Exhibit 11.12   **Subjects covered in a comprehensive orientation program.**

- To explain the various services that exist for all employees, identify who staffs them, and describe how one can take advantage of them

   The orientation program's goals may be communicated and achieved in small, face-to-face situations or in group lectures and presentations. In many large firms, corporate managers from many levels and departments are introduced and may conduct some of the orientation sessions. This is most often the case when large numbers of new employees are to be welcomed to their new environment. In any case, your company is depending on you to fulfill the promises of its orientation effort in the everyday job setting.

Induction

Induction
The planning and conduct of a program to introduce a new employee to her or his job, working environment, supervisor, and peers

Induction includes the planning and conduct of a program to introduce your new person to his or her job, working environment, supervisor, and coworkers. Induction is your responsibility as the new person's supervisor. Planning for it begins as soon as an offer of employment is accepted. Following the final selection interview, you must begin to tailor your induction activities to fit the needs of your subordinate. Specific goals must be set, and a timetable must be worked out to achieve them.

   In chapter 6 we discussed theories X, Y, and Z and the Pygmalion effect. You will recall that these talked about assumptions that managers make about their new people and how those assumptions can affect the treatment of new subordinates. You must assume the best about your new people until they prove your assumption to be incorrect. You must have faith in their ability to learn their new responsibilities. You needed that faith to offer them employment, and you will need it to structure your approaches to them during induction and training.

It is essential to get your people started with a positive set of experiences from their first day on the job. A warm welcome and immediate successful experiences will reassure the new person and help to remove the anxiety and insecurity that comes with a new job. Studies done at the Texas Instruments Company confirm the following:

1. The first several days on a new job are stressful and disturbing to the new employees.
2. New employee initiation activities conducted by the employee's peers often intensify his or her anxiety.
3. Anxiety in new people interferes with their ability to function properly in training and often leads to turnover.[18]

Because of such findings, induction becomes a very important program that can and does affect the short- and long-term performance of new employees. Induction can give people a proper start or sow the seeds for early failure and employee turnover.

It is important to shield your people from negative initial experiences by introducing them to successful employees and experiences and by keeping the malcontents away from them until they have firmly established their attitudes and mastery over their tasks. You must control their environment by controlling their exposures to it and in it. Keep this in mind as you construct your induction activities and timetable.

Induction Goals

Your induction program can have as many goals as you think proper and can take as long as you feel is necessary. Among the typical induction goals are the following:

- To instill a favorable impression and attitudes about the work section, its operations, and its people
- To remove as many sources of anxiety as possible, by helping the new person meet his or her needs for security, competence, and social acceptance
- To design and provide initial experiences that foster motivation and promote early success
- To begin to build a human relationship that is based on trust and confidence

	Yes	No
1. Have you reserved time for proper introductions to coworkers?	——	——
2. Are the tools, equipment, supplies, and other things on hand for the newcomer's first day?	——	——
3. Have you obtained up-to-date copies of the newcomer's job description?	——	——
4. Are needed identification forms and personnel forms available and scheduled to be filled out by the newcomer?	——	——
5. Have you reserved time with others that the newcomer should meet during his or her induction?	——	——
6. Are copies of the company's employee handbook, policy manual, and union contract ready for the newcomer?	——	——
7. Have you planned to give the newcomer a really positive experience the first day?	——	——
8. Have you planned a systematic introduction of the new person's duties to him or her?	——	——
9. Have you talked with the newcomer's coworkers, paving the way for a friendly welcome?	——	——
10. Have you reserved enough time to spend with the newcomer in the first few days on the job?	——	——

Things left to do: _____

_____

_____

Exhibit 11.13   **Checklist for planning your induction program.**

In order to accomplish these goals, base your planning on them. Your planning should be concerned with the construction of an induction program whose procedures and practices will enable you to achieve each of the above-mentioned goals. In light of these goals, determine what specific steps you wish to accomplish and in what sequence you wish each step to occur. Then determine what resources and facilities you require. In short, you must decide what to do, how to do it, and who to have assist you. You may wish to delegate some of the tasks to your most reliable assistants. Exhibit 11.13 contains a checklist that may prove useful to you as you plan your program.

Making Arrangements

The personnel department must be contacted, and the necessary forms, passes, booklets, and so forth must be procured so that they are available on the first day. As the newcomer's supervisor, you will want to brush up on the forms and content of the booklets so that you can guide the employee through the maze of paperwork effectively and can smooth out the wrinkles that might otherwise interfere with a constructive first impression.

The person's work area must be prepared so that the basic inventory of tools, equipment, supplies, and materials is on hand. It must be put into a clean and polished state of readiness so that the new employee starts off with the desirable standards of housekeeping and maintenance firmly in view. Everything must be in its place and in working order so that there are no surprises waiting for the new person or for you.

Arrangements must be made for the new person to join one or another of the formal groups of workers in your department. It is a good idea to get someone to act as the new employee's *mentor*—a guide and tutor who will be available to answer questions and help once you have finished your induction. A mentor should be a volunteer who knows the ropes and whose judgment and abilities you respect. This person can provide immediate acceptance and social companionship on the job and off (during breaks and lunch).

Prior to the new person's arrival, the formal group must be informed about his or her qualifications. Share all the positive features you know about the new person that are not confidential. Pave the way for his or her acceptance by the positive group or groups, to help in shaping his or her attitudes. There is much to do, so do not waste time and put things off too long. What happens the first day may make the difference between a successful career employee and one who will quit in the near future.

If the new employee is in need of training, the details of the training must be thought through and outlined. A training schedule needs to be drawn up, and the goals that the newcomer is to achieve must be established. All the necessary aids and materials have to be obtained in advance, and the people to be involved in the training must be given advance notice about the parts they will play, so that they can prepare for the training sessions by brushing up on the skills they will need to demonstrate. Chapter 12 examines training in more detail.

The Socialization Process

Socialization
The process a new employee undergoes in the first few weeks of employment through which he or she learns how to succeed and cope

When people enter a new organization to take up a new job, they go through a number of experiences that familiarize them with their new environment—its people, goals, processes, and systems. **Socialization** is the process through which both the new person and the organization learn about each other. Ultimately this leads to a "contract" that both parties can live with. Through socialization, new employees find out what restrictions exist on their freedom, how to succeed and cope, and what place exists for them in the new environment.

Psychological contract
An unwritten recognition of what an employer and an employee expect to give and to get from one another

After all the new employee's questions are answered, a **psychological contract** forms between employer and employee. It is not written but understood by all concerned, and it summarizes what both expect to give to and get from the other. The terms on the contract evolve as time passes and experiences increase. A sense of fairness or equity must exist between employee and employer: each must believe that the other is doing his or her part and giving in proportion to what he or she expects to receive.[19]

Not all new employees will survive long enough to forge a psychological contract. And after the contract is formed, conflicts can arise where one person believes that its terms are being violated by the other. During orientation and induction, certain promises may be made and then broken. Such is the case when a job is oversold and puffed up into something it is not. A supervisor can tell the new person to produce at one level—the only one the supervisor says will be acceptable—and then tolerate a lower level of output from the new person or from others.

As you participate in orientation and induction programs and activities, make certain that you know what is and is not likely to happen to the new person once installed on the job. Be honest and sincere and clear up any misconceptions that you sense the new person has. Don't promise or let your company promise more than you know it can deliver. Now let's return to induction and the specific questions that newcomers have on their minds. How you help them answer these questions will shape their views of the terms of their psychological contract.

The Five Basic Questions

As soon as the new employee arrives, the induction or initiation procedure begins. The typical induction answers the following five basic questions for the new worker:

1. Where am I now?
2. What are my duties?
3. What are my rights?
4. What are my limits?
5. Where can I go?

Where Am I Now?

After greeting the new arrival warmly, you should explain in words and graphic form just where he or she fits into the entire company's operations. By starting with a copy of the company's organization chart, you can move from his or her slot in your department all the way up the chain of command to the chief executive. Explain the jobs performed in your department and in the departments adjacent to it. Name the personalities involved in each, with particular emphasis on those the new employee is most likely to encounter. Give the newcomer a good idea as to how his or her job and department relate to the ultimate success and profitability of the company.

This initial explanation can be followed by a tour of the department and a look at the work area. Introduce the person to his or her coworkers and mentor and give them a chance to chat. Next, familiarize the new person with the facilities within the department that he or she will need to use from time to time—storage areas, supply room, toolroom, washroom, water fountain, and the like. This is also a good time to point out the bulletin board, time clock, and various signs that are posted about the area. Give the newcomer a chance to ask any questions that relate to what he or she sees. Anticipate the likely problem areas and, if he or she does not get to each of them, be certain that you do.

From the tour of the immediate work area and your department, take a walk through the adjacent areas and explain the functions that go on in each. Introduce the newcomer to people you meet along the way in such a manner as to demonstrate your enthusiasm and pride in having him or her join your operation. Something like this should do the trick: "Bill, I'd like you to meet Howard Kramer. Howard, this is Bill Watkins. Howard has just joined our team, and we are lucky to have him." This gives your new worker a chance to know your true feelings about his or her decision to come aboard. The newcomer will quickly begin to sense that he or she is respected and well thought of, as well as needed. Howard will not remember the names of all those to whom he has been introduced, but he will remember your enthusiastic welcome. When he meets these people later, chances are that they will remember him and exchange a greeting.

During your walk through the company, you should have an excellent opportunity to review the company's history and to reinforce the company's orientation program. By sharing knowledge of the company, you will give the new person the sense of being an important part of a big operation. There is tremendous value in this, as we all like to feel we belong to groups that are bigger and more powerful than ourselves. Review the company's line of products or services, and point out the major events in the company's history that have contributed the most to its present position. Pass on all the positive information you have that is not confidential so that a positive image is created of the company, its people, and its future.

When you tour the cafeteria or lounge area, treat the new arrival to a cup of coffee. Some companies pick up the tab for the first day's snacks and lunch and some do not. If your company does not, why not pay for the coffee yourself? It is hard to think of a better way to say "welcome." Lunchtime is a good time to visit in a relaxed and personal way and to assess the impact of the morning's events on your new person. It gives him or her a chance to clear up any questions.

A student once told me that he has a simple philosophy about induction and orientation. In his words, "I just treat them like I would an old friend I haven't seen for some time. There's so much to talk about and share that conversation is never a problem."

What Are My Duties?

After you return from your tour, take the new person back to the work area. All the supplies, materials, tools, and equipment needed will be there because you made sure they would be. The area will be clean and orderly, thus demonstrating the standards of housekeeping and maintenance you expect the employee to maintain.

Give a copy of the job description to the new person, and go over each duty. Explain the details implied by the general listing, and check his or her understanding of each. Wherever you can, demonstrate each duty—either by performing it or by giving specific examples.

Issue any passes or identification cards needed for parking, entering the cafeteria, obtaining tools, and the like. Help the newcomer fill out all the necessary forms, which are sometimes a bit confusing and difficult to follow. By answering questions for your new worker, you will be helping to accomplish all the goals of your induction program.

What Are My Rights?

By *rights* we mean receiving what is owed or due each employee. All workers are entitled to receive their wages according to a prearranged schedule. Explain the pay periods and how pay is calculated. Explain fringe benefits such as group life- and health-insurance plans, the company's profit-sharing plan, paid holidays, incentive awards, the suggestions plan, and the like. In particular, communicate the eligibility requirements (where they exist) for each benefit.

If there is a union, be certain to introduce the steward and explain the rights a person has in regard to union membership. Where this is voluntary, say so. Do not give your views about unions. Simply advise the newcomer of what he or she needs to know.

Review the overtime procedures you follow, and explain how workers become eligible for overtime. Go over the appraisal process, and specify what will be rated in it. If there is a union, explain the grievance process and how to file a grievance complaint.

Cover all the areas that you know from past experience have been sources of misunderstanding in the area of workers' rights. For instance, workers often confuse sick days with personal-leave days. Be sure that your employee knows the difference and understands the company policy with regard to these matters.

What Are My Limits?

Your first and most important duty regarding discipline is to inform each employee about the limits or boundaries placed on their conduct and performance (see chapter 15). Discipline starts with the induction and orientation of each person. The *do's* and *dont's* that you intend to enforce should be explained, along with the penalties attached to each. Each employee should have copies of the company regulations and department rules.

Pay particular attention to the areas affecting safety. Each worker should know not only the rules but company policy as well. If safety equipment is needed, be sure that it is issued or purchased, whichever is required. Then be certain to emphasize safety throughout the newcomer's training. Instill respect for safe working habits and conduct right from the start. Enforcement then becomes easier.

Where Can I Go?

This question involves the opportunities for advancement that exist for each new person. Explain his or her eligibility for training and advanced programs that increase both work skills and the opportunities for promotions. State the criteria you use for making promotion and transfer decisions. People need to know what is required of them in order to advance. Finally, explain the standards he or she must meet in order to qualify for a raise.

Following Up

Plan a follow-up interview to talk with the newcomer about the first day's experiences and answer any questions that may have accumulated. See if you can get a handle on how he or she really feels.

At the end of the first week, schedule another informal meeting with the new person, and determine if he or she is making an adequate adjustment to the new job. Your personal daily observations should tell you if he or she and the group are getting along and if any personal problems are beginning to surface. Watch for warning signals such as fatigue, chronic complaints, lack of interest, or sudden changes from previous behavior patterns. If you spot any of these signals, be prepared to move swiftly to uncover the causes.

You must be prepared for the possibility that the new person may not work out. He or she may not, in spite of your efforts and those of the personnel department, be cut out for the type of work that has been assigned. If your observations and his or her responses seem to indicate this, get together with your boss and discuss the matter. You may be able to work something out, such as a transfer to a different job within or outside your section. It may also be possible to redefine duties to compensate for the difficulties. You want to try your best to salvage the new arrival and to avoid costly termination and replacement proceedings.

All you have to do is to treat the new person like a guest in your home whom you wish to impress favorably. If you have his or her welfare uppermost in your mind, you will not go wrong. Be honest. Keep the channels of communication open. Through adequate planning, a warm welcome, and a constructive induction program, you will be doing all that you can do or are expected to do.

Probation

Most organizations make it clear to new employees that their first weeks are a probationary period—a period of adjustment for both the new person and the organization—after which a more permanent commitment by both can be made. Most union contracts allow for this and will not extend the protection of the union to a new person until a period of time has elapsed—usually about thirty days. Find out what your company's policy is on this, and let the new person know it.

During the probationary period you must do your best to ensure that the new person settles in and adjusts as well as possible. If you recommended the new arrival or gave the offer of employment, it is in your best interest to do so. It is during the probationary period that most of the new employee's attitudes about work, the company, you, and the coworkers are formed. During probation, you have the time to note the new person's strengths and weaknesses. Praise the person for the former, and help the person remove the latter. Your opinion of the new person will probably be the deciding factor in confirming or denying continued employment. If the new person works out, you can take pride in the fact that you have played a part. If the new person is let go, you will have to take part of the responsibility for that as well.

Instant Replay

1. A proper selection process involves the supervisor of the worker who will be hired, usually as the interviewer in the final selection interview.

2. Supervisors should make the final selection because their commitment to the success of new employees is vital.

3. People interviewed in a final selection interview should be pre-screened by personnel or the human resource management department, using proper selection devices.

4. Selection devices include any interview, form, or other instrument that will be weighed or used in making the decision to hire.

5. Selection devices and procedures should not adversely affect minorities and women, and they should have validity.

6. The selection process is both an information-gathering and an information-giving process.

7. Errors in the selection process can be expensive both in fines and court costs connected with discrimination charges and in replacing a person who should not have been selected.

8. Orientation programs are usually conducted by the personnel or human resource management departments and are designed to welcome new employees to the enterprise as a whole.

9. Induction programs are usually conducted by the supervisor of the new employee and are designed to welcome new employees to a specific job, working environment, and peer group.

10. Orientation and induction programs are normally tailored to fit the specific needs of different groups of new employees.

11. Studies show that the first few days on a new job are extremely important and determine to a great extent the future performance and careers of newcomers.

12. The supervisor of a new person, more than any other factor at work, can mean the difference between success and failure on the job.

13. Both orientation and induction programs should be designed to

remove sources of anxiety and to help new employees satisfy their needs for competence, security, and social acceptance.

Directive interview an interview planned and totally controlled by the interviewer. It follows a script of questions written out in advance.

Disparate impact the existence of a significantly different selection rate between women and/or minorities and nonprotected groups.

Induction the planning and conduct of a program to introduce a new employee to his or her job, working environment, supervisor, and peers.

Interview a conversation between two or more people that is under the control of one of the parties. (Interviews are usually more private and more confidential than other kinds of meetings and are designed to screen and hire, share appraisal results, instruct, gather information, and sell ideas.)

Job description a formal listing of the duties (tasks and activities) and responsibilities that make up a formal position (job) in an organization.

Job specification the personal characteristics and skill levels required of an individual to execute a specific job.

Minority according to the EEOC, the following groups are members of minorities protected from discrimination in hiring and other employment decisions: Hispanics, Asians or Pacific Islanders, blacks not of Hispanic origin, American Indians, and Alaskan natives.

Nondirective interview an interview planned by the interviewer but controlled by the interviewee. It makes use of open questions designed to uncover the interviewee's true feelings and opinions with regard to specific areas of interest to the interviewer.

Orientation the planning and conduct of a program to introduce a new employee or groups of new employees to their company—its policies, practices, rules, and regulations that will affect the employees' lives immediately.

Psychological contract an unwritten recognition of what an employee and an employer expect to give and get from one another.

Selection the personnel or human resource management function that determines who is hired and who is not.

Socialization the process a new employee undergoes in the first few weeks of employment, which teaches the new person what the restrictions are, how to succeed and cope, and what place exists for him or her in the new environment.

Validity the characteristic that a selection device has when it is predictive of a person's performance on a job. The degree to which a selection criterion measures what it is supposed to measure.

Questions for
Class Discussion

1. Can you define this chapter's key terms?

2. What is the proper role for a supervisor to play in the process that will select his or her new subordinate?

3. What will a personnel or human resource management department normally do during the selection process?

4. What are the major selection devices used in a typical selection process?

5. How should you prepare to give a selection interview?

6. What are the major pitfalls in the selection process?

7. What are the goals of a good orientation program?

8. What are the goals of a good induction program?

9. What happens to an employee who passes through the socialization process?

10. What are the five basic questions that new employees want answered?

11. How can you link what you know about motivation to the orientation and induction programs' goals?

Incident

Purpose To give you the experience of creating an orientation program.

Your Task Create an outline for an orientation program to introduce a new student to your school, college, or current institution. Use your chapter's guidance and your own experiences to create your program. Be sure to include your induction efforts as well. Compare your program to those of your classmates.

Case Problem 11.1   Belle's First Job

Ever since the First Trust and Savings Company hired Belle Walker for the summer, she has been a thorn in Kay Farrel's side. As head cashier, Kay is responsible for supervising the bank's eight tellers. Three weeks before Wilma Banks was to retire, Belle was hired as Wilma's replacement, without any consultation with Kay. Kay was openly critical of the way in which Belle had been hired, because it was a significant departure from past practices and company policy.

Kay had inquired why exceptions were made in Belle's case but was given only terse and evasive answers. After some checking on her own, Kay discovered what she believed to be the real reason. James B. Walker, Belle's father, is one of the most important merchants in town. He keeps large personal and business accounts at the bank and is a member of its board of directors.

Kay does not have any serious doubts about Belle's ability to become a good teller. Belle is a high-school graduate and has been an above-average student for most of her school years. She is a bright and personable young lady and is very good with customers. Her instructor for her first three weeks was Wilma Banks, the best teller at First Trust and Savings Company.

During the first two weeks of training Belle, Wilma mentioned on several occasions that Belle's heart did not seem to be in her work. She would often say she understood but then make some simple mistake when left on her own. She enjoys talking to the customers more than she does handling their banking transactions, and more than a few times they let Belle know this. Belle is also fond of saying that she really does not need this job or the money it pays but wants to work for the experience and to meet new people. She is headed for college in the fall and wants to fill some time.

This week, the first week Belle was on her own, she was unable to balance out at the end of her shift on Tuesday and Thursday. She had a significant excess of cash she could not explain on Tuesday and a shortage of cash on Thursday. Kay is also concerned about Belle's tardiness—another departure from her behavior pattern of the first two weeks on the job. Twice this week she has been late in opening her window. This creates problems for the other tellers, who do not hesitate to let Kay know how they feel about it. When Kay spoke to Belle about her tardiness on Monday, she was assured it would not happen again. But Belle was late again today.

Kay knows that Belle will be around only for another eight weeks and wonders if it is worthwhile to raise the problem about her performance. She has doubts about her boss's willingness to stand behind her in any attempted disciplinary action. He has let her down before, even when a big depositor's daughter was not involved. Kay is afraid, however, that letting things go unchecked might lead to more serious problems in her department.

Questions

1. What special treatment has Belle already received? What are the consequences?
2. Suggest a selection system that might have avoided this problem.
3. What should Kay do now?

Case Problem 11.2   Black Tuesday

"You people in personnel don't have to supervise them, so it is all well and good that you can hire a person so quickly. If that's your final decision, then don't blame me if Hilda doesn't work out. I've told you no, and I'm on record." After this statement Alice Bartlett hung up her phone. She began to think back over the past week when the whole unpleasant incident began.

Joan Hasbrook had given notice that she would quit on the fifteenth of the month. She and her husband were moving to Florida. Alice had immediately notified personnel of her need for another billing clerk in the credit department. It was an important position in Johannson's downtown store, the largest women's store in Edwardsboro. Customer billing exceeded $2 million last year and would be closer to $2.5 this year. Nearly 70 percent of all retail purchases were done through charge cards, the store's own and several bank credit cards. Joan's replacement would be responsible for processing all customer accounts, A–G. This group accounted for nearly one-fifth of all purchases on credit at Johannson's.

Joan had agreed to stay until her replacement was hired to assist the new employee in initial training and orientation. Two days after Alice notified personnel, three candidates were interviewed. Alice selected Jane Vlasoff but was overruled by personnel. They had hired Hilda Clayborn, who was due to report for work tomorrow morning, Tuesday. Alice had just received a day's notice to that effect.

Alice sat down with Joan for lunch and began to detail her unhappiness.

"Well, Joan, I guess they weren't kidding with that memo last month about emphasis being placed on hiring minorities. I interviewed three applicants for your job, and they picked a black woman over two qualified white people."

"I had a feeling we would see one here sooner or later," said Joan. "Has this black got any credit experience at all?"

"No. She doesn't even have retail experience. What gets me is that they let me interview these people, and then they go against my recommendation. What's the purpose of sending them to me if they are going to ignore my choice?"

"Wait until Suzy finds out we've got a Negro," sighed Joan. "You know how outspoken she is against them. She had better watch that big mouth of hers."

Questions

1. Who has the authority to hire in this company?
2. How does this case illustrate the concept of functional authority?
3. Who has the responsibility for Hilda's training?
4. If Hilda quits, how might this adversely affect Alice and her department?

Notes

1. Carol Kleiman, "Personnel Office Tasks Growing but Staffing Isn't," *Chicago Tribune* (April 19, 1987), §8: 1.
2. Equal Employment Opportunity Act of 1972, Subcommittee on Labor of the Committee on Labor and Public Welfare, United States Senate (March 1972), 3.
3. Glen Elsasser, "Supreme Court Expands Rights of Ethnic Whites," *Chicago Tribune* (May 19, 1987, §1: 1–2.
4. Ibid.
5. Tony Mauro, "Big Boost for Affirmative Action," *USA Today* (March 26, 1987): 1A.
6. Lawrence A. Johnson, "Employing the Hard-Core Unemployed," Research Study No. 98 (New York: American Management Association, 1969).
7. Kleiman, note 1.
8. Robert Half, *On Hiring* (New York: Crown, 1985), 67.
9. "Uniform Guidelines on Employee Selection Procedures," *Federal Register* 43, #156 (August 1978): 38295-309.
10. Thomas Melohn, "Screening for the Best Employees," *Inc.* (January 1987): 104–5.
11. Ibid., 105–6.
12. Ibid., 105.
13. Ibid.
14. Ibid.
15. Ibid., 106.
16. Ibid.
17. "How Employers Say a Formal 'Hello,' " *Chicago Tribune* (October 12, 1977).
18. E. R. Gomersall and M. S. Meyers, "Breakthrough in On-the-Job Training," *Harvard Business Review* (July–August 1966): 64. See also R. D. Scott, "Job Expectancy: An Important Factor in Labor Turnover," *Personnel Journal* 51 (1972): 360–63.
19. Edgar H. Schein, *Career Dynamics: Matching Individual and Organizational Needs* (Reading, Mass.: Addison-Wesley, 1978): 94–97.

Suggested Readings

Gatewood, Robert D., and Field, Hubert S. *Human Resource Selection*. New York: Dryden Press, 1987.

Half, Robert. *On Hiring*. New York: Crown, 1985.

Jenks, James M., and Zevnik, Brian L. P. "ABCs of Job Interviewing." *Harvard Business Review* (July–August 1989): 38–39, 42.

Ledvinka, James, and Scarpello, Vida G. *Federal Regulation of Personnel and Human Resource Management*. 2d ed. Boston: PWS-Kent Publishing Co., 1991.

Libbin, Anne E.; Mendelsohn, Susan R.; and Duffy, Dennis P. "Employee Medical and Honesty Testing." *Personnel* 65 (November 1988): 38–48.

Loden, Marilyn, and Rosener, Judy B. *WorkForce America: Managing Employee Diversity as a Vital Resource*. Homewood, Ill.: Business One Irwin, 1991.

Nuventures Consultants, Inc. *America's Changing Workforce*. LaJolla, Calif.: Nuventures Publishing, 1990.

Sugiura, Hideo. "How Honda Localizes Its Global Strategy." *Sloan Management Review* (Fall 1990): 77–82.

Tully, Shawn. "GE in Hungary: Let There Be Light." *Fortune* (October 22, 1990): 137–138, 142.

Weiss, Donald H. *How to Be a Successful Interviewer*. New York: AMACOM, 1988.

12 Training

Outline

Objectives

After reading and discussing this chapter, you should be able to do the following:

1 Define this chapter's key terms.
2 List at least three advantages that a supervisor receives from training a subordinate.
3 List at least three advantages that a trainee receives from training.
4 List the three basic requirements that a trainer must satisfy in order to train.
5 List the five basic requirements a trainee must satisfy in order to learn.
6 List and briefly describe the seven principles that govern training.
7 List and briefly describe the four parts of the training cycle.
8 List and briefly describe the five pitfalls in training.

Key Terms

behavior modeling	reinforcement
individualism	response
motivation	subjects
objective	training
realism	training objective

Introduction

This chapter is concerned with how you can help your subordinates acquire new skills, improve their existing ones, and improve their abilities to handle their jobs. The process of training is concerned with improving employees' performances in their present jobs. It helps them acquire the attitudes, skills, and knowledge they need to execute their present duties and the duties that will be coming their way in the near future.

Training becomes necessary by the very fact that you have subordinates. Whether they are old-timers, newcomers, or a mix of the two, you must continually see to it that they are functioning effectively and to the best of their abilities. If they are not, training is called for. Whether you train or rely on others to help you with training, you are responsible for seeing to it that your people are properly trained.

According to a recent study by the U.S. Department of Labor and the Rand Corporation, 40 percent of U.S. workers have taken part in training programs while on their current jobs. The study also notes that training increased earnings for workers, as well as reducing the likelihood of their becoming unemployed.[1] American corporate spending for training and development programs away from the office and from shop floors amounts to about $30 billion per year, according to the Washington-based American Society for Training and Development. It has been estimated that American corporations spend in excess of $1 billion each year on basic education—attempts to bring workers' skill levels up to basic literacy standards by teaching the three R's. This figure is expected to be about $10 billion by the year 2000.[2]

The Subjects of Training

Training
The activity concerned with improving employees' performances in their present jobs by imparting skills, knowledge, and attitudes

Training imparts attitudes, knowledge, and skills. It is an ongoing process governed by basic principles and provided by people with the aid of machines and methods specially suited to the subjects to be covered and the persons to be taught. Training, like daily living, increases our knowledge and understanding of the people and things that surround us.

Attitudes

Much has already been said about *attitudes,* and all of it is related to the training process. You must remember that, when you train, you are attempting to instill positive attitudes—either as replacements for improper ones or as useful additions to fill a void in the minds of your trainees. Attitudes are taught primarily through your own example and secondarily through your words. Workers learn an attitude by observing what you do. If you talk about safety but act in an unsafe manner or lightly skip over safety during the training period, your workers will adopt the same casual attitudes. The most important attitudes that you must help form in trainees are those that involve their job and their safety.

Knowledge

Knowledge is the body of facts, ideas, concepts, and procedures that enable people to see or visualize what must be done and why. If trainees can understand the whole job and its relationship to the work of others, they have a better chance to master their own jobs. They must understand the theory (fundamental principles and abstract knowledge) that governs their work before they can adequately perform their own tasks. Then they must (with your help) translate the theory into practice through the training process. Knowing what to do is one thing, but applying the knowledge is the most important thing.

Skills

When we apply knowledge, we are exercising some type of *skill:* technical, human, or conceptual. Technical skills require muscular coordination—based on knowing what to do, why, and how to do it—that we can use to operate tools, machines, and equipment. Conceptual skills involve mental processes such as those used in problem solving, learning, and communicating (reading, writing, calculating, and imagining).

The best way to teach a skill is to involve the trainees as quickly as possible in performing the skill. Practice and more practice are keys to the successful acquisition of motor skills. Moving from an in-depth understanding of the tools, equipment, or machinery to an actual working knowledge of the trade or craft, the trainees experience a controlled exposure to both the technical side and the manipulative side of their jobs.

Early successes are essential, and extremely close supervision must be exercised so that improper work habits are not acquired and so that confidence is instilled as soon as possible. Often you may have to ask the trainees to unlearn certain procedures or habits acquired by earlier experiences before you can substitute the proper methods. This is a difficult and time-consuming task that requires a great deal of patience from both you and your trainees.

Tom Peters, co-author of *In Search of Excellence* and *A Passion for Excellence,* offers several suggestions to managers who want their companies to survive in today's business climate.[3] First, he says, workers must be trained to accomplish the following goals:

- Learn many jobs (twenty to thirty).
- Perform many tasks (maintenance, repair, budgeting, and quality control).
- Perform many skills (problem cause-and-effect analysis, listening, interpersonal dynamics—team problem-solving skills).
- Function as a member of a ''business team,'' with team leadership rotating among its members.

Second, he says, managers must be trained and developed to achieve the following ends:

- Be better listeners.

- Believe in the virtually unlimited potential of every worker.

- Become true facilitators for the teams they must lead.

- Recognize and pay for productivity increases and quality improvements. Above-average base pay and team-based incentives tied strictly to measurable performance improvement are essential.

The problem is, however, that about 20 percent of current and new employees lack the basic literacy skills they need to succeed in their jobs. Aetna Life and Casualty has created a basic education program for its primarily white-collar work force. It found that it could no longer assume that a high school graduate can write an intelligible sentence. Their program costs about $700,000 per year.[4] R. J. Reynolds invested about $2 billion in automating its factory in Winston-Salem, North Carolina, before discovering that its work force lacked the reading skills necessary to operate and maintain the new equipment. Of its 6,000 workers, 1,300 had to be put through a basic literacy program.[5] Finally, IBM offered a free, college-level course in algebra to its employees only to discover that 30 out of 280 workers who signed up were able to read and calculate at the twelfth grade level (a prerequisite for taking the course).[6]

Advantages of Training for the Supervisor

Just what do you yourself get out of training a subordinate? What is in it for you? The following are but a few of the many benefits you receive when you train your people properly:

1. *You get to know your subordinates.* When you are dealing with new employees, you hasten the process of learning about their needs, wants, and potentials. With your other subordinates, you get a chance to update your knowledge of each person, thereby making your personnel decisions and recommendations easier with regard to promotions, raises, transfers, and the like.

2. *You further your own career.* As your people grow in abilities, proficiency, and reputation, so will you. As each individual increases his or her efficiency and effectiveness, the whole group benefits. As your subordinates look better, feel better, and perform better, they strongly affect your reputation as a supervisor and leader. As we have stated before, your reputation is largely a product of their performance.

3. *You gain more time.* As a result of training, your people become more self-sufficient and confident. You will find that, as their performances improve, you have more time for the essentials. You will spend less time on corrections and deficiencies and more on planning, organizing, controlling, and coordinating. You may be able to shift from an autocratic style of supervision (so necessary during the training) to a less time-consuming style.

4. *You promote good human relations.* One of your primary roles in developing good human relations with your people is that of educator. You give them logical reasons to support sound working relationships with you and their peers. They gain self-confidence, pride, and security through their training, which promotes cooperation and respect for you. Many will see you as the cause of their improvement and will rely on you more for advice and direction in the future.

5. *You reduce safety hazards.* By emphasizing safety rules, procedures, and attitudes through your proper conduct and words, you reduce the likelihood of violations and the resulting accidents and injuries. How tragic it would be to have to live with the knowledge that a subordinate's injury might have been prevented if you had done all that you should have in the area of safety.

Advantages of Training for Subordinates

Training gives your workers as many advantages as it gives you (if not more), including the following:

1. *They increase their chances for success.* Through training, workers gain new knowledge and experiences that help reduce the risks of personal obsolescence and increase their value to themselves and to the company. By exposure and practice, workers gain new techniques that enhance their abilities and their enjoyment of work. By successfully completing training, workers confront change, meet challenges, and decrease fears.

2. *They increase their motivation to work.* Through successful training experiences and proper guidance, individuals experience a greater measure of achievement. They find ways to reduce fatigue, increase contributions, and expend less effort to accomplish their tasks. These accomplishments tend to fortify a desire to work harder. We

all need the security that comes with knowing our jobs so well that we are free to learn new skills and to advance in our careers. We all need a sense of competence.

3. *They promote their own advancement.* As workers become more proficient, they earn the right to receive additional duties, either through delegation or through a job change. By proving themselves through the learning process, they justify the investment of additional company time and money in their development. They become more mobile members of the organization.

4. *Their morale improves.* Mastery of new responsibilities inevitably leads to new prestige and importance. This newfound pride can be translated into higher earnings, a greater commitment to the company, and a renewed self-image. As the spirits of group members rise, they can and often do spread throughout the group. Workers see themselves as necessary and more valuable parts of the whole and as greater contributors to the group's success.

5. *Their productivity increases.* Their output becomes less problem-ridden, exhibits less wasted effort and materials, and results in higher-quality production and a greater return to themselves and the company.

Some or all of these benefits will accrue to everyone who takes part in training. The degree to which an individual receives such benefits is a variable that cannot be predicted. But training does tell your people of both your company's interest and your personal interest in their welfare and development. Just be sure to let trainees put their training to use as soon after its completion as possible.

Requirements for Trainers

Ideally, you as the supervisor should plan and execute the essential function of training. This is true primarily because of the many personal benefits available to you when you do. After all, the workers on your team are your responsibility.

There are times, however, when you cannot train subordinates. You may lack either the time or the first-hand knowledge of the job to be taught (or both). In such cases, you may have to delegate the training duties to a subordinate or rely on the various staff specialists your company can provide. Either way, you are accountable for their actions and the results. Therefore, it would be wise for you to assist, when you are able, in the planning of the training and to check up on its execution periodically. Better one ounce of prevention than pounds of cure.

Regardless of who does the training, he or she should meet the following basic requirements:

- Be willing to conduct the training.
- Know the body of knowledge, attitudes, and skills to be taught.
- Know how to train—posses a working knowledge of the ways in which people learn, the principles that govern training, and the several kinds of training methods, along with their respective advantages and disadvantages.

Every trainer must want to do the best job possible and must recognize that his or her actions and enthusiasm will teach as much as if not more than the words spoken during training. Training is an art that can be learned.

Kenneth Blanchard, chairman of Blanchard Training and Development and co-author of *The One-Minute Manager*, believes that a positive relationship with workers is a powerful motivator. "To gain the respect and loyalty of employees, a manager should emphasize the positive aspects of someone's performance and de-emphasize the negative."[7] Such a manager builds a relationship of *TRUST* with subordinates:

T stands for *time*—taking time to provide feedback on performance.

R stands for *respect*—respect that grows from relationships based on trust.

U stands for *unconditional positive regard*—trainers should have the best interests of trainees at heart.

S stands for *sensitivity*—the best trainers learn to anticipate the feelings and needs of trainees.

T stands for *touch*—trainees need a pat on the back and a pleased "Well done!"

Behavior modeling
A visual training approach designed to teach attitudes and proper modes of behavior by involving supervisors and others in real-life performances

Behavior Modeling

The case problems given in this text at the end of each chapter show, for the most part, supervisors in trouble and usually doing the wrong things. Sometimes they simply do not know what to do, and sometimes their attitudes get in the way. Such cases help you spot a failure and search for the causes of it. **Behavior modeling,** on the other hand, teaches attitudes and proper modes of behavior to supervisors by involving them in real-life situations and providing immediate feedback on their performances.[8] By watching a film, a videotape, or live role-playing sessions, supervisors are shown proper ways to deal with true-to-life situations. Participants, by watching, discussing, and then trying to apply what they see, can and do experience behavioral changes.

Behavior modeling can be used to teach human relations: how to deal properly with employee complaints, how to conduct training, and how to do virtually anything supervisors are likely to have to do. Participants in behavior modeling are usually called upon to act out what they believe to be proper conduct, given specific situations and persons to deal with. Their performances are usually taped or filmed and then discussed by all concerned on playback.

If your company offers it, this technique can help you learn how to be a better trainer. You can use its techniques to help your trainees duplicate behaviors, as well. It is always a good idea to rehearse your training lessons before you attempt to perform for real. Watching yourself on film or listening to your delivery on tape can greatly improve your timing and delivery of vital information.

Requirements for Trainees

In general, people who are about to go through training should meet the following requirements:

1. They should be informed about what will be taught and why.
2. They should recognize that they need what is to be taught.
3. They should be willing to learn what is to be taught.
4. They should have the capabilities to learn what is to be taught.
5. They should see the advantages to them in mastering what is to be taught.

Given trainees who meet these preconditions and a trainer who meets his or her preconditions, genuine learning and meaningful change can take place. Learning theory tells us that, without motivation or the incentive to learn, no real learning will take place. When learning does take place, motivated trainees and trainers are the central reason for it. The principles that follow will enable you to design and execute a successful training program.

The Principles of Training

There are several established and proved principles that you should keep in mind while planning and conducting a training program. These principles should be used as a checklist to make certain that you have not overlooked anything important. They are summarized by the acronym *MIRRORS,* to help you to remember them:

Motivation

Individualism

Realism

Response

Objective

Reinforcement

Subjects

These principles are interdependent and interrelated.

Motivation

Motivation
The training principle that requires both trainer and trainee to be favorably predisposed and ready to undergo training

Unless both you and the trainee are motivated, the training process will achieve something less than is desired. Your **motivation** should come easily, as you have much to gain from training. If you delegate to a subordinate, you again should have no problem with motivation because he or she willingly accepted the responsibility. It is the trainee who poses the greatest concern. New employees are usually anxious to get through training successfully, so as to gain some level of independence and security. Old-timers may be less than enthusiastic, however.

Remember that training imparts a sense of competence. If people know what is expected of them, believe that they are capable of mastering those expectations, see the rewards that lie ahead, and want those rewards, they will be motivated.

Individualism

Individualism
The training principle requiring a trainer to conduct training at a pace suitable for the trainee

The principle of **individualism** states that the training you prepare and present must be tailored to meet the needs and situations of individuals. In order to do this, you must know what skills, knowledge, and attitudes the people already possess, so you can start from there in designing your program. By building on what they already know, you can use their past experience as a frame of reference. What is to be added can be linked to their present abilities.

NEWS
You Can Use

America's work force is aging. According to the U.S. Bureau of Labor Statistics, the forty-five to fifty-four year old age group will represent 22 percent of America's work force by the year 2000. As our population ages, fewer young people will be entering the work force and higher education. Employers in some industries are already facing a shortage of knowledgeable workers and more will be in the future. To make up for this shortfall, employers are turning increasingly to recruiting and hiring older workers. Early retirement incentives will be cut back in the future, encouraging people to stay on the job longer.

Mature (over-fifty year olds) people bring a number of benefits with them to work. Studies have shown them to be better educated, more experienced, less prone to tardiness and absenteeism, and much less likely to have a drug addiction or alcohol problem. Many work out of necessity, but many return to the work force because of boredom and frustration with retirement. Some lose their spouses and return to work to seek human companionship. These people generally become part of our permanent part-time work force. About 1.5 million people work for temporary employment agencies and employee-leasing firms. These firms are meeting a growing need for well-trained, experienced workers as employers seek to reduce their payroll and benefits costs.

While some industry studies show a resistance to training among older workers and an unwillingness to spend training dollars on them, most employers will have no choice but to keep their work force members current through regular, ongoing training and to retrain those whose skills become obsolete. William St. Clair, McDonald Corporation's director of store employment, echoes many personnel specialists' opinion when he says, "We've developed an awareness and sensitivity to older people among our management. Older people are as trainable as younger ones."*

*Source: Carol Kleiman, "Firms Find That, with Retraining, Older Is Better," *Chicago Tribune* (February 4, 1990) sect. 8, p. 1.

By individualizing your approach, you can adjust the sequence of what is to be taught to fit present conditions most appropriately. For instance, if people already know how to operate a particular piece of machinery that is similar but not the same as the one they must now operate, begin by pointing out the similarities, and then show the differences or exceptions.

Finally, this principle states that you must vary your presentation of material to fit people's ability to assimilate it. Let the trainees advance at a comfortable rate, and do not give too much at once; you will only frustrate and confuse them if you do.

You are probably experiencing exposure to older employees. By the year 2000, the average worker in America will be thirty-nine years old, and the ''baby boomers'' will be in their fifties. When older employees go through training, you can individualize your approach by relying on thoroughness rather than speed. Use older employees' backgrounds and experiences as connecting links to the new information or methods. By providing constant feedback to keep them abreast of their progress, you help to overcome some of the fear of failure that older workers have when facing the new and different.

Realism

Realism
The training principle that requires training to simulate or duplicate the actual working environment and behavior or performance required of the trainee

Make the learning process as close to the real thing as you can. In most training situations, you should teach people on the job, using the actual equipment, tools, or machinery that must be mastered. In the case of office or clerical employees, use the actual forms, manuals, procedures, and practices. This **realism** is not always possible, because of various limitations. Noise levels may interfere with proper communications; space may not be adequate for proper demonstrations or explanations; equipment or machines may not be available for training use because they are being fully utilized in current production. When you cannot train on the job, or deem it wiser not to do so, set up conditions that are as close to the actual working situation as you can. Use examples and situations that accurately reflect actual problems the worker is likely to encounter. Then move from the simulated conditions to the actual environment as soon as possible.

A medium-size manufacturer in the Midwest was reluctant to purchase and install the latest manufacturing equipment in its plant because it lacked skilled workers who could operate and maintain it. The solution was to find a community college that had the computer-integrated equipment in its facilities and to send a select group to learn the equipment. After the group was trained, the workers returned to train others in the plant on the equipment that was then being installed.

Response

Response
The principle of training that requires feedback from trainees to trainers

The principle of **response** reminds you to check on the trainee's receptiveness and retention regularly. Involve the trainees in a two-way conversation. Ask questions and encourage them to do the same. It is only by frequent checking that you can be sure that lasting progress is taking place.

Response also includes the concept of evaluation. Besides oral questions and answers, you can evaluate or measure the trainees' progress by conducting performance tests or written quizzes. Use whatever means you believe will yield the information you seek. Involve the trainees in feedback throughout the training process. Share the results of trainees' regular evaluations with them. One member of a corporate training program put it this way: "I like the daily quizzes my instructor gives. They let you know right away how well you have caught on to the material covered. It keeps you on your toes and forces you to review each night. I need this course. It means another twenty-five dollars per week."

Objective

Objective
The training principle that requires trainer and trainees to know what is to be mastered through training

The principle of the **objective** states that trainees and trainers should always know where they are headed at any given point in the training process. As a trainer, you have to set goals for the training program and for each of the individual training sessions you conduct. These must be communicated to the trainees so that they know where they are headed and can tell when they get there.

The trainees' goals are targets to shoot for during each session, as well as throughout the entire program. They should be realistic, specific, and within the trainee's ability to achieve. They tell employees that their training is planned and professional. There will be more about objectives later in this chapter.

Reinforcement

Reinforcement
The training principle that requires trainees to review and restate knowledge learned

According to the principle of **reinforcement,** if learning is to be retained, it must involve all of the senses—or as many as possible. When you first explain an idea, you may involve both sight and hearing, using a demonstration coupled with an explanation. Then you can let the trainees try out their understanding by repeating the demonstration and explanation in their own words. They will then be using sight, touch, and hearing and will be reviewing the concepts as well. By using frequent summaries and by reviewing key points, you will be practicing reinforcement. By repetition and practice, you lend emphasis and greatly increase retention.

Try to put the knowledge and skills that must be learned to work in a real situation as soon as possible. Studies reveal that we retain about 50 percent of what we hear immediately after we hear it and about 75 percent of what we experience immediately after the event. As time passes without further reference to our knowledge or to the application of our skills, our retention of them diminishes still further. More than one training supervisor knows the truth behind the old adage "Tell them what you are going to tell them; tell them; then tell them what you told them."

Subjects

Subjects
The principle of training that requires trainers to know the subject being taught and to know the trainees' needs

The principle of **subjects** is two-sided: you must know as much about the trainees as possible, and you must have a mastery of the subject to be taught. By research and rehearsal before the main event, you will be aware of the likely trouble spots both in the presentation and in the learning of the material.

In determining what you wish to teach—the subjects of your training program—you have several areas to consider. If you are preparing to teach an entire job, you will want to consult the job description and its corresponding job specifications. Next you will need to know what skills and knowledge the job holder has, in relation to what he or she needs. Then you can construct a program to teach the skills, knowledge, and attitudes the new person needs. Be certain that the description of the job accurately outlines the job and its duties as they presently exist, not as they once were.

To determine the subjects to teach to your current subordinates, consult their most recent performance evaluations, your current observations, and the workers themselves. Disciplinary actions and records may point out the need for training. So may the results of exit interviews conducted with voluntarily departing subordinates. Common complaints may signal common problems that can be eliminated, through training, for those who remain employed.

A company recently switched from one brand of computers to another and introduced the use of several new software programs throughout one of its divisions. After a few weeks, work began to fall off in quality. It became obvious to the division manager that many departments were having trouble with the new software. On investigation, the division chief discovered that several supervisors were unable to teach the new software because they had not learned it. Several other supervisors knew the software but seemed unable to teach it to their team members. The division chief got together with the personnel head of training and constructed two courses: "training the trainer to train" and a course on the uses and applications of the software. In the latter course, help was obtained from the vendor of the new computers. A skilled analyst was dispatched to the company, the course was taught to supervisors and videotaped, and the rest of the troubled workers took the course by watching the video presentation and working along with it.

The Training Cycle

Exhibit 12.1 shows the four parts of a successful training effort. Training, like planning, demands that you know your destination before you plan your trip. The first step is to identify where training is needed. Once areas are identified, objectives can be written to specify what is to be taught,

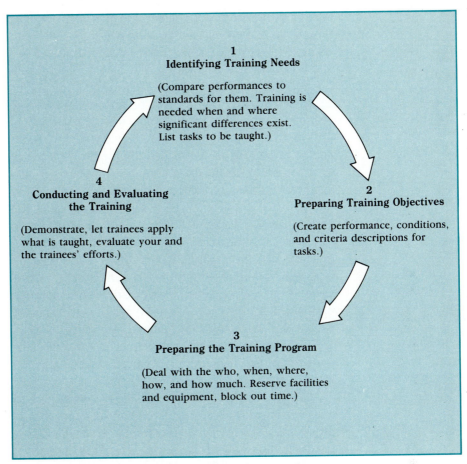

1
Identifying Training Needs

(Compare performances to standards for them. Training is needed when and where significant differences exist. List tasks to be taught.)

4
Conducting and Evaluating the Training

(Demonstrate, let trainees apply what is taught, evaluate your and the trainees' efforts.)

2
Preparing Training Objectives

(Create performance, conditions, and criteria descriptions for tasks.)

3
Preparing the Training Program

(Deal with the who, when, where, how, and how much. Reserve facilities and equipment, block out time.)

Exhibit 12.1   **The four basic components of the training cycle.**

under what conditions, and how the learning can be verified. Unless all persons undergoing the training have no knowledge of what is to be taught, a pretest is called for to determine who knows what and to what extent they know it. A training plan can then be constructed to answer the questions of who, when, where, how, and how much about the training. The program is then put into action, and the results are evaluated to determine areas that were successful and the need for improvements or repetition of some lessons.

Part 1. Identifying Training Needs

You know that you or your people need training when things are not as they should be. Your efforts at control and supervision should tell you when performances are not meeting expectations or standards. Training is always needed to some degree with the addition of new subordinates to your area. As new equipment is arranged for, people have to be trained to use and maintain it. When new procedures are to be established, people should be warned in advance and taught how to execute them.

Let's assume that you are a restaurant manager faced with the arrival of a new employee who must be trained in your restaurant's methods, attitudes, and skills as they relate to being a waiter. How would you start to determine what should be taught? It would make sense to turn to your copies of the waiter's job description and job specification. You have these, they are up to date, and you have already used them to conduct your recruiting and interviewing prior to your decision to hire. They contain a list of duties and tasks, as well as a list of the personal qualities demanded of a waiter. From each task listed on the job description, you can determine the specific skills needed to execute the task. The task of greeting customers cordially after they are seated by the host requires language and interpersonal skills. The task of serving customers their orders requires manual dexterity and coordination—mental as well as physical. Once you know what types of performance are expected of the waiter, you have the raw material necessary to assess possible training needs. If the new person is experienced, you will probably have to teach your particular restaurant's applications of skills already possessed to some degree.

The day has arrived. Ben, your new waiter, has two years of experience with the job. Your earlier and present contacts with Ben will tell you the areas in which he needs training. After induction, you show Ben the job description and talk through each of the duties with him, making sure to point out any differences that may arise between what Ben has been doing elsewhere and what he will be expected to do for you. Now that Ben is familiar with his tasks, you are ready to try him out on each and monitor his performance. But before monitoring, you must have a clear understanding of each task, of the conditions that surround its performance, and of the criteria by which you will judge the quality of performance. These three items constitute what is called a **training objective.**

Training objective
A written statement containing what the trainee should be able to do, the conditions under which the trainee is expected to perform, and the criteria used to judge the adequacy of the performance

Part 2. Preparing Training Objectives

Before you can train or a person can learn, both parties must have common objectives in front of them. These should be in writing to avoid confusion and to ensure mastery. All objectives should state three things as clearly as possible: (1) what the trainee should be able to do (the *performance* expected); (2) the *conditions* under which the learner is expected to do it; and (3) how well the task must be done (the *criterion* or criteria).[9] Let's look at each of these in more detail.

Performance The specific things you want a trainee to do are usually outlined or summarized under the major headings of tasks listed in a job description. But each task may and usually does have a series of minor tasks connected to it. For example, Ben's job description states, "takes orders from patrons." What subtasks or other duties are connected to this one? One might be that the waiter be able to write the orders on a prescribed form in a prescribed manner so that the kitchen people can properly interpret it. Before an order can be taken, patrons need to know what is available. Consequently, menus must be distributed and specials for the day announced. All of these subtasks must be understood and stated, if they are to be taught. Finally, certain skills are connected with these tasks. They, too, must be identified, described, and (in some cases) taught.

Your immediate concern with Ben will be to decide which tasks he can perform, and you cannot do that until you have listed all the tasks in all their detail. Before you can train Ben or evaluate how much he already knows, you have to possess a *complete* list of required tasks, skills, and attitudes.

Objectives usually state the performance needed by using active verbs such as *construct, list, identify,* and *compare.* These specified behaviors can be observed or evaluated fairly easily. The more specific the duty, the easier it will be to find out if the trainee has mastered it. Stay away from verbs such as *know, understand, appreciate,* and *believe;* these actions are far too vague to be taught or evaluated with precision.

Conditions Objectives should contain a listing of the items needed by the trainee to execute the performance and any limits or constraints that will be placed on performance. In our ongoing example of Ben, the new trainee, you already know that he will need the restaurant's prescribed order forms, a writing instrument, and a knowledge of the kitchen staff's "shorthand" for taking orders from patrons. But there is a time restraint as well at your restaurant. Ben must take the order within a fixed period of time after patrons are seated or, if they are undecided at his first visit, he must return to the table within five minutes of his first contact (at which he announced the specials of the day).

When preparing to write the conditions for a task, consider the following questions:

1. What equipment will the trainee need and be allowed to use?

2. What resources will be denied to the trainee (equipment, manuals, materials, and so on)?

3. What time restraints should be listed?[10]

Conditions usually begin with the word *given*. For example, "Given the restaurant's order form, a ballpoint pen, and a working knowledge of the restaurant's order shorthand, the waiter should be able to. . . ." Each learning objective at the beginning of each chapter in this text begins with a specification of the conditions that are considered necessary for a student to demonstrate each performance listed. The two conditions are to read and to discuss each chapter. Only then can a student be expected to perform each objective. In a business setting, some objectives may begin with a statement about what will be denied to a trainee. For example, "Given no direct supervision . . ." or "Without the aid of tools, the trainee should be able to. . . ." Such a condition is understood to exist when you as a student take most of your tests. You understand that you are to answer the questions asked *without* the aid of notes, texts, or other classroom learning materials, unless they are specifically authorized for use.

Each major task listed on Ben's job description can be broken down into subtasks. A performance and condition for each can then be written. For example, the subtasks related to "taking a customer's order" may break down as follows:

1. Visit the table.
2. Greet the customer cordially.
3. Introduce yourself and the specials of the day.
4. Offer to take the customer's order.
5. If the customer is undecided, leave and return to take his or her order.
6. Write the customer's order.
7. Deliver the order to the kitchen.

Each of these subtasks is involved in the major task of taking a customer's order. Each has a condition or two attached to it. Writing your restaurant's policies and procedures into the first performance will give you the following:

1. Visit the table within one minute after the customer is seated by the hostess, armed with the restaurant's order forms, a ballpoint pen, a knowledge of the kitchen shorthand and daily specials, a clean uniform, and a smile on your face.

The performance expected is to visit the customer's table. The conditions surrounding that performance include a one-minute time limit, possession of equipment and knowledge, and a warm and friendly demeanor. Each of the other six subtasks may be given conditions as well. If they are all to be taught together, the conditions in number 1 will be understood to exist in numbers 2, 3, 4, and 6. A new time limit may be required for number 5.

The key to writing descriptions of conditions is to be detailed enough to ensure that the desired performance will be executed in the way you as a trainer desire it to be. Add as much description as you feel you must to communicate your intent to the trainee. When in doubt, describe. With detailed lists of tasks and their conditions, both you and the trainee can progress in an orderly manner, leaving little to chance.

Criteria Criteria state the standards that a trainee must be able to meet in order to give a satisfactory performance. When speed, accuracy, and a quality of performance can be stated, they should be made a part of the training objective. In this text, the learning objectives at the front of each chapter do not specify criteria for measuring the adequacy of your performance. That is a job for your instructor to decide. The questions at the end of each chapter ask you to demonstrate your performance in the learning objectives. But the quality, speed, and accuracy factors and what you will be allowed to use while performing them have been left up to your instructor to determine.

Criteria need not always appear in a training objective. Sometimes they are part of the conditions. Ben's first performance required him to visit a table within one minute of the customer's being seated. In this case, the time limit is both a limit and a criterion for evaluating Ben's performance.

Some criteria are best demonstrated or shown. You as a trainer can do this, pointing out the quality of performance you desire through personal demonstrations or by using the behavior modeling techniques of film or videotape. Nothing need be written into the training objective in this case.

As long as you and the trainee know what makes a performance acceptable, you have met the requirement for including criteria in your training objectives. If you cannot find some words or ways to determine acceptability of performance, perhaps you should reconsider its importance to you and to your trainee.[11] It may be of such minor importance that it should not be treated formally in training.

Part 3. Preparing the Training Program

You have determined the needs you have for training. You have identified the tasks to be taught and have written solid training objectives. These answer the questions ''Why should there be training?'' and ''What will be taught?'' The rest of your training program will answer questions relating to who, when, where, how, and how much (see Exhibit 12.2).

The **Who:**	Who will do the training? Who will receive it?
The **When:**	What times will be set aside for training?
The **Where:**	What specific physical areas and equipment will be needed to conduct the training?
The **How:**	In what chronological order will the tasks be taught? What methods of instruction are best for each task?
The **How Much:**	How much money will be needed to ensure a successful training effort? How much time and equipment will be needed to teach all the objectives?

Exhibit 12.2   Checklist to help you plan your training program.

Who You answer this question by determining the specific people who will conduct the training and who will learn from it. In our example, you are the trainer and Ben is the trainee.

When The answer to this question blocks out specific time periods for conducting training. Since you run a busy restaurant, the best times for training are before the doors open to customers, during between-meals times, and after closing.

Where Specific areas must be designated and reserved for training use.

How Two answers are needed for the following question: In what order will the objectives be taught, and by what methods? Priorities and a training schedule must be constructed to guarantee that all items are included, in an order of presentation that makes sense to the trainee. Many techniques can be used to deliver your training. Exhibit 12.3 lists the major techniques and specifies where they are most appropriately utilized. Each has positive and negative features, and one is usually more appropriate than the others for teaching specific performances. All of them can be classified under one of three headings: a buddy system, a machine-based system, and group sessions.

Buddy Systems. The *buddy system* is a person-to-person or one-on-one method of training. It may also be known as the *teacher-pupil method* or the *master-apprentice method*. Regardless of what it is called, this method utilizes one trainer and one trainee; a person who knows the job teaches someone who needs to know it. Instruction usually takes place "on the job," using the actual workplace, tools, and equipment

Method	Definition	Strengths	Weaknesses
1. Lecture	Speech by the instructor, with very limited discussions.	Clear and direct method of presentation. Good if there are more than 20 trainees. Materials can be provided to trainees in advance, to help in their preparation. Trainer has control over time. Cost-effective (cheap).	Since there is no discussion, it is easy to forget. Sometimes it is not effective. Requires high level of speaking ability. Requires quick understanding by trainees.
2. Group discussion (conference)	Speech by the instructor, with a lot of participation (questions and comments) from the listeners. Sometimes instructor not necessary; however, a leader is needed.	Good if the participants are small groups. Each participant has opportunity to present own ideas. More ideas can be generated.	Sometimes they get away from the subjects. Some group leaders or instructors do not know how to guide discussions. Sometimes one strong individual can dominate others.
3. Role playing	Creating a realistic situation and having trainees assume parts of specific personalities in the situation. Their actions are based on the roles assigned to them. Emphasis is not on problem solving, but rather on skill development.	Good if the situation is similar to the actual work situation. Trainees receive feedback that gives them confidence. Good for interpersonal skills. Teaches individuals how to act in real situations.	Trainees are not actors. Trainees sometimes are not serious. Some situations cannot be implemented in role playing. Uncontrolled role playing may not lead to any sufficient results. If it is very similar to actual life, it may produce adverse reactions.

Exhibit 12.3 **Comparisons of basic training methods.** (*Source:* Sulaiman M. Al-Malik, unpublished paper. Georgia State University, Winter 1985; published in Lloyd L. Byars, Ph.D., and Leslie W. Rue, Ph.D., *Human Resource Management*, Homewood, Ill.: Irwin, 1987, 2nd ed., pp. 237–240.)

Method	Definition	Strengths	Weaknesses
4. Sensitivity training (laboratory training)	Used for organizational development. Creating situations and examining the participants' reaction and behavior, then having feedback about behavior. Group members exchange thoughts and feelings in unstructured ways.	Helps individuals find the reasons for their behavior (self-insight). Helps individuals know the effects of their behavior on others. Creates more group interactions.	People may not like information about their behavior, especially if it is negative. May lead to conflict and anger within the group. May not be related or transferable to jobs.
5. Case study	A written narrative description of a real situation, issue, or incident that a manager faced in a particular organization. Trainees are required to propose suitable solution or make appropriate decision.	Cases are usually very interesting. High group discussion and interaction about many solutions, since there is no absolute solution. Develops trainees' abilities in effective communication and active participation. Develops trainee's ability to figure various factors that influence their decision building. Develops trainees' ability to make proper decisions in real-life situations (transfer of learning).	Slow method of training. Often difficult to select the appropriate case study for specific training situation. Requires high level of skills by both trainees and trainer, as the discussion can become boring. Can create frustration on part of trainees, especially if they fail to arrive at specific solution.
6. Management games	Giving the trainees information about the organization and its environment; then	Develops practical experience for the trainees. Helps in transferring	Often, it is difficult to study the results of each team's decision. Some teams may not

	Description	Advantages	Disadvantages
	dividing into teams. Each team is required to make operational decision and then evaluate its decision.	knowledge and in applying administrative thoughts. Helps to evaluate and correct the trainees' behavior.	take it seriously. May be a slow process.
7. Simulation exercises	Same as management games, except a digital computer is used to input information and analyze the team decisions. Results of trainees' actions are evaluated.	Same as management games.	Same as management games. Very costly. Difficult to simulate very complex system.
8. Wilderness training	Several managers meet out of the workplace and live in cabins or tents for up to seven days. They test their survival skills and learn about their own potential—for creativity, cooperation, etc.	People learn limits and capabilities.	Very costly. May not be transferable.
9. In-basket training	Creates the same type of situation trainees face in daily work. Trainees observed: how they arrange the situations and their actions regarding them. Trainees evaluated on the basis of the number and quality of decisions. Used for MD and assessment centers.	Effective for corrective action or reinforcement. Widely used in assessment centers for measuring supervisory potential.	Tendency to be or become overly simplistic.

Exhibit 12.3 (cont.)

Method	Definition	Strengths	Weaknesses
10. Incident process (problem solving)	Simple variation of the case study method. The basic elements are given to the trainee, who then asks the instructor for the most sufficient information that will help him in making his decision. The instructor will only give the requested information.	Has an immediate feedback from the instructor. Develops supervisory skills in seeking facts and decision making.	Requires high degree of instructing skills in forming answers.
11. Vestibule training	Setting up training area very similar to the work area in equipment, procedures, and environment but separated from the actual one so trainees can learn without affecting the production schedule. Used for training typists, bank tellers, etc.	Fast way to train employees. Trainees can get the most from this method.	Very expensive.
12. Apprenticeship training	Trainee works under guidance of skilled, licensed instructor and receives lower pay than licensed workers.	Develops special skills: mechanical, electronic, tailoring, etc. Extensive training.	Takes a long time.

	Description	Advantages	Disadvantages
13. Internship training	According to agreement, individuals in these programs earn while they learn, but at a lower rate than if they worked full-time.	More chance for trainees to apply what they have learned. Trainee gets exposure to both organization and job.	Takes a long time.
14. Projects	Like group discussion method. Trainees together analyze data and reach conclusion.	Helps trainees to know more about the subject.	Requires instructor's time to ensure the group is going in the right direction.
15. Videotapes and movies	Recording and producing certain events or situations with clear descriptions in order to cover certain subjects. Can be shown many times, then reviewed and discussed to help trainees understand more fully.	Tapes can be played many times to ensure individual's understanding. Many events and discussions can be put on one tape. Because length of time is known, presentation and follow-up can be scheduled.	Recording and producing has to be done by professionals to get good quality. Expensive (a typical 20- to 30-minute cassette costs $50, without projector or screen).
16. Multiple management	Lower- and middle-level managers participate formally with top management in planning and administration.	Helps top management to identify top management candidates. Enhances employees' participation in the organization.	

Exhibit 12.3 (*cont.*)

during regular working hours. When the person doing the training is properly prepared, the buddy system has the following major advantages:

1. *It is flexible.* Learning can take place in a classroom, in a laboratory, or on the job. Changes can be introduced quickly. The system can be tailored in pace and content to meet the individual needs of the trainee.

2. *It provides for immediate feedback.* The teacher/trainer works directly with the trainee and can evaluate his or her progress or lack of progress personally and quickly, offering corrections and reviews to improve retention and mastery.

3. *It is personal.* It humanizes the training process and allows for questions and answers, reviews, and additional drills or practices at any time. Personalized corrections may be made, and personalized instructions may be given throughout the duration of training. The system frequently helps the trainees to satisfy some of their social needs.

The primary disadvantages of the buddy system are the following:

1. *It is costly.* The salary or wages of the trainer go to pay for the training of just one trainee during any training sessions. Expensive equipment and machines are tied up and utilized by only one trainee at any given moment. The time and talents of the trainer are utilized by only one trainee per session.

2. *It is difficult to prepare for and conduct adequately.* If the real advantages of the buddy system are to be realized, the instructor must adequately assess the needs of the trainee, tailor the instruction to meet those needs, and avoid passing along attitudes, prejudices, and shortcuts that differ from what the trainee needs and what management wants taught.

Machine-Based Systems. Computer-based or programmed instruction methods are referred to as *machine-based systems of instruction and training* because they rely heavily on a machine to relay information and evaluate trainee responses. Computers, through their video display terminals and programs, and machines that use filmstrips, videotapes, audiotapes, records, and the like can enhance the learning environment and enrich the kind of training that takes place. But all machine-based instruction requires people: (1) to prepare the learner and materials; (2) to monitor the training process by keeping track of time and handling questions or making adjustments to the equipment; and (3) to evaluate the progress or lack of progress made by each trainee. This method is more often used to supplement other types of training than to substitute for them. It works well when used to complement the other methods.

The advantages of machine-based training include the following:

1. *It is uniform.* It ensures that the same material is presented in exactly the same way to each trainee.

2. *It is flexible.* It can be adjusted, or can adjust itself, to fit the needs and pace of the trainees. It involves the learners in the learning process. It frees trainers for other duties and allows them to handle more than one trainee per session. By periodically checking on each person's progress and by remaining available to each trainee, the trainer will often be able to accomplish other tasks while the machines do part of the instructing.

3. *It is inexpensive.* While the materials and machines may be expensive to prepare, install, and keep in repair, these costs can be spread over dozens or hundreds of trainees and over a long period of time; and such costs can be slowly absorbed as an operating expense through allowances for their depreciation. Vendors of equipment such as word processors and computers often provide machine-based training and/or trainers and materials free or at a reasonable cost at the time of purchase and before or just after equipment deliveries.

The disadvantages of machine-based training are the following:

1. *It is impersonal.* Machines cannot fully replace the need for human interaction. They cannot provide the warmth of a smile and a compliment from an instructor for a job well mastered in training. They cannot sense an employee's fear or frustration or the lack of comprehension of a video or verbal message.

2. *It requires expertise.* Learning materials demand a great deal of money, know-how, and time to prepare. To be economical, they must use materials that will not require frequent changing and will not become obsolete in a short period of time.

3. *It can be boring.* For trainees with short attention spans, for those who learn quickly, and for those who already know a significant portion of the material to be mastered, the teaching machine method of training can become frustrating and boring.

4. *It needs to serve many trainees in order to be economical.* Computer programs and videotapes cost too much to prepare if only a few trainees are to use them.

Group Sessions. Lectures, conferences, and role-playing sessions can be quite effective methods of training more than one person at each session. Lectures present basic principles and individual points of view, and they can be used to introduce, summarize, or evaluate training sessions or performances. Conferences and discussions can inform, solve problems, clarify situations, and help participants critically evaluate their opinions, attitudes, and methods. Role playing helps people act out a situation to what they see as its logical conclusion. Participants see one another in different lights and have a chance to evaluate the solutions of others while trying out their own solutions on the group. All group sessions deal with two or more trainees and require expert planning and leadership if they are to be successful.

The major advantages of the group-sessions method are the following:

1. *It is uniform.* Two or more people are exposed to the same material in the same way at the same time.
2. *It is inexpensive.* Compared to other training methods, group sessions offer savings in hours and salaries for training purposes.

The major disadvantages of the group-sessions method are the following:

1. *It is impersonal.* It does not allow for individual differences, individual participation, or close involvement in the training.
2. *It magnifies errors.* The impact of each involuntary mistake or bit of misinformation is magnified by the number of trainees.

Natasha Josefowitz, management consultant and author of two books on management, notes that people have preferred ways of learning and teaching. Basically, we all learn by seeing, hearing, and doing. People who prefer to learn by hearing should be talked through operations and the reasons for them. People who prefer to learn by seeing should be shown the execution of tasks, examples of why they are necessary, and the finished results expected. People who learn best by hands-on doing should be given ample time to perform with you as you demonstrate each operation. But people learn best when more than one of these methods is used in training.[12] Exhibit 12.4 presents a model to help you conduct your training programs.

In designing your training program, try to utilize more than one method of training. For most types of training, a single method will not do. A blend or mix will probably suit your purposes better. When you know what has to be taught and what human and material resources you have available, think about which methods should work best for you and your trainees.

Step 1: Preparation of the Learner

1. Put the learner at ease—relieve the tension.

2. Explain what is being taught, and why.

3. Create interest, encourage questions, find out what the learner already knows about his or her job or other jobs.

4. Explain the why of the whole job and relate it to some job the worker already knows.

5. Place the learner as close to the normal working position as possible.

6. Familiarize the worker with the equipment, materials, tools, and trade terms.

Step 2: Presentation of the Operation

1. Explain quantity and quality requirements.

2. Go through the job at the normal work pace.

3. Go through the job at a slow pace several times, explaining each step. Between operations, explain the difficult parts, or those in which errors are likely to be made.

4. Again go through the job at a slow pace several times, explain the key points.

5. Have the learner explain the steps as you go through the job at a slow pace.

Step 3: Performance Tryout

1. Have the learner go through the job several times, slowly, explaining to you each step. Correct mistakes, and if necessary, do some of the complicated steps the first few times.

2. You, the trainer, run the job at the normal pace.

3. Have the learner do the job, gradually building up skill and speed.

4. As soon as the learner demonstrates ability to do the job, let the work begin, but don't abandon him or her.

Step 4: Follow-up

1. Designate to whom the learner should go for help if he or she needs it.

2. Gradually decrease supervision, checking work from time to time against quality and quantity standards.

3. Correct faulty work patterns that begin to creep into the work, and do it before they become a habit. Show why the learned method is superior.

4. Compliment good work; encourage the worker until able to meet the quality/quantity standards.

Exhibit 12.4   **A four-step outline for conducting training.** (*Source:* Gary Dessler, *Personnel Management,* 4th ed., copyright 1988, pp. 254–255. Adapted by permission of Prentice Hall, Englewood Cliffs, New Jersey.)

How Much This question needs two answers. You must determine how much time you will need to teach your performances and how much money you will have to spend. You will need to incorporate your time into your training schedule. You may need approval for spending money that is not already in your budget for training. Needed training equipment and supplies must be ordered ahead of time and must be in place when training begins.

Break the job into learnable units—units small enough to be effectively taught and absorbed in one session. If the units are too big, the trainee will be unable to digest them. It is far better to have less material—leaving ample time for review and practice—than to have too much. A good rule of thumb is to attempt to teach no more than three performances in every sixty-minute session.

Part 4. Conducting and Evaluating the Training

When you are finished with your planning, execution begins with the preparation of the training area. Have everything on hand and in working order so that the session can flow smoothly and without interruption. Have the area properly arranged and in the same condition you expect your workers to keep it in. Prepare yourself through rehearsals—trial run-throughs—to check on your timing and command of the material.

Prepare the workers in the following ways:

1. Put them at ease.
2. State the objectives to be achieved during the session.
3. Point out the advantages to be received from the training.
4. Explain the sequence of the events that are about to follow.

You should stress the fact that when you and the company take the time and make the effort necessary to train workers, it is positive proof of concern for the workers and an expression of confidence in their abilities. Training is costly, and the trainees should know the costs and why management is willing to incur them. If eligibility for training was competitive, let each trainee know of your pride in his or her selection. Let your trainees know that there is no harm in making mistakes. In fact, we learn more by analyzing our mistakes than we do by listening to a teacher who says all the right things. It is by examining our failures or incorrect examples that we discover their causes and can prevent their recurrence.

Demonstrating During the demonstrating phase of your training presentation, you have the opportunity to show and tell. You can perform as your objective specifies or let experienced help demonstrate the tasks for you. In Ben's case, you may want to call upon your trusted and skilled old-timers to do what they do best. Or you may videotape performances and let the trainee view the film, commenting on what is being shown and asking and answering questions. If your trainee has no questions, ask some of your own. Check on Ben's understanding of each critical performance. Remember that training involves communication and communication requires feedback.

Application   The application phase of training asks the trainee to get his or her feet wet. In this case, Ben will be asked to duplicate the performance that he has just witnessed. You may want to show Ben more than one performance before asking him to repeat it. However, don't try to include too many behaviors before you let the trainee try them out. By mixing the demonstration with applications, you provide the trainee with immediate feedback and highlight both what he or she has mastered and what he or she has not. You will be applying the principle of reinforcement, as well as providing the early and measured successes that are so important to the mastery of performances and the motivation of the trainee. You may be able to videotape the trainee in his or her performance and use the tape in playback to review his or her efforts.

Evaluation   The evaluation phase determines if the trainee has mastered performances and if the training effort was successful. The basic question here is: "Can the trainee perform, under the prescribed conditions and to the necessary degree of quality, all the essential tasks taught?" Evaluation may take place at any point in a demonstration or during a trainee's application of lessons. Performance tests, written or oral quizzes, and the trainer's own observations are the most frequently used devices for evaluating performances.

Provide trainees with frequent and immediate feedback. Let them know when they are correct and ask them to spot their own mistakes. Let them examine the product of their efforts and try to spot any defects. Once they discover an error, explain, or get them to explain, just how it can be prevented from happening again. Point out how one error—the one just made, for example—can lead to others. Use each mistake as a point for review, and then conduct a critique to summarize the entire lesson.

Through evaluation you can quickly ascertain the need for reteaching a point. You will also realize just how fast you can place people on their own, free from your strict supervision and control. Put people on their own, but gradually. Do not let them feel that when the training ends, it is sink or swim. Be available to them, and let them know that you are.

Simply make your visits and observations less frequent as each person demonstrates an ability to perform to standards. Your follow-up should tell you whether lasting effects have been achieved or whether an individual needs additional training.

There is a technique of great merit in use in different types of apprenticeship programs. The master mechanic or teacher bugs a machine by deliberately planting a problem within it. The student must troubleshoot the item to uncover its problem and then correct the deficiency. This technique may fit your needs, so give it some thought. Just be sure that the bug you plant does not permanently damage the equipment!

Pitfalls

Besides violations of any of the aforementioned principles of training, the following are the major pitfalls:

1. *Letting George do it.* By delegating or using the assistance of staff specialists, you may hope that proper training will take place. Since you are not directly involved, you tend to wash your hands of the process and rely on their efforts. Remember that you have accountability and must participate in both the planning and the execution to the extent necessary to know what is being done and what goals are being achieved. You will be stuck with the results, so make them as beneficial as possible.

2. *Making assumptions.* A trainer sometimes makes the mistake of assuming that, because trainees were told to read about a concept, they will understand it on their own—or that, because the trainer presented the material according to plan, all of it has been assimilated. There is an old axiom that bosses would be wise to cite to their subordinates: when you assume anything, you make an *ass* out of *u* and *me*. Rely on facts and observations that can provide you with the basis for a proper evaluation of the program and its effectiveness, not on assumptions.

3. *Fearing a subordinate's progress.* Some people fear the successes and increasing abilities of others because they view them as threats to their own security. Have you known a manager who refused to train a subordinate because he or she was afraid that, if someone else could do the job, he or she might lose it? Managers may refuse to delegate in order to keep their people dependent on them and

may deliberately deny subordinates the chance to advance, fearing that the subordinates may challenge their position. Keep in mind that, unless you have a trained successor, you are locking yourself into your present position. Training is the job of every manager who has subordinates. By not doing it, you are neglecting a very important duty. This neglect will be reflected in your ratings.

4. *Getting too fancy.* Trainers may get too caught up in methods and training aids and lose sight of what it is they must teach. There may be too much flash and too little substance. Have you ever listened to a speaker or lecturer who talked for hours and said nothing? If you have ever seen a fireworks display, you know what this error is like.

5. *Substituting training for proper selection processes.* Training is not a substitute for proper selection procedures. Selection (chapter 11) involves trying to procure the best available person to fill a vacancy. It requires skills in such areas as interviewing, testing, and recruiting. Some employers treat selection as an unimportant activity and rely on the training of new employees to impart the skills required to execute a job properly. This is especially true in areas where keen competition for qualified people exists among employers, such as in data processing. But some skills cannot be taught effectively by employers, such as the abilities to read and write effectively in English or any other language. Companies cannot afford to conduct such training and lack the qualified personnel to do so. Selection should make certain that people brought into the organization only lack skills, knowledge, and attitudes that the employer is willing to teach.

Instant Replay

1. Training is the supervisor's responsibility. It may be delegated, but the supervisor is accountable for it.

2. Training imparts skills, knowledge, and attitudes needed by trainees now or in the near future.

3. Training benefits you, your trainees, and your employer. Be certain that trainees know what they are to learn and why.

4. You are judged on your performance and on the performances of your subordinates. The better they do, the better you all look to each other and to superiors.

5. Anyone may train if he or she possesses the body of knowledge, skills, and attitudes to be taught, knows and follows the principles that govern training, and wants to train.

6. The training cycle asks you to identify your training needs, to prepare performance objectives, to create a training program, and to conduct the training.

7. The central purpose behind training is to get performances up to standard—to make certain that they turn out as planned.

Glossary

Behavior modeling a visual training approach designed to teach attitudes and proper modes of behavior by involving supervisors (and others) in real-life situations and providing immediate feedback on their performances.

Individualism the training principle requiring a trainer to know the individual trainee's levels of skills and knowledge, to understand the trainee's attitudes, and to progress in training at a pace suitable for the individual trainee to master the material being taught.

Motivation the training principle that requires both trainer and trainee to be favorably predisposed and ready to learn before and during training.

Objective the training principle that requires trainers and trainees to know what it is that must be taught and mastered. Objectives describe the behavior or performance expected from a trainee as a result of training. They are set with specific conditions in mind, and their mastery is verified through the use of specific standards.

Realism the training principle that requires training to simulate or duplicate, as closely as possible, the actual working environment and behavior or performance required of a trainee.

Reinforcement the training principle that requires trainees to review and restate knowledge learned, to practice skills, and to involve as many senses as possible in the learning process.

Response the principle of training that requires feedback from trainees to trainers in the form of questions, practical demonstrations, and evaluation exercises.

Subjects the principle of training that requires trainers to know the subject being taught and to know the trainees—their existing levels of skills and knowledge, their attitudes, and their predispositions to learn.

Training the activity concerned with improving employees' performances in their present jobs by imparting attitudes, skills, and knowledge needed now or in the near future.

Training objective a written statement containing what the trainee should be able to do (performance), the conditions under which the trainee is expected to perform, and the criteria used to judge the adequacy of the performance.

Questions for Class Discussion

1. Can you define this chapter's key terms?
2. What are three advantages that a supervisor receives when he or she trains a subordinate?
3. What are three advantages that a trainee receives through training?
4. What are three basic requirements that a trainer must satisfy?
5. What are five basic requirements that a trainee must satisfy in order to get the most out of training?
6. What are the seven principles of training, and what does each mean to a trainer?
7. What are the four major steps in the training cycle?
8. What are the five pitfalls that a trainer should be aware of?

Incident

Purpose To create and conduct a brief training program, following the four basic parts to training as shown in Exhibit 12.1.

Your Task Create a training program through which you teach another person *your way* of assembling a flashlight (including batteries) from a collection of parts. After you have created your learning objective(s), chosen a method, reserved a location, and gotten a volunteer, write down each step, noting the standards you wish to teach and use to evaluate the learner's performance. Set a time limit and conduct your training session in class, following the steps outlined in Exhibit 12.4. When you have taught the lesson, evaluate your efforts through the learner's and the class's comments. Don't be surprised if the learner or the class comes up with a better way to assemble your flashlight!

Case Problem 12.1 **John Paul Jones**

John Paul Jones is general manager of the Gier Variety Store in Boston. Bentley Gier founded that store in 1981 and now personally manages another newer store, while entrusting the Boston store to Jones. Jones receives a salary of $25,000 annually and a bonus of 1.5 percent of his store's annual sales. He directly supervises all of his store's eleven employees, ten of whom are salespeople. He pools merchandise orders with Mr. Gier on a regular basis.

The Boston store's annual gross sales amounted to $1.2 million last year, an increase of $65,000 over the preceding year. Both stores carry a wide line of inexpensive household items as well as medium-priced goods in leather, small appliances, and children's wear. Prices range from a few pennies to $200. Since

1. Explain the time card and attendance policy to each trainee.
2. Familiarize each trainee with the store's entire inventory.
3. Teach the store's method of pricing goods, and explain the price tag information and coding.
4. Train the trainee to handle cash, credit, and discount sales.
5. Teach basic salesmanship techniques and how to greet customers.
6. Teach register operations and wrapping.
7. Welcome each person to the Gier Team!
8. Instruct each person on the merchandise requisitioning procedures.
9. Compliment the trainees when they are right and criticize them when they are not.
10. Introduce them to the other salespeople and to our store policies.
11. Emphasize housekeeping!
12. Keep the trainees supplied with the supplies they need.
13. Keep Mr. Jones posted on the trainees' progress or lack of progress.

Exhibit A   Sales trainer's duties.

Jones took over the management of the Boston store in 1988, sales have climbed steadily, averaging a 5 percent increase per year.

Personnel has been J.P.'s most frustrating challenge over the past three years. The annual average turnover of sales personnel has averaged 60 percent. Jones has shown a preference for hiring persons of middle age and older. He has attempted to hire experienced salespeople to avoid the need for training, but this has become increasingly difficult.

Sales personnel receive an average hourly wage of $4.95 and work a forty-hour week. Recently the store has been forced to remain open for twelve additional hours each week to include Sundays. This has caused a rearrangement of work schedules for the experienced staff and has necessitated the addition of two new workers this week, both of whom are inexperienced at selling.

Jones has designed a training program in which the two new employees are assigned to an experienced saleswoman for on-the-job training. The training is to last as long as the trainer deems it necessary. A description of the trainer's duties as determined by Mr. Jones is shown in Exhibit A.

Prior to this year, Mr. Jones personally trained each new employee, but lately his duties have become more time consuming. When the two new and inexperienced persons joined the staff, he felt that the new arrangement would be best. He chose the trainer, Blanche Hecker, on the basis of his personal knowledge of her performance and because he considered Blanche to be his best salesperson. She knew the merchandise and had been with the store longer than anyone else. After talking his proposal over with her (and using some salesmanship tactics of his own), Blanche agreed to try the training assignment. Mr. Jones assured her that she would have no difficulties because in his words, "I'll be right here if you need help. Don't hesitate to ask for it."

In designing the program Jones drew heavily on the years of selling experience that he acquired with Mr. Gier from 1986 to 1988. Both men felt and now feel that unless an employee has to give something for what he or she gets, it will not be appreciated. As a result, the new workers are required to spend one hour each day for a week with Ms. Hecker learning the store's inventory before the store opens. This they are to do with no pay. After the first week's training the three will return to their normal shift hours, continuing to train on the job.

Blanche Hecker is forty-seven, single, and impeccable in both dress and manner. She has been with the store since 1982 and has established a sales record never equalled by any other employee. She has been in retailing since graduating from high school and has had over seventeen years of selling experience. Although she has never trained anyone before, she has been through the sales-training program offered by H. R. Croft and Company, one of Boston's largest department stores.

Questions

1. What do you think are the chances for success of Jones's program? Why?
2. Are Blanche's qualifications adequate for the position of trainer? If not, why not?
3. Analyze the list of Blanche's duties. What is on it that should not be? What has been left off, if anything?
4. To what factors might you attribute Jones's inability to attract trained salespeople?
5. What factors may account for the 60 percent average annual turnover?
6. Which principles of training has Jones overlooked?

Case Problem 12.2   Terminal Illness

Richard Boscok, the supervisor of the accounting department, was hard-pressed to know what his next move should be. In two weeks, the new computers would be arriving, and none of his people knew how to operate them. Top management wanted them on line "as soon as possible," which Richard's boss had translated to mean within one week of arrival. Richard had some pretty able people on the old equipment, but the procedures would have to be redone in line with the new equipment's capabilities. This, he thought, would surely slow his people's transfer of work to the new machines and software.

As he looked through the operator's manual for the new computers, he realized that about half the machine functions would be slightly different from the ones his people had been using. Keys and keying operations were different, and new capabilities built into the computers would make existing procedures obsolete. It dawned on Richard that the switch was going to be tough for the old-timers. He remembered how hard it had been to get them used to the current machines five years ago. Some operators were new and had not yet finished learning the existing equipment. He wondered if he should stop their training immediately and wait for the new equipment to arrive. "No," he thought, "they would just be idle for two more weeks."

Richard decided on a two-phase plan. First, he would map out his training program over the next two weeks; in it, he would start with the similarities and then teach the differences. Second, when the equipment was installed, he would teach a select group of fast-learners, and they in turn would teach the others in their sections. When Richard shared his plan with his boss, however, he received a big shock. The plan for installing the new equipment called for removing the old equipment over the weekend preceding the delivery. Richard would not have the luxury of two computers for each operator—one old and one new model. As plans stood now, all the old computers would be out before the new ones were installed. Then within two working days after delivery, the nine new machines would be operational.

Questions

1. What should Richard do over the next two weeks to prepare his people for the new computers?

2. What might go wrong with Richard's plan to teach a small group of fast-learners who would then teach the others in their groups?
3. On the basis of Exhibit 12.3 and your own experience, what methods would you recommend to Richard to teach the operations of the new computers to both new and experienced employees?

Notes

1. Michael Brody, "Helping Workers to Work Smarter," *Fortune* (June 8, 1987): 86–87.
2. Ron Grossman, "The Three R's Go to Work," *Chicago Tribune* (October 29, 1989), sect. 4, p. 1.
3. Tom Peters, "Bosses Must Keep the Ball Rolling to Stay on Top of Their Competition," *Chicago Tribune* (August 10, 1987), 4: 7.
4. Ron Grossman, op. cit., p. 1.
5. Ibid., p. 4.
6. Ibid.
7. Kenneth Blanchard, "Moby Dick Management," *Success!* (June 1987): 24.
8. Bernard L. Rosenbaum, "A New Approach to Changing Supervisory Behavior," *Personnel* 52, 2 (March–April 1975): 37–44.
9. Robert F. Mager, *Preparing Instructional Objectives,* 2d ed. (Belmont, Calif.: Pitman Learning, 1984), 21.
10. Ibid., 51.
11. Ibid., 86–87.
12. Natasha Josefowitz, *You're the Boss!* (New York: Warner Books, 1985), 151.

Suggested Readings

Bartlett, Christopher A., and Ghoshal Sumantra. *Managing Across Borders.* Boston: Harvard Business School Press, 1989.

Clark, Ruth C. "Nine Ways to Make Training Pay Off on the Job." *Training,* 23, 11 (November 1986): 83–87.

Goldstein, Irwin L. *Training in Organizations: Needs Assessment, Development, and Evaluation.* 2d ed. Monterey, Calif.: Brooks/Cole Publishing Co., 1986.

Hicks, William D., and Klimoski, Richard T. "Entry into Training Programs and Its Effects on Training Outcomes: A Field Experiment." *Academy of Management Journal,* 30, 3 (September 1987): 542–552.

Jones, Gareth R. "Socialization Tactics, Self-Efficacy, and Newcomers' Adjustments to Organizations." *Academy of Management Journal,* 29, 2 (June 1986): 262–279.

Kuzmits, F. E. "Train Your New Managers with LCI." *Personnel* (April 1985): 69–72.

Mager, Robert F. *Preparing Instructional Objectives.* 2d ed. Belmont, Calif: Pitman Learning, 1984.

Shook, Robert L. *Honda: An American Success Story.* New York: Prentice Hall Press, 1988.

Zemke, Ron. "The Rediscovery of Video Teleconferencing." *Training,* 23, 9 (September 1986): 28–36.

Zemke, Ron. "What Is Technical Training, Anyway?" *Training,* 23, 7 (July 1986): 18–22.

13 The Appraisal Process

Outline

Objectives

After reading and discussing this chapter, you should be able to do the following:

1 Define the key terms.
2 List six major purposes in appraising your subordinates.
3 Explain why clear objectives and standards are needed in order to prepare proper appraisals.
4 List and give examples of three types of appraisal methods.
5 List and give examples of five pitfalls in the appraisal process.

Key Terms

appraisal process   standard (in appraisals)

computer monitoring

Introduction

Appraisal process
Periodic evaluations of each subordinate's on-the-job performance as well as his or her character, attitudes, and potential

One of your primary duties as a supervisor is to appraise or evaluate the on-the-job performance of each of your subordinates periodically. During the **appraisal process** you must make judgments about the person—his or her character, attitudes, and potential—as well as about his or her performances and their outcomes. This process is often referred to by several different terms such as *merit rating, employee performance evaluation* (or *review*), and *performance appraisal*. Regardless of the name it goes by, the process is intended to help you fortify your relationships with your people and to give you a better understanding of each of them.

The formal appraisal process may take place once or twice a year. The informal appraisal process, however, takes place daily. Both of these help the individual employee of any formal organization determine where he or she stands with the boss and the company. They help satisfy the need to know, and they help remove fear and misunderstanding. It is through your daily appraisals that you build your case for the formal one. In the performance of your daily routine and through your daily observations, you are best able to critique a subordinate's performance and offer him or her constructive criticism and suggestions for improvement.

Goals of Appraisals

The following are the major goals of employee appraisals:

- To measure employee performance
- To measure employee potential
- To assess employee attitudes
- To further the supervisor's understanding of each subordinate
- To fortify supervisor-subordinate relationships
- To analyze employee strengths and weaknesses—providing recognition for the former and ways to eliminate the latter
- To set goals for the improvement of performance
- To substantiate decisions about pay increases and eligibility for promotion, transfer, or training programs
- To verify the accuracy of the hiring process
- To eliminate hopelessly inadequate performers

If the appraisals you make on each subordinate are to accomplish these goals, they must be as objective and accurate as you can make them. They must reflect a true and definite image of the man or woman, in line with company policy and standards. This requires you to be fair in your evaluation efforts.

What to Appraise

When appraising subordinates, you can focus either on their output (results and outcomes of their actions and efforts) or on their behaviors (the kind and quality of their activities). The first approach focuses on the end product and quantity measures. The second focuses on the way in which work is done. Production counts may be useful indicators of performance if all other factors, such as relative difficulty of the tasks being performed, are considered. But their use is mostly limited to positions that process substantial amounts of standardized, repetitive work.[1] Most appraisal programs try to measure both outcomes and behaviors.

As a supervisor, you will be appraised on the quality of your behaviors—decision making, planning, communicating, and problem solving—and the outcomes of those behaviors, as well as on the behaviors of your subordinates. For example, the appraisal of you will consider the amount, timeliness, and quality of work produced by your section or department. Your appraisal, therefore, is partly in the hands of your subordinates.

Exactly what you appraise in your subordinates will be dictated by the forms and approaches your company asks you to use. Look at the forms you will use, and determine how much of them is devoted to appraising outcomes and what part of them is concerned with behaviors. Keep this division in mind as you informally evaluate your people each day. The best producers from among your subordinates should be the ones to receive the greatest financial rewards you have to give. Those who demonstrate weaknesses in one or more of their expected behaviors should be scheduled for training to relearn and strengthen those behaviors.

Standards

Standard
A quantity or quality designation that can be used as a basis of comparison for judging performances

Whether you are appraising outcomes or behaviors in your subordinates, you must do so with well-defined and mutually understood criteria or **standards.** You will recall from chapter 12 that training objectives required criteria so that both trainer and trainee could tell when a behavior was being demonstrated with sufficient mastery. Appraising people in different categories or by different factors also demands such criteria. Regardless of the forms you use in your appraisals, be certain that the words on them have clear and precise meanings to you and to your subordinates. What does *good* or *excellent* or *satisfactory* mean? You had better have an explanation for their meanings if you intend to use them in your appraisals.

When you appraise performances, turn to job descriptions and to the training materials developed to teach tasks. The criteria you used in training will allow you to pass informed and mutually understood judgments in discussions with your people. When appraising outcomes or output, be certain that the standards of quantity and quality you use are taught to your people before they are used to appraise them. Keep in mind that standards will vary in proportion to the employee's time on a job and to the training he or she received to perform the job to standard. You should not expect the same output from a new person that you expect from a seasoned veteran. When selecting criteria, consider the following guidelines:

1. *Relevance.* This refers to the extent to which criteria relate to the objectives of the jobs.

2. *Freedom from contamination.* When comparing the performance of production workers, for example, the appraiser must allow for differences in the type and condition of the equipment they are using. Similarly, a comparison of the performances of traveling salespeople is contaminated by the fact that territories differ in sales potential.

3. *Reliability.* This aspect of a criterion refers to its stability or consistency. In the case of job performance, it refers to the extent to which individuals tend to maintain a certain level of performance over time. In ratings it may be measured by correlating two sets of ratings made by a single rater or by two different raters.[2]

In addition to these technical considerations in selecting criteria, there are also the requirements that the criteria be acceptable to management, and be considered fair by those subjected to them.[3]

You as an Appraiser

Before you can appraise your people properly, the following must be true:

1. You must know the job responsibilities of each of your subordinates.
2. You must have accurate, first-hand information about each subordinate's performances.
3. You must have established clearly understood standards by which to judge outcomes and behaviors.
4. You must be able to communicate the evaluations to your subordinates, along with the criteria you used to make your judgments.[4]

If you feel uncomfortable or unsure of yourself when it comes to appraising subordinates, try to determine why you do. If you do not have enough first-hand knowledge about your people it is because you are not with them enough and do not oversee their work as much as you should. If you are stuck with an appraisal system that you and your people do not believe in, get together with your peers who feel as you do and work with higher authorities to change things. If an appraisal system that is in place has no support from either the appraised or the appraisers, it will be worthless and will create negative results for all concerned. If more training for you, the appraiser, is called for, it may be obtainable from inside or outside authorities. But if you need help, seek it. Appraisals are far too important to you, to your subordinates (or should be), and to your organization to let them be considered a waste of time and effort.

Your duty to rate each subordinate cannot be delegated. It is much too important a task to be entrusted to another. The results must be kept confidential and are not to be shared with your subordinate's peers. Only you, your subordinate, your boss, and a select handful of staff managers should have access to the results of these formal appraisals. Since you have the primary interest and knowledge needed to evaluate your people properly, only you should be responsible for preparing their appraisals.

Appraisal the Japanese Way

In Japanese companies, a worker's job description is kept somewhat vague. An individual's responsibilities are not defined with precise clarity for two major reasons: first, workers are taught to take a team and family approach to their work and sections; second, when something goes wrong, it is considered "bad taste" to try to find out who made mistakes. Efforts are made to find out what went wrong and how to avoid a similar situation in the future. People pursue the investigation with no fear, and lessons learned by all will help to prevent mistakes in the future. No person is held up to ridicule, no feelings are hurt, and no reputations are damaged beyond repair.[5]

While your organization may want to pin the blame for things that go wrong on a particular person, keep in mind that you will most probably have to continue to live and work with the person who gets the blame. At the same time, that person will have to continue to live and work with you and his or her coworkers. Name calling and blame placing are not the purposes of appraisals; showing a person what went wrong and how to correct a situation are. An appraisal goes well if it rewards the good performances, helps the individuals involved learn from past errors, and points the way toward improvement.

Legal Concerns When Appraising Workers

Federal, state, and local laws deal with employment discrimination. The federal laws listed and explained in chapter 11 bear to some extent on the appraisal process—in particular, the Equal Pay Act of 1963, the Age Discrimination in Employment Act of 1967, and Title VII of the 1964 Civil Rights Act. Karen Clegg, Counsel at Allied Bendix Aerospace and a member of the Commerce Clearing House Advisory Board on Human Resources Management, offers guidelines for avoiding charges of discrimination linked to the appraisal of subordinates. According to Clegg, a good performance appraisal system will have the following characteristics:

- Be in writing
- Contain specific procedures
- Include specific instructions for supervisors
- Provide for training supervisors in how to evaluate employees
- Utilize standardized forms for related groups of employees (for example, one form could be used for appraising supervisory employees, another for appraising hourly employees)

NEWS You Can UseAn analysis of U.S. Supreme Court rulings over the past twenty-five years reveals that performance appraisals are likely to be illegal if:

- Like tests, the instruments used are not valid;
- Standards are not job-related and objective (quantifiable and observable);
- The results of the process have a disparate impact on women, the handicapped, or minorities;
- Scoring of factors used is not standardized;
- Like people in like jobs are evaluated differently, using different forms, factors, or processes;
- Factors or criteria are not developed in line with the EEOC guidelines;
- Employees are not warned of declining or substandard performances;
- The evaluation is not based on the most recent, up-to-date content of the job.

In addition to the above, employers should have an adequate representation of women, the handicapped, and minorities in the ranks of the appraisers.

- Be thoroughly communicated to employees
- Be given annually
- Evaluate specific work behavior, not personal traits or characteristics
- Be continually monitored by equal opportunity staff personnel for its impact on protected groups
- Include reviews of subordinates' appraisals (made by their supervisors) by persons more senior than the supervisors[6]

Appraisal Methods

Your company is probably making use of one or more of the currently popular methods of appraising workers. Each of these methods has its own advantages and disadvantages. Which one you may have to use and which will be used on you by your boss is decided by company policy.

Instructions to Rater: List your subordinates by their overall rating in one or another of the categories below. Use their complete initials and do not exceed the percentages listed.

Percentage	Category	Subordinate(s)
5%	Superior	GBH
12.5%	Above Average	SAB, RFL
65%	Average	PTC, BCT, LH, NPB, SDO
		LMR, GSW
12.5%	Below Average	
5%	Unacceptable	PBC, TFM

Exhibit 13.1   **Percentage-ranking method of worker appraisal.**

Ranking or Forced-Distribution Method

You may be required to rank your people from most productive to least productive or from most valuable to least valuable. Often such rankings are based on a normal distribution curve, requiring that no more than a certain percentage of your people fall into one or another of the categories listed. Exhibit 13.1 illustrates a typical ranking approach.

You may be required to make a simple list of your subordinates, ranking one over another as to their abilities and contributions. This will force you to say that one man or woman is better as an employee than another.

The major disadvantage of the *ranking method* or *forced-distribution method* is that it requires you to compare your people to one another. That might be tolerable if all of your workers perform identical tasks. If they do not, the system requires you to compare apples and oranges. Also, it may prevent a supervisor with a disproportionate number of above-average (or below-average) performers from listing them as such because of the rather arbitrary percentage limits established for each category.

The forced-distribution method can be helpful if used in conjunction with one or more of the other methods. It does force you to make a choice and to picture your people as you may never have done before.

Checklist or Forced-Choice Method

One of the most prevalent methods used in industry today is the *checklist method* or *forced-choice method* of appraisal. In it, you are asked to pick the one block and statement that best describes your subordinate's stand-

Factor	Superior	Very Good	Average	Fair	Poor
Quantity of Output	Extraordinary Volume and Speed of Output	Above-Average Output	Expected Output— Normal Output	Below-Average Output	Unsatis-factory Level of Output
	☑	☐	☐	☐	☐

Exhibit 13.2   Forced-choice appraisal method.

ing with regard to the factor listed. These types of forms work well for summarizing the degrees to which a person has or lacks certain characteristics or traits desired. Exhibit 13.2 shows a sample.

Picking the one best choice may be difficult, especially when your workers perform many different tasks that have differing standards of output and that demand different types of skills and experiences. Fitting this type of form to young, inexperienced workers typically puts them at a disadvantage, as they appear in a bad light when contrasted to the others. Some way of compensating for these shortcomings should be designed into the system.

Critical-Incident or Narrative Method

The most flexible method, but clearly the most demanding way of appraising workers, is the *critical-incident method* or *narrative method*. In this method the supervisor must make reference to specific situations that highlight or illustrate a worker's abilities, traits, or potentials. Using the essay approach, the rater writes personal observations and comments about both positive and negative occurrences, in order to dramatize the particular point under examination. Exhibit 13.3 gives such a description.

This method offers the maximum degree of expression possible for precise and informative evaluations. It is difficult, however, because it demands an in-depth knowledge of subordinates' behaviors and attitudes, which can only come from frequent and regular observations and a recording of the results. It demands that a supervisor be with subordinates daily. Although this is highly desirable, it is not always possible. Many subordinates work physically separated by great distances from their supervisors. Salespeople, construction workers, research people, and staff specialists are a few examples. In their cases, comments from the people they serve may prove quite helpful. This method applies best to managers who are rated by other managers.

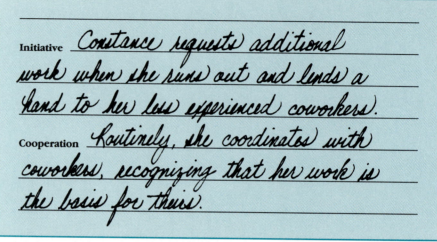

Initiative *Constance requests additional work when she runs out and lends a hand to her less experienced coworkers.*

Cooperation *Routinely, she coordinates with coworkers, recognizing that her work is the basis for theirs.*

Exhibit 13.3   Critical-incident or narrative appraisal.

Behaviorally Anchored Rating Scales

The *behaviorally anchored rating scale* (BARS) method of appraisal uses statements that describe both effective and ineffective job performance. The statements used are constructed by people who know very well the job that will be evaluated. Statements are created to describe a behavior that the rater is expected to be able to evaluate. The statements then run along a scale that includes degrees of acceptable and unacceptable performances. A point value is assigned to each statement. The rater chooses statements that best describe the ratee's performances and totals the points attached to each. The following three statements illustrate the use of BARS for rating a trainer's punctuality while conducting training sessions:

- The trainer always arrives for each training session before the session is scheduled to begin.   (5 pts.)
- The trainer usually arrives for each training session before the session is scheduled to begin.   (3 pts.)
- The trainer infrequently arrives for each training session before the session is scheduled to begin.   (0 pts.)

Notice that these statements combine the forced-choice method and the critical-incident method. Such a rating list could also be used by the trainer's supervisor and by the trainees. For each behavior considered crucial to successful performance on any job, statements like the ones above can be constructed. Input from those who will be rated should be sought during construction of the statements, to ensure that a complete list of essential behaviors is included and to help enlist the support of those who will be rated under the BARS method.

While BARS offers specific behavior statements that can be discussed between supervisor and subordinates, it focuses mainly on a person's activities and not on the results that they lead to. Under BARS, you may find yourself with an employee who performs all the activities well but does not achieve the desired results.

Field-Review Method

The *field-review method* requires that interviews be conducted between a supervisor and personnel staff assistants (either singly or in groups). Questions—usually requiring a *yes* or *no* answer—are asked by the specialists with regard to each of the supervisor's subordinates. The staff aides record the answers and write the formal appraisals. After reading them, the supervisor must either approve them with a signature or disapprove them with comments.

This method was designed to relieve supervisors of the burden of paperwork accompanying the appraisal process. It does require, however, that each supervisor be as completely prepared for the interview as if he or she had to fill out the ratings himself or herself. If he or she is not well prepared, extensive revision and rethinking may have to take place before accurate appraisals can be communicated to each worker.

Scale Method

The *scale method* combines the ranking and forced-choice methods. The rater must decide where each person stands in relation to his or her peers on the basis of a scale, with or without a specific description to go by. Two types of scales are illustrated in Exhibit 13.4. Some scales may attach a point value to the supervisor's choice, and total points may be used to sum up a worker's standing in his or her group. Once again, supervisors are forced to pick one that may not be exactly what they would or could say if allowed freedom of expression.

All of these systems are subjective: they allow the rater to let personal interests, preferences, and prejudices flavor the rating given to each person. Even the critical-incident or narrative method records the situation from the supervisor's point of view and in his or her own words. No system has yet been devised that will completely eliminate this. It is up to you, the rater, to be as objective as you can by making every effort to leave personal bias and personality clashes out of each rating. Your emphasis should be first and foremost on the subordinate's performance on the job,

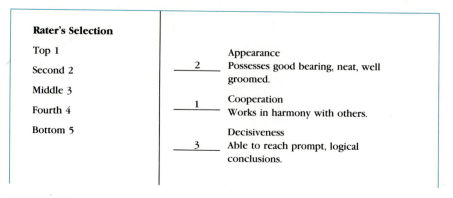

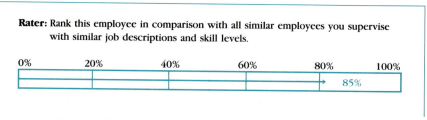

Exhibit 13.4   Scale method of appraisal.

in accordance with the standards established for that job. Only secondarily are you concerned with a subordinate's character and potential. State as clearly as you can what each person did, how well it was done, and what you believe the person is capable of doing.

Management by Objectives

In chapter 4, you were introduced to management by objectives (MBO) as it related to planning.[7] In this chapter, MBO becomes a useful method for appraising the performance of subordinates. Superior and subordinate determine, through *mutual* discussions, what is needed in order to improve the individual and the situation. While there are many approaches to MBO as an appraisal method, most managers agree that it is useful because it involves individuals in the determination of what is needed to make themselves and their operations better. Managers' primary hope, with regard to MBO, is that people will be more committed to achieving goals they have had a role in setting.

     The objectives or goals that individuals set through interaction with superiors are determined by the individuals' job descriptions and current situations. Performance objectives relate directly to a person's job—the area of routine and specialized duties normally pursued by that individual. They represent statements of intention to improve in the execution of one's position or job. Personal development objectives are statements of intention to improve one's skills, attitudes, and competencies.[8]

When you meet with a superior or with one of your subordinates to set goals, keep in mind that goals are ends or end states that are attained through the performance of activities; consequently, they usually require the expenditure of means. They may or may not result in change. For example, a goal may be to ensure that no change occurs. However, MBO works best when changes for the better are sought.[9]

A proper objective has the following characteristics:

1. It is clear, concise, and unambiguous.
2. It is accurate in describing the true end state sought.
3. It is consistent with policies, procedures, and plans as they apply to the unit.
4. It is within the competence of the man or woman or represents a learning and development experience for the person.
5. It is interesting, motivating, and/or challenging whenever possible.
6. It requires an acceptable expenditure of resources.[10]

Appraising with MBO

Approaches to appraising by MBO differ widely. Most involve the commitment of top management to the program, and efforts to introduce MBO begin with top managers learning to use it. Gradually, as the upper echelons gain the expertise they need, MBO is used at progressively more levels. If you do not have the permission of your superior to use MBO, you should not use it.

Exhibit 13.5 outlines a series of distinct steps that can make MBO work for you. It represents only one of many approaches, but it is a comprehensive method that can prevent some of the major problems others have encountered in their early MBO efforts.

Step 1: Setting Goals

As was stated earlier, goals are ends or end states that have to do with a person's or a unit's growth and development. If they are to be meaningful, they should meet the hallmarks set forth above. They must be set through a dialogue or discussion between superiors and subordinates.

Step 1. **Setting goals.** Ends must be mutually determined through discussions between supervisors and subordinates. Areas for improvement can be determined from past appraisals, current situations, job descriptions, and the rated person's ambitions to improve and gain higher responsibilities.

Step 2. **Identifying resources and actions needed.** The amount of time, money, and materials required to reach an objective need to be determined. To obtain any goal, the efforts of the goal setter and others may be required. Accurate predictions must be made.

Step 3. **Arranging goals in priorities.** Both the rater and the ratee need to agree as to the importance of each goal and as to how and in what order they should be pursued.

Step 4. **Setting timetables.** Precise times need to be set for the completion of actions and the attainment of goals. These times will allow formative evaluations on progress to be made and will permit adjustments in either the means or the ends.

Step 5. **Appraising the results.** The summary judgment as to successes and failures that occurs at this step sets the stage for a return to step 1. Thus, the cycle repeats.

Exhibit 13.5   **Basic steps in appraising through MBO.**

They must be based on the goal setter's recognition of their importance and commitment to their acquisition.

Step 2: Identifying Resources and Actions Needed

Before superiors and subordinates can agree on goals, the means to achieve them must be examined and determined to be within the organization's and the individual's abilities to execute or utilize. Resources include human energy and effort, time, money, and materials. Actions may be required of one person or unit or several. If these are possible and reasonable, success is probable.

Step 3: Arranging Goals in Priorities

Which goal should be worked on first, second, and so on? What end state is considered by both parties to be the most essential or important? One guideline for answering these questions is the cost in money or lost time that currently exists and awaits a cure. An attack on the most expensive areas of waste or problems could be planned first on the list of objectives. Lesser areas of waste could be attacked simultaneously or at later dates.

In addition to the achievement or nonachievement of a goal, consider the following when evaluating performances:

1. How has the subordinate grown through the effort to achieve the goal or goals?
2. Was the subordinate effective—doing the right things in a proper sequence?
3. Was the subordinate efficient—using only those resources needed and in their proper amounts?
4. Was the individual a help or a hindrance to fellow workers?
5. Were due dates met? Were goals achieved earlier than planned?
6. Were the obstacles met dealt with in the proper ways—some being overcome, some being circumvented?
7. Were the goals easy to achieve or difficult?
8. Is the subordinate getting better at choosing goals and setting priorities and timetables?

Exhibit 13.6   Some additional criteria to consider when appraising with MBO.

Step 4: Setting Timetables

Besides agreeing on priorities, both boss and subordinate must agree on the times by which each goal is to be achieved. Time estimates must be made, and calendars must be prepared for future reference. Dates for completion become guideposts and serve as checkpoints to determine progress and problems. As these dates arrive, boss and subordinate coordinate to determine if any adjustments are necessary. New times may be needed, new or different approaches may be required, or new goals or refinements to the original ones may have to be made.

Step 5: Appraising the Results

At the regular intervals dictated by your company, you and your subordinate meet to discuss the progress and events that have taken place since the last formal evaluation. Your formal appraisal of your subordinates' efforts is not based solely on their goal achievement or lack of achievement. Your appraisals should consider both means and ends (see Exhibit 13.6).

Each cycle in MBO is time-consuming and requires patience and tolerance from both parties. But as the number of cycles increases, so will the proficiency of the parties involved and the accuracy of their estimates. When used properly by people who have been taught to use it, MBO can improve individuals and organizations. It is more difficult to learn and to use with workers than are other kinds of appraisal methods, but it can spark motivation and win commitment to growth and change.

Appraising by Computer

According to the National Institute of Occupational Safety and Health, 13 million people operate video display terminal (VDT) equipment, and 8.6 million of them are monitored by their computers.[11] The computer industry estimates that by the year 2000, 75 percent of all jobs in the United States will involve some time in front of a computer.[12]

Computer monitoring
Using computers to measure how employees achieve their outputs—monitoring work as it takes place—and to keep track of their total outputs

Computer monitoring measures how employees achieve their outputs—monitoring work as it takes place—in addition to keeping track of their total outputs. It counts such things as the number of keystrokes per minute, the use of individual machines per hour, and the number and kinds of items processed by a sales clerk per customer per hour. Computer monitoring allows employers to rate employees' levels of productivity and to rank them according to how completely and effectively they use each minute of each working hour. By taking averages, new time standards for all kinds of work can be created and used to evaluate individual performances.

"A small computer—aptly named Tripmaster—installed on the dashboard of a truck can record speed, gear shifts, how long the truck idles and how long a driver stops for lunch or a coffee break. . . . Electronic leashes track the activities of delivery and repair people who work in the field far from a central office."[13] Company supervisors can now monitor telephone use throughout their companies and time that workers spend away from their workstations. From management's point of view, computer monitoring helps to control costs, improve security, increase productivity, and obtain more precise information needed for objective appraisals.

Critics of computer monitoring argue that it creates additional worker stress, fatigue, and turnover. Many workers feel that it is or can be dehumanizing—making their jobs more machinelike and less challenging.[14] But the nationwide movements to eliminate annual across-the-board pay increases and to create meaningful pay-for-performance systems of compensation demand specific and quantifiable standards of performance, which computer monitoring can provide. Those who meet and beat fair standards can be justly compensated, while corrective and training actions can be taken for those who fall below the standards. Above-average performers need no longer feel ignored or relegated to a par with below-average workers. ·

Pitfalls

Several common types of errors can be made by raters. If you know about them, you can consciously try to prevent their occurring in your appraisals of your subordinates. Committing any one of them will render your rating inaccurate. Some of the pitfalls discussed here were also discussed in chapter 11 with regard to rating new applicants and existing employees.

The Halo Effect

One of the most frequent errors committed by raters is known as the *halo effect.* The rater allows one outstanding positive or negative trait or incident about a person to color the overall rating and image of that subordinate. Because one of your people dresses well and has good manners and bearing, you may tend to let this overshadow his or her other traits or the whole work performance record. Conversely, if the most recent incident you can recall about a person is his or her commission of a major mistake, you might allow this to obscure his or her many fine qualities. Your formal ratings are supposed to reflect the whole person. You must guard against letting isolated events or appearances dominate your total impression and objectivity toward a worker.

Rating the Person—Not the Performance

There is a strong tendency for a rater to give a person high ratings if the rater and the individual get along and low ratings if they do not. Human nature is such that we perceive in a favorable way people we like most and tend to dismiss those we dislike as worthless persons. A rater's personality and attitudes may clash with those of a subordinate; then, even though that worker's performance and potential are above average, he or she may receive an overall unsatisfactory rating. If you do this, you are not being honest or fair. Your job in appraisals is to rate each person according to his or her performance in a particular job. Unless an individual's personality traits are interfering with his or her work or are a great asset to him or her, there is no reason for you to bring them into the formal appraisal. You may not like an individual, but in fairness you still may have to rank him or her as superior. Leave your personal biases and prejudices out of the picture you paint of the person. Avoid personal attacks.

In order to keep your actual or potential biases in check, you should avoid the following specific behaviors in appraising subordinates:

1. *Stereotyping:* choosing to ignore a person's uniqueness and individuality by assuming that any member of a specific group must have the characteristics that conform to a predetermined image of that group's members: Bill is a salesperson, and therefore Bill is . . . ; or Jane is Hispanic, and therefore she is. . . . Our perceptions of a member of any specific group may or may not be rooted in fact.

2. *Projecting:* accusing others of the very faults you yourself possess. Examine most of the anger you express toward another person and beneath it you will find a particular way in which you have played a part in the situation.

3. *Screening:* noticing only the negative aspects of a person or his or her performance; interpreting events in the most negative way possible; recording only events that support a preformed judgment about a person; ignoring positive contributions.

Rating Everyone as Average

This error, which is often referred to as the *central tendency,* occurs when you rate everyone as average. You may be tempted to do so because you lack sufficient data to do otherwise or because you see this as the safest, least controversial method of handling your appraisals, since you will not have to justify a high or a below-average rating.

Quite often, raters fear that if they rate a subordinate as above average, the subordinate will get a big head and become more difficult to direct or control. Or they may fear that if they rate a person below average, they will face a confrontation at the appraisal interview or criticism from their boss for allowing a poor performance. In other words, supervisors may fear that, when they are appraising their people, they themselves are being appraised—that the major purpose of appraisals is to find out how good a boss the supervisor has been and not primarily to evaluate the workers. If you have cause to believe that this is the case where you work, you have a very unfortunate appraisal system. How well your people perform does influence your future. But making out phony appraisals that show them all as average or above average cannot be justified by the facts, and your boss will know it. Simply saying someone is good does not make it so. If you falsify their ratings, your people will know it, too. And if you think it might be hard to supervise an employee who earns a good rating and is told about it, how much more difficult will it be to supervise an employee who feels that you have been dishonest with him or her?

Saving Up for the Appraisal

Some supervisors spot a deficiency, record it, and save their discussion of it for the formal appraisal. No criticism should be a surprise to the rated employee; rather, each should have been discussed when it happened. The formal appraisal interview should provide a *review* of past events that exhibits a concern for preventing the recurrence of past infractions, as well as offering a focus for improvement in the future.

The only safe road to travel is that of integrity. Arm yourself with the facts by careful and frequent observations. Be with your people as often as you can, and make on-the-spot corrections and comments about their work and their attitudes. Let them know where they stand with you regularly. Be open and available; if you are, there will be no shocks or surprises at the appraisal interview. Your informal appraisals will have prepared them for what you will say, they will expect what they receive, and you will have the facts and events to support their ratings.

The Rush Job

Related to most other appraisal errors is the last-minute, hurry-up job of rating that occurs at midnight, on the day before the interviews, or at lunch or breaks on the day when you must relay the results. Whether you have two subordinates or twenty, you have to give yourself enough lead time for thinking things through and searching your memory and your files for tangible data upon which to prepare your case. How would you like it if your boss summed up your past six months at work with a fifteen-minute effort on your appraisal form?

A great deal rides on your formal appraisals. Your people know that it represents in writing your opinion of them and their performances. They know that what you say will directly affect their futures and their earnings. They also know that you go on record with your superiors in these appraisals. Your relationships and credibility are at stake. Do not muff this great opportunity to cement your relations; pass out deserved praise, and build programs for their improvement. This should be a task that you tackle with great concern and eagerness. You are laying foundations that will have to support future plans and programs. Make those foundations firm and strong.

Comparisons

If you try to rate a worker by comparing him or her with another, you are making a big mistake. We know that people are unique and dynamic. No two subordinates look alike, think alike, or act alike. Even if your people have the same job, they cannot be compared because their experiences, training, education, attitudes, and skill levels are different. To say that Paul is better than Peter has no meaning unless you know exactly how good Paul is and should be. The questions then arise, "How long has Peter had a chance to be as good as Paul?" and, "Has he the potential to be so?" For these reasons, the ranking and forced distribution methods are not recommended.

The only comparisons that you should make are to the standards that have been established for each job and for worker conduct. You can say that Suzy meets the standards of her job while Helen does not, or that Joe exhibits the cooperative spirit necessary for success in his job while Jess does not. These are not comparisons of one person to another; instead, they are comparisons of each person to the standards and expectations you have for each subordinate in relation to his or her duties.

Not Sharing the Results

We have assumed that, whatever your formal appraisal of a worker is, it will be discussed with that worker. To do otherwise defeats the whole purpose behind appraising people—to better their performance individually and collectively. Yet some companies promote systems for evaluating employees that actually prohibit or discourage communicating the results to the rated individuals. They do so because they assume that the daily appraisals have said all that needs to be said or because they see the formal appraisal as primarily a communications device between supervisor and middle manager or between line and staff. This unfortunate perception of the process denies the supervisor and every other manager the opportunity to accomplish all of the goals we have mentioned previously. If this situation exists in your company, you must realize how it affects your workers. A sense of fear and distrust is created by this secrecy, and frustration will result from not knowing what the formal reports about a person's abilities have to say. Work for a change in policy if you function under such a system.

Lack of Proper Training

All too often, companies sow the seeds for management failures by neglecting to provide each supervisor with the training he or she needs to appraise people properly. A supervisor who has not been taught how to appraise, how to prepare for an appraisal interview, and how to conduct such an interview will make mistakes that could have been prevented. If you are uncertain about how to do your appraising, seek counsel from your peers and superiors. If the company fails to give you the proper training in this vital area, it will be up to you to fill the gap by yourself. Self-study, conferences with your boss, college courses in personnel management, and management seminars are all good ways to establish or improve your skills in this area.

Lack of Standards of Performance

Unless supervisors have clearly defined and properly communicated standards of performance to refer to as they gather information and make observations of their subordinates, they will not be capable of making and sharing an adequate appraisal. Your people must know what is expected of them. You must know how they perceive their jobs. Unless both the supervisor and the rated employee know these standards ahead of time, the appraisal process and its accompanying interview will yield something less than the goals listed at the beginning of this chapter.

Lack of Proper Documentation

When you attempt to criticize an employee's performance, you must be prepared to give specific information. You must have concrete evidence to back up your observations and criticisms. In noting an employee's tardiness, be specific by giving the dates and the amount of time missed.

Appraisals are used as a basis for decisions about promotions, demotions, raises, and discharge. Federal equal employment opportunity guidelines require you to appraise specific performances that are essential for good overall performance and to document your substantiation for your ratings. You could someday find yourself a party to a lawsuit claiming that you were unfair or discriminatory in your appraisal if you do not justify your ratings.

The Error of Recent Events

Supervisors often find that recent events inordinately influence their judgments about subordinates, especially if they are strongly negative or positive. You must guard against letting the most recent events overshadow those of the previous months. The best defense is to keep accurate records of individuals' performances, recording significant events as they occur.

Your appraisal should give equal consideration to all that has occurred over the appraisal period.

The Appraisal Interview

Your daily contacts should provide you with the facts you need to prepare and support your formal evaluations. The big event for both you and your worker is the appraisal interview, where you both can discuss the judgments you have made. This meeting should occur in private and without interruption.

There are three stages related to sharing the results of your appraisal efforts: the preparation for the interview, the conduct of the interview, and the follow-up to check on its results.

Preparation

The interview should not just happen. It must be planned with the same thoroughness you would apply to the planning of any important event. Then you can foresee and prevent most of the problems and misunderstandings that could permanently damage your relationship (see Exhibit 13.7).

Be certain that you review each rating in detail before you attempt to meet and discuss it with your worker. Even though you wrote it, you probably wrote several others at the same time, and it is amazing how easily you can confuse them in your own mind. Anticipate the areas or individual remarks that might give rise to controversy. Be clear in your own mind about why you rated a person below average on a given point, what led you to that conclusion, and what supports it now. If you have recorded a failure that the person has overcome and is not likely to repeat, be sure that you have so stated on the rating. You do not want to put much emphasis on such a situation, however. After all, most of our learning takes place through trial and error, and we learn best by analyzing our mistakes.

Imagine students who are first introduced to the mathematical process called *addition*. They receive an explanation of the process and are guided through several examples. Then they are asked to add the numbers 3 and 6. The students try, and they get the wrong answer. The instructor reviews the process and the students' individual application of it to find out where and how they made their errors. When the errors in application are pinpointed, the students try again. This time they get the correct answer.

1. Evaluators should develop their own style, so they feel comfortable in an interview. If an interview makes the evaluator feel uncomfortable, the employee being evaluated probably will feel uncomfortable too. An evaluator should not try to copy someone else or follow a rigid format if it does not feel comfortable and natural.

2. Both parties should carefully prepare for the interview beforehand. Employees should review their performance and assemble their own information documenting how well they have done. Evaluators should gather relevant information about each employee's past performance and should compare it against the objectives for the period. Lack of preparation for the interview by either party is an obvious indication of disregard and disinterest.

3. The evaluator should clarify the purpose of the interview at the very beginning. The employee should know whether it is a disciplinary session, a contributions appraisal, or a personal development appraisal. In particular, the employee should understand the possible consequences of the interview so that he or she can prepare appropriate responses. For example, an employee's responses during a contributions appraisal can appropriately be a bit guarded and defensive. But in a personal development appraisal, such responses would greatly reduce the effectiveness of the interview.

4. Neither party should dominate the discussion. The superior should take the lead in initiating the discussion, but the employee should be encouraged to express opinions. The superior should budget the time so that the employee has approximately half the time to discuss the evaluation.

5. The most popular format for the interview is the "sandwich" format—criticism sandwiched between compliments. The rationale for this format is that positive comments made at the beginning and end of the interview create a positive experience. The opening compliments should put the employee at ease for the interview. The closing compliments should leave the employee feeling good about the interview and motivated to do better.

6. An alternative format is the problems-recognition-future planning format. This approach is very direct and to the point. The supervisor begins by saying, "There are _____ problems I'd like to talk with you about: _____, _____, and _____." Each problem is briefly identified at the beginning, before the supervisor discusses the problems in detail. An employee immediately knows what the "charges" are and does not sit in uncertainty waiting for the next bomb to fall. After the problems have been discussed by both superior and subordinate, the discussion focuses on accomplishments for which the employee deserves recognition. The superior should describe specific actions deserving recognition and be as complimentary as the behavior merits. The interview should not end until the superior and subordinate have discussed plans for future performance. Future goals and objectives should be clarified, and plans for personal development and performance improvement should be discussed.

Exhibit 13.7   **Guidelines for conducting effective performance appraisal interviews.**
(*Source:* David J. Cherrington. *Personnel Management: The Management of Human Resources* (Dubuque, Ia: Wm. C. Brown Publishers, 1983), 313.)

After adding for several days they master the process and never repeat their original errors. Would you now hold their initial error against them? You would not and should not. The students' more recent performance indicates quite strongly their mastery of the concepts, and they have proved that they will not fall victim to those errors again.

Having analyzed your subordinate's weaknesses as probable points for discussion and questions, construct a list of his or her strong points. Label what he or she does extremely well. Identify favorable personality traits. These represent excellent introductory material to get the interview going. Some managers use what is referred to as the *sandwich approach*. This technique gives the worker a strength, then a weakness, then a strength, and so on. It tends to soften the blows to a person's ego and to promote confidence in the person being rated. Use whatever approach you feel is best for both you and your worker. Watch his or her reaction, and be ready to adjust your approach as necessary.

Finally, set down a list of goals or objectives that you would like to see the person set for himself or herself. These should relate most specifically to improving his or her performance and growth. Then determine the possible ways in which he or she might go about achieving each one. For example, suppose that your subordinate has recurring difficulty in making logical and practical decisions. Be ready to get his or her views as to how he or she might improve. Have a suggested plan on hand, and recommend that the subordinate follow it if he or she does not have a plan. For every weakness, you should stand ready with a suggestion for improvement. Let us hope that your subordinate will concur. Most appraisal interviews are a mixture of the problem-solving meeting and the informational meeting and fluctuate between directive and nondirective interviews (see chapter 11). Pick the approach you think best for each individual. Prepare your script carefully and be prepared to stick to it.

Conducting the Interview

Make arrangements for adequate time and facilities, and ensure that you will be free of unnecessary interruptions. This is time for just you two and should not be interfered with.

Begin the interview by emphasizing that its purpose is to promote improvement in both the individual and the department. Then move into the specifics. Keep it short and to the point.

One good approach is to begin with some rather general questions such as, "Well, Tom, how would you rate yourself on your progress since our last interview?" or, "If you had to appraise yourself for the past six months, what would you say about your performance?" This method gets your subordinate talking and gives you additional insights into his or her way of perceiving things. Also, it makes the point that this interview

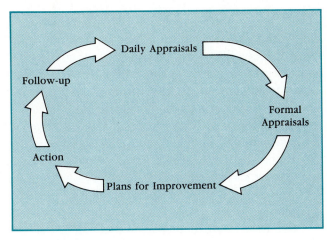

Exhibit 13.8 The appraisal cycle.

is supposed to be a dialogue and an exchange of points of view. Avoid the lecture format, and get your subordinate's feelings and observations into the open. You should work for mutual agreement and accord.

At some point during the interview, give the worker a copy of the appraisal. Allow him or her time to read it and to understand its contents. Ask him or her for reactions, and take each as a lead into the why behind the rating. With each weakness noted, give a validation of it. Then discuss how it can be overcome. If your subordinate sees no immediate way to attack it, introduce your thoughts on the matter.

Finally, set some specific short-range goals with your subordinate to remedy the list of shortcomings. These should tackle the questions of what should be done, by what time it should be completed, and how each goal should be reached. You will be instilling hope in each person you interview, and, more concretely, you will be showing a way out of the present difficulties. Here again is a chance to convince your subordinate of your honest concern for his or her welfare and progress.

Follow-up

After the interview and as part of your normal performance of your duties, check on each person's progress toward the goals set in the interview. If Ann said she would brush up on her basic skills, visit with her to see if she has. If Wally said he was going to try a new method, find out how well he is doing. Your people will soon realize, as you do, that appraisals are daily routines that are only periodically summarized through the formal appraisal report and interview. This realization should cause them to give their best regularly and not just at appraisal time. Exhibit 13.8 shows this concept as a cycle that never ends and always repeats itself.

Rewards

How much you can do to provide tangible rewards for your people who excel is related to many factors, including the extent of your authority, your control over the purse strings through budget requests, and your boss's willingness to delegate to you. Often all you can do from a dollar-and-cents point of view is to recommend a fixed amount as a raise. A worker who is near or at the top of the wage rate may only be eligible for a token increase. Until a worker gets a promotion to a higher pay grade, he or she will have peaked out. The incentive to hasten the promotion may be sufficient to impel that person to work at an above-average pace. Or, if he or she is trapped by being the least-senior person, it could mean frustration.

You have many intangible awards you can give each person, however: the pat on the back for a job well done; the frequent appreciation you show each person both in public and in private. Your demonstration of your dependence on each team player goes a long way toward satisfying his or her need for esteem and status. Sending a letter of commendation upstairs for the exceptional contributions your people give when they do not have to, passing over an outstanding performer when some occasional dirty jobs come along, and granting time off if you have the authority to do so can go a long way toward proving to your people that you are aware of each of them and of the value of their individual efforts. Besides the other things we have discussed, the appraisal process should make you keenly aware of which of your subordinates are carrying the load in your department and just how dependent you really are on them.

Negative Results

Just as your subordinates' appraisals can lead to rewards and tangible improvements, they can lead to negative consequences if warranted. When performance has been judged to be below standard, certain restrictions on privileges, requirements for additional training, and denials of positive benefits may be in order. No raise, a token raise, no promotion, or a possible demotion could be appropriate under management policy or union agreement. In extreme cases where people can but will not perform, termination may result. Let your people know what good and bad effects can follow from their performance appraisals. Be certain that the link between performance and rewards and punishments is clear to each of your subordinates.

As a summary to appraising and before you begin the appraisal process, review the checklist in Exhibit 13.9. Keep in mind that appraisals can either help or hinder the development of good human relations between you and individuals or groups you supervise. Make the appraisals

1. Am I with my people regularly? If not, have I some way of measuring their performance, attitudes, and potential?
2. Do I often let them know how they stand with me? Am I honest when I do so?
3. Do I really know each of my people as individuals? If not, what am I doing about it?
4. Can I detail in writing each of their specific duties? Would my list agree with theirs?
5. Do my appraisals emphasize an individual's performance on the job? Am I using established and approved standards for comparison?
6. Can I back up my opinions with facts? With specific incidents?
7. Have I commented on my subordinates' potentials?
8. Have I planned well to share the results with each person?
9. Have I thought about ways that each can improve his or her rating?
10. Is this rating something I will be proud to put my signature to?

Things left to do: _____

_____

_____

Exhibit 13.9   **Checklist to help you prepare for the appraisal effort.**

you perform positive experiences to cement team spirit and individual morale. Lock away any biases you may have and stick to the facts. Use observable, job-related standards to rate people on their performances. Use your appraisal interview to coach and counsel as well as to praise and to criticize.

Instant Replay

1. Efforts to evaluate subordinates take place daily. Formal appraisals usually take place once or twice each year.
2. The appraisal process is too important for a supervisor to delegate.
3. Appraisals look at a person's personal growth and changes in performance capabilities.
4. Appraisals must be based on known standards and linked to definite rewards and punishments.
5. The many approaches and methods of appraising subordinates all have advantages and disadvantages. All allow for personal bias and subjective judgments.

6. By being aware of the pitfalls in appraising individuals, you can act to prevent their occurrence in your appraisals.

7. The real value of appraisals lies in sharing them with the rated individual. Supervisors get to know their people better and vice versa. Specific problems and achievements can be noted, and plans can be made for improvement.

8. The appraisal process is a cyclical one. As old problems are corrected, new ones appear. Change is inevitable and requires new methods and approaches to routine and special tasks that everyone faces.

Glossary **Appraisal process** periodic evaluations, both formal and informal, of each subordinate's on-the-job performance, as well as of his or her character, attitudes, and potential.

Computer monitoring using computers to measure how employees achieve their outputs—monitoring work as it takes place—in addition to keeping track of their total outputs.

Standard (in appraisals) a quantity or quality designation that can be used as a basis for comparison for judging performances. Something used by mutual agreement to determine if things are as they should be or were meant to be.

Questions for Class Discussion

1. Can you define this chapter's key terms?

2. Why do supervisors appraise their subordinates? What in the process will benefit supervisors? What will benefit their subordinates?

3. Why are clear objectives and standards needed in the appraisal process?

4. Which of the appraisal methods described in this chapter would you as a supervisor prefer to use? Why?

5. What are the major pitfalls in the appraisal process?

6. How often are you appraised at work? How often in your management course? Would you like to be appraised more often? Why?

Incident **Purpose** To experience the difficulties connected with the use of vague, general, usually unobservable traits as rating criteria.

Your Task Listed below are several traits sometimes used by companies when rating their employees. After each of the traits, write as specific a definition as you can. When you have finished, compare your definitions with those of your fellow students. Then make a list of reasons why rating on the basis of traits is not a valid substitute for rating with clear, observable, job-related standards for work performance.

1. Integrity: _____

_____

2. Judgment: _____

_____

3. Tact: _____

_____

4. Sensitivity: _____

_____

5. Ambition: _____

_____

Case Problem 13.1   The Annual Review

"Well, Gary, how did it go?" asked Ron Latham.

"Man, that supervisor is somethin' else. I thought he would be full of praise. I haven't heard a criticism in months. But Old Bobby really laid it on me. He told me everything that was wrong with me and my performance, and he had me dead to rights on every one of 'em."

"I got the same treatment. He must have eyes in the back of his head. When I read the things he wrote about me, I realized he knows a lot more about us than he lets on. Bob told me about some mistakes I made months ago. I didn't even know he knew about 'em."

"Old Bobby dug up some memos he wrote to himself and read them to me. He had the dates, the times, and the facts down real good. Hell, he ain't no supervisor, he's a *snoopervisor.* I don't know where he gets his info but someone must be cluein' him in."

"You know what gets me, Gary, is that the first you hear about a mistake is six months after it happens. That guy is a better bookkeeper than he is a manager."

"All I know is that from now on I'm going to watch what I say around here."

"Old Robert ought to work for the F.B.I., interrogatin' prisoners or somethin'. He came on real strong right from the beginning. First he asks me to read his write-up on me and keeps on talkin' while I'm trying to read. When I asked him about a couple of points, he gets real red in the face. You know, like he's real mad or somethin'. After two minutes in that office all I wanted to do was get out."

"At least you had some time with him. All the time I was in there the damn phone was ringing, or he was talking to someone on it. He just shoved my rating at me and told me to read it. He asked me if I had any questions and gave me a list of things for me to correct. Then he tells me not to make the same mistakes twice. I'm going to try my best to correct the things on that list the best way I know how."

"Well, it's over for another year. Hey, there's the big man now. Look . . . he's postin' somethin' on the bulletin board."

After Robert Knutson returned to his office, Ron and Gary walked over to the board.

"Cripes!" yelled Ron. "He posted our rankings! Will you look at that."

Questions

1. What style of supervision is Bob using on Ron and Gary?

2. How do you suppose Bob gets his information for his ratings?
3. What errors can you identify in the way Bob conducted his appraisal interviews?
4. Comment on the statement: "I'm going to try my best to correct the things on that list the best way I know how."

Case Problem 13.2   It's Results That Count

Six months ago, Jane Farley set her performance goals in a meeting with her supervisor, Phyllis Johnson. Ten specific goals had been set and were to have been achieved within the six months just passed. Jane had accomplished six of the goals and felt strongly that two more would be reached within the next thirty days. She had begun to view the other two goals as unrealistic, given that time and circumstances had changed so drastically since the two were set. As she walked to Phyllis's office, Jane hoped that her supervisor would feel the same way. She would know in a few minutes, when her appraisal interview should begin.

"Sit down, Jane," said Phyllis. "It's that time again. It's been a few months since we last talked about your progress. Let's start with your summary of what goals you have accomplished and which ones remain."

As Phyllis began to review her list of Jane's goals, Jane recited a list of her successes and failures. Phyllis listened intently, making notes throughout Jane's recitation. When Jane had finished, Phyllis began her comments.

"You know how I feel, Jane. It's results that count. You and I agreed six months ago that the ten goals in front of us could and should be accomplished by today. Six of your goals have been reached. That gives you a 60 percent score by anyone's math. Today you tell me that you need another thirty days for two of your goals. Contrary to your feelings, I do not feel that the last two goals you mentioned are impossible to attain. What I want to

know now is, why have you waited until today to tell me of your feelings and failures? When you first realized that your goals were unattainable, why didn't you come to me and discuss it?"

"Phyllis, I honestly thought that I would have eight goals accomplished by today until about two weeks ago. You were on vacation until last week so that would have been the earliest we could have talked. I thought that, since we were meeting today, that would be soon enough. We disagree on the possibility of reaching two goals. I think that your budget cuts and the loss of my coworker, Abrams, has delayed work output enough to make these last two goals impossible until Abrams is replaced and overtime is restored to our section."

"Well, you have not done the kind of job I expected from you. You will be rated below average. The two goals you say you need thirty days more for will be our starting point for your next six month's performance plan. Abrams left five weeks ago and personnel has not moved to find a replacement. Times are tight, and overtime is not planned for at least the next six months, so you will have to apply yourself more. You may find as others have that eight hours on the job are not enough. If you do, your goals are still the same in number, and extra effort may be required during those eight hours each day or on your own time. Now let's get started on your next set of goals for the next six months."

Questions

1. What do you think of Phyllis's statement, "It's results that count"?

2. Using Exhibit 13.6, how has Phyllis failed in her execution of the supervisor's role in MBO?

Notes

1. Priscilla Levinson, *A Guide for Improving Performance Appraisal* (Washington, D.C.: U.S. Office of Personnel Management, 1980), 25.
2. Ernest J. McCormick and Joseph Tiffin, *Industrial Psychology,* 6th ed. (Englewood Cliffs, N.J.: Prentice-Hall, 1974), 36–40.
3. H. J. Chruden and A. W. Sherman, Jr., *Personnel Management: The Utilization of Human Resources,* 6th ed. (Cincinnati: South-Western Publishing, 1980), 236.
4. David J. Cherrington, *Personnel Management: The Management of Human Resources* (Dubuque, Iowa: Wm. C. Brown, 1983), 293.
5. See Akio Morita with Edwin M. Reingold and Mitsuko Shimomura, *Made in Japan: Akio Morita and Sony* (New York: E. P. Dutton, 1986).
6. CCH Editorial Staff with George S. Odiorne, *Performance Appraisal: What Three Companies Are Doing* (Chicago: Commerce Clearing House, 1985), 31–34.
7. The first specific application of the MBO process to appraisals is generally attributed to Peter F. Drucker through his important book, *The Practice of Management* (New York: Harper & Row, 1954), chap. 11.
8. H. L. Tosi, John R. Rizzo, and Stephen J. Carroll, "Setting Goals in Management by Objectives," *California Management Review* 12, #4 (1970): 70–78.
9. Ibid.
10. Ibid.
11. Haya El Nasser, "Video Terminals Watch Workers," *USA Today* (July 7, 1986): 6B.
12. "VDTs Allow Boss to Become Big Brother," *Chicago Tribune* (November 28, 1986), 3:2.
13. Gary T. Marx, "The Company is Watching You Everywhere," *New York Times* (February 15, 1987): E21.
14. Carey W. English, "Pay for Performance—Good News or Bad?" *U.S. News & World Report* (March 11, 1985): 66.

Suggested Readings

Bernardin, H. John, and Beatty, Richard W. "Can Subordinate Appraisals Enhance Managerial Productivity?" *Sloan Management Review* 28, #4 (Summer 1987): 63–73.

————. *Performance Appraisal: Assessing Human Behavior at Work.* Boston: Kent-Wadsworth, 1984.

Dipboye, R. L. "Some Neglected Variables in Research on Discrimination in Appraisals." *Academy of Management Review* 10 (January 1985): 116–27.

Ewing, David W. *Justice on the Job.* Boston: Harvard Business School Press, 1989.

Gordon, R. F. "Does Your Performance Appraisal System Really Work?" *Supervisory Management* 30 (February 1985): 37–41.

Longenecker, Clinton O.; Sims, Henry P., Jr.; and Gioia, Dennis A. "Behind the Mask: The Politics of Employee Appraisal." *Academy of Management Executive* (1987): 183–193.

Lowe, Terry R. "Eight Ways to Ruin a Performance Review." *Personnel Journal* (January 1986): 60–62.

Schneier, Craig E.; Beatty, Richard W.; and Baird, Lloyd S. "Creating a Performance Management System." *Training and Development Journal* 40 (1986): 74–79.

14 Discipline

Outline

Objectives

After reading and discussing this chapter, you should be able to do the following:

1 Define the key terms.

2 Differentiate between positive discipline and negative discipline.

3 Explain the role of punishment in the exercise of discipline.

4 List and briefly explain four principles of discipline.

5 List and briefly explain four common pitfalls that can affect a supervisor's efforts at discipline.

6 Explain what it means to be fair when you discipline your subordinates.

7 Describe why supervisors should know themselves and their subordinates well before they attempt to discipline their subordinates.

Key Terms

discipline

employment at will

negative discipline

positive discipline

progressive discipline

sexual harassment

whistleblower

Introduction

Discipline
The management duty that involves educating subordinates to foster obedience and self-control and dispensing appropriate punishment for wrongdoing

By **discipline** we mean two distinct and related concepts: education and training to foster obedience to reasonable rules and standards (called *positive discipline*), and the dispensing of appropriate punishment for wrongdoing (called *negative discipline*). Both approaches are necessary to accomplish the primary purpose of disciplinary actions: to promote reasonable and safe conduct at work, so as to protect lives and property and to sustain acceptable performances that promote individual and group success.

Nearly everything we have been exploring since chapter 1 relates to this chapter. Your human relations role as judge requires you to administer discipline. As a supervisor, you are the person closest to your subordinates and are thus the member of management best suited to deal with them when they become guilty of misconduct or violate rules. You are the person responsible for preparing up-to-date job descriptions and specifications that can be the cause of problems in employee behavior. You play a role in selecting new people. If you bring people into your environment, you should be thinking about how well they will fit into it, and you should help keep potential problem workers out. Your training and appraisals can either prevent problems or be the causes of them. Both can either foster self-discipline and self-control in subordinates or sow the seeds for future performance problems. And, most important, what you say and how you act set the tone for employees' behaviors at work.

The Supervisor and Discipline

Paul M. Magoon and John B. Richards, authors and lecturers, have conducted supervisory workshops and seminars for many years. From over 2,000 supervisory participants and their ideas, Magoon and Richards have identified four major emotional job-security needs of employees:

1. The need to know what the boss expects in the way of work performance and conduct on the job
2. The need for the boss's regular feedback on their performances to include praise as well as censure
3. The need to be treated fairly and impartially by the boss
4. The need to be judged on the basis of facts and standards rather than on the basis of opinions and assumptions[1]

Subordinates depend on their superiors to satisfy their need in these areas. When superiors fail to help subordinates, others stand ready to do so. Unions, cliques, and other employees are three such groups.

Item 1 on the preceding list stresses the need to be careful in planning the work given to subordinates. The work and limits on its execution must then be carefully explained to those who will be responsible for it. Policies, rules, and procedures may need to be taught, explained, or reviewed. Standards must be communicated, and needed support or training must be arranged for. By knowing what is expected of them, your people know what will be used to assess their contributions.

Items 2, 3, and 4 on the list remind us that we appraise our subordinates daily, informally, whenever we are with them or have the chance to observe the results of their efforts. By recording your observations, you will have a list of critical incidents available to draw from when you formally appraise subordinates. You must be ready with compliments when they are earned. You must be ready to give counsel, corrective training, or earned punishment when they are called for. Whether they are being appraised informally or formally, subordinates have a right to expect that they will receive what they have earned.

By recognizing your own and your employees' needs for job security, you can do your part to meet them. By doing so, you will avoid a major cause of employee turnover and job dissatisfaction and simultaneously take a big step toward instilling self-control and self-discipline in your subordinates.

You are forced by the nature of your position to make judgments about your people and their conduct. When you become aware of an infraction or improper behavior, you are expected to act. You are the chief enforcement officer where workers are concerned, and you cannot escape that duty. You must get all the facts that relate to the offense. Then you must act as both judge and jury, determining the degree of guilt and deciding on an appropriate penalty to fit the wrongdoing. Knowing yourself and your people well will prevent a great deal of trouble for you in your role as disciplinarian. Practicing sound human relations and demonstrating established leadership principles and traits to your subordinates should minimize your need for punitive actions.

Subordinates and Responsibility

Effective discipline is contingent on many things, not the least of which is the individual employee's willingness to accept responsibility for work assignments. Too many organizations rely on controls outside the individual to enforce compliance with orders and assignments. But when individuals accept responsibility for their own output—its quality and quantity—job security and pride in achievement are part of the daily routine.

Peter Drucker points to three prerequisites that managers must provide to subordinates if they expect them to take responsibility for their work:

1. Productive work
2. Feedback information
3. Continuous learning[2]

These three elements point out the link between planning work and doing it. While planning and execution are separate activities, they can and should involve the same people. Those who do the work are the fountainheads of information and the best judges of just how productive it really is. Workers need to know why they are being asked to do certain work and how that work fits into the total scheme of things.

In order to take responsibility, workers and work groups require an accurate source of information, direction, and arbitration, and a channel through which information to and from various experts can flow. Workers and work groups also need positive and negative discipline. Supervisors must tailor work for subordinates, let them know how well they are doing, and help them grow and progress to avoid obsolescence. In Drucker's words, a supervisor is a "resource to the achieving worker and his (her) work group. . . ." The proper role for a supervisor includes the following: "knowledge, information, placing, training, teaching, standard setting, and guiding."[3]

If your workers like their jobs and respect you as their supervisor, they have the best reasons for avoiding the need for punitive action on your part. Such workers are bent not on disruption but on construction. Workers who appreciate that your concern is for their welfare will not let you down intentionally.

A Fair and Equitable Disciplinary System

As is the case with appraisal systems, unless you and your subordinates view the disciplinary system you must work with as both fair and equitable, it will cause more problems for you than it can cure. You and your company's efforts at discipline must consider a person's dignity, his or her legal rights, and the union agreement where one exists. A fair and equitable disciplinary system has the following characteristics:

1. It has reasonable and needed policies, rules, and procedures that govern human conduct at work. These exist to prevent problems, and they do not violate any federal, state, or local laws.

2. It communicates the above information and the consequences that one can expect when guilty of a deliberate violation.

3. It has consistent enforcement of rules, policies, and procedures, along with consistent applications of punishments for infractions.

4. It has progressively severe punishments for repeated infractions by the same party.

5. It places the burden of proving guilt on management.

6. It considers the circumstances surrounding an infraction.

7. It has an appeals procedure as a check on punishments.

8. It has a short memory—purges the memories of wrongdoing after a reasonable time and avoids holding a grudge.

Evaluate the disciplinary system you live with by these standards. If you suspect or know that there are problems, get together with your fellow supervisors and go to those who can change things. You cannot expect to enjoy the respect of your subordinates if you have to violate the preceding standards when executing your role as judge.

The Hot Stove Concept

Professor Douglas McGregor (who gave us Theories X and Y) offers a useful analogy to keep in mind when approaching disciplinary tasks and handing out earned punishment. Called the *hot stove concept,* it compares the hot stove to the organization's disciplinary system and the burn victim to the employee who has earned punishment. Professor Raymond L. Hilgert from Washington University puts it this way:

> The first element is advance warning; just as everyone knows that if he touches a hot stove he'll be burned, so should every employee know the rules and work standards. Second, the pain should be immediate; the boss shouldn't wait to respond. Third, discipline should be consistent: anytime you brush up against the stove, you get the message. . . . Finally, hot stoves are impersonal, and the boss should be too.[4]

Anyone who touches the hot stove will receive the same result. Initially, the victim will feel anger and hostility toward the stove, but normally this reaction is a result of the realization that the angry person is wrong or has acted incorrectly. The anger fades in time, and the victim learns respect for the stove. The victim's behavior will change in the future.

So it should be with your disciplinary actions. They should be immediate when they are earned by wrongdoers. People should not be in doubt that burns will occur when rules, procedures, standards, and policies are violated. Make sure that they know the stove is hot and that it will burn anyone who fails to respect its heat.

An Example An associate during my high-school teaching days told me about his method for handling cheating in his classroom. He began each new term by defining his policy on cheating. Anyone caught cheating on an exam, project, or quiz would receive a failing grade for it, and his or her parents would be notified to this effect. If a student were caught cheating twice in the same course, he or she would receive a failing grade for the course, and his or her parents would again be notified. For most students, a warning in such clear terms would be sufficient. However, there are always a few people who either do not believe you or who feel that cheating is worth the risk.

When my friend caught a student cheating, he would simply take up the student's paper and ask the student to see him after class. Before he picked up a paper, however, the teacher would make certain in his own mind that cheating had occurred. When they met after class, the teacher would tell the student what he had witnessed and ask the student to verify his observations. If the student would not admit the offense, the teacher was prepared to let him or her complete the exam. In point of fact, however, my friend was never confronted with this situation. In every case during the five years he used this system, the student readily admitted his or her wrongdoing. In no case did that student, once caught, do it again.

This method is simple and direct. The teacher practiced it without exception. At no time during five years did this teacher have two students who were caught cheating in the same class. Word got around that this teacher meant what he said. He was a "hot stove" in action, and the students respected him for it. The honest students felt secure that their hard work and study would pay off and not be jeopardized by the cheating of their dishonest fellow students. The grades in this teacher's class reflected each student's ability and not someone else's. Not once did parents complain about this system. In fact, some of them expressed their complete agreement with it and indicated that they were more involved with their children as a result. Eventually, this teacher's methods were adopted by the school as policy.

One lesson from this story is that you must start out firmly with your people. You cannot afford to be too lenient or permissive. Do not look the other way when you witness an improper situation, but do not go looking for trouble either. You certainly do not want to be accused of spying or setting traps for your people. That is totally improper. Get your subordinate to admit his or her mistake and to accept the punishment. If you get yourself into a swearing match (where it is his or her word against yours), you have a poor case indeed. Get a witness or at the very least an admission of guilt on which to build your case. And remember, criticize the action—not your subordinate as a person.

Progressive Discipline

Progressive discipline uses advance warnings about what is and is not acceptable conduct; specific, job-related rules; punishments that fit the

Progressive discipline
A system using advance warnings about what is and is not acceptable conduct; specific, job-related rules; punishments that fit the offense; punishments that grow in severity as misconduct persists; and prompt, consistent enforcement

- Specific rules
- Job relatedness
- Clearly defined punishments
- Punishments that fit the severity of the offense
- Punishments that increase with repeated infractions
- Careful investigation
- Prompt enforcement
- Consistent enforcement
- Documentation of offenses committed and punishments given
- Effective communication of standards, what happens when they are violated, and during disciplinary interview
- Disciplinary actions performed in private
- An appeals process established
- Follow-up to prevent recurrence and to cement relations

Exhibit 14.1   **Characteristics of a progressive discipline system.**

offense; punishments that grow in their severity as misconduct persists; and prompt, consistent enforcement. Exhibit 14.1 highlights the hallmarks of a progressive discipline system in more detail.

Managements lose respect from their employees and lawsuits in court when they attempt to enforce vague rules, punish in an inconsistent manner, fail to follow their own disciplinary procedures, and fail to warn employees of changes and unacceptable conduct. The progressive discipline system is formal; it is known by all who are governed by it. It does restrict management actions and thereby its flexibility to deal with problem employees. It must be applied to all in a just and fair way. But it does offer the best defense for accusations of bias and discrimination.[5]

Positive Discipline

Positive discipline
The part of discipline that promotes understanding and self-control by letting subordinates know what is expected of them

Positive discipline promotes understanding and self-control. The primary aim of discipline by any manager at any level in the hierarchy should be to prevent undesirable behavior or to change it into desirable behavior. You must communicate what is expected of each individual with regard to his or her behavior on the job. This process begins with the arrival and induction of each new employee and continues throughout his or her employment.

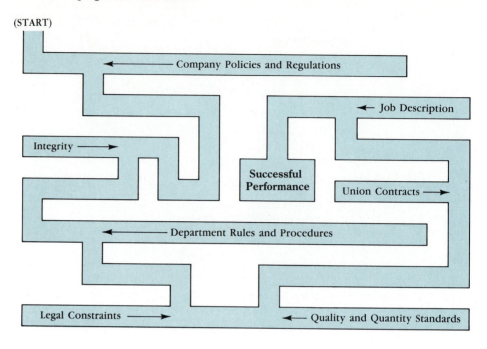

(START)

Company Policies and Regulations

Job Description

Integrity

**Successful
Performance**

Union Contracts

Department Rules and Procedures

Legal Constraints

Quality and Quantity Standards

Exhibit 14.2   The path to successful job performance is surrounded with restrictions.

The subject of your communications should be the limits placed on each individual by company policies and regulations, departmental rules and procedures, the person's job description, and the union contract (if one exists). By communicating before any infraction occurs the expectations you have of each worker and the limitations under which he or she has to work, you forewarn your subordinate about the type of conduct you want him or her to exhibit while on the job (see Exhibit 14.2). If employees stay within these boundaries, they risk nothing; but if they step outside them, they can expect management to react in certain predictable ways. Once established, these boundaries need to be maintained by regular review of their usefulness and by the judicious application of fair punishments.

Each person is evaluated at work by certain standards and norms. Most situations involving the need for discipline center on a failure to communicate these standards adequately. The need for punishment arises because of an individual's failure to meet one or more of the standards set up to govern his or her performance and conduct.

When employees know their jobs and the standards they must meet, they gain security. They are aware of the degree of freedom allowed and have definitive limits that they know they must not overstep. If they cross one or another of these limits, they know that a punishment will follow the violation.

Positive discipline can be illustrated by a police officer traveling in the flow of traffic in a well-marked, easily identifiable police car. He or she is visible to other motorists, serves as a reminder to obey traffic regulations, and represents a warning that violators will be apprehended and given a penalty. There is nothing sneaky or subterranean about his or her behavior, and the officer's main purpose is to prevent violations from occurring. Contrast this with an unmarked squad car parked out of the view of passing motorists. In this case prevention is deemphasized and detection and punishment are emphasized.

One example of positive discipline comes from a Florida company, Tampa Electric. Since 1979, the company has had a procedure it calls a "discipline-making leave day." When an employee below the rank of top management commits an offense or series of offenses that would ordinarily lead to a suspension, the company gives the employee one day's suspension *with* pay. The employee is given that day to think seriously about whether or not he or she wants to continue to work for Tampa Electric. Since the procedure has been used, 150 leave days have been handed out, and attendance problems have been cut in half. Supervisors who had been reluctant to give an earned suspension now see it as a positive step toward improving conditions.[6]

Do not leave your people guessing about the limits imposed on them or about their chances of getting caught in wrongdoing and being punished. Be visible and obvious, and let them have no doubts about your intentions and your punitive powers. You are not trying to trap anyone. Rather you are serving to inform them by your actions and words that you wish to promote reasonable behavior and prevent any unacceptable conduct.

People resent rules that they consider unnecessary or unfair. It is often insufficient to issue prohibitions. People need to know why they cannot do certain things. For example, if employees cannot smoke in Department A, the supervisor should explain why they cannot. If your subordinates are not to use company tools at home on a loan basis, tell them why not. Resentment follows from a lack of understanding or a misunderstanding of the need for rules or regulations. Be sure your people have adequate explanations so that their obedience will be based on logic. This procedure should provide an incentive to cooperate.

Legal Concerns

Chapter 11 introduced you to the various laws that govern the hiring and selection processes. The equal employment opportunity laws also affect disciplinary and dismissal decisions. It is unlawful to discipline, deny employment rights to, or fire someone because of his or her race, color, religion, sex, national origin, age, or handicap status. Worker compensation laws from the fifty states prohibit disciplining and terminating employees who make compensation claims. The Occupational Safety and Health Act (discussed in more detail in chapter 16) protects employees from terminations and other disciplinary actions when they exercise their rights under the act. Labor laws (discussed in chapter 15) prohibit the disciplining of workers for involvement in efforts to unionize and for engaging in lawful union activities.

Whistleblower
An employee who makes known to authorities the violations of laws and actions committed by his or her employer that are contrary to public policy

A number of federal and state laws protect **whistleblowers**—employees who make known to authorities the violations of laws and actions committed by their employers that are contrary to public policy (the good of society). It is generally unlawful to punish individual employees in any way for refusing to engage in or to conduct unlawful activities. In addition, some towns and cities have enacted such legislation and laws that prevent discrimination on the basis of one's sexual preference or orientation.

The above points out the need for some person in every organization to be a specialist in the area of the law and discipline. Check with your personnel or human resource specialists before you decide to take any disciplinary actions.

Resolving Complaints

Although chapter 15 has detailed information on handling employee complaints, a few words are in order here. Complaints should be a warning to you that something is not right for your people. They can be symptoms of deep-seated or long-standing problems with work or its environment. If they are not dealt with in a fair and equitable way, they can lead to employee misconduct. A person's job may be so boring and unfulfilling that she seeks conversations with others at work, disrupting their work and taking her away from her own.

When your subordinate or team member comes to you with a complaint, give it a fair hearing. Show sincere interest and give the person time enough to say what he or she thinks and feels. Listen without passing judgment. Get the person's perspective. If you can do something to help, do it. If you cannot, find someone who can. Send the complaint and/or the complainer to another person for assistance. Let people know that you and the company don't want dissatisfied employees.

Some companies have "open door" policies that encourage employees to go beyond their supervisors, all the way to the top, if necessary. Others have committees or one neutral individual to guarantee a fair hearing for complaints that can't be solved on the lowest levels of management. Use the paths created in your organization and the people who populate them. Do what you can to prevent a minor problem from becoming a major headache.

Employee Assistance Programs

Programs created to help employees with personal and job-related problems at work are collectively called employee assistance programs (EAPs). A person with a family, health, financial, or stress-related problem may need immediate help. Drug intervention programs offer the addict a way to overcome the addiction and to keep a job. Exercise, diet, and access to medical professionals offer employees a way to handle a variety of problems, which, if left unattended, can lead them into disciplinary troubles. People unable to cope with their problems will become problems for themselves and others at work. Some of the symptoms of troubled workers are absenteeism, tardiness, lateness in handling assignments, difficulties in working with others cooperatively, and turnover.

The hospitality industry is one suffering from high rates of absenteeism and employee turnover. Some hotels experience as much as 100 percent turnover in a year. The Chicago Hilton and Towers has reduced its turnover rate to about 38 percent due in large part to its EAPs focused on wellness: smoking cessation, diet, exercise, training in interpersonal relations, and regular meetings with new hires and staff.[7] If your people are showing signs of trouble, play your counselor role and get them the help they need before disciplinary actions are called for.

Creating a Team of Interdependent Individuals

Johnsonville Foods in Wisconsin operates almost entirely through employee teams whose members are responsible for hiring, defining their jobs, inspecting their output, scheduling their own production, and disciplining their own members. CEO Ralph Stayer puts it this way: "We believe discipline is the problem of people who have to work with other individuals, peers. We think any work area should set up its own standards and rules and enforce them. It's part of our overall philosophy. People are in charge of their own areas: setting budgets, hiring, firing, training, and discipline."[8]

Companies that have tried team disciplining of their members find mixed success. In general, people who are made to feel responsible for their work (those who feel they own their jobs) tend to take more pride in performing their duties. More pride usually means less problems with their work and with them. In addition, most people take criticism from their peers with greater reluctance than they do the criticism from their bosses. Think about it. You goof up on the job and your team members turn to you and say, "You sure blew it this time. Look at the problems you caused." How would you feel? One disadvantage of such control over discipline is that it cuts the supervisor out of the picture, tending to undermine his or her formal authority. But if the results are better—less need for discipline and better work performances—the good outweighs the bad.

Negative Discipline

Negative discipline
The part of discipline that emphasizes the detection and punishment of wrongdoing

Negative discipline emphasizes the detection of wrongdoing and punishment. It can become bureaucratic and impersonal, relying heavily on records, rules, and procedures, but it need not be this way. It is often characterized by a lack of trust in subordinates, by demands for blind obedience, and by willful disobedience of rules and regulations on the part of the employees. Many employees play a game with their supervisors when they work in such an environment. They become covert and sneaky in their behavior. They deliberately plot to break rules to see if they can beat the system and get away with it or simply to keep management off-balance and irritated. They do so because they resent the approach to discipline taken by their employer and supervisors, and they take delight in frustrating their efforts. They have not developed the attitudes that support a willing compliance with and obedience to their organization's rules.

A climate in which negative discipline thrives—one in which the need for punishment is frequent—should be examined and restructured to promote willing obedience and positive discipline. Individual counseling is absolutely essential in order to turn the situation around. Human relationships need development, nourishment, and maintenance. Supervisors must initiate and properly play their roles in human relations. Rewards and merit awards should be established for the good performers. The disciplinary system must become more professional and worthy of the respect and confidence of the employees.

Punishment

An important aspect of discipline has to do with the punishment of wrongdoers. Sometimes, as with controls, prevention devices and actions may fail; then the need for prompt and fair action takes over. Your power to take action in dealing with infractions is probably limited. Typically, most supervisors can do any of the following:

Illegal Activities	Gambling; verbal and physical assaults among workers; failing to report physical injuries or intentional damage to property; theft of common property; sexual harassment; possession of forbidden substances
***Rule Violations**	Tardiness; leaving early; unexcused absence; unacceptable language; horseplay; excessive break times; minor safety and security violations

Exhibit 14.3 **Disciplinary problems supervisors can expect to encounter at work.**
*Note: These offenses and violations may be considered minor when they occur infrequently and when their consequences can be considered inconsequential or less than serious by the company and the parties directly involved. Each offense has the potential of becoming serious, however, if left unnoticed and if allowed to be repeated by the same individuals.

1. Give an oral warning.
2. Issue a written reprimand.
3. Suspend a person from the job without pay.

Whether you have the powers mentioned above or not depends largely on your job description, your company's policies, and the union contract's stand on this issue, if your company has a union. Often the union contract will have much to say about your powers to discipline and about management's powers in this area. Be certain that you know the limits placed on your disciplinary powers and that you stay within those limits.

Common Problems

As a supervisor, you will face one or more of the problems identified in Exhibit 14.3 during a given year. Illegal activities may require immediate suspension or dismissal as well as criminal prosecution. Rule violations may be less serious, at least until they become "normal" behaviors for your subordinates. They usually carry the penalty of a verbal reprimand for the first offense, a written reprimand for the second, and a suspension without pay for a third violation. Of course, the person's intentions, his or her work history, and the circumstances surrounding the offense must be considered before any punishment can reasonably be given.

Two of the problems you are likely to run into are absenteeism (most companies say it is their biggest problem) and sexual harassment (a growing concern for many companies). There are some things you should know and some actions you can take with regard to these areas.

Absenteeism People are missing from their jobs for a variety of reasons each day. Some of these reasons mean that you have some work to do to cut down on lost time. If the employee has a legitimate excuse, the first time it happens you may just let him or her know you are concerned. If there is a possibility that the reason will recur, discuss it and try to prevent it from doing so. Suppose that Jill, a single parent, has not been late or absent in the past. Yesterday she called in with a request to take the day off because her babysitter was not available. Is this a legitimate reason? Maybe. But it can recur, and Jill should be working on an alternative to her regular sitter.

Sometimes your company may be to blame for absent employees. Suppose your company offers five sick days each year that cannot be "banked" and if not used are lost. Suppose employees with legitimate gripes are experiencing job-related stress about which the company has done nothing. At some point the stress becomes too much to deal with, and the employee feels a real need to escape the source of the stress, at least for a time. Finally, suppose your subordinate has come to you with a plea to enrich his job. If you fail to deal with your worker's boredom and loss of motivation, you may find an absent worker in the not too distant future.

Treat all absentees seriously. Talk to each when he or she returns. Keep an eye open for patterns in absenteeism—for example, Jack is always out the third Friday of every month. Be sure that you are setting a good example through your own attendance before you decide to discipline others for poor records.

Stay in touch with all your people on a regular basis. Greet them warmly when they come in each day. Listen to their concerns and deal with their problems promptly. Give those who can handle it a bigger say in what they do and how they do it. Through thoughtful delegation you empower people to become more responsible and to take more pride in themselves and their work.

Sexual harassment
Unwelcomed sexual advances, requests for sexual favors, and other physical and verbal conduct of a sexual nature

Sexual Harassment   Under Title VII of the Civil Rights Act, **sexual harassment** is unwelcomed sexual advances, requests for sexual favors, and other verbal or physical conduct of a sexual nature when:

1. Submission to such conduct is made either explicitly or implicitly a term or condition of employment;
2. Submission to or rejection of such conduct by an individual is used as a basis for employment decisions affecting that person or third parties;
3. Such conduct has the purpose of unreasonably interfering with an individual's work performance or creating an intimidating, hostile, or offensive working environment.[9]

Examples

- Unwelcome touching, patting, or pinching
- Sexually offensive language, pictures, or objects
- Derogatory, sexually based humor
- Pressure to engage in sexual activity
- Disparaging remarks to a person about his/her gender

- References to an assumed or desired sexual relationship
- Suggestive references about a person's body or appearance
- Unsolicited, unwanted notes, graphics, calls, company, requests for dates
- Obscene gestures

Victim Responses

- Say "no." Sexual harassment is a pattern of behavior that continues after you say "no."
- Don't blame yourself. It's not your fault.
- Don't ignore it. The behavior is likely to continue.
- *Do* tell someone.

Supervisory Responses

- Confront the perpetrator.
- Report findings to superiors.
- Do not ignore the behavior.
- Follow up on superiors' decisions.

Ideally, you can tell the other person to stop and he/she will. Keep a record of what is going on and what you have done to stop it.

Exhibit 14.4   **Examples of sexual harassment and what should be done when they occur.**

Thousands of cases go to the EEOC each year (about 8,000), and thousands more appear in civil actions through the state courts. The average award for persons claiming sexual harassment can run into six figures with damages, court costs, and lost time from work. As a supervisor, you could be named in a sexual harassment suit or complaint, making you liable for damages. If you know about a case of sexual harassment at work (see Exhibit 14.4) and fail to take any action, you are liable for the consequences. You and your company need to take a strong, clear stand against sexual harassment. You need to deal with it as soon as you become aware of it. A company policy stating what sexual harassment is and what will be done about it if it occurs must be written and communicated to all employees. There should be a specific procedure to follow in filing a complaint. Anyone who feels the need to complain should be allowed to do so with privacy and dignity. There should be no implied or expressed penalty or fear of retribution connected with filing a complaint.

Before Taking Action

Just what action you take when your subordinates violate rules and regulations should be governed by the following principles:

1. Know each subordinate, his or her record, and the nature and causes of the offense.
2. Know your powers as laid down in your job description; when in doubt, check with your boss and your peers.
3. Check on the precedents, if any, that governed similar situations in the past.
4. Be consistent: if you have given an oral warning on the first minor offense as a general rule, do so in every like case.
5. Consider the circumstances surrounding the misconduct. Was it willful or accidental? Was the person aware of the limits placed on his or her conduct? Is this his or her first offense? Get the facts.
6. If a subordinate has made the same mistake more than once, make the punishment progressively more severe. Generally you progress from an oral warning to a written reprimand and eventually to a suspension.
7. Coordinate with the other supervisors on enforcement. Every manager should enforce every policy, rule, standard, and procedure with equal weight and effort. It is better not to have a rule that is unenforced or unenforceable.
8. Be reasonable and fair.

   Being fair means many things, but the most important aspect of it involves basing your decisions on the circumstances. What may be an appropriate punishment for one party to an infraction of the rules may not be so for another. For example, suppose that you find two of your people in a shoving match; before you can break it up, one of them hits the other. Both people are guilty of fighting, but can you think of reasons justice might dictate for coming down harder on one than on the other? Consider the circumstances and the motives underlying the action you observed. Someone started the fight. Shouldn't that person be dealt with more severely than the person who was provoked? What if one of the people had done this before while the other had a clean record? Wouldn't these facts influence your decision?

Being fair does not mean treating everyone the same. You are not a machine that operates automatically or in the same manner with everyone. When we talk about precedents, we mean treating like offenses in a like manner. But the key word is *like*. Be careful that what you are dealing with and the people you are dealing with are sufficiently similar to warrant concern for precedents. An old-timer who should and does know better should not receive the same treatment as a new employee. One has learned while the other is learning; one has more responsibility to set a good example than the other.

When you punish, you must look at the person and the circumstances. This does not mean that you do so in order to exercise prejudice or to get even. If you are vindictive or carry a grudge, you are bound to attack people personally. They will know it, even if you do not admit it: you will be basing your actions on a personal dislike for them and not on their actions. As in making appraisals, you must be as objective as you can in order to prevent criticism of your motives or intent. Your job and your reputation are too valuable to risk on immature behavior.

Do not be the cause of your subordinates' mistakes either. Set the example, and let them know you mean what you say. Give them the security that comes with knowing what they must do and why.

A man who audited stores for a large retail chain for over thirty years once told me that, where he uncovered dishonest employees, there was usually a dishonest manager who seemed to encourage them. This type of manager would, on the way out of the store each day, help himself or herself to a handful of peanuts or candy. At other times, such a manager might be too lenient in enforcing rules or regulations or deal weakly with dishonest employees. Honest employees began to resent the extras enjoyed by their peers and decided to get into the action too. It may start with a pen or pencil, but it may not end until the take reaches some pretty high figures.

Keep in mind that you are not the final voice in matters of discipline. Your company and the union may have procedures providing for review of your decision, as matters of discipline are often considered too important to entrust to any one manager. Chapter 15 has much more to say on this matter. If you are wrong, you will be overruled. If not, you should be able to count on your boss for backing. Your subordinates will hear about your disciplinary decisions, too. Do not jeopardize your relations with them by hasty or irrational actions. You could damage your relationships with other workers and their groups if you are unfair. Be sure that you have the facts and that you have put them together properly. Consult with superiors before you act.

Consider the case of a supervisor named John who has given an oral order to a subordinate, Harry. Harry has failed to respond. Orders are intended to provoke an immediate positive response and usually do if they are not overutilized, so John immediately assumes that Harry is being insubordinate. Without any further investigation, John suspends Harry for one week while he and the company decide whether to fire Harry or not. But wait a moment. Aren't there several legitimate reasons Harry could have for not following the supervisor's order? Here are but a few:

1. Harry did not hear the order.
2. Harry was told to do something illegal.
3. Harry was told to perform a task outside his job description or beyond his capabilities or training.
4. John was unclear in his order, and Harry did not understand it.

All of these and more could get Harry off the hook. If John goes solely on his observations, without any further investigation, he is likely to make an improper decision and be reversed. In that case, Harry will be back at work, with pay for his time off. Meanwhile, John will have damaged his reputation and alienated Harry, among others. It pays to get the employee's point of view.

Giving the Reprimand

You have studied the case of wrongdoing, gathered your facts, touched bases with experts, and reached the conclusion that disciplinary action is called for. The penalty has been chosen to fit the offense, and you have scheduled a meeting with the offender. Now begins one of the least pleasant parts of being a supervisor. Here are some tips to make that disciplinary session as productive as possible.

- Choose a time and place that ensures privacy and freedom from interruptions.
- Have your facts in writing and your mind clear about the who, what, when, where, and how.
- Be businesslike and serious. The meeting is not the time or place for discussion about anything other than the offense and the consequences of it.
- Take charge of the meeting. Lay out your case with specifics. Get agreement on essentials and listen for any new information.
- Be clear about the fact that the behavior is in question, not the person.
- Once you have given the reprimand, don't "rub it in."

> **NEWS**
> **You Can Use**
>
> **Flying High**
>
> In October 1990, three former Northwest Airlines flight crew members were sentenced to serve jail terms for violating a federal aviation regulation. The pilot and his two crew members admitted to drinking to intoxication through the night before they flew their jet on an early morning run from Fargo, North Dakota, to Minneapolis, Minnesota. The pilot admitted to drinking more than 15 rum and cola drinks while the two crew members shared at least six pitchers of beer.
>
> Northwest Airlines has a regulation forbidding its flight crews from drinking within 12 hours of a flight. For violating that regulation, the crew lost their jobs. For violating the federal aviation regulation of no alcohol within 8 hours of a flight, the crew lost their freedom. These three people knowingly endangered their own lives and the lives of their 91 passengers. At his sentencing, the pilot said: "I accept full responsibility for the incident and if anyone bears the brunt of it, I do. It is my hope that never again will three pilots be in this courtroom."
>
> Source: "Pilots Who Flew Drunk Get Prison," *Chicago Tribune* (October 27, 1990), sect. 1, p. 2.

- Try to get a commitment from the offender for improvement and for no repetitions of the offense.
- Both of you should return to your duties.

The Decision to Fire

The decision to fire a person usually rests with the person or persons who have the authority to hire. In most disciplinary cases, this is the course of last resort and should only be followed when *all* else has failed. Some situations, however, usually demand that the guilty party receive an immediate dismissal. These include the following cases:

1. Gross insubordination such as refusal to obey a direct, lawful order
2. Drunkenness on the job
3. Willful destruction of company property
4. Serious cases of dishonesty or theft
5. Being found guilty of or pleading guilty to a felony (crime punishable by more than one year in a federal or state penitentiary)
6. Engaging in conduct that is totally unacceptable, given the employee's position and responsibilities

Certainly there will be exceptions, even in these extreme situations, and whatever circumstances surround each of these exceptional cases must be considered. It is nevertheless true that a large majority of companies require that the penalty for these infractions be automatic dismissal.

Legal Concerns   Along with employment discrimination laws and the other federal laws already discussed in this chapter, nearly all the states have some laws that restrict an employer's right to fire anyone for any reason. The courts have added to these restrictions. Prior to 1980, the "employment at will" rule from the common law prevailed. **Employment at will** means that both the employer and the employee have the right to terminate the employee's employment at any time, with or without just cause. In 1980, the California Court of Appeals ruled that employers had a duty to deal fairly and in good faith with employees and could be held accountable for discharging employees without having good cause.[10] Since that time more than forty states have allowed exceptions to the employment at will rule under specific conditions. Discharged workers can recover losses and regain their jobs by proving that an implied or expressed contract was violated, that an implied or expressed promise of continued employment was violated, or that the firing was contrary to public policy.[11] As a result, employers who wish to retain the power to terminate employees at will must refrain from making any promises, guarantees, or covenants that may lead the employee to believe that some right to long-term employment exists.

Puerto Rico has created the Discharge Indemnity Act, which details just causes for terminating an employee. It is shown in Exhibit 14.5. Several states are now drafting their own laws using Puerto Rico's act as their model.

Employment at will
The common law doctrine that holds that employment will last until either employer or employee decides to terminate it, with or without just cause

Pitfalls

As is the case with the pitfalls we discussed in the previous chapters, the major problems you may encounter when you attempt to carry out your disciplinary duties can be eliminated or at least minimized if you are aware of each of them and consciously try to prevent them from interfering with your efforts.

Starting Off Soft

Supervisors, especially those who are new at the job, are apt to associate being lenient with being liked. They sometimes feel that, if they look the

> ## Sec. 185b. Discharge without just cause
>
> Good cause for the discharge of an employee of an establishment shall be understood to be:
>
> (a) That the worker indulges in a pattern of improper or disorderly conduct.
>
> (b) The attitude of the employee of not performing his work in an efficient manner or of doing it belatedly and negligently or in violation of the standards of quality of the product produced or handled by the establishment.
>
> (c) Repeated violations by the employee of the reasonable rules and regulations established for the operation of the establishment, provided a written copy thereof has been timely furnished to the employee.
>
> (d) Full, temporary or partial closing of the operations of the establishment.
>
> (e) Technological or reorganization changes as well as changes of style, design or nature of the product made or handled by the establishment and in the services rendered to the public.
>
> (f) Reductions in employment made necessary by a reduction in the volume of production, sales or profits, anticipated or prevalent at the time of the discharge.
>
> A discharge made by mere whim or fancy of the employer or without cause related to the proper and normal operation of the establishment shall not be considered as a discharge for good cause. . . .

Exhibit 14.5   Definition of "just cause" in Puerto Rico's Discharge Indemnity Act. (*Source:* P. R. Laws Ann. tit. 29, Sec. 185a–185*i*.)

other way on occasion or mete out less than a deserved penalty for an infraction, they will endear themselves to their subordinates. Nothing could be farther from the truth. In actuality, their leniency will be the cause of more trouble. If Mary arrives late and you say nothing, she will be encouraged to do it again. So will the others who witness the event and your failure to take constructive action.

We have stated before in this book that, when you take office, your people will adopt a wait-and-see attitude toward you. They can be expected to test you on numerous occasions and in numerous ways. Each of them wants to know if you mean what you say. They need to know the limits and where the hard-and-fast boundaries lie. They want to know specifically what to expect if they commit a violation. If you talk one kind of game and play another, or if you promise punishment and do not deliver, you will adversely affect your relationships for months to come.

It is always easier to start out tough, with an emphasis on the letter of the law. As you gain self-confidence and additional knowledge about your duties and your people, you can shift the emphasis to the spirit of the law as well, tempering your judgment within the framework of your understanding of your people, their personalities, and the group pressures at work on them. This is what is meant by justice. Each person and most events are unique and should be dealt with as such.

If you are soft, those who toe the line will resent you for it. They will see no tangible reward for proper behavior, while they witness some for improper conduct. Your softness will be interpreted as weakness, and you can expect more testing on their part to find the limits.

Incomplete Research and Analysis

Let us assume that you see a man stretched out on a packing crate 30 feet away and, because he has his eyes shut, you jump to the conclusion that he is sleeping on the job or, at the very least, goofing off. You should know by now—from your past experience and from this book—that appearances do not always reveal the whole truth. It takes more than one observation to make a sound case, where discipline is involved. Unless you go to the man (preferably with a witness you can count on) and ask him some questions, you cannot really be sure that your observations are correct.

If you intend to punish someone, be certain that you have a firm case that will stand up to a review by higher authority. Have the details clearly in mind and make some notes of your observations for later reference. The mind loses certainty and eliminates details with the passage of time between a disciplinary action and the appeal of that action. Answer questions such as who was there and what was said by each. If all you have is a swearing match, you will lose the case, especially when a union is involved.

Acting in Anger

How many times have you wished you could take back remarks made to another in anger? If you are like most people, the answer is *too often*. With emotions influencing your observations and judgment, you will seldom make a sound decision. Too often you will have to back down and apologize for a demonstration of your lack of self-control.

Count to ten or to one hundred if necessary, but cool down before you decide anything. It helps to move physically away from the situation and the environment of a wrongdoing, in order to regain your composure. Tell the guilty party to report to you in your office in a few minutes. This will give you both time to recapture your sense of composure.

Disciplining in Public

If you have some critical remarks for an individual, pass them along in person and in private. Each person has a reputation to uphold both with you and with his or her peers. He or she has pride and self-esteem, which need protection. He or she does not wish to be subjected to ridicule or embarrassment. It may not be punishment that your people fear but your way of dispensing it. Your methods may make the difference between a constructive and a destructive kind of discipline.

Exceeding Your Authority

Keep in mind that, like your people, you have limits on your power and conduct. To paraphrase an oil company's slogan, you have "power to be used, not abused." Check with your boss and your peers when you are in doubt about what course of action to take. There is no legitimate excuse for falling into the trap of exceeding your authority; there are too many avenues open to you that can prevent it.

Being Vindictive

The best defense one of your subordinates can have in a disciplinary case is that you are picking on him or her or making a personal attack. Be sure that the reasons behind your action and words are not based on personality clashes or personal prejudice. Put your biases aside, or they will shine through with a neon brilliance for all to see. If you single out one person for disciplinary action, and your methods rest in your personal biases, you will certainly lose your case and will face the wrath of those who must review your actions.

Like your subordinates, you have likes and dislikes. It would not be reasonable to expect you to like all your people. But you are being paid to serve all of them, regardless of their personal feelings toward you or yours toward them. Unless a subordinate's personality is defective and interferes with his or her performance, you cannot in conscience hold it against that individual. You are not out to win your subordinates over as friends or to socialize with them. It is tough to be fair to those whom we dislike, but if we are to be of service to our company and ourselves, we must make every effort to do so.

Leaving It to Others

Like appraising your people, disciplining them is your exclusive right and duty. You cannot be asked to part with it if you are expected to control and direct your workers properly. Some companies allow the personnel department or some other outside authority to mete out discipline. This reduces the supervisor's role to that of an arresting officer. Your subordinates will soon realize that you cannot punish but can only report violations. As a result, your status will be greatly reduced. This represents a tremendous handicap to a supervisor. While some managers prefer this arrangement because it releases them from a difficult responsibility, they fail to see that giving up this power makes them impotent and subjects them to additional and needless harassment from above and below.

Even worse than losing disciplinary powers to a higher authority is giving them away to a top worker or straw boss—someone acting with your authority on your behalf. Knowing how difficult it is to discipline properly, how much more likely do you think it is that such people might make a mess of it? Remember, these people are extensions of yourself and, as such, represent you to your other subordinates. Do not give them the power to cause you and themselves trouble. You and only you are responsible for your people and accountable for their actions. If your top worker or straw boss made the wrong decisions, you would have to correct them, thus injuring their already difficult position, possibly beyond repair. Most straw bosses do not want such authority, but if they try to assume it, make it clear to them that they cannot have it.

Failing to Keep Adequate Records

In order to gain and keep a perspective on each of your people, you should keep records of their performance appraisals, reprimands, peculiarities, and needs. These files will prove quite helpful when you face tough personnel decisions. They also come in very handy when you want to justify your opinions or take specific disciplinary actions.

Instant Replay

1. Both positive discipline and negative discipline are needed if reasonable and safe conduct at work is to be promoted, along with a sense of responsibility for one's work.

2. When an organization or an individual supervisor tolerates a poor performer, the organization or the supervisor cannot, in conscience, discipline anyone whose performance exceeds the poor performer's.

3. The best kind of disciplinary system is one based on the individual employee's sense of responsibility for his or her own work and on each employee's self-control.

4. People need to know what is expected of them and how well they are or are not doing; they have a right to expect consistent enforcement of necessary rules, policies, and standards.

5. People need to know that good work will be rewarded and that poor performance will earn swift and predictable responses from management.

6. People do not resent punishment that they know they deserve. They do resent being punished for something they did not know was wrong—for not being forewarned.

7. The majority of your subordinates will not need negative discipline if the positive side of discipline has been developed.

8. Discipline is either an easy task or a hard one, depending on how well you have built your relationships with your subordinates and how well you have instilled a measure of self-control in each of them.

Glossary   **Discipline**   the management duty that involves educating subordinates to foster obedience and self-control and dispensing appropriate punishment for wrongdoing.

Employment at will   the common law doctrine that holds that employment will last until either employer or employee decides to terminate it, with or without just cause.

Negative discipline   the part of discipline that emphasizes the detection and punishment of wrongdoing.

Positive discipline   the part of discipline that promotes understanding and self-control by informing subordinates of what is expected of them with regard to on-the-job behavior.

Progressive discipline   a system using advance warnings about what is and is not acceptable conduct; specific job-related rules; punishments that fit the offense; punishments that grow in severity as misconduct persists; and prompt, consistent enforcement.

Sexual harassment   unwelcomed sexual advances, requests for sexual favors, and other physical and verbal conduct of a sexual nature.

Whistleblower   an employee who makes known to authorities the violations of laws and actions committed by his or her employer that are contrary to public policy.

Questions for Class Discussion

1. Can you define this chapter's key terms?

2. What is the difference between negative and positive discipline? In what ways are they similar?

3. What is the purpose of punishment in a disciplinary system?

4. What are the basic principles of discipline?

5. What are the major pitfalls a supervisor can fall victim to when carrying out disciplinary functions?

6. What does it mean to be fair when disciplining subordinates?

7. Why should you know yourself and your subordinates well before attempting to discipline or punish them?

Incident

Purpose To test your knowledge about and ability to spot the existence of sexual harassment in a work setting.

Your Task After each of the following, indicate if you agree or disagree with the statement. The answers are shown below. Don't look at them until after you have tried the quiz.

	Agree	Disagree
1. If I don't mean to sexually harass a person, sexual harassment does not exist.	_____	_____
2. A sexually harassed person who does not complain is not a problem for managers.	_____	_____
3. Men cannot be sexually harassed.	_____	_____
4. About all a supervisor can do when he or she witnesses sexual harassment is to ask the harasser to stop.	_____	_____
5. When a woman starts work in what has been an all-male environment, behaviors will usually have to be changed.	_____	_____
6. If a supervisor does not hear about any cases of sexual harassment, none are occurring.	_____	_____
7. If a member of management is being sexually harassed, he or she should handle the matter by himself or herself.	_____	_____
8. Sexually suggestive visuals or objects at work cannot constitute sexual harassment unless a person complains	_____	_____

(answers: all are "disagree")

Case Problem 14.1   **What Should Be Done?**

After reading each of the following situations, decide what you would do if you were the supervisor. Your options include the following: seeking more information; counseling with the person; referring the person to another authority; giving additional training; giving an oral warning or reprimand; giving a written reprimand; or recommending a suspension without pay. You may decide to use a combination of options, and you must give reasons for your choices.

Situation 1. You overhear your subordinates talking about the big pro games coming up this weekend. You notice Wally tearing sheets of paper, writing on them, and placing them in his hat for others to draw out. Several $5 bills are piled on Wally's desk, and Jim and Al are adding to the pile. Company rules forbid gambling.

Situation 2. On your rounds through the shop, you notice that Sally is not wearing her protective gloves. She is at her workstation where she handles sharp-edged sheets of metal, but her machine is not operating. Sally has had two minor injuries in the last six months, and you have warned her twice in the last two weeks to wear the required gear. Company rules state that, while at one's workstation, one must wear safety gear.

Situation 3. Your subordinate, Hazel, reports to your office twenty minutes late. She explains that her daughter missed the bus this morning and she had to drive her to school. Hazel has been late three times this month but has always had a different excuse. She has never been late by more than forty minutes and has taken only two sick days in the past twelve months.

Situation 4. Betty arrives in your office crying. She calms down enough to tell you that a worker from another department confronted her in the employee cafeteria and used foul and abusive language to her, embarrassing her in front of several others. Betty claims that she gave the other person no cause to behave the way he did and refuses to tell you who he is.

Situation 5. Bob reports to you to tell you about the theft of a transistor radio from his desk. Bob used the radio at work for several months and always left it on his desk during working hours. Each night he locked it in his desk. The radio disappeared during his coffee break this morning. The radio is old and cost $15 when new. Company rules encourage securing all personal property, unless it is in clear view of its owner. Coffee breaks are routinely taken away from the workstation.

Situation 6. Rita, a coworker and friend of Ruth's, tells you at lunch that Ruth is being sexually harassed by a supervisor in another department. Both Ruth and Rita are your subordinates and the supervisor in question is a close personal friend of yours. Both the supervisor and Ruth are married, but not to each other.

Case Problem 14.2 A Real Bind

Lance Cooper is superintendent for the Los Angeles plant of Weller and Sons Bindery. He is pondering his next move regarding Gil Wainwright, who is the best production supervisor he has ever had. The last time Lance counseled Gil, he was careful to be gentle. However, Gil took the criticism the wrong way and has been hypersensitive ever since.

Wainwright is production supervisor for the plant's three shifts, each of which is directed by an outstanding worker. Prior to being hired for his present job, Gil was a top worker in a competing bindery. He left because, as he put it, "My boss was a career supervisor." Within a month after joining Weller

and Sons, Wainwright boosted production to a record level and introduced several cost-reduction programs. His most notable achievement was with the third shift. Its production had consistently been below that of the other two shifts. With some employee shuffling and a new top worker, Gil brought its production level to equal that of the first shift. By the end of six months, production increased by 18 percent and the marketing department was hard pressed to fill the slack time that resulted.

The old methods of production scheduling have gone "out the window," and Lance now relies on Gil to schedule production for him. Little by little, Lance found that he can turn

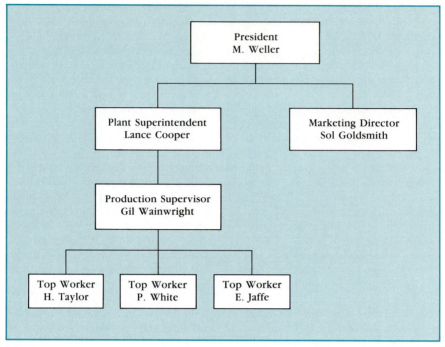

Exhibit A

over many of his traditional duties to Gil and has done so.

Lance's present problem began when Sol Goldsmith, the marketing director, tried to reach Ed Jaffe, the top worker on the third shift. According to Mr. Weller, marketing should run production. As a result, Sol was in the habit of talking directly with the top workers. During the early morning hours on Tuesday (today), Sol called twice. Each time he got one of the workers and left a message for Ed to return his call. Ed did not do so until this morning at 9:30 A.M. Goldsmith had wanted to be certain that his customer's order would be ready for pickup by the customer at 8:00 A.M. as scheduled. It was not, and the first-shift top worker, Harry Taylor, indicated that he could not promise it by the end of his shift, 4:00 P.M.

After Sol finished talking with Ed, he called Lance. Sol expressed his displeasure and reminded Lance that this was not the first time that the third shift had wrecked his relation-

ship with a customer. He cited two very recent cases with which Lance was all too familiar. Sol ended the conversation by stating, "Don't worry about chewing Jaffe out. I've done that for you."

After this conversation Lance called Ed. Ed tried to explain to Goldsmith that the machinery broke down during the early part of his shift, and he was so involved in getting it running that he had no time for anything else. He had six idle workers and he believed he should give them priority. After all, talking about the problem at 3:00 A.M. would not help things any. Ed explained that the machinery was tired and overworked. Besides, he felt that the other two shifts were not pulling their maintenance as scheduled.

Lance began to wonder if he had been too lenient with Gil—giving him free reign and nearly absolute control over production scheduling. Twice before Gil had promised to deliver orders early and had not been able to do so. It seemed there was always an excuse—

too many workers out with the flu or faulty equipment. On the other hand, other shifts used the same equipment, and they didn't have as many problems as the third shift had.

Lance made his decision. He would meet with Gil this afternoon and give it to him straight. No more promises about early production unless he is absolutely sure it can be done. And from now on, Gil would be made to look in on the third shift and its operations at least once each week.

The company's chain of authority is shown in Exhibit A.

Questions

1. Comment on Mr. Weller's philosophy that marketing should run production.
2. Do you believe that Lance has been "too lenient" with Gil? If so, in what way?
3. What do you think about Lance's decision?
4. If you were Gil Wainwright, what would you think about all this?
5. Briefly discuss the relationship each boss in this case has with his subordinates.

Notes

1. Paul M. Magoon and John B. Richards, *Discipline or Disaster: Management's Only Choice* (Jericho, N.Y.: Exposition Press, 1966), 15–16.
2. Peter F. Drucker, *Management: Tasks, Responsibilities, Practices* (New York: Harper & Row, 1974), 270–271.
3. Ibid., 281.
4. Walter Kiechel III, "How to Discipline in the Modern Age," *Fortune* (May 7, 1990): 180.
5. James Ledvinka and Vida G. Scarpello, *Federal Regulation of Personnel and Human Resource Management,* 2d ed. (Boston: PWS-Kent, 1991), 315–25.
6. "Disciplining Employees with Dollars," *Success!* (April 1987): 25.
7. Carol Kleiman, "Employee Turnover a Bottom-Line Issue," *Chicago Tribune* (October 21, 1990), sect. 8, p. 1.
8. Walter Kiechel III, op. cit.
9. Brian S. Moskal, "Sexual Harassment '80s-Style," *Industry Week* (July 2, 1989): 24.
10. Donald C. Bacon, "See You in Court," reprint of article from *Nation's Business* (July 1989): 4.
11. Ibid.

Suggested Readings

Campbell, David N.; Fleming, R. L.; and Grote, Richard C. "Discipline Without Punishment—at Last." *Harvard Business Review* (July–August 1985): 162–178.

Ewing, David W. *Justice on the Job.* Boston: Harvard Business School Press, 1989.

Grothe, Mardy, and Wylie, Peter. *Problem Bosses.* New York: Facts on File, 1987.

Leap, Terry L., and Crino, Michael D. "How to Deal with Bizarre Employee Behavior." *Harvard Business Review* (May–June 1986): 18–22.

Ledvinka, James, and Scarpello, Vida G. *Federal Regulation of Personnel and Human Resource Management.* 2d ed. Boston: PWS-Kent, 1991.

Sovereign, Kenneth L. *Personnel Law.* 2d ed. Englewood Cliffs, N.J.: Prentice-Hall, 1989.

Zarandona, Joseph. "A Study of Exit Interviews: Does the Last Word Count?" *Personnel,* 62, #3 (March 1985): 47–50.

IV Special Concerns

Part IV contains an in-depth look at two areas that are of special concern for supervisors: dealing with employee dissatisfaction in both union and nonunion environments and protecting against several different kinds of hazards.

Dealing with worker complaints in a union or nonunion environment is the topic of chapter 15. It outlines the major prohibitions on union and management conduct as set forth in the most important pieces of federal labor legislation. A step-by-step process is included to help you deal with worker grievances in both small and large organizations. Through the discussion in this chapter, you will find that there are far more factors at work to bring labor and management together than there are to drive them apart.

Chapter 16 covers security of physical facilities, as well as preventing and coping with work-related accidents, illnesses, and injuries. Various steps, checklists, and procedures are outlined and included to help supervisors with these important duties. The essentials of the federal Occupational Safety and Health Act (OSHA) and its inspection procedures are explained in this chapter.

15 Complaints, Grievances, and the Union

Objectives

After reading and discussing this chapter, you should be able to do the following:

1   Define this chapter's key terms.
2   List the five steps for handling complaints, and comment about what happens in each.
3   List four prohibitions of the Wagner Act.
4   List four prohibitions of the Taft-Hartley Act.
5   Compare the role of supervisors and stewards in labor relations.
6   Outline typical grievance procedures for a large organization and a small organization.

Key Terms

arbitration

collective bargaining

complaint

employee association

grievance

grievance processing

labor relations

mediation

steward

union

Introduction

About 16.4 percent of American workers belong to unions. This translates into about 17 million working people. Both these percentages have been shrinking over the past decade due in part to the following:

■   The number of persons working in the traditional unionized areas (blue-collar/manufacturing jobs) has steadily declined or experienced no growth as the work force has grown.

■   The primary growth areas in our economy contain vast numbers of jobs that are traditionally nonunion.

■   Industry jobs have moved offshore and to the South and Southwest, traditionally nonunion areas.

■   Workers have shown a trend to decertify their unions, moving from unionized to nonunionized status.

- Many of the foreign-owned companies that have come to America to establish production facilities have created nonunion work forces.

- Enlightened, people-focused enterprises have created work environments built on trust, mutual respect, and genuine concern for the welfare of their employees, removing major causes why unions form.

Unions are still a force, both political and economic, in our economy. They have achieved some success in replacing their lost blue-collar employees with white-collar, service and professional employees. Increasingly, unions have become partners with management, working to remove barriers to productivity and to quality. They have done so out of necessity to preserve employment opportunities for their members. They have shown a willingness to trade restrictive work rules and past economic gains for job security.

This chapter discusses the proper ways of dealing with the complaints of employees. First, we take up how to handle complaints you might encounter in a company where there is no union. Next, we discuss briefly what unions are and why workers join them. Finally, we learn how complaints are handled in a company where there is a union contract.

Complaints

Complaint
Any expression of unhappiness with working conditions or on-the-job relationships that comes to a manager's attention

For our purposes, a **complaint** is any expression of unhappiness with working conditions or on-the-job relationships that comes to a manager's attention. Complaints may be based on a worker's assumption that he or she has been treated unfairly or inequitably. Complaints often begin with a worker's perception that he or she has been or is being treated differently from others in similar circumstances.

Complaints may involve (1) objects that can be seen and touched (the switch is broken, or the machine needs adjustment); (2) sensory experiences other than touch and sight (the ventilation is poor in here, or the office is too noisy); or (3) nonsensory situations (my pay is too low, or they do not reward experience around here). Complaints that fall into the first of these categories are easily dealt with by personal observations and inspection. Each complaint is either true or not true and offers little difficulty in resolution. The other two types of complaints are different, however, as they are difficult to pin down and verify.

Complaints may be symptoms of a very different problem from the one they seem to state. The worker may be complaining about his or her level of pay or job classification, but the real issue may be dissatisfaction with the job—even though the worker may feel that more pay or a higher job classification will make the job more bearable. Therefore, even after a careful explanation of why a certain level of pay goes with the labor grade, the worker will remain dissatisfied because the real problem has not yet been dealt with.

Some complaints are imaginary. Take the case of an old, high-ceilinged plant structure that had been recently air-conditioned. Both before and after this renovation, the workers complained about feeling too hot and working in a stuffy atmosphere. The air-conditioning ducts had been mounted nearly 20 feet above the plant floor, and the individuals in the area could not feel any cool air circulating. In fact, many of them accused management of not turning the system on. They were convinced that it was not functioning.

Management's answer was to install thermometers on the plant pillars and to tie colored streamers to the air outlets. The workers could now see for themselves that the temperature was proper and that the air was in fact circulating. Their complaints stopped immediately. Seeing was believing.

Handling Complaints: A Company-Wide Systems Approach

Research done by Mary P. Rowe (a labor economist and full-time mediator of nonunion employees' complaints) and Michael Baker (a social scientist, researcher, and business consultant) indicates that only about one-third of U.S. employers have developed formalized complaint systems for both managers and workers.[1] If you are lucky, you work for such a company and have clear guidelines to follow and steps to take. After looking at what these employers are doing, we shall turn our attention to what you can do if you work for a company from among the other two-thirds.

Qualities of an Effective Complaint System Companies that have designed formal complaint systems usually try to make them accessible, safe, and credible. An *accessible* system gives employees a number of options. Things such as complaint hotlines, personnel counselors, complaint committees, and in-house surveys and suggestion systems are designed and made available. A *safe* system guarantees anonymous or confidential access to those who can help. It forbids reprisals against complainers and takes punitive action when reprisals do occur. A *credible* system assures complainers of a fair and objective hearing from truly neutral parties who have power to investigate and to recommend possible courses of action and ways to proceed.[2]

If a complaint system is to be effective—providing those who have complaints with a safe, credible, and just hearing and an objective resolution—it must guarantee the supervisors of complaining employees that their sensible decisions will be supported by higher-ups and that they will have a face-saving way out of their improper decisions regarding complaints. It must encourage the complainer and that person's supervisor to take up complaints initially and to pursue them jointly to an equitable solution. Finally, it must remove the common sources of fear in employees so that the system will be used and will function properly.[3]

If employees believe that their complaint will not get a fair hearing, or if they fear the system or the act of complaining or its consequences, they can become negative influences at work. Some turn hostile to management. Others waste time, infect others with negative attitudes, and actively work to harm their companies. Do what you can to remove employee fears and encourage your people to air their complaints. Accept the complaints of employees as a fact of working life and as a chance to mold better employees and working environments.

The Five Functions of an Effective Complaint System   Effective complaint systems have the following five functions:

1. *Personal communication with individuals:* anonymous and confidential ways to seek accurate information
2. *Confidential counseling with individuals:* people with authority and professional training who are available to help parties define problems and determine ways to find solutions
3. *Investigation, conciliation, and mediation:* experts who can help determine facts and encourage the parties to reach agreement on what is needed to resolve complaints
4. *Adjudication:* a person or group with the powers needed to render a decision or judgment when the parties to a complaint cannot agree on a resolution.
5. *Upward feedback:* people and methods to keep management informed as to employee concerns, complaints, and the resolutions of them[4]

Exhibit 15.1 identifies the various people, methods, and devices (structures) used by companies with formal complaint systems to achieve these five functions. Spend time with this table, and identify which functions you can execute and which structures you have available.

Handling Complaints: Developing Your Own Approach

Even if you are not fortunate enough to work in an environment that has instituted the preceding system for handling complaints, you still must deal with them—and more or less on your own. What follows can help you to formulate your own approach. Keep in mind that you want to include as many of the aforementioned qualities and functions as you can.

To begin with, your attitude toward the complaints of your workers should be to treat them seriously. Your subordinates think that their complaints have merit, or they would not bring them to your attention. Often you may overhear a complaint of your workers. Their actions as well as their words will provide you with clues about their true feelings. Watch for any sudden changes in established patterns of behavior. If complaints are not dealt with as soon as they are discovered, they can spread quickly to other workers and begin to interfere with your department's cooperation, production, and morale.

An open-door policy (letting subordinates know that you are available and eager to discuss their problems) is the best way to prevent trouble from getting out of hand. If your people feel that you care about them, will act swiftly, and have sound judgment, you will find them willing to air their irritations and observations. This can only come about, however, after you have established solid human relations with them as individuals and as a group. So do not be discouraged if you only hear about gripes through the grapevine: it takes time to develop proper attitudes and relationships. If you find that your people do not come to you, it means that you have more work ahead of you. Find out why, and then go to work on the problems.

Your four roles of educator, counselor, judge, and spokesperson come into play in handling complaints. As a trainer, you teach the essentials for success on the job. Retraining or additional training may be needed to remove the cause of a task-related complaint. As a counselor, you should be experienced enough to know where to send someone with a complaint that you cannot resolve. As a judge of your employees' performances and behaviors, you are able to appraise their efforts, formally and informally, discovering and dealing with their complaints as you do so. As a spokesperson, you can represent the complaining subordinates to higher or outside authorities, in order to seek fair treatment of their complaints.

A Recommended Approach

The steps that follow will help you to deal effectively with your subordinates' complaints. You should find them useful if your company does not have prescribed complaint procedures.

Functions / Typical Structures	Communication with Individuals (may be on a confidential basis)	Counseling with Individuals (may be on a confidential basis)	Investigation, Conciliation, and Mediation	Adjudication	Upward Feedback: Management Information*
Line supervision	●	●	●	●	●
Personnel/human resources/employee relations	●	●	●	●	●
Multistep appeal systems			●	●	●
Equal opportunity counselors	●	●	●		●
Open-door investigators	●	●	●		●
Ombuds practitioners	●	●	●		●
Work problems counselors	●	●	●		●
In-plant counselors	●	●	●		●
Communications managers	●	●	●		●
Employee coordinators	●	●	●		●
Employee councils		●			●
Advisory boards	●				●
Suggestion-processing committees					●
Standing working groups			●		●

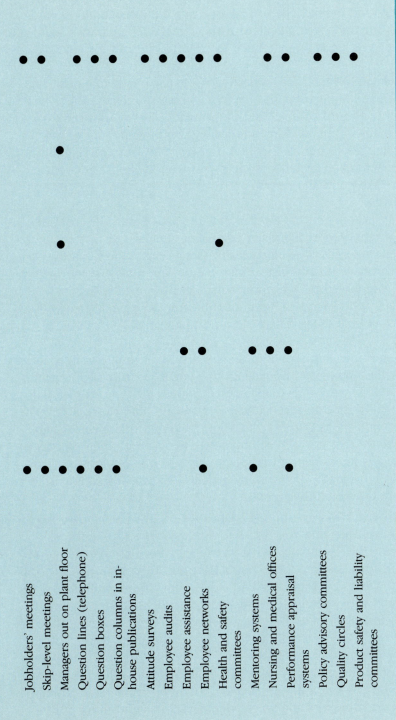

Exhibit 15.1 Typical structures and functions in complaint systems. *Data usually offered in the aggregate to protect confidentiality and privacy. [Reprinted by permission of *Harvard Business Review*. An exhibit from "Are You Hearing Enough Employee Concerns?" by Mary P. Rowe and Michael Baker, *Harvard Business Review* (May–June 1984). Copyright 1984 by the President and Fellows of Harvard College. All rights reserved.]

1. *Listen to the complaint: determine its causes and the complainer's feelings and motives.* Be prepared to give the complaining subordinate your undivided attention. If the complainer's timing is not right for you, set up an appointment as soon as you can for your discussion.

   Remain calm. If the complainer is agitated and emotional, you should be the opposite. You cannot counsel effectively unless you are in control of yourself and the situation. Try to uncover what the complainer is thinking and feeling, by allowing him or her to verbalize his or her feelings and motives. But avoid passing judgment. What you are after is the person's perceptions, not your own. Take notes and reserve your opinions and facts for later in the meeting.

   By listening attentively and drawing people out, you may find that what began as the major complaint gradually slips away as the real and underlying issue comes to the surface. When that happens, you will have hit pay dirt. It may be the first time that the workers were able to express what was really on their minds. Gradually all the facts will emerge in your subordinates' words, and the problem will come into focus. Then and only then can it be intelligently resolved.

   Remember that people frequently just want to talk with someone about their problems. By talking, they are expressing confidence in you and showing respect for your opinion. Often the workers know that the solution to their difficulty is beyond both their control and yours. In discussing such a situation, we often find a clarity and perspective that it is almost impossible to discover alone. The workers may come to realize that the problem is not as serious as they originally thought, or they may actually discover a solution as they attempt to explain their views.

2. *Get the complainers' solutions.* Once your subordinates have talked themselves out, and you feel that you know the real issues, ask them for their solutions. What would they do if they were in your shoes? What do they think would be a fair disposition of their complaint? What you want to know is what they think will make them happy. If it is within your power to grant such a solution, and if you believe it to be a wise one, then do so. If you need more information or wish to check out their side of the story, defer your answer and give them a specific time for receiving it.

   Try to find mutually beneficial solutions that will leave you both better off. Seek a win-win situation where no meaningless compromises are necessary and where no one will have to think of himself or herself as a loser.

3. *Make a decision and explain it.* Before you can make a decision you need to consider who is best qualified to make it. If it is yours to make and you have all the facts you need, give your subordinate your decision and the reasons for it. If higher authorities are involved, identify them. If rules, policy, or procedures are involved, explain their meanings and their applicability to the situation. Your subordinate may not receive the answer that he or she was looking for, but he or she will know that you have done your homework. Let him or her know that you have done your best.

4. *Explain how to appeal.* If your workers are dissatisfied with your decision and want to pursue the matter further, tell them how to do so. Let them know whom they should see and how they can make an appointment. If your workers decide to appeal your decision, you should not hold that action against them, and you should let them know that you do not.

5. *Follow up.* Regardless of the outcome, it is sound management practice to get back to the people who have made a complaint within a reasonable time after its resolution. Assess their present attitudes, and make it clear that you want your people to come to you with their gripes. Be sure you keep a record of the proceedings for future reference.

By being sincere, listening attentively, asking exploratory questions, and acting on each complaint promptly, you will minimize conflicts and reduce barriers to productivity and cooperation.

Maintaining a Nonunion Environment

Essick Air Products employed 150 people in Arkansas when its president, Harry Gaffney, was presented with a petition for an election to certify the United Auto Workers as its union. In the three months—June through August—between the petition and the election, Gaffney mobilized management's efforts to defeat the union. A law firm specializing in labor relations was hired to advise management and to ensure that no labor laws were violated. A formal appraisal system was established, along with improvements in communications between management and workers. Union backers in the company were identified and their arguments countered. The negative aspects of union membership were identified and discussed with workers. Management won the election, and the employees won a new sensitivity to their needs and complaints.[5] Many of the improvements promised by the union were made a part of the company's working environment.

Fred K. Foulkes, professor of management at Boston University's School of Management, has studied the twenty-six largest nonunion industrialized companies in the United States to determine their common attributes, attitudes, and policies. The results are shown in Exhibit 15.2. Together they summarize a strong management concern for employees. Managers at every level have more flexibility to try the new and different. There is no adversary relationship between managers and workers. There is a strong climate of cooperation between the two groups.[6]

Labor Unions

So far in this chapter we have discussed complaints and gripes in companies where there is no union. Let us now shift to companies that are unionized. Before we consider what happens in a company with a union contract, however, we need to take a brief look at unions in the United States.

Union
A group of workers who are employed by a company or an industry or who practice the same skilled craft and have banded together to bargain collectively with their employers

A labor **union** consists of a group of workers who are employed by a company or an industry or who are practicing the same skilled craft and have banded together to bargain collectively with employers for improvements in their wages, hours, fringe benefits, and working conditions. *Craft* or *trade unions* are composed of workers in the same skilled occupation. For example, the International Brotherhood of Electrical Workers (IBEW) and the International Brotherhood of Teamsters, Chauffeurs, Warehousemen, and Helpers of America (usually called the *Teamsters*) are unions organized to represent skilled craftspeople and tradespeople. *Industrial unions* include all workers in a company or an industry, regardless of their specific occupations. The United Auto Workers (UAW) and the United Food and Commercial Workers are two examples of industrial unions.

Employee Associations

Employee association
A group that bargains collectively with management but has given up or has been barred from the right to strike

In addition to the growing number of white-collar workers in unions, about 2.5 million others now belong to **employee associations.** Salaried and professional employees have traditionally resisted attempts to unionize them, but this reluctance has diminished in recent years. Police and fire personnel, nurses, teachers, and university professors have increasingly turned toward *collective bargaining* through the formation of employee associations. These associations differ from unions primarily

1. **A sense of caring.** Top management's commitment to employees is demonstrated not only symbolically but also through certain policies and practices. Hewlet-Packard, for example, is committed to job security, innovative training programs, promotion from within through job posting, cash profit sharing, an attractive stock purchase plan, widely granted stock options, and flexible working hours.

2. **Carefully considered surroundings.** Several situational factors are also important both in fostering an effective personnel program and in encouraging a climate of trust and confidence. These factors include, among others, plant location and size and the handling of "sensitive work" and particular employee groups.

3. **High profits, fast growth, & family ties.** Certain financial and ownership characteristics seem to have an important bearing on personnel policies. Most of the companies studied are profitable—some, extremely so. Many are high technology growth businesses, have dominant market positions, and are leaders in their industries. Growth enables them to offer many promotion opportunities, provide full employment, and make profit sharing pay off. Another important company characteristic is close ties between ownership and management.

4. **Employment security.** Many of these companies attempt to minimize workers' usual nagging uncertainty regarding future employment. . . . methods of weathering peaks and troughs in the work load include hiring freezes and the use of temporary or retired workers. . . . Permitting employees to bank their vacation time can also ensure some flexibility in lean times.

5. **Promotion from within.** A policy of promoting from within—accompanied by training, education, career counselling, and (frequently) job posting—is most attractive when a company's growth rate opens up many advancement opportunities.

6. **Influential personnel departments.** Not only are the personnel departments of the companies studied usually extremely centralized, they also have access to and in many cases are part of top management.

7. **Competitive pay and benefits.** As might be expected, the 26 companies in my sample work hard to ensure that employees perceive their pay and benefits policies as equitable. All of them, therefore, compensate their employees at least as well as their unionized competitors do.

8. **Managements that listen.** The companies studied use a variety of mechanisms to learn employees' views on various matters. Attitude surveys "take the temperature" of the organization and expose developing employee concerns. Some companies regularly conduct "sensing sessions," or random interviews to understand employees' sentiments.

9. **Careful grooming of managers.** Managers in these companies know that effective management of people is an important part of their jobs. Many of the companies studied avoid bonuses that reward short-term performance. Instead, they emphasize long-term results, including successful employee relations.

Exhibit 15.2   **Nine common attributes, attitudes, and policies of twenty-six large nonunion industrialized companies.** (*Source:* From Fred K. Foulkes, ''How Top Nonunion Companies Manage Employees,'' *Harvard Business Review* (September–October 1981). Copyright 1981 by the President and Fellows of Harvard College. All rights reserved.)

because they lack the legal right to strike. Although these groups have occasionally struck in major cities such as New York, Chicago, and San Francisco, they usually do not have the legal right to do so and frequently have been ordered back to work through court injunctions or orders. According to the AFL-CIO, a confederation of our country's largest unions representing about 13 million people, the largest employee associations are the following:

National Education Association

New York State Employee Association

American Nurses Association

Fraternal Order of Police

California State Employee Association

About 40 percent of America's public service employees belong to employee associations. In 1962, President Kennedy signed Executive Order 10988, which required federal agencies to recognize and bargain with the associations that represented a majority of their employees, as determined by secret-ballot elections. Executive Order 11491, issued by President Nixon, further encouraged and improved collective bargaining rights for federal employees. In 1981, President Reagan fired 11,000 air-traffic controllers from our nation's airport control towers for taking a strike action, something they are forbidden by federal law to do.

Why Employees Band Together

Workers join employee associations and unions for many reasons. They want equity, job security, more pay, and better benefits. By banding together, they improve their bargaining position with employers and are better able to avoid unfair and discriminatory treatment.

Better Bargaining Position   Compared with their employers, individuals have little bargaining power. A company can simply make an offer on a take-it-or-leave-it basis—or make no offer at all. The employee is free to say *yes* or *no*. The individual's bargaining power rests on his or her ability to refuse to accept an employment offer or to quit when dissatisfied. But where all of the employees at a company in a trade or department bargain as one with the employer, the business would have to shut down or operate under severe handicaps if the whole group of workers were to strike.

Fair and Uniform Treatment   Pay raises, transfers, promotions, and eligibility requirements for company training programs can be quite arbitrary without union checks on management's prerogatives. Favoritism and discrimination can influence these decisions, resulting in inequities with little hope for appeal. Unions have increasingly pushed for a greater reliance on uniform published procedures when management makes such decisions; thus, there is a heavy reliance on seniority provisions when management is firing, promoting, and the like. The best man or woman may not always get the benefit, but objectivity will bear on the decision. Workers are constantly trying to protect themselves and their financial futures from insecurity.

One of our most basic needs is for safety and security. Safer working conditions have been brought about through union demands and through state and federal legislation. Fringe benefits such as insurance and pension plans are major examples of unions' quest for greater security for their members.

Union Security Provisions

Unions have fought for years to win recognition from employers. They want to increase their strength by requiring all employees to belong to a union once it is recognized as their legitimate bargaining agent. In an election for certification, a union may only win by a slim majority. Those workers who voted against it may not be willing to join the union voluntarily. To counter this resistance, various types of shop agreements have been formulated and won through favorable types of legislation and collective bargaining.

With a *union shop* agreement, all current employees must join the union as soon as it is certified as their legitimate bargaining agent. Newcomers have to join after a specified probationary period—normally thirty days. The majority of union contracts with employers call for a union shop. The union shop is illegal in the twenty states that have enacted right-to-work laws—so named for granting people the right to work with or without membership in a union.

In a *modified union shop,* employees may elect not to join the union that is representing an employer's employees. Part-time employees, students in work-study programs, and people employed before a specified date may refuse to join. At the time that the modified union shop is won through collective bargaining, all members who belong to the union must remain members or lose their jobs. Nonmembers at that time may refuse to join.

In a *maintenance-of-membership shop,* employees who voluntarily join a union must remain in the union during the lifetime of the labor agreement with an employer. It also may provide an escape period during which those who wish to do so may drop their memberships.[7]

Employees do not have to belong to the union under an *agency shop,* but they must pay a fee to the union. The reason for this is that union negotiations benefit all employees—members and nonmembers alike. Since all employees benefit, each should pay his or her share of the costs of winning those benefits.

In an *open shop,* membership in the elected union is voluntary for all existing and new employees. Individuals who decide not to join the union do not have to pay any dues to the union.

A *closed shop* requires an employer to hire only union members. This kind of shop is forbidden by the Taft-Hartley Act (described later in this chapter), but it does exist because of hiring practices in many skilled-craft areas. If a construction company needs skilled tradespeople, it will generally contact a union's hiring hall to fill its employment needs.

Labor Legislation

From colonial days until the 1930s, unions and employee associations were prosecuted and banned by the courts as illegal conspiracies in restraint of trade. Courts uniformly held, in case after case, that these groups of employees wrongfully interfered with the right of employers to run their businesses as they saw fit. Nearly every employee hired during this period accepted as a condition of employment that he or she would not join a union or engage in union activities. A worker who did join was considered to have breached the contract of employment and was subject to immediate dismissal.

In the 1890s, an additional burden was placed on unions by their inclusion under the provisions of the Sherman Antitrust Act (1890) and related antimonopoly legislation. Courts took the position that unions might be considered monopolistic, and their efforts at collective bargaining were viewed as attempts to interfere with a free-market mechanism. This was the first instance in U.S. history that any federal law dealt with the rights of workers to bargain collectively with their employers. Actually the Sherman Act did not specifically state that unions were monopolistic, but its wording was so general that unions could be (and were) construed to fall under its provisions. In 1914, however, the Clayton Act removed unions from the jurisdiction of antitrust laws.

Norris-LaGuardia Act (1932)

Further relief came in 1932 with the enactment of the Norris-LaGuardia Act, which severely restricted the use of court orders (*injunctions*) against

organized labor engaged in labor disputes with employees. It also out-
lawed the use of *yellow-dog contracts* by which employees were forced to
agree not to join a union. No laws, however, required an employer to
recognize an employees' union or prevented an employer from starting a
company union. Employers began to require that new employees join the
company union, which was controlled by the management and operated
for its benefit. The union leaders achieved for their members only the
benefits that management wanted them to.

The Norris-LaGuardia Act did not attack the practice of blacklisting,
nor did it forbid the discharge of employees for union activities. Companies were still in control, and by locking their employees out of their shops
(*lockouts*), they could outlast, in most cases, the workers' enthusiasm for
unionization. Since many workers lived on subsistence wages, they could
not hold out for very long.

National Labor Relations Act (1935)

As the Great Depression dragged on, Congress began to analyze its causes
and soon realized that the mass impoverishment of so many workers had
been a significant factor. To achieve a balance of power between labor and
management, the National Labor Relations Act (often called the *Wagner
Act*) was passed as one of the measures of the New Deal. It has often been
referred to as organized labor's Magna Carta (great charter or birth certificate), because it guaranteed the rights of unions to exist free from legal
prosecution. It gave the individual worker the right to join a union without fear of persecution by his or her employer. In the words of Section 7
of the act:

> employees shall have the right to self-organization, to form, join or as-
> sist labor organizations, to bargain collectively through representatives of
> their own choosing, and to engage in concerted activities for the purpose
> of collective bargaining or other mutual aid or protection.

The Wagner Act also listed as unfair practices the following management activities by employers:

- Restraining employees from joining a union
- Contributing financially to or interfering in any way with union
  operations
- Discriminating in any way against a worker because of his or her
  union affiliation
- Punishing union members who reported management violations of
  the act

■ Refusing to bargain in good faith with a duly elected union of their employees

The second and third prohibitions above are most significant to supervisors. These provisions have been interpreted as forbidding management from making threats or promises of financial gain to employees who are considering union affiliation or who are about to engage in an election to determine a bargaining agent.

The Wagner Act also established the National Labor Relations Board (NLRB), consisting of five members appointed by the president of the United States and empowered to investigate alleged violations of the act and to oversee elections to determine a bargaining unit. Its decisions have the power of law and bind both unions and employers. The Wagner Act was challenged in the courts, but it was declared constitutional by the Supreme Court. It was so prolabor, however, that it eventually had to be amended to curb some of the labor excesses it helped to create.

Labor-Management Relations Act (1947)

During the years between the passage of the Wagner Act and the end of World War II, the country witnessed a phenomenal growth in union membership and also in abuses of union power. Organized labor grew from about 4 million members in 1935 to about 15 million (35 percent of the work force) by 1947. Unions were becoming a powerful force and were exercising financial and economic power that was almost totally unchecked. Postwar strikes threatened the economy. While management's hands had been tied, organized labor's hands had not.

Congress again felt compelled to balance the two forces. Despite the protests of labor and a veto of the bill by President Truman, it passed the Labor-Management Relations Act, usually called the *Taft-Hartley Act*. The act was intended to curb many of the abuses that organized labor had been guilty of in the 1930s. It amended the Wagner Act to include a list of provisions against specific practices by unions:

1. Workers could not be coerced to join or not to join a union.
2. The closed shop was prohibited.
3. Unions were required to bargain in good faith.
4. Complex restrictions were placed on certain kinds of strikes and boycotts. The *secondary boycott,* by which the union forces an employer to stop dealing with or purchasing from another company not directly involved in a labor dispute, was prohibited. (A *primary boycott* is the union's refusal to deal with a company with which it

NEWS
You Can Use

Replacing Striking Workers

Since 1938, companies experiencing strikes have been legally entitled to replace striking workers with permanent new hires. The practice was not widespread until the 1980s, beginning with the 1981 firing of the air-traffic controllers who were systematically replaced over a period of years when they went on strike. Following soon after, Phelps Dodge and Continental Airlines broke their unions by hiring nonunion replacements for their striking employees. In 1989, the Supreme Court ruled 6–3 that striking workers are not legally entitled to get their jobs back once their positions have been filled by nonstrikers with less seniority. In 1990, Greyhound began hiring replacement drivers even before its negotiations with the Amalgamated Transit Union were at an impasse. After a bitter and long strike, thousands of drivers for Greyhound had no jobs to return to. The increasing use of this tactic by companies has discouraged several unions from striking, agreeing instead to continue talking once the contract runs out. Not every employer can hire replacements because many need the kinds of employees that are in short supply, especially during times of low unemployment.

does have a labor dispute.) Also prohibited were jurisdictional strikes, which were designed to force an employer to give work to one union rather than to another.

5. Unions could not charge their members excessively high initiation fees.

6. Employers were not required to pay for services not performed (*featherbedding*).

The Taft-Hartley Act also gives management the right to sue a union for violating collective bargaining agreements. Other provisions require unions to make annual disclosures of their financial records and allow states to enact right-to-work laws.

An emergency provision in the Taft-Hartley Act allows the president of the United States, through the attorney general's office, to seek a court injunction to stop a strike or lockout that threatens the nation's general health or welfare. The injunction can last for up to eighty days. During this cooling-off period, the federal government attempts to mediate the disputes that are separating the parties. The National Labor Relations Board can hold a secret-ballot vote among the striking or locked-out union members after the injunction is sixty days old, to see if the company's latest offer is acceptable.

Representation Elections

The National Labor Relations Board (NLRB) has established procedures that must be followed by both management and workers when the latter express their desire to be represented by a union. The *certification* process (the process of getting the NLRB to certify a particular union as the legitimate bargaining agent for employees) begins when at least 30 percent of the workers sign authorization cards calling for a union to represent them. Then the workers can ask the NLRB to schedule a representation (certification) election.

Once the NLRB determines that the company falls within its jurisdiction (some companies may have too small a sales volume), it must determine how to form appropriate bargaining units. Separate unions may be called for to represent such groups as general service and maintenance workers, office and clerical workers, and technicians. An election for each will then be scheduled and conducted by NLRB representatives. Once the election is held, the results tabulated, and the disputes settled, the NLRB certifies a bargaining agent. The employer is then obligated to enter into negotiations with the certified union toward a collective bargaining agreement.

The effort by employees to get rid of their bargaining agent (union) works in the same way as the process of obtaining such an agent. *Decertification,* as it is called, first requires 30 percent of the bargaining agent's members to call for a decertification election.

The Supervisor's Role During Representation Elections

Your job is the same as any other manager's during employee certification or decertification elections: remain neutral and preserve an atmosphere in which workers can express their uninhibited choices. In general, do nothing that is not expressly OK'd by higher management. Do not express your opinions—pro or con—toward unions or union membership by your subordinates. Make no threats and make no promises. Do not give or announce any increases in pay or benefits just before or during representation elections, unless the increases are totally unrelated to the election campaigns.

You may point out to workers the economic costs that are connected to union membership. Such costs include the dues paid to support union officers and activities, the costs of processing employee complaints through the union contract's complaint procedures, and the costs connected with strikes that take people off the payroll. You may also point out that both the union contract and its constitution place restrictions on workers. Rules and punishments are prescribed in both.

Labor Relations

The area of **labor relations** includes all the activities within a company that involve dealings with a union and its members, both individually and collectively. Specifically, two main areas are the most important and time consuming: **collective bargaining** (arriving at a contract that covers workers' wages, hours, and working conditions) and **grievance processing** (dealing with complaints that allege violations of the collective bargaining agreement).

Collective Bargaining

Bargaining collectively—the union representatives on one side of a table, management's representatives on the other—is the traditional way in which labor disputes are settled and labor-management agreements are formed. Some time in advance of the expiration date of a labor contract, the two groups begin a series of meetings that ultimately lead to the signing of a new agreement. Bargaining may take place on the local level, where only one local union and employer are involved, or on an industry-wide basis, where the agreement sets the standard for the industry— as in the automotive and trucking industries.

The usual process involves a specialist in labor relations from the company's labor relations department (usually at the vice-presidential level) and the union's negotiating committee. Both sides employ labor lawyers who are well versed in the most recent developments in labor law and who help them in hammering out specific contract provisions and wording.

Both sides bring to the bargaining a list of demands and, in their own minds, assign to each a priority that will become apparent as negotiations develop. Some demands are made merely to serve as trading material. Negotiating involves give and take, so each side must be prepared to bargain away some of its demands in order to obtain others.

Each side attempts to resolve the many minor issues as quickly as it can, reserving the major issues for the final meetings immediately preceding or following a strike. It is then that the pressure for a settlement is greatest. Ultimately, through compromises and trading, a new contract emerges. No one is anxious to be labeled a winner or a loser. Rather, both sides seek to improve their positions and eliminate problem areas that stand in the way of harmony and efficient output. The agreement is then offered to the union membership, who vote to accept or reject it. A simple majority vote is usually required.

The union contract with management spells out in rather precise terms the rights of workers with regards to rates, hours, and conditions of employment. It is a formal written document that both managers and union members must thoroughly understand. It can and does limit management's authority. Both parties must operate within the restrictions it lays down if they are to avoid costly and time-consuming work stoppages and disagreements. As always, outside experts stand ready to help supervisors and union members with interpretations of the contract.

Enforcing the Labor Contract

Enforcement of the terms of the agreement worked out through collective bargaining depends on communication of the contract provisions and of the demands they make on labor and management. Managers—especially those who direct workers—must be made aware of their rights and duties. Copies of the agreement are made available to each manager, along with an explanation that is easy to understand. Any questions that may arise in a manager's mind can quickly be answered by consultation with the personnel department and with labor-relations officials.

The union also must make its members aware of their rights and duties. Copies of the contract are distributed to each member, and meetings are held locally to explain the contract's terms. At the plant and department levels, workers may turn to their steward for guidance in understanding the contract and in dealing with any alleged violations of it.

The Supervisor and the Steward

Steward
The union's elected or appointed first-line representative in the areas in which workers are found

The **steward** is first of all an employee and a worker. He or she has the additional responsibilities of a union office because the union members have elected or appointed him or her. Stewards receive release time from work to carry out their duties. Exhibit 15.3 lists the differences and similarities that exist between the roles of supervisor and steward. More points draw them together than keep them apart.

Just as a supervisor is management's spokesperson, a steward is labor's spokesperson. He or she has the duty to represent workers in the early stages of the grievance process. The steward must be able to interpret the contract both to the supervisor and to fellow workers, if he or she is to carry out the role intelligently. A worker's complaint usually cannot win the union's backing without the steward's consent.

Stewards, like managers, have a difficult and demanding position. They are workers and must conform to company standards or risk disciplinary action. On the other hand, they have the status of elected union officers who, if they wish to retain their posts, must be effective represen-

Supervisors	Stewards
Know the contract	Know the contract
Enforce the contract	Enforce the contract
Look out for the welfare of subordinates	Look out for the welfare of constituents
Are spokespersons for both management and subordinates	Are spokespersons for the union and constituents
Settle grievances fairly (in line with management's interpretation of the contract)	Settle grievances fairly (in line with union interpretations of the contract)
Keep abreast of grievance solutions and changes in contract interpretation	Keep abreast of grievance solutions and changes in contract interpretation
Maintain good working relationships with stewards	Maintain good working relationship with supervisors
Keep stewards informed about management's decisions and sources of trouble	Keep supervisors informed about union positions and sources of trouble
Protect management rights	Protect labor rights

Exhibit 15.3 **The responsibilities of supervisors and stewards in labor relations.**

tatives of and counsels to their constituents. They may, therefore, feel a good deal of pressure to push complaints to grievance status, even when their own best judgment says they should not. In circumstances where there are few complaints or grievances, some stewards feel the need to dig for some issues or manufacture some discontent in order to justify their position and to prove that they are serving a useful purpose.

Just how stewards behave is largely an individual matter, influenced in part by their supervisors and by the kind of relationship they have. Where there is room for interpretation, stewards are bound to take the union's view, just as supervisors are bound to accept management's. Therein lies the stuff of which grievances are made.

Handling Grievances

Grievance
Any alleged violation of the collective bargaining agreement as filed by management or labor

When a worker is dissatisfied with a supervisor's disposition of a work-related complaint, he or she may appeal that decision by filing a formal charge called a **grievance.** All grievances allege that a violation has occurred to one or another of the provisions of the labor agreement. A complaint that is improperly handled can and usually does become a grievance. Managers should consider every gripe about wages, hours, and

DOs

- Begin by considering every complaint to have merit.
- Give the grieving employee your time and listen carefully to each word.
- Identify the specific contractual wording that the grievance alleges was violated.
- Visually check out the location where the grievance supposedly took place.
- Interview every person who may have knowledge of the grievance, the parties to it, the event, the location, and the circumstances.
- After gathering all your facts, check out all past grievances that have a bearing on this one.
- Hold all your interviews and discussions with concerned parties in private.
- Before giving any answer to the grievance, touch base with your boss.
- Give your answer as completely as you can within any time limit prescribed by the union contract.
- Keep written records of all your findings, your interviews, and your answers.

DON'Ts

- Settle any grievance outside the terms of the written contract.
- Engage in trading one grievance settlement for the withdrawal of another.
- Engage in bargaining over issues that are not part of the written contract.
- Agree to any changes in the precise wording of the contract.
- Fail to deliver any remedy endorsed by the parties as a settlement for the grievance.

Exhibit 15.4   **Dos and dont's for the supervisor when handling a grievance.**

working conditions a potential grievance. Managers, as well as workers, can and do file grievances.

A grievance is not a personal attack on or an insult to a supervisor; it is a problem to be solved. The first thing you must do is keep calm and listen. Do not start an argument. Grievance discussions can become heated debates, and words may be said that will be regretted later. Grievances that are not properly settled in their early stages can grow into very costly and damaging disputes. Exhibit 15.4 contains do's and dont's for you to follow while handling a grievance.

If the details of the grievance are not clear to you after you hear the complaining employee's case, ask questions. Find out the what, when, where, why, and how. Find out exactly what the person believes will make him or her happy and what provisions of the labor contract are involved.

Conduct your own investigation to determine whether or not the facts presented to you are complete and true. If they are not or if you are

1. *Who is affected?* List the names, numbers, and departments of all workers and management representatives involved.

2. *What is it about?* Lost time? Pay shortage? Seniority violation?

3. *Is it a contract violation?* If so, state the clause and how company or union action violates it.

4. *When did it happen?* Report the exact time or period when the grievance was suffered. If it concerns lost time or retroactive pay, report the exact dates for which time or pay is due.

5. *Where did it happen?* This is especially important in cases involving a health or safety hazard.

6. *Why did it happen?* Was the incident simply a clerical error? Was a worker unjustly penalized?

7. *What is the demand?* What specific action or remedy did the worker and the steward request?

8. *Did you obtain signatures and dates?* If any written petition was handed in, did you obtain the signatures and dates of the writer and steward?

9. *Did you distribute copies to the proper persons?* If you prepared a report on the grievance incident, have you made certain that all the interested parties have a copy of it?

Exhibit 15.5 **A checklist to be used when putting a grievance into writing.**

uncertain about any of them, list your questions and gather the evidence needed to clarify the situation. If you are unsure about the proper interpretation or application of the specific language of the labor contract, seek counsel from the labor-relations specialists.

If you determine that the grievance is without merit, give the worker and the steward your facts, your (management's) interpretation and application of the labor-contract provisions, and your specific reasons for denying the grievance.

Your oral answer to the complaining employee may not be acceptable to him or her or to the steward. If it is not, your involvement may be far from ended. You will probably be given a written copy of the complaint and asked to spell out in specific language the answer you gave orally. You will probably be questioned by various labor-relations people and union officials during later phases of the grievance procedure.

If your oral answer is accepted by the complaining employee and the union steward, prepare a written record of the complaint and your disposition of it. Just be certain that the remedy you grant is within your power to give and has your boss's approval.

When writing up a grievance, use the checklist in Exhibit 15.5 to make certain that you have included the necessary information. It often becomes necessary to refer to your written records later, when similar situations arise or when the grievance advances beyond your influence.

The Grievance Procedure

Where a union and a labor agreement exist, a formal procedure for handling grievances will be outlined and explained in the collective agreement. Exhibit 15.6 shows typical procedures for small and large unionized companies. The following procedure applies to large organizations:

1. *The supervisor meets with the steward and the employee filing the grievance.* After the steward has agreed with a worker that the handling of his or her complaint was inadequate and that there is the possibility of an infringement on the contract terms, the steward brings the formal grievance back to a supervisor and attempts to work out a solution.

   Every effort is made in this initial step to resolve the conflict. Both the union and management want to eliminate the time and expense of further discussion and debate.

   If, after hearing them out, the supervisor believes nothing new has been added to change the situation, he or she will stick to the original decision. It is understood, however, that the manager has researched the issue carefully and consulted with the various specialists available before reaching the decision that led to the grievance.

2. *The supervisor's immediate superior and/or a representative from the labor-relations department meets with the chief steward.* A middle manager, usually with the counsel of a labor-relations expert, sits down with the company's chief steward—the person who is in charge of all the other stewards and who speaks on behalf of the union. Issues are examined to determine if any precedents (agreed-to settlements from earlier grievance processing) apply. If no solution can be agreed on, the grievance advances to the next step.

3. *The labor-relations director and/or the plant and division manager meets with the union committee members.* The union grievance committee is usually composed of several stewards, including the chief steward, and one or more representatives from the union local. Costs and time devoted to the problem are increasing, and both sides will want to solve the issues as quickly and as equitably as they can.

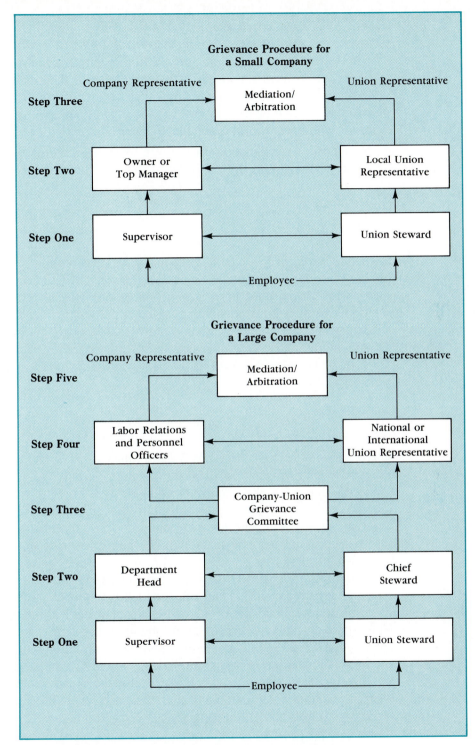

Grievance Procedure for a Small Company

Step Three — Company Representative — Mediation/Arbitration — Union Representative

Step Two — Owner or Top Manager ↔ Local Union Representative

Step One — Supervisor ↔ Union Steward

Employee

Grievance Procedure for a Large Company

Step Five — Company Representative — Mediation/Arbitration — Union Representative

Step Four — Labor Relations and Personnel Officers ↔ National or International Union Representative

Step Three — Company-Union Grievance Committee

Step Two — Department Head ↔ Chief Steward

Step One — Supervisor ↔ Union Steward

Employee

Exhibit 15.6 **Typical grievance procedures for a small and a large unionized organization.** (*Source:* Reprinted with permission of the authors from *Personal and Industrial Relations,* 3d ed. by John B. Miner and Mary Green Miner. Copyright © 1977 Macmillan Publishing Company.)

4. *A member or members of top management discuss the issues with a representative or group from the national or international union that chartered the local union whose member initiated the grievance.* If a local independent union is involved that has no affiliation with a national or international union, the local's attorney and business agent will meet with management's representatives.

5. *Mediation or arbitration is carried out.* A neutral third party intervenes, meeting with the personnel involved in the dispute at steps 1 through 4.

Mediation

Mediation
The use of a neutral third party in a labor/management dispute to recommend a solution to the issues that divide the parties

Mediation brings in the expertise of a neutral outsider who is allied with neither labor nor management. He or she is invited to try to bring the two sides together and, after hearing both points of view, to recommend a solution. The decision is not binding on either party. Often the mediator is a distinguished public official, such as a mayor or a judge, who has a fine reputation and whose insights, wisdom, and power are respected by both sides. He or she usually serves in the public interest, without pay of any kind.

Arbitration

Arbitration
The use of a neutral third party in a dispute between management and labor to resolve the areas of conflict

In **arbitration** a neutral third party is again called in. He or she is a professional arbitrator recommended by the American Arbitration Association (AAA), the Federal Mediation and Conciliation Service (FMCS), or one of the various state agencies set up for this purpose. Arbitrators usually serve with pay. In a typical year, the AAA and the FMCS process about 23,000 grievances through arbitration. About as many grievances are arbitrated through other agencies.

The arbitrator conducts hearings into the dispute, calling witnesses, recording testimony, and, in general, conducting the proceedings in much the same manner that a court of law uses to conduct a hearing. It may be quite informal, however, depending on the arbitrator's style. When he or she announces a decision, it is binding on both union and management.

Normally, grievances are not put into writing until they progress from the first step to the second. This is especially true in large corporations, where the number of grievances is quite large and where the majority are usually solved at the steward-supervisor level. From this step on, the number of people involved increases, as does the need for precise language. Since the complainant and the steward are not present in the later steps, their thoughts and those of the supervisor must be put in writing.

Instant Replay

1. Complaints are serious matters to be dealt with in a serious way. In a unionized organization, complaints can and often do turn into grievances.

2. Handling complaints requires honesty, sincerity, and an open discussion of all the relevant facts and emotions involved. As a supervisor, you must treat them seriously. Your subordinates do.

3. The grievance procedure begins when you and a subordinate or the union steward meet to discuss a formal complaint alleging a violation of a union contract and cannot agree on a solution.

4. When you manage in a union environment, you must know your labor agreement's provisions and the results of grievances that act to explain and define its limits.

5. You need to know federal and state laws that regulate your treatment of employees in all matters—not just in labor-relations areas.

6. Develop a cooperative relationship with your steward. You are not enemies or adversaries. Both of you are paid to look out for special interests and to reach accommodations when it is in your mutual interests to do so.

7. Unions exist to serve their members. In many companies, they are a fact of life.

Glossary **Arbitration** the use of a neutral third party in a dispute between labor and management to resolve the areas of conflict. It may be binding and compulsory.

Collective bargaining the process of negotiating a union agreement that will govern wages, hours, and working conditions for employees who are union members.

Complaint any expression of unhappiness with working conditions or on-the-job relationships that comes to a manager's attention.

Employee association a group that bargains collectively with management but has given up or has been barred by law from the right to strike.

Grievance any alleged violation of the collective bargaining agreement as filed by management or labor.

Grievance processing settling an alleged violation of the collective bargaining agreement in accordance with the method outlined in the labor agreement.

Labor relations   management activities that are created by the fact that the organization has a union or unions to bargain with. The two major labor-relations duties are collective bargaining and grievance processing.

Mediation   the use of a neutral third party in a dispute between labor and management to recommend a solution to the issues that divide the two parties. The recommendations of a mediator are not binding or compulsory.

Steward   the union's elected or appointed first-line representative in the areas in which workers are found.

Union   a group of workers who are employed by a company or an industry or who practice the same skilled craft and have banded together to bargain collectively with their employers with one voice—the union's. A union possesses the right to strike.

Questions for Class Discussion

1. Can you define this chapter's key terms?
2. How should a supervisor handle complaints in a logical way?
3. What does the Wagner Act prohibit?
4. What does the Taft-Hartley Act prohibit?
5. In what ways are the supervisor and the steward similar? In what ways are their labor-relations roles different?
6. Can you outline a typical grievance procedure for a large organization? What might be left out in a small company?

Incident

Purpose To determine what your attitudes are toward unions.

Your Task After each statement below, indicate if you agree or disagree with it. After you have taken the quiz, check the key that follows and discuss your choices with your classmates. Try to discover why you feel as you do.

	Agree	Disagree
1. Without unions, most managements would act in an arbitrary and unfair manner toward their workers.	_____	_____
2. Unions, for the most part, are helping companies to become more productivity and quality oriented.	_____	_____
3. The standard of living enjoyed by most American workers today is in large part a result of the power and influence of unions.	_____	_____
4. Today, unions are more concerned with their own survival than with improving the competitiveness of the areas they have organized.	_____	_____

5. Union members generally have more rights and freedoms on the job than do their nonunion counterparts.   _____   _____

6. Without unions, employees would have little influence over management decisions.   _____   _____

7. The primary reason why people elect to join unions is to gain more economic benefits for themselves.   _____   _____

8. Most unions are controlled by their leaders, not by their members.   _____   _____

9. Unions are still necessary in some industries and working environments to help to guarantee just and fair treatment for employees.   _____   _____

10. The supervisor's job would be much easier if he or she did not have to worry about a union and its contract.   _____   _____

Scoring: You are prounion if you answered seven or more questions as follows: (1) agree, (2) agree, (3) agree, (4) disagree, (5) agree, (6) agree, (7) disagree, (8) disagree, (9) agree, (10) disagree.

Case Problem 15.1   An Intoxicating Experience

Red Hastings entered the break area and noticed Pauline Brown in an animated conversation with her peers. Pauline was talking in a very loud voice that seemed to pierce the air. When she laughed, it felt as though the room's mirror would break. Red thought that her words were slurred and that she looked and was behaving as though she was intoxicated. As Pauline's supervisor, he was concerned. If she was loaded, he thought, she would have to return to the office for an additional two hours of work. Sloppy work on her part could cause his department real problems.

Red sat across the room from her until her break ended and she and her coworkers began to leave. He signaled for her to stay and talk but she hastily left the area. He followed, only to see her enter the women's locker area. He waited for nearly fifteen minutes until she emerged. Red confronted Pauline as follows:

"You have been drinking, haven't you?"

"I have not," Pauline replied.

"Don't lie to me, Pauline. I watched you

on break and you were a textbook example of a drunk."

"I resent being called a drunk," Pauline answered as she took off at a fast pace to her work station. Red felt that he had smelled the distinct odor of alcohol on her breath as she passed him. Red followed her to the office and watched her carefully for nearly one-half hour. He did not talk with her again but did check her work as she generated it and it was perfect.

Red was puzzled. Pauline had worked for him for over eleven months and he had never noticed the kind of behavior she exhibited today. He had had many conversations with her and had never smelled alcohol on her breath.

After all the office personnel had left, Red decided to check Pauline's work area. He found a large bottle of mouth wash in her bottom drawer. Its label read: "12% alcohol." In her wastebasket he found a crushed paper bag. As he unfolded it a receipt fell from the bag. It was from the local liquor store and in the amount of $3.79. "Just enough for a pint," he thought.

Red returned to his office to check the company's policy manual. "Just as I thought," he said to himself. ". . . an employee who reports to work intoxicated can be fired."

Questions

1. If you were Red, what course of action would you pursue if the company had no unions?

2. How might your course of action change if you were Red and worked in a union environment?

3. What alternatives does a company have when faced with an employee with an alcohol problem?

Case Problem 15.2   Suspension with Pay?

Lennie Dawson swung around in his swivel chair to greet Shirley Masters and Ruby Blake.

"Sit down, Shirley and Ruby. Now what has gotten into you two lately? Shirley, you have been with us two months, and I don't have any record of trouble with you before this morning. How come all of a sudden you get yourself in trouble?"

"I haven't been myself lately, Mr. Dawson. My husband and I are having difficulties. My mind can't seem to concentrate on anything else."

"And what's your excuse, Ruby?" asked Lennie.

"Shirley has been getting on my nerves lately. She's become unbearable. We work side by side, and all day long she mutters and mumbles to herself under her breath. I ask her a simple question and she won't answer. I can't take it anymore. You have to separate us."

"Look here, you two, I've got a department to run and have no time for petty squabbles. Ruby, you can't get along with anyone, so far as I can see. Two months ago it was Hazel Dumbrowski, and before that you picked a fight with Liz Turner."

"Mr. Dawson, you know I tried to get on with them. I really did. It's not my fault that they were jealous of my bonus checks and higher salary. They just resented the fact that I earned more than they did."

Lennie was getting upset and beginning to show it.

"That's ancient history. What I want to know, Ruby, is did you or did you not throw Shirley's purse at her?"

"Yes, but . . ."

"That's all I need to know. Take three days off without pay, starting now. The next time you goof off, I'm going to make it a week. I . . ."

"Mr. Dawson," Shirley interrupted, "it was really my fault. I started it by telling Ruby to shut her face, and when she didn't, I pushed her work off her desk. That's when she threw my purse."

"Shirley, it is noble of you to try to get Ruby off the hook. But she has had too many of these incidents before. Her file has several warnings for similar occurrences. She needs time off to cool off. Now, since this is your first offense, Shirley, I am going to give you a written reprimand which will go into your personnel file downstairs. If you get involved with Ruby like this again, you will join her with a week at home."

Ruby then turned to Lennie and asked, "Are you going to separate us?"

"No. You two have got to learn to get along."

The two women left the office together.

"Ruby, why didn't you tell him I started the whole thing?"

"Listen, Shirley, you're new here. Once that guy gets something on you, he never forgets it. He had already made up his mind that I was at fault. There's no use arguing. I'll see the shop steward and file a grievance. Don't worry! I'll get three days off with pay."

Questions

1. Using Exhibit 15.5, put Ruby's grievance in writing.
2. Using Exhibit 15.3 and assuming the role of Ruby's union steward, indicate which responsibilities you consider most important in this case.
3. Evaluate Lennie's efforts at getting the facts.
4. Do you think Ruby will win her grievance? Why?
5. Assuming a nonunion environment in this case and ignoring the last three sentences of the case, what would you do if you were Lennie's boss and Ruby came to you with her complaint?

Notes

1. M. P. Rowe and M. Baker, "Are You Hearing Enough Employee Concerns?" *Harvard Business Review* (May–June 1984): 130.
2. Ibid., 130–33.
3. Ibid., 128–30.
4. Ibid., 133–34.
5. Harry Gaffney, "We Beat the Union," *Inc.* (November 1980): 62–68.
6. Fred K. Foulkes, "How Top Nonunion Companies Manage Employees," *Harvard Business Review* (September–October 1981): 90.
7. H. J. Chruden and A. W. Sherman, Jr., *Personnel Management: The Utilization of Human Resources,* 6th ed. (Cincinnati: South-Western Publishing, 1980), 387.

Suggested Readings

Baer, Walter E. *Grievance Handling: 101 Guides for Supervisors.* New York: American Management Association, 1970.

Caruth, Don, and Mills, Harry N. "Working Toward Better Union Relations." *Supervisory Management* 30 (February 1985): 7–13.

Foegen, J. H. "Labor Unions: Don't Count them Out Yet!" *Academy of Management Executive,* 3 (1989): 67–69.

Fossum, J. A. *Labor Relations: Development, Structure, Process.* 4th ed. Dallas: Business Publications, 1989.

Freeman, Richard B., and Medoff, James L. *What Do Unions Do?* New York: Basic Books, 1984.

Fruhan, William E., Jr. "Management, Labor, and the Golden Goose." *Harvard Business Review* (September–October 1985): 131–41.

Kerr, Steven, and Hill, Kenneth D. "The First-Line Supervisor: Phasing Out or Here to Stay?" *Academy of Management Review* 11 (1986): 105–8.

Kochan, Thomas A.; Katz, Harry C.; and McKersie, Robert B. *The Transformation of American Industrial Relations.* New York: Basic Books, 1986.

Sibbernsen, Richard D. "What Arbitrators Think About Technology Replacing Labor." *Harvard Business Review* (March–April 1986): 8–16.

Tidwell, Gary L. "The Supervisor's Role in a Union Election." *Personnel Journal* 62 (August 1983): 640–45.

16 Security, Safety, and Health

Outline

Objectives

After reading and discussing this chapter, you should be able to do the following:

1 Define the key terms.

2 Outline security measures that supervisors can take to safeguard the office and shop from theft by employees.

3 Describe a supervisor's duties in the event of a fire and with regard to fire prevention.

4 Outline procedures open to supervisors to prevent loss from vandalism.

5 Describe the purposes of the Occupational Safety and Health Act.

6 Describe the enforcement procedures and an employer's rights with regard to OSHA inspectors.

Key Terms

accident

computer virus

ergonomics

health

OSHA

safety

security

vandalism

workers' compensation

Introduction

As the title of this chapter implies, we are concerned here with the supervisor's duties in the following areas:

Security
Efforts at protecting physical facilities and nonhuman assets from loss or damage

- **Security**—protecting physical facilities and nonhuman resources from loss or damage

- **Safety**—protecting people from accidents and injuries

Safety
Efforts at protecting human resources from accidents and injuries

- **Health**—the general condition of a person physically and emotionally, and efforts at preventing illness and treating injuries when they occur

Our focus will be on prevention—the ways in which supervisors can head off trouble and minimize damage to their company's human and

Health
The general condition of a person physically, mentally, and emotionally and efforts at preventing illness and treating injuries when they occur

material resources. We shall explore what supervisors are expected and required to do to help protect these resources. Your duties with regard to security and safety begin with the screening of new applicants and continue on a daily basis as you carry out your managerial functions. Keep in mind that supervisors usually have assistance in the areas of safety, security, and health from various staff managers. The larger the company, the more assistance supervisors can expect.

In directing the employees, you can help them avoid accidents and prevent theft through training and discipline. In organizing your department, you can build a structure for preventing accidents and enforcing safety rules. In planning, you can design programs, procedures, and practices that will help carry out management policies and coincide with state and federal safety standards. You can construct effective preventive, diagnostic, and therapeutic controls to deal with safety and security problems. Through effective communications, committee action, and peer-group cooperation, you can ensure the coordination of safety and security efforts throughout the company.

Physical Security

Each year businesses lose billions of dollars through thefts by customers, employees, owners, and outside criminals. Thefts of employee property cause suspicion, low morale, dollar losses, and employee turnover. Thefts of a company's assets result in increased costs, a loss in productivity, and higher prices for the products and services it has to sell. Keeping their employees' and their own property secure from theft costs employers billions of dollars each year.

Employee Theft

The largest cause of loss to most American businesses is employee theft. Surveys routinely disclose that companies from every industry have experienced employee theft. In May 1991, the U.S. Attorney for the northern district of Illinois announced indictments for three high-ranking former First National Bank of Chicago executives, charging them with operating a multimillion-dollar kickback scheme involving local real estate developers and a former Chicago official.[1] In December of 1988, Du Pont Corporation received an ultimatum from an industrial spy: deliver $10 million or competitors would learn the company's secrets for making the artificial fiber Lycra. With the help of the FBI, Swiss police caught the spy and his accomplices, all former Du Pont employees. A study done recently showed that 48 percent of 150 companies surveyed have experienced similar black-mail attempts.[2] The motivations given by thieving employees range from taking an "extra" reward for working a tough shift to taking revenge for what an employee perceives as too low a wage.[3]

As the above paragraph indicates, employees steal money and secrets. For money and other motives, employees steal vital information about product designs, marketing plans, customers, finances, and research projects. This information in the competition's hands can do great harm. Such losses of information occur through managers who talk too much to the wrong people, the careless disposal of trash and waste paper, the failure to use computer access codes, and uncontrolled access to information by visitors and vendors. Finally, much information is lost to competitors when they hire away knowledgeable employees.[4]

Electronic thieves working from within a business steal as much as $3 billion each year through a variety of schemes. Computer criminals can siphon money from business accounts into their personal accounts; they can create phony charges from nonexistent vendors and then authorize payment of those charges. Most computer crimes are committed by programmers, computer operators, clerks, bank tellers, executives, and disgruntled or fired employees. Losses to computer thieves tend to be much larger than losses to "conventional" thieves. According to Ernst & Whinney's recent report on computer fraud, 51 percent of the 240 companies surveyed had been victims of computer crime, and the average loss amounted to $600,000.[5] The accounting firm's survey also indicates that computer crime is increasing because there are more computers and because criminals are getting more sophisticated each year.

Computer virus
A rogue computer program that can reproduce itself endlessly, destroying stored data

Two recent problems have surfaced in regard to electronic security: the computer virus and the bugging of facsimile machines. A **computer virus** is a rogue computer program (usually planted by a disgruntled employee or a computer "hacker") that can reproduce itself endlessly, thus displacing and destroying stored information. It usually hides in computer software until triggered by routine computer uses or by the arrival of a specific time. In January 1990, the most infamous inventor of a computer virus was found guilty of unleashing a virus that crippled a nationwide network of thousands of computers. A 1986 federal computer fraud and abuse law was used to convict the former graduate student, resulting in a five-year jail sentence and a $250,000 fine.[6]

Facsimile (fax) machines use telephone lines to transmit printed copy. These machines can be tapped into by making a secret connection with the telephone lines of the party whose fax messages are to be intercepted. Readily available equipment is sold through most electronics stores. Imagine the theft that is possible today by tapping into and receiving messages from a competitor's facsimile machines.[7]

Employees also steal time from their employers, and that means a loss of dollars and productivity. According to Robert Half International, an executive recruiting firm, employee theft of time translates into a loss of $170 billion per year. The 330 executives surveyed indicated that the average employee "steals" 4 hours and 29 minutes each week. Of those surveyed, 84 percent believed that workers under 30 steal the most time.[8]

Cures For controlling theft by employees, a "corporate policy and guidelines are the first lines of defense . . . experts say."[9] Microprocessor-controlled cash registers virtually eliminate chances to steal from these machines, but preventing theft by computers is more difficult. August Bequai, a Washington, D.C., attorney and author specializing in computer crime, offers five major tips for prevention:

- **Put out the word:** Managers must warn employees that the company frowns on computer crime, whether it be theft of a floppy disk or information from a data base, and that it will prosecute offenders. When a crime occurs, you have to make good on your word.

- **Name a contact:** Employees should have somebody to talk to if they suspect crimes. If you don't have a security director, you should. He or she must be a high-level person reporting directly to the chairman.

- **Create a code of ethics and give every employee a copy:** State explicitly what the company regards as computer crime and what it considers unethical. Tell employees these actions are grounds for dismissal or prosecution.

- **Educate top management:** Studies have shown that when the top executive understands the use and abuse of computer systems, employees commit fewer crimes.

- **Institute data security:** There should be at least three levels of security. Passwords should be changed every thirty days. Don't leave access codes and passwords lying around.[10]

Since computers emit radio waves when they are used, computer facilities can be made safer with walls and windows that prevent radio waves from leaving. More than fifty makers of computers and allied equipment now make leak-proof models; these cost about 30 percent more than their leaking counterparts.[11]

Since many businesses depend on an unfailing source of electricity to keep their offices and operations going, backup sources in the form of generators and batteries are important. Burglar alarms and fire alarms are often computer-controlled, as are the machine tools and physical environments of many labs and workrooms. Power failures can cause loss of data and essential life-support systems.

As a supervisor, you may have to enforce backup copy rules to avoid the loss of data. Let your computer users know the importance of copying important data onto a second disk and putting it in a secure place. Your job may also entail enforcing procedures designed to control who accesses and uses data. "A number of commercial software packages, through identification and password requirements, protect an individual microcomputer against unauthorized access. Once the password gives access to a database, the holder can read or write only in files specifically authorized for him."[12]

As a defense against computer viruses and the bugging of fax machines, several manufacturers have produced software and devices that work. There are several virus scanners available, and IBM upgrades their scanner regularly to help detect new viruses. Some software packages contain virus detection programs and can even remove them. Newer fax machines use code systems to defend the information transmitted. They scramble messages, making them unreadable to hackers. Check on your office's computer and fax security systems. They may be badly behind the times and leaking valuable information.

Regardless of policies and procedures, all security efforts and programs depend on management personnel at all levels for their implementation and enforcement. The quality of enforcement ultimately depends on what employees perceive to be the company's response in backing up informants and enforcers and in dealing with thieves. Ideally, all employees should be taught that theft prevention and detection depends on their cooperation as individuals and as a group.

Selection and Prevention

Preventing crimes committed by employees begins with the selection of each new employee. In most companies, supervisors are involved in the selection of new employees, as they certainly should be. During the screening process, both the supervisors and members of the personnel department should be alert for telltale signs of a potentially dishonest employee (see Exhibit 16.1). In addition to this list of clues, you should check the applicant's life-style for any hints that the person is living above his or her level of income. Be certain that all new employees know your company's policy on and penalties for dishonesty.

Ask for and verify a recommendation from the applicant's most recent employer. This precaution will not always uncover a person with a history of theft or willful destruction of company property, however, because many employers simply ask an employee caught stealing to resign. They

1. Gaps in employment	Be sure to fill in these gaps during the employment interview.
2. Criminal record	A criminal record check must be job related. Don't hire anyone who has a criminal conviction that will bear on the job to be filled.
3. Lies on the application	Significant falsehoods on an employment application signal falsehoods to come.
4. Frequent job changes	Changes that indicate the person does not know what he or she wants (no focus or common ground connects the past jobs) usually predict a short tenure with your organization.
5. Financial problems	A strong focus on money issues by the applicant may mean overextension and temptations to profit at others' expense.
6. Overqualified	Someone seeking a job for which he or she is overqualified may be on a search for a temporary, stopgap job just to make ends meet.

Exhibit 16.1   Some warning signs of a potentially dishonest applicant.

often do not fire such an employee or prosecute him or her in the courts, because they do not want to air their dirty linen in public. Few employers pass negative information about a former employee on to a potential new employer because they fear being accused of violating that person's civil rights and having a lawsuit filed against them. In addition, courts have been notoriously lenient toward white-collar criminals, who have often received only small fines or jail terms of less than a year following convictions for thefts amounting to thousands of dollars in cash or goods.

Office Security

Most companies have on their premises tangible assets to protect such as office machines and equipment, as well as valuable, highly sensitive information. To protect these assets, some basic, common-sense approaches work well alongside sophisticated and sometimes quite expensive equipment.

The biggest problem in protecting office equipment, machines, and sensitive information involves preventing access by unauthorized personnel. People must be separated into two groups in the minds of office supervisors: those who belong, and those who do not.

It should not be possible for someone to enter an office without being screened at the entrance. To make this screening process easier, many offices have only one entrance; it is usually the only nonfire exit, as well. Someone such as a receptionist should be on hand at all times to greet visitors from the moment the office is opened until it is closed for the day. People who have no legitimate reason to go farther should not be allowed to do so. People admitted beyond the reception area should have a specific destination. In the case of messengers and delivery people, the receptionist should accept the parcel or message or should request that the addressee come forward to receive it, if a specific signature is required. Parcels should be checked into a central cloak room or, if this is not practical, should be periodically spot-checked by security personnel. Briefcases, packages, lunch pails, and similar objects can easily be used to carry company property or sensitive information out of an office.

The protection of the employees' personal property can be best achieved by alerting people to the ever-present dangers of loss and theft. Office personnel should be asked to keep their valuables with them or safely locked away. A purse or a pocket calculator left on a desk is just too big a temptation for some people, whether strangers or regular employees. Advise your people to take their valuables home after work, especially when the office is to be left unoccupied over a weekend or long holiday period (when a burglary or fire is most likely to occur). Unfortunately, warnings are not enough for some people, and losses are almost certain to happen.

When a theft occurs, an investigation is called for on your part. It should involve security people if they are available. Use any past experience as a reminder that losses have occurred. There is nothing quite so effective as an actual loss to drive home the need to safeguard one's own property. Exhibit 16.2 gives a short security checklist to follow at the end of each day. Whoever is in charge of securing the office should refer to such a list before leaving.

Shop Security

Shop or plant security has some definite parallels to office security. Again the prevention of access by unauthorized personnel is the biggest problem standing in the way of safety and security. Controls can be exercised over people who enter the area in similar ways. Personal belongings can be secured in employee lockers or checked with the company's security personnel upon entering the plant or shop.

But there are some related problems that go along with plant and office security. Besides protecting property and information from theft, you must be concerned with the prevention of vandalism and fires.

Vandalism is generally considered to be wanton or willful destruction or damage to another's property. Sometimes it is done by disgruntled

Vandalism
Wanton or willful destruction or damage to another's property

---

Daily Security Checklist

1. File cabinets locked.   ☐
2. Safe locked.   ☐
3. Personal valuables secured.   ☐
4. Windows locked.   ☐
5. Machines off.   ☐
6. Night lights on.   ☐
7. Nonessential lights off.   ☐
8. People out.   ☐
9. Doors secured.   ☐
10. Alarm on.   ☐

Remarks: _____

_____

_____

Date: _____ Time: _____

Checklist completed by: _____

Exhibit 16.2   **Daily security checklist for closing an office.**

employees and sometimes by outsiders. Regardless of who does the damage, some simple precautions can help prevent or minimize losses.

To begin with, control over and security for all equipment, machines, tools, and other expensive pieces of company property should be the responsibility of specified people. Portable pieces of equipment should be issued only upon request and should be returned by the persons to whom they were issued. The responsibility for levels of maintenance should be associated with the operator and the maintenance department so that each item will be properly cared for and its condition checked periodically. Any damage or changes should be reported immediately, their causes determined, and blame or responsibility (financial and otherwise) fixed.

Physical facilities must be kept clean and under observation at regular and irregular intervals. Storage areas require extra security measures if they contain sensitive or highly valuable materials. Illumination of inside and outside areas helps avoid trouble and unwelcome visitors. Closed-circuit television, guards, proximity devices, and alarm systems are popular but expensive prevention and detection measures. Locks, however, remain the primary means of security used by any business firm; and they cannot prevent trouble or vandalism if they are not used properly. Locks and guard routes should be changed periodically. Finally, remind subordinates that damage means costs to them and to the company in time and money. Damaged equipment and facilities are unavailable for production. This often means lost revenues and wages.

Shoplifting

According to the National Retail Merchants Association, retailers lose about 2 percent of their revenue each year to shoplifters. That amounts to between $40 and $60 billion a year.[13] We all lose because stores must raise prices and spend more money to prevent thefts by customers. When stores raise their prices, they become less competitive. The dollars lost are then not available to make the businesses more productive and profitable.

Cures Most experts agree that training employees to look out for shoplifters can and does cut such losses. Such training also reminds employees that no one, not even employees, should steal. Mass merchandisers such as K-Mart and Sears have experienced reduced losses to shoplifting as their spending on employee training has risen.[14]

As a supervisor of retail salespeople, you can train your people never to leave a customer alone long enough to pocket merchandise. You can train your people to catch credit-card thieves and users of invalid credit cards by teaching and enforcing proper clearance procedures. Finally, you can enforce antitheft procedures such as keeping display cases locked and displaying one item to one customer at a time.

Your employer has other remedies and prevention measures to offer, as well. Rewards can be paid for catching shoplifters and for recovering stolen or void credit cards. Store detectives can be used to pose as shoppers and, along with closed-circuit TVs, monitor shoppers. Tagging merchandise with price tags that self-destruct when tampered with or with tags that only store personnel can remove also helps. Some stores have tags that trigger alarms when the customer leaves the store—indicating that the tag, which should have been removed at purchase, has not been removed. Checkpoint Systems Inc., an electronic security firm from New Jersey, manufactures electronic circuits that set off alarms at exits. Such circuits are quite small and can be built into a product's packaging or affixed to a piece of paper and inserted into a product. Target Stores, a Midwestern mass merchandiser, has installed the Checkpoint system in about one-fourth of its stores. It paid for the cost of installation within one year through loss prevention.[15]

Cub Foods in Colorado Springs had a big shoplifting problem until it created and installed two cardboard cops in its aisles. Each is a 6-foot stand-up photograph of a real cop in uniform. The figures are placed in aisles that have experienced losses to shoplifters. Since their installation, shoplifting is down 30 percent. According to Bob Demetry, loss-prevention manager at the store, the figures remind would-be shoplifters of what the consequences can be.[16]

Fire Prevention

According to the National Fire Protection Association, public fire departments fought 2.4 million fires in 1988. These fires killed 6,215 people and cost about $8.4 billion in property losses.[17]

While you are not expected to be a professional firefighter, you are expected to minimize the risks of having a fire start in any area over which you have control. The job is not yours alone. You must have the support of management, your peers, and your subordinates. Without their cooperation, your efforts will be ineffectual.

Most fires result from carelessness and can be prevented. Piles of rubbish, oily rags, the improper use of smoking materials, and inflammable liquids represent hazards whose potential harmfulness people with good common sense should recognize. Proper training of personnel in fire prevention and in how to extinguish various kinds of fires can go a long way toward reducing and eliminating fire hazards. A concern for fire prevention begins with the initial training of each new employee and continues to be reinforced by fire-prevention programs throughout the year.

Every department should conduct regularly scheduled inspections. All of your people represent potential causes of fires, just as they also represent detection and prevention devices. All employees should be made to feel that fire prevention and detection depend on them personally. Such attitudes are instilled through actions and words and by responding in a positive way each time a subordinate tells you about a potential fire hazard or takes time to remove one. Exhibit 16.3 shows a sample hazard checklist.

Be certain that all pieces of fire-fighting equipment such as extinguishers and hoses are visible, accessible, and in proper working order, and make sure that you and your people know where they are and how to use them. Different kinds of fires require different kinds of fire-fighting equipment. The wrong type of extinguishing agent—such as water used on a grease fire—can spread the fire and increase the likelihood of injuries and property damage. Periodic but unpredictable fire drills will prepare your people for the worst and will reinforce proper evacuation procedures and routes.

Fire Protection

	OK	Needed
1. Are portable fire extinguishers provided in adequate number and type?	☐	☐
2. Are fire extinguishers inspected monthly for general condition and operability and noted on the inspection tag?	☐	☐
3. Are fire extinguishers recharged regularly and properly noted on the inspection tag?	☐	☐
4. Are fire extinguishers mounted in readily accessible locations?	☐	☐
5. If you have interior standpipes and valves, are these inspected regularly?	☐	☐
6. If you have a fire alarm system, is it tested at least annually?	☐	☐
7. Are plant employees periodically instructed in the use of extinguishers and fire protection procedures?	☐	☐
8. If you have outside private fire hydrants, were they flushed within the last year and placed on a regular maintenance schedule?	☐	☐
9. Are fire doors and shutters in good operating condition?	☐	☐
Are they unobstructed and protected against obstruction?	☐	☐
10. Are fusible links in place?	☐	☐
11. Is your local fire department well acquainted with your plant, location and specific hazards?	☐	☐

12. Automatic Sprinklers:

Are water control valves, air and water pressures checked weekly? _____

Are control valves locked open? _____

Is maintenance of the system assigned to responsible persons or a sprinkler contractor? Who? _____

Are sprinkler heads protected by metal guards where exposed to mechanical damage? _____

Is proper minimum clearance maintained around sprinkler heads? _____

Exhibit 16.3   **Sample checklist for fire prevention.** (*Source: OSHA Handbook for Small Businesses.*)

If and when a fire occurs, you have three jobs to do in a hurry:

1. Get your people out of danger.
2. Call the fire department.
3. Fight the fire if you know how to and have the proper means and training to do so without putting yourself in jeopardy.

Protecting People

Protecting people from illness, accidents, and injuries is not only smart business—it is required by law, as well. By law, a business is responsible for injuries suffered by its employees if the injuries occur during or arise as a result of the employee's employment.

Accident
Any unforeseen or unplanned incident or event

An **accident** is defined as any unforeseen or unplanned incident or event. Damage to people or property need not occur to have an accident. Workers who slip on a wet floor but do not suffer any injury are still victims of an accident. People who pound a nail into a wall and miss the nail without damaging themselves or the wall are also victims of an accident.

While accidents are usually unforeseen, many are not unforeseeable. Planning and safety programs can and do yield significant decreases in accidents. Through the three Es of accident prevention established by the National Safety Council—engineering, education, and enforcement—the probability of accidents can be reduced and their severity can be minimized. Engineering has to do with **ergonomics**—how to design work sites, machinery, equipment, and systems to minimize stress and injury on the job. Education means teaching people what they need to know to prevent illness, injury, and death. Enforcement means making rules, regulations, and procedures work to that same end. More about the three Es of accident prevention will be discussed later in this chapter.

Ergonomics
Concern about the design of work sites, machines, equipment, and systems to minimize stress and job-related injuries

Illnesses, Injuries, and Deaths

In 1989, according to the U.S. Department of Labor, there were 284,000 cases of occupational illness, 6.3 million job-related injuries, and about 3,600 work-related deaths. Repetitive trauma illnesses, such as carpal tunnel syndrome—a malady affecting the wrists and forearms in those who repeat the same motions throughout the day—increased by 32,000 cases.[18] The leading cause of death on the job for women was homicide. The leading cause of death for men was vehicle accidents.[19] The costs connected with these numbers are huge. They include dollars lost in wages, medical bills, insurance premiums, and the increased costs in other areas that companies must incur to survive and cope with their losses.

Although each working environment is unique, each has certain hazards and types of accidents that can be identified and removed or neutralized so that they cause a minimum amount of damage and human suffering. Federal studies over the years have found the following basic elements in workplaces that have good accident prevention programs and records:

1. The top manager assumes the leadership role.
2. Responsibility for safety and health activities is clearly assigned.
3. Possible accident causes are properly identified and either eliminated or controlled.
4. Appropriate safety and health-related training is instituted.
5. An accident record system is maintained.
6. A medical and first-aid system is ready for possible use.
7. There is continued activity designed to foster on-the-job awareness and acceptance of safety and health responsibility by every employee.[20]
8. People are forewarned about and told how to cope with the hazards they must face on the job.

Regardless of the size of your organization, all of these elements can be utilized to prevent work-related accidents and possible injuries and illnesses.

When followed, this eight-point approach to safety and health in your company will reduce human misery and losses in dollars and hours. You can begin in your own area by identifying present hazards; taking responsibility for enforcement of standards, rules, and procedures; teaching safety and practicing it; and developing regular routines for all your subordinates.

Warning Signs Many symptoms exist in the workplace to let you know that you have a problem or will have in the future. Some obvious signs are accident and injury statistics, employee illnesses that are linked to the workplace, and absentee figures related to these. A company can analyze accident statistics, looking at categories of accidents (accidents to the eyes or fingers, for example) to determine if safety programs of a particular category or type are required. Not-so-obvious signals include labor turnover, excessive waste or scrap, increases in the number of near

No Smoking

No smoking by any employee, on or off the job. That's the policy of the Blackwood/Formall Corporation in Knoxville, Tennessee. Since the founding of the company in November 1988, the company and its employees have been smokeless. Any employee hired is given ninety days to quit the habit. Signing a no-smoking pledge is a condition of employment. Only one employee has been fired for breaching the pledge. "I am told my ban is legal," says Roger Blackwood, owner. "I've also believed for years that employers could get sued for not providing a smoke-free atmosphere."*

Ford Motor Company is one of a growing number of companies to ban smoking on company property. An increasing number of companies are not hiring smokers. Many businesses force their smokers into undesirable areas and out of doors to engage in their pastime. Hotels now offer smoking and nonsmoking rooms to guests. Federal clean air legislation has severely restricted smoking in public places.

According to the Secretary of Health and Human Services, Louis Sullivan, smoking costs America more than $52 billion each year in health care costs and lost productivity. In his 1990 report, Sullivan claims that smoking-related diseases cost each American $221 a year, largely in health-care and insurance costs. Roger Blackwood says that with the company he owns, smokers are absent 80 percent more than nonsmokers. John Banzhaf, director of Action on Smoking and Health (a national legal action antismoking group), estimates that each smoker represents $5,000 per year to his or her employer.

*Source: "Company Posts No-Smoking Sign—On or Off Job," *Chicago Tribune* (July 16, 1989), sect. 8, p. 1.

misses that could have caused injuries or property damage, and the pending receipt of new equipment and new employees (these last two signal a need for safety training).

A rising concern for most employers is the presence of indoor pollution in the plant and office. What has become known as sick-building syndrome (SBS) may be caused by one contaminant or by several acting in concert. Many indoor locations are chemical and bacterial "nurseries," trapping such contaminants as asbestos, radon gas, formaldehyde, carbon monoxide, cigarette smoke, and fungi and bacteria of all sorts. Currently, more than 65,000 chemicals are used or manufactured in the workplaces of America with about 1,500 new ones introduced each year. Only about 10 percent of these are tested by the Environmental Protection Agency. Of these, about 2,000 have been identified as leading to occupational diseases

Before Moving to New Quarters

1. Check the site history. What have been the past uses for the premises? Who have been the tenants/owners?

2. Check with the neighbors. Ask them if there have been any pollution problems in the past with your proposed location and the immediate area.

3. Check with the local city hall. What have been the past zonings for the property? Has there been any problem with the occupants or the facilities?

4. Check the building's plans. Track down the construction drawings and specifications for building materials to spot hidden problems like foam insulation or asbestos.

5. Have the duct work inspected. Look for mold, fibrous particles, humid conditions, and general state of repair and efficiency of operation.

6. Get a certification of habitability from the owner. Get the landlord or seller to guarantee in writing that the premises are not contaminated.

Dealing with Your Existing Pollution

1. Get reliable help. You need professionals to search and to cure most problems. Find an expert to inspect the premises.

2. Give smokers their own ventilation system or restrict use of the premises to nonsmoking.

3. Periodically air out the indoor areas. Provide some means for periodic venting.

4. Keep all duct work clean and dry. Bacteria and fungi grow in dark, moist places.

5. Remove and avoid installing anything that gives off unpleasant, irritating odors. An unpleasant smell generally means complications down the road.

6. Provide lots of plants to absorb carbon dioxide and odors. They give off oxygen as well.

Exhibit 16.4   Avoiding and dealing with indoor air pollution.

if exposures are high enough.[21] Indoor air pollution has become a larger problem as more structures are built or renovated to become more energy efficient. Exhibit 16.4 gives you some advice on avoiding or cleaning up indoor pollutants.

The symptoms exhibited by those in a polluted environment include redness and tearing of the eyes, congestion, nose bleeds, difficulty with breathing, tiredness, headaches, runny noses, and other flulike symptoms. A study by the Walter Reed Institute of Medical Research in Washington concluded that absenteeism increases about 50 percent in poorly ventilated buildings. Conversely, when buildings are cleaned up, absenteeism and productivity improve, according to environmental consultant Laurence B. Molloy.[22]

Drugs and Employees

Employees whose performances are affected by dependency on alcohol or other drugs are a danger to themselves and to others. They are usually incapable of delivering satisfactory levels of output, and they can cause all kinds of losses to their employers. The drug-dependent employee may steal from the employer or from fellow employees to get the money needed to support his or her habit. Small mistakes can become major problems and can lead to accidents, injuries, and worse.

While drug testing of new applicants for jobs is rapidly becoming the norm with employers, routine drug testing for existing employees is an issue loaded with controversy. As of 1988, about 30 percent of America's largest corporations were using some form of drug testing.[23] Every employer should make it clear that use of unlawful drugs in the workplace will not be tolerated.

In the federal government, routine, random drug testing has been the rule in the armed services for military and some civilian employees since the early 1980s. The Transportation Department began urine tests for drug and alcohol use during annual physicals about the same time and began random testing of air-traffic controllers, aviation and railway safety inspectors, electronic technicians, and employees with top secret clearances in 1987.[24]

In a recent poll by *USA Today,* 81 percent of those polled said that some or all workers should be tested for drugs, and 88 percent said that they would agree to be tested. Of the remaining respondents, 13 percent said that no one should be tested, and only 4 percent said that the tests should be voluntary.[25]

Drug testing raises questions of invasion of privacy, and some state and local laws put restrictions on testing in the workplace. False test results can keep people from employment or can cause them to lose employment. And drug testing with the more accurate tests is expensive—$75 to $100 per test. Many companies that do test their employees offer those who test positive some form of or access to treatment, thus avoiding lawsuits and the loss of experienced employees.[26]

State and local laws tend to limit drug testing of employees. For example, a Connecticut statute allows random testing only in certain, highly restricted circumstances. But when drug testing is used selectively and in sensitive work settings and testing is done in ways that collect, safeguard, and test samples properly, the courts have been able to endorse it. Some questions management should ask before testing employees for drugs are:

- What problem are we trying to solve?
- Is there adequate business justification for the costs and burdens involved?

- Are we avoiding the appearance of indifference to employee sensibilities?
- What will we do with a positive result?[27]

According to the National Institute on Drug Abuse (NIDA), 29 percent of workers in the twenty to forty age bracket have improperly or illegally used drugs (not including alcohol) in the past twelve months; 19 percent use such drugs regularly.[28] Robert DuPont, the former director of NIDA and a consultant to industry on drug abuse, estimates that drug-using employees cost American employers $33 billion annually in lost productivity. This breaks down to about $1,000 for every worker on the payrolls in America.[29] When compared to their drug-free counterparts, drug-using employees have the following record:

- They have three to four times more on-the-job accidents.
- They file five times as many workers' compensation claims.
- They cost employers three times as much in medical expenses.
- They are absent from work three times as often.
- They are more likely to steal from their companies and coworkers.[30]

Employee-Assistance Programs

Most major employers recognize that it is very costly to keep employees who are unproductive because of their personal and drug-related problems. But they also know that it is costly to lose well-trained, experienced people, especially in job categories where there is a shortage of talent. As a result, many companies have initiated employee-assistance programs, using a variety of specialists both inside and outside their work forces. These programs offer troubled employees the same kinds of employer consideration that is given to those with physical illnesses. Financial consulting, access to alcohol- and drug-abuse programs, psychiatric care, and fitness or well-being programs are just a few of the employee-assistance operations that are being made available.

The Supervisor's Role

Nearly all efforts at promoting safety and identifying and getting help to the troubled worker depend on you as a supervisor. Safety programs, regulations, procedures, and committees need your input and enforcement efforts to work effectively and efficiently. Exhibit 16.5 outlines your role in efforts at safety promotion and enforcement.

Many sources of help are available to you for identifying problem

The safety-minded supervisor:

1. Takes the initiative in telling management about ideas for a safer layout of equipment, tools, and processes.

2. Knows the value of machine guards and makes sure the proper guards are provided and used.

3. Takes charge of operations that are not routine to make certain that safety precautions are determined.

4. Is an expert on waste disposal for housekeeping and fire protection.

5. Arranges for adequate storage and enforces good housekeeping.

6. Works with every employee without favoritism.

7. Keeps eyes open for the new employee or the experienced employee doing a new job.

8. Establishes good relations with union stewards and the safety committee.

9. Sets good examples in safety practices.

10. Never lets a simple safety violation occur without talking to the employee immediately.

11. Not only explains how to do a job, but shows how and observes to ensure continuing safety.

12. Takes pride in knowing how to use all equipment safely.

13. Knows what materials are hazardous and how to store them safely.

14. Continues to "talk safety" and impress its importance on all employees.

Exhibit 16.5   Typical profile of a supervisor with low accident and injury rates.
(*Source:* U.S. Department of Labor.)

areas and for taking corrective actions. Exhibit 16.6 lists the most important areas to consider when conducting your investigations. You may be able to add areas of importance to it, based on your own working environment. When you have identified the hazards, you are ready to set up and implement controls to prevent, eliminate, or deal with each. These controls get rid of a hazard or effectively eliminate or restrict its potential to cause harm. Dangerous machines can be eliminated or fitted with proper safeguards. Operators can be thoroughly trained and drilled in the safety procedures required. Personal protective gear can be purchased, issued, and checked regularly to see that it works and is being used correctly. Access to hazards can be carefully controlled by restricting it to those who are aware of and equipped to deal with hazardous situations.

Your role as a supervisor is crucial in spotting troubled workers who need special assistance and in getting them started on a program designed to meet their needs. Look for warning signs such as changes in an em-

Processing, receiving, shipping, and storage—Equipment, job planning, layout, heights, floor loads, projection of materials, materials handling, storage methods.

Building and grounds conditions—Floors, walls, ceilings, exits, stairs, walkways, ramps, platforms, driveways, aisles.

Housekeeping program—Waste disposal, tools, objects, materials, leakage and spillage, cleaning methods, schedules, work areas, remote areas, storage areas.

Electricity—Equipment, switches, breakers, fuses, switch boxes, junctions, special fixtures, circuits, insulation, extensions, tools, motors, grounding, NEC compliance.

Lighting—Type, intensity, controls, conditions, diffusion, location, glare and shadow control.

Heating and ventilating—Type, effectiveness, temperature, humidity, controls, natural and artificial ventilation and exhausting.

Machinery—Points of operation, flywheels, gears, shafts, pulleys, key ways, belts, couplings, sprockets, chains, frames, controls, lighting for tools and equipment, brakes, exhausting, feeding, oiling, adjusting, maintenance, lock out, grounding, work space, location, purchasing standards.

Personnel—Training, experience, methods of checking machines before use, type clothing, personal protective equipment, use of guards, tool storage, work practices, method of cleaning, oiling, or adjusting machinery.

Hand and power tools—Purchasing standards, inspection, storage, repair, types, maintenance, grounding, use and handling.

Chemicals—Storage, handling, transportation, spills, disposals, amounts used, toxicity or other harmful effects, warning signs, supervision, training, protective clothing and equipment.

Fire prevention—Extinguishers, alarms, sprinklers, smoking rules, exits, personnel assigned, separation of flammable materials and dangerous operations, explosive-proof fixtures in hazardous locations, waste disposal.

Maintenance—Regularity, effectiveness, training of personnel, materials and equipment used, records maintained, method of locking out machinery, general methods.

Personal protective equipment—Type, size, maintenance, repair, storage, assignment of responsibility, purchasing methods, standards observed, training in care and use, rules of use, method of assignment.

Exhibit 16.6 **Typical scope of a self-inspection program.** (*Source: OSHA Handbook for Small Businesses.*)

ployee's routines and behaviors. Increases in an employee's tardiness, absenteeism, ineffectiveness, or need for disciplinary action may signal that the employee has a personal or drug-related problem. Employees who suddenly isolate themselves from fellow workers and who become argumentative with their peers are asking for help.

When you think you have a troubled employee on your hands, let him or her know what you think, and recommend or refer the person to those in your company who can help. If drug use is suspected, your company should have a policy that is in line with your state's laws. A mandatory physical examination or drug test may or may not be approved in your state. Your company's medical department will work with the individual or refer him or her to an appropriate agency for treatment. Failure to comply with the company's directives may leave the employee subject to disciplinary measures and termination. You need to keep your people aware of the help that is available to them, and your company should have an ongoing educational program to expose employees to the dangers of drug abuse. Whatever programs your company provides should guarantee confidentiality to all who take part in them. This encourages voluntary compliance and helps avoid possible legal problems later on.

Success Stories

In 1989, Chrysler, in cooperation with the United Auto Workers (UAW) and the Occupational Safety and Health Administration (OSHA), reached an agreement that is designed to reduce repetitive motion injuries at Chrysler's plants. A pilot study began in 1990 at the Belvidere plant in Illinois to find the causes and solutions for ergonomic problems leading to carpal tunnel syndrome and other cumulative trauma conditions. The agreement calls for Chrysler to hire an ergonomic consultant to conduct the study and to implement engineering and work-practice controls to reduce identifiable hazards. The company also began a training program for workers and medical personnel to help them recognize cumulative trauma disorders. What is learned will be transferred to Chrysler's other plants.[31] In 1990, General Motors reached a similar agreement with the same parties—the United Auto Workers union and OSHA.[32]

Ford Motor Company has traveled a different route but has been after the same results. In 1982, Ford contacted the University of Michigan's Center for Ergonomics to help it reduce the injuries to its workers. In 1987, Ford's contract with the UAW called for development of ergonomic committees in about eighty plants, the result of the university research. These committees now routinely tackle complaints about pain from workers and are made up of both workers and managers.[33]

Nypro Inc. of Clinton, Massachusetts, makes safety the first topic at every meeting whether with managers or with managers and workers. When an accident occurs, it is examined and discussed in detail. The result of this persistence? The company has an annual accident rate of between 1 and 2 percent and has cut its workers' compensation insurance bill from $500,000 to $100,000.[34]

The Occupational Safety and Health Act (1970)

OSHA
The federal agency called the Occupational Safety and Health Administration

In 1970 Congress passed the Occupational Safety and Health Act, which created the **Occupational Safety and Health Administration (OSHA)** "to assure so far as possible every working man and woman in the nation safe and healthful working conditions to preserve our human resources." The law, which became effective in April 1971, applies to all employers engaged in any business affecting commerce and employing people. Its terms apply to all the states, territories, and possessions of the United States but do *not* apply to government employees or to working conditions protected under other federal occupational safety and health laws such as the Federal Coal Mine Health and Safety Act, the Atomic Energy Act, and the Migrant Health Act.

According to OSHA, each employer has the duty to furnish employees a working environment free from recognized hazards that cause or are likely to cause death or serious physical harm. Each employee has a duty to comply with safety and health rules and standards established by the employers or by OSHA. Administration and enforcement of OSHA are vested in the secretary of labor and in the Occupational Safety and Health Review Commission, a quasi-judicial board of three members appointed by the president. Research and related functions are vested in the secretary of health and human services, whose functions will for the most part be carried out by the National Institute for Occupational Safety and Health. The institute exists to develop and establish recommended occupational safety and health standards; to conduct research and experimental programs for developing criteria for new and improved job safety and health standards; and to make recommendations to the secretaries of labor and health and human services concerning new and improved standards.

Occupational Safety and Health Standards

In general, job safety and health standards consist of rules aimed at preventing hazards that have been proved by research and experience to be harmful to personal safety and health. Some standards—such as fire protection standards—apply to all employees. A great many standards, however, apply only to workers engaged in specific types of work, such as handling inflammable materials.

Various safety and health standards have been issued by OSHA and are available to you through your company or from one of the many local OSHA offices in major cities around the country. Exhibit 16.7 shows a representative OSHA regulation. All help to define protective measures or

1910.151 Medical services and first aid.

(a) The employer shall ensure the ready availability of medical personnel for advice and consultation on matters of plant health.

(b) In the absence of an infirmary, clinic, or hospital in near proximity to the workplace which is used for the treatment of all injured employees, a person or persons shall be adequately trained to render first aid. First-aid supplies approved by the consulting physician shall be readily available.

(c) Where the eyes or body of any person may be exposed to injurious corrosive material, suitable facilities for quick drenching or flushing of the eyes and body shall be provided within the work area for immediate emergency use.

Exhibit 16.7   **Sample OSHA standard dealing with medical services and first aid.** *(Source: General Industry Standards, USDOL-OSHA 2206.)*

ways in which to deal with an identifiable hazard. The activities of OSHA are discussed in more detail at the end of the chapter.

It is not enough to warn and instruct employees about safety hazards. Supervisors must also *enforce* instructions and *remove* or *eliminate* hazards. Supervisors who ignore company or OSHA safety rules and standards can cause a doubling of the OSHA-prescribed penalties if accidents are the result of such behavior.

All employers and supervisors are obligated to familiarize themselves and their subordinates with the standards that apply to them at all times. Any person or business adversely affected by a government standard may challenge its validity by petitioning the U.S. Court of Appeals within sixty days after the new standard is imposed. Variances from standards may be granted to employers if extra time is needed to comply or if an employer is using safety measures as safe as those required by federal standards.

Compliance Complaints

Employees who believe that a violation of a safety or health standard exists that threatens them with physical harm may request an inspection by sending a signed written notice to the Department of Labor. A copy should be provided to the employer. The names of the complainants will not be revealed to the employer. If the department finds no reasonable grounds for the complaint and a citation is not issued, the complainants will be notified in writing. Employee complaints may also be made to any local OSHA office. Complaining employees may not be persecuted in any way by their employers.

Since the *Whirlpool Corporation* v. *Marshall* case in 1980, workers have had the right to refuse a job assignment or to walk off the job ''because of a reasonable apprehension of health or serious injury coupled with a reasonable belief that no less drastic alternative is available.'' This wording and other words in the Supreme Court decision have been interpreted to mean that workers may refuse to perform work that constitutes a clear and present danger, in their minds, to their safety. Employers are not required to pay workers who do not perform such work, but they may not reprimand them in any way.

OSHA Inspections

Since October 1981, OSHA may only target for regular inspection visits firms with ten or more employees, firms with below-average safety records, and firms with complaining employees. Since the 1979 Supreme Court decision in *Marshall* v. *Barlow's, Inc.,* employers do not have to admit OSHA inspectors who do not have a search warrant. But all companies (except those with ten or fewer employees) must keep OSHA-required accident and illness records and records on employee exposure to potentially toxic materials or other harmful physical agents. Since August 1987, 59 million workers have had the right to demand information about hazardous chemicals at their work sites. They can demand to know the identities and compositions of chemicals that they are exposed to at work. Public employees still do not have these rights.

When OSHA compliance officers (inspectors) call, they may be on a routine inspection or they may be responding to an employee's complaint. In the latter case, the inspectors need not limit their visits to the complaint. Other areas may be investigated as well.

An OSHA inspector may ask the supervisor or any person in charge of an area to accompany him or her on an inspection, or the inspector may conduct the inspection alone. Employers do not have an absolute right to accompany inspectors. It is a good practice for any supervisor to tag along on any inspection that involves his or her work area. You may spot violations that the inspector does not, and you will be present to give explanations and to make on-the-spot corrections of minor problems.

OSHA inspections consist of an opening conference between the compliance officer and the employer, an inspection tour, and a closing conference. At the closing conference, the compliance officer reviews the findings and may issue a citation stating the standard(s) violated and specifying a time limit for correcting each violation. Citations for most violations are usually sent by registered mail from the area director of the OSHA office. Citations must be posted in a prominent place until the violations they cite are corrected. Fines may be assessed for failing to post the citation, for removing it prematurely, and for exceeding the time limit mentioned in the citation for correcting violations. When an employer feels that a citation is unfair or incorrect, it may appeal the citation within fifteen working days after receipt.

On-Site Consultation

OSHA has developed a free, on-site consultation service that is available to any employer upon request. An OSHA consultant will visit a business and tour the facilities, pointing out what operations are governed by OSHA standards and how to interpret them. If violations are found, they are pointed out and suggestions are offered on how to correct them. No citations are issued, but—as part of the decision to accept a consultation— the employer must agree to eliminate all hazards discovered within a reasonable time.

State Programs

When the Occupational Safety and Health Act was passed in 1970, many states already had their own state safety laws. Some of these laws were criticized for their weak standards, ineffective administration, and lax enforcement. Others were considered quite acceptable. The federal safety law offered states the opportunity to develop and administer their own safety and health programs, provided that the states could demonstrate that their programs were "at least as effective" as the federal program. State safety and health programs have to be approved by OSHA; if they are approved, OSHA will pay 50 percent of their operating costs.[35]

To obtain approval from OSHA, a state must demonstrate that its standards for safety and health are adequate and that it is capable of enforcing them. A state is given a three-year probationary period to demonstrate that it has adequate standards, enforcement, appeal procedures, protection for public employees, and trained safety inspectors. About half of the states have developed and are administering their own safety and health programs. OSHA continues to evaluate the state programs to ensure that they meet acceptable standards. If a state program fails to meet the standards, OSHA has the authority to withdraw approval of the program.[36]

Workers' Compensation

Prior to 1910, workers were injured frequently on the job. Their lost wages and medical bills were usually their own problems, unless they could prove in a court of law that their employers were the sole force or cause of their injuries. If a worker contributed in any way to the injury suffered or if a worker knew his or her work to be dangerous, the employer could usually avoid legal responsibility for damages.

Workers' compensation
Federal and state laws designed to compensate employees for illnesses and injuries that arise out of and in the course of their employment

Today **workers' compensation** laws exist at both the federal level and the state level. If a worker suffers an illness or injury on the job, he or she can file a claim with the state's compensation board. An employer is directly responsible and liable for accidents and illnesses that arise out of and in the course of a worker's employment. Benefits are paid to individuals according to schedules of benefits containing fixed maximums that may be awarded by compensation boards. Most business firms carry some kind of workers' compensation insurance of the type sold by nearly every casualty insurance company.

States have either compulsory or elective workers' compensation laws. Under elective laws, a company may provide the protection the law requires on its own. But if the company rejects the law, it loses its common-law defenses against claims of negligence. Employees (or their families) would then therefore be free to sue the employer for damages for injuries, illness, or death.

Under compulsory workers' compensation laws, every employer within the state's jurisdiction must accept the application of the law and provide the benefits required. They may self-insure to provide the benefits of workers' compensation insurance policies. When the company provides on its own the protection required by law through workers' compensation insurance, the employee who suffers an injury or illness may not sue.

Benefits from workers' compensation insurance compensate employees for medical and disability expenses, as well as for income loss because of illness or injury. The cost of this insurance varies, depending on a company's history of worker claims. The more claims filed against a company, and the more benefits paid by an insurance company, the greater the premium charged for workers' compensation protection. Most businesses, therefore, try to insure workers' safety through the latest in equipment devices and work safety rules—not only to protect its workers from injury but also to protect its profits from the drain of insurance premiums and self-insurance funds. See Exhibit 16.8. Note the "management responses" portion in particular.

Instant Replay

1. The security of your company's and subordinates' assets is partly your responsibility.

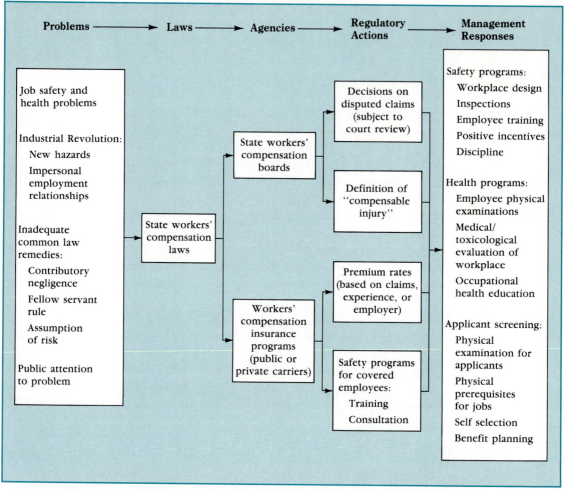

Exhibit 16.8   Regulatory model of the workers' compensation system. (*Source:* James Ledvinka, Vida G. Scarpello. *Federal Regulation of Personnel and Human Resource Management*, 2d ed. Boston: PWS-Kent, 1991, 193.)

2. Your people depend on you and the company's policies, programs, and procedures, along with their own efforts, to protect them from recognized and recognizable hazards.

3. While safety and security are everyone's legitimate concern, your organization depends on you and its other managers for planning, implementing, and enforcing proper programs.

4. Engineering, education (training), and enforcement are the keys to successful safety and security efforts.

5. Since 1971, over 40 million working Americans have depended on regulations and enforcement inspections provided by the Occupational Safety and Health Administration, along with their

employers' efforts and their own actions, to make the workplace a less hazardous environment.

6. Supervisors who really care about safety and security listen to their employees, look for hazards, fix responsibility for safety and security, enforce standards and procedures, and discipline violators of safety and security policies.

Glossary

Accident any unforeseen or unplanned incident or event. An accident may or may not lead to personal injuries or property damage.

Computer virus a rogue computer program that can reproduce itself endlessly, thus destroying stored data.

Ergonomics concern about the design of work sites, machinery, equipment, and systems to minimize stress and injury on the job.

Health the general condition of a person physically, mentally, and emotionally and efforts at preventing illness and treating injuries when they occur.

OSHA the federal agency whose full name is the *Occupational Safety and Health Administration*. Less frequently *OSHA* is an abbreviation for the Occupational Safety and Health Act of 1970.

Safety efforts at protecting human resources from accidents and injuries.

Security efforts at protecting physical facilities and nonhuman assets from loss or damage.

Vandalism wanton or willful destruction or damage to the property of another.

Workers' compensation federal and state laws designed to compensate employees for illnesses and injuries that arise out of and in the course of their employment.

Questions for Class Discussion

1. Can you define this chapter's key terms?

2. As a supervisor, how would you go about the task of safeguarding your office or shop environments?

3. What are a supervisor's duties with regard to fire prevention? with regard to fighting a fire?

4. How can a supervisor act to prevent losses from vandalism?

5. What are the major purposes of the Occupational Safety and Health Act? When did it become effective in enforcement efforts? How does it enforce its regulations?

6. What are an employer's rights with regard to OSHA inspectors? In general, how does an OSHA inspector conduct inspections?

Incident

Purpose To give you practice in identifying unsafe conditions in your school or place of work.

Your Task Using the checklist that follows, inspect the public access areas either where you work or where you take this course. Record your findings and make recommendations to correct any unsafe area or condition you discover.

Checklist	OK	Action Needed
1. Are all exits visible, marked, and free of obstructions?	_____	_____
2. Are stairs free of obstructions and equipped with sturdy handrails?	_____	_____
3. Are portable fire extinguishers readily available and marked as to their locations?	_____	_____
4. Do the fire extinguishers have inspection tags?	_____	_____
5. Do the inspection tags indicate that the extinguishers have been recently (within sixty days) inspected?	_____	_____
6. Do you find people smoking in posted "no smoking" areas?	_____	_____
7. Are trash receptacles covered and emptied regularly?	_____	_____
8. Are public hallways clear of obstructions to the flow of people?	_____	_____
9. Are floors clean, dry, and free of irregular surfaces?	_____	_____
10. Is there a first-aid station, properly equipped and staffed, on the premises?	_____	_____

Case Problem 16.1   Safety First

"Our regulations clearly state that employees may not walk off the job or refuse to perform a job just because they think it is unsafe," said Amy Price, the personnel manager of Hadley Products Company.

"That's right," said Andy Prachak. "As the foreman out in that yard, I know what those men go through every day. I don't blame Ed for wanting safer conditions. But I draw the line at open protests and insubordination to get them."

Rick Sczebo, head of the union's grievance committee, interrupted. "You two are talking about firing Ed for leaving a hazardous job. You ought to be grateful Ed hasn't complained to OSHA about conditions out in that yard. There have been two serious injuries already, due mainly to the company's refusing to fix known hazards. Does someone have to be killed or permanently injured before people do something about safety?''

''Don't cloud the issue, Rick,'' said Amy. ''We are talking about a serious breach of discipline. If we let Ed get away with a clear case of insubordination, Andy will have to suffer for it for a long time to come. Ed was given a direct order to finish stacking those skids with his forklift. He refused and left the yard before quitting time and without a pass. What's worse, he refused in front of three other workmen who heard Andy's order.''

''Look, Amy, this is not a case of insubordination. Andy will be the first to tell you that Ed is a good worker. Right, Andy?''

''Right, one of the best. That's why I'm shocked at his leaving like he did. It just wasn't like him.''

''Well,'' said Rick, ''that ought to tell you how bad things must have been in Ed's mind. You were asking him to risk his life and limb. As the grievance says, and I quote Ed's words, 'Those skids were broken and piled in a dangerous way. They were stacked badly and were already too high. When the foreman told me to add another layer, I knew they would be too unsteady to stay up for long. I wasn't going to put my buddies and myself in any more danger by adding another layer.' ''

''You see,'' Rick continued, ''Ed saw a clear danger and acted the way any normal person should. He refused to carry out a stupid order that never should have been given in the first place.''

''Now see here,'' said Andy, ''I resent that. If Ed thought the job was that dangerous, why didn't he tell me what he thought? He didn't explain anything until he wrote that grievance in response to his firing. All I know is that I don't want him back in the yard. He's fired now, and if he's rehired, I'll quit.''

''Wait a minute, Andy. Let's not lose our heads here,'' said Amy. ''Let's have a cup of coffee and relax a minute. I'll get some. Be back in a minute.''

Amy left the room. Andy and Rick glared at each other through a long silence. Then Rick spoke up.

''The union tells me that any worker can leave his job if he believes there is a *real* danger of death and serious injury.''

''Well, what your union doesn't say is what OSHA cases have said: that a worker can leave *only* when the company knows about the hazards *and* refuses to do anything about them. Ed never told me what he thought. I'm not a mind reader.''

Amy returned with three steaming cups of coffee for two steaming employees. Amy spoke as she set the cups down. ''What's it going to take to settle the case, Rick?''

''Amy, what the union wants is to correct the bad conditions out in the yard as soon as possible, and to reinstate Ed with back pay and seniority. If we don't get some action soon, we're going to call in the OSHA inspectors.''

''If you do,'' replied Amy, ''you could shut this place down with violations. Your members would be out of a job for Lord knows how long. You know how government red tape can foul things up. Let me propose a compromise here. If it's OK with Andy, we will get started on a safety program and fix the problems your boys think are the most serious ones. Give us a list, and we will do as much as we can as fast as our budget will allow. Second, we will bring Ed back with no back pay for the two weeks he's been fired and give him his seniority minus those two weeks. What do you say, Andy?''

''OK, if that's the best we can do.''

''What do you say, Rick?''

Questions

1. Comment on the union's and the company's views of OSHA.

2. What are the central issues in this case?

3. If you were the union's spokesperson, how would you answer Amy's suggested compromise?

4. Comment on the supervisor's view of the importance of safety versus the importance of maintaining discipline.

Case Problem 16.2   Good Housekeeping

As the supervisor of a woodworking shop, you are responsible for enforcing standards of safety and health. You have held meetings with your people regularly to discuss health and safety. For the most part your people want to assist you in keeping the shop clean and safe, and all of them know the rules. But every week a few of the workers get sloppy or forget about basics. It is Friday, and your workers have left for the weekend. In making your daily inspection you find and record the following conditions:

a. Dirty clothes and rags overflowing the laundry cart
b. Empty packing boxes and crates piled in the toolroom and the toolroom door left unlocked
c. An exit light burned out above the back door
d. A power drill left out on Harry's workbench
e. Oil spilled while Sam was filling his machine's oil cup has made an aisle slippery

Questions

1. Which of the above conditions was/were caused by your workers?
2. As the supervisor, how could you have prevented each of the above?
3. Which of the above can wait until Monday morning?

Notes

1. "3 Ex-Execs Charged at 1st National," *Chicago Tribune* (May 30, 1991), sect. 3, p. 1.
2. "Du Pont Doesn't Cotton to Blackmail," *Business Week* (March 13, 1989): 46.
3. "Cost of Employee Theft Hits $21 Billion a Year," *Chicago Tribune* (June 30, 1986), §5: 19.
4. "Information Thieves Are Now Corporate Enemy No. 1," *Business Week* (May 5, 1986): 120–21, 123.
5. "Average Take of Computer Fraud $600,000," *USA Today* (May 7, 1987): 6B.
6. "Invader of Computer Network Is Convicted," *Chicago Tribune* (January 23, 1990), sect. 3, p. 1.
7. A. E. Cullison, "Fax Machines an Open Book to Hackers," *Chicago Tribune* (September 9, 1990), sect. 7, p. 11B.
8. "Clocking Time Stolen from Our Jobs," *USA Today* (November 26, 1986): 4B.
9. Jack B. Rochester, "Insiders Lead the List of Electronic Thieves," *USA Today* (June 8, 1987): 8E.
10. August Bequai, "Ethics, Education Key to Crime Prevention," *USA Today* (June 8, 1987): 8E.
11. John Hillkirk, "They're Plugging the Leaks in Our Computers," *USA Today* (June 8, 1987): 8E.
12. Karen Berney, "The Cutting Edge," *Nations Business* (April 1986): 57.
13. Valerie Reitman, "Alarm Sounded on Shoplifting," *Chicago Tribune* (January 28, 1990), sect. 7, p. 12.
14. Mark Memmott, "Training Cuts Shoplifting, Employee Theft," *USA Today* (December 3, 1986): 9B.
15. Reitman, op. cit., p. 13.
16. Ann Hagedorn, "It's Why Employees Don't Want the Boss's Portrait on the Wall," *The Wall Street Journal* (November 29, 1990): B1.

17. *The World Almanac.* New York: Pharos Books, 1991, p. 851.

18. ''More Workers Fall Prey to Repetitive Motion Ills,'' *Chicago Tribune* (November 15, 1990), sect. 2, p. 3.

19. ''Homicide at Job a Danger for Women,'' *Chicago Tribune* (August 18, 1990), sect. 1, p. 4.

20. Occupational Safety and Health Administration, U.S. Department of Labor, *OSHA Handbook for Small Businesses,* rev. ed. (1979), 2.

21. Merrill Goozner, ''Job Diseases Remain a Major Cause of Death,'' *Chicago Tribune* (August 31, 1990), sect. 1, pp. 1, 14.

22. Faye Rice, ''Do You Work in a Sick Building?'' *Fortune* (July 2, 1990): 87.

23. James Ledvinka and Vida G. Scarpello, *Federal Regulation of Personnel and Human Resource Management,* 2d ed. (Boston: PWS-Kent, 1991), 306.

24. ''Bid to Stall Drug Testing Fails,'' *Chicago Tribune* (September 5, 1987), §1: 3.

25. Memmott, note 14.

26. Ibid.

27. Ledvinka, op. cit., pp. 308–309.

28. ''Help's on the Way with Drug Treatment Programs,'' *Chicago Tribune* (January 3, 1988), §19: 45.

29. Ibid.

30. Ibid.

31. Merrill Goozner, ''Repetitive Motion Injuries Target of Chrysler Accord,'' *Chicago Tribune* (November 3, 1989), sect. 3, p. 3.

32. Maryanne George, ''Autoworkers Get Helping Hand,'' *Chicago Tribune* (December 3, 1990), sect. 4, p. 12.

33. Ibid.

34. ''Safety First,'' *Inc.* (January 1989): 107.

35. David J. Cherrington, *Personnel Management: The Management of Human Resources* (Dubuque, Iowa: Wm. C. Brown, 1983), 623.

36. Ibid.

Suggested Readings

DeReamer, Russell. *Modern Safety and Health Technology.* New York: John Wiley & Sons, 1980.

Hammer, Willie. *Occupational Safety Management and Engineering.* 3d ed. Englewood Cliffs, N.J.: Prentice-Hall, 1985.

Ledvinka, James, and Scarpello, Vida G. *Federal Regulation of Personnel and Human Resource Management.* 2d ed. Boston: PWS-Kent, 1991.

Lutness, John. ''Self-Managed Safety Program Gets Workers Involved.'' *Safety and Health,* 135, #4 (April 1987): 42–45.

National Safety Council. *Supervisor's Safety Manual.* 5th ed. Chicago: National Safety Council, 1975.

———— . *Fundamentals of Industrial Hygiene.* 2d ed. Chicago: National Safety Council, 1979.

Peterson, Dan. *Safety Supervision.* New York: AMACOM, 1976.

———— . *Techniques of Safety Management.* New York: McGraw-Hill, 1978.

Rice, Faye. ''Do You Work in a Sick Building?'' *Fortune* (July 2, 1990): 86–88.

Appendix

How to Present a Case in Class

A. GETTING THE FACTS

1. Read the entire case through.

2. Before reading the questions that follow it, ask yourself where the problems lie. If you have no clear insights, reread the case. Recall that the case appears in conjunction with a chapter in the text. The major purpose of a case is to dramatize an incident within which you can apply the knowledge you have gained from that chapter and the ones preceding it.

3. Read all the questions following the case. Consider each in a sequence that you feel makes the most sense. Use your experience to help you resolve each issue. Where you read about a person taking action, ask yourself, "What will be the effect of that action on the people in the case?"

4. Where a question calls for your opinion, back it up with specific examples from your own experiences when possible.

5. When you feel that you cannot answer a question without additional information, try to read into the case and between its lines. Look for clues that will allow you to deduce or create what is probably true from what you are given. Most cases give you symptoms rather than a disease. Try to get under the surface of the wording. This will become easier for you with each new case.

6. Make notes on your answer to each question. Quote from the case and cite specific references from the chapter(s) that relates to the case.

B. PRESENTING THE CASE IN CLASS

1. Start with a capsule summary of the facts as you see them. Identify the key persons in the case and put their names and titles on the blackboard so that you can refer to them as you speak.

2. When answering each question, be as specific and factual as you can. State your decision and give the audience the benefit of your research and analysis. Cite your references and quote from the case to prove a point. Let the class know where you are when you do so, so that they can follow your argument.

3. Keep in mind that there is no one right answer to the case's questions. There are many wrong ones, however. You are far better off to base your conclusions on facts than to guess. You can expect the greatest resistance and objections from the class when you state decisions that required deductions or assumptions. If you can show the group your logic, they will probably accept your reasoning. Be prepared for different sets of assumptions—possibly as valid as yours—with the corresponding different conclusions. Allow time for questions. If you are stuck, defer the answer to a classmate or volunteer.

Glossary

Accident any unforeseen or unplanned incident or event. An accident may or may not lead to personal injuries or property damage.

Accountability having to answer to someone for your actions. It makes us answer to our superiors for the quality of our performance and for the ways in which we choose to perform our duties.

Appraisal process periodic evaluations, both formal and informal, of each subordinate's on-the-job performance, as well as of his or her character, attitudes, and potential.

Arbitration the use of a neutral third party in a dispute between labor and management to resolve the areas of conflict. It may be binding and compulsory.

Attitude a person's manner of thinking, feeling, or acting toward specific stimuli.

Authority a person's right to give orders and instructions to others as a result of the position he or she occupies. Authority is also called *formal authority.*

Autocratic style a management style characterized by the retention of all authority by the leader, who keeps subordinates dependent on the leader for instructions and guidance.

Behavior modeling a visual training approach designed to teach attitudes and proper modes of behavior by involving supervisors (and others) in real-life situations and providing immediate feedback on their performances.

Belief a perception based on a conviction that certain things are true, or based on what seems to be true or probable in one's own mind (opinion).

Bureaucratic style a management style characterized by the manager's reliance on rules, regulations, policies, and procedures to direct subordinates.

Career a sequence of jobs leading to higher levels of pay and responsibility. These jobs require differing skills, competencies, and areas of specialization.

Career path a route chosen by an employer or employee through a series of related horizontal and vertical moves to jobs of ever-increasing responsibilities.

Clique an informal group of two or more people who come together by choice to satisfy mutual interests or to pursue common goals. Cliques can be vertical, horizontal, or mixed.

Collective bargaining the process of negotiating a union agreement that will govern wages, hours, and working conditions for employees who are union members.

Communication the transmission of information and common understanding from one person or group to another through the use of common symbols.

Complaint any expression of unhappiness with working conditions or on-the-job relationships that comes to a manager's attention.

Computer monitoring using computers to measure how employees achieve their outputs—monitoring work as it takes place—in addition to keeping track of their total outputs.

Computer virus a rogue computer program that can reproduce itself endlessly, destroying stored data.

Controlling the management function that sets standards—both managerial and technical—that are then used to evaluate and monitor the performances of people and processes in order to prevent, identify, and correct deviations from standards.

Counselor the human relations role in which a supervisor is an adviser and director to subordinates.

Delegation the act of passing one's authority, in part or in total, to another. Only managers can delegate, and only authority is delegated.

Democratic style a management style characterized by the sharing of authority and decision making with subordinates through problem-solving sessions, delegation, and the development of a team spirit.

Direction in communication, the flow or path a message will take in order to reach a receiver. The four directions are upward, downward, diagonal, and horizontal.

Directive interview an interview planned and totally controlled by the interviewer. It follows a script of questions written out in advance.

Discipline the management duty that involves educating subordinates to foster obedience and self-control and dispensing appropriate punishment for wrongdoing.

Disparate impact the existence of a significantly different selection rate between women and/or minorities and nonprotected groups.

Educator the human relations role in which the supervisor is a builder of skills and a developer of potentials in subordinates.

Employee association a group that bargains collectively with management but has given up or has been barred by law from the right to strike.

Employment at will the common law doctrine that holds that employment will last until either employer or employee decides to terminate it, with or without just cause.

Ergonomics concern about the design of work sites, machines, equipment, and systems to minimize stress and job-related injuries.

Ethics a field of philosophy dealing with the rightness of human conduct in society.

Feedback any effort made by parties to a communication to ensure that they have a common understanding of each other's meaning and intent.

Force-field analysis a method for visualizing the driving and restraining forces at work within an individual so as to assess more accurately what is needed to make a change in his or her attitudes.

Foreman traditional term for a supervisor engaged in managing production or workers engaged in manufacturing.

Formal group two or more people who come together by management decision to achieve specific goals.

Formal organization an enterprise that has clearly stated purposes and goals, a division of labor among specialists, a rational design or organization, and a hierarchy of authority and accountability (management).

Functional authority the right that a manager of one department (usually a staff department) has to make decisions and to give orders that affect another department. For example, the personnel department can dictate hiring practices to all other departments.

Goal the objective, target, or end result expected from the execution of specific programs, tasks, and activities.

Grapevine the transmission of information and/or misinformation through the use of informal channels at work.

Grievance any alleged violation of the collective bargaining agreement as filed by management or labor.

Grievance processing settling an alleged violation of the collective bargaining agreement in accordance with the method outlined in the labor agreement.

Group two or more people who are consciously aware of one another, who consider themselves to be a functioning unit, and who share in a quest to achieve one or more goals or some common benefit.

Health the general condition of a person physically, mentally, and emotionally, and efforts at preventing illness and treating injuries when they occur.

Hierarachy the group of people picked to staff an organization's positions of formal authority—its management positions. Members of the hierarchy oversee all the people and activities of the organization.

Human needs physiological and psychological requirements that all humans share and that act as motives for human behavior.

Human relations the development and maintenance of sound on-the-job relationships (educator, counselor, judge, spokesperson) with subordinates, peers, and superiors.

Individualism the training principle requiring a trainer to know the individual trainee's levels of skills and knowledge, to understand the trainee's attitudes, and to progress in training at a pace suitable for the individual trainee to master the material being taught.

Induction the planning and conduct of a program to introduce a new employee to his or her job, working environment, supervisor, and peers.

Informal group two or more people who come together by choice to satisfy mutual needs or to share common interests (a clique).

Information   any facts, figures, or data that are in a form or format that makes them usable to the person who possesses them.

Interview   a conversation between two or more people that is under the control of one of the parties. Interviews are usually more private and confidential than other kinds of meetings and are designed to screen and hire, share appraisal results, instruct, gather information, and sell ideas.

Job description   a formal listing of the duties (tasks and activities) and responsibilities that make up a formal position (job) in an organization.

Job enlargement   increasing the number of tasks or the quantity of output required in a job.

Job enrichment   providing variety, deeper personal interest and involvement, greater autonomy and challenge, or increased amounts of responsibility in a job.

Job rotation   movement of people to different jobs, usually for a temporary period, in order to inform, train, or stimulate cooperation and understanding between and among them.

Job specification   the personal characteristics and skill levels required of an individual to execute a specific job.

Judge   the human relations role in which the supervisor enforces company policies and departmental rules and procedures, evaluates subordinates' performances, settles disputes, and dispenses justice.

Labor relations   management activities that are created by the fact that the organization has a union or unions to bargain with. The two major labor-relations duties are collective bargaining and grievance processing.

Leadership   the ability to get work done through others while winning their respect, confidence, loyalty, and willing cooperation.

Leading   the management function involving the specific actions of staffing, training, offering incentives, evaluating, and disciplining.

Line manager   a member of the organization's hierarchy who oversees a department or activity that directly affects an organization's success (profitability), such as production, finance, or marketing activities.

Linking pin   key individual who is a member of two or more formal groups in a business organization, thus linking or connecting the groups.

Maintenance factor   according to Herzberg, a factor that can be provided by an employer in order to prevent job dissatisfaction.

Management   (1) an activity that uses the functions of planning, organizing, leading, and controlling human and material resources for the purpose of achieving stated goals; (2) a team of people (the hierarchy) that oversees the activities of an enterprise in order to get its tasks and goals accomplished with and through others.

Management by exception   a control principle asserting that managers should spend their time on only matters that require their particular expertise.

Management by objectives (MBO)   a control principle that encourages subordinates to set goals for their performances that are in line with unit and organizational goals and are approved by their supervisors. These mutually agreed-upon goals become the standards by which the subordinates' performances are evaluated.

Management by wandering around (MBWA)   a principle of management that tells supervisors to get out of their offices regularly so that they can communicate with customers, suppliers, subordinates, and others who affect their operations and whose operations they affect.

Management skills   categories of basic abilities required of all managers at every level of the organization.

Manager   a member of an organization's hierarchy who is paid to get things done with and through others by executing the four management functions. Managers always have formal authority, but to be effective they should also possess power (informal authority).

Mediation   the use of a neutral third party in a dispute between labor and management to recommend a solution to the issues that divide the two parties. The recommendations of a mediator are not binding or compulsory.

Medium   a channel or means used to carry a message in the communication process.

Mentor   a volunteer guide and tutor who will act as an immediate companion for a new employee, providing social acceptance and a source for accurate information.

Message   the transmitter's ideas and feelings that form the content to be transmitted to a receiver.

Middle management   members of the hierarchy below the rank of top management but above the supervisory level. Their subordinates are other managers.

Minority   according to the EEOC, the following groups are members of minorities protected from discrimination in hiring and other employment decisions: Hispanics, Asians or Pacific Islanders, blacks not of Hispanic origin, American Indians, and Alaskan natives.

Mission statement   the formal statement of the central purpose behind the existence of an organization—its reason for being.

Motivation   1. the drive within a person to achieve some goal. Human wants and needs fuel our drives. 2. the training principle that requires both trainer and trainee to be favorably predisposed and ready to learn before and during training.

Motivation factor   according to Herzberg, a factor that has the potential to stimulate internal motivation to provide a better-than-average performance and commitment from those to whom it appeals.

Negative discipline   the part of discipline that emphasizes the detection and punishment of wrongdoing.

Networking   using one's friends, family, and work-related contacts to help find employment or advance in one's career.

Nondirective interview   an interview planned by the interviewer but controlled by the interviewee. It makes use of open questions designed to uncover the interviewee's true feelings and opinions with regard to specific areas of interest to the interviewer.

Objective   the training principle that requires trainers and trainees to know what it is that must be taught and mastered. Objectives describe the behavior or performance expected from a trainee as a result of training. They are set with specific conditions in mind, and their mastery is verified through the use of specific standards.

Obsolescence   the state that exists when a person or machine is no longer capable of performing up to standards or management's expectations.

Operating management   the level of the hierarchy that oversees the work of nonmanagement personnel (workers).

Opinion   a belief based on a perception of what seems to be true or probable in one's own mind.

Organization development   a planned, managed, systematic process used to change the culture, systems, and behavior of an organization to improve its effectiveness in solving problems and achieving goals.

Organizing   the management function that requires (1) determination of tasks to be accomplished, (2) establishment of a framework of authority and accountability (hierarchy) among the people who will do and oversee the tasks, and (3) allocation of resources needed to accomplish the tasks.

Orientation   the planning and conduct of a program to introduce a new employee or groups of new employees to their company—its policies, practices, rules, and regulations that will affect the employees' lives immediately.

OSHA   the federal agency whose full name is the *Occupational Safety and Health Administration*. Less frequently *OSHA* is an abbreviation for the Occupational Safety and Health Act of 1970.

Peer   person at the same level of the organization as you are, in terms of formal authority and status in the organization.

Planning   the management function that attempts to prepare for and predict the future. Plans construct goals, programs, policies, rules and procedures.

Policy   a broad guideline constructed by top management and intended to influence managers' approaches to solving problems and dealing with recurring situations.

Positive discipline   the part of discipline that promotes understanding and self-control by informing subordinates of what is expected of them with regard to on-the-job behavior.

Power   the ability to influence others so that they respond favorably to orders and instructions. Power comes to people through their personalities and jobs. It is often called *informal authority,* and it cannot be delegated.

Problem-solving meeting   meeting conducted in order to reach a group consensus or solution to a problem affecting the group. It uses the discussion format, which allows members to participate actively under the direction of a chairperson.

Procedure   a general routine or method for executing the day-to-day operations of a unit or organization.

Productivity the measurement of the amount of input needed to generate any given amount of output. A basic measurement of the efficiency of a business.

Program a plan developed at every level of the management hierarchy that lists goals and the methods for achieving them. Programs usually contain the answers to *who, what, when, where, how,* and *how much.*

Progressive discipline a system using advance warnings about what is and is not acceptable conduct; specific job-related rules; punishments that fit the offense; punishments that grow in severity as misconduct persists; and prompt, consistent enforcement.

Psychological contract an unwritten recognition of what an employee and an employer expect to give and get from one another.

Quality the totality of features and characteristics of a product or service that bear on its ability to satisfy stated or implied goals.

Quality of work life a general label given to various programs and projects designed to help employees satisfy their needs and expectations from work.

Realism the training principle that requires training to simulate or duplicate, as closely as possible, the actual working environment and behavior or performance required of a trainee.

Receiver the person or group intended by transmitters to receive their messages.

Reinforcement the training principle that requires trainees to review and restate knowledge learned, to practice skills, and to involve as many senses as possible in the learning process.

Response the principle of training that requires feedback from trainees to trainers in the form of questions, practical demonstrations, and evaluation exercises.

Responsibility the obligation each person with authority has to execute all duties to the best of his or her ability.

Résumé an employment-related document submitted by the applicant and containing vital data such as the person's name, address, employment goals, and work-related education and experience.

Role ambiguity a situation that occurs whenever a manager is not certain of the role he or she is expected to play at work.

Role conflict a situation that occurs when contradictory or opposing demands are made on a manager.

Role prescription the collection of expectations and demands from superiors, subordinates, and others that shapes a manager's job description and perception of his or her job.

Rule a regulation or limit placed on the conduct of people at work. Rules specify what is or is not to be tolerated in people's behavior.

Safety efforts at protecting human resources from accidents and injuries.

Sanction negative means, such as threats or punishments, used by superiors or the organization to encourage subordinates to play their roles as prescribed by superiors or the organization.

Security efforts at protecting physical facilities and nonhuman assets from loss or damage.

Selection the personnel or human resource management function that determines who is hired and who is not.

Sexual harassment unwelcomed sexual advances, requests for sexual favors, and other physical and verbal conduct of a sexual nature.

Socialization the process a new employee undergoes in the first few weeks of employment, which teaches the new person what the restrictions are, how to succeed and cope, and what place exists for him or her in the new environment.

Spectator style a management style characterized by a strong reliance of the supervisor on the skills, knowledge, and initiative of subordinates, with the corresponding development of a high level of independence and pride among the subordinates.

Spokesperson the human relations role through which a supervisor represents management's views to workers and subordinates' views to management.

Staff manager a member of the organization's hierarchy who renders advice and assistance to all other managers or departments in his or her area of expertise.

Standard a device for measuring or monitoring the behavior of people (management standard) or processes (technical standard).

Standard (in appraisals) a quantity or quality designation that can be used as a basis of comparison for judging performances. Something used by mutual agreement to determine if things are as they should be or were meant to be.

Steward the union's elected or appointed first-line representative in the areas in which workers are found.

Stress worry, anxiety, or tension that accompanies situations and problems we face and makes us uncertain about the ways in which we should resolve them.

Subjects the principle of training that requires trainers to know the subject being taught and to know the trainees—their existing levels of skills and knowledge, their attitudes, and their predispositions to learn.

Supervisor a member of the operating level of the management hierarchy who directs the activities of nonmanagement employees (workers).

Synergy cooperative action or force of two or more elements pulling together that yields a result greater than the sum of the results that could be achieved separately by the elements.

Syntality a group's "personality"—its collection of traits, strengths, and weaknesses that make it unique.

Team adviser supervisor managing a team of people who share his or her authority and who jointly run their operations in terms of decision making and problem solving.

Theory X a set of attitudes traditionally held by managers that assumes the worst with regard to the average worker's initiative and creativity.

Theory Y a set of attitudes held by today's generation of managers that assumes the best about the average worker's initiative and creativity.

Theory Z a set of approaches to managing people based on the attitudes of Japanese managers about the importance of the individual and of team effort to the organization.

Top management the level of the hierarchy that includes the chief executive and his or her subordinates.

Training the activity concerned with improving employees' performances in their present jobs by imparting attitudes, skills, and knowledge needed now or in the near future.

Training objective a written statement containing what the trainee should be able to do (performance), the conditions under which the trainee is expected to perform, and the criteria used to judge the adequacy of the performance.

Transmitter the person or group that transmits or sends a message to a receiver.

Union a group of workers who are employed by a company or an industry or who practice the same skilled craft and have banded together to bargain collectively with their employers with one voice—the union's. A union possesses the right to strike.

Validity the characteristic that a selection device has when it is predictive of a person's performance on a job. The degree to which a selection criterion measures what it is supposed to measure.

Value an activity, condition, or object that we feel has merit or worth in our lives.

Vandalism wanton or willful destruction of damage to the property of another.

Whistleblower an employee who makes known to authorities the violations of laws and actions committed by his or her employer that are contrary to public policy.

Worker any employee who is not a member of the management hierarchy.

Workers' compensation federal and state laws designed to compensate employees for illnesses and injuries that arise out of and in the course of their employment.

Work ethic people's attitudes about the importance of working, the kind of work they choose or are required to perform, and the quality of their efforts while performing work.

Index